GLOBAL ENTREPRENEURSHIP AND INNOVATION

T0323335

Sara Miller McCune founded SAGE Publishing in 1965 to support the dissemination of usable knowledge and educate a global community. SAGE publishes more than 1000 journals and over 800 new books each year, spanning a wide range of subject areas. Our growing selection of library products includes archives, data, case studies and video. SAGE remains majority owned by our founder and after her lifetime will become owned by a charitable trust that secures the company's continued independence.

Los Angeles | London | New Delhi | Singapore | Washington DC | Melbourne

GLOBAL ENTREPRENEURSHIP AND INNOVATION

Sarika Pruthi
& Jay Mitra

Los Angeles | London | New Delhi
Singapore | Washington DC | Melbourne

Los Angeles | London | New Delhi
Singapore | Washington DC | Melbourne

SAGE Publications Ltd
1 Oliver's Yard
55 City Road
London EC1Y 1SP

SAGE Publications Inc.
2455 Teller Road
Thousand Oaks, California 91320

SAGE Publications India Pvt Ltd
B 1/I 1 Mohan Cooperative Industrial Area
Mathura Road
New Delhi 110 044

SAGE Publications Asia-Pacific Pte Ltd
3 Church Street
#10-04 Samsung Hub
Singapore 049483

Editor: Matthew Waters
Editorial assistant: Charlotte Hanson
Production editor: Nicola Marshall
Copyeditor: Tom Bedford
Proofreader: Derek Markham
Indexer: Judith Lavender
Marketing manager: Kimberley Simpson
Cover design: Francis Kenney
Typeset by: C&M Digitals (P) Ltd, Chennai, India
Printed in the UK

Library of Congress Control Number: 2022944484

British Library Cataloguing in Publication data

A catalogue record for this book is available from the British Library

ISBN 978-1-5264-9446-7
ISBN 978-1-5264-9445-0 (pbk)

To my students for your curiosity, receptivity and global diversity.

To my family for your love, patience and support.

To the memory of Mike Wright, my revered teacher, advisor, mentor and co-author who tragically passed away in 2019. Thank you, Mike, for introducing me to the idea of entrepreneurship and innovation, and for your motivation and inspiration for as long as I can recall. Your astute knowledge and swift guidance, restless energy and cheerful humour, are all greatly missed. The rich legacy of work that you have left behind continues to spur me on and reinforces my faith in the value and purpose of academic scholarship.

– Sarika Pruthi

To Gill for all that is best in life and love, to Daniel for showing how love remains.

To my parents for their belief in me.

To my students for their curiosity and reach across the globe.

– Jay Mitra

TABLE OF CONTENTS

ONLINE RESOURCES

This textbook is accompanied by online resources to aid teaching and support learning. To access these resources, visit: **https://study.sagepub.com/pruthi**. Please note that lecturers will require a SAGE account in order to access the lecturer resources. An account can be created via the above link.

For Instructors

- **PowerPoints** that can be downloaded and adapted to suit individual teaching needs
- **Additional Case Study Material** providing real-world examples to use with students
- **Multiple Choice Questions** and **Application Questions** that can be used for both formative and summative student assessments

ABOUT THE AUTHORS

Sarika Pruthi

Sarika Pruthi is Associate Professor in Entrepreneurship at the School of Global Innovation and Leadership, Lucas College & Graduate School of Business, San Jose State University (SJSU), California, USA. Sarika's research is situated at the intersection of international and immigrant entrepreneurship, and international business. Her research interests are in the areas of immigrant and social entrepreneurship, international venture capital and private equity finance. She is passionate about ethnic and immigrant, transnational and returnee entrepreneurs, their start-up motivations, and the role of their social ties in the founding and growth of their ventures, especially in the context of rapidly growing start-ups and born global firms. Her work spans both developed and emerging economy contexts, in particular the US, UK and India due to her personal experience of living and working in all three countries.

Sarika's work has appeared in top peer-reviewed entrepreneurship and international business journals including the *Asia Pacific Journal of Management, International Business Review, International Journal of Management Reviews, Entrepreneurship & Regional Development, Small Business Economics, Foundations and Trends in Entrepreneurship*, and *Strategic Management Journal*, among others. She has reviewed for top academic journals including the *Journal of Management* and the *Journal of World Business*. For over ten years, Sarika has reviewed for the Entrepreneurship Division at the Academy of Management, and the Academy of International Business, the two highest ranked management conferences in the world, where she has also presented papers, chaired competitive paper sessions and co-hosted professional development workshops and teaching symposia. Sarika serves on the executive board of the Academy of International Business West Chapter and the editorial board of the *Journal of Entrepreneurship and Innovation in Emerging Economies*.

Sarika teaches introductory and advanced courses in entrepreneurship and international business. These include Introduction to Entrepreneurship, Global Entrepreneurship, Developing Your Entrepreneurial Potential, Global Dimensions of Business, and Entrepreneurship (MBA). She was recently invited to teach on a transformative, new interdisciplinary (HonorsX) learning program at SJSU, of which she is also one of the co-founding members. Envisioned as a program for future change makers and leaders, the goal of HonorsX is to empower students from a variety of disciplines to propose innovative solutions to pressing global problems, and build complementary skills and practical knowledge outside of their major areas of study to implement proposed solutions. Sarika is extremely passionate about the cause of student success. She organizes the

Silicon Valley Innovation Challenge, an annual business ideas competition at SJSU, leads the International Programs and Students Committee, and Student Success Committee, and serves the International House Executive Board in an advisory role at SJSU.

Sarika has won several awards and honors for her research, teaching and service. These include the 'extremely competitive' Sybil Weir-John Galm Award for her research contributions, and Master Teacher Awards (2015–16, 2018–19, 2020–21, 2021–22) for exemplary teaching at SJSU. In Spring 2022, she was selected to receive the 2022 Lucas College of Business Distinguished Teaching Award. She has received recognition for her outstanding service to the Academy of International Business (2022 Best Reviewer Award; International Entrepreneurship track), and the Academy of Management (five years of outstanding service to the Teaching & Learning Conference, probably the biggest and most successful teaching conference in the world). In 2019, she received the Dean's nomination for the Outstanding Professor Award at SJSU.

Prior to joining SJSU, Sarika taught and researched at King's College London, University of London (UK) (ranked 6th in the UK; QS World University Subject Rankings 2022, and #33 in Best Global Universities), and the University of Nottingham (UK) where she also earned her MA and PhD.

Jay Mitra

Jay Mitra is Professor of Business Enterprise and Innovation and Director of the Venture Academy at Essex Business School, University of Essex. He has acted as a Scientific Adviser to the OECD (Organisation for Economic Cooperation and Development) as the Head of the Scientific Committee on Entrepreneurship for the OECD's Centre for Entrepreneurship and the LEED (Local Economic and Employment) Programme at its Trento Centre and in Paris. He is a Visiting Professor at the University of Luneburg, Germany, and has acted in that capacity at Bayero University, Nigeria, University Externado, Colombia, the Institute of Management Technology, India, the School of Management, Fudan University and the School of Public Policy at Jilin University, both in China, at Bologna University, Italy and EDHEC Business School, France. He is a Fellow of the Royal Society of Arts in the UK.

Jay Mitra also leads the International Entrepreneurship Forum (IEF), a unique network and forum for researchers, policy makers and business practitioners working on entrepreneurship, innovation and regional development issues. The IEF has organized 18 international refereed conferences to date around the world bringing together academic researchers, reflective practitioners and dynamic policy makers.

Educated at Presidency College, Calcutta University, Jadavpur University, both in Kolkata, India, and at University of Stirling, UK, Professor Mitra trained in the private sector in the UK, worked as a Principal Officer for local government also in the UK, specializing in economic and business development, and taught at three other universities in the UK before joining the University of Essex. At Essex he established the unique School of Entrepreneurship and Business (SEB) in 2005 where he developed an original portfolio of postgraduate programs on entrepreneurship and innovation and their significance for the private, public and social sectors together with the first doctoral program in Entrepreneurship at the University. Later SEB merged with another school to become Essex Business School.

Professor Mitra's teaching, research, development and knowledge exchange interests include micro aspects of new venture creation, entrepreneurship, innovation and economic development, migrant entrepreneurship, entrepreneurship policy, entrepreneurship education and training, socially driven entrepreneurship, gender and entrepreneurship, and citizen engagement in entrepreneurship. He is the editor of the new *Journal of Entrepreneurship and Innovation in Emerging Economies* published by Sage. He is a member of various editorial boards of international refereed journals. His latest book is *Entrepreneurship, Innovation and Economic Development* 2nd edn (2020) published by Routledge which follows the recent publications of *The Business of Innovation*, published by Sage in 2017, and *Entrepreneurship and Knowledge Exchange* (2015), also by Routledge.

He has also set up two new businesses and has been directly involved in supporting the creation of numerous new ventures in the UK, including those of his students. He is a Board member of the International Network for Small and Medium Sized Enterprises (INSME), based in Rome, Italy, and has acted as a member of the Ethical Investment Committee of the European Business Angel Network.

ENDORSEMENTS

'This new text on Global Entrepreneurship by Sarika Pruthi and Jay Mitra breaks new ground in our understanding of the frontiers and forces of globalization and how that generates prospects for entrepreneurship and innovation. For too long books on the subject have confused internationalization with globalization assuming that a firm's internationalization strategy corresponds to its place in a globalized environment. The authors demystify this confusion deftly and explore a comprehensive range of topical issues affecting business creation and growth in different contexts where globalization has not necessarily meant a flat world of economic, social, and technological development. The chapters on globalization and migration, in particular, together with those of migrant and returnee entrepreneurs, the local and global nexus, and digitization offer a smart and nuanced approach to thinking about the trajectories and flows of entrepreneurial capability across the world. A very interesting array of case studies bring the discourse to life. The book is a must read by all students of entrepreneurship, reflective practitioners and policy makers looking to develop new strategies and policies in a complex global environment.'

Sergio Arzeni, President, International Network for SMEs (INSME), Rome, Italy, and former Director of the OECD Centre for Entrepreneurship, Small and Medium-sized Enterprises (SMEs) and Local Development, Paris, France

'This book is an excellent contribution to our understanding of global entrepreneurship and innovation. Most importantly, it is a timely contribution as it proposes a thorough analysis of some current topics of a critical importance such as immigrant and returnee's entrepreneurship, digitalization in entrepreneurship in a global context, but also the global and local paradox of global entrepreneurship. In this regard, this book complements very well the existing titles. It is a book of a great value for research scholars and instructors in global entrepreneurship.'

Elie Chrysostome, Professor of International Business, Ivey Business School at Western Ontario, Canada, and Editor-in-Chief, Journal of Comparative International Management (JCIM)

'This book provides a very useful and informative foundation in entrepreneurship, on a global scale. The book explains the various dimensions of international entrepreneurship, and highlights the role of innovation and key drivers of this phenomenon, critical to the success of national economies worldwide. Noting that educational materials in global entrepreneurship and innovation are quite limited, the text provides a practical and useful guide for students and practitioners alike. The book addresses significant and challenging issues. The writing is clear and highly accessible, providing information and knowledge that are useful, interesting, and engaging. The contents are comprehensive, covering all the key aspects of international entrepreneurship, including globalization, small firms, venture capital, strategy, with a particular focus on migration and immigrant entrepreneurship. The book is a must-read primer for anyone interested in international entrepreneurship. Written by top scholars in the field, Pruthi and Mitra have a flair for excellent writing and an arsenal of amazing facts and information that are state-of-the-art on international entrepreneurship. The book fills a major gap in an important area, vital to individual entrepreneurs, entrepreneurial firms, and nations seeking economic advancement. Bravo to the authors for writing such an engaging, informative, and useful volume.'

Gary Knight, Professor of Global Management, Helen Simpson Jackson Endowed Chair of International Management, Atkinson Graduate School of Management, Willamette University, USA

'An excellent book that offers a unique and timely exploration and review of the global entrepreneurship and innovation fields incorporating, inter-alia, highly topical issues of migration, globalization, digital technology, and local-global dynamics. This is a must-read book by academic scholars, students at both the undergraduate and postgraduate levels, entrepreneurs, policy-makers and other stakeholders who are interested in understanding issues related to globalization and internationalisation and their association with innovation of differently sized firms, economic growth and societal wellbeing.'

George Saridakis, Professor of Small Business and Entrepreneurship, University of Kent, UK

'Pruthi and Mitra's *Global Entrepreneurship and Innovation* offers a thoughtful, timely and comprehensive coverage of major issues in the field. It addresses issues related to the role of global entrepreneurship in economic and comparative development as well as local and regional forces shaping international entrepreneurship. I especially like the discussion on immigration and ethnic returnee entrepreneurship. The book is a great contribution to the literature and contemporary debates about the effect of digitalization, deglobalization , and decoupling. It is well written, well presented and supported by the best research results. The book will undoubtedly serve as a major reference for scholars all over the world. I compliment the authors on a job well done.'

Shaker A Zahra, Professor, Robert E. Buuck Chair of Entrepreneurship, Strategic Management & Entrepreneurship Department, Carlson School of Management, University of Minnesota, USA

ACKNOWLEDGEMENTS

Sarika Pruthi

This book is the culmination of years of my research and teaching in the exciting field of international and global entrepreneurship. I feel humbled to consolidate my knowledge and experience in this way and sincerely acknowledge the support of many in this rewarding endeavor.

First and foremost, I thank my students for alerting me to the opportunity for this book. The idea for this book was conceived in my Global Entrepreneurship class at San Jose State University (SJSU) where I have been teaching this course for the past several years. The inconvenience of assembling a custom reading pack from several disparate sources in the absence of a single, user-friendly textbook covering the key issues led to the discovery of a market gap. The relative difficulty of navigating the material for students and hence the need for a real solution to the problem was equally hard to ignore. If entrepreneurs are those who spot gaps and find solutions, then perhaps I became one thanks to my students. So glad to be able to finally practice what I preach!

This book would not be possible without the contribution of several individual entrepreneurs and venture capital investors from three different continents – the US, UK and India – who, over the years, graciously agreed to being interviewed and generously volunteered their time and valued insights related to their entrepreneurial pursuits. Thank you all for the diversity of your personal and professional, ethnic and national, backgrounds, and the richness of your experiences and perspectives that has lent a truly global flavor to the text and brought the otherwise mundane theoretical concepts to life. I am grateful for your cooperation and permission.

My co-author, Jay Mitra, deserves a special mention for introducing me to the prospect of producing a textbook, a new scholarly endeavor for me. The experience of writing this book has opened my mind to unexplored possibilities and novel forms of academic inquiry and expression. Jay, I am grateful for your promise and collaboration, especially in the face of grave personal tragedy that you have recently encountered.

I also wish to thank the editorial team – Matthew Waters, Charlotte Hanson and Lyndsay Oliver – at SAGE Publishing for your dedicated support and guidance throughout the seemingly endless process of drafting this manuscript. This book has greatly benefitted from the constructive comments and expert feedback of four anonymous reviewers and subject specialists from across the world whom your proficient team helped to judiciously select.

I must not forget the able research assistance of Monica Appiano, SJSU student at the time of writing this book. Thank you, Monica, for your availability and timely support that greatly eased my burden and helped me to inch closer to the finish line. Your good-natured self made it a real pleasure to work with you. You'll be happy to know that the book is finally complete.

Last but not least, I owe a debt of gratitude to my family. To my husband, Deepak, for your eternal wisdom, patience and perseverance that I often take for granted, and both our children, Arushi and Aditya, whose unconditional love and boundless energy brightens up my life and makes everything so much more worthwhile.

Jay Mitra

The sources of my knowledge and inspiration for co-writing this book are large, various and across different domains. What I write about a topic is not simply a function of knowledge gleaned from established researchers who have already provided us with significant content on the subject. For me, the writing of something new is driven by the intersectional and eclectic ideas, insights, empirics experiences and the curiosity of the global academic community, industry practitioners, consultants, a range of policy makers, my international students, the wide array of global entrepreneurs with whom I have worked and shared happy times in lively formal and informal exchanges. There are so many of them. I hope I am excused for not mentioning all in a celebrity list here. And always, music and poetry.

Over the years, some people have stayed the course with me as mentors, colleagues and friends. They are the architects of my global canvas. They include Sergio Arzeni, formerly of the OECD and now President of the International Network for SMEs in Rome; Zoltan Acs of George Mason University in the USA; David Storey of Sussex University in the UK; John Edmondson, publisher and editor of *Industry and Higher Education* journal; Alan Barrell, the unofficial, entrepreneurial mayor of Cambridge; and Piero Formica of Maynooth University, Ireland, and Bologna, Italy, for the wisdom and friendship of wise men. To understand the wonder and buzz of global enquiry as lived experience I owe a lot to Su-Hyun Berg of Flensburg University in Germany, a global business consultant. For the spirit of cooperation, support, and their distinctive European openness I thank Ursula Weisenfeld of Luneburg University in Germany, Silke Tegtmeier at Sonderborg University, Denmark, and Mariusz Sokolowicz and Agnieszka Kurczewska both of Lodz University in Poland. How creativity, music and art take inno-vation seamlessly from the urban to the rural, this I could learn from Amitava Bhattacharya, the founder of the Banglanatak.com, India. A brave new world of entre-preneurship in Nigeria together with other forays in entrepreneurial research was enabled by Yazid Abubakar of Bahrain University, and Murtala Sagagi, Bayero University, Nigeria. Then there is the community of the robust young, my students, current and past, who keep me on my toes. I mention a few of my former students: Imran Hossain, Asma Rauf, Neha Gopinath, Janja Tardios, all now in the first flush of promising academic careers. Add to that the kindness and wisdom of strangers. I am indebted to all of them.

Special thanks to my co-author Sarika Pruthi who persevered with me in the best of scholarly traditions and friendship. To her goes most of the credit for this new book. The team of editors at Sage led by the patient and wise Matthew Waters and including Charlotte Hanson, Lyndsay Oliver and Nicola Marshall for their forbearance, guidance and interest.

The fount of all my inspiration and love for writing, the reason for being hungry for new ideas and knowledge, is a remarkable woman, my wife and soul mate, Gill. I am a poorer writer without her presence now, but I know her power, the glory and the passion (plus the meticulousness) are all around me. My son, Daniel, my new Prospero, in whose magic I find strength, and whose indulgence sets me free.

1

INTRODUCTION

International entrepreneurship has become a topic of substantial interest in recent years. Both developed and developing countries are benefitting from a surge in entrepreneurial activity and innovation. In 2018, small businesses in the US created 55% of all jobs and 66% of all net new jobs (USBA, 2018). According to Startup Genome (2020), the global start-up economy created around $3 trillion in value from 2017 to the first half of 2019. This figure is at the same level as the gross domestic product of a G7 economy. Consider a few more statistical high notes:

- Different ecosystems around the world (around 84 of them) produced start-ups with over $1 billion in valuation (the unicorns of this world) in 2019 (Startup Genome, 2020).
- The global trend suggests a spatial shift and spread in the concentration of these start-ups. Around 30 different global centers around the world are expected to follow Silicon Valley, still ranked number one among the top 30 ecosystems. These include New York, London, Beijing and Boston, and with around 30% of them in the Asia Pacific region compared to 20% in 2012. In fact, the Asia Pacific region posted the highest market valuation, $971.37 billion, for unicorns worldwide, over $100 billion more than the valuation of North American unicorns which showed a valuation figure of $857.57 billion. Europe lagged behind by a considerable margin with $125.86 billion in valuation (Statista, 2020a).
- The top ten performing cities boast capturing about 74% of the value from start-ups globally. In their survey of 18 start-up hubs, PricewaterhouseCoopers (2019) show that Stockholm is the best place for start-ups, followed by Oslo and Tel Aviv.
- The most successful and highly valued unicorn is not located in the USA or in Europe but in China. ANT Group, the Chinese fintech company, is valued at $125 billion as of January 2020. The unicorn ByteDance, occupying second place and valued at $75 billion, is also Chinese (Statista, 2020c, 2021).[1]

---

[1]Data shown here also cited in Finances Online: https://financesonline.com/startup-statistics/#:~:text=-Global%20Startup%20Statistics%20The%20global%20startup%20economy%20has,the%20gross%20domestic%20product%20of%20a%20G7%20eAb

International small and medium enterprises controlling and managing value-added activities in more than one country are becoming increasingly important for developing home grown global players (Ibeh et al., 2004). What the data indicates is that entrepreneurship has emerged as a robust global phenomenon. So much so that we could be confident about referring to the term 'global entrepreneurship', which includes but also differentiates itself from the notion of 'international entrepreneurship'. Internationalization suggests a process of venturing in the global marketplace following patterns of trade and investment taking firms mainly in the West (the USA and Europe) to other parts of the world. We now see the emergence of multiple landscapes of entrepreneurial activity which challenges any idea of Western hegemony over entrepreneurship (see below for a fuller explanation of this movement).

Geography alone does not explain the global entrepreneurship phenomenon. There are other trends worth noting. The entrepreneurs, themselves, are not the same as they were before, and what they achieve in terms of creating new stocks of firms, new jobs, products and services, augment the global value of enterprise creation. Immigrants, for example, are increasingly having a major positive impact on the economies of 'host' nations. Noteworthy is the job creation potential of immigrant enterprise (Zolin and Schlosser, 2013). In the UK, migrant-founded enterprises employ 1.16 million people and contribute to 14% of job creation in small and medium-sized firms (Johnson and Kimmelman, 2014). The job creation potential of immigrant enterprise is especially high among skilled immigrants who are more likely to start firms with more than ten employees than comparable natives with only primary education (Hunt, 2011; 2015). Many of the innovative start-ups such as Uber and eBay that have become indispensable to our daily lives are founded by immigrant entrepreneurs. These firms significantly contribute to economic growth, accounting for as many as 50% of gross jobs created annually between 1980 and 2010 (NVCA, 2019).

Whereas US policy makers are increasingly recognizing the role of small businesses for supporting jobs and reducing trade deficits, those in emerging economies like China are considering entrepreneurship as a key means to address the challenges of inequality, ill-health and pollution resulting from the rapid economic growth of the past two decades (Bosma and Kelley, 2018). They are also tapping into the potential of their skilled diaspora abroad for local development (Nazareno et al., 2019). Firms founded by Chinese American and Taiwanese Americans in Southern California, for example, employ more than 440,000 people and generate $70 billion in taxable revenues. These businesses have expanded business opportunities and contributed to the development of China's information and communication technology industries (Saxenian, 2002; Zhou and Hsu, 2010). There is growing evidence that immigrant entrepreneurs permanently returning home to start-up contribute to innovation, competition and development of an entrepreneurial culture in their home country (Tynaliev and McLean, 2011; OECD, 2017).

As specialized suppliers of equity finance to high-growth prospects, also significant in the global entrepreneurial domain is the presence of venture capital (VC) firms.

According to Gornall and Strebulaev (2015), 42% of US companies that went public between 1974 and 2015 were venture-backed. These companies represented 63% of the market capitalization and 85% of the total research and development (R&D) of all public companies. At the end of 2018, US venture-backed companies including Microsoft ($780 billion), Apple ($746 billion), Amazon ($737 billion), Alphabet ($727 billion), and Facebook ($374 billion) accounted for five of the six largest publicly traded companies by market capitalization.

Altogether, the phenomenon of global entrepreneurship is of significant interest and impact. In this introductory chapter, we explain the concept of international and global entrepreneurship and innovation, and outline the drivers of international entrepreneurial activity. We also introduce the readers to the structure and scope of the rest of this book.

From International to Global Entrepreneurship and Innovation: Concepts and Drivers

International entrepreneurship is the process of creatively discovering and exploiting opportunities that lie outside a firm's domestic market in the pursuit of competitive advantage (Zahra and George, 2002). Oviatt and McDougall (2005) define international entrepreneurship as the discovery, enactment, evaluation and exploitation of opportunities across national borders to create future goods and services.

The study of international entrepreneurship has emerged from the confluence of two interrelated but separate research streams: entrepreneurship and international business. **Entrepreneurship** is the study of new ventures. According to Shane and Venkataraman (2000), entrepreneurship is the scholarly examination of how, by whom and with what consequences opportunities to create future goods and services are recognized, formed, evaluated and exploited. Integral to the concept of entrepreneurship is the idea of innovation. **Innovation** reflects firms' endeavors to utilize unexploited opportunities by developing new products and business models, improving processes or generating novelty by creating new combinations from existing components. As the sum of creativity and commercialization, innovation is the means by which entrepreneurs either create new wealth-producing resources or endow existing resources with enhanced wealth-creating potential (Drucker, 1993).

Although definitions and forms of innovation vary, they stress the commercialization of new knowledge or technology to generate increased sales or business value (Hansen and Birkinshaw, 2007). Whereas **marketing innovations** are aimed at better addressing customer needs, opening up new markets, or newly positioning a product on the market with the objective of increasing the firm's sales, **product innovations** entail the introduction of goods or services that are new or significantly improved with respect to their characteristics or intended uses, and which are created from diverse knowledge inputs. Innovation is a necessity for firm survival in free market economies (Baumol, 2002). Innovating firms have higher productivity, grow faster and are more profitable than non-innovating firms.

The field of **international business** spans organizations crossing national geographic borders to do business in foreign countries. Thus, international entrepreneurship is the phenomenon of early and rapid internationalization of new and small firms. In their seminal paper, Oviatt and McDougall (1994) define international new ventures (INVs) as business organizations that, from inception, seek significant competitive advantage from the use of resources and the sale of outputs in multiple countries. These rapidly growing firms have the potential to transform into global start-ups characterized by the dispersal of multiple value-chain activities across the globe *and* extensive coordination of those activities in multiple countries.

As an area of study, international entrepreneurship is relatively new. Early beginnings of the field were marked by interest in foreign market opportunities for new ventures. Until two decades ago, a substantial body of research was published on established firms, both domestic and international, and on domestic new ventures. In contrast, research on new ventures that are international was sparse. According to Oviatt and McDougall (2005), there are two branches to the study of international entrepreneurship: cross-national comparisons of domestic entrepreneurship (e.g. differences in entrepreneurial activity rates across countries), and entrepreneurial internationalization (e.g. cross-country differences in the drivers of new venture internationalization). Whereas the former is focused on the cross-national border comparison of entrepreneurs, their behaviors and the circumstances in which they are embedded, the latter is about the cross-national border behavior of entrepreneurial actors.

International entrepreneurship began with the study of new and small firms that are also international in scope. However, the study of international entrepreneurship is not limited to new and small ventures. A growing number of participants, including established firms, are embracing entrepreneurship, especially in emerging economies. International entrepreneurial activities also occur in large, well-established companies pursuing entrepreneurial activities. Further, scholars have researched knowledge-intensive firms and family businesses as contexts for international entrepreneurship. They cover both mini-national and multinational companies across a range of industry sectors.

Accordingly, the definition of international entrepreneurship has evolved over time to consider several types of firms that exhibit entrepreneurial behavior abroad, regardless of the type of international activities they embrace or contexts in which they operate. Zahra et al. (2014) further extend the definition of international entrepreneurship as 'the recognition, formation, evaluation, and exploitation of opportunities across national borders to create new businesses, models, and solutions for value creation including financial, social, and environmental' (pg. 138). Their definition refers to multiple forms of value creation, beyond for-profit or commercial outcomes. In this textbook, we focus on new and small firms as the context of international and global entrepreneurship.

Drivers of International and Global Entrepreneurship

The forces of globalization, especially in the last two decades, have played a key role in driving the interest in new and small firms that are also international in scope (Zahra et al., 2014). Political, economic and social developments, and the increasing complexity of technological development, namely digital technologies, have unleashed new opportunities around the world to seek solutions to global problems. Add to this migration and cross-border movements of people, and the proliferation of equity financing outside of developed markets that have shaped the landscape for entrepreneurship and innovation in terms of the availability, range and location of opportunities, actors engaged in the identification and exploitation of those opportunities, and hence the form of their entrepreneurial endeavors. We examine each of these forces in turn below.

The globalization of entrepreneurship can be explained in part by the need to respond to major political, economic, social and technological changes across the world. These universal phenomena, bolstered by public agitation and interest, have generated a universal demand for new products and services created and promoted by different types of individuals and networked firms across the world. Political and economic forces including the move to privatization and deregulation have opened up new opportunities for entrepreneurs in various parts of the world. The formerly state-controlled and centrally planned countries such as those of Eastern Europe, China and Vietnam, for instance, are now fertile grounds for founding and growing small businesses. Entrepreneurs in all parts of the world are increasingly expected to tackle global challenges such as poverty, energy consumption and climate change. Troubled, allegedly, by corruption, difficulties in doing business (according to the World Bank), and, apparently, a low-quality entrepreneurial environment, some countries in Africa are nonetheless now home to entrepreneurs of all ages solving a range of pressing problems in health care, infrastructure and poverty alleviation.

Driven by the forces of technology and competition, the production of knowledge has become a worldwide enterprise. The phenomena of offshoring and outsourcing have created an abundance of opportunities for new firm creation in the form of sourcing, sales or partnerships. The ability to disperse and coordinate value-chain activities across the globe means that entrepreneurship is becoming prevalent in a larger number of countries than ever before. Individuals can build on innovations developed by others or join in the creation and discovery of new products and technologies anywhere in the world.

Since 2005, the number of internet users has soared from 900,000 to more than 3 billion, while new technologies have enabled the number of connected digital devices to triple to nearly 21 billion. The 'new oil' of our times, global data flows have grown by tenfold over the past decade. The current 20,000 gigabits of data that travels around the world per second is expected to triple by the start of the third decade of this century (Bhattacharya et al., 2017). The power of the internet has made it possible for entrepreneurs to easily cross geographic borders and sell outside of their home market. In some cases, small firm founders are forced to internationalize due to external environmental pressures, leaving them little choice but to look abroad in order to survive. Thus, entrepreneurs are no longer confined to domestic markets; they are increasingly crossing geographic borders to do business. Entrepreneurs operating in countries with varying levels of economic development can more easily seize opportunities outside of their domestic markets and exploit global distribution channels and the coordination of value-chain activities in multiple countries.

Another influential world trend that is shaping the dynamics of international entrepreneurial activity is the changing nature of migration, in particular skilled migration, especially in the developed West. Four countries – the US, UK, Canada and Australia – are home to nearly 73% skilled migrants in all OECD countries (Kerr et al., 2016). Increasing recognition of the central role of human capital in economic growth and the rising pursuit of foreign education by young people are among the key factors underlying this trend. Immigrants in developed economies are displaying a disproportionately high propensity toward entrepreneurship and new firm formation (Desiderio and Mestres-Domènech, 2011). In the US, self-employment and new business formation rates among immigrants are increasing, whereas those among natives are decreasing (Fairlie and Lofstrom, 2014). Alongside this, forms of immigrant enterprise have evolved from local, labor-intensive enterprises to global, knowledge-intensive and diverse professional services (Nazareno et al., 2019).

Businesses owned by immigrant or ethnic group members, especially in the knowledge-intensive industries, are more engaged with their counterparts in their home countries to pursue entrepreneurial opportunities than ever before (Nazareno et al., 2019; Saxenian and Sabel, 2008). Traversing host and home country borders, these transnational entrepreneurs leverage their knowledge and social networks of the two countries to found new ventures. Several new immigrant and transnational entrepreneurs are even permanently returning home to start up (Drori et al., 2009). Since 2000, there has been a steady increase of approximately 500 returnee-founded enterprises each year in China (Zhou, 2008). These transnational and returnee entrepreneurs have become key players in bridging their homeland's domestic capital with technological expertise gained from abroad, and even establishing linkages with the global market. Many of the rapidly growing new and small firms are founded or co-founded by highly skilled immigrant entrepreneurs who have a link with another country outside of their country of origin.

Finally, the introduction of new financial instruments and innovative forms of finance, in particular equity finance, has made it easier for small and international entrepreneurs originating in any part of the world to form global start-ups. Although substantial as a proportion of total global venture capital investment, the US share of global capital invested and exited has dropped precipitously over the past 15 years. Several parts of Asia and the developing world outside of developed Western markets have witnessed a rise of VC Associations (NVCA, 2019). Israel, for example, is considered one of the biggest VC centers in the world, with Tel Aviv considered the fifth best city for entrepreneurs, after Silicon Valley, New York, Los Angeles and Boston (IFC, 2018). According to Pricewaterhouse Coopers, global VC funding increased nearly 50% year on year, with $254 billion invested across nearly 15,300 deals in 2018 (NVCA, 2019). Powered by new communications technologies, the growing reach and supply of venture capital beyond developed markets has made it possible for entrepreneurs to implement their ideas in a broader range of countries across international boundaries with growing ease (Iriyama et al., 2010).

These alterations in the dynamics of international entrepreneurship activity, driven by political, economic, social, technological and financial forces, push us towards examining international entrepreneurship from a different, overarching perspective, a global perspective; hence the term 'global entrepreneurship'.

Scope and Structure of this Book

The global student base of entrepreneurship courses necessitates exposure to, and critical appreciation of, diverse environments, and the practice of international and global entrepreneurship and innovation. Yet, teaching and learning resources for courses in global entrepreneurship and innovation are currently limited. Although there are several entrepreneurship texts on the market, most focus on the new venture creation process, typically in a domestic context. Few textbooks offer a nuanced global dimension in their contents. International business texts seldom cover international and transnational entrepreneurship issues. Identifying and assembling relevant instructional material and learning resources from disparate sources is tedious and time-consuming for both instructors and students.

In consolidating a broad range of themes specifically relevant to the research and practice of entrepreneurship and innovation from a global perspective, we fill this gap. Our aim is to examine the global scoping and international development of entrepreneurship and innovation, including the behavior of new and small firms in the global context. We present examples from both the commercial and the social sectors, referring to the global contexts of international entrepreneurship. Using a combination of theory, and illustrative, multi-country case studies in a user-friendly format, we trace the role of new and small firms' characteristics in their international, and global, growth. We include such topics as distinctive features and growth challenges of small firms; international entrepreneurship and innovation ecosystems and global circuits of knowledge exchange; motivations and foreign market entry strategies of international entrepreneurs; immigrant entrepreneurs; INVs and born globals; and international venture capital and private equity finance.

We expect that this book will be of value to entrepreneurship instructors, research scholars seeking to learn about key issues in international and global entrepreneurship as a field of study, as well as potential individual entrepreneurs embarking on their entrepreneurial journey in an increasingly globalizing world. It is intended for both introductory and advanced courses in global entrepreneurship at the undergraduate and graduate, doctoral and executive (MBA, MSc, MA Management and PhD) levels. Such courses typically explore the opportunities that entrepreneurs create, encounter and change in the global and cross-cultural arena. They also examine how entrepreneurs adapt to and succeed in a global economy, and how institutional networks and availability of venture capital finance facilitate global and immigrant entrepreneurship.

This book complements existing titles to include such novel topics as types of immigrant entrepreneur and their role in the founding and growth of new, global start-ups. We also extend previous titles on comparative entrepreneurship and internationalization of small and medium enterprises to incorporate comparative venture capital, and internationalization of both rapidly growing entrepreneurial ventures and their providers of finance.

Broadly consistent with other introductory texts, we offer 15 chapters in this book. We have organized these chapters into three parts. The first part is about entrepreneurship and small firms, international development of entrepreneurship and innovation, and international entrepreneurship. Chapter 2 begins with introducing the concept and context of entrepreneurship. We outline the significance of entrepreneurship and small firms, identify forms of entrepreneurship and small firms, and explain theories of entrepreneurship. We outline the distinctive features of small firms and discuss the implications of those features for their growth.

Chapters 3 and 4 are devoted to a comparative development of entrepreneurship and innovation (Chapter 3), and local and regional systems of international entrepreneurship (Chapter 4). In Chapter 3, we use evidence from the Global Entrepreneurship Monitor to compare and contrast the global environment for the development of international entrepreneurship. Using illustrative examples, we evaluate the role of political, economic, socio-cultural and technological factors in the founding of new ventures in different countries. We also discuss key issues in drawing international comparisons of entrepreneurship. One of the paradoxes of global entrepreneurship is the equally important factor of the local and regional economic context for firms going global. The more global the new firm the stronger its presence in a local economy in the country in which it originates. We examine this paradox and study the local and regional factors that enhance the scope of globalization of both the firms and the locales of their start-up activities in Chapter 4.

Next, we examine the motivations and internationalization strategies of international entrepreneurs. We discuss alternative theoretical explanations for small firm internationalization in Chapter 5. Here, we outline the incidence and relevance of small firm internationalization, and compare and contrast three seminal theories of small firm internationalization. We then draw on the theoretical background outlined in this chapter to examine the factors influencing small firms' internationalization strategies in Chapter 6. First, we explain the core elements of small firms' internationalization strategy. Then we evaluate the factors influencing international entrepreneurs' choice of foreign market and entry mode strategies.

The second part of the book is devoted to immigrant entrepreneurship and global start-ups. One of the ways in which we can better understand immigrant entrepreneurship is by critically reviewing the role of migration in global economic and social development. In Chapter 7, we explore the migration issue, what enables and induces migrants to become entrepreneurs, what impedes their opportunity realization, and how they overcome barriers to engage in transnational activity. We subsequently elaborate on ethnic (Chapter 8), transnational (Chapter 9) and returnee (Chapter 10) entrepreneurs as the three types of immigrant entrepreneurs to emphasise the critical role that these entrepreneurs play in the global venturing landscape. In Chapter 8, we present an overview of migration and immigrant communities engaged in entrepreneurship in developed host countries. We outline the distinctive characteristics of ethnic entrepreneurs as a type of immigrant entrepreneur and evaluate alternative theoretical explanations for the emergence of immigrant enterprise. We also present evidence on the diversity of immigrant enterprise, and on the performance and impact of immigrant firms.

In Chapter 9, we review evidence related to the migration of skilled personnel in developed host countries. We identify the distinctive human and social capital resources of the new immigrant entrepreneurs. We also introduce transnational entrepreneurs as a type of new immigrant entrepreneur and review their motivations for the founding of their ventures in host and home countries. Finally, we discuss the performance and impact of the new immigrant and transnational entrepreneurs. We chart broad trends in, and discuss the drivers of, returnee entrepreneurship in Chapter 10. Using illustrative examples, we identify the distinctive human and social capital resources of returnee entrepreneurs and evaluate the role of these resources in venture creation before concluding with the issues of performance and impact.

Chapters 11 and 12 are about globalization, and INVs and global start-ups, respectively. In Chapter 11 we explore directly the phenomenon of globalization, its entrepreneurial contents and its disconnects. Understanding globalization is central to our appreciation of the new, path-breaking changes in how entrepreneurship obtains in the global landscape, and why appreciating the differences in contexts, global firm dynamics and policies is essential to a more nuanced analysis of global entrepreneurship. In Chapter 12, we draw on Oviatt and McDougall's (1994) seminal work to explain the phenomenon of rapid internationalization of new and small firms. We outline the distinguishing features of INVs and explain key elements of the theory of INVs. We then compare and contrast diverse types of INVs. Finally, we outline the distinguishing features of global start-ups.

No study on entrepreneurship and innovation is complete without a critical consideration of the value of new technologies, especially digitization, and their impact on global entrepreneurial endeavour. We study digitization and global entrepreneurship in

Chapter 13, navigating our way through a review of the digital technologies that spur on global entrepreneurship, the implications of the use of technologies for new firm formation and the structure of new firms. Crucially, we look at how digitization facilitates global connectivity of firms and other stakeholders in entrepreneurial, and across different global, ecosystems.

Finally, the last part of the book is focused on the supply of investment capital for rapidly growing small and new firms. In Chapter 14, we compare and contrast venture capital firms and business angels as formal and informal sources of equity finance, respectively, for high-growth prospects. We evaluate the significance of venture capital and discuss its role in the development of entrepreneurship. We introduce the topic of internationalization of venture capital/ private equity firms in Chapter 15. Here we chart broad trends in both the international development of VC and cross border flows of venture capital investment, and outline the reasons for the internationalization of VC firms. Finally, we review the challenges to VC firms in conducting investment operations in foreign markets.

References

Baumol, W.J. (2002) 'Entrepreneurship, innovation and growth: The David-Goliath symbiosis', *Journal of Entrepreneurial Finance*, 7(2): 1–10.

Bhattacharya, A., Khanna, D., Schweizer, C. and Bijapurkar, A. (2017) *Going Beyond the Rhetoric: The New Globalization*. Boston Consulting Group. Available at www.bcg.com/publications/2017/new-globalization-going-beyond-rhetoric (last accessed 20 July 2022).

Bosma, N. and Kelley, D. (2018) *Global Entrepreneurship Monitor 2018/2019 Global Report*. Santiago: Grafica Andes.

Desiderio, M.V. and Mestres-Domènech, J. (2011) 'Migrant entrepreneurship in OECD countries'. International Migration Outlook: SOPEMI. Available at www.oecd.org/els/mig/Part%20II_Entrepreneurs_engl.pdf (last accessed 27 September 2022).

Drori, I., Honig, B. and Wright, M. (2009) 'Transnational entrepreneurship: An emergent field of study', *Entrepreneurship Theory and Practice*, 33(5): 1001–1022.

Drucker, P.F. (1993) 'The rise of the knowledge society', *The Wilson Quarterly*, 17(2): 52–72.

Fairlie, R.W. and Lofstrom, M. (2014) 'Immigration and entrepreneurship', in B.R. Chiswick and P.W. Miller (eds.), *Handbook of the Economics of International Migration: The Impact*, Vol. 1. Oxford: North-Holland, pp. 877–911.

Gornall, W. and Strebulaev, I.A. (2015) 'The Economic Impact of Venture Capital: Evidence from Public Companies', *Stanford Graduate School of Business*, Working Paper No. 3362, 1–22.

Hansen, M.T. and Birkinshaw, J. (2007) 'The innovation value chain', *Harvard Business Review*, 85(6): 121.

Hunt, J. (2011) 'Which immigrants are most innovative and entrepreneurial? Distinctions by entry visa', *Journal of Labor Economics*, 29(3): 417–457.

Hunt, J. (2015) 'Are immigrants the most skilled US computer and engineering workers?' *Journal of Labor Economics*, 33(S1): S39–S77.

Ibeh, K., Dimitratos, P. and Johnson, J.E. (2004) 'Micromultinationals: Some preliminary evidence on an emergent "star" of the international entrepreneurship field', *Journal of International Entrepreneurship*, 2(4): 289–303.

International Finance Corporation (IFC) (2018) 'Sustainability report redefining development finance'. Available at www.ifc.org/wps/wcm/connect/3aa05003-d634-40f9-8af4-35b8c8a87248/IFC-AR18-Full-Report.pdf?MOD=AJPERES&CVID=moNw5we (last accessed 27 September 2022).

Iriyama, A., Li, Y. and Madhavan, R. (2010) 'Spiky globalization of venture capital investments: The influence of prior human networks', *Strategic Entrepreneurship Journal*, 4(2): 128–145.

Johnson, L. and Kimmelman, D. (2014) 'Migrant entrepreneurs: Building our businesses, creating our jobs'. A Report by Centre for Entrepreneurs and DueDil. Available at https://centreforentrepreneurs.org/cfe-research/creating-our-jobs/ (last accessed 27 September 2022).

Kerr, S.P., Kerr, W., Ozden, C. and Parsons, C. (2016) 'Global talent flows'. Working Paper 17-026, *Harvard Business School*, pp. 1–25.

National Venture Capital Association (NVCA) (2019) *Yearbook*. Data Provided by Pitchbook. Available at https://nvca.org/wp-content/uploads/2019/08/NVCA-2019-Yearbook.pdf (last accessed 27 September 2022).

Nazareno, J., Zhou, M. and You, T. (2019) 'Global dynamics of immigrant entrepreneurship: Changing trends, ethnonational variations, and reconceptualizations', *International Journal of Entrepreneurial Behaviour and Research*, 25(5): 780–800.

OECD (2017) 'Capitalizing on return migration by making it more attractive and sustainable', in OECD (ed.), *Interrelations between Public Policies, Migration and Development*. Paris: OECD Publishing. Available at http://doi.org/10.1787/9789264265615-12-en

Oviatt, B.M. and McDougall, P.P. (1994) 'Toward a theory of international new ventures', *Journal of International Business Studies*, 25(1): 45–64.

Oviatt, B.M. and McDougall, P.P. (2005) 'Defining international entrepreneurship and modeling the speed of internationalization', *Entrepreneurship Theory and Practice*, 29(5): 537–553.

PricewaterhouseCoopers. (2019) *PwC European Startup Survey: A Research Study of 18 startup hubs in Europe*. London: PricewaterhouseCoopers.

Saxenian, A. (2002) 'Silicon Valley's new immigrant high-growth entrepreneurs', *Economic Development Quarterly*, 16(1): 20–31.

Saxenian, A. and Sabel, C. (2008) 'Roepke lecture in economic geography venture capital in the "periphery": The new argonauts, global search, and local institution building', *Economic Geography*, 84(4): 379–394.

Shane, S. and Venkataraman, S. (2000) 'The promise of entrepreneurship as a field of research', *Academy of Management Review*, 25(1): 217–226.

Startup Genome. (2020) *The Global Startup Ecosystem Report 2020*. Startup Genome, 25 June. Available at https://www.statista.com/statistics/893954/number-fintech-startups-by-region/

Statista. (2020a) 'Number of Fintech startups worldwide from 2018 to February 2021, by region'. *Statista*, 17 March.

Statista. (2020b) 'Number of financial technology startups worldwide 2020, by industry'. *Statista*, 1 December. Available at https://www.statista.com/statistics/1056200/number-of-financial-technology-companies-worldwide-by-industry/

Statista. (2020c) 'Number of insurtech startups worldwide 2019, by business category'. *Statista*, 10 December. Available at https://www.statista.com/statistics/1056761/number-of-insurtech-startups-worldwide/

Statista. (2021) 'Market valuation of unicorns in Europe as of April 2021, by industry (in billion U.S. dollars)'. *Statista*, 11 January. Available at https://www.statista.com/statistics/1094241/market-valuation-unicorns-europe-by-industry/#:~:text=Published%20by%20Statista%20Research%20Department%2C%20Jan%2011%2C%202022,and%20telecommunications%20unicorns%20at%2026%20billion%20U.S.%20dollars

Tynaliev, U.M. and McLean, G.N. (2011) 'Labour migration and national human resource development in the context of post-Soviet Kyrgyzstan', *Human Resource Development International*, 14(2): 199–215.

USBA Office of Advocacy (2018) *Annual Report of the Office of Economic Research, FY 2017*. Available at www.sba.gov/advocacy/2018-small-business-profiles-states-and-territories (last accessed 27 September 2022).

Zahra, S.A. and George, G. (2002) 'International entrepreneurship: The current status of the field and future research agenda', in M.A. Hitt, R.D. Ireland, S.M. Camp and D.L. Sexton (eds.), *Strategic Entrepreneurship: Creating a New Mindset*. Oxford: Blackwell Publishers, pp. 255–288.

Zahra, S.A., Wright, M. and Abdelgawad, S.G. (2014) 'Contextualization and the advancement of entrepreneurship research'. *International Small Business Journal*, 32(5): 479–500.

Zhou, J. (2008) 'New look at creativity in the entrepreneurial process', *Strategic Entrepreneurship Journal*, 2(1): 1–5.

Zhou, Y. and Hsu, J.Y. (2010) 'Divergent engagements: Roles and strategies of Taiwanese and mainland Chinese returnee entrepreneurs in the IT industry', *Global Networks*, 11(3): 398–419.

Zolin, R. and Schlosser, F. (2013) 'Characteristics of immigrant entrepreneurs and their involvement in international new ventures', *Thunderbird International Business Review*, 55(3): 271–284.

2
ENTREPRENEURSHIP AND SMALL FIRMS

The focus on health and, in particular, on hygiene and sanitation, has never been so pronounced than in the grave situation of the COVID-19 global pandemic. Yet, the consequences of the lack of proper hygiene are dismal in more ways than one. According to the World Health Organization (WHO), about 16,000 children under the age of five die every day, a quarter of whom succumb to pneumonia and diarrhea, both of which are largely preventable with proper hygiene.

Source: images.pexels.com

Against this backdrop, the wastage of soap, a commodity that is taken for granted by most of us, could be deeply disturbing. Studies show that roughly around 5 million bars of soap per day are thrown away by hospitality establishments worldwide. Shawn Seipler, an entrepreneur, wondered about the fate of such used bars of soaps. He went ahead to understand more about the scale of soap wastage and came across the re-batching process to produce new soap out of old and used soap.

Shawn Seipler initially started out in his garage in Puerto Rico, where he cooked soap from discarded bars using readily available kitchen utensils. The initial cooking sessions raised suspicion among the police. After overcoming several ordeals, Seipler's dream company, Clean the World (CTW) was born.

(Continued)

CTW is based in Orlando and hosts around 20,000 volunteers who help in recycling soaps that consequentially reduce the waste at local landfills. Today, CTW partners with about 5,000 hotels in the US (20%). The list includes Disney's properties, most of the Vegas Strip, and a handful of establishments from New York and Chicago.

CTW has plants in locations such as Las Vegas, Hong Kong, Montreal, India and the largest one in Orlando. At these facilities, used soap bars are melted down to make new soap. These newly produced bars are then sent to impoverished countries. In 2016, CTW sent out 400,000 hygiene kits and made more than 7 million bars of soap.

Source: images.pexels.com

Source: pixabay.com

The hotels partnering with CTW pay 50 cents per room per month to recycle the toiletries. CTW provides logistics support for the pickup, delivery and shipping of the soaps. Moreover, the organization trains the housekeeping staff to separate the soap and put the bars in a special bin. Placards and information cards are placed in rooms to let the guests know how the unused soaps are changing the lives of less privileged individuals.

It is encouraging that CTW has been working towards recycling soaps for the last ten years. NGOs and charities like the Red Cross and Salvation Army are some of the recipients of boxes of new bars of soap produced by CTW. Many other companies are following in the footsteps of CTW and are pitching in toward this cause. In 2017, United Airlines decided to donate unused first-class items towards hygiene kits. CTW is also trying to partner with cruise lines and hospitals to reduce waste.

Although Seipler's company has come a long way in recycling soaps and has tracked with a worldwide decline in the number of child deaths, he believes that he has just scratched the surface and there is a lot more to be done to harness the full potential of the effort.

Source: adapted from Meltzer (2017)

Learning Outcomes

After studying this chapter, you should be ready to:

- **LO1**: Discuss the significance of entrepreneurship and small firms
- **LO2**: Explain the meaning, context, and forms of entrepreneurship and small firms
- **LO3**: Distinguish between entrepreneurial firms and small businesses as types of small firm
- **LO4**: Explain the theories of entrepreneurship
- **LO5**: Identify the distinctive features of small firms and assess their implications for small firms' growth

Introduction

Some years ago, economists predicted that small entrepreneurial businesses would be largely replaced by a much smaller number of large businesses. Despite the fact that large firms can benefit from economies of scale, especially in some industries, the exact opposite has happened. Entrepreneurial firms have found a renewed economic footing. In fact, they have grown very rapidly. Entrepreneurial businesses found new opportunities in the 1970s and early 1980s due to global competition and the decline of large multinational enterprises. They have since continued to thrive.

Entrepreneurship is often called the engine of the economy. In the US, small businesses have been the backbone of economic success. Since the 1970s, small businesses have provided 55% of all jobs and 66% of all net new jobs (USBA Office of Advocacy, 2018). Innovative entrepreneurs, or those who state that their products or services are new to all or some customers, and for which there are no or few competitors, substantially contribute to society. Examples include Facebook, Google, Amazon or Uber, whose services have become indispensable in our daily lives.

The population of malll firms is heterogeneous. Small firms are found in a variety of contexts. Not all small firms grow into large businesses. Entrepreneurs have varying motivations to found and grow new ventures, and these motivations have implications for the type of firms that they create.

In this chapter, we introduce the concept of entrepreneurship and describe the various contexts in which it exists. We also identify forms of entrepreneurship and small firms, and explain the theories of entrepreneurship to address the question of why individuals engage in entrepreneurship. Next, we identify the distinctive features of small firms, and assess the implications of those features for their growth. Finally, we discuss the significance of entrepreneurship and small firms.

Performance and Impact of Entrepreneurship and Small Firms

Small firms contribute to the economy and society. Small firms have significant wealth and job creation potential (Bosma and Kelley, 2018). Although small in size, small firms outnumber large firms and play a dominant role in the ability of nations to make economic progress. Additionally, entrepreneurs introduce innovations into their societies, contributing to the emergence and growth of industries.

Economic Impact

As a type of start-up firm, entrepreneurial firms are unique in terms of the growth aspirations of their founders, and hence their potential ability to grow. Small firms have the potential to grow into large firms that dominate world business, and hence provide substantial profits to their owners. There are countless stories of entrepreneurs who have grown their ventures into successful large firms in every community around the world (Bamford and Bruton, 2016).

In the US, for example, despite the fact that the self-employed make up fewer than 20% of workers, almost two-thirds of millionaires are self-employed. Close to 50% of these millionaires are entrepreneurs. Examples include Sergey Brin and Larry Page (Google), Bill Gates (Microsoft), Mark Zuckerberg (Facebook) and Richard Branson (Virgin).

The rapid growth potential of small firms is especially true of high-tech ventures that are often the foundations for global businesses. The failure rate of high-tech ventures is much lower than that of other new start-ups (MacKenzie and Jones-Evans, 2012). Every business in the Fortune 500, for example, started as a new venture (Bamford and Bruton, 2016). Each one was the brainchild of a single individual or a small group of people.

Entrepreneurs contribute to employment through job creation. According to Bosma and Kelley (2018), the Europe and North America regions demonstrate high-growth expectations among entrepreneurs, particularly in the US and Turkey. Entrepreneurship has the potential to contribute substantially to employment in these countries.

In the US, whereas big businesses have eliminated 4 million jobs since 1990, new entrepreneurial firms have added 8 million new jobs (Bamford and Bruton, 2016). Small businesses in the US accounted for 64% of the net new jobs created between 1993 and 2011 (Liberto, 2019). The Association for Enterprise Opportunity estimates that more than 25.1 million microenterprises with five or fewer employees contribute to 22% of all private employment in the US.

ECONOMIC IMPACT OF
SMALL BUSINESSES IN THE US

According to the United States Small Business Administration (USBA) Office of Advocacy (2018) (Figure 2.1):

- In 2014, the 600,000-plus franchised businesses in the US accounted for 40% of all retail sales and some 8 million jobs
- In 2015, US small businesses employed 58.9 million people, or 47.5% of the private workforce
- Firms with fewer than 100 employees have the largest share of small business employment. In 2015, small businesses created 1.9 million net jobs. Firms employing fewer than 20 employees experienced the largest gains, adding 1.1 million net jobs. The smallest gains were in firms employing 100 to 499 employees, which added 387,874 net jobs
- In 2018, small businesses provided 55% of all jobs and 66% of all net new jobs since the 1970s

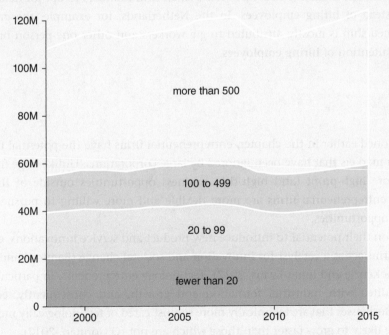

Figure 2.1   United States employment by business size (employees)

Source: USBA Office of Advocacy (2018)

The importance of SMEs is not limited to the US. SMEs contribute roughly 45% of total employment and 33% of GDP in the OECD countries. Between 2002 and 2012, SMEs created 77% of new jobs in Canada, nearly the same percentage as in most emerging economies.

As per Bosma and Kelley (2018), entrepreneurs in the Latin America and Caribbean region, Guatemala, Chile and Colombia expect to add six or more jobs in the next five years. The highest proportion of entrepreneurs expecting to create six or more jobs in the next five years (2020–25) are in the United Arab Emirates (UAE) and Colombia. Despite low rates of entrepreneurship, over half of entrepreneurs in the UAE project the highest level of job creation. This demonstrates that entrepreneurship can exert substantial impact even when it is less prevalent in a society.

At the same time, however, entrepreneurial firms have relatively lower job creation potential in some regions of the world. Except for Taiwan, the proportion of entrepreneurs with high-growth expectations in East and South Asia, for instance, is relatively low. The lack of qualified labor or constraints related to hiring and maintaining workers are some of the factors underlying this observation. It could also reflect work preferences or business models where, instead of hiring internally, entrepreneurs operate as part of a value network, often enabled by technology.

In other cases, incentive structures cause small firm founders to opt for flexible contracts instead of hiring employees. In the Netherlands, for example, the growth of entrepreneurship is mostly attributed to gig workers and other one-person businesses with no intention of hiring employees.

Societal Impact

As mentioned earlier in the chapter, entrepreneurial firms have the potential to garner profits in markets that have been ignored by large corporations. Unlike large firms that may ignore high-profit (and high-risk) business opportunities outside of their core domain, entrepreneurial firms are more flexible and more willing to pursue a wider range of opportunities.

Based on their potential to introduce new product and service innovations, entrepreneurial firms act as a catalyst for innovation and societal change (Bamford and Bruton, 2016; MacKenzie and Jones-Evans, 2012). Technology entrepreneurs, in particular, have been credited with industrial formation and growth, and consequently, economic growth. Businesses that are technically more sophisticated or technologically more innovative are likely to grow faster than those which are not (O'Gorman, 2012).

According to Bosma and Kelley (2018), innovative entrepreneurs, or those who state their products or services are new to all or some customers, and for which there are no or few competitors, substantially contribute to society in the US and Canada.

In Luxembourg and Chile, 48% of entrepreneurs, and 47% of entrepreneurs in India, report introducing new products or services through their ventures that are not generally offered by competitors.

At the same time, however, small firms face a number of disadvantages in trying to be innovative. The lack of financial, human and technical resources restricts the development of customer-driven innovations in small firms. Small firms, because of their financial and human constraints, might find it difficult to legally defend patents, and hence might be reluctant to invest in IP protection. As compared to large firms, small firms are more likely to be involved in patent-related litigations and court proceedings. However, due to their liabilities of newness, they have fewer repeated interactions with other parties, and hence fewer incentives to cooperatively solve issues.

It is also argued that in some industry sectors like biotechnology, firms of all sizes have similar propensities to innovate (Blackburn, 2003). Moreover, small firms remain less innovative than large firms in some countries. The advantages and disadvantages of small size for innovation are summarized in Table 2.1 below.

Table 2.1   Advantages and disadvantages of small firms for innovation

Advantages	Disadvantages
Entrepreneurial motivation and dynamism	Lack of scale and scope economies
Informal structure and organization	Financial constraints
Market proximity and informal customer relationships	Human resource constraints
	Lack of market control

Entrepreneurship and Entrepreneurs

The earliest use of the term **entrepreneurship** was in an economic context. It was used to refer to a class of economic actors who are financially dependent on others (Pittaway, 2012). They are set up with capital to conduct their enterprise, or are undertakers of their own labor without capital. **Entrepreneurs** are individuals who start new business ventures. Unlike employees who earn a living from directly working for someone else's business, entrepreneurs start their own business. They work for themselves. Unlike in large organizations where ownership is dissociated from control, entrepreneurs are both owners and managers of their own business. They own the profit that they earn, and may choose to reinvest it in the business or take it as payment.

Later thought evolved to define entrepreneurs as coordinators who act as intermediaries between the other agents of production, taking on the risk and uncertainty inherent in the process. The word entrepreneur is a French word that is derived from two words: 'Entre' and 'Prendre'. 'Entre' means 'risk' and 'prendre' means 'to take'. The word 'entrepreneur' was used to describe someone who undertook any project that entailed risk.

According to the French economist, Jean Baptiste Say, entrepreneurs 'add value to scarce resources'. Resources are inputs that are used to produce products or services. Entrepreneurs share the common goal of capturing sustained value from the use of scarce resources. They are actors who make profits as a reward in return for the risk and uncertainty that they undertake for coordinating production.

According to Schumpeter's seminal idea of **creative destruction**, entrepreneurs introduce innovations to the market. They make possible 'new combinations' of production. These new combinations take the form of introduction of a new good or a new quality of a good to the market; introduction of a new method of production; opening a new market; developing a new source of supply or raw materials or half-manufactured goods; or the carrying out of a new organization of any industry.

In introducing innovations, entrepreneurs destroy existing markets and create new ones. New technologies, new kinds of products, new methods of production and new means of distribution make old ones obsolete, forcing existing companies to quickly adapt to a new environment or fail. Schumpeter's idea of creative destruction is considered to be the vital force behind capitalism. Punctuated by long and short waves, major advances occur every 50 or 100 years bringing a new set of technologies and industries into existence.

Small Firms: Context and Forms

A key element of entrepreneurship is ownership; however, paths to business ownership are varied. People can be entrepreneurial in many different ways and in multiple contexts (Bosma and Kelley, 2018). Whereas **solo entrepreneurs** operate on their own, without any co-founders, others co-found ventures in teams. Often, solo entrepreneurs have no intention to employ others.

Novice entrepreneurs are individuals with no prior or minority or majority firm ownership experience, either as a firm founder or as purchaser of an independent firm, who currently own a minority or majority equity stake in an independent firm that is either new or purchased (Wright et al., 2012). In contrast, **habitual entrepreneurs** hold or have held a minority or majority ownership stake in two or more firms, at least one of which was established or purchased. Habitual entrepreneurs are fairly young when they start their first business, and have accumulated more diverse resource pools than novice entrepreneurs, which can impact their subsequent behavior and performance.

They also tend to be more highly educated and have higher levels of managerial human capital than novice entrepreneurs.

Some individuals start their ventures from the **ground up**. Creating a new venture from the ground up means starting it from scratch, that is, identifying an innovative new business opportunity, and acquiring the necessary resources to develop it. Amazon, Facebook, Microsoft, Sun Microsystems and Google are examples of how promising ideas developed in this manner have transformed into high-growth ventures.

Others may **buy** an existing company, secure **franchise rights**, **license** or **purchase** critical technology or methods, or even **inherit** a company. Each of these forms provides incomes to individuals and their families and contributes to national economies.

Initially, the context of entrepreneurship was narrowly defined to include new venture creation in an independent context. Since the 1990s and 2000s, the entrepreneurial context has been expanded to include corporate entrepreneurship, technology entrepreneurship and social entrepreneurship. All these approaches hold in common the Schumpeterian notion that entrepreneurship is an innovative process. However, the entrepreneurial processes of each are very different from those used in many established businesses.

As against starting up new ventures in an independent context, individuals can also start up as employees of large organizations. **Corporate entrepreneurship** refers to formal or informal activities aimed at creating new products or businesses, new business models or international organization structures in established companies through product and process innovations and market developments. Thus, corporate entrepreneurship is the infusion of entrepreneurship thinking into large bureaucratic structures.

Corporate entrepreneurship is also called 'intrapreneurship'. An **intrapreneur** is an employee of a large organization who has the entrepreneurial qualities of drive, creativity, vision and ambition but who prefers, if possible, to remain within the security of an established company (Tseng and Tseng, 2019). Unlike in an independent context, employees of large organizations have access to financial and human capital resources from the organization to develop their ideas. At the same time, however, the lack of flexibility, ownership or commitment to the business on the part of the organization poses barriers to corporate entrepreneurship.

Large firms like GE and Motorola are increasingly employing entrepreneurial thinking to enhance their futures. Known for brands like Scotch tapes, Scotch-Brite, cleaning products, and Post-it repositionable products, 3M (Minnesota Manufacturing and Mining Corporation) is an excellent example of corporate entrepreneurship. More than 75,000 3M employees work at the company to create more than 500 new products every year. The company is recognized as one of 'America's Most Admired

Corporations'. During 1985–2000, 3M appeared on the Fortune top-three rankings for innovativeness more often than all other companies except Rubbermaid. Additionally, in 1995, 3M was awarded the National Medal of Technology, the US government's top award for innovation.

Underlying the company's great success is a corporate culture that promotes intrapreneurship by tolerating failure and rewarding success (see Box below). Also compelling are its policies and philosophy such as the 15% Option and 30% Rule. Equal advancement opportunities through both technical and management career ladders and the availability of seed capital from the parent company to develop new product ideas at the business unit level are other incentives.

FOSTERING INNOVATION AT 3M: SELECTED POLICIES AND PHILOSOPHIES

15 Percent Option

Employees spend 15% of the week pursuing their choice of individual projects without disclosing or justifying to manager

30 Percent Rule

30% of business unit revenue comes from products less than four years old

Dual Ladder Career Path

Employees can follow technical or management career paths with equal advancement opportunities to stay focused on research and professional interests

Seed Capital

Product inventors can request seed capital from Business Units or Genesis Grant worth up to $50,000

Tolerance for Failure

Team members are guaranteed their previous jobs if the venture does not succeed

Rewards for Success

Employees receive raises, promotions, and recognitions like The Golden Step Award when the ventures achieve expected goals

Source: adapted from Achtmeyer, W.F. (2002) '3M corporation'. William F. Achtmeyer Center for Global Leadership, Tuck School of Business at Dartmouth, No. 2-0002. Available at http://mba.tuck.dartmouth.edu/pages/faculty/chris.trimble/osi/downloads/20002_3M.pdf (last accessed 27 September 2022).

3M offers multiple avenues for individuals to obtain the seed capital necessary to pursue their innovative ideas. With business units required to contribute towards innovation projects, employees are free to pitch their ideas to any business unit and request a grant. The company also offers seed capital in the form of a Genesis Grant of up to $50,000 for about 90 ideas every year in the field of research, product development and test marketing. After obtaining the grant, the employee behind the idea, or the product 'champion', can choose the team to develop the product.

3M believes that failures are mere teachers, hence the company does not penalize its employees for any failed ideas. They can return to their previous jobs in such situations. Sometimes, failed products lay the foundations for innovations in a different field. For example, an adhesive project that failed for not being strong enough resulted in the birth of Post-it notes.

The firm rewards deserving employees by offering raises, promotions and recognitions. The Golden Step award is presented to the products that create revenue worth $2 million in the US or $4 million globally. Furthermore, the Carlton award, commonly known as The Nobel Prize of 3M, celebrates employees who contribute towards breakthrough technical innovations. Each new product that surpasses the sales target gets its own department for development. After exceeding another cut-off, a separate business unit, led by the product 'champion', is formed which gets split up once the profit reaches $200 to $300 million.

Source: adapted from Achtmeyer (2002)

Dyson, the company famous for vacuums and hand dryers, is another excellent example of a company that is in the business of making things. The company has a history of inventing new ways to build common devices that we use every day. Recently (early 2020), the company moved remarkably fast to make ventilators to help fight the COVID-19 global pandemic (see Box below).

COVID-19 AND DYSON: INNOVATING QUICKLY TO SOLVE A BIG PROBLEM

The grave COVID-19 pandemic in early 2020 strained the health care system as thousands of patients daily battled for life in hospitals around the world. The disease also led to a sudden growth in demand for life-sustaining devices like ventilators. Ventilators are sophisticated life-support systems that enable critically ill patients to breathe. However, these devices are also complicated to build. Governments predicted that it

(Continued)

would take weeks, if not months, to fill gaps in demand. Yet, the luxury of time was not something anyone could afford given the life and death situation confronting many COVID-19 patients.

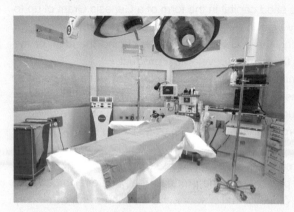

A UK-based company, Dyson, rose to the challenge by designing and building ventilators in a short period of time. Dyson collaborated with a Cambridge-based science and innovation company, The Technology Partnership, to introduce a battery-operated and bed-mounted ventilator 'CoVent' for use in makeshift hospitals around the world. The device was swiftly manufactured on a large scale.

Source: www.needpix.com

Its efficiency was tested in various clinical settings to address the specific needs of COVID-19 patients.

These ventilators were largely useful in places facing an extreme shortage of beds. Dyson received an order for 10,000 units from the UK government and the company planned to donate several units to other countries as well.

It is remarkable that a company like Dyson, known for innovative products like vacuum cleaners and hairstyling solutions, was able to solve a problem of such magnitude in a crisis situation.

Source: adapted from Aten (2020)

In this textbook, we focus on entrepreneurs who are engaged in starting up and growing their businesses from the ground up in an independent context, either solo or with others.

Technology entrepreneurship refers to entrepreneurship in the technologically advanced industries (MacKenzie and Jones-Evans, 2012). It entails the creation of new, independent, technology-based ventures, or spin-offs from either university departments or large organizations.

Technology entrepreneurs are a combination of inventors and entrepreneurs. Typically, technical entrepreneurs have a degree of technical expertise, and related skills and experience. They may have invented new processes or products. In addition, they have an entrepreneurial side to them, which enables them to bring this experience to the market in the form of their new organization. To that end, the lack of management experience of technical entrepreneurs can pose a constraint to their ability to commercialize new innovations.

Technology entrepreneurs can be found in a number of different industries and environments. James Watt and Abraham Lincoln are perhaps two of the oldest technical entrepreneurs who introduced the steam engine and telephone, respectively. More recent examples include Larry Page, co-founder, Google, and Jeff Bezos, founder, Amazon.

Social entrepreneurship entails solving a social problem for the wider good. Social problems may be such problems as poverty, lack of food, or potable drinking water (Chalmers and Fraser, 2012). Whereas traditional enterprises create value for their customers, social ventures create value for the community. Success, in turn, is measured by the creation of societal wealth rather than economic wealth of traditional enterprises.

Social entrepreneurs operate at the nexus of the government, civil society and the market to create sustainable solutions for both global and niche social problems. They play the role of change agents in the social sector by adopting a mission to create and sustain social (not just private) value. They recognize and relentlessly pursue new opportunities to serve that mission, engaging in the process of continuous innovation, adaptation and learning, and acting boldly without being limited by the resources currently in hand.

Social entrepreneurs are so passionate about the social cause driving their ventures that they wish for the underlying problem to be eradicated someday, which would effectively mean the end of their business. Also influential in social entrepreneurship is the role of funders of social entrepreneurship, some of whom have successful commercial and technological backgrounds. Bill Gates (Bill & Melinda Gates Foundation), Larry Page and Sergey Brin (Google.org), and Jeff Skoll (Skoll Foundation), are some well-known examples.

Although social entrepreneurship is more about creating social impact rather than making a profit, sometimes there exists a dual tension between profits and mission in social ventures. Thus, social ventures are conceptualized on a continuum, ranging from purely charitable businesses to for-profit and commercial ventures. Between each extreme are a multitude of organizational forms and structures that blend varying levels of economic and socially driven activity.

Social enterprises, for example, serve a social mission but with a profit motive. Social enterprises fulfil needs that are simultaneously unmet by existing institutions and are unattractive to the market. They do so by adopting revenue-generating business models of commercial entrepreneurship. Their primary goal is to meet social needs, but for a profit. Thus, they have the dual goal of achieving beneficial returns for society as well as profitability. Featured in the opening profile, Clean The World is a social enterprise.

Another form of social entrepreneurship is **green entrepreneurship**. Green entrepreneurship refers to enterprise activities that avoid harm to the environment or help to protect the environment in some way (Saari and Joensuu-Salo, 2019). Green entrepreneurship can create jobs as well as generate new entrepreneurship opportunities. In either form, the goal of green entrepreneurship is to conserve natural resources and save money. It helps to increase energy efficiency, decrease harm to workers' health and enable existing or new businesses to tap into new sources of funding. Known as ecopreneurs, green entrepreneurs identify environmental innovations and their market opportunity and successfully implement those innovations resulting in new products and services.

Green entrepreneurship can be seen as a focal component of sustainable development. According to the World Commission on Environment and Development (WCED, 1987), sustainable development is an attempt to reconcile economic growth with environmental and social issues. It seeks to resolve the environmental problems of affluence and the social problems of poverty within a transformed approach to the process of development. Therefore, a concept typically used in the context of green entrepreneurship is the triple bottom line, which refers to economic, environmental and social as the three pillars of sustainability.

The term 'entrepreneurial firms' is sometimes used interchangeably with '**small businesses**'. Although both are small firms, they are not the same. Entrepreneurship focuses more on the context (e.g. start-up process) where innovative effort is required. As discussed above, entrepreneurship is applied to multiple entrepreneurial contexts – e.g. new venture creation, corporate, technology or social ventures.

'Small business', in contrast, focuses on established small firms that may not fit any of these categories. A **small business** is defined by the United States Small Business Administration's (USBA's) Office of Advocacy as having fewer than 500 employees and selling less than $5 million worth of products and services annually (USBA, 2018). The Internal Revenue Service classifies small businesses as companies with assets of $10 million or less, and large businesses as those with over $10 million in assets (Liberto, 2019). Examples of small businesses include a corner grocery or bakery shop, a neighborhood restaurant, a laundromat, a dry-cleaning shop or a lawn-mowing company.

Whereas corporate America has been downsizing, the number of small businesses in the US has increased 49% since 1982. As per USBA (2018), 30.2 million small businesses in the US comprise:

- 99.9% of all US firms
- 99.7% of all US firms with paid employees
- 47.5% of private sector employees
- 40.8% of private sector payroll

In this textbook, we use the term small firms to refer to both entrepreneurial firms and small businesses.

Theories of Entrepreneurship

Entrepreneurs have varied motivations to start a business. Several theories of entrepreneurship, namely personality, psycho-sociological and cognitive theories, have been proposed to explain why some individuals are entrepreneurs compared to others.

Personality Theory

According to the **personality theory**, individual characteristics of personality influence opportunity recognition. Individuals are likely to be entrepreneurs because of their personality. Entrepreneurs are 'born', not 'made'.

According to Vas Bhandarkar, serial entrepreneur and founder of multiple ventures in enterprise software and mobile/ internet space in the US, the 'restlessness' in his personality and incessant desire to 'change the world' played an important role in motivating him to start up:

> Entrepreneurship is in your genes. I think that there was that certain restlessness in your personality that causes you to be an entrepreneur. You are never satisfied with your status quo. I think an entrepreneur wants to change the world, have an impact on the world. That's an entrepreneur. That partly motivates me. (Vas Bhandarkar, Founder, Global Logic, California)[1]

Earlier research focused on two personality traits that were linked to the propensity to be a successful entrepreneur. These are the **locus of control** and **risk-taking propensity** (Delmar and Witte, 2012). Whereas the former refers to the extent to which individuals attribute events to factors within their control (as opposed to external, environmental factors), the latter implies the willingness to assume risks in the entrepreneurial process and venture into the unknown.

The risk of failure is one major drawback of entrepreneurship. About one in five new businesses fails in the first eight years of its founding. Another third close because entrepreneurs become discouraged and give up. Entrepreneurs risk losing not only their own money, but also the financial investment of others. Individuals who have a higher internal locus of control and higher willingness to take risks are more likely to be entrepreneurs.

Studies have also considered other personality traits such as the **desire for independence/autonomy** and **need for creativity**. Entrepreneurs desire to be their own boss. Studies have established that the motivations of entrepreneurs are largely concerned with their professional contentment and being their own boss rather than profit-seeking. Technology entrepreneurs, in particular, are motivated by the desire for autonomy, besides the wish to exploit a market opportunity.

Entrepreneurship gives individuals freedom and flexibility regarding the use of their time and setting of their own work schedule. Unlike employees, entrepreneurs make their own decisions; they are not forced to take orders from someone else. They can create a work environment that reflects their values. They may hire others to do the tasks they may not themselves like or are not so good at. Bill Gates, for example, liked to design software. Therefore, he hired people to manage Microsoft's operations and to market and sell its products.

---

[1]Quotes from entrepreneurs throughout are from the authors' own research.

Some entrepreneurs feel that they can control their future, taking an active role in directing their companies through their strategic vision and controlling their time – a particularly important factor for female entrepreneurs (Bamford and Bruton, 2016). In reality, although entrepreneurs have the flexibility to choose their work hours, they end up investing very long hours into their business on a daily basis. As a result, entrepreneurs often experience stress in their personal lives. Long hours of work take a toll on their health, as well as on their relationships with other friends and family.

Entrepreneurship is a **creative** endeavor. It allows the possibility for entrepreneurs to exercise creativity in what they do. Entrepreneurs get a **strong sense of fulfillment** from founding something from scratch and seeing it grow and mature into a successful business. According to Barringer and Ireland (2016), passion for the business is one of the key characteristics of successful entrepreneurs. Successful entrepreneurs are passionate about their business and excited and fulfilled by their work. They are motivated by the need to reach their full potential.

Although useful as a starting point to think about the motivations of entrepreneurs, there are some shortcomings of personality theory. There is no conclusive evidence of which of the many personality traits explains entrepreneurial behavior (Delmar and Witte, 2012). Studies exploring traits use varied samples. They often struggle to define the entrepreneur in a common way and find it difficult to justify the criteria used to define 'entrepreneurial success'.

Psycho-Sociological Theory

According to the psycho-sociological theory of entrepreneurship, not all entrepreneurs start a new business for positive, pull-based factors. Entrepreneurs are displaced or socially marginal people who have been supplanted from their familiar way of life and have somehow been forced into an entrepreneurial way of life due to their circumstances (Delmar and Witte, 2012). Although displacement comes from both positive and negative forces, it is typically attributed to negative, external forces, which are beyond the power of the individual to influence.

For technical entrepreneurs, for example, **disgruntlement** is often a motivation to start up. Becoming disillusioned with their previous employment or being forced into entrepreneurship due to a tight labor market are among the push factors. Often, redundancy or a period of unemployment forces individuals into self-employment as an answer to their period of difficulty.

Vikas Vij, a UK-based founder of Ideas Exchange, cited dissatisfaction as a reason for first starting his own entrepreneurial venture. Vikas qualified as a chartered accountant in the UK. His first job after graduation was at Arthur Anderson, followed by Prudential in the UK. Both firms were known for their work in the areas of strategy and finance, but Vikas did not enjoy it. He did not wish to do the work despite the high salary earned.

No, I didn't really like the finance or corporate tax work, or career option of being a chartered accountant. I couldn't imagine doing that for the rest of my life... despite the security of good pay and career prospects, and all that corporate stuff. I didn't want to do that forever. (Vikas Vij, Founder, Ideas Exchange, UK)

Vikas decided to try something completely different after gaining five years of work experience. He teamed up with a friend to start a company called mypencil.com, a one-stop solution for corporates to obtain all their office requirements, including stationery, IT equipment and printing.

Cognitive Theory

Cognitive theories of entrepreneurship propose that entrepreneurs **perceive market gaps** or identify **unnoticed opportunities** (Kirzner, 1973). They recognize the opportunity to start a business that other people may not have noticed. Thus, entrepreneurship is not only the propensity to efficiently pursue goals, but also the drive and alertness required to identify which goals to pursue in the first place.

According to Jeffry Timmons, skillful entrepreneurs can shape and create opportunities where others see little or nothing – or see too early or late. Thus, **opportunity recognition** is a cognitive process. Entrepreneurs observe political, economic, social and technological trends in the environment to spot gaps between what is available and what is possible (Barringer and Ireland, 2016). Sometimes, entrepreneurs recognize problems and find ways to solve those problems. Solutions could be to personal problems arising from daily life (e.g. Dropbox), problems due to advances in technology (e.g. antivirus software) or problems associated with emerging trends (e.g. security).

For VS Joshi, founder, TrintMe, an online dating app, finding a solution to a personal problem motivated venture creation (Pruthi, 2016). The idea for TrintMe was born at an alumni meeting in Mountain View, California, when one of Joshi's former classmates wondered why Joshi had never asked her out while at college. At that moment, Joshi realized he had missed an opportunity. Two individuals who had the same feelings for each other had not been able to express themselves because of the fear of rejection. Joshi developed an application, TrintMe, to solve the problem.

Yet, alertness is largely a learned, rather than an innate, skill. People who are more knowledgeable in an area, for instance, are more alert to opportunities in that area than others. Therefore, cognitive theories draw attention to entrepreneurs' **human capital** such as **education** and **prior experience** as key factors influencing their ability to identify opportunities. Some earlier studies show that entrepreneurs have comparatively fewer qualifications than the general working population (Delmar and Witte, 2012). However, on average, technical entrepreneurs are more highly educated than other types of entrepreneurs.

Both **prior work experience** and **prior start-up experience** influence opportunity recognition. Various researchers have shown that previous work experience can be a major factor in influencing the success of start-ups. Prior industry-specific experience, for example, provides knowledge about the gaps in that industry, and hence potential business opportunities to exploit those gaps. Ravi Kulasekaran, a California-based founder of Stridus, discovered the opportunity for his first entrepreneurial venture, Simplify, while working at Oracle Corporation. He was 'baffled' as to why the ERP (Enterprise Resource Planning) implementation process was so time consuming and expensive, and lacked integration with another application. He also discovered that the clients he serviced at Oracle faced a constant challenge of retaining their internal IT staff who often left in search of better opportunities. He teamed up with one of his colleagues to solve the problem and develop a solution to standardize the implementation of ERP software in organizations. The software led to a significant reduction of IT infrastructure, and Ravi and his team captured 60% of the mid-market business in Silicon Valley, also serving clients nationwide.

SIMPLIFY: ROLE OF PRIOR WORK EXPERIENCE IN OPPORTUNITY RECOGNITION

Ravi Kulasekaran took a master's in Manufacturing Systems Engineering with a thesis in semiconductor packaging at Lehigh University, Pennsylvania, USA. A few years after graduating, he took up a position at Oracle Corporation. Ravi's job in the consulting division at Oracle was to implement the Oracle Applications ERP solution for clients. During the first two years of working in this role, Ravi could not comprehend why the implementation process was so time consuming and expensive. Clients desired a customized solution and integration with other applications, which was deemed as an 'additional piece of work' by the service providers. He also discovered that the clients he serviced faced a constant challenge of retaining their internal IT staff who often left in search of better opportunities.

At that time, several new companies were being formed and the internet had just taken off, making it possible to remotely manage applications. Ravi thought of a better way to implement the software solution and teamed up with a colleague to start his first venture, Simplify. The idea of Simplify was to standardize the implementation of ERP software in organizations. Ravi and his co-founder provided a turnkey solution to clients through their application. They helped them to install and configure the software, after which they provided maintenance and follow-up support services at a predictable price.

Ravi proposed to become an IT partner, rather than just a service provider, which meant building deeper relationships with clients on an ongoing basis. He and his team took it upon themselves to deal with Oracle Support to resolve problems reported by the client. Additionally, he offered a breadth of expertise in areas as diverse as supply chain planning and management, financials, human resources, manufacturing, sales and marketing, and customer relationship management, each of which needed starkly different skill sets in order to be effective.

Ravi also aimed to bring down costs by way of standardization. Customers were given multiple pre-set options from which to select, and consultants were put through several implementation cycles in order to enhance their expertise and knowledge sharing capabilities between multiple projects. Such standardization of procedures helped to ensure that the installation process and functioning of the software were not highly dependent on the skills of the specific persons who installed the application.

The solution brought a paradigm shift in the marketplace because of an innovative approach to delivery and accurate projections of demand. The services led to a significant reduction of IT infrastructure as it eliminated the need for organizations to invest in hardware or huge data centers for storing data. As the company gained traction, Ravi and his team captured 60% of the mid-market business in Silicon Valley and several clients nationwide.

Prior to founding MallforAfrica (www.mallforafrica.com) and MallfortheWorld, an online e-commerce company that enables US and UK e-commerce sites and brands to reach and sell to individuals and companies in Africa, Chris Folayan was the CEO of OCFX Inc., an application, web development and design company focused on converting web or application ideas and needs from concept to actual product. With over 20 years of web, application and multimedia game design and development experience in both large and small firms serving clients like Adobe, Quantum, Cisco and Sony, he helped launch many start-ups prior to the founding of his first venture. Additionally, Chris founded and owned many web-based income-generating companies, patenting work of his own and helping companies develop patent worthy applications, which contributed to the launch of his own ventures.

Using data from CPS (Current Population Survey), Lazear (2004) hypothesizes that entrepreneurs are generalists who are good at a variety of skills, although not necessarily excellent at any one. As the Box below shows, individuals who take up a variety of jobs in the current gig and sharing economy represent a pool of potential entrepreneurs ready to start their own ventures.

POTENTIAL ENTREPRENEURS IN THE GIG AND SHARING ECONOMY

The **gig economy** is about finding online or on-site service jobs (such as translations, deliveries or dog-sitting) via internet-based platforms, whereas the **sharing economy** is about making available to others parts of one's own goods and services, possibly for money. People may be employed elsewhere, but supplement their income with gigs or sharing. Although often facilitated with app-based platforms, gig and sharing options can operate without technology applications.

According to the GEM Adult Population Survey (Bosma and Kelley, 2018), the highest rate of gig and sharing economy activity is in the Republic of Korea, with one in every five adults involved in such activities. Israel, Chile, Ireland and the United States also report high rates of involvement in the gig and sharing economy. High gig rates are also seen in a low-income country like Sudan. In contrast, gig entrepreneurs are nearly absent in some other low-income countries like Indonesia and Madagascar that otherwise display high entrepreneurial activity.

As per Bosma and Kelley (2018), many gig workers have intentions to start a business in the near future, or are, in fact, setting up a business. Gig workers thus represent an interesting pool of potential entrepreneurs.

Source: Bosma and Kelley (2018)

The relative lack of business skills of technology entrepreneurs is one of their greatest weaknesses (MacKenzie and Jones-Evans, 2012). Although the majority of high-tech firms are founded by engineers and scientists, and in-depth knowledge of technology is a source of strength, the lack of familiarity with business and managerial skills of these entrepreneurs constrains their ability to commercialize their innovations.

By virtue of their prior business ownership experience, habitual entrepreneurs, who currently own multiple ventures, or have owned at least one venture prior to their current venture, are more alert to opportunities than novice (or first time) entrepreneurs (Wright et al., 2012). Based on their experience, habitual entrepreneurs are more likely to become experts in processing information relating to potential entrepreneurial opportunities. In contrast, inexperienced, novice entrepreneurs with less market knowledge are more likely to engage in extensive searches to identify opportunities.

According to De Vries (1977), entrepreneurial behavior can also be linked to individuals' family life and early family relationships. Familial influence, along with education and prior entrepreneurial experience, plays a particularly important role for technology entrepreneurs (MacKenzie and Jones-Evans, 2012). Much of the literature suggests that owner-founders tend to have fathers who are themselves entrepreneurs, and this is a major factor influencing the decision of their children to enter into entrepreneurship.

Research findings on entrepreneurial alertness are mixed. Some researchers believe that alertness goes beyond noticing things and involves a more purposeful effort. For example, one scholar concludes that the crucial difference between entrepreneurs and non-finders is their relative assessments of the marketplace. Compared to other individuals, entrepreneurs are better at sizing up the marketplace and inferring the likely implications.

Financial rewards, moreover, can be a strong motivator for entrepreneurship. Founders of salary-substitute businesses, for instance, are driven by the need to earn an income that can substitute their earnings from a full-time job. Such entrepreneurs use the income from their businesses to fund gaps in household income, pay for college or support extraordinary expenses through their business endeavors.

At the same time, however, not all entrepreneurs are motivated by money (Wright et al., 2012). Monetary reasons may be more important for first-time entrepreneurs, but less so in subsequent ventures, particularly if owners of second or later ones generally desire less novel ventures.

Small Firms: Distinctive Features and Implications

Small firms have distinctive **quantitative** and **qualitative** characteristics. The **quantitative** aspects of small firms refer to the small number of employees and small initial capital requirements.

Small and Medium-Sized Enterprises (SMEs) is a widely used term in the context of small businesses, especially by the European Union (EU), the United Nations and the World Trade Organization. SMEs are businesses that maintain revenues, assets or number of employees below a certain threshold (Liberto, 2019). In the US, SMEs are frequently referred to as **small-to-mid-size businesses**. Elsewhere, in Kenya, they go by the name MSME, short for micro, small and medium-sized enterprises, and in India, the term MSMED, or micro, small and medium enterprise development, is used.

Each country has its own definition of what constitutes an SME. Certain size criteria must be met and, occasionally, the industry in which the company operates is also taken into account. As per the EU, an SME is a company with fewer than 50 employees and a medium-sized enterprise is one with fewer than 250 employees.

In the US, the SBA classifies small businesses according to their ownership structure, number of employees, earnings and industry. For example, in manufacturing, an SME is a firm with 500 or fewer employees. However, businesses that mine copper ore and nickel ore can have up to 1,500 employees and still be identified as an SME.

Most small businesses are founded as **microenterprises**, which are defined as businesses with five or fewer employees (typically, microenterprises employ up to ten employees), initial capitalization requirements of less than $50,000, and the habitual operational involvement of the owner (USBA, 2018). Like the EU, however, the US distinctly classifies companies with fewer than ten employees as a small-office-home-office (SOHO). According to the SBA, more than 60% of all US firms are SOHO, having four or fewer employees.

Small firms are also **qualitatively** different from large firms. Although the core principles of running a large and small business are the same, the operations of a small firm are not the same as those of a large one. This is because of differences in the nature of ownership and control. Unlike in large firms where ownership is dissociated from control and owners delegate responsibility to professional managers, small firm owner-founders are also managers who are themselves responsible for the conduct of various functions within the firm. Thus, small firms also have an informal culture as they are not burdened by bureaucracy, policies and procedures, unlike their large firm counterparts (Bamford and Bruton, 2016).

Although they can be run by successor owners, or franchisees, and are often registered with local, state and federal agencies, small businesses are typically **family businesses** that are owned and/or operated by founder-entrepreneurs and successive generations of family members. Thus, as different from entrepreneurial firms, small business typically refers to routine business experience, that is, running a small business (Haworth and Hamilton, 2012). The unit of analysis in small business research is the firm as opposed to the individual entrepreneur, and research is typically focused on key aspects of managerial practice (e.g. marketing or human resource management) inside a small firm or key contextual issues that may impact small firms.

The unique quantitative and qualitative features of small firms have implications for how operations are run, and for their dealings with various stakeholders such as employees and customers. The distinctive features of small firms also have implications for their growth. As explained below, small size has both advantages and disadvantages for growth.

Advantages of Small Size

As compared to large firms whose strengths are mainly material, arising from economies of scale and scope due to financial and technological resources, the strengths of small firms are mostly behavioral in terms of entrepreneurial motivation and dynamism, informal structure and organization, and proximity to the market. These strengths translate into greater potential for innovation, more opportunities for progression, and greater influence over customers' behavior.

Entrepreneurial Motivation and Dynamism

Large firms typically ignore business opportunities if they believe the results are not likely to yield profit. In contrast, entrepreneurial firms have the potential to garner profits in markets that have been ignored by large corporations (Bamford and Bruton, 2016). Thus, they offer a high potential for innovation. This is because of the founder's willingness to take risks and garner necessary resources to realize their ideas. By virtue of the owner-founders' passion for the product/service idea, entrepreneurial firms are more willing to pursue a wider range of opportunities as compared to small firms. They are also able to exercise cost-control in production.

Informal Structure and Organization

Most small firms are characterized by a 'simple structure' (Mintzberg, 1979). Typically, owner-founders are actively involved in the founding of their businesses and the direct production or provision of services. As key decision makers, they also play a significant role in the day-to-day management of their businesses and the growth of their firms. Therefore, their personality traits, skills and attitudes are influential in the growth path of small firms. The benefit of the simple structure is that entrepreneurs are in close contact with the key issues of the business, and 'on the spot' in dealing with problems, and maintaining quality standards through direct supervision and control. As compared to their larger counterparts, small firms can also more easily implement an informal culture based on socialization and teamwork.

Sometimes, small firms offer more opportunities for progression by virtue of the small size of their top management team, and the need to quickly replace people in the event of a layoff. Manish Chandra, Founder, Poshmark, an online platform for buying and selling fashion, chose to join a start-up, an innovative, small database company located in Berkeley, California, as a young engineer. He was attracted to its urban location in Berkeley at a time when there was no technology industry in San Francisco. He recalled that the start-up ran out of cash every now and then, even though it was a small, 80-person company. It also had high turnover, having laid off 20% of the workforce at the time of Manish's joining the company. Yet, the set-up presented an excellent opportunity for progression. Manish was able to quickly fill a leadership gap and progress to team leader within a year of joining the company, which presented a rapid path of progression for him:

> There were four database companies. I had offers from all four. I chose the database company that was the most innovative in its technology… they were an 80-person company… I joined this company. I was a young engineer. They had just laid off a bunch of people which means there was a whole vacuum for

leadership. I was quickly able to go from a 20-something fresher to becoming a team leader within a year. That whole set of processes led to a lot of rapid progression. (Manish Chandra, Founder, Poshmark, California)

Market Proximity and Informal Customer Relationships

Without corporate layers of management and public stakeholders, new and small firms are free to put all their energy into satisfying the needs of their customers. Small business owners, for instance, are able to exert influence over their customers' purchasing behavior based on informal relationships with them. The success of small firms often occurs because they are simply more focused on their customers than their large corporate counterparts. Friendly and convenient shop locations/ store layouts help to reinforce a customer service attitude and cultivate informal relationships with customers. The ability of founders to respond more quickly to their customers can lead them to operate more effectively, which has also led to a growth in the number of entrepreneurial firms over the years (Bamford and Bruton, 2016).

Disadvantages of Small Size

Although there are several advantages of being small, small size constrains growth due to the lack of scale and scope economies, limited human resources of the owner-founder, and the lack of market control.

Lack of Scale and Scope Economies

Unlike their large counterparts, small firms are unable to benefit from economies of scale. Large firms can sometimes do things more efficiently because of their ability to operate on a larger scale than can small firms. For example, large firms can get discounts for bulk purchases of raw materials from their suppliers. Similarly, in manufacturing industries, the unit cost of production falls with increasing volumes. Therefore, it is often cheaper to produce quantities in large scale than to manufacture small volumes.

Financial Constraints

Most small firms are under- and inappropriately capitalized in terms of both a high debt-equity ratio and an over-reliance on short-term debt (O'Gorman, 2012). Poor capitalization may be due to low levels of profitability and the difficulties of raising finance that small firms face. Financial constraints prevent investment in physical plant and equipment, and/or manufacturing facilities, which restrict the ability to grow. In the extreme, inadequate and inappropriate capitalization are significant contributory factors to the high levels of failure among new businesses.

Sometimes, small firm owner-founders substitute cheaper sweat equity for financial capital. They may consciously choose to maintain a high level of personal equity investment due to their desire for control and reliance on insider knowledge for evaluating the likelihood of success. Low levels of investment might result in non-value-maximizing behaviors such as high CEO salaries.

Human Resource Constraints

Small firm owner-founders' tendencies such as short-term focus, desire for control, and obsession with quality can be detrimental to the growth of their firms. Small firms may be limited in their growth potential due to the owner-founders' short-term focus. Often, small firms are founded to provide only part-time employment for their owners, or enable them to enjoy a certain lifestyle (Bamford and Bruton, 2016). **Salary-substitute firms** allow their owners to earn a living as they would earn from working for someone else. Examples of these firms include corner shops, small family restaurants and laundromats. **Lifestyle firms** are microenterprises that permit their owners to follow a desired pattern of living based on their passion. Examples of lifestyle businesses include tour guides or coaches who start up on their own to build a business around a pursuit they deeply enjoy.

Thus, although more fluid than other types of businesses, microenterprises may not be intended as long-term enterprises and may not have the goal of growing larger. Often, they are planned as only temporary ventures to provide income during periods of unemployment or to supplement household finances for a particular purpose.

The founders' overarching desire for control may translate into centralization of decision making and lack of delegation of responsibility. As a result, owner-founders may be unwilling to adopt innovative production practices, expand in new geographic locations or professionalize management. Often, small firm owner-founders have an unflinching focus on the quality of their goods and services. Such obsession with quality can lead to small batch production, and lack of automation and mechanization in the production process.

By virtue of their predominant reliance on the owner-founders, and a small number of employees, small firms are constrained in available skills and expertise, and even their awareness and use of external, more professional sources of information and support. Small firms are especially limited in their capacity to investigate and evaluate new technical developments that might impact their competitive position (O'Gorman, 2012). Thus, in many cases, they operate in sectors that have a stable technological trajectory, allowing them to pursue a reactive strategy.

Lack of Market Control

As they are small, small firms lack control of markets in which they operate, and therefore, likely underinvest in growth. For example, SMEs may be discouraged from training their personnel because they are concerned about other firms, particularly large firms, poaching their employees at high salaries. This results in a 'free-rider' problem where the non-training firms gain cost advantages over the firm that trains. SMEs are less able to protect themselves from these challenges.

Chapter Summary

LO1: Small firms have the potential to grow into large firms that dominate world business, and hence provide substantial profits to their owners. The rapid growth and **wealth creation potential** of small firms is especially true of high-tech ventures that are often the foundations for global businesses. Small firms have significant **job creation potential**. Additionally, entrepreneurs **introduce innovations** into their societies, contributing to the emergence and growth of industries. At the same time, however, financial, human and technical resource constraints restrict the development of customer-driven innovations in small firms.

LO2: The earliest use of the term **entrepreneurship** was in an economic context. It was used to refer to a class of economic actors who are financially dependent on others. They are set up with capital to conduct their enterprise, or are undertakers of their own labor without capital. **Entrepreneurs** are individuals who start new business ventures. Unlike employees who earn a living from working directly for someone else's business, entrepreneurs start their own business. Whereas **solo entrepreneurs** operate on their own, others co-found ventures in teams. Whereas **novice entrepreneurs** have no prior or minority or majority firm ownership experience, **habitual entrepreneurs** hold or have held a minority or majority ownership stake in two or more firms, at least one of which was established or purchased. Some individuals start their ventures from the **ground up**, others **buy** an existing company, secure **franchise rights**, **license** or **purchase** critical technology or methods, or even **inherit** a company. The entrepreneurial context includes corporate entrepreneurship, technology entrepreneurship and social entrepreneurship. **Corporate entrepreneurship** refers to formal or informal activities aimed at creating new products or businesses, new business models or international organization structures in established companies through product and process innovations and market developments. **Technology entrepreneurship** is entrepreneurship in the technologically advanced industries. **Social entrepreneurship** entails solving a social problem for the wider good. **Green entrepreneurship** is defined as enterprise activities that avoid harm to the environment or help to protect the environment in some way.

LO3: Entrepreneurship focuses more on the context (e.g. start-up process) where innovative effort is required. 'Small business' focuses on established small firms that may not fit any of these categories. A **small business** is defined as having fewer than 500 employees and selling less than $5 million worth of products and services annually.

LO4: According to the **personality theory**, individual characteristics of personality influence opportunity recognition. Individuals are likely to be entrepreneurs because of their personality. Entrepreneurs are 'born', not 'made'. According to the **psycho-sociological theory** of entrepreneurship, not all entrepreneurs start a new business for positive, pull-based factors.

Cognitive theories of entrepreneurship propose that entrepreneurs perceive market gaps or identify unnoticed opportunities.

LO5: Small firms have distinctive **quantitative** and **qualitative** characteristics. The **quantitative** aspects of small firms refer to the small number of employees and small initial capital requirements. Distinctive **qualitative** features of small firms are their informal culture, and the role of family, due to lack of dissociation of ownership from control. The strengths of small firms are entrepreneurial motivation and dynamism, informal structure and organization, and proximity to the market. However, small size also constrains growth due to the lack of scale and scope economies, limited financial and human resources, and the lack of market control.

Review Questions

1. Explain what you understand by the term 'entrepreneurship'. What are the different contexts for entrepreneurship as described in this chapter?
2. What is the significance of entrepreneurship and small firms for a) wealth creation, b) job creation, and c) innovation? Discuss the performance and impact of small firms based on what you have learned in this chapter.
3. Explain what you understand by the following terms. Give examples to support your answer:
   i.   Corporate entrepreneurship
   ii. Technical entrepreneurship
   iii. Social entrepreneurship
4. 'Entrepreneurs are born, not made'. To what extent do you agree/disagree with this statement? Discuss.
5. Explain what you understand by the term 'small businesses'. What is the relationship between small businesses and entrepreneurship?
6. What are the distinctive features of small firms? Explain the quantitative and qualitative features of small firms based on the material covered in this chapter.
7. What are the advantages of small firm size? What are the disadvantages? To what extent does small firm size constrain small firms' ability to grow? Discuss.

Case 2.1

In the Company of Stars: Small Businesses in Beverly Hills, California

If one were to visit the posh neighborhood of Beverly Hills, they would find that more than 80% of the shopping companies are small businesses. These businesses, some of them several decades old, cater to the residents and tourists that flock to this

(Continued)

neighborhood. Contrary to one's belief, these businesses are favored by the neighborhood's first-rate municipal services and celebrity encounters.

Nevertheless, high rents, strict anti-advertising regulations, and the presence of well-known shopping brands such as Armani, Christian Dior etc., make it difficult for these small businesses to stand out. Three small mom-and-pop businesses in the neighborhood, Arturo's Shoe Fixx, Pioneer Hardware and Edelweiss Chocolates, provide additional services such as credit accounts and home delivery to build and retain customer loyalty, and market themselves via word of mouth.

Arturo's Shoe Fixx

Arturo's Shoe Fixx, located in Beverly Hills, prides itself on offering difficult shoe and accessory repairs. The store is well known for its culture of personal customer service and relationship, and accommodates unusual requests like dyeing a white Celine purse neon pink or transforming a Chanel single-strap purse into a double strap.

The store was founded by Arturo Azinian, and has now been running for over 30 years. Prior to opening the repair shop, Arturo owned a shoemaking business. Currently run by the grandson of the founder, Ari Libaridian, the duo carries on

with the legacy of superior artisanship and is well known for making special efforts to be warm and friendly to customers. Ari, who took over from his grandfather after working at the store for more than two decades, continues the family tradition of fine workmanship. He also continues to respect the shop's valued culture of personal customer service based on informal relationships. Unlike their more impersonal luxury emporia in the area, Ari and his grandfather are known for going out of their way to be warm and friendly, even when faced with demanding customers. Using ideas from designer magazines and social media posts, they accommodate difficult requests for more aesthetic rather than practical alterations.

Source: www.needpix.com

Apart from normal customers, the store also caters to productions such as Fox's 9-1-1 by providing repairing and cleaning services to their footwear. The store gets referrals from large shoe companies such as Gucci's and Barney's, and has been graced by several famous clients like Donatella Versace and Jennifer Lawrence.

Despite being successful, Arturo's Shoe Fixx has been impacted by rising rents in recent times, forcing them to change location. However, thanks to Arturo Azinian and his grandson's loyal customer base, the store continues to thrive and stand out from other luxurious emporia in the upmarket Beverly Hills neighborhood.

Pioneer Hardware

Pioneer Hardware is run by Joseph Tilum, a second-generation owner and operator of the family business. Tilum, a one-time mayor of Beverly Hills, purchased Pioneer Hardware from its former owner when the latter retired, combining it with his New York-based Lucerne Hardware business.

Located on the east of Rodeo Drive in Los Angeles, the store is known for its customer relations. Each customer gets personalized treatment with an employee greeting them at the door, often by name and escorting them inside. Tilum believes in a hands-on approach and helps his customers to find the items they are looking for. Unlike his larger counterparts on Rodeo Drive, employees are also trained to offer to answer their clients' questions at all times. The personalization does not end here, as the store also offers credit services with options to settle the account at the end of the month.

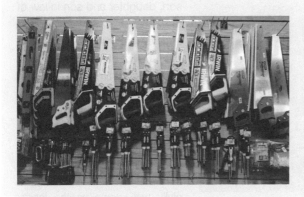

Despite having the term 'hardware' in its name, Pioneer Hardware is more of a general store. It stocks essentials such as light bulbs, rat traps, key chains and screws, as well as premium items such as fancy steel dish racks, and exclusive guest towels. Some of the trinkets on its shelves like key chains and sodas are priced for as little as 50 cents to a dollar. Others like screws can be had for a nickel, a dime or a quarter. Pioneer Hardware embodies a rustic feel by retaining the hand-cranked cash register and wooden ladder by the rails.

Source: www.needpix.com

Edelweiss Chocolates

Founded by a Montana expatriate named Grace Young, Beverly Hills' Edelweiss Chocolates has been graced by countless celebrity customers like Katherine Hepburn, Frank Sinatra, Dean Martin, Reese Witherspoon, Ben Affleck, Oprah Winfrey and Madonna since its inception in 1942. One of the main selling points of the confectionery store is that it allows customers to present their choice of molds and accepts orders requesting chocolate replicas for special events.

(Continued)

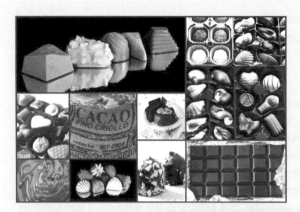

Source: ww.needpix.com/photo/759412/

Edelweiss Chocolates is well known for their trademark chocolate-covered pretzels, and nine varieties of flavored marshmallows. The chocolates are handcrafted on-site by seven of the company's twelve employees using the finest ingredients and with great attention to detail. This explains the high price of $52.95 per pound.

The store is currently owned by the couple Madlen and Steve Zahir, who bought it from actress Shirley Jones and her husband Marty Ingels in 2000. The family had no prior bonbon experience; however, they now stand strong with all five members of the family – including the son, daughter and son-in-law of the Zahirs – actively running the business. While the business has always been family-owned, this is the first time it is seeing the involvement of the second generation. Daniel Zahir, the son of its owners, is the creative director of Edelweiss.

Source: pixabay.com

Edelweiss Chocolates attracts numerous customers. It is especially well-known as the facility where actress Lucille Ball spent weeks in the 1950s while preparing for her role in the popular show, *I Love Lucy*, and where she accidentally immersed herself in chocolate during one of her visits.

Source: adapted from Buchanan (2019)

Discussion Questions

1. Why are the Beverly Hills businesses profiled above small businesses? Based on the material covered in the chapter, explain the distinctive a) quantitative and b) qualitative characteristics of these businesses. Cite examples from all three businesses to illustrate your answer.
2. What is the role of family in small firms? Use examples from the Beverly Hills businesses to discuss your answer.

3. According to the chapter, small firms lack control of the markets in which they operate. Do you agree with this statement? Why / why not? Give examples from the Beverly Hills businesses to illustrate your answer.
4. To what extent do you believe the Beverly Hills businesses have limited growth potential? Is there anything the founders can do to overcome these challenges? Discuss.

References

Achtmeyer, W.F. (2002) '3M corporation'. William F. *Achtmeyer Center for Global Leadership, Tuck School of Business at Dartmouth*, No. 2-0002. Available at http://mba.tuck.dartmouth.edu/pages/faculty/chris.trimble/osi/downloads/20002_3M.pdf (last accessed 27 September 2022).

Aten, J. (2020) 'In just 10 days, Dyson designed a completely new ventilator specifically for Covid-19 patients', *Inc. Magazine*. Available at www.inc.com/jason-aten/in-just-10-days-dyson-designed-a-completely-new-ventilator-specifically-for-covid-19-patients.html (last accessed 27 September 2022).

Bamford, C.E. and Bruton, G.D. (2016) *Entrepreneurship: The Art, Science, and Process for Success* (2nd edn). New York: McGraw Hill Education.

Barringer, B. and Ireland, R.D. (2016) *Entrepreneurship: Successfully Launching New Ventures* (5th edn). Harlow: Pearson.

Blackburn, R.A. (ed.) (2003) *Intellectual Property and Innovation Management in Small Firms*. London: Routledge.

Bosma, N. and Kelley, D. (2018) *Global Entrepreneurship Monitor 2018/2019 Global Report*. Santiago: Grafica Andes.

Buchanan, L. (2019) 'Even the rich and famous of Beverly Hills need to buy hardware and produce: Here's where they shop', *Inc. Magazine*. Available at www.inc.com/leigh-buchanan/beverly-hills-hollywood-celebrity-favorites-small-business-week-2019.html (last accessed 27 September 2022).

Chalmers, D. and Fraser, S. (2012) 'Social entrepreneurship', in S. Carter and D. Jones-Evans (eds), *Enterprise and Small Business: Principles, Practice and Policy* (3rd edn). Harlow: Financial Times Prentice Hall, pp. 289–301.

Deakins, D. and Freel, M. (2003) 'Entrepreneurship and small firms', *International Journal of Business and Technopreneurship*, 5(3): 397–406.

Delmar, F. and Witte, F.C. (2012) 'The psychology of the entrepreneur', in S. Carter and D. Jones-Evans (eds.), *Enterprise and Small Business: Principles, Practice and Policy* (3rd edn). Harlow: Financial Times Prentice Hall, pp. 152–178.

De Vries, K. (1977) 'The entrepreneurial personality: A person at the crossroads', *Journal of Management Studies*, 14(1): 34–57.

Haworth, C. and Hamilton, E. (2012) 'Family businesses', in S. Carter and D. Jones-Evans (eds), *Enterprise and Small Business: Principles, Practice and Policy* (3rd edn). Harlow: Financial Times Prentice Hall, pp. 232–251.

Kirzner, I.M. (1973) *Competition and Entrepreneurship*. Chicago, IL: University of Chicago Press.

Lazear, E.P. (2004) 'Balanced skills and entrepreneurship', *The American Economic Review*, 94(2): 208–211.

Liberto, D. (2019) 'Small and mid-size enterprise (SME)'. Available at www.investopedia.com/terms/s/smallandmidsizeenterprises.asp (last accessed 27 September 2022).

MacKenzie, N.G. and Jones-Evans, D. (2012) 'Technical entrepreneurship', in S. Carter and D. Jones-Evans (eds), *Enterprise and Small Business: Principles, Practice and Policy* (3rd edn). Harlow: Financial Times Prentice Hall, pp. 268–279.

Meltzer, M. (2017) 'Your used bar of soap has a surprising afterlife', *Thrillist*. Available at www.thrillist.com/travel/nation/hotel-bar-soap-clean-the-world-orlando-charity (last accessed 27 September 2022).

Mintzberg, H. (1979) *The Structuring of Organizations*. Englewood Cliffs, NJ: Prentice Hall.

O'Gorman, C. (2012) 'Strategy and the small firm', in S. Carter and D. Jones-Evans (eds), *Enterprise and Small Business: Principles, Practice and Policy* (3rd edn). Harlow: Financial Times Prentice Hall, pp. 386–403.

Pittaway, L. (2012) 'The evolution of entrepreneurship theory', in S. Carter and D. Jones-Evans (eds), *Enterprise and Small Business: Principles, Practice and Policy* (3rd edn). Harlow: Financial Times Prentice Hall, pp. 9–26.

Pruthi, S. (2016) 'TrintMe: Perseverance a friend or enemy?' *Journal of Critical Incidents*, 9: 16. ISSN 2380-6664 (Online/Email). ISSN 2380-6648 (Print). ISSN 1943-1872 (CD-ROM).

Saari, U.A. and Joensuu-Salo, S. (2019) 'Green Entrepreneurship'. In: Leal Filho, W., Azul, A., Brandli, L., Özuyar, P. and Wall, T. (eds.) *Responsible Consumption and Production. Encyclopedia of the UN Sustainable Development Goals*, Springer, Cham. https://doi.org/10.1007/978-3-319-71062-4_6-1

Tseng, C. and Tseng, C.C. (2019) 'Corporate entrepreneurship as a strategic approach for internal innovation performance', *Asia Pacific Journal of Innovation and Entrepreneurship*, 13(1): 108–120.

USBA Office of Advocacy (2018) *Annual Report of the Office of Economic Research, FY 2017*. Available at www.sba.gov/advocacy/2018-small-business-profiles-states-and-territories (last accessed 27 September 2022).

WCED (1987) *Our Common Future*. Oxford: UN, Oxford University Press.

Wright, M., Westhead, P. and Ucbasaran, D. (2012) 'Habitual entrepreneurs', in S. Carter and D. Jones-Evans (eds), *Enterprise and Small Business: Principles, Practice and Policy* (3rd edn). Harlow: Financial Times Prentice Hall, pp. 252–267.

3

GLOBAL ENTREPRENEURSHIP MONITOR AND COMPARATIVE DEVELOPMENT OF ENTREPRENEURSHIP

OPPORTUNITIES AND CHALLENGES FOR FEMALE ENTREPRENEURSHIP IN THE PALESTINIAN TERRITORIES

Aya Kishko, 26 years old, is the founder of an enterprise built on upcycling discarded wooden crates into high-value furniture in Gaza. An architectural engineering graduate, she is among a small but growing number of rising female innovators in non-traditional and high-impact fields in the Palestinian territories.

Aya's example is compelling in an environment that is fraught with several challenges for skilled women. Untapped supply of talent and human capital, largely characterized by female and youth, is a striking feature of the Palestinian labor force. Educated men have

(Continued)

an advantage over women, especially in the private sector. According to the World Bank, if a Palestinian female worker were to be compensated as equally as her male counterpart with equal human capital endowments and labor market experience, she would earn between 68 to 76% more than she currently does.

Women face multiple barriers to entry into the labor market, including wage discrimination. About three out of every four post-secondary graduate women across the Palestinian territories are in the labor force; yet, close to half are unemployed. In contrast, unemployment among educated males in the labor force is much lower at 18%. There are also large disparities by region. As compared to 28% men, 60% of the economically active women who hold post-secondary degrees in Gaza, for example, are unemployed.

Educated women continue to face challenges regarding their choice of industry sector. In 2015, 48% of educated women worked as teaching professionals, compared with only 15.2% of educated men, even as the unemployment rate for this profession reached 68%. The private sector is characterized by blocked opportunities for female career mobility and progression. In 2013, the percentage of females who became top managers in the formal private sector was only 1.2%, compared with an average of 5.1% for the Middle East and Africa region and 19% globally.

According to the World Bank, many of the discriminatory practices against women are due to the absence of laws that can safeguard against implicit and explicit forms of discrimination. The law currently does not mandate equal pay for work of equal value or non-discrimination in hiring based on sex. The government also does not prohibit employers from asking about family status. Laws that require employers to fully cover maternity benefits, with no mandated paternal benefits, contribute to discouraging firms from hiring women. The concentration of women in certain fields also reveals other barriers. These include the lack of affordable and high-quality child care, no measures against sexual harassment in the workforce, as well as Israeli mobility restrictions and the lack of reliable transportation networks.

Investing in female entrepreneurs in the Palestinian territories means more jobs for women in better positions not just in the Palestine territories, but also globally. Women owners tend to hire more women as employees and in leadership positions. Aya, for instance, endeavors to provide opportunity and hope to several unemployed Gazan youth, and inspire more women in a field that is largely male-dominated. She also wants to establish a women's training center to involve them in a range of functions including design and marketing, manufacturing and implementation.

However, closing the gender gap requires tackling all identified constraints in a comprehensive manner, and adopting and implementing new, targeted policies. This includes reforming laws that do not treat men and women equally, and enforcing a discrimination-free environment surrounding employment in the private sector.

The Palestinian Authorities are taking steps to advance women's rights at the national level in an effort to improve the local environment for female entrepreneurship.

The World Bank is also focusing on creating productive opportunities for women in the Palestinian territories by creating incentives for increased investments in women-owned enterprises, promoting e-work among Gazan youth with valuable work experience, and supporting formalization of home-based businesses, which is particularly important due to mobility constraints in the region. The true impact and effective implementation of policy initiatives on the ground remains to be seen.

Source: The World Bank (2019)

Learning Outcomes

After studying this chapter, you should be ready to:

- **LO1**: Describe the importance of the Global Entrepreneurship Monitor (GEM) for global entrepreneurship
- **LO2**: Analyze patterns in the international development of entrepreneurship based on the GEM findings
- **LO3**: Evaluate the role of the external environment in the international development of entrepreneurship
- **LO4**: Discuss key issues in comparing the international development of entrepreneurship

Introduction

The 1990s have seen increased appreciation for entrepreneurship and, in particular, for the role of start-ups (Bosma and Kelley, 2018). Current economic policy in China, for example, is focused on dealing with the challenges of inequality, health and pollution that have been brought about as a consequence of economic growth in the past two decades. Entrepreneurship can be a key means of addressing these challenges.

As discussed in Chapter 2, the need for power or achievement is one of the reasons individuals found new ventures. However, motivational change, by itself, is not enough to engage in entrepreneurial behavior. It is important that the external environment in which entrepreneurs live supports personal effort and initiative. As the opening profile suggests, labor market challenges such as high unemployment and discrimination against women limit available start-up opportunities for women entrepreneurs in the Palestinian territories.

In this chapter, we use evidence from the Global Entrepreneurship Monitor (GEM) to compare and contrast the international environment for the development of entrepreneurship across different parts of the world. Using illustrative examples, we evaluate the role of political, economic, socio-cultural and technological factors in the founding of new ventures.

For individual entrepreneurs, an assessment of opportunities and challenges for entrepreneurship in the external environment can help them to select an optimal geographic location for founding their ventures. For policy, a comparative assessment of the international environment can help to identify gaps in the underlying conditions for the development of entrepreneurship and take steps to address those gaps.

The structure of this chapter is as follows. We begin by describing the significance and objectives of the GEM study. Then we analyze key patterns in the international development of entrepreneurship based on the GEM findings. In the following section, we evaluate the role of the external environment in the development of entrepreneurship. Finally, we discuss key issues in comparing the international development of entrepreneurship.

Global Entrepreneurship Monitor: Key Objectives and Findings

The GEM is one of the most comprehensive studies of global entrepreneurship, conceived as a joint initiative by Babson College, Massachusetts, United States, and the London Business School, UK, in 1999. Available data on businesses in different countries in the 1990s primarily captured registered businesses, which vastly underestimated actual business activity in many economies, and made it difficult to study entrepreneurship and start-ups in some countries. The objective of GEM when it was first conceived was to improve the relationship between perceptions of entrepreneurship, entrepreneurial activity and national economic growth.

GEM initially planned to explore the following three questions about entrepreneurship:

1.　Does the level of entrepreneurial activity vary amongst countries and, if so, to what extent?
2.　Does the level of entrepreneurial activity affect a country's rate of economic growth and prosperity?
3.　What makes a country entrepreneurial?

Over time, GEM has revised its objectives to measuring differences in the level of entrepreneurial activity between economies and uncovering the factors underlying these differences. The study also aims to establish the link between entrepreneurship and economic growth and, hence, economic development over a longer period of time. The revised objectives of GEM are to:

1. Measure differences in the level of entrepreneurial activity amongst countries
2. Uncover factors determining national levels of entrepreneurial activity
3. Identify policies that may enhance the national level of entrepreneurial activity

GEM was designed as a long-term longitudinal research case study involving international comparisons between the G7 (US, UK, Canada, Japan, France, Germany, Italy), and initially three other (Denmark, Finland and Israel) countries. Further additions raised the total number of countries involved to 42 by the year 2007, and 49 by 2018. The study is conducted using both surveys and face-to-face interviews, especially in emerging economies like India, China and Uganda.

For the purpose of the GEM study, entrepreneurship is defined as 'an attempt to create a new business enterprise or to expand an existing business by an individual, a team of individuals or an established business' (Bosma and Kelley, 2018). As some regions of the world have individual economies that are not formally recognized as separate countries, the results of the study refer to 'economies' rather than 'countries', unless the regions being discussed are classified as countries. The findings of the 2018 study are based on a survey of 164,269 adults in 49 economies.

GEM set out to explore a number of questions relevant to the study of entrepreneurship. Even though it has not answered all of them, GEM has assembled a considerable amount of data about entrepreneurship in a wide range of countries, which indicates that the level of entrepreneurship does considerably differ across countries. The main findings of two decades of GEM research, as documented in the 2018–19 GEM report, are summarized below.

Variations in Levels of Entrepreneurship across Countries

GEM developed a measure called the **Total Entrepreneurial Activity (TEA) index** to indicate differences in the levels of entrepreneurial activity across countries (Bosma and Kelley, 2018). The TEA index value shows for each country the percentage of the adult population who have taken some action towards creating a new business in the past year or who are owner-managers of an active business less than 42 months old. The TEA index is made up of two measures:

- Nascent start-up rate (those in the process of creating a new business)
- New firm or new business ownership rate (those actually owning and running early stage businesses). It is entrepreneurial activity that is centered on the period preceding and immediately after the actual start of a firm

According to the GEM findings, 12.6% of entrepreneurs are engaged in total early-stage entrepreneurial activity and 8.4% have established businesses.

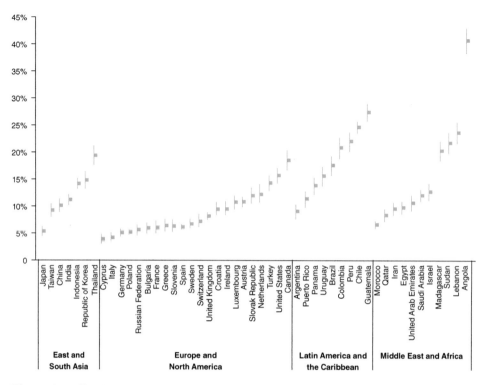

Figure 3.1   Total early-stage entrepreneurial activity (TEA) rates among adults (18–64) in 49 economies, in four geographic regions

Source: Bosma and Kelley (2018)

The highest TEA rates are found in Angola (41%), a low-income economy (Figure 3.1). High rates are also found in middle- and higher-income economies, Guatemala and Chile, reporting 28 and 25%, respectively. The lowest overall TEA rates are found in North America and countries in Europe, which consists of mostly high-income economies. Most countries show less than 10%, with Canada and the US exhibiting the highest rates. Overall, there is significant variation in the rate of business formation by world regions as measured by the TEA index.

The GEM study also reports variations by entrepreneurship type, industry sector and gender. Further, there exist differences across countries in the motivations for engaging in entrepreneurial activity.

Variations by Entrepreneurship Type

Whereas 18.6% of TEA is in **family businesses**, 8.0% of TEA is **solo businesses**. Solo entrepreneurs are found in all regions and at all development levels. As per Bosma and Kelley (2018), Brazil has the highest proportion (53%) of solo entrepreneurs, followed by Madagascar (30%). Many European countries also display solo entrepreneurship, notably, the Netherlands, UK, Italy, Germany and Sweden. In East and South Asia, Thailand shows a high proportion of solo entrepreneurs, as well as high TEA rates.

Variations by Industry Sector

According to GEM findings, the industry profiles of early-stage entrepreneurs are related to national income levels across countries. The decline in wholesale/retail activity, and increase in services and technology, is the most noticeable trend moving from low- to high-income groups. Wholesale/retail businesses account for more than half of early-stage entrepreneurs in every low-income economy. In contrast, only 4 of 31 high-income economies report more than half of early-stage entrepreneurs operating in this sector.

Few entrepreneurs in low-income economies start finance / real estate / business services or ICT businesses. In contrast, 20% or more of the start-up activity in over half of the high-income economies is in finance / real estate / business services. Service and technology business show high levels in Europe, with Austria exhibiting the highest percentage of health / education / government / social and consumer services early-stage entrepreneurs (33%), and Switzerland the highest proportion of early-stage entrepreneurs in finance / real estate / business services (30%). Ireland shows the largest percentage of entrepreneurs in ICT (13%).

Variations by Gender

Across the world, men are twice as likely to start a business as women; the 2018–19 GEM study reports seven women entrepreneurs for every ten men founders. Only six countries (Indonesia, Thailand, Panama, Qatar, Madagascar and Angola) show equal TEA rates between men and women. The Europe and North America region has many economies with a lack of gender equality. In six countries (Slovenia, Greece, Sweden, Switzerland, United Kingdom and Turkey), the start-up rate among women is half that of men. No country in this region shows equal levels between the genders.

The Middle East and Africa is unique in having countries which display both gender equality and gender inequality. In Angola and Madagascar, equal participation between genders boosts overall TEA rates. In Lebanon and Sudan, on the other hand, women participate at high levels, but men account for a disproportionate share of overall entrepreneurship activity.

Varying Motivations for Entrepreneurship

In 2001, the GEM study was widened to explore two sub-sets within entrepreneurship: **opportunity entrepreneurs** and **necessity entrepreneurs** (Bosma and Kelley, 2018). Whereas the former starts a business to exploit a business opportunity

(opportunity entrepreneurs), the latter is motivated by the need to sustain themselves because all other options for work are either absent or unsatisfactory (necessity entrepreneurs). Such a classification allows for differentiation according to the reasons that motivate entrepreneurial behavior.

Figure 3.2 illustrates the proportion of necessity and opportunity entrepreneurs among economies in four regional groups.

The proportion of opportunity entrepreneurs, or those seeking higher income or greater independence, accounts for an average of 37% of entrepreneurs in the low-income economies. This increases to 42% on average among middle-income economies, and 51% in the high-income economies.

Entrepreneurs in low-income economies are more likely motivated by necessity than in developed economies. An average of 35% entrepreneurs in low-income economies start their businesses because they have no better option for work. The level of necessity entrepreneurship drops as economic development level increases.

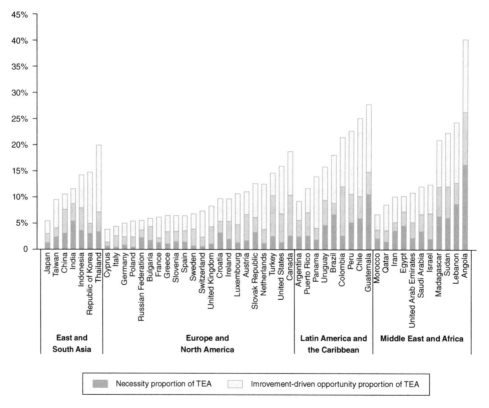

Figure 3.2   Total early-stage entrepreneurial activity (TEA) rates among adults (18–64) in 49 economies, in four geographic regions, showing necessity and improvement-driven opportunity

Source: Bosma and Kelley (2018)

At the same time, however, there are economies with high necessity motives in both low- and high-income groups. In the middle-income group, 40% of entrepreneurs in Russia, for example, are necessity driven. In the high-income group, 32% of entrepreneurs in Croatia report these motives.

Overall, the usefulness of categorizing entrepreneurship as either necessity or opportunity has been questioned. Empirical evidence does not always support necessity theory. Some GEM reports have indicated that entrepreneurs might fall into both categories.

Relationship between the Level of Entrepreneurial Activity in a Country and its Rate of Economic Growth

In the first three years of its work, the GEM study reported a statistically significant association between entrepreneurial activity and national economic growth as indicated by a growth in GDP. However, the strength of the association tended to vary depending on the countries included in the survey and the nature of the entrepreneurial activity.

When the GEM study first looked at necessity and opportunity entrepreneurship, it reported that the prevalence rate of necessity entrepreneurship was positively associated with national economic growth and this association was strongest when countries highly dependent on international trade were excluded. In contrast, opportunity entrepreneurship was not associated with any measure of national economic growth. Since 2004, the GEM study has reported a U-shaped relationship in which:

1. For low-/middle-income countries, the level of entrepreneurship is relatively high, but it reduces as income levels rise
2. For high-income countries, necessity entrepreneurship is low but opportunity entrepreneurship starts to increase as income levels rise

It must be noted that such a relationship does not imply any specific causal relationship between entrepreneurial activity and economic development.

Factors Influencing the International Development of Entrepreneurship

The issue of what makes a country entrepreneurial was the original question that the GEM study sought to address. Over the years, this question in its original form has been dropped. Instead, the GEM study has been aimed at uncovering the factors determining the levels of entrepreneurial activity across the world, and identifying the policies that may enhance the level of entrepreneurial activity.

Each economy has its own entrepreneurship profile in terms of activity rates across various phases of the entrepreneurship process, characteristics of entrepreneurs and their businesses, and their attitudes and perceptions. Each economy also has its own environmental profile, containing enabling factors entrepreneurs can leverage, as well as challenges they must overcome to start new ventures.

Broadly, these influences can be ascribed to political (P), economic (E), socio-cultural (S) and technological (T) aspects of the external environment. We use the PEST framework to evaluate the influence of the external environment on the level of entrepreneurship (Figure 3.3).

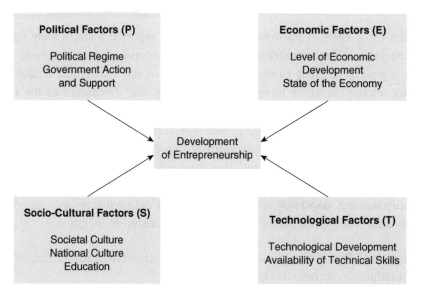

Figure 3.3 External environmental influences on the level of entrepreneurship: PEST framework

Political Factors (P)

Governments influence the level of enterprise in more than one way. Both the type of political regime and the nature of government action and support are influential.

Political Regime

The size of the state sector negatively impacts entrepreneurship (Aidis et al., 2010). In contrast, freedom from corruption positively and significantly impacts entrepreneurial entry. The former communist countries of the Soviet Bloc, for example, shared a common political system – that of communism and central planning. Some of these countries like the former Czechoslovakia and Hungary were quite enterprising before central planning was imposed in the communist regime (Bridge et al., 2003). However, attitudes changed when these countries became a part of the Soviet Bloc. Entrepreneurial behavior in the communist system was viewed with considerable suspicion; entrepreneurs were perceived as antisocial and self-seeking, and frequently as acting unethically. Disparities in income and wealth furthered the perception of enterprise as a destabilizing force in society relative to the sense of equality that is characteristic of communist regimes.

In the present day, the Palestinian territories are an example of how the lack of sovereignty poses a serious constraint to the emergence of enterprise. As a country that is occupied by another country, Palestinians face restrictions on their right to movement on a daily basis, which discourages businesses, daily life and logistics. A survey by the United Nations Office for the Coordination of Human Affairs (2015) shows that the government of Israel deployed 91 new checkpoints to restrict Palestinian vehicular movement in 2015, which added to the pre-existing 452 checkpoints from the previous year. Importing raw material and resources into Palestinian lands requires the Israeli government's approval and the threat of illegal confiscation is high, which discourages private business enterprise.

Government Action and Support

Government intervention to promote entrepreneurship can take two forms: setting the conditions for enterprise, and direct measures to support the entrepreneurial process. Governments around the world have pursued entrepreneurship as an explicit policy objective to set the **conditions for enterprise** (Bennett, 2012). Governments have introduced tax reforms, regulations such as time to set up and register new businesses, low interest rates, and less stringent listing requirements for new and small firms.

Tax reforms in Sweden in the 1990s, for example, led to a cut in corporate taxes, thus encouraging people to start up businesses (Bosma and Kelley, 2018). In Brazil, the government's emphasis has moved from pegging the value of the *real* to the US dollar and privatizing public services and state-owned companies, to an emphasis on combating income inequalities. TEA rates rose in 2009 and 2010, with an all-time high in 2015, accompanied by a high proportion of necessity-motivated entrepreneurship.

More recently, there is a risk that the UK will become less of an attractive destination for European Union (EU) tech migrants due to restrictions on the freedom of movement in the wake of Brexit (Mazour, 2019). Such barriers have implications for the entry of potential high-tech entrepreneurs in the UK. They also impact small firms' access to high-skilled employees from across the border. The UK government has taken away the fee to apply for 'settled' or 'pre-settled' status in order to ensure continuity in the immigration status of EU citizens and their families in a post-Brexit future. This move has somewhat lowered the barriers for the entry of highly skilled workers to the UK. While entrepreneurs may have to expand their search for talent, and encourage a culture of openness, innovation and excitement to attract the best talent, the government's move has ensured that the conditions are still attractive for technology talent and entrepreneurship in the UK.

Governments also **directly intervene to promote enterprise**. They do so by providing financial support, setting up public enterprise agencies, subsidizing enterprise R&D, education, advice and training, and setting up science parks and incubation workspaces.

An example of high government support is the Yozma Group created by the Israeli government to increase the **supply of funds** for entrepreneurs in Israel (Bosma and Kelley, 2018). Established in 1993 with $100 million of capital, and co-invested with ten funds modelled as limited partnerships from outside of Israel, the group originated from an Israeli government program aimed at promoting venture capital (VC) investments in high-growth companies in strategic sectors, namely communications, information technologies and life sciences (IFC, 2018). The group is considered as one of the key factors underlying the country's entrepreneurial success.

Chile has received a lot of attention for its Start-up Chile program that pays foreign entrepreneurs to spend six months in the country as an effort to build global skill connections and a mini-Chilean 'diaspora' (Kerr and Kerr, 2016). The program now supports 200–250 new ventures per year and Chile has even launched sister programs based upon the success.

The 2005 Vocational and Technical Entrepreneurship Act in the US, and the Entrepreneurship Action Plan in Wales, UK, are examples of **public enterprise agencies** offering financial and non-financial incentives to start-ups. The EU has introduced a variety of initiatives to create a friendly business environment, provide access to finance, support competitiveness and innovation, provide key support networks and information for SMEs.

For example, the Small Business Act for Europe (SBA) provides a comprehensive SME policy for the EU and individual EU countries. The SBA promotes the 'Think Small First' principle and promotes entrepreneurial spirit among European citizens. The Entrepreneurship Action Plan supports entrepreneurship education, and provides support tools for aspiring entrepreneurs. The European Commission's 'Start-Up and Scale Initiative' aims to give Europe's many innovative entrepreneurs every opportunity to become world leading companies through access to venture capital investment, insolvency law, taxation and more (Figure 3.4).

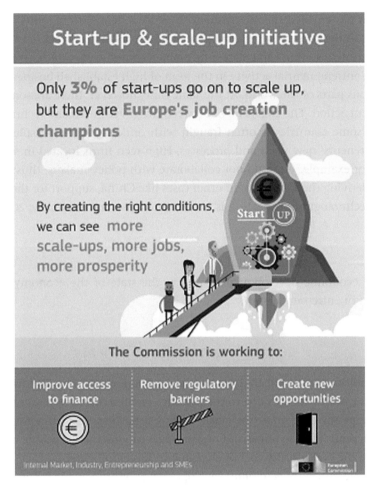

Figure 3.4 Entrepreneurship and small and medium-sized enterprises

Source: European Commission (n.d.)

Government intervention can spur entrepreneurship through **investment in R&D**. EU policy has focused on promoting innovation in small firms as part of the wider Lisbon Agenda designed to close the competitiveness gap between Europe and the US. Aimed at creating a more competitive and resource-efficient European economy based on knowledge and innovation, the Executive Agency for Small and Medium-Sized Enterprises (EASME) has been set-up by the European Commission to manage on its behalf several EU programs. These programs are designed to encourage SMEs to undertake collaborative R&D and improve innovation capability.

Israel has a long history of developing new civilian and military technologies, in part because of the country's high level of investment in R&D (IFC, 2018). Israel spends 4.25% of its GDP on R&D, more than any other country in the world. Such a project-rich environment has enabled the government to create a demand for equity capital, thus contributing to the success of the entrepreneurial ecosystem in Israel.

The government's efforts to create a favorable economic climate have resulted in a high level of entrepreneurial activity in the form of high established business ownership rates in various parts of the world. At the same time, however, there are some criticisms of government action. The engagement between the government and technology entrepreneurs in some countries is often fraught with difficulty due to challenges arising from entrepreneurs' new ideas and processes. High-tech firms located in science parks in the UK, for example, often do not collaborate with policy makers, thus refuting the purpose underlying their creation. In other cases like China, support for the service sector or non-technological innovation is less common (Bosma and Kelley, 2018).

Economic Factors (E)

The level of economic development as well as the state of the economy impact the development of entrepreneurship.

Level of Economic Development

GEM has traditionally found that developed economies tend toward lower entrepreneurship rates, at least in part due to the presence of alternative job options and higher levels of competitiveness that can make starting a business less attractive. Economic development tends to raise wages and higher wages can discourage people from starting up by raising the opportunity cost of engaging in self-employment.

However, the impact of economic development on entrepreneurship is contentious. Since the 1970s, per capita income has had a positive impact on the self-employment rate, at least in developed countries (Bridge et al., 2003). The birth rate of businesses is higher in economically less developed countries; however, the continuity of business is higher in developed countries than their less developed counterparts. In countries where environmental uncertainty is high, businesses are viewed as 'temporary projects' that are mainly aimed at making money in the short term. People work on their businesses to earn money as long as possible until a more attractive project appears.

In economically stable countries, in contrast, motivation is not limited to earning a living, and the continuity of the business can be of primary importance to the entrepreneur. Also, in less developed countries, most businesses are started by entrepreneurs rather than bought or inherited, and more entrepreneurs have had more than one business. Risk-avoidance behavior is also more pronounced in these countries where entrepreneurs are more likely to cash out in the short run given long-term uncertainty.

Moreover, entrepreneurship acquires a different meaning in economically developed and less developed countries. Developing countries in Asia and Africa are increasingly becoming known for some of the most powerful and scalable social innovations (Chalmers and Fraser, 2012).

Founded in 1976 by Professor of Economics Muhammad Yunus, Bangladesh's Grameen Bank is one such example (see Box below). The principle of providing micro-finance or small loans to the poor in Bangladesh through the Grameen Bank unlocked the entrepreneurial potential of the region and has proved to be a model rapidly adopted in areas of extreme poverty. Over 7.5 million individuals have accessed funds directly from the Grameen Bank, allowing the organization to expand and diversify into other socially innovative activities.

Examples of social ventures also abound in other developing economies. Founded in Egypt, organizations such as Sekem have matured from providing agricultural solutions to creating educational centers, schools, a university and a medical center. In Brazil, Vila das Canoas has launched a community-based tourism venture that enables travelers to lodge with local residents. This has enabled villagers to earn a revenue stream while sharing their knowledge and culture with foreign visitors.

MICROFINANCE AND SOCIAL ENTREPRENEURSHIP IN BANGLADESH

Definitions of innovation vary from country to country. Innovation in developed econo-mies like the US is often considered to be synonymous with technology entrepreneur-ship. Innovation can take many different forms, especially in developing economies. It can be coming up with a more cost-effective way to design a product, configuring a business model or creating social change. In some developing economies, innova-tion can even mean devising a way for people to make payments via low-cost mobile phones or building ultrasound scanners using off-the-shelf parts.

As discussed in Chapter 2, social entrepreneurship is the use of entrepreneurial principles to found ventures that solve pressing social problems and create social change. Unlike their commercial counterparts, social entrepreneurs assess the suc-cess of their business in terms of their impact on society.

One example of social entrepreneurship is microfinance. Microfinance consists of extending financial services to individuals to establish or expand a small, self-sustain-ing business. One of the components of microfinance is microcredit – the extension of small loans to individuals who are too poor to qualify for traditional bank loans. Micro-finance institutions often offer business advice and counseling, and facilitate peer sup-port between clients in order to facilitate the transition out of poverty. Microfinance specifically targets women. This is because women are more likely to reinvest their earnings in the business and in their families.

The idea for microfinance began in 1976 when Professor Muhammed Yunus loaned the equivalent of $27 from his own pocket to 42 stool makers in a tiny village

(Continued)

in Bangladesh. These individuals simply needed enough credit to purchase the raw material for their trade. Yunus's loan allowed them to break out of the cycle of poverty. The Grameen Bank was formally established in 1983.

Microfinance is considered one of the most effective and flexible strategies for fighting poverty. It is sustainable and can be scaled up to respond to the urgent needs of the world's poorest. Microfinance has helped to generate employment. Since inception, the Grameen Bank has lifted millions of people in developing countries out of poverty. It has also helped to elevate the status of women, especially in developing countries. In 2006, Mr. Yunus won the Nobel Peace Prize for enabling economic and social development through microcredit.

Source: http://clarke.dickinson.edu

State of the Economy

Factors such as the state of the economy and levels of employment impact entrepreneurial activity. The United States shows an interesting pattern in that TEA rates went down after the financial crisis during the years 2009 and 2010 (Bosma and Kelley, 2018). TEA picked up in 2011, after GDP grew in 2010. Likewise, evidence from Iran suggests that favorable internal market dynamics and free and open markets are critical for both entrepreneurs and business owners, especially those who sell domestically.

The availability of jobs signals the presence of fall-back options for those whose entrepreneurial efforts do not work out. In China, GEM evidence from the last two decades shows that entrepreneurial activity (both early-stage and in the established phase) has diminished over time probably due to the increased scale of growth of many companies as a consequence of sustained economic growth, and hence the many opportunities for employment that they offer.

Similarly, the apparent decline in TEA in Iran in 2018 may be partly caused by an increase in job opportunities following sanctions relief. In contrast, high TEA rates in the US in the late 2000s coincided with a period of high unemployment (3.8% in mid-2018), a level not seen since the year 2000.

STUDENT-LOAN DEBT AND BUSINESS FOUNDING IN US

According to the Wall Street Journal, the share of people under 30 years of age who own private businesses has fallen to a 24-year low. Students in this age group likely face financial challenges, which impact their willingness to take risks. Rising student debt is a key factor underlying this trend. Total student-loan debt outstanding increased 9.6% in the third quarter of 2014 over the same period a year earlier, according to the Federal Reserve Bank of New York.

According to the US Small Business Administration (SBA), entrepreneurs under age 40 with student-loan debt are less likely to apply for a business loan. Student loans force entrepreneurs to abandon their start-up dreams or radically reshape their business plans. Compared with 27% of those without student loan debt, just 17% of households with a young self-employed member that had student loan debt had applied for a business loan in the last five years in 2012.

Founders with student loans also have fewer employees. According to the SBA, young self-employed individuals without student loan debt employed on average about nine workers in 2010, while those with student loan debt employed just two workers.

Source: Simon (2015)

Additionally, key global events and evolving features of the world economy in the last two decades, including the start of the new millennium, the profound financial crisis starting in 2007 and increased worldwide tensions over international trade agreements, have influenced entrepreneurial behavior (Bosma and Kelley, 2018).

More recently, the post-Brexit environment has had implications for entrepreneurship in the UK. While businesses of all sizes struggle to picture what a post-Brexit Britain may look like, Brexit is significant for entrepreneurs. It brings with it concerns about how founders will navigate waters such as funding, data laws, talent and trade.

Source: www.needpix.com/photo/1424864/

According to recent research from KPMG Enterprise, the UK remains Europe's prime investment destination for venture capitalists even after the Brexit vote (Mazour, 2019). The funding will continue to come if businesses in the UK can keep proving to be investment worthy. At the same time, however, European funds face an inherent risk that the trajectory of their British start-up investees may be stalled post-Brexit. Thus, entrepreneurial businesses need to prove their worth more than ever in order to make the capital follow them.

Social-Cultural Factors (S)

The cultural context plays an important role in influencing enterprise and innovation. There are wide variations in societal understanding, perceptions, attitudes and behaviors across countries. National culture also impacts the propensity to found new entrepreneurial ventures. Recognition of such differences is important to gaining global acceptance of enterprise as a positive concept, as well as for founders to function effectively in other cultures.

Societal Culture

The GEM study measures **societal attitudes** as signals of the beliefs about the status of entrepreneurship and the presence of potential entrepreneurs in a society (Bosma and Kelley, 2018). **Societal attitudes** include whether people think that successful entrepreneurs are conferred high status, whether they believe that starting a business is a good career choice, and the extent to which entrepreneurship receives media attention. Media attention generates awareness and can increase acceptance and interest in entrepreneurship across a society. It also includes whether people think it is easy to start a business in their locale.

As per the GEM study, there are both consistencies and wide differences between a) whether successful entrepreneurs are admired in a society and b) whether people think entrepreneurship is a good career choice. Between two-thirds to three-fourths of people in most countries in North America and Europe believe successful entrepreneurs have high status. However, more people in these countries believe that entrepreneurs have high status than think entrepreneurship is a good career choice.

Moreover, there are cultural differences even across the US and Europe. Entrepreneurs in Europe are perceived to suffer from an 'aspiration gap' (Bose and Glynn, 2008). Some investors believe that unlike their US counterparts, European entrepreneurs don't have role models to look up to, and often do not recognize the full potential of their ideas, which necessitates investors to tweak business plans and proactively make necessary introductions to develop those ideas. Inspired by success stories, especially in Silicon Valley, US entrepreneurs, in contrast, face a 'reality gap', often showing impatience to become billionaires within a short span of time.

Early-stage entrepreneurs and established business owners also appear to have an important role in Iranian society (Bosma and Kelley, 2018). High perceptions about the status of entrepreneurs based on events and competitions conducted by universities, government ministries and chambers of commerce support the notion that entrepreneurship has value in Iranian society.

The opposite pattern appears in Latin America and the Caribbean, where in most economies, more people think entrepreneurship is a good career than believe it affords high status. Less than half of those in Croatia and Spain similarly think successful entrepreneurs have high status.

National Culture

National culture also impacts risk-taking and proactiveness. Hofstede's cultural dimensions provide a useful context for exploring the meaning and nature of enterprise. According to Hofstede (2001), five dimensions of 'national culture', namely, **power distance**, **masculinity/femininity**, **uncertainty avoidance**, **long-term orientation** and **individualism-collectivism**, are a key determinant of the degree of enterprise in a country. Each of these dimensions poses interesting questions about whether countries with specific cultural orientations are more likely to be enterprising.

Power distance defines the extent to which the less powerful members of institutions and organizations expect and accept that power will be unequally distributed. A large power distance country may be expected to be less enterprising. This is because subordinates in organizations in such a country may be more likely to accept inequality and hierarchy and, hence, acquire attitudes inimical to entrepreneurship. In some countries, deeply entrenched socio-economic divides rooted in the caste system, and hence the perceived superiority of some groups, are a deterrent to entrepreneurship.

For Anshu Gupta, founder of Goonj, a social venture devoted to the cause of clothing in India, such attitudes stood in the way of growth of his entrepreneurial venture (Pruthi,, 2012). Founded in 1999, the premise of Goonj was the redistribution of surplus clothing, collected from mainly urban donors, to the poor, residing predominantly in rural parts of the country.

As per the business model of Goonj, instead of 'getting' clothes for free, recipients in rural areas were expected to 'earn' them in return for performing developmental work within their local communities. The biggest challenge to the growth of Goonj, in Anshu's words, was the mindset of people, both donors and recipients. In India, people perceive giving away their possessions as a 'donation' or 'favour' to those who receive it. Recipients, in turn, feel entitled to receiving for free, by virtue of their underprivileged position in society.

According to Anshu, it was important to change these perceptions. Rather than thanking themselves for making a donation, it was critical that donors, or people parting with used clothing, acknowledged it as their 'discard', and thanked the recipients for accepting their waste. On the demand side, the challenge entailed making a case for 'earning' rather than 'getting' discarded clothes in return for labor, thus forcing the poor to attach a sense of dignity and self-respect to accepting discarded clothing.

Masculinity/femininity defines the extent to which social gender roles in the society are clearly distinct. In masculine societies, men are supposed to be assertive and focused on material success, and women to be more modest and tender, and concerned with quality of life. Femininity pertains to societies where gender roles overlap. Traditionally, attributes of the feminine gender are viewed to be less likely to lead to enterprising behavior.

Just like other Arab countries, Palestine, for example, is a masculine society that favors men over women. As mentioned in the opening case, although these attitudes are gradually changing, they have been reflected in discriminatory labor market practices that have historically discouraged female entrepreneurship. According to a recent (2019) World Bank report, a prevalent view among employers is that men are more deserving of a job than women. Such employer discrimination against women has thwarted women's leadership and created wage disparities despite comparable human capital endowments and labor market experience.

According to Hofstede (2001), two national cultural values, namely, uncertainty avoidance and long-term orientation, are particularly strongly correlated with the entrepreneurial attitude of the population. **Uncertainty avoidance** defines the extent to which members of a culture feel threatened by uncertain or unknown situations. It refers to society's avoidance of uncertainty stemming from an unknown future and cognitive ambiguity. The fear of failure is high in countries where uncertainty is high, which is inimical for risk-taking and entrepreneurship.

As per GEM, Latin America stands out for its low fear of failure rate (Bosma and Kelley, 2018). Fewer than one-third of those seeing opportunities in every economy in this region state that fear of failure would prevent them from starting a business. Although highest (64%) in Morocco in the given sample, the fear of failure is the lowest (17%) in Angola in the Middle East and Africa region.

In contrast, entrepreneurs in some developed countries like Switzerland, for example, are not big risk takers. According to GEM (2013), Swiss entrepreneurs prefer to 'stay on the safe side', perfecting their products within a small circle rather than seeking rapid growth and expansion. Socio-cultural attitudes like 'have a no nonsense approach to business', and an undaunting belief in high product quality as a long-lasting Swiss tradition, makes them self-confident and unwilling to adopt aggressive selling tactics. Unlike in Silicon Valley where the idea that 'if you fail, fail fast' is the norm, 'take a step slower but take it controlled and perfect' is the entrepreneurs' guiding philosophy in Switzerland.

Long-term orientation is the tendency to prioritize the long term. Long-term orientation defines a country in terms of its trade-off between short-term and long-term gratification of needs (long-term orientation emphasizes values such as perseverance and thrift). On the one hand, taking a long-term view may likely lead to caution and conservative behavior. On the other hand, uncertainty accepting and long-term oriented cultures are more positively associated with innovativeness, proactiveness and autonomy, thus fostering a higher rate of new business formation.

Finally, the **individualism-collectivism** cultural dimension reflects the extent to which it is the interest of the individual or the interest of the group that prevails. Personal initiative plays a significant role in the highly individualistic West. Thus, entrepreneurs in Western countries are expected to be more entrepreneurial than their counterparts elsewhere. The highly individualistic European countries, for instance, display self-confidence in their entrepreneurial ability.

In contrast, in highly collectivist countries such as Japan and Indonesia, the insight and initiative of someone else is very important, which might deter individual initiative, which is so intrinsic to entrepreneurship in the West. Where individualism is counter-cultural, as in Japan, entrepreneurship may be less likely to be manifested in the form of independent, small ventures founded by individuals.

As compared to 34 hours of American workers and 26 of their German counterparts, the average worker in collectivist South Korea spent 42 hours a week on the job in 2010, the highest in the OECD (Organization for Economic Cooperation and Development) (Chafkin, 2011). The core value of a strong work ethic is also reflected in the work culture at both large companies and small entrepreneurial start-ups where sleeping arrangements in the office are commonplace.

Founded by 32-year-old Brian Park in Seoul in 2011 with $40,000 in seed capital from Ticket Monster's Shin and another $40,000 from the South Korean government, the seven-person X-Mon Games is one such example. The company that makes games for mobile devices put up beds in their conference room to allow their managers and employees to take naps given their long work hours. CEOs often 'live' in their offices, sleeping on small, foldup futons next to their desks for months at a stretch.

Yet, despite this outward show of dynamism, South Korea remains deeply conservative. The idea of young entrepreneurs from wealthy backgrounds willing to assume risks to start up is still viewed with suspicion by the seriously conservative older people. In part, this is because of the country's history mired in the Asian financial crisis of 1997 that nearly destroyed the economy and took great hardship to overcome. The Chaebol, Korea's family-owned conglomerates, a symbol of certainty and stability, and provider of the best jobs, remains highly regarded for this reason. The threat of nuclear or chemical attack from the North Korean border in the present day continues to evoke a sense of extreme caution. Thus, to many South Koreans, being an entrepreneur, that is to say, going against the system that made the country rich, is seen as rebellious or even deviant.

Education

Universities foster the emergence of entrepreneurial firms by providing knowledge, conditioning mindsets and providing support infrastructure like incubation and support networks. Alumni of MIT (the Massachusetts Institute of Technology) in the US, for example, have created 25,800 active companies employing about 3.3 million people and generating annual world revenues of $2 trillion, producing the equivalent of the 11th largest economy in the world (MacKenzie and Jones-Evans, 2012). The University of Waterloo, Canada, is another outstanding example of an entrepreneurial university that has produced over 250 spin-offs.

In some fields such as technology, higher education provides the expertise, environment and networks that enable technology entrepreneurs to hone their business skills and create new ventures. The education system also plays an important role in conditioning mindsets. Entrepreneurship education in universities is often focused on creating awareness and enthusiasm for entrepreneurial activities.

At the same time, however, the purpose of education is perceived differently from society to society (Bridge et al., 2003). An individualist society aims at preparing the individual for a place in the society of other individuals. This means learning to cope with new and unknown situations. A collectivist society, in contrast, emphasizes tradition, and adaptation to the skills and virtues necessary to be an acceptable group member. In some countries like Iran, less attention is paid to entrepreneurship education, especially at the post-school level (Bosma and Kelley, 2018). Yet, entrepreneurs in Iran are highly educated, with 71% having earned at least a bachelor's degree.

Access to a well-educated, skilled workforce to support operations in the home country is especially important for immigrant entrepreneurs wanting to re-establish business links with their country of origin (Pruthi et al., 2018). The ability to utilize value-chain advantages based on the prior experience of working and living in India, for example, motivates entrepreneurs of Indian origin in the US to operate in both the US and India. Their access to a young and well-educated workforce, especially technical talent, in India due to the culturally high value placed on education in India, reinforces these motivations.

Educational institutions including both universities and research centers / institutes also offer technical assistance and support infrastructure to new ventures in the early stages (MacKenzie and Jones-Evans, 2012). The world's first science park, the Stanford Industrial Park (now Stanford Research Park), a forerunner to the creation of Silicon Valley in the US, is built on the grounds of Stanford University. Geographic clusters such as these are known for creating social networks that enable entrepreneurs to exchange information related to their innovations, customers and sources of funding with large organizations and educational institutions, investors and other stakeholders.

Universities are playing an increasingly important role in encouraging entrepreneurship through the provision of incubator space, mentoring and expert business support and advice, often at reasonably priced rates. Universities also enable new and young ventures to attract investment, which is suggested to be a positive factor in their smoother operation, and hence their higher probability of survival (Anderson et al., 2010).

Technological Factors (T)

Technical developments such as information and communication technology (ICT) have enhanced opportunities for entrepreneurs in various parts of the world (Bosma and Kelley, 2018). Technological developments enable entrepreneurs to connect with their markets/ customers. Technology also helps to coordinate activities at a distance, thus making it possible to sell in markets outside of the entrepreneurs' home market. The advancement of digital ICT, for instance, has enabled new forms of entrepreneurship and networking.

Although technology-creation capabilities in Europe are equal to those in the US, many Western European entrepreneurs lack experience in translating technology into customer value propositions (Bose and Glynn, 2008). According to Bruce Dunlevie at Benchmark Capital, a Silicon-Valley-based VC firm, European entrepreneurs often do not have the rigor to select the right combination of technical features while building their products, which necessitates investor intervention to transfer such skills:

> It takes not only that spark of genius, but also a lot of detailed decision making processes. For example, if there are 1,000 potential features that could go into a product, but if I'm only going to put 400 of them in, which 400 should I pick? If the last five are wrong, the product could be a failure. It's that trade-off rigor that I don't think exists inherently in a lot of European businesses. (Bruce Dunlevie, Partner, Benchmark Capital, in Bose and Glynn, 2008, p. 9)

Although technology entrepreneurship is not spatially bound, particularly with the rapid development of ICT, certain conditions can encourage technical entrepreneurs. As technology entrepreneurship, in particular, is a highly uncertain process that requires information sharing to keep abreast of technical developments, as well as a strong supporting infrastructure including access to sources of financing, the location of the new firm that creates a favourable ecosystem for entrepreneurial activity is one of the most important factors impacting the emergence of technical entrepreneurship (MacKenzie and Jones-Evans, 2012). Areas with a strong presence of other high-tech firms and technology-focused specialist venture capital investors often establish a reputation for the quality of their local specialist support for nascent firms, which can be vital in the early stages of technical entrepreneurs' decision to create a new venture.

Developed as a result of the actions of a few individual firms, regional clusters such as Silicon Valley in California, Route 128 in Boston, Massachusetts, and Cambridge, UK, have drawn attention to technical entrepreneurship in these regions over the last 50 years. Due to the prevalence of technology infrastructure and the physical proximity of top class educational and research institutions, large and small high-tech firms, and venture caplitalists, Silicon Valley is one of the most favourable regions for starting up in the world.

With the exception of three companies (Massachusetts-based Moderna Therapeutics, Maryland-based Tenable, and Utah-based PluralSight) from outside of the region, all of the ten largest IPOs for US venture-backed companies in 2018 hailed from California (NVCA, 2019). Helped by the presence of MIT and Harvard universities, the supportive environment of Route 128 in the Boston area has similarly contributed to a high incidence of spin-off entrepreneurs.

Countries like Sweden are also credited with a strong technology infrastructure, translating into high start-up emergence rates. According to the OECD, Stockholm produces the second-highest number of billion-dollar tech companies per capita after Silicon Valley (Bosma and Kelley, 2018).

New technologies and mobile connectivity in developing countries are also leading to tremendous growth in entrepreneurship and innovation in these countries. The use of the M-Pesa mobile payments system in Kenya, for example, has made the country a leader in mobile payments technology (Bright and Hruby, 2015; Kohli, 2015). This improvement in connectivity has helped lay the foundations for Africa's 'Silicon Valley' called 'Silicon Savannah' in Nairobi. This region has attracted a range of technology start-ups and venture capital firms.

Issues in International Comparisons of Entrepreneurship

PEST factors impact the development of entrepreneurship across countries and economies as discussed above. However, drawing comparisons of the international development of entrepreneurship between different countries is not straightforward. This is because of ambiguity in the impact of specific external factors, interdependence of various external factors, differing forms and goals of entrepreneurship, as well as regional variations in the development of entrepreneurship.

Ambiguity in the Impact of Specific External Factors

The influence of any single external factor on the development of entrepreneurship is not clearly understood. Little is known, for example, about how different dimensions of culture interact to reinforce or negate each other (Bridge et al., 2003). Economically successful nations exhibit significantly different scores on each of Hofstede's cultural dimensions, suggesting that there are no easily defined 'right' or 'wrong' conditions for entrepreneurship.

Much also depends on how the outcome variable is defined. Positive outcomes can emerge from a wide range of contexts, even if those contexts are not necessarily amenable to small firm emergence and development. Societal norms supporting the acceptance of authority and discipline (high power distance), and association of individuals with the collective good of the group (collectivism) in countries like Korea and Japan, for example, underlie the success of some of the world's leading conglomerates originating in these countries.

GEM findings affirm that the connection between start-up rates and external environmental conditions is not obvious. In some cases, entrepreneurs thrive in economies with seemingly poor support. They operate in the informal sector, navigate poor external environments through their own social networks or even succumb to corruption.

Interdependence of External Factors

In this chapter, we have used the PEST framework to explain the influence of external factors on the development of entrepreneurship. However, PEST categories are not water tight and various external influences are interdependent (Bridge et al., 2003). For example, political, economic and cultural influences are interrelated (Hofstede, 2001). Less developed countries typically have unstable and unpredictable environments, which impacts business longevity. Entrepreneurs in developed European countries are the most individualistic and display self-confidence in their entrepreneurial ability. In developed Western countries, the firm is seen as an institutionalization of work; entrepreneurs in less developed countries, in contrast, ascribe more importance to the firm as a family institution.

Likewise, beliefs towards entrepreneurship may depend on the availability of other career options (Bosma and Kelley, 2018). Entrepreneurship may appear less attractive if, for example, good jobs are available in a society, and especially if the potential for rewards is low or unpredictable.

More recently, Brexit and the challenge of data transfers between the UK and EU has illustrated the intersection of political, economic and technological influences on the development of entrepreneurship. Data is one of the most crucial ways for small, innovative businesses to directly deliver, or enable their clients to deliver, personalized services to their customers (Mazour, 2019). The ability to understand and implement an effective data strategy differentiates small businesses from their competition. The UK government expects to maintain the stability of data transfers between the EU member states and the UK. However, given that around 75% of the UK's cross-border data flows are with EU countries, the lack of detail on how the government plans to deliver this outcome is a major concern.

Differing Forms (and Goals) of Entrepreneurship

According to the GEM study, it is not appropriate to assess the effect of the external context solely on start-up rates or assume a single depiction of an entrepreneur (Bosma and

Kelley, 2018). Entrepreneurship is manifested in a variety of forms, and different types of entrepreneurs contribute to achieving economies that are both stable and dynamic.

Enterprise and entrepreneurship in collectivist Asian countries, for example, happens in large organizations (Bridge et al., 2003). We discussed the concept of corporate entrepreneurship in Chapter 2. The notion of 'trust' explains why Japanese and Koreans can handle very large organizations efficiently. The collectivist tradition and culture of subordinating personal to group interests, cooperation and group harmony raises the question of whether entrepreneurial behavior is exhibited by the group itself, by individuals working through the group, or by breaking group norms.

In some cases, large, established organizations may have a disproportionate influence and access to key resources, enabling them to thrive in unfavorable environments, often to the exclusion of other newer and smaller businesses (Bosma and Kelley, 2018). At the same time, however, these constraints may create conditions for small business entrepreneurship. They may lead to an inefficient business environment, generating gaps leading to entrepreneurial opportunities.

The definition of enterprise typically used to compare external influences on entrepreneurship is that of enterprise in the private sector. This is because private businesses are most studied and analyzed. Enterprise can also manifest itself in other ways, especially in economies where external conditions for mainstream enterprise are far from ideal. As discussed in Chapter 2, businesses are also started for social reasons. Thus, social ventures or businesses created with the goal of solving social problems must also be considered.

Regional Variations in the Development of Entrepreneurship

According to GEM, variations in societal attitudes to entrepreneurship among economies within a region are much higher than differences in averages across the regions (Bosma and Kelley, 2018). Despite similar levels of economic development, three innovation-driven economies in East and South Asia, for example, show different levels on the two indicators – whether people think that successful entrepreneurs are conferred high status and whether they believe that starting a business is a good career choice – related to societal perceptions about entrepreneurship.

Japan shows low levels on both indicators, particularly relative to whether entrepreneurship is considered a good career. People in Taiwan, on the other hand, are more likely to think entrepreneurship is a good career than to believe successful entrepreneurs have high status. The Republic of Korea shows higher levels on the status indicator than these two economies, suggesting successful entrepreneurs are held in high regard, but entrepreneurship is in general not as highly regarded as a career choice.

Regional variations in the development of entrepreneurship can be attributed to the heterogeneity of culture and differing goals within regions. The ways of doing business in Asia, for instance, are subtly different from those of the West. Moreover, they are different within the region itself (Bridge et al., 2003). Each form is embedded in the cultures and development histories of its own society, and has differing goals and outcomes.

Bridge et al. (2003) argue that the concept of a common culture applies more to societies than to countries. Some authors define culture as a set of historically evolved learned values, attitudes and meanings shared by the members of a given community that influence their material and non-material way of life. Members of the community learn these shared characteristics through different stages of the socialization processes of their lives in institutions, such as family, religion, formal education and society as a whole.

According to Hofstede (2001), shared values typify a society, and 'the collective programming of the mind distinguishes the members of one group or category from another'. Almost everyone belongs to a number of different groups and categories of people at the same time, and carries within themselves mental programming corresponding to different levels of culture.

Different cultures are likely to produce different working models better suited to their group values and beliefs. Thus, a single indicator, namely, new start-up rate, may not be sufficient to assess the development of entrepreneurship in an economy. While Taiwan, for example, has lower start-up rates than its regional neighbors, its established business rates and employee entrepreneurship rates are high (Bosma and Kelley, 2018). Qatar also shows low TEA rates, but high employee entrepreneurship. In addition, despite these low levels, Qatar has a high proportion of growth-oriented and international entrepreneurs. India displays low TEA but stands out for its high proportion of innovative entrepreneurs.

Similarly, in Japan, the large, complex organization is known as the Kaisha. The Kaisha is a large, professionally managed and highly complex enterprise with wide ownership. Unlike the large American corporation that exists to return wealth to shareholders, the driving reason for the existence of the Kaisha is to employ people.

In South Korea, the Chaebol, or a huge family business run like a regiment, derives much of its dynamism from its contribution to the national development goals of Korea. Where doing business in Asia needs strong local knowledge and connections, as in China, the instrument of wealth creation is the family business. The Chinese family business is a small business networking to escape the limitations of its size. It exists primarily to create and sustain family fortunes.

Overall, the relationship between the environment and entrepreneurship is complex. GEM introduces a composite index, the National Entrepreneurship Context Index (NECI), to assess the environment for entrepreneurship in an economy. The NECI is derived from 12 framework conditions including political factors such as government policies, bureaucracy and support programs, economic factors such as market dynamics or entry regulations, socio-cultural and social norms, and the availability of infrastructure such as education and entrepreneurial finance. These factors are weighted based on the importance experts place on them. NECI results can help to identify areas where there are gaps between the ratings on the framework conditions in different economies, particularly in relation to the importance placed on them.

Figure 3.5 and Table 3.1 show the lowest and highest ranking economies by region based on the NECI score for 54 economies completing GEM's National Expert Survey in 2018. NECI results are consistently high in the East and South Asia region. Three of the top ranked economies – India, Taiwan and Indonesia – are in this region.

Conversely, the Latin America and Caribbean region shows consistently low results, with no economies making the top 20, and with Panama and Puerto Rico among the lowest five ranked of all economies completing the survey. In Europe, a ranking of 3 in the Netherlands contrasts with that of 53 in Croatia. The Middle East and Africa region shows the most variation with both the highest ranked (Qatar) and lowest ranked (Mozambique) countries.

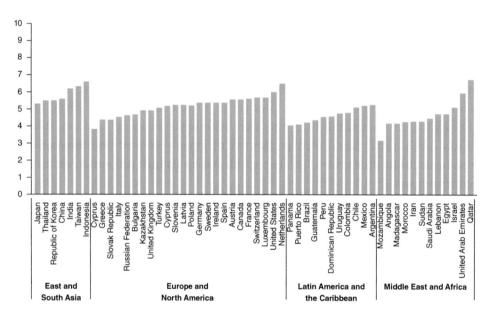

Figure 3.5   National Entrepreneurship Context Index results for 54 economies in four geographic regions

Source: Bosma and Kelley (2018)

Table 3.1   National Entrepreneurship Context Index rankings and scores for 54 economies

Income Level	REGION	Economy	NECI Rank	NECI Score (out of 10)
high income	Middle East and Africa	**Qatar**	1	6.7
low income	East and South Asia	**Indonesia**	2	6.6
high income	Europe and North America	**Netherlands**	3	6.5
high income	East and South Asia	**Taiwan**	4	6.3

Income Level	REGION	Economy	NECI Rank	NECI Score (out of 10)
low income	East and South Asia	India	5	6.2
high income	Europe and North America	United States	6	6.0
high income	Middle East and Africa	United Arab Emirates	7	5.9
high income	Europe and North America	Luxembourg	8	5.7
high income	Europe and North America	Switzerland	9	5.7
high income	Europe and North America	France	10	5.6
middle income	East and South Asia	China	11	5.6
high income	Europe and North America	Canada	12	5.5
high income	Europe and North America	Austria	13	5.5
high income	East and South Asia	Republic of Korea	14	5.5
middle income	East and South Asia	Thailand	15	5.5
high income	Europe and North America	Spain	16	5.4
high income	Europe and North America	Ireland	17	5.4
high income	Europe and North America	Sweden	18	5.4
high income	Europe and North America	Germany	19	5.4

Source: Bosma and Kelley (2018)

An examination of the top-ranked economies shows the importance of healthy conditions across all aspects of the environment affecting entrepreneurship. Qatar and Taiwan are the top-rated economies that exhibit high ratings on every framework condition, while Indonesia, India and the Netherlands have high ratings on all factors except one (inadequate physical infrastructure in Indonesia and India, and inadequate internal market dynamics in the Netherlands). These results show that strong contexts for entrepreneurship may have differing effects on entrepreneurship profiles.

Chapter Summary

LO1: The **Global Entrepreneurship Monitor (GEM)** is one of the most comprehensive studies of global entrepreneurship. Conceived in 1999, the objective of GEM was to improve the relationship between perceptions of entrepreneurship, entrepreneurial

(Continued)

activity and national economic growth. Over time, GEM has revised its objectives to measuring differences in the level of entrepreneurial activity between economies and uncovering the factors underlying these differences. The study also aims to establish the link between entrepreneurship and economic growth and, hence, economic development over a longer period of time.

LO2: GEM developed a measure called the **Total Entrepreneurial Activity (TEA) index** to indicate differences in the levels of entrepreneurial activity across countries. The TEA index value shows for each country the percentage of the adult population who have taken some action towards creating a new business in the past year or who are owner-managers of an active business less than 42 months old. There is significant variation in the rate of business formation by world regions as measured by the TEA index. The findings of the GEM study also report variations by entrepreneurship type, industry sector and gender. Whereas 18.6% of TEA is in **family businesses**, 8.0% of TEA is **solo businesses**. The industry profiles of early-stage entrepreneurs are related to national income levels across countries. Across the world, men are twice as likely to start a business as women. Further, individuals start a business for two main reasons: to exploit a business opportunity (opportunity entrepreneurs), or to sustain themselves because all other options for work are either absent or unsatisfactory (necessity entrepreneurs). The proportion of opportunity entrepreneurs increases from an average of 37% of entrepreneurs in the low-income economies, to 42% in middle-income economies, and 51% in the high-income economies. Entrepreneurs in low-income economies are more likely motivated by necessity than in developed economies.

LO3: Political, economic, socio-cultural and technological (PEST) aspects of the external environment in each economy influence its entrepreneurship profile. Government intervention to promote entrepreneurship can take two forms: setting the conditions for enterprise, and directly intervening to support the entrepreneurial process. Both the level of economic development and the state of the economy, societal culture and national culture, influence the development of entrepreneurship. Hofstede's five dimensions of 'national culture', namely, **power distance**, **masculinity/femininity**, **uncertainty avoidance**, **long-term orientation** and **individualism-collectivism**, are a key determinant of the degree of enterprise in a country. Technical developments such as information and communication technology enable entrepreneurs to connect with their markets/customers and coordinate activities at a distance, thus making it possible to sell in markets outside of the entrepreneurs' home market.

LO4: Drawing comparisons of the international development of entrepreneurship across countries is not straightforward due to ambiguity in understanding the impact of specific external factors, the interdependence of various external factors, differing forms and goals, as well as regional variations in the development of entrepreneurship.

Review Questions

1. What is the GEM? What are the objectives of the GEM?
2. How does the GEM study contribute to our understanding of the international development of entrepreneurship? Explain the key patterns in the international development of entrepreneurship based on the GEM findings.
3. How does the external environment influence the development of entrepreneurship? Explain the role of a) political, b) economic, c) social and d) technological factors in the development of entrepreneurship in any country of your choice. Give examples to support your answer.
4. How can governments intervene to promote the development of entrepreneurship? Discuss the forms of government intervention outlined in the chapter. Give examples to support your answer.
5. According to the chapter, 'entrepreneurship acquires a different meaning in economically developed and less developed countries'. To what extent do you agree/ disagree with this statement? Discuss.
6. According to the chapter, 'Hofstede's cultural dimensions provide a useful context for exploring the meaning and nature of enterprise'. To what extent do you agree/ disagree with this statement? Name Hofstede's five dimensions of national culture and discuss their relevance for the international development of entrepreneurship.
7. What role do educational institutions play in the development of entrepreneurship? Explain.
8. According to the chapter, 'technical developments such as information and communication technology (ICT) have enhanced opportunities for entrepreneurs in various parts of the world'. Using examples, explain the role of technology in the international development of entrepreneurship.

Case 3.1

Entrepreneurship in Spain: Moving Out of the Dark Ages?

Europe has produced business pathbreakers, such as Spain's Amancio Ortega, co-founder of Zara-owner Inditex SA, the world's largest fashion retailer by sales, and Janus Friis and Niklas Zennstrom, the Scandinavian founders of the internet phone company Skype, which was acquired by Microsoft for $8.5 billion in 2011. However, the external environment in the Eurozone raises questions about its attractiveness for potential entrepreneurs.

Legal and Regulatory Environment

There are several examples of government action and support for entrepreneurship in the Eurozone. The Spanish government, for example, has passed legislation to

(Continued)

encourage hiring by making it cheaper to fire workers. An 'Entrepreneurship Law' includes tax breaks, steps to limit entrepreneurs' liability in case of bankruptcy and programs to teach entrepreneurship in schools. Lately, Spain has been making a case for reduced documentation requirements and red tape for entrepreneurs. It has tried streamlining business registration by electronically linking the government agencies involved in the new firm start-up process.

One long-standing government program allows the jobless to claim all or part of their unemployment benefits in a lump sum for starting a business (Fig. 3.7). According to the Labor Ministry, around a million Spaniards have used their benefits in this way since the country plunged into recession in 2008. Many of these ventures are making strides. For example, Francisco Javier Gómez, 38, and his brother used about $30,000 in unemployment benefits to bootstrap a tech company, Qualica-RD, which exports its automatic identification technology.

Despite these initiatives, the OECD ranked Spain second worst in a survey on barriers to entrepreneurship in 29 nations in 2013. In 2015 World Bank rankings on the ease of starting a business, Spain placed 74th out of 189 countries, right behind Egypt, Saint Lucia and Trinidad and Tobago.

There are several underlying reasons for these numbers. First, government initiatives to aid entrepreneurs are uneven and tend to be dispersed among different agencies, with much of the responsibility left to local governments or educational institutions. Gerard Vidal formed a data-encryption firm, Enigmedia, when he couldn't find an employer looking for a PhD in physics. But even a physicist was perplexed by the paperwork involved in starting a company in Spain, and the launch was delayed months by a process he believes was inefficient and frustrating.

Second, regulations related to incorporation are cumbersome. According to the World Bank, it takes an average of 13 days to start a business in Spain. The average for OECD countries is 9.2 days, and in an efficient country like the Netherlands, the average is four days.

Incorporating a company is also expensive. In the six months that Diana and Arantxa Fernández needed to obtain the multitude of permits required to open up a nursery school last year, the sisters burned through most of the capital they had husbanded from taking lump-sum unemployment.

Finally, government policy is excessively focused on emergency self-employment measures such as the lump-sum payments, rather than tax-code revisions specifically aimed at high-potential start-ups.

Economic Environment

Recent government budget cuts and corporate layoffs have left more than 18 million people out of work in the Eurozone. The COVID crisis is expected to further worsen the unemployment situation. The only way for individuals to find work in this scenario is to create their own jobs. Layoffs in Spain and the Eurozone have forced others to follow suit, however inexperienced entrepreneurs might not find it easy to tread the entrepreneurial path in the current economic climate.

For instance, Juan Pedro Mellinas, a Spanish entrepreneur, started Eternalia, a company that tends to grave sites, after losing a white-collar marketing job in 2011.

Eternalia now has franchises in six cities, but he struggles to pay employees to do the cleaning at his local cemetery.

Banks are still holding back on lending as they shore up balance sheets damaged during years of recession (Fig. 3.6). When David Fito tried to open a gluten-free bakery after getting laid off by a bank a few years ago, 30 banks refused to lend him the €100,000 he needed. He got the credit only after his parents pledged their apartment as collateral and seven other wage earners agreed to co-sign.

Cesar Martin started a digital education venture, Sapeando, after losing his photo-editing job. Although the site was a hit, he couldn't find sufficient advertisers or a bank lender, forcing him to quit his venture. An uptick in lending to smaller businesses in recent months may soon be reversed due to the COVID-19 pandemic. The level of credit is still far lower than what it was before the crisis and below the level needed.

Socio-Cultural Environment

On the one hand, there are signs that attitudes to entrepreneurship in Spain are changing. Propelled by massive job destruction in Spain's public and private sector, co-working centers are now popping up, as are reality TV shows featuring the enterprising leaders of 'los start-ups', and bookstores sell volumes such as *From Unemployed to Businessman*.

Another encouraging development is the surge of business accelerators and incubators. According to a study by Telefonica SA, the Spanish telecommunications giant, the number of these business launchpads between 2007 and 2013 increased by nearly 400%, to 260, in ten leading European economies. The Creapolis business incubator near Barcelona is one such example. It is described as a 'creativity park' aimed at nurturing entrepreneurs.

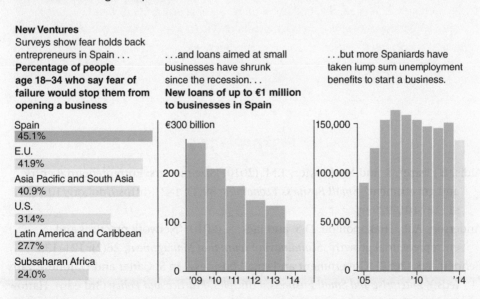

New Ventures

Surveys show fear holds back entrepreneurs in Spain . . .
Percentage of people age 18–34 who say fear of failure would stop them from opening a business

Spain
45.1%

E.U.
41.9%

Asia Pacific and South Asia
40.9%

U.S.
31.4%

Latin America and Caribbean
27.7%

Subsaharan Africa
24.0%

. . .and loans aimed at small businesses have shrunk since the recession. . .
New loans of up to €1 million to businesses in Spain

€300 billion

. . .but more Spaniards have taken lump sum unemployment benefits to start a business.

Figure 3.6 New ventures in Spain

Source: Moffett (2014)

(Continued)

According to Nick Drandakis of Athens, founder of Taxibeat, an app that provides passenger ratings on taxi drivers, the fear of failure is less of an issue in Spain. This is because of the perpetual economic hardship in the country that people feel accustomed to. The learning curve for novice entrepreneurs is steep.

At the same time, however, according to academic surveys, the fear of failure remains a bigger impediment to entrepreneurship in Spain compared to other regions in the Eurozone (Fig. 3.6). Entrepreneurship education is not commonly included in taught school curricula at the elementary and middle school levels. For example, María Alegre, 29-year-old CEO and co-founder of Chartboost Inc., a 130-employee company that helps mobile game developers find new users and monetize games, started selling home-made jewelry at the age of 13. However, she had never heard the word 'entrepreneurship' until her fifth year at a Spanish business school. She feels she did not get encouragement until she was studying at the University of Michigan. The Spanish culture in her view is one of being risk-averse and not dreaming big enough.

Source: Moffett (2014)

Discussion Questions

1. What aspects of the political environment impact the development of entrepreneurship in Spain as described in this case? Evaluate the political environment for entrepreneurship in Spain.
2. How favorable is the economic environment for starting a new business in Spain? Discuss.
3. According to the case, the 'culture of being against risk and not dreaming big enough' is amiss in Spain. To what extent do you agree/disagree with the statement? Discuss.
4. Do you think Spain is 'moving out of the dark ages in entrepreneurship'? Why / why not? Give reasons to support your answer.

References

Aidis, R., Estrin, S. and Mickiewicz, T.M. (2010) 'Size matters: Entrepreneurial entry and government', *Small Business Economics*, 39(1): 1–21. https://doi.org/10.1007/s11187-010-9299-y

Anderson, A.R., Drakopoulou, D.S. and Jack, S. (2010) 'Network practices and entrepreneurial growth', *Scandinavian Journal of Management*, 26(2): 121–133.

Bennett, R.J. (2012) 'Government and small business', in S. Carter and D. Jones-Evans (eds.), *Enterprise and Small Business: Principles, Practice and Policy* (3rd edn). Harlow: Financial Times Prentice Hall, pp. 46–77.

Bose, K.R. and Glynn Jr., J. (2008) 'Benchmark capital: The international expansion of a Silicon Valley venture capital firm'. *Stanford Graduate School of Business*, Case No. E218.

Bosma, N. and Kelley, D. (2018) *Global Entrepreneurship Monitor 2018/2019 Global Report*. Santiago: Grafica Andes.

Bridge, S., O'Neill, K. and Cromie, S. (2003) 'Enterprise: The external influences', in S. Bridge, K. O'Neill and S. Cromie (eds.), *Understanding Enterprise: Entrepreneurship and Small Business* (2nd edn). New York: Palgrave Macmillan, pp. 104–133.

Bright, J. and Hruby, A. (2015) 'The rise of Silicon Savannah and Africa's tech movement', *TechCrunch*, 23 July. Available at https://techcrunch.com/2015/07/23/the-rise-of-silicon-savannah-and-africas-tech-movement (last accessed 27 September 2022).

Chafkin, M. (2011) 'The returnees', *Inc. Magazine*, December. Available at www.inc.com/magazine/201112/the-returnees.html (last accessed 27 September 2022).

Chalmers, D. and Fraser, S. (2012) 'Social entrepreneurship', in S. Carter and D. Jones-Evans (eds), *Enterprise and Small Business: Principles, Practice and Policy* (3rd edn). Harlow: Financial Times Prentice Hall, pp. 289–301.

European Commission (n.d.) 'Internal market, industry, entrepreneurship and SMEs'. Available at https://ec.europa.eu/growth/smes_en (last accessed 27 September 2022).

Global Entrepreneurship Monitor (2013) 'Report on Switzerland, School of Management Fribourg'. Available at http://repository.supsi.ch/4782/1/GEM_Switzerland_2013_DEF.pdf (last accessed 27 September 2022).

Hofstede, G. (2001) *Culture's Consequences: Comparing Values, Behaviors, Institutions, and Organizations across Nations*. Thousand Oaks, CA: Sage.

International Finance Corporation (IFC) (2018) 'Sustainability report redefining development finance'. Available at www.ifc.org/wps/wcm/connect/3aa05003-d634-40f9-8af4-35b8c8a87248/IFC-AR18-Full-Report.pdf?MOD=AJPERES&CVID=moNw5we (last accessed 27 September 2022).

Kerr, S.P. and Kerr, W.R. (2016) 'Immigrant entrepreneurship', Working Paper 22385. Cambridge, MA: National Bureau of Economic Research.

Kohli, T. (2015) 'Why Kenya, home to Africa's "Silicon Valley", is set to be the continent's ultimate tech hub', *Mail & Guardian Africa*, 24 February. Available at http://mgafrica.com/article/2015-02-19-why-kenya-is-africas-tech-hub (last accessed 27 September 2022).

MacKenzie, N.G. and Jones-Evans, D. (2012) 'Technical entrepreneurship', in S. Carter and D. Jones-Evans (eds), *Enterprise and Small Business: Principles, Practice and Policy* (3rd edn). Harlow: Financial Times Prentice Hall, pp. 268–279.

Mazour, I. (2019) 'A post-Brexit future for entrepreneurs: How to navigate an uncertain climate', *Entrepreneur Europe*, 4 April. Available at www.entrepreneur.com/article/330705 (last accessed 27 September 2022).

Moffett, M. (2014) 'New entrepreneurs find pain in Spain: Startups face cratered consumer market, scarce capital, dense bureaucracy and culture averse to risk'. *The Wall Street Journal*, 27 November. Available at www.wsj.com/articles/new-entrepreneurs-find-pain-in-spain-1417133197 (last accessed 27 September 2022).

National Venture Capital Association (NVCA) (2019) *Yearbook*. Data provided by Pitchbook. Available at https://nvca.org/wp-content/uploads/2019/08/NVCA-2019-Yearbook.pdf (last accessed 27 September 2022).

Pruthi, S., (2012) 'Process of social entrepreneurship in India: The case of Goonj', in Underwood, S., Blundel, R., Lyon, F. and Schaefer, A. (eds.) (2012) *Social and Sustainable Enterprise: Changing the Nature of Business, Contemporary Issues in Entrepreneurship Research*, 2(1): 1–24.

Pruthi, S., Basu, A. and Wright, M. (2018) 'Ethnic ties, motivations, and home country entry strategy of transnational entrepreneurs', *Journal of International Entrepreneurship*, 16(2): 210–243.

Simon, R. (2015) 'Why Chile and Colombia are startup savvy? Study shows the Latin American nations are leaders in entrepreneurship'. *The Wall Street Journal*, 7 January. Available at www.wsj.com/articles/why-chile-and-colombia-are-startup-savvy-1420675782 (last accessed 27 September 2022).

United Nations Office for the Coordination of Human Affairs. (2015) 'Movement restrictions on West Bank roads tightened, OCHA survey: 20 per cent increase in closure obstacles'. Available at https://goo.gl/JypiQP (last accessed 27 September 2022).

The World Bank (2019) 'Palestinian women entrepreneurs forging paths for women and men'. World Bank, 7 March. Available at www.worldbank.org/en/news/feature/2019/03/07/palestinian-women-entrepreneurs-forging-paths-for-women-and-men (last accessed 27 September 2022).

4
THE LOCAL AND REGIONAL DIMENSIONS OF INTERNATIONAL ENTREPRENEURSHIP

---Learning Outcomes---

After studying this chapter, you should be able to:

- **LO1**: Understand critically the value of local and regional aspects of entrepreneurship for international business and entrepreneurship
- **LO2**: Map and define the unique features as part of carrying out a critical overview of the contextual features of local and regional entrepreneurship and economic development that have a bearing on international entrepreneurship
- **LO3**: Understand critically how local and regional strategies contribute to internationally focused entrepreneurial identities of local regions
- **LO4**: Observe, understand and evaluate the journey that local regions take to connect with cross-border regions and become transnational regions through growth corridors
- **LO5**: Critique underpinning concepts and theories of local and regional entrepreneurship development and their relevance for global entrepreneurship and innovation

Introduction

It may sound like a contradiction or a paradox, but understanding global entrepreneurship is partially dependent on appreciating and observing critically the differences and commonalities of the varied, local entrepreneurial contexts or ecosystems which make up the global environment for entrepreneurship. Businesses trade, make strategic alliances, network, invest overseas and set up offshore operations not simply on the basis of specific contacts with counterparts in other countries, but also on the information they collect about the alternative, attractive regions, the local skills and knowledge base, the local supplier and distribution networks, local policies and regulations, the strength and resilience of these places to engage in international business, and even their social environment. Part of the reason for obtaining useful, relevant information about other places is based on the increasing dependency on international supply and value chains, the relative strengths of the international value chain partner and the acceleration of pace with which products are made and sold to multiple customers worldwide. These considerations have become even more critical in an interconnected global economy. The corresponding entrepreneurial capacity of a range of partners or suppliers in a region many distant miles away from home, the ability to switch between them at short notice, and their capability for adding value to products and services sold worldwide are all factors which guide businesses when they explore international opportunity.

There is another normative paradox that underlies the significance of local regions for international entrepreneurship and business activity. The more global a region is in economic terms, the greater the likelihood that it is also a powerful local economy. This is not just a hypothesis for research exploration. It is almost a truism. Witness California and New York in the USA, London, Cambridge and the South East in the UK, Tel Aviv and Herzliya in Israel, Berlin and Badden Wuttenburg in Germany, Leuven in Belgium, Gothenburg and Stockholm in Sweden, Paris in France, Bangalore and Mumbai in India, Beijing, Shanghai and Guandong in China, Mexico City in Mexico and so on. They are a mix of cities and regions which thrive economically at the local level and are seen as innovative hotspots to draw in or export finance, talent and other resources while making a range of alliances with their counterparts in other parts of the world. That is when regions move from being local to becoming global.

One final, good reason for understanding the value of the local and regional is that they exist in their own right. Just knowing how different locales function and change technologically, economically and innovatively is central to our understanding of how firms in different parts of world engage in international entrepreneurship and business. Even when businesses do not interact with others in specific regions in the world, it helps to know how other firms, potential competitors, operate in those environments. It is good to be enlightened about what is going on in other parts of the world. Policy makers studying alternate economic environments can evaluate what could be emulated and adjusted to support their local industries.

To try to comprehend what local issues are critical to local and international development enabling international business, we will work with several concepts and terms which are used in the various literature on international entrepreneurship, regional development and innovation, and globalization. We will explore terms such as knowledge spillovers, institutional thickness, absorptive capacity and others as we navigate our way through the regions of the world. These concepts are part of the standard terminology in discussions and critiques of entrepreneurship, development, internationalization and globalization.

The chapter starts with a brief explanation of what constitutes regions ending with a proposal for a liberal and flexible approach to this concept. It then introduces the reader to the important concept of spillovers, especially knowledge spillovers which underpin our understanding of how many regions evolve, especially in today's knowledge economy. The chapter concentrates mainly on cities as regions of knowledge creation entrepreneurship and international development, and we travel from Berlin in Germany to Singapore, and Leuven in Belgium, to allow for some interesting contrasts between these rather different locations. All three cities represent spaces for negotiating the interplay between talented people, new technologies, strategic purpose, new enterprise and knowledge creation, internationalization and governance structures. They are local places whose identities have been established by local factors that distinguish their locale, the uniqueness of which has global appeal. All three cities are at the forefront of global knowledge production and new forms of business creation, and the mini case studies have been prepared to provide insights into this frontier. We end the chapter by stretching the regional concept to examine how the reach of regions exceeds their local and national borders when they connect with other regions in neighboring countries. These are physical connects that facilitate business and economic development. They are referred to as growth corridors.

The Region as a Starting Point

Regions are a good point to start. References to innovative regions around the world and the cities and towns that form part of those regions are quite common. But what do regions mean? From a theoretical point of view, they are associated with governance of policies of institutions facilitating economic development, social cohesion and environmental welfare, as part of the making and distribution of public and private goods. The term varies by country but it tends to focus on the level of a sub-national administrative unit, as for example the Administrative Region of Quebec in Canada or the 'Autonomous Community of Murcia' (Region de Murcia) in Spain. Regions can encompass countries such as when reference is made to the European Region or Community (an economic and quasi political union). The Brazilians group their 'estados' – the primary administrative divisions – into 'grandes regioes' or greater regions for statistical purposes (Mitra, 2020). There is an inherent fuzziness about the nomenclature, its use and its meaning for citizens or entrepreneurs, not least because a region's identity is based on critical arrangements and reconfigurations of beliefs, values and cultural perceptions of groups of people. They are difficult to define in terms of size, and often confused with smaller 'districts' or 'quarters' such as the cultural quarter of Hoxton in London or the creative district of Tianzifang in Shanghai. Both 'regions' draw their spatial identity from the natural or engineered concentration of specific creative indus-tries, respectively, in those geographical areas.

Cities are often large enough to have a regional identity because they dominate the geographical space where they are situated due to the critical mass of economic and social activities in those cities. Cambridge in the UK is often regarded as a proxy of the wider political, administrative unit of Cambridgeshire because the focus of interest tends to be on the disproportionate concentration of technological, scientific and entre-preneurial prowess in that city, compared to the surrounding area. Travel to work distances are often considered a good metric for identifying a region, but in our fast changing world where so much of our productive work is carried out worldwide or per-formed at home, it is problematic to use that proxy as a definite guide.

For our practical purpose, we will adopt a flexible approach and take the term 'region' to include cities, towns, urban and rural districts, or areas with a definable and tangible critical mass of people, technologies and networks, supported by a structure of govern-ance. While many of these 'regions' will have different economic and social compositions, they will invariably involve different stakeholders, the creation and availability of different sets of opportunities mediated by entrepreneurs and by the dif-ferent institutions that are responsible for their governance. Our interest is in the mechanisms and processes that contribute to the achievement of this optimal mix for entrepreneurship and economic development that help these regions to grow and locate themselves in a global map of connectivity with other regions in the world.

The Significance of the Regional Dimension

The European Union and the OECD have been advocating the role of entrepreneurship in benchmarking and catching-up for under-performing regions in Europe (House of Lords, 2003; OECD, 2000, 2010) for some time now. There has been much interest in 'regional innovation systems' and 'regional competitiveness' and both before and with the emergence of globalization. The argument that regions compete globally for the loca-tion of Foreign Direct Investment, innovation, skills and business opportunities (Martin and Tyler, 2000) is well rehearsed. Researchers have provided theoretical insights and empirical observations of connected regions such as California (Silicon Valley), Bangalore, Mumbai, Shanghai, Beijing, Tel Aviv and Taipei, with their flows of capital, technologies and circulation of brain and talent (Mellander and Florida, 2007; Saxenian, 2006).

Starting with the USA

It is almost a reflex that we think of the USA as the bastion of entrepreneurship. Between 1996 and 2004 it created an average of 550,000 small businesses every month (The Economist, 2009). Looking at more granular information offered by the US Census Bureau, by way of business formations within four quarters (BF4Q), a forward-looking measure made up of business applications that effectively convert into businesses with employees within four quarters of application, BF4Q fell sharply during the Great Recession, with the decline starting long before 2007. There was a slight recovery starting in 2014, as BF4Q rose to nearly 80,000 per quarter, after falling to approximately 70,000 in 2012. What this data tells us is that business formations remain well below their pre-recession levels. In 2006, before the recession of 2008, the majority of the western states together with those on the East Coast were deemed 'hot' in that they performed relatively well in terms of new employer business formations per capita. Unfortunately, a relative weakness in BF4Q was already noticeable in some states, including the Midwest. By 2010, three years after the Great Recession started hitting the economy, business formations per capita had fallen substantially for many states. Projected business formations per capita based on 2017 business applications show that improvements have been hard to obtain since 2010, and that many states were only likely to create new firms at much lower rates than the pre-recession levels of 2006 (Dinreloz, 2018).

Why does the information about start-ups in the USA matter? Understanding the dynamics of change makes it possible to grasp the fact that even in the most fertile of environments for entrepreneurship, circumstances make it problematic for both businesses and the regions in which they are located to retain or attract new formations. In these declining conditions, international business activity suffers, as evinced in the fall in overall trade between the USA and other countries around the world, during and after the recession. What the data helps researchers and policy makers do is to measure and monitor changes in the environment for start-ups, the relationships between entrepreneurial activity, business cycles and new business formation, and the consequent effect of local economic development policies on new business activity. If decisions are going to be made about the stock and flow of international business activity it does pay to examine what is happening in potential places of collaboration and engagement. From a commercial point of view observing the trends in business formation in regions enables entrepreneurs and businesses to evaluate whether they can work with dynamic, innovative firms, whether the region has absorptive capacity to host new entrants in the market, and whether there are choices available in terms of identifying the most appropriate partners or investment opportunities. Policy makers too may need to recalibrate local strategies for attracting new firms and supporting new innovative firms which are more likely to seek international opportunities.

The vast economic machine of the USA and the established infrastructure in large parts of the country have allowed unknown rookie firms to grow rapidly and become leading organizations in their industry, remaining in their coveted positions for decades to come. Walmart was founded only in 1962, and only went public about ten years afterwards. Google, Facebook and YouTube were the minnows a decade ago. The apparent strength of entrepreneurship in America is considered to be a function of flexible employment structure (the ease of hire and fire), structural advantages created by the world's most mature venture capital (VC) industry, significant R&D capacity, close working relations with universities, an open immigration policy which allows for 52% of Silicon Valley start-ups being founded by immigrants, a critical mass of firms which work across numerous and sometimes technology frontiers, and the willingness of consumers to try new products. Add to that the creative environment of artists, musicians, architects and their bohemian consorts who provide fertile ground for creative entrepreneurs to pursue their new venture ideas.

Beyond the USA

But India and China are also creating billions of entrepreneurs today (Khanna, 2007), and in rather different ways. While India relies on the top end of its higher education system, the ideal of meritocracy, its technology-savvy expatriate entrepreneurs, and more recent attempts at deregulating the economy with handsome start-up initiatives, China has developed over time a relentlessly fast moving state machinery which creates or boosts state-owned and private enterprises together with highly innovative, technology-based new entrepreneurs to enhance its entrepreneurial mettle. Israel, Denmark and Singapore also rely on a focus on technology, foreign investments and systematic government intervention to promote entrepreneurship.

Is It All the Same?

The reference to the geographic spread of entrepreneurship across different countries might suggest the adoption of a homogenous model of entrepreneurship. In reality it masks the variations in entrepreneurial opportunities and outcomes in different parts of those countries. Certain regions are almost inevitably more entrepreneurial than others. The importance of specific regions to the growth of entrepreneurship and innovation can best be understood by recognizing the differences in those regions, sometimes in the same country. Detroit is not New York in the USA, Berlin is not Bremen in Germany, and Bangalore is not Patna in India! The German example is a particularly interesting one. Although Bremen is a large port city with advanced shipping facilities, it is one of the poorest cities in Germany. It contributes the least GDP among German states. In 2015, the state had a GDP of €31.6 billion, and according to the Cologne Institute for Economic Research, one in every four adults and one in every three children are considered poor (Rohl, 2016; Rohl and Schroder, 2017).

The Concept of Spillover

What makes a local, regional environment conducive to entrepreneurship development can be studied from a number of different perspectives using different concepts and theories. One such concept is that of 'knowledge spillover', which refers to the significance of local linkages for the creation of a firm's own knowledge and learning base. Knowledge created in any one organization can be leaky, especially when we consider information and communication technologies, making it easy for rival organizations to appropriate some of that knowledge for their own use without having to create it in the first place. Employees changing jobs, difficulties in securing intellectual property rights, knowledge exchange with universities, informal collaborations among firms and the necessity for sharing know-how across value chains, all contribute to these spillovers.

Knowledge spillovers are defined as 'knowledge externalities bounded in space', which means that firms operating in proximity to key sources of knowledge, intelligence and data are better able to introduce innovations at a faster rate than rival firms located elsewhere (Breschi and Lissoni, 2001). Knowledge takes the form of local human capital, business R&D and government R&D (Acs and Karlsson, 2002; Knudsen and Lien, 2007; Stuart and Sorenson, 2003). Levels of innovation and new firm creation in a region can be distinguished by the extent to which knowledge is created and spilled over from one firm to another, or from a university to a business. The presence of universities and R&D institutions together with a stock of firms that can use the research and learning at those organizations heightens the spillover effect.

Additional spillover momentum gathers pace when there is a concentration of similar or related firms because they can, potentially, share knowledge, technologies, talent and services due to their close proximity to each other. A cluster of innovative firms also attracts venture capital together with suppliers and other service firms in these clusters. Like all experiences of excess, when the concentration of firms, support agencies and institutions reach a threshold it is no longer economic to have such concentrations because of congestion or negative path-dependent factors such as 'lock-in' (of ideas, beliefs, codes of practice, knowledge) which prevent firms from seeking new knowledge from elsewhere (Mitra, 2020).

Something more than abstract knowledge or tangible know-how augments the spillover effect. When creative firms with creative talent concentrate in specific regions what tends to spur their development is the availability of physical, institutional, social and socio-psychological factors, which help to establish appropriate framework conditions for entrepreneurship and wealth creation. The chicken and egg question about what comes first – firms or institutional factors – is a difficult one to resolve. But is it? There is no clear logical explanation to recommend what prevails before the other can emerge. What we do know, however, is the tendency for a positive association between a creative economic and social environment and the presence of creative talent. This association contributes to economic prosperity and civic well-being, as evinced throughout history from the flourishing communities of the Indus Valley civilization in the Indian sub-continent to Medici Florence right down to today's Berlin in Germany or Hoxton and the City in London.

Let us now go for a short but promising visit to Berlin.

GLOBAL CITY EMERGING – BERLIN'S CREATIVE ENVIRONMENT AND ENTREPRENEURIAL DEVELOPMENT

No visitor to Berlin can miss the ambience created by artists, designers, musicians and writers who form part of a creative environment that is as attractive to them as it is conducive to entrepreneurs, social activists and even policy makers. Berlin is after all the capital city of Germany! However, it has not always been like this.

Dramatic changes have taken place in Berlin ever since 1989 with the fall of the Berlin Wall. The geographical and ideological divide which the wall created led to a number of economic challenges for the city within a new, reunified Germany. The aid-dependent and vulnerable economic structure of West Berlin met the trials and tribulations of privatization of enterprises in East Germany, while manufacturing withdrew with the dawning of free and open global markets (Bernt et al., 2013, p. 16; Häußermann and Kapphan, 2002, p. 91). A major phenomenon that occurred was that of 'cultural squatting' in historical buildings of the inner cities of East Berlin. This was the beginning of Berlin's unique cultural and creative urban change. Cultural squatting made a direct contribution to the attractiveness of the district and led to gentrification especially around Kunsthaus Tacheles in the former Mitte district between the late 1990s and the early 2000s (Ikeda, 2019), and in the former Prenzlauer Berg district in the mid- to late 2000s (Bernt and Holm, 2013; Holm, 2010; Levine, 2004).

Gentrification itself had three stages (Ikeda, 2019):

1. The transformation of a district marked by functional, social, structural and symbolic upgrading that took place in the late 2000s with the temporary utilization of the vacant stores by artists, with the shift in cultural change gradually contributing to the doubling of average rents and the emergence of a new social structure. Revitalisation from the end of the 2000s to the early 2010s was characterized by functional and structural upgrading along with a social upgrading

2. The influence of gentrification on symbolic upgrading played a significant role generating other appreciations of, for example, the commercial environment. Artists, cafes, bars, retail and service businesses, and new residents were part of a new, chic, 'place to be' environment of enhanced lifestyles and consumption

3. The third finding is the transitionality of these, which we could also read as an evolutionary process of change. In terms of activities that dominated the scene during the different stages of the gentrification process, we find that the arts and arts-related events were the first to enter the changing local scenario, prompting a unique mode of local development. It was not that the

arts started a renewal of the district at this juncture alone. After the early 2000s it was the arts studios, galleries and ateliers that moved in, attracted by the cheap rent. The related businesses of cafes and bars consolidating the early bohemian landscape followed later, after the arrival of the new retail and service businesses. We can see what Ikeda (2019) means when he states that it was a particular kind of artistic community – the more commercially oriented ones tuned to the needs and benefits of the wider public that curated the original gentrification process, with the cafes and bars that followed extending the mix of bohemian life with commercialization by encouraging a thriving nightlife in the neighborhood and transforming what was regarded as a problematic district of the 20th century to an internationally focused, gentrified haven by the 21st

Twenty-first century Berlin has acquired a global reputation, alongside London, as a rapidly mushrooming creative city with more than one in ten jobs in Berlin being created in the various sub-sectors of the creative industry in the first decade (Merkel, 2008), and a growth of 33% of creative industry firms in just six years from 2000 to 2006.

Since that monumental time of the fall of the Berlin Wall in 1989, a combination of cheap rent, open spaces and loose town planning arrangements seeded a creative, cultural industry that was characterized both by the flash of bohemian, experimental and alternative life and work styles (the early transformation) as well as the industrialization of the creative arts in the form of the creative industries (Ebert and Kunzmann, 2007; Lange et al., 2008). This was an economic and social transformation occurring in an open laboratory where entrepreneurs, artists and other creative people carved out their special relationship with their tolerant, open and dynamic local environment minus any interference from government, particularly in the two districts of Pankow and Friedrichshain-Kreuzberg. The economic and social networks fostering creative and commercial diversity was what drew a growing body of entrepreneurs to locate in these districts, with Prenzlauer Berg (a brewery district in the 19th century) attracting the artists and designers and Kreuzberg being the magnet for architects and entrepreneurs in the fields of media and entertainment (Senatsverwaltung, 2008). The Media Spree Project emerged to help redevelop the waterfront area into a media cluster and a fresh, energized, economic and cultural location which gradually saw the arrival of the Universal record company followed by the broadcasting company MTV.

What made the global firms referred to above move to these burgeoning artistic areas? Perhaps the creative atmosphere itself was a big draw, but as with all global firms seeking foreign pastures, the red carpet of money and incentives (often a mix of subsidies and tax breaks) from the Berlin Senate Department of Urban Development could not be ignored (Bader and Scharenberg, 2010; Lange et al., 2008). Securing an anchor such as Universal or MTV meant that an army of smaller creative businesses also set up shop in the Kreuzberg quarter around the Oberbaum bridge.

(Continued)

Creativity soon became a symbol of change and development in Berlin with new initiatives being realized in fields other than the arts or media, boosting local economic development, the networks and the quality of place creating opportunities, a local identity with a global reach, not to mention the growing credibility of local, creative entrepreneurs. One could discern a representational perspective of geographical proximity underpinning the clustering of facilities and talent supported by notions of trust, socialization and informal exchanges, and untraded interdependencies. There is also a non-representational perspective, highlighting the specific experience and substance of the urban environment, including the sense of a local buzz (Berg, 2017) or the Marshallian 'something in the air' (Marshall, 1920). These perspectives help to explain the function of 'knowledge spillover' theories, referred to earlier, that is the gradual progression of city development as one set of ideas and resources (tangible and intangible) spilled over and across the city.

One cannot ignore the tangible reasons that lie behind the decision of entrepreneurs and established firms to locate in these areas. These include the availability of inexpensive space and well-established contacts and knowledge of people (colleagues and friends) in the city. "Over time it becomes inevitable that a network base expands beyond local circles, as established firms and entrepreneurs seek new employees with a new skills-set, and opportunities for contracts or collaboration with other potential partners, and interestingly, playgrounds, nurseries and good schools for the children of their employees."

The utilitarian value of place manifest in clubs, bars and cheap premises, necessary for establishing oneself, gives way to the symbolic value of local space, the look and feel of a place with a reputation, historical value or fashionable architecture, alongside the presence of other creative people. The stability of their environment is not just dependent on formal institutions, but on their organic recognition of opportunities, learning, the development of routines and creation of trust-based credibility. This place-space, hard and soft nexus underpins the spillover effect.

The emergence of the arts, underground music, counter-culture cafes and bars, and the annual techno festival went hand in hand with the renovation of over 170 museums, to welcome migrants and refugees, boost tourism and embed an entrepreneurial culture in Berlin. Creative economies attract and give space to immigrants (Florida, 2002), and Berlin has seen a rapid influx of foreigners who now make up 1 in 7 of its 3.5 million people. They populate the region and start creative businesses because they find the opportunity to do so. The city government has identified talent and capabilities and has been encouraging local start-ups particularly in the fashion industry. Yet it is not simply urban policy measures which have provided for authentic, creative environments. Rather, it is the mix of symbolic and utilitarian values of places and neighborhoods that create the capacity for entrepreneurs to generate new ideas, new firms, new technologies and new goods and services that are born local but have global reach and significance.

Sources: adapted from Ikeda (2019); Heebels and Van Aalst (2010); and other authors cited in the case study above

This first case study charts the evolution of Berlin as a global city through the development of specific districts that lent themselves to an open, liberal approach to different kinds of entrepreneurship. This is an important consideration because what ignited the city's creative hub at the start of the German unification project was not trade and commerce but art, artists and a bohemian way of life, enabled in part by cheap property and creative, community-oriented activity. The gradual expansion of the creative talent base and the frugal, liberal lifestyle were huge attractors as established music and media firms moved in with the help of local government largesse to grow that talent base. Civic, institutional governance, consolidating the creative forces, followed the organic development of social networks, social capital and spaces where people could experiment and nurture new ideas in a place that was conducive to creative entrepreneurship. The place represented the local geography of belonging for creative people who opened up spaces for internationalization, with the eventual support of larger established firms and the local authority.

The Role of Entrepreneurship in the Space-Place Nexus

How did entrepreneurship grow in Berlin? How did that growth become both symbolic and a manifestation of global knowledge creation? To try to answer these questions we will stay in Berlin and reflect on the story of one of the most exciting technology companies in the world.

THE MITTE DISTRICT OF BERLIN AND ROCKET

The Mitte district in Berlin is a mini-world of creativity. Once a drab district in central Berlin it has become part of the continuous change and redefinition of the city. Spurred on in the early stages by inexpensive accommodation and an ambience of frugality it has drawn in creative people, migrants and subsequently the trendy, well-heeled art or nerdy technological types to its fold. As the physical spaces of the city opened up so did the mental space of people who became part of its creative landscape.

To suggest that Berlin suddenly found a creative star lighting its way would be to fictionalize the city's evolution. Other more prosaic terms, such as path dependency (following and building on past capabilities) better explain the creative and counter-culture urban environment. West German punks and gays objecting to military service sought

(Continued)

refuge in the city during the Cold War era. The subsequent settlement by government of the city as the administrative capital of the country may have dimmed some of the anarchic sparkle, but the individual creativity and the growing social mobility and gentrification has not been stopped, as the sales of $400 Trippen boots testify. What was also taken from the past was the notion of physical elegance. The Uter den Linden, a tree-lined boulevard, was Berlin's answer to Paris's Champs Elysees. After the devastation of the Second World War, the new developments hold the tension between the old and the new, between an attempt to create a different, environmentally conscious, sustainable city and a new technology-driven creative hub (Mitra, 2020).

Berlin's entrepreneurial ecosystem has become the envy of many cities around the world. When the investment firm Sequoia made a $19 million investment in Wunderlist, it ushered in a new gold rush for the city by a throng of international investors. Much of the start-up scene was dominated by the almost exponential success of Rocket Internet, the giant accelerator, company builder or entrepreneurial clone factory for e-commerce companies, which created a portfolio of star-performing start-ups, and which was valued at €6 billion in 2016. Its move to the historic site of Checkpoint Charlie (where the East of the city meets the West) signaled its arrival on the global stage as the largest online conglomerate outside the USA and China. It achieved its unicorn status by building e-commerce companies quickly, investing heavily in its own creations and other start-ups which became market leaders rapidly, and recruiting highly competent business school and technology graduates who worked very hard to execute agreed plans. Capital was raised quickly and effectively from German investors gung-ho about digital strategies, enabling Rocket to establish its unique selling proposition of accelerated investment strategy and high talent recruitment, raising capital quickly to build its business model. Soon it was investing in start-ups globally, jumpstarting the city's technology and entrepreneurial ecosystem.

The Rocket-led incubation process did not, however, last long. The ability, or perhaps hubris, of start-ups to internationalize early (note the recent phenomena of similar downfalls of firms seeking poorly timed IPOs, such as Uber and Airbnb) burst the Rocket balloon. In the first six months of 2016 it had posted losses of €671 million (close to $700 million). Life before its IPO (Rocket went public in 2014 at a valuation of around €8.2 billion – £7.3 billion or $9.8 billion) was a different story, but its 2016 value had bottomed at €3 billion. Although Rocket is one of Berlin's biggest tech success stories having launched and taken to IPO tech giants such as Zalando, Europe's biggest e-fashion platform, as well as Delivery Hero, HelloFresh and Home24, it has struggled to keep the flow of success running. In 2020, Rocket Internet (RKET.DE) announced it planned to delist from the Frankfurt and Luxembourg stock exchanges, following the decline in the value of its stock by approximately 13% that year. It cited the diminishing significance of the capital markets as a source of finance.

Rocket's decline has not necessarily driven the entrepreneurial impetus away from Berlin. Other accelerators with a different approach, such as AXA Springer supported by the marquee car manufacturer Porsche, have occupied key positions in the financing and support of high-tech start-ups. Rocket laid the groundwork for a thriving technology start-up scene. Unlike other high-tech environments such as Silicon Valley, the new start-ups are more interested in building their own niche boutique firms or empires than in copying established technology giants, providing a new frontier to Germany's traditional strength in engineering with more creative technology firms. The art and designer studios remain but the new urban flourishing is seen in the rise in firms in diverse sectors such as artificial intelligence, mobility, food technology, cyber-security, digital health, fintech and eco fashion. Take 'Elektroculture' created by Lisa Lang, an engineer, who founded the fashion technology firm concentrating on light wearables, such as LED jewelry and clothes that glow in the dark (for example a jacket that changes colors when it receives texts!), which has attracted business from Lufthansa, IBM and Intel. Consider Relayr, founded in 2013, with its expertise in creating a platform for the 'Internet of Things', and which is working with Bosch to develop sensors that set up machinery such as kitchen appliances, elevators (lifts) and espresso machines, so that they can send data to and received instructions from owners. A firm that is well known to academics around the world is 'Research Gate', a social network for academic and other researchers and scientists. Founded in 2008 it has attracted the interest and investment of none other than Bill Gates ($35 million) and some other investors. With over 10 million members storing and accessing data, searching for research and collaborating with other researchers, the firm has earned the accolade of being the 'coolest start-up in Germany'. As another example, in just over six months since its launch in late 2014, Dubmash's short selfie-style videos synchronized with audio clips from pop culture created a sensation in social media. App users record themselves with their favorite songs and 100 million of them have done so creating 35 videos per second. The firm's president Suchit Dash argues that a lot of the content is very conversational and to that end it launched Dubchat, a messaging service on its own platform (Mitra, 2020).

Sources: adapted from Bock (2016, pp. 10–12); Vasagar (2015, p. 12); The Economist (2016, p. 69)

The Rocket story is a salutary one of clever, streetwise entrepreneurship development that used the early success of a creative business and social model to scale up as quickly as it could. Except that accelerated scaling up is hard to do. Scaling up operations in international markets with very different contexts with large amounts of financial capital sourced widely can mean diverting attention from the core purpose of the venture. It can also subject such an organization to the vagaries of the global capital market and also the grand failure of that market as evinced in the recession of 2008.

However, Rocket had planted the seed of classy, high-end technological incubation and growth underpinned by masses of creative talent and, subsequently, a local governance infrastructure. Following Rocket there is now New Space Vision, APX Axel Springer

Porsche Gmbh, Beyond 1435, Hardware, The Family, German Acclerator South-East Asia and a host of others generating a support infrastructure of VCs, incubators and accelerators, popping up around the city and vying to catch the next big unicorn. Berlin now boasts some of the most successful accelerators alongside, for example, Massachusetts in the USA, Hong Kong and Singapore to provide thousands of entrepreneurs access to capital and expertise, together with social capital through the establishment of networks, since the founding of the first accelerator in 2005 in the USA.

The creative technology capital of Germany is as engaged in internationalization of businesses and globalization as one of its hottest rivals, London in the UK. Affordability and attractiveness across the spectrum of leisure, technology and commerce makes it one of the most desirable capital cities in the world. While newcomers can find learning the complexities of the German language and access to accommodation not necessarily easy, they find a responsive ecosystem of culture and technology embracing their interest in making the city their place of work and play. 'Technology-enabled firms in Berlin have specialist staff whose primary responsibility includes troubleshooting for new workers in the city, including the provision of German language training, recreational facilities and even a flea market for foreign employees. Berlin may not be able to compete on salaries or lifestyle choices that their better-funded US start-ups offer, but there is a European, and particularly German, attraction of a good work-life balance (Mitra, 2020) and a growing fund of social capital.

Social Capital or Human Capital: What Makes Creative Environments and Creative People Build Global Cities and Regions

Implicit in the case studies above is the significance of social capital and its key component of trust, networks and institutions which help to spur on innovation and seed the entrepreneurial capital of different environments. The capacity of an environment to attract such talent, to tolerate the diversity of talented people irrespective of their gender, color race or sexual orientation, fuses with the capabilities for invention and development of new technologies and innovation. As Florida (2002) observes, the talent, technology and tolerance that distinguish the community of artists, designers, engineers, entertainers, musicians, scientists, engineers and others are the critical props of a creative environment.

What then of human capital? Glaser (2005), echoing Romer and Becker, reckons it is human capital that is the key to economic growth especially in urban areas. Additionally, Acs (2008), shows that if Florida's 3Ts of tolerance, talent and technology are included in a regression along with human capital the creativity variables become insignificant. Therefore, human capital matters most and education is the key instrument for creating a successful economic environment. Countries or regions making clever use of local factors together with the improvement or attraction of human capital demonstrate an innovative approach to creating a growing, entrepreneurial economy.

However, two other authors, Davidsson and Honig (2003), are of the view that social capital has a more integral role to play than human capital in entrepreneurial success because it enables the harnessing of contributions of people other than the individual entrepreneurs, namely the networks and the relationships of the people connected within those networks. An entrepreneurial region thrives because of the interactions between people enabled by social networking or social capital, its diversity and human capital. The cultural diversity that obtains in urban networks facilitates the inflow of different kinds of human capital, which mixed together, promote innovation, accelerate information flow and foster new ideas leading to a higher rate of new firm formation (Lee et al., 2004).

How does the creative space enabling the accumulation of human and social capital underpinning the creative agenda of cities become international?

Internationalizing the Region, Addressing a Global Agenda

We can review another short case study of a global city region, Singapore, and how it has created a unique innovation space for addressing critical problems associated with one of our foremost necessities in life. What makes this case study poignant is that it addresses a major global issue associated with climate change. This is a story about water. It is also a story about the global awareness of the future scarcity of water across the world, and how it takes talent, creativity and global partnerships to find technological breakthroughs, capturing the essence of international entrepreneurship and innovation in a city state.

SINGAPORE – INTERNATIONALIZING TALENT AND CREATIVITY CAPITAL

Climate change, carbon emissions and the constant depletion of natural resources have been top priorities for governments, corporate board rooms, researchers and indeed the wider community across the globe for some time now. Despite the feeble attempts of climate deniers and autocrats with vested interests, the subject has engaged minds actively searching for solutions to the problems of resource depletion

(Continued)

and scarcity of the world's strategic resources – oil, coal, land and water. Each of these resources, their use and importance have been the subject of fundamental political, economic, geographic and ecological debates and controversy. Water's perennial natural presence in our lives is probably the most important resource. Countries fret over reduced water supply and contamination, among other considerations, with convoluted arguments about water being a natural, public good or a utilitarian commodity.

The island city of Singapore, a country surrounded by the Johore Strait, which separates it from the Malay Peninsula – on the southeast by the Singapore Strait and on the southwest by the Strait of Malacca – has quietly and strategically positioned itself to be a center for water excellence. The country has no natural lakes and its only source of fresh water is rainfall. To ensure adequate levels of water supply it has built reservoirs and water catchment areas to store fresh water. Land reclamation with earth from its own hills, the seabed and neighboring countries has featured among major capital projects, resulting in the land area growing substantially over time to 724.2 square kilometers today. Rising sea levels have led to the construction of sea polder and barrage with the consequence of a further increase in the land area.

Singapore recognizes that climate change in the decades ahead will have major implications for the island nation. Research on and experiments with water follow a three-pronged approach to climate change. The focus of the Centre for Climate Research Singapore is on: a) researching what and how the nation might be affected by climate change, b) implementing mitigation measures, and c) adapting to the coming changes. The government of Singapore has promoted the country as a global hydro hub and facilitated experiments with reclaimed seawater, waste-water treatment and recycling. To scale up this work quickly it has attracted the big names in the industry, including Siemens Water Technologies, Black and Veatch, GE Water and the Norit Group, which have based their regional headquarters in the city-state and set up R&D centers too. A range of engineering, manufacturing support and other services forms part of a $13 billion regional market for water and water technologies. This forms part of a holistic approach to water management based on the availability of competitive research programs, the provision of testing facilities and the attraction of talent.

What made a global big hitter such as The Dutch Norit Group locate in Singapore? According to the company the cultural and technological and diversity, which underscore its engineering and management excellence, is what makes Singapore a genuine knowledge hub. Add to the mix of strategic and holistic action for water Singapore's ability to take advantage of spillover effects of tackling climate change and its commitment to other key areas of climate issues. It was the first country in South-East Asia to introduce a carbon tax, at US $5 per ton, levied on the largest carbon-emitting corporations that produce more than 25,000 tons of carbon dioxide per year. It is now building one of the world's largest floating solar farms with a 60 MW capacity at Tengeh Reservoir in Tuas. This will help to purify water for almost 9% of the world's population.

Like all humankind, Singapore does not live by water alone. But its creative and strategic approach to climate change has other spillover effects. Fusionopolis is an innovative cluster of R&D activities located at the One-North business park in Singapore. The cluster is a state-of-the art hub for information, communications and media talent, dedicated to the digital future enabled by the convergence of info-communications and new media. Although Singapore has built up a reputation in the hard sciences and process-driven technology services, we now find that focus on excellence spreading, as its robust physical and technological infrastructure together with talent leadership is catapulting it to become a major creative economy especially in the world of digital media.

The French company Ubisoft, one of Europe's largest distributors of video games, established its 18th development studio in Singapore, creating high-profile game titles such as *Teenage Mutant Ninja Turtles: Turtles in Time Re-Shelled*, which rose to number one in the video game charts in August 2009. Other recent productions include *Assassin's Creed 2* and *Prince of Persia: The Forgotten Sands*. Its decision to locate in South-East Asia was prompted by Singapore's strong commitment to this and other technological industries and the relatively easy sourcing of high talent. The expansion plans will make it the largest games development studio in the region. Yet another games company, Double Negative Visual Effects (DNVE) one of Europe's top providers of visual effects for films, also set up shop in Singapore in 2009, citing talent as the country's major draw. DNVE's claim to fame lies in its production of the Hollywood blockbuster *Iron Man 2* with Lucasfilm, Industrial Light and Magic.

Source: talentcapital.sg; collectivecreativity.ft.com; Financial Times, Tuesday July 20, 2010 and August, 4, 2010; Straits Times (2018, 2019, 2020), Mitra, 2020

Human, Social and Entrepreneurial Capital and Governance: Enabling Entrepreneurship and Internationalization

Understanding Singapore's attraction as a global city is to realize the city-state's entrepreneurial vision centered round the availability of highly skilled human capital supported by a strong physical and learning infrastructure. This vision acts as a magnet for high-tech global firms. Its erstwhile reputation on banking and financial services was also built around technological prowess and talent. That capability remains. The belief in enterprise and technology and human talent has now added the new layer of opportunities in new markets such as the youth market for video games and the creative arts.

While it is tempting to think of human capital as being the main driver for entrepreneurship and technology development in Singapore, it is important to pause and reflect on the strategic role of the Singapore government to create a fertile environment for the convergence of talent, technology, finance, international venturing and a rich hard and soft infrastructure of support. Good governance in terms of entrepreneurship development and talent generation and attraction has given Singapore the local edge above neighboring countries such as Malaysia and Indonesia to establish its international reputation. This amalgam of institutions, talent and technology could be regarded as creative entrepreneurial capital. Audretsch et al. (2008) suggest that entrepreneurship capital can be explained as a form of composite capital and defined at the economic (region and industry), organizational and personal (team and individual) levels of analysis. Our interest is in entrepreneurship capital being created and utilized at the regional level, in other words the formation of the entrepreneurial capital of a local or regional economy. The idea of entrepreneurship capital of a region can be understood as comprising a regional milieu of agents and institutions where the social acceptance of entrepreneurial behavior is complemented by the willingness of individuals and firms to create new firms, products and services. The demand side players do not create entrepreneurial capital on their own. The organic social embedding of their activities invariably involves service providers, including financial institutions and government agencies, which share some of the burden of risk and the ensuing benefits associated with the new project formation and development and the ensuing competitive strength of regions.

Developing Competitive Strength

One of the key objectives for pursuing a regional development strategy is to increase its competitive capacity that is drawn from the nexus of place and space, and that cocktail of human, social, technological and entrepreneurial capital, and governance. As we have noted in the examples above when we refer to the competitiveness of a city or a region we tend to highlight the creation or existence of conditions that enable firms in particular regions to compete in their chosen markets at home and abroad, and for the economic and social value that these firms create to be captured within those regions (Huggins, 2010). So how regions attract firms, and sustain and retain them there, is seen as a distinct capability for regional competitiveness. The expectation is that this would enhance the quality of life of people living in those regions and especially of people who participate in the wealth creation process. The distributive effect of that wealth creation process and its value is, however, not always a critical consideration when compared to the use of other traditional metrics like share of GDP or employment in assessing competitive strength. Also, the factors that drive growth may not necessarily be found locally. Often, they are imported, as is the case with foreign direct investment (FDI) or talent and technology transfer.

The drivers of growth will vary across geographical space as a result of the strength of their institutions, social capital, technological capability, infrastructure and talent, and, therefore, the growth rates of different regions will vary (Audretsch and Keilbach, 2004). Instead, therefore, of relying on traditional metrics of GDP and employment alone, the combination of these regional assets and their strength or value is generally regarded as a good way of measuring regional competitiveness (Huggins et al., 2014; Malecki, 2004, 2007).

It is important to distinguish between regional competitiveness and firm-level competitiveness. Regions do seek to attract FDI, and the various rankings of regions and countries in terms of their share of global FDI distribution suggests that any one government is constantly working on policies that can help their region to outcompete another for capital or talent. However, the nature of this kind of competition does not guarantee regional growth. Economic value is derived if the creation of facilitative conditions is conducive to the growth and competitive capability of individual firms or sectors in different markets. At best regional competition is centered round making provisions for effective and efficient platforms for high levels of productivity, employment and wealth creation by firms (Huggins et al., 2014). In some cases, regions of different countries work jointly to create economic growth corridors or clusters of regions to enable a critical, geographical mass for the production of goods based on unique regional capabilities and formation of value chains connecting different firms.

Growth Corridors

For decades now, one of the ways in which regional competitiveness has been secured by national governments, often in conjunction with multilateral organizations, including the International Monetary Fund, the World Bank, the Africa Development Fund and others, is through the promotion of growth corridors. A good example is China's Belt and Road Initiative which resurrects the great Silk Route corridor connecting Asia with Africa and Europe.

What are growth corridors? How are they constituted? The literature suggests that corridors are the mix or bundles of infrastructure, including rail links for passengers or freight transport and highways, that connect two or more urban areas in the same country or across adjacent countries. Often, and especially in modern times, the infrastructure of corridors is enhanced by ICT infrastructure, electricity power lines and cables, as well as pipes for drinking water, natural gas, crude oil, electricity and sewage (Dannenberg et al., 2018; Priemus and Zonneveld, 2003).

Growth corridors are instruments with which to boost economic development drawn from deliberations at the World Economic Forum, and through the World Bank's World Development Reports. Part of the strategy was to support economic growth in emerging and developing economies as explained in the Africa and the G20 report 'The Compact with Africa' that was showcased at the G20 Finance Ministers' and Central Bank Governors' Meeting in 2017.

But why should countries select certain regions as growth corridors and not others? To answer this question we need to go back a few decades to Hirschman's (1958) theory of unbalanced growth which posits that it is not possible to allocate equal amounts of sufficient capital and organizational capability for making decisions across all sectors or regions of a country at any given period of time. It is only those regions and sectors with a high potential for inducing growth in related sectors that demand attention by policy makers.

Corridors can be limited to single countries or run across urban and rural areas in one or more countries. These corridors can be specialized in one sector or be diversified, with a variety of funding sources from local and national governments, private firms, public-private partnerships, multilateral agencies and even non-governmental organizations.

Types of Growth Corridors

Growth corridors are often referred to as development corridors by multilateral agencies trying to promote global linkages. They often start as transport routes facilitating the movement of goods and people, evolving, gradually, into a trade, technology and business nexus of social and economic development. They vary in their structure from those that develop a particular sector of the economy, such as an agricultural corridor, to others whose remit might stretch to supporting wider social development and economic growth at the sub-national or a cross-border region. The latter type is assumed to have acquired the status of a fully-fledged economic corridor. Table 4.1 provides a typology of growth and development corridors often used in research and policy circles.

Table 4.1 A typology of growth corridors

Type	Description
Development Corridor	Includes all corridors at any stage of evolution from a simple transport route through to a fully established economic corridor.
Domestic Trade Corridor	The World Bank defines a domestic trade corridor as a designated route within a national transport network. This route, which includes different modes of transport together with nodes that link up different modes and service areas, consist of links and nodes used to distribute goods inside a country and within the country. These corridors usually straddle across provincial borders and are generally established through national legislation.
Foreign Trade Corridor	The World Bank refers to foreign trade corridors as those corridors which are used to transport the imports and exports of a country. Therefore, these corridors have an endpoint located at either a border crossing or as part of an international gateway. Essentially, the locations of the production of exports and the consumption of imports determine these corridors. The national legislation of countries allowing the movement of goods under the supervision of customs authorities stipulates the locations where foreign trade may enter and exit the country.

Type	Description
Transboundary Corridor	Often used interchangeably with the term 'transnational corridor', a transboundary corridor refers to paths used by wildlife (for example the movement of animals along their predatory or traditional migratory routes), according to the World Wildlife Fund. Sometimes transboundary corridors are referred to in the context of a region containing development corridors, resulting in some degree of confusion over their identity.
Transit Trade Corridor	These corridors, which are marked by a border crossing at one end and an international gateway (or a border crossing) at the other, help to shift the cargo of other countries. The routes may be determined by specific national legislation. What passes as governance of the movement of transit goods is generally coordinated with neighboring countries by way of bilateral agreements or in some cases through regional agreements.
Transnational Corridor	Any development corridor that cuts across national borders is known as a transnational corridor

Note: The shaded corridor is an unusual mix of the wider environment of people and wildlife movements, suggesting ways in which trade and economic activity can form part of ecological considerations and enquiry.

Source: adapted from Hope and Cox (2015)

Growth Corridors as Evolving, Cross-Border Spatial Initiatives

When it comes to economic corridors the objective at the very outset is to achieve a mix of hard infrastructure, transport and logistics services, institutional arrangements and protocols and wider community involvement. This mix is expected to yield a broad-based development project to tap unrealized economic potential. Seen as conscious and deliberate planning, the first such attempt to develop such an initiative was put together by the South African government in the mid-1990s. A variety of public and private sector and community stakeholders were brought together in a structured network as part of a spatial planning approach or what was referred to as a spatial development initiative (SDI). It was first applied to the Maputo Development Corridor (MDC) from 1996, and its broad success led to the New Partnership for Africa's Development enabling replication throughout Africa (Hope and Cox, 2015). The SDIs constituted a specific African approach to development corridors. In Asia, the planning of corridors adopted a strategic framework approach.

What drives the development of a corridor is the economic potential of a basic transport route. Once this potential is established, the hard infrastructures supporting the transport modes allows for the development of a transport corridor. Subsequently, an increasing volume of freight and people moving along the corridor calls for the improvement of logistics, legal, institutional and management support making up the soft infrastructure to ensure the effectiveness and efficiency of operation of the corridor. The ripple effect of efficiency in operations stimulates further economic activity attracting new investment, leading to the evolution of an economic corridor. This is summarized in Figure 4.1, which shows the evolution of the different corridors over time.

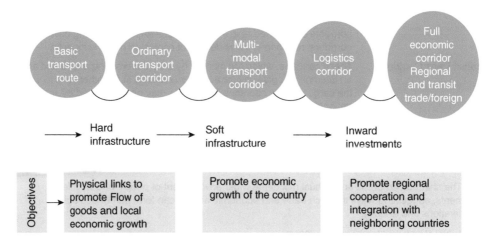

Figure 4.1   Growth corridors and their evolution

Source: adapted from Hope and Cox (2015)

THE MAPUTO DEVELOPMENT CORRIDOR IN AFRICA

The MDC opens up the landlocked regions of the Mpumalanga, Gauteng and Limpopo provinces, as it runs along the highly industrialized and productive regions of Southern Africa. It is a typical transportation corridor that includes road, rail, border posts, port and terminal facilities which has evolved into an economic corridor.

The MDC was launched in 1996 as part of a new investment strategy of the South African government, known as the strategic development initiative. Four important objectives informed the development of this fully-fledged economic corridor. First, the MDC was seen as a strategic initiative to rehabilitate primary infrastructure along the corridor including road, rail, port and border posts. Second, the idea was to maximize investment in inherent corridor potential to attract global capital and facilitate the development of regional markets and regional economic integration. Third, the socio-economic objective of maximizing social development, employment opportunities, entrepreneurship and increased participation of the historically disadvantaged communities was woven into the strategy. Fourth, a key issue was that of ensuring sustainability through the development of policies, strategies, frameworks and instruments to ensure an inclusive, participatory and holistic approach to environmentally sustainable development.

Taking each landlocked region at a time, we find the rationale and value behind the interlocking of the regions.

GAUTENG PROVINCE TO PORT MAPUT

As a traditional heartland for gold production, Gauteng, a Sotho-Tswana word for 'Place of Gold', is regarded as the manufacturing engine of the sub-continental economy, producing around 40% of South Africa's GDP. Traversing South Arica's capital city of Pretoria, the MDC connects this industrial and commercial hub of the Witwatersrand, which includes the urban, metropolitan areas of Ekurhuleni on the East Rand, Johannesburg, and Mogale City Municipality on the West Rand, with its nearest deep water port in Maputo, Mozambique.

THE LIMPOPO PROVINCE TO PORT MAPUTO

At the northernmost point of the country is where the province of Limpopo is located. It is South Africa's third largest mining producer, generating 9% of the country's income arising from mining activities. In this sector, diamonds, gold and the platinum group of precious metals make up the major mineral deposits. Given that its borders are with Botswana, Zimbabwe and Mozambique, Limpopo is also the transit point for most of the trans-South African freight headed to and from landlocked Zimbabwe, Zambia and Malawi. The MDC links this landlocked part of South Africa with its nearest deep water port via the Phalaborwa Spatial Development Initiative. Phalaborwa also happens to be the site of major petrochemical production.

MPUMALANGA PROVINCE TO PORT MAPUTO

The lion's share of the Maputo Corridor runs through Mpumalanga, South Africa's Japan, the 'place where the sun rises' as the word isiTsonga translates. This is where one can find the majority of South Africa's electricity-generating coal-fired power stations, with the province accounting for 76% of South Africa's coal mining output and 50% of national coal reserves. A significant amount of that coal is exported via the Matola Coal Terminal in Matola Port, Maputo. Mpumalanga's status as an important energy producing province is enhanced by its closeness to the gas fields of the Mozambican coast and the closest port to the South African northern hinterland. With the completion of the gas pipeline running from the Temane and

(Continued)

Pande gasfields near Moatize in Mozambique to Sasol's plant in Secunda together with the construction of liquid petrochemical pipelines along similar routes, the province's contribution to the MDC has acquired considerable significance. Additionally, important centers for South Africa's coal, vanadium and stainless steel mining and production plus principal areas of maize production in the province's agricultural sector, forming a vast industrial and agro-production sector, as in the Nkangala District Municipality and the cities and towns of Delmas, Witbank and Middelburg, are covered by the MDC.

Further east in the corridor, a modern motorway and rail track run through the wilderness area and gorges before reaching the Lebombo / Resanno Garcia Border Posts and the Lebombo Dry Port in the border town of Komatipoort.

SOUTH AFRICAN / MOZAMBICAN BORDER TO PORT MAPUTO

Once the MDC crosses the Lebombo / Resanno Garcia border into Mozambique's Maputo Province, it connects the northern hinterland of South African with Mozambique's capital, Maputo, and its two deep-water ports of Maputo and Matola. This connection is made possible by a 92 kilometer fast and efficient national road, known as the EN4 on the Mozambican side, that drives straight to Port Maputo before ending close to the downtown area of the capital city.

In common with many development corridors, it is the government (in this case the governments of both South Africa and Mozambique) that has established the MDC as a classic SDI to foster sustainable growth and development based on bilateral policies and substantial public and private sector investments. The future sustenance of the corridor is now left to the private sector which will need to continue private-public partnerships, seek routine improvement of the management of border procedures and operational hours together with the development and coordination of investment zones, the organization of efficient and enhanced transport services, increased capacity, higher levels of services including modern information services, and the setting of competitive rates for road, rail, port, terminals and shipping lines.

Sources: adapted from Hope and Cox (2015); www.portmaputo.com/maputo-development-corridor

The MDC case study is a good example of an engineered initiative led by the public sector to harness economic capacity in the region and extend the scope to adjoining regions, in this case crossing the national border of one country to another. The absence of specific data on new business creation in the corridor might restrict us from making the case for entrepreneurship in these environments. Data deficiencies can be a problem but that should not necessarily hinder understanding the efforts made to promote entrepreneurship in a region. Such an understanding could help to promote the need for gathering relevant data.

One of the functions of public policy is to create facilitative conditions for new business creation and, critically, for existing organizations to avail themselves of new opportunities through trade, alliances, infrastructure support and the easier movement of goods and services, and to search for new opportunities across borders. Connecting key hubs in the corridor stretching from a landlocked area in South Africa to the port of the capital city of Maputo in Mozambique opens up possibilities for enhanced connectivity between the hubs and for new and existing businesses to identify new opportunities, mobilize resources and realize economic and social gains, at a global scale. We could argue that the corridor itself is an entrepreneurial unit which sponsors and supports numerous innovative activities.

Limitations of Corridors

The economic impact of these corridors, which are essentially spatial development initiatives, is not entirely clear. Some researchers argue that growth corridors induce a form of disequilibrium at both the spatial and sectoral levels. In other words, they upset the routine arrangements for the flow of goods and services in a region. Corridors are meant to attract investment without institutional constraints, which could deprive other regions of investment. This disequilibrium releases opportunities for targeted investment leading potentially to unbalanced growth aimed intentionally at creating a spatial and/or sectoral disequilibrium to encourage further investment. However, the expected spread effects from an unbalanced growth impetus (Hirschman, 1958) are not realized automatically. Referring to countries in the Global South, Murphy (2008) and Mold (2012) have pointed out that the induced disequilibrium approach often fails to generate the planned regional development and the benefits of spillover, trickle down and positive externalities, because of backwash or displacement effects, leading to new regional inequalities.

In common with most evolutions, growth corridors have mutated over time along with significant changes in the way trade, private investment and globalization has influenced economic activity and social accommodation. Global value chains have overtaken interest in regional economic corridors, with the former representing the integration of international value chains of individual and connected sectors, public-private partnerships, multiple forms of cross-border investment, trade hubs and gateways, and associated public policies (Baxter et al., 2017; Dannenberg et al., 2018; Gálvez Nogales, 2014).

Chapter Summary

LO1 to **LO3**: The discussion on the evolution of growth corridors provides us with an opportunity to make the interesting connection between regions in any one country to their counterparts in other countries. We have seen how regions, and in particular cities, become international hubs or focal points of global economic and cultural activities by cultivating different forms of human, social, creative and entrepreneurial capital alongside the necessary developments of infrastructure and institutions. These combine to secure a symbolic space for the cultivation of talent, technology and capabilities and a representational place for different types of businesses, institutions, networks and support services. The way the place-space relationship in cities and regions generates unique, sometimes inimitable characteristics for the regions. These features become attractive to both people looking for new opportunities in their lives and for firms seeking new partnerships, alternative business models and a global presence.

LO2: While the nature of regional development may follow an organic path (Berlin) or emerge as strategic centers of excellence established by interventionist government policy (Singapore), their critical mass is partly a function of internationalization or globalization. They can be described as centripetal spaces and places which bring the world outside to their local environments. Local corridors, on the other hand, are dependent on the physical extension of a region to enable cross-border economic activity (in their most powerful formation) through engineered government policy. Emerging as they do as international corridors they enable extended and improved trade, commerce, infrastructure development and the movement of people across national borders through targeted policies and regulations.

We are now entering the complex and vast territory of globalization, which is the subject of Chapter 11.

Review Questions

1. Why is the study of regions and cities important for understanding international business and entrepreneurship?
2. What are the essential features of cities that create possibilities for international entrepreneurship activities?
3. How can different forms of capital available in cities be best utilized for international connectivity?
4. What are growth corridors and what is their significance?
5. How do the different types of growth corridors facilitate internationalization while improving the competitiveness of local regions?

References

Acs, Z.J. and Karlsson, C. (2002) 'Introduction to institutions, entrepreneurship and firm growth: From Sweden to the OECD'. *Small Business Economics*, pp. 183–187.

Audretsch, D.B. and Keilbach, M. (2004) 'Entrepreneurship capital and economic performance'. *Regional Studies*, 38: 949–959.

Audretsch, D.B., Bönte, W. and Keilbach, M. (2008) 'Entrepreneurship capital and its impact on knowledge diffusion and economic performance'. *Journal of Business Venturing*, 23: 687–698.

Bader, I. and Scharenberg, A. (2010) 'The sound of Berlin: Subculture and the global music industry', *International Journal of Urban and Regional Research*, 34(1): 76–91.

Baxter, J., Howard, A.C., Mills, T., Rickard, S. and Macey, S. (2017) 'A bumpy road: Maximising the value of a resource corridor' *The Extractive Industries and Society*, 4(3): 439–442.

Becker, G.S. (2009) Human capital: A theoretical and empirical analysis, with special reference to education. Chicago: University of Chicago Press.

Berg, S.H. (2018) Local buzz, global pipelines and Hallyu: The case of the film and TV industry in South Korea. *Journal of Entrepreneurship and Innovation in Emerging Economies*, 4(1): 332–352.

Bernt, B. M. Grell, A. and Holm (Eds.), (2013) *The Berlin reader: A compendium on urban change and activism*. Verlag: Bielefeld.

Berry, C. R. and Glaeser, E. L. (2005) 'The Divergence of Human Capital Levels Across Cities', *Papers in Regional Science*, 84: 407–444.

Bock, P. (2016) 'Berlin', in *Europe's 100 Hottest Start-Up Cities. A Wired supplement in association with Pictet*, October, pp. 10–12.

Breschi, S. and Lissoni, F. (2001) 'Knowledge spillovers and local innovation systems: A critical survey'. *Industrial and corporate change*, 10(4): 975–1005.

Dannenberg, P., Diez, J.R. and Schiller, D. (2018) 'Spaces for integration or a divide? New-generation growth corridors and their integration in global value chains in the Global South'. *Zeitschrift für Wirtschaftsgeographie*, 62(2): 135–151.

Davidsson, P. and Honig, B. (2003) 'The role of social and human capital among nascent entrepreneurs'. *Journal of Business Venturing*, 18(3): 301–331.

Dinreloz, E. (2018) *Business Formation Statistics: A new Census Bureau Product that takes the pulse of early-stage US business activity*. US Census Bureau. Business and Economy, Center for Economic Studies (CES) and Expenses and Expenditures. Available at www.census.gov/newsroom/blogs/research-matters/2018/02/bfs.html (last accessed 1 October 2020).

Ebert, R. and Kunzmann, K.R. (2007) 'Kulturwirtschaft, kreative Räume und Stadtentwicklung in Berlin'. *DisP-The Planning Review*, 43(171): 64–79.

The Economist (2016) 'The freaks are coming: Berlin's tech scene'. *The Economist*, 420(9008), 24–30 September, p. 69.

Florida, R. (2002) *The Rise of the Creative Class*. New York: Basic Books.

Gálvez Nogales, E. (2014) 'Making economic corridors work for the agricultural sector' Food and Agricultural Organisation (FAO)'. United Nations. Rome.

Häußermann, H. and Kapphan, A. (2002) 'Arbeiterviertel und Villenkolonien: Die Herausbildung sozialräumlicher Strukturen vor 1945'. In *Berlin: Von der geteilten zur gespaltenen Stadt?* (pp. 25–56). VS Verlag für Sozialwissenschaften, Wiesbaden.

Heebels, B. and Van Aalst, I. (2010) 'Creative clusters in Berlin: Entrepreneurship and the quality of place in Prenzlauer Berg and Kreuzberg'. *Geografiska Annaler: Series B, Human Geography*, 92(4): 347–363.

Hirschman, A. (1958) *The Strategy of Economic Development*. New Haven: Yale University Press, 1958).

Hope, A. and Cox, J. (2015) *Development Corridors*. Coffey International Development, EPS Peaks. Available at https://theasiadialogue.com/wp-content/uploads/2017/04/Topic_Guide_Development_Corridors.pdf (last accessed 27 September 2022).

House of Lords. (2003) *The Commission's Green Paper: Entrepreneurship in Europe: Selected Evidence*. Select Committee on the European Union, S2002-03 34th Report. London: House of Lords

Huggins, R. (2010) 'Regional competitive intelligence: benchmarking and policy-making'. *Regional Studies*, 44(5): 639–658.

Huggins, R., Izushi, H., Prokop, D. and Thompson, P. (2014) 'Regional competitiveness, economic growth and stages of development'. *Zbornik radova Ekonomskog fakulteta u Rijeci: časopis za ekonomsku teoriju i praksu*, 32(2): 255–283.

Ikeda, M. (2019) 'Role of culture and consumption in the process of gentrification: Case study of the Reuter Quarter in the former West Berlin Neukölln' (English Translation). *Geographical Review of Japan Series B*, 92(1): 10–32.

Khanna, T. (2007) *Billions of Entrepreneurs: How China and India are Reshaping their Futures and Yours*. Boston, MA: Harvard University Business School Press.

Knudsen, E.S. and Lien, L.B. (2015) Hire, fire, or train: innovation and human capital responses to recessions. *Strategic Entrepreneurship Journal*, 9(4): 313–330.

Lange, B., Kalandides, A., Stöber, B. and Mieg, H.A. (2008) 'Berlin's creative industries: governing creativity?' *Industry and Innovation*, 15(5): 531–548.

Lee, S.Y., Florida, R. and Acs, Z. (2004) 'Creativity and entrepreneurship: A regional analysis of new firm formation'. *Regional studies*, 38(8): 879–891.

Malecki, E.J. (2004) 'Jockeying for position: What it means and why it matters to regional development policy when places compete', *Regional Studies*, 38(9): 1101–1120.

Malecki, E.J. (2007) 'Cities and regions competing in the global economy: Knowledge and local development policies', *Environment and Planning C: Government and Policy*, 25(3): 638–654.

Marshall, A. (1929) *Principles of Economics*. London: Macmillan.

Martin, R. and Tyler, P. (2000) 'Regional employment evolutions in the European Union: a preliminary analysis'. *Regional Studies*, 34(7): 601–616.

Mellander, C. and Florida, R. (2007) 'The creative class or human capital? explaining regional development in Sweden' (No. 79). Royal Institute of Technology, CESIS-Centre of Excellence for Science and Innovation Studies.

Mitra , J. (2020) *Entrepreneuship, Innovation and Regional Development: An Introduction* (2nd ed). Abingdon: Routledge.

Mold, A. (2012) 'Will it all end in tears? Infrastructure spending and African development in historical perspective'. In: *Journal of International Development*, 24(2): 237–254.

Murphy, J.T. (2008) 'Economic geographies of the Global South: Missed opportunities and promising intersections with development studies'. *Geography Compass*, 2(3): 851–873.

OECD. (2000) *Enhancing the competitiveness of SMEs in the global economy: Strategies and policies*, Workshop 2, Local Partnership, Clusters and SME Globalisation, Conference for Ministers Responsible for SMEs and Industry Ministers, Bologna, Italy, 14–15 June.

OECD. (2010) *SMEs, Entrepreneurship and Innovation*. OECD Studies on SMEs and Entrepreneurship. Paris: OECD Innovation Strategy.

Priemus, H. and Zonneveld, W., 2003. 'What are corridors and what are the issues? Introduction to special issue: The governance of corridors'. *Journal of Transport Geography*, 11(3): 167–177.

Röhl, Klaus-Heiner (2016) 'Entrepreneurial culture and start-ups: Could a cultural shift in favour of entrepreneurship lead to more innovative start-ups?', IW Policy Paper, No. 2/2016E, Institut der deutschen Wirtschaft (IW), Köln.

Rohl, K.H. and Schroder, C. (2017) Regionale Armut in Deutschland: Risikogruppen erkennen, Politik neu ausrichten IW-Analysen No. 113: Institut der deutschen Wirtschaft (IW), Köln. (http://hdl.handle.net/10419/157160. Last accessed 20 January 2021).

Romer, P.M. (1989) 'Human capital and growth: Theory and evidence'. The NATIONAL BUREAU OF ECONOMIC RESEARCH Cambridge, MA 02138 November 1989. Available on ehttps://www.nber.org/system/files/working_papers/w3173/w3173.pdf (last accessed 15 March 2020).

Saxenian, A. (2006) 'International Mobility of Engineers and the Rise of Entrepreneurship in the Periphery' (No. 2006/142). WIDER Research Paper.

SENSTADT–SENATSVERWALTUNG F.S.B. (2008) Digitaler Umweltatlas Berlin. 06.01 Reale Nutzung der bebauten Flächen 06.*02 Grün-und Freiflächenbestand (Ausgabe 2008)*. URL: http://www.stadtentwicklung. berlin. de/um welt/umweltatlas/e_text/kc601.pdf (gesehen am 22.12. 2011).

Straits Times. (2018) 'Singapore Budget 2018: Carbon tax of $5 per tonne of greenhouse gas emissions to be levied'. *Straits Times*, 19 February. Available at www.straitstimes.com/singapore/singapore-budget-2018-carbon-tax-of-5-per-tonne-of-greenhouse-gas-emissions-to-be-levied (last accessed 27 September 2022).

Straits Times. (2019) 'National Day Rally 2019: Three-pronged approach for Singapore to tackle climate change'. *Straits Times*, 18 August. Available at www.straitstimes. com/politics/national-day-rally-2019-three-pronged-approach-for-singapore-to-tackle-climate-change (last accessed 27 September 2022).

Straits Times. (2020) 'Work begins on Singapore's largest floating solar farm in Tuas'. *Straits Times*, 18 August. Available at www.straitstimes.com/singapore/environment/work-begins-on-singapores-largest-floating-solar-farm-in-tuas (last accessed 27 September 2022).

Stuart, T. and Sorenson, O. (2003) 'The geography of opportunity: Spatial heterogeneity in founding rates and the performance of biotechnology firms'. *Research Policy*, 32(2): 229–253.

The Economist, The United States of Entrepreneurs, America still leads the world. (2009) https://www.economist.com/special-report/2009/03/14/the-united-states-of-entrepreneurs (last accessed 20 January 2021).

Vasagar, J. (2015) 'Baffling Berlin decoded, startups: German culture shock'. *Financial Times*, 14 January, p. 12.

5
THEORIES OF SMALL FIRM INTERNATIONALIZATION

Source: www.needpix.com/photo/326991/

Italian makers of delicacies such as prosciutto, specialty cheese and wine are facing increasing pressure to venture into foreign markets for their products. Among the key underlying reasons is the domestic market recession that has engulfed the country in recent years.

With the country facing its third recession in six years as recently as 2015, consumer spending has fallen 13% since 2008. Small food businesses have been among the worst hit due to falling prices. Due to a decline in eating out, the return on the sales of wine at the point of consumption, a common and high-margin marketing strategy in the industry, dropped a third since 2007.

Falling consumer spending has forced hard-pressed supermarkets to squeeze their small suppliers. Even specialty stores, known for their product differentiation and

(Continued)

high margins, have not been able to maintain their margins or be kind to their small suppliers. Relying on specialty wine stores in the domestic market instead of large super-markets for their custom, several high-end wineries have felt the brunt of the downturn, suffering from as much as a 15% decline in margins.

With a rise of hard discounters in the wake of the recession, small food makers are also facing stiff competition at home. In 2013, for example, 14% of Italians shopped at hard discounters, up from 10% in 2011.

Some small food makers have been forced to curtail supplies in the face of falling demand. According to research by Bocconi University, since 2008, one in eight small food producers have gone bust as a consequence. Faced with a drop in prices due to declining demand, the consortium of makers of Parmigiano-Reggiano cheese, for instance, decided to withdraw 90,000 wheels from the market.

Source: www.needpix.com/photo/1675981/

THE INTERNATIONALIZATION CHALLENGE

Selling outside of the domestic market can enable Italian food makers to survive these trying conditions. The food industry makes up about one-seventh of Italy's economy, however just 12% of Italian food producers sell abroad at all. Total Italian food exports are half those of Germany. Even though there is a huge demand for Italian food abroad, Italian entrepreneurs have not been able to figure out how to sell abroad.

There are several reasons for the inability of Italian small businesses to venture abroad. A vast majority of Italy's food businesses are small firms. Food companies with more than 50 workers constitute only 1.5% of Italy's total cohort of small businesses. By virtue of their small size, these companies face severe financial and human resource constraints, often lacking the money, vision and managerial expertise to break out of the domestic market. In some cases, owner-founders are also unwilling to share profits with importers who could help them to penetrate foreign supermarkets and high-end restaurants abroad.

Italy's relatively backward retail sector is another factor. As compared to their French or German counterparts like Carrefour SA or Metro that took local foodstuffs with them when they ventured abroad, big Italian supermarket chains have been unable to step into international markets. Thus, unlike small food businesses in France or Germany that benefitted from the international expansion of big supermarket chains, Italian food makers have been largely confined to the domestic market. The recessionary conditions have only aggravated their plight, with virtually all retailers imposing tougher conditions on their suppliers.

Some small food businesses, especially wineries, decided to expand abroad several years ago, managing to strike deals with importers in the US. Establishing a foothold in international markets makes them better positioned than if they were selling only in Italy. US cities like New York, for instance, offer great visibility to small brands. However, small firms' efforts to break into the New York City market have not been successful as importers too demand steep discounts. Even though some small companies earn more than half of their revenues from foreign markets, their overall sales are flat.

In a push to expand abroad, some small food businesses have ventured elsewhere, including foreign markets like Russia. However, sanctions on importing in Russia have put their plans to a halt. Emulating the success of Italy's luxury-goods sector, other food producers have attempted to move up the price ladder, developing their own retail networks or latching on to high-end gourmet vendors. However, narrow product lines have limited their possibilities, at least at the beginning.

Venchi, a Turin-based chocolatier, for instance, tried for years to open its own foreign retail network in order to escape a declining domestic market. At first, the company ventured into retail selling only its chocolates. As such a narrow product line wasn't enough to support a big investment, it tried again six years later, adding chocolate beverages, ice cream and other products. It also upgraded its locations and store designs, replacing cheap furniture with tonier pieces, and hired more experienced sales staff.

In yet other cases, partnering with fancy Italian supermarkets abroad has borne fruit. A sensation in foreign markets due to its array of Italian delicacies and in-store restaurants, the Eataly supermarket, for instance, allows its small Italian suppliers to earn much higher margins than traditional supermarkets. Eli Prosciutti, a family-run maker of Italian ham, has flourished with Eataly, earning higher (as much as five times) unit prices for its products abroad.

Source: Mesco (2015)

───Learning Outcomes───

After studying this chapter, you should be ready to:

- **LO1**: Compare and contrast the theories of small firm internationalization
- **LO2**: Describe the stages model of internationalization and evaluate its role in explaining small firm internationalization
- **LO3**: Identify different types of social networks and evaluate their role in small firm founding and growth
- **LO4**: Identify small firms' resources, and evaluate the role of internal (firm-specific) and external (environmental) factors in small firm internationalization

Introduction

Small firms are no longer confined to their domestic market. International small and medium-sized enterprises (SMEs) first began to gain prominence because of the difficulties experienced by Western multinational enterprises (MNEs) in the late 1970s and early 1980s (Carter and Jones-Evans, 2012). Developments such as the oil crisis of 1974, depressed global demand, intense international competition from Japan and the newly industrializing countries, and privatization and de-regulation programs led MNEs to lose their grip on world trade during this period.

More recently, trends of outsourcing and demand for services and microelectronics have spurred small firm internationalization (Scarborough, 2014). Most small firms see internationalization as imperative. Both large and small companies have also increasingly embraced internationalization as a way of leveraging technology (Ibeh, 2000).

Internationalization has many benefits for small firms. As compared to their non-international counterparts, international small firms selling products or services in other countries generate more sales revenue, are more profitable and have higher levels of productivity. Additionally, international small firms positively impact the economy. Policy makers in the US are increasingly recognizing that small business exports can support jobs and reduce trade deficits. According to the shipping firm UPS, small firms engaged in global trade produce 20% greater job growth and are 20% more productive when compared to non-exporters (Gerwin, 2015).

As discussed in Chapter 2, small firms face pressing financial and human resource constraints, which impedes their ability to grow. Yet, as the opening profile suggests, small firm founders may be forced to internationalize due to external environmental pressures, leaving them little choice but to look abroad in order to survive. In this chapter, we discuss alternative theoretical explanations for small firm internationalization (we draw on the theoretical framework outlined here to examine the factors influencing small firms' internationalization strategies in the next chapter).

Below, we outline the incidence of small firm internationalization and explain its relevance for small firms. Next, we compare and contrast three small firm internationalization theories, namely stages mode, social network theory and the resource-based view of the firm.

Small Firm Internationalization: Incidence and Relevance

The term **internationalization** refers to the process of increasing involvement in international operations. It describes the continuum that stretches from import activity or domestic internationalization (through extra regional expansion) to full globalization (Luostarinen, 1994).

Measurement difficulties prevent an overall picture of the extent of small firm internationalization. In many economies, only basic data on the number of SMEs and SMEs' economic contribution is collected, while data on SMEs' involvement in international trade and investment is scarce.

More than half of APEC members, for example, do not have data on SME exports and investment abroad (APEC, 2015). SMEs are usually not part of any representative business association promoting their interests, and many of them do not necessarily keep detailed records of their activities. Constantly evolving business patterns also make it difficult to find a sound methodology to measure the degree of internationalization across time.

Despite these difficulties, there are some notable efforts to measure the incidence of small firm internationalization. These include the Global Entrepreneurship Monitor (GEM) and the SME working group of the APEC (Asia Pacific Economic Cooperation). According to Bosma and Kelley (2018), entrepreneurs are international when 25% or more of their sales are from customers outside their economies. In general, SME internationalization is greater in small, open economies and less in large, more self-contained economies.

Figure 5.1 displays the percentage of international entrepreneurs by country in different parts of the world.

The Middle East and Africa region contains economies with the highest levels of international entrepreneurship, with 59% entrepreneurs in Lebanon and 55% in Morocco stating that 25% or more of their sales are to international customers. High internationalization also occurs in Qatar, UAE and Saudi Arabia. In Canada, 44% entrepreneurs are international. Countries with the highest internationalization rates in Europe, except Switzerland, are all members of the European Union (EU). However, this is not the case for all EU countries; less than 10% of entrepreneurs in European countries such as Poland, Bulgaria, the Netherlands and Spain are international.

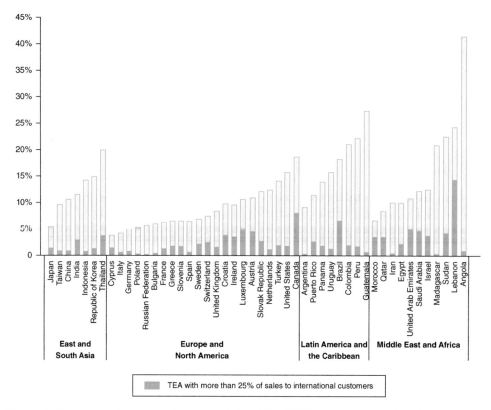

Figure 5.1 Total early-stage entrepreneurial activity (TEA) rates among adults (ages 18–64) in 487 economies in four geographic regions, showing the proportion of international TEA

Source: Bosma and Kelley (2018)

The Latin American and Caribbean region is the least international of the regions, with almost no entrepreneurs classified as international in Brazil. The highest level of internationalization in this region is observed in Puerto Rico, which conducts most of its trade with the United States.

In the US, SMEs are a vital contributor to US exports to the world. According to the US Department of Commerce, over 400,000 US SMEs engaged in goods trade in 2016, representing 98% of exporters and accounting for 33% of the value of exports (The Year in Trade, 2019).

SMEs are also important contributors to US services trade. More than 95% of all US firms that exported services in 2015 had fewer than 250 employees, and such firms accounted for almost half of the total value of US service exports in that year. Further, firms with fewer than ten employees accounted for almost a quarter of the total value of US services exports in 2015.

Benefits of Small Firm Internationalization

Internationalization has many benefits for small firms. Internationalization allows entrepreneurs to **access foreign markets**, and **increase sales and profits**. Entrepreneurs who enter international markets can **offset declining sales in the domestic market**. They can also benefit from **improved product quality** based on improved operational efficiency to tap their production potential and meet the demands of foreign customers.

Internationalization helps SMEs to **disperse business risk** across different markets. In some cases, the easily measured physical manufactured small firm exports are accompanied by significant **related international service** activity including customer service, design, distribution and marketing.

Internationalization also offers the benefits of **economies of scale**. Economies of scale refers to lower unit costs of production with increase in volume. International entrepreneurs can benefit from lower costs of production by spreading fixed costs over a large number of units. Doing so can help them to enhance their competitive positions compared to other businesses.

International small firms are more **resilient** (Gerwin, 2015). They are less likely to fail than those that limit their sales to the domestic market. In fact, evidence shows that internationally active SMEs **grow faster** than their domestic counterparts, especially right after entering the foreign market (Carter and Jones-Evans, 2012). During the turbulent period from 2005 to 2009, small manufacturers that exported grew by 37%, while non-exporters declined by 7%. Those in niche markets and new, high-tech industries constitute the fastest growing segment (20%). Internationalization generates more revenue to invest in technology and production, which is key to SMEs' growth.

Internationalization has advantages for not only individual firm founders, but also for the economy. According to research by the European Commission, innovation and internationalization share a positive causal effect in competitiveness (APEC, 2015). Internationalization is closely linked with industrial development strategies aimed at improving economic competitiveness.

At the same time, however, small firms are disproportionately underrepresented in the international market. A significant proportion of SMEs with exporting potential restricts themselves to domestic operations in the flawed belief that size is a disadvantage in internationalization. Only a very small share of all US services firms export, service SMEs being less likely than larger services firms to engage in trade. Internationalizing SMEs in some APEC countries constitute a miniscule proportion of total SMEs (APEC, 2015). In Japan and Korea, SMEs investing abroad account for only 0.1% and 0.03% of total SMEs, respectively.

Internationalization Motives: Explaining Small Firm Internationalization

Until relatively recently, internationalization was regarded as the domain of large corporations. It is necessary to understand the factors influencing small firm internationalization in order to encourage small firm internationalization. Three theoretical approaches have been advanced to explain SME internationalization. These are the stages model of internationalization, network theory and resource-based theory. Each of these theories is explained below.

Stages Model of Internationalization

The stages model is used to explain the process of small firms' development along the internationalization route. The main premise of the stages model is that small firm internationalization is a sequential, 'staged' process. This model is based on Johanson and Vahlne's (1977) model of knowledge development and increasing foreign market commitment, which in turn is built on Johanson and Wiedersheim-Paul's (1975) study of the internationalization behavior of four Swedish firms from their early beginnings. Johanson and Wiedersheim-Paul found that the internationalization process of the four large Swedish firms was the consequence of a series of incremental decisions, rather than large, spectacular foreign investments.

The stages model explains firms' choice of both foreign markets and foreign entry modes to penetrate those markets. According to the stages model, psychic distance has a significant impact on the time ordering of establishing foreign operations in new foreign countries (Johanson and Vahlne, 1977). **Psychic distance** refers to the extent of proximity in language, culture, political systems and business factors like industry structure and competitive environment. Firms start internationalization with markets that are most easily understood and where perceived uncertainty is low, venturing only at a later stage into new markets with successively greater psychic distance.

The stages model is also called the Uppsala model of internationalization. This is because the model originated from the Uppsala University in Sweden. Sometimes, it is also referred to as the Innovation-Related model that presents small firms' export development as an innovation adoption cycle. Small firms first sell their products/services outside of their local region, prior to crossing country borders to sell in a foreign market.

Psychic distance also affects the choice of entry mode through its impact on resource commitments (Hill et al., 1990). The development of entry mode within a given target market follows a **chain of establishment** (Johanson and Vahlne, 1977, 1990; Johanson and Wiedersheim-Paul, 1975). Firms' international involvement exhibits four different sequential stages including no regular export, export via independent representation (agents), sales subsidiaries and production/manufacturing. Firms start with no export activities in their selected market, followed by exports via independent representatives, and later through a sales subsidiary. Manufacturing facilities are established last in order. The commitment of resources to a chosen foreign market is incremental, based on acquiring successively greater foreign market knowledge and learning.

According to the stages model, cultural similarity reduces the transaction costs of setting up and managing foreign subsidiaries; it increases the desire for full-control entry modes (Erramilli and Rao, 1993; O'Farrell and Wood, 1994). When cultural values, language, social structure and ways of life of the target country are strikingly different from those of the home country, decision makers are more fearful of their capacity to manage foreign operations (Root, 1994). Subsequent expansion of operations in a host country may be based on the gradual acquisition and use of experiential knowledge about operations there as well as incrementally increasing resource commitments to foreign markets (Johanson and Vahlne, 1977).

The stages model has been subject to several criticisms. One of them is the **psychic distance paradox**. There is no concrete evidence to show that high resource commitments increase the costs of full-control modes when psychic distance is high (Erramilli and Rao, 1993). Factors like the availability of more efficient means of supplying information, less fragmented nature of markets, need for rapid growth in a dynamic industry context, and speedy commercialization of applications, especially in the service sector, may be more crucial than psychic distance alone. These factors may provide a rationale for entering psychically distant markets at an early stage of the internationalization process.

Another criticism of the stages model is that not all small firms are the same. The population of small firms is heterogeneous. Madsen and Servais (1997) classify small firms into three types: **traditional exporters**, **late starters** and **born global** firms, that display varying internationalization patterns. Traditional exporters internationalize in an incremental manner, in accordance with the main tenets of the stages model. The late starters are those that sell in the domestic market for several years, before taking a sudden leap into a distant foreign market. This type of small firm leapfrogs stages.

A rapid pace of internationalization, or time between inception and first entry into a foreign market, is a defining feature of born global firms. Founders of born global firms use their social networks to identify opportunities that are global in scope and implement those opportunities by rapidly penetrating a large number of foreign markets irrespective of psychic distance (Autio et al., 2000; Madsen and Servais, 1997). We explain more on rapidly internationalizing and born global firms in Chapter 13.

The applicability of the stages model also depends on the nature of the product or service in question. Service firms have special characteristics that distinguish them from manufacturing firms (Buckley et al., 1992; Knight, 1999). Two key features of services are **intangibility** and **inseparability**. Unlike manufacturing firms that produce tangible, physical products, service firms have intangible offerings that are not amenable to stockpiling or selling in physical form. Knowledge, the intrinsic intangible component of several services, can be easily combined with existing physical assets in many industries, and in different countries, at low cost. More recently, information technology (IT) is also impacting upon the nature of services as well as the way in which they are delivered.

Also unlike manufacturing, services are characterized by simultaneous production and consumption of their offerings at the point of sale or customer contact. These features of intangibility and inseparability mean that traditional modes of entry to penetrate foreign markets do not apply to services. Therefore, the conventionally used frameworks of internationalization may not explain the behavior of all internationalizing service firms.

In some cases, small firms follow their domestic customers abroad in order to retain their customer base. Customer followership or customer-driven internationalization is especially prevalent in high-tech, knowledge-intensive sectors where success in entering foreign markets is more dependent on firms' existing relationships with customers in their domestic markets.

In other cases, internationalization may be more than just a reactive response to a set of circumstances that necessitates changing the normal course of business. It is important to take into account the aspirations of entrepreneurs. A key criticism of the stages model is that it does not acknowledge the role of strategic decision making of owner-founders. Entrepreneurs may go abroad to actively seek new markets or customers. Such 'market seeking' may be motivated by the need to exploit attractive opportunities in foreign markets based on market research or a considered assessment of their external environment.

Network Theory of Internationalization

The concept of social networks has been used to explain the creation and growth of small firms. In this section, we first explain the concept of social networks and identify different types of networks. Then we examine the role of social networks in both small firm founding and internationalization.

Social networks are defined as the pattern of relationships, or actual set of links, between individuals. A network is a social structure, comprised of a set of relationships between individuals, groups and organizations, which is greater than the sum of its parts. In formal network analysis, the actors are called nodes and the links between them are called ties (Oviatt and McDougall, 2005). Social networks are different from **networking**, which is the activity by which network relationships are built, nurtured and mobilized, and the flows through these relationships, such as information, money, power and friendship.

Defined as the strength and quality of relations within an entrepreneur's network (Jack, 2005), **social ties** include personal ties such as family and friends, **industry ties** such as business colleagues or **intermediary ties** based on participation in networking and alumni associations.

In the absence of organizational and strategic processes, new entrepreneurial firms, unlike large firms, typically rely on the social capital of entrepreneurs for resource acquisition (Gilbert et al., 2006). Defined as the actual set of links amongst a set of individuals, social networks provide **social capital**, that is, the actual and potential resources embedded within, available through and derived from social networks (Nahapiet and Ghoshal, 1998).

Social network theory postulates that social networks of entrepreneurs (or who they know) influence their ability to create, develop and grow their firms (Aldrich and Zimmer, 1986). Founders' motivations and hard work alone are not sufficient; extensive and diverse social networks provide considerable financial, legal, business and emotional support, and help to overcome formidable odds in both venture creation and growth. Social networks also enable the building of technological competence in small firms.

Research has established the importance of social networks across a broad range of industry sectors including computing and IT, wine, specialist cheese, business services and oil. Studies have also indicated the importance of social networks to entrepreneurial activity across a wide range of countries including the US (Saxenian, 1985), the UK, Japan, Greece, Norway, Sweden, Italy, Belgium, Slovakia and Sri Lanka (Carter and Jones-Evans, 2012).

For Ujjal Kohli, Silicon-Valley-based founder of Meru Networks, networks were a 'huge part' of what he had been able to accomplish as an entrepreneur. Ujjal had 500 names in his Outlook account and another 2,500 on LinkedIn at the time of this research. According to Ujjal, they were not random names but people he had all met and knew; he did not accept a request to connect from anyone he did not know. He could easily reach out to these people because of the credibility of his network. His social network helped him to find co-founders and build teams, as well as locate venture capital (VC) investors for his ventures:

> Networks had been a huge part of whatever I have been able to accomplish...
> I have in my Outlook I have 500 names... these are all people I have met and I
> know..., and on LinkedIn I have 2,500 names... when people are two apart, you
> can easily reach out to them... it's through all these networks that I always built
> the teams, found my co-founders, found the VCs. (Ujjal Kohli, Founder, Meru
> Networks, California)

Social networks also help to monitor opportunistic behavior. As Ujjal explained, one of his classmates from Harvard Business School was a VC investor in one of the portfolio companies that Ujjal was also an investor in. Ujjal was aware that his classmate's presence on the board of the portfolio company acted as a check on his own behavior. As he had known his classmate for 20 years, any inappropriate act on Ujjal's part would come at a 'huge cost':

when VCs are looking at various entrepreneurs they want to invest in people that they know have the energy, the talent, the motivation, the integrity that they can trust, so this guy has known me for 20 years you know we were classmates at Harvard Business School, and certainly if I were to do anything inappropriate it would be at a huge cost… so he knows that and so it creates huge trust. (Ujjal Kohli, Founder, Meru Networks, California)

Types of Social Networks

Dimensions of Networks

Entrepreneurship research on the role of networks in venture creation and growth explores the full breadth of relationships or dimensions of networks in which small firms are involved. These dimensions are network size, diversity, density, stability and strength.

Network size refers to the number of actors participating in the network. Network size can be large or small depending on the number of participant actors. **Diversity** refers to the number of different types of actor in the entrepreneurs' network. Diversity may be measured along a number of different dimensions such as age, gender, education, etc.

Density or connectedness of a network refers to the extensiveness of ties between actors (Carter and Jones-Evans, 2012). It is the number of actual linkages in the network as a ratio of the total number of possible linkages. Actors have sparse networks when the nodes to which they are tied are, for the most part, not tied to each other (Oviatt and McDougall, 2005). For example, if a Swedish new venture has a link to two businesses in Australia, but those businesses have no ties to each other, then the network of the Swedish venture is less dense than it would be if the two Australian businesses were directly linked in some way.

Dense networks are believed to be inefficient at producing unique information, while sparse networks are believed to be more efficient (Oviatt and McDougall, 2005). Sparse networks are believed to produce new information better than dense networks because the sparse networks link disparate nodes while the dense networks link nodes through redundant ties.

For example, if the two Australian businesses sell to distinctively different product markets, the Swedish venture has a chance to learn information about both markets. Alternatively, if the two Australian firms sell to each other in addition to those distinctive product markets, then the Swedish venture has redundant links through which it may get information about both Australian firms and the markets that they serve.

At the same time, however, the redundant links of dense networks have the advantage that there are more links and, therefore, more interaction among all the actors in the network. Thus, monitoring of behavior is more efficiently accomplished and reputations are more quickly communicated to all actors in the network. Business behavior regarded as illegitimate in a dense network is quickly detected, widely known and punished. Thus, trust is stronger in a dense network than in a sparse one because there are penalties for opportunistic behavior.

Stability is the degree to which a network pattern changes over time. A large number of entrepreneurship studies are devoted to the **strength** of social ties (e.g. Elfring and Hulsink, 2003, 2007; Jack, 2005). **Strength** refers to the distinction between strong and weak ties. **Strong ties** bind people in long-term relationships. Strong ties between nodes or actors are durable and involve emotional investment, trust, reliability and a desire to negotiate over differences in order to preserve the tie.

Weak ties refer to a diverse set of persons in different contexts with whom there is some business connection and infrequent contact (Starr and MacMillan, 1990). Weak ties are relationships with customers, suppliers and others that are friendly and business-like. Weak ties are far more numerous than strong ties because they require less investment. Their number can grow relatively quickly, and they are important because they are often vital sources of information and know-how.

The entrepreneurial processes of opportunity recognition and resource acquisition require different combinations of strong and weak ties. Differences in tie strength underlie differences in the nature of information entrepreneurs are exposed to and hence the opportunities that they perceive (Arenius and De Clercq, 2005). Although important in the early stages, **strong ties** are fraught with the risk of 'overembeddedness'. This means that they do not supply the diverse knowledge necessary for growth and development (Uzzi, 1997).

Formed as indirect contacts like friends of friends, and characterized by infrequent interaction, weak ties based on business networks and support agencies become more effective at later stages of development (Deakins et al., 2007). Weak ties give better access to novel and diverse information compared to strong ties that are fraught with the risk of 'overembeddedness', or insulation from external information (Uzzi, 1997).

The case of James Dyson, accomplished designer, innovator and entrepreneur, and founder of the Dual-Cyclone vacuum cleaner, illustrates the use of different types of informal social networks in the founding and growth of his business ventures (Carter and Jones-Evans, 2012). Dyson made use of his extensive and diverse network to access finance and legal advice, social and emotional support, and marketing and public relations services, as well as talented young design engineers.

The creation of Dyson's business ventures was also heavily dependent on both family and friends (strong ties), as well as acquaintances and serendipitous meetings (weak ties). Strong ties such as family and friends provided him with financial and knowledge-based resources that helped to ensure that he was able to turn his various novel ideas into successful business ventures. Weak ties such as contacts made on an airplane, in business meetings and in seminars played an important role in the international growth of his venture.

Studies have also explored the distinction between personal and industry ties. **Personal or friendship ties** include strong networks of family and friends. **Industry or professional ties** comprise contacts with former colleagues, buyers or suppliers within a given profession such as medicine or education, and are bound by 'professional ethics of co-operation'. The workplace forms a natural environment for opportunity recognition since this environment allows people to spot opportunities in their own industries (Arenius and De Clercq, 2005) and build network contacts based on relationships with industry players such as other firms, buyers, suppliers or customers (Nahapiet and Ghoshal, 1998).

The entrepreneurship literature also mentions **intermediary ties** (Crick and Spence, 2005; Ozgen and Baron, 2007). These ties refer to professional forums, conferences or events that entrepreneurs attend and that might enable the formation of strong or new ties. Evidence shows that the educational level of the entrepreneur and growth orientation of the firm can positively impact the use of certain forums of interaction such as trade fairs and business seminars.

Some entrepreneurs feel less confident about the sustained value of prior work-based connections. According to Vas Bhandarkar, a Silicon-Valley-based serial entrepreneur, relationships with former colleagues are often short-lived. The value of those relationships quickly goes down upon exiting a former employer to join another company. Just because a project with a former colleague worked well in the past does not necessarily mean that it would also succeed in the future. In Vas's view, it was important to be 'forward looking' and seek out other networks besides former colleagues:

> Former colleagues, those networks, you have to be very careful how you use them. Let's say I've been working with you for five years. And then for whatever reason I left and joined another company. Within six months, the value of that relationship goes down by half... you may have worked with that person in one field in one project, but that does not necessarily mean you'll be good in another project... that's quite backward... you seek out people who are forward looking. You partner with them and then you bring people in. (Vas Bhandarkar, Serial Entrepreneur, California)

TYPES OF SOCIAL NETWORKS
THE CASE OF UJJAL KOHLI

Ujjal Kohli, Founder, Meru Networks, California, identified five types of social networks that were relevant to him as an entrepreneur. These included alumni networks in his host and home countries, a professional networking organization, former colleagues and networks of contacts in his role as an angel investor:

1. One of his key networks was his alumni (IIT) network from his home country, which was very strong in Silicon Valley.
2. The second network was a professional networking organization for entrepreneurs (TiE) in Silicon Valley where he met one of his co-founders:

I had three or four networks that have helped me a lot so one network is of course the IIT network and that's very strong in Silicon Valley, and the second network, if you know, TiE has been very helpful at that time I met one of the co-founders at TiE in this case.

3. The third network was his alumni network in the host country, which was probably his strongest network. This was for two reasons: first, it was a large network; and second, networking among students was part of the institution's culture:

Harvard Business School is probably the strongest network… First of all because the numbers are large… Harvard graduates at least (at that time) 800 students a year… Also, Harvard business school has a strong cultural networking into their students…the clear message was it doesn't matter what you know, what matters is who you know and who's going to take your call and who is going to do something because you called them. They just pound that into you.

4. The fourth network was his network of former colleagues in the host country. This 'extremely large' network, from mainly 'three or four companies' in Silicon Valley where he had previously worked, had been very valuable to Ujjal:

So that Harvard network is priceless but McKinsey alumni is another network I use and it's a really strong network and very large because you know over the years I think four out of five people who join McKinsey not many people stay for very long. So, the alumni network is extremely large and very well placed in corporate America so that's been a huge help to me…

Then my first job was at Intel, and if you chart the growth of Silicon Valley there are three or four companies that have produced massive alumni networks that became entrepreneurs later. So Intel is one like that, Hewlett-Packard is another one… in more modern times PayPal has been one company and a lot of PayPal alumni have started companies and all these data guys have done extremely well.

5. The fifth network was through Ujjal's investing activities. His investment in 12 companies over the years had connected him to probably 20–30 VCs who were co-investors in the same companies and sat on the board with him:

(Continued)

> And then through my investing activities in any one company we have four, five, up to ten or even more sometimes so those two–three years in investing were very useful because I got connected to many VCs. I invested in about 12 companies and just through that probably got to know 20–30 VCs who were co-investors in the same companies and sat on the board with me.

Source: authors' own research

Role of Social Networks in Internationalization

Social networks are important for firm growth. Social networks provide resources such as foreign market information and experiential knowledge, business contacts and local sales and distribution channels that positively impact the internationalization of new and small firms (Coviello and Cox, 2006). They also enable small and new ventures to rapidly internationalize and display a variety of entry modes. Evidence suggests that small businesses of more than ten employees and growth-oriented small firms have a lower bias towards local networks.

According to Oviatt and McDougall (2005), three key aspects of networks, namely a) the strength of network ties, b) the size of the network and c) overall density of the network, influence the rapid internationalization of small firms. Different types of social ties, namely personal and professional, are also influential.

Strength of Network Ties

Evidence on the relative role of strong and weak ties in internationalization is sparse. Nevertheless, existing research suggests that strong ties are not the most important type for internationalization. This is because of their small number and investment required. Entrepreneurs are most dependent upon strong ties at start-up. Cross-border weak ties positively and significantly influence the speed of venture internationalization. If an entrepreneur already has weak ties when he or she discovers or enacts an opportunity, the initial foreign entry may occur with unusual speed.

Network Size

The size of an entrepreneur's network is the second key aspect influencing the speed of internationalization. The more direct or indirect cross-border weak ties that an entrepreneur has established, the greater the potential country scope of internationalization, and hence greater possible speed for increasing that scope. Larger entrepreneurial networks are associated with faster venture internationalization and more rapid increases in country scope. Furthermore, with a large network in place, a relatively large portion of venture revenue comes rapidly from foreign sources, and the venture, therefore, has more rapid commitment to internationalization.

Network Density

Dense networks can be seen as a partial substitute for strong ties across national borders. Since successful international business operations are dependent upon reliable interaction among actors in multiple foreign countries, dense cross-border networks provide relatively efficient support for internationalization. Entrepreneurs who have already established such networks can internationalize rapidly. Unlike in strong ties, however, trust in dense networks is established by their monitoring potential of actors linked by weak ties, rather than by the emotional investment present in strong ties.

Network Type (Personal, Professional and Intermediary Ties)

Entrepreneurs' personal or professional contacts can enable their entry into foreign markets (Loane and Bell, 2006). Research finds that highly educated entrepreneurs are significantly more likely to have personal networks that span national boundaries (Donckels and Lambrecht, 1997).

Rishi Khosla, a London-based founder of the Softbank-backed Oak North Bank, launched in late 2015, built his first venture from the bottom up with the help of one of his former international classmates at the London School of Economics (LSE). Rishi brought in his Colombian classmate, who had recently exited his own venture, as a co-founder, and they hired interns from different nationalities prior to targeting foreign market entry. Rishi's own familiarity with India helped him to penetrate the country using his family home in Delhi to set up an office:

> I then brought in my business partner who was a Columbian guy. Erm, who again he was a classmate at the LSE, he'd just sold the business in Miami, to WPP group... I convinced him that we should start this business together, he moved over to London...and then we started hiring interns over here... we went to Oxford, Cambridge, the LSE... when we got to about 20 interns or so, we said okay we need to, we've now got some revenue coming through so we took a group of these interns... and took them to India... we'd establish in Delhi, because that's where my family house was so we'd have somewhere to stay. (Rishi Khosla, Founder, Oak North Bank, London)

For Vikas, a Silicon-Valley-based founder, his foreign entries in China and Latin America were dictated by the personnel on his management team. As they belonged to the foreign target countries in question, these personnel facilitated the entry of Vikas's venture in those markets. In all cases, these members of the top management team were either his friends or ex-workers whom he previously knew:

> There are people in the management team that come from China, Latin America, yes. They came from friends or ex-workers from these areas who I know. That's how I entered these places. Singapore, they approached us. But other entries are through contacts. (Vikas, Entrepreneur, Silicon Valley, California, USA)

Sometimes, entrepreneurs leverage **intermediary networks** to penetrate foreign markets. Vijay Maheshwari, co-founder of Verismo Networks, California, said that his customers in Europe found him through conferences that he and his team attended in Europe. He recalled that he relied on databases, industry publications and websites to get the necessary information about clients in the early stages of his start-up when he did not have money to go to conferences. Then he would search for industry experts and potential customers in order to contact them.

More recently, customers from Europe had begun to approach him further to meeting with him at information booths that he and his team set up at the conferences they attended in Europe. Several people frequented the booths to learn more about the product and then approached Vijay and his team in the US on that basis:

> And we have customers in Europe so I go to Europe… They [customers] found us through conferences. We go to a bunch of conferences… Previously when I started I did not have money to go to conferences but then I used to get the databases or the publication or you can go to website and figure out who gave a lecture and who gave a talk and… figure out which company they were and then get connected to them. Because the guy is writing a paper and giving so he has to know what he is doing. (Vijay Maheshwari, Co-founder, Verismo Networks)

Vikas explained that he tried to use social media in addition to direct contacts in his efforts to seek out clients. He encouraged his employees to put up news about the company on Facebook and Twitter. As his was a small company, social media helped to get the 'buzz' out and establish a semblance of familiarity with the large clients when he eventually reached out to them to pitch his company. It also enabled him to establish credibility in his personal circle of family and friends, some of whom were employees of these large companies that he wished to target:

> And we try to use direct contact and also social media. So any good news about our company, I do put onto Facebook… On LinkedIn, again the same thing. Any positive news on Twitter make sure it's part of the headlines… and the whole idea is that we are a small company we need to get the word or buzz out subconsciously that we are doing well. So when we approach them we would like to pitch this to their company. (Vikas, Entrepreneur, Silicon Valley, California)

Social networks are important to not just enter foreign markets, but also to manage operations in those markets. When Ujjal Kohli first entered India for his venture, turnover was extremely high. The engineers he hired were prone to regularly changing jobs in order to get a quick salary raise. In his view, employees recruited through referrals were more likely to be loyal and less likely to leave in response to a slightly better salary offer:

> So also at that time in India… people wanted 30–40% raises every year and engineers figured out a way to do that was to change jobs every year. People who had networks in India tend to bring in the first set of employees through their contacts. So when people are through your contacts…, they indulge in less abusive behavior. They just don't take off or accept the job and not show up because then you know people are going to find out or whatever so we didn't have any of that. (Ujjal Kohli, Founder, Meru Networks, Silicon Valley, California)

Resource-Based Theory

The **resource-based theory (RBT)** postulates that firms are collections of productive resources and the heterogeneity of resources provides them with unique, idiosyncratic characteristics that contribute to competitive advantage. Founders may possess some of the most valuable, unique and hard-to-imitate resources.

Resources include financial and human resources. Whereas **financial resources** are tangible resources like money or financial savings, **human resources** are intangible resources like decision makers' education, knowledge, skills, experience or networks. Resources that are valuable, rare, inimitable and non-substitutable enable firms to conceive of and implement strategies that improve their efficiency and effectiveness.

Dynamic capabilities refer to firms' ability to combine and re-combine resources, and to use their resource base in ways that confer a competitive advantage over a long period of time. The idea of dynamic capabilities extends the previously static viewpoint of RBT to allow for the dynamic component of firm-specific advantages. According to RBT, resources must have value not just at any one point in time, but over a long period of time.

From a resource-based lens, internationalization decisions are taken within a coordinated framework of resources and capabilities, as well as environmental (including competitive) realities. Firms have a different mix of resources/competencies/capabilities and resource/competency/capability gaps, and their strategic responses to these gaps allow for the possibility of different paths to growth and internationalization.

Small firms enter foreign markets to exploit their firm-specific, internal resources and capabilities in the light of external, environmental constraints. Established as a merger of biological and pharmaceutical companies, the Bioclon Institute, an SME formed to research and develop antivenins in Mexico in 1990, is an excellent example of the use of a conscious resource-based strategy to leverage the company's internal resources and capabilities for international growth (see Box on the following page).

BIOCLON INSTITUTE
USING A RESOURCE-BASED STRATEGY
FOR SUCCESS

Established as a merger of biological and pharmaceutical companies in 1990, the Bioclon Institute, a research-focused SME in Mexico, was started with the aim of using new biotech developments to become a worldwide leader in the R&D of antivenins. Scorpion sting, for example, can be life threatening, especially in children, and the condition is 1,000 times more common in Mexico than in the USA.

With fast growing sales, the company gained around 7% of the global market of antivenins by the mid-2000s. It was the only company that had obtained an 'orphan drug' status from the Food and Drug Administration (FDA) of the United States at the time (medicines that are designated as orphan drugs must fulfil certain criteria so that they can benefit from incentives such as protection from competition once on the market). The company initiated clinical trials to get approval for its third drug, ANALATRO, designed to treat black widow spider envenomation. In May 2015, the company received FDA approval to commercialize ANAVIP, their second drug approved by the FDA after ANA-SCORP. Both are commercialized in the US by the Rare Disease Therapeutics, Inc.

These competitive advantages have been the result of a conscious strategic plan developed to strongly leverage the company's own internal resources and capabilities. The firm has developed state-of-the-art products, equipment and processes. It has also pioneered innovative internal, operations and IP management, development strategies and organization technologies. Moreover, the company has engaged in continual product and process innovation.

The company's efforts to harness its resources and capabilities have led to the development of a technology management model incorporating links with customers. This model has also been supported by a strong academic-industrial connections program focused on promoting modernization and leading to national-level research through grants, stimuli for researchers and the development of providers.

Source: Solleiro et al. (2006)

Unlike network theory, the RBT is focused on strategic decision making. As mentioned earlier in the chapter, one of the key criticisms of the stages model is that it does not allow for strategic decision making or the proactive role of the owner-founder. The RBT addresses these shortcomings in suggesting that entrepreneurs strategically leverage their tangible and intangible resources to plan their firms' foray into foreign markets.

Manish Chandra, founder of Poshmark, an online platform for buying and selling second-hand fashion, envisaged his foreign market entry to be a strategically planned process based on evaluating market feasibility rather than responding to the presence of network connections abroad. As he had connections 'everywhere', he felt that he could potentially enter any country. What was more important in his view was to plan the process given the high level of investment involved and the large number of approvals needed, all considering the sophisticated nature of his platform:

> I have connections everywhere. Between me, our investors, our advisors, I can get into any country, if we needed to. It won't be an accident. It'll be very well planned. It's very expensive to enter a market. We have to do full top down. You have to make an investment. You have to get the board approval. It's not a casual thing because of the way our platform is structured. You have to handle payments, you have to handle shipping. (Manish Chandra, Founder, Poshmark, California)

Small firm founders must assess both internal and external factors in order to internationalize. Whereas **internal factors** include firms' resources and capabilities, **external factors** are foreign market size, and competitive and institutional environments in the home and foreign markets. Below, we explain the role of both internal, firm-specific factors and external, environmental factors in internationalization.

Internal (Firm-Specific) Factors

Financial resources refer to sales revenues or capital available for investment. Often, entrepreneurs or small firm founders use their own personal savings in firm founding. As foreign market entry is expensive in terms of costs of R&D, or setting up foreign offices, small firms' ability to internationalize may depend on the availability of financial capital reserves.

According to the RBT, both the quantity and quality of **human resources** impact the propensity to internationalize and the choice of internationalization strategy. Whereas the quantity of human resources pertains to the number of employees/turnover, quality encompasses education, knowledge, skills, wide ranging experience and even social networks of the decision maker.

The number of employees is often an indicator of firm size. Empirical findings about the impact of firm size on internationalization are mixed. As a general rule, large firms are more likely to internationalize than small firms; however, the correlation between size and internationalization does not appear to hold beyond a certain minimum size.

Although evidence is mixed, human capital, often measured as **age** and years of formal **education**, is used as a predictor of an individual's ability to identify and develop entrepreneurial opportunities (Lundberg and Rehnfors, 2018). Entering a foreign market also requires a great deal of **knowledge** about that market. Firms without such knowledge, especially small firms, are typically thought to be unlikely to entertain foreign market entries. Knowledge of specific markets acquired through learning by doing from initial market entry reduces the perceived uncertainty of market entry

(Johanson and Vahlne, 1990). Gaining knowledge rarely appears in the list of reasons why a business goes international, and yet it is of crucial importance. Small firms that do not internationalize are more vulnerable to failure due to lack of knowledge of foreign markets. International competition exposes small firms to the need for excellence. By cooperating with foreign enterprises, SMEs can gain access to more advanced technology and improve innovative capacity.

Eriksson et al. (1997) identify three types of **experiential knowledge** in an international business context: experiential knowledge of clients, market, and competitors (foreign business knowledge); experiential knowledge of government, institutional frameworks, rules, norms and values (foreign institutional knowledge); and experiential knowledge of the firm's capability and resources to engage in international operations (internationalization knowledge). Taken together, they have been called a person's **international orientation**. International orientation is variously defined as foreign education or work experience, travel, foreign birth, world mindedness. The balance of empirical evidence suggests that founders of internationalized SMEs are likely to have spent part of their lives abroad and are accustomed to dealing with uncertainty.

Vas Bhandarkar reaffirmed the importance of knowledge in internationalization. According to Vas, personal networks are not necessarily helpful; they are just a means to an end. It is not networks, but how one operates that is critical to the international growth of a small firm. Skills and expertise about foreign markets where small firms want to sell is often critical to selling in those markets. Sometimes such expertise could be obtained by acquiring teams that had the expertise of selling in new markets, as well as of markets where new products could be built:

> It is not the network per se, it's how you operate. You don't necessarily need to have a network. You can always try to source these teams. You can always decide strategically that you want to grow. Then you grow. So it's important. Personal networks are not going to help. They are means to an end. They are nice to have but not a must have. If you want to build a truly global business, you want to acquire teams that have expertise in selling into new markets but also where your products can be built, in those markets. (Vas Bhandarkar, Serial Entrepreneur and Founder, GlobalLogic, California)

The human capital of entrepreneurs based on **prior work or start-up experience** is also positively associated with both entrepreneurial discovery and exploitation (Mosey and Wright, 2007; Shane, 2000). Human capital derived from prior work experience enables entrepreneurs to build ties with industry players such as other firms, customers or suppliers, and to improve the effectiveness of the resultant social capital in spotting or exploiting opportunities (Nahapiet and Ghoshal, 1998).

Altogether, increased knowledge and experience expand the capability to manage institutional contextual influences. They boost the cultural intelligence of entrepreneurs, and help them to form an international mindset and develop personal cross-cultural competence (Johanson and Vahlne, 2009; Zahra et al., 2005). Migrant entrepreneurs, in particular, develop their cognitive alertness for effectively scanning and interpreting international opportunities as a result of confronting two different contexts (Kirzner, 1979, pp. 142–143). Migration experience gives entrepreneurs an extraordinary creative, social and cultural capital (Terjesen and Elam, 2009). Bridging different national contexts has been found to be favorable for opportunity recognition and venture creation (George et al., 2016).

As mentioned earlier in the chapter, decision makers who have **international networks** are more likely to exploit foreign market opportunities than those who lack such relationships. Some studies have also considered founders' attitudes towards exporting, dynamism and self-confidence of the decision maker. The overall conclusion of these studies is that decision makers' perceptions impact the internationalization potential of their firms. Decision makers who perceive foreign markets as less risky, less expensive and of higher profit potential as compared to the domestic markets are more likely to internationalize.

External Factors

Besides internal factors, the external environment of the firm in both home and foreign markets influences internationalization. The external environment of firms includes their competitive and institutional environment in both home and foreign markets.

Competitive environment refers to the size, intensity and structure of competition in the market. A few decades ago, small companies concerned themselves mainly with competitors who were perhaps a few blocks away; today, small firms face fierce competition from businesses that may be several time zones away. As a result, entrepreneurs find themselves under greater pressure to expand into international markets and to build businesses without borders.

In some cases, a declining home market can push small firms abroad. As mentioned in the opening case, world-renowned Italian food producers are caught in a painful squeeze at home, forcing them to look abroad to sell their product. Entrepreneurs in countries with small populations such as Luxembourg, Cyprus, Slovenia and Qatar often seek customers beyond their small internal markets.

In contrast, a large domestic market dissuades entrepreneurs from selling abroad. Although there are some exceptions (for example, India, with over one-fourth of entrepreneurs selling outside the country's borders, despite a large domestic market), countries with large populations such as China, the United States, Indonesia and Brazil provide large and diverse, as well as familiar, internal markets that may be sufficient for most entrepreneurs (Bosma and Kelley, 2018).

Manish Chandra explained that even though Japan was a large and attractive market for fashion and mobile, it was just one fourth the size of the massive $300 billion dollar a year US domestic market. Although he was attracted to Japan, he wanted to fully exploit the local market before venturing abroad:

The market that everyone is really excited for fashion and mobile, is Japan. Some investors have introduced me to a few Japanese companies. I haven't made a decision as to when we can go there…We are still focused on the local market. We are still very young. We have to prove out many things before we go beyond the US market. Fashion in US is about a 300 billion dollars a year, it's a trillion in the world. So the nearest market is one fourth the size of US in fashion. It's massive just doing US. (Manish Chandra, Founder, Poshmark, California)

Institutional Environment

Institutional environment is about the political, legal and regulatory environment in the home or foreign market. Support from domestic governments enables entrepreneurs to enter foreign markets. For example, federal grants from the government in Las Vegas, Nevada, USA, have led small businesses to enter foreign markets. By traveling to foreign markets to meet with their customers, small business owners in Las Vegas have been able to grow sales and develop new products. Benefitting from the Small Business Administration's (SBA's) grant program, these businesses have been able to generate more than $1.7 million in revenue. The relationships that they have developed with overseas customers have also enabled them to generate jobs and strengthen Nevada's economy.

Nature of Product / Service

In addition to internal, firm-specific factors and external, foreign market environmental factors, decision makers must also consider the nature of their **product or service** in planning foreign market entry. Empirical studies on small firm internationalization point to the role of **technological intensity**, R&D competencies, market research and product development, advertising and sales promotions as impacting internationalization.

The RBT is especially useful to explaining the internationalization of small service firms, which, compared to manufacturing firms, are diverse in nature. Knowledge-intensive small firms, for example, even in traditional industries, are increasingly using the power of technology and marketing and e-commerce skills to rapidly enter foreign markets. **R&D intensity and product/service attributes** are more important than size in explaining small firm internationalization.

While SMEs in industries characterized by low skill levels and high transportation costs are less likely to internationalize, those in sectors marked by short lifecycles are motivated to accelerate their entry into the international markets. For services that are tradable, location choice is dependent upon the need to adapt to local market conditions, economies of scale in production, the availability of factor inputs such as suitably qualified personnel, as well as the degree of vertical integration within the firm. In some cases, even the **history of small firms**, including their efforts to expand outside of their region, influences their propensity to internationalize.

Overall, the RBT offers an integrative platform for explaining small firm internationalization. It presents a holistic view of the firm, and reinforces the point that internationalization is affected by multiple influences.

Chapter Summary

LO1: Internationalization has many benefits for small firms. Internationalization allows entrepreneurs access to foreign markets, which can offset declining sales in the domestic market. They can also benefit from improved product quality, and the ability to disperse business risk. Internationalization also offers the benefits of economies of scale or lower unit costs of production with increase in volume. International small firms are more resilient and grow faster than their domestic counterparts. Three theoretical approaches have been advanced to explain SME internationalization. These include the **stages model of internationalization, network theory** and **resource-based theory**.

LO2: The main premise of the **stages model** is that small firm internationalization is a sequential, 'staged' process. Firms start internationalization with markets that are most easily understood and where perceived uncertainty is low, venturing only at a later stage into new markets with successively greater psychic distance. The commitment of resources to a chosen foreign market is also incremental, based on successively greater foreign market knowledge and learning. Firms perform no export activities in their selected market, followed by exports via independent representatives, and later through a sales subsidiary. Manufacturing facilities are established last. The stages model has been subject to several criticisms. The applicability of the stages model to the service sector depends on the nature of the product or service in question. There is no concrete evidence to show that high resource commitments increase the costs of full-control modes when psychic distance is high. It is also important to take into account the role of technology and the aspirations and networks of entrepreneurs.

LO3: **Social networks** are defined as the pattern of relationships, or actual set of links, between individuals. Social network theory postulates that social networks of entrepreneurs (or who they know) influence their ability to create, develop and grow their firms. Entrepreneurship research on the role of networks in venture creation and growth explores the full breadth of relationships or dimensions of networks in which small firms are involved. These dimensions are network size, diversity, density, stability and strength. **Network size** refers to the number of actors participating in the network. **Diversity** refers to the number of different types of actor in the entrepreneur's network. Density or connectedness of a network refers to the extensiveness of ties between actors. **Stability** is the degree to which a network pattern changes over time. A large number of entrepreneurship studies are devoted to the strength of social ties. **Strong ties** bind people in long-term relationships. Strong ties between nodes or actors are

(Continued)

durable and involve emotional investment, trust, reliability and a desire to negotiate over differences in order to preserve the tie. **Weak ties** refer to a diverse set of persons in different contexts with whom there is some business connection and infrequent contact. **Personal or friendship ties** include strong networks of family and friends. Industry or **professional ties** comprise contacts with former colleagues, buyers or suppliers within a given profession. **Intermediary ties** refer to professional forums, conferences or events that entrepreneurs attend and that might enable the formation of strong or new ties. Social networks are important for firm growth. Social networks provide resources such as foreign market information and experiential knowledge, business contacts and local sales and distribution channels that positively impact the internationalization of new and small firms. They also enable small and new ventures to rapidly internationalize and display a variety of entry modes.

LO4: The **resource-based theory (RBT)** postulates that firms are collections of productive resources and the heterogeneity of resources provides them with unique, idiosyncratic characteristics that contribute to competitive advantage. Whereas **financial resources** are tangible resources like money or financial savings, **human resources** are intangible resources like decision makers' **age**, **education**, **knowledge**, **skills**, **experience and networks**. From a resource-based view, key internationalization decisions are taken within a coordinated framework of resources and capabilities, as well as environmental realities. Firms have a different mix of resources/competencies/capabilities and resource/competency/capability gaps, and their strategic responses to these gaps allow for the possibility of different paths to growth and internationalization. In addition, decision makers must also consider the **nature of their product or service**, and **history** in planning foreign market entry. Overall, the RBT offers an integrative platform for explaining small firm internationalization.

Review Questions

1. What is the relevance of small firm internationalization? Based on what you have read in this chapter, explain the importance of internationalization for a) international entrepreneurs/small firms and b) the economy.
2. What is the stages model of internationalization? To what extent does the stages model explain internationalizing firms' choice of a) foreign market and b) foreign entry mode strategy? Discuss.
3. Explain what you understand by the term social networks. Define the different types of social networks outlined in this chapter.
4. What is the role of social networks in the a) founding and b) internationalization of small firms? Give examples to explain your answer.
5. What is the resource-based theory of internationalization? What are the different types of resources that influence small firm internationalization?
6. How do firm-specific resources and capabilities influence small firm internationalization, according to the resource-based theory of internationalization? Use examples to explain your answer.

Case 5.1

Leveraging the Social Network for Innovation: The Case of James Dyson

After leaving school, where he studied humanities at 'A' level, James Dyson went to art school in London, UK, and later to the Royal College of Art (RCA) where he earned a master's degree in design. Dyson's subsequent business career was roughly split into three major phases corresponding to the development of three product innovations. This case traces the role of Dyson's social ties in the founding of these ventures.

Innovation #1: Sea Truck

While a student at the RCA, Dyson built a prototype of one of his innovative ideas – the 'Sea Truck'. The Sea Truck was a flat-hulled, high-speed water-craft that could land without a harbour or jetty. Dyson patented the idea. Dyson met Joan Littlewood, a theatre and film personality, at the RCA who invited him to design a new theatre that she was planning to build. Dyson sought financial support from British Aluminium where one of the managers introduced him to an entrepreneur named Jeremy Fry. He began to work for Jeremy Fry who manufactured motorized valve actuators for pipelines. Fry encouraged him to adopt a practical approach to design and set up a subsidiary of his company – 'Rotork' – to manufacture Dyson's product.

Dyson's wife, Deidre, stepped in to help with marketing when Dyson realized his message to potential buyers was too complicated. She designed a brochure for each function and the Sea Truck began to sell. More than 250 Sea Trucks were sold at a turnover of many millions, but Dyson soon began to feel the need to return to the drawing board.

Innovation #2: Ball Barrow

While working for Rotork, Dyson and his family moved from London to a 300-year-old farmhouse in the Cotswolds. Undertaking most of the re-building work himself, Dyson conceived the idea of re-inventing the wheelbarrow by replacing the wheel with a ball, and left Rotork to set up his own manufacturing company Kirk-Dyson to manufacture the ball barrow.

Although he had made money from the Sea Truck, he needed financial support to establish a company to manufacture the ball barrow. He turned to his family. He went to see a lawyer friend of his brother-in-law. The lawyer, Andrew Phillips, provided legal advice to help with the formation of the company. He also persuaded Dyson's brother-in-law, Stuart Kirkwood, to invest in production equipment for the venture.

Dyson had a friend called Gill Taylor whom he had met at badminton and happened to have been Miss Great Britain in 1964. He convinced the beauty queen to tour the garden centers of the West Country to promote ball barrows.

Gradually, the partners managed to make the ball barrow a success and began considering ways in which they could expand the business. They wanted to increase output by acquiring a factory and investing in some injection-molding equipment.

(Continued)

George Jackson, a local property developer, provided £100,000 in exchange for a third share in the company.

In addition, Dyson brought in an old friend of his father's, Robert Beldam, for industrial expertise. Robert was chairman of the CBI small companies section, and even though his presence on the board created some resentment, Dyson was grateful for the moral support that he provided. The product became a commercial success; however, a US company stole the idea and Dyson was voted out of the company after losing a legal case to fight the claim.

Innovation #3: Dual-Cyclone Vacuum Cleaner

Next, Dyson came up with the idea of a cyclone vacuum cleaner. He found that the household vacuum cleaner needed only a thin layer of dust inside the dust bag to clog the pores and reduce performance. Using an old vacuum cleaner, cardboard and industrial tape, he constructed a prototype for the Dual-Cyclone – the world's first bagless cleaner.

Dyson needed finance to proceed, and thus sought a partner to invest in the setting up of the Air Power Vacuum Cleaner Company. Dyson launched the vacuum cleaner business with £25,000 from Jeremy Fry and £25,000 from his own personal savings (£18,000 of which he raised by selling his vegetable garden at Sycamore House and the rest borrowed with his home as security).

Over a three-year period, he built around 5,000 prototypes and, by 1982, he had a Dual-Cyclone that was 100% efficient, but debts of more than £80,000. He had also spent a considerable amount of time trying to persuade various European companies, including Hoover, Hotpoint, Electrolux, AEG and Zanussi, to manufacture his vacuum cleaner, but to no avail. The Fry connection once again proved invaluable, as Fry persuaded Rotork's Chief Executive, Tom Essie, to provide further funding. However, Rotork did not proceed with manufacture of the Dual-Cyclone when Tom Essie was replaced by another executive.

Dyson established a deal with a Canadian company that took over responsibility for the North American market. The company was run by an Englishman, Jeffery Pike, with whom Dyson had become acquainted after sitting next to him on an airplane in May 1986, and both turned out to be reading the same novel by Fay Weldon.

As the product was about to be launched onto the US market, 'Amway', a US company, unlawfully launched their own version. Dyson was once again embroiled in a long-running and extremely expensive legal battle. In 1991, Dyson decided that he would set up production in the UK himself but, as before, was constrained by the lack of capital. Again, he was able to make use of his extensive network to resolve the problem. He approached a man called David Williams who owned Linpak, Britain's biggest plastic producer (and who he had met during the founding of the ball barrow), to build his tooling. He recouped the money in installments as he began to sell. He finally successfully launched the first 'DC-01' Dual-Cyclone vacuum cleaner in the UK 15 years after he had conceived the original idea.

As plans for the manufacture of the Dual-Cyclone in the UK progressed Dyson was keen that it embody the very latest technological developments. By this time he had a healthy stream of royalties from Japan and the US and could afford to hire designers from his Alma Mater. About the time he was planning the 'DC-02', Dyson was at the RCA degree show as he had since become an internal examiner on their product design course, and offered one or two of the graduates jobs at his venture. The team consisted of four design engineers from RCA – Simeon Jupp, Peter Gammack, Gareth Jones and Mark Bickenstaffe – all in their 20s.

The RCA connection continued to be of value to Dyson after the company became highly successful; by 1995 demand meant that he had to move out of the Chippenham factory because it had a limited capacity of 30,000 units per week. His old tutor, Tony Hunt, and an accomplished architect called Chris Wilkinson, designed a brand new factory for him. However, the business expanded so fast that it had outgrown the factory even before it was built. Wilkinson and Hunt returned to draw up plans to treble the 90,000 square foot factory space a year later.

By 1996, Dyson was considering ways in which he could extend into the increasingly global market for consumer products. After considering the attractions of Germany and France as the first step in his expansion he eventually settled on Australia. He got a call from a man called Ross Cameron. Cameron was an Australian who had attended Dyson's presentation at Johnson-Wax in Racine, Wisconsin, and agreed to start up in Australia. Yet again, Dyson's social network (see Table 5.1) proved to have a major impact on the direction and fortunes of his business venture.

Table 5.1 James Dyson's social network

Name	Brief Profile	Relationship	Resources Provided	Type of Network
Jeremy Fry	Entrepreneur	Introduced by manager at British Aluminum	Financial support	Professional
Deirdre Dyson	Marketer	Wife	Emotional support; marketing (brochure design)	Family
Andrew Phillips	Lawyer	Brother-in-law's friend	Legal advice	Professional
Stuart Kirkwood	Investor	Brother-in-law	Investment in production equipment	Family
Gill Taylor	Miss Great Britain	Friend	Marketing; toured the garden centers with ball barrows	Personal
Robert Beldam	Chairman of the CBI small companies' section	Father's friend	Moral support and industrial expertise	Personal

(Continued)

Table 5.1 (Continued)

Name	Brief Profile	Relationship	Resources Provided	Type of Network
Jeffrey Pike	Owner of Canadian company that took over responsibility for the North American market	Co-passenger on airplane flight	Business development	Professional
Tony Hunt	Engineer	Old tutor	Designed brand new factory	Professional
Chris Wilkinson	Architect	Friend	Designed brand new factory	Personal
Ross Cameron	Australian vendor in the US	Attended Dyson's presentation at Johnson-Wax, Racine, Wisconsin	Global marketing for consumer products in Australia	Professional

Source: adapted from Conway and Jones (2012a)

Overall, Dyson's extensive and diverse social network provided him with considerable financial, legal, business and emotional support. It is unlikely that Dyson would have overcome pressing hurdles in the founding of his ventures without these networks.

Source: adapted from Conway and Jones (2012b)

Discussion Questions

1. Based on the material covered in this chapter, which different types of social networks did Dyson use in the creation of his ventures?
2. What were the strong ties that Dyson leveraged in his entrepreneurial career? What was the role of these ties in the a) founding and b) growth of his ventures? Discuss.
3. What weak ties did Dyson use? How did Dyson benefit from these ties in the a) founding and b) growth of his ventures? Discuss.
4. Do you agree that 'it is unlikely that Dyson would have overcome formidable odds in the founding of his ventures without these networks'? Based on the chapter, do you believe factors other than social networks influenced Dyson's success? If so, what were those factors and what role did they play in Dyson's success? Discuss.

References

Aldrich, H. and Zimmer, C. (1986) *Entrepreneurship through Social Networks: The Art and Science of Entrepreneurship*. Cambridge: Ballinger.

APEC (2015) 'SME internationalization and measurement', *APEC Policy Support Unit – Policy Brief No. 12 March 2015*. 20.500.12592/s80tg2.

Arenius, P. and De Clercq, D. (2005) 'A network-based approach on opportunity recognition', *Small Business Economics*, 24(3): 249–265.

Autio, E., Sapienza, H.J. and Almeida, J.G. (2000) 'Effects of age at entry, knowledge intensity, and imitability on international growth', *Academy of Management Journal*, 43(5): 909–924.

Bosma, N. and Kelley, D. (2018) *Global Entrepreneurship Monitor 2018/2019 Global Report*. Santiago: Grafica Andes.

Buckley, P.J., Pass, C.L. and Prescott, K. (1992) 'The internationalization of service firms: A comparison with the manufacturing sector', *Scandinavian International Business Review*, 1(1): 39–56.

Carter, S. and Jones-Evans, D. (2012) *Enterprise and Small Business: Principles, Practice and Policy* (3rd edn). Harlow: Financial Times Prentice Hall.

Conway, S. and Jones, O. (2012a) 'Entrepreneurial networks and the small business', in S. Carter and D. Jones-Evans (eds.), *Enterprise and Small Business: Principles, Practice and Policy* (3rd edn). Harlow: Financial Times Prentice Hall, pp. 338–361.

Conway, S. and Jones, O. (2012b) 'Retelling the story of Dyson from a social network perspective', in S. Carter and D. Jones-Evans (eds.), *Enterprise and Small Business: Principles, Practice and Policy* (3rd edn). Harlow: Financial Times Prentice Hall, pp. 345–351.

Coviello, N.E. and Cox, M.P. (2006) 'The resource dynamics of international new venture networks', *Journal of International Entrepreneurship*, 4(2–3): 113–132.

Crick, D. and Spence, M. (2005) 'The internationalization of "high performing" UK high-tech SMEs: A study of planned and unplanned strategies', *International Business Review*, 14(2): 167–185.

Deakins, D., Ishaq, M., Smallbone, D., Whittam, G. and Wyper, J. (2007) 'Ethnic minority businesses in Scotland and the role of social capital', *International Small Business Journal*, 25(3): 307–326.

Donckels, R. and Lambrecht, J. (1997) 'The network position of small businesses: An explanatory model', *Journal of Small Business Management*, 35(2): 13–25.

Elfring, T. and Hulsink, W. (2003) 'Networks in entrepreneurship: The case of high-technology firms', *Small Business Economics*, 21(4): 409–422.

Elfring, T. and Hulsink, W. (2007) 'Networking by entrepreneurs: Patterns of tie-formation in emerging organizations', *Organization Studies*, 28(12): 1849–1872.

Eriksson, K., Johanson, J., Majkgård, A. and Sharma, D.D. (1997) 'Experiential knowledge and cost in the internationalization process', *Journal of International Business Studies*, 28(2): 337–360.

Erramilli, M.K. and Rao, C.P. (1993) 'Service firms' international entry-mode choice: A modified transaction-cost analysis approach', *Journal of Marketing*, 57(3): 19–38.

George, N.M., Parida, V., Lahti, T. and Wincent, J. (2016) 'A systematic literature review of entrepreneurial opportunity recognition: Insights on influencing factors', *International Entrepreneurship and Management Journal*, 12(2): 309–350.

Gerwin Jr., E. (2015) 'Small business exports can drive big growth'. *Longitudes*. Available at www.ups.com/us/en/services/knowledge-center/article.page?kid=bf86c7a0 (last accessed 27 September 2022).

Gilbert, B.A., McDougall, P.P. and Audretsch, D.B. (2006) 'New venture growth: A review and extension', *Journal of Management*, 32(6): 926–950.

Hill, C.W.L., Hwang, P. and Kim, W.C. (1990) 'An eclectic theory of the choice of international entry mode', *Strategic Management Journal*, 11(2). 117–128.

Ibeh, K.I.N. (2000) 'Internationalization and the small firm', in S. Carter and D. Evans (eds.), *Enterprise and Small Business: Principles, Practice and Policy*. Harlow: Financial Times and Prentice Hall, pp. 434–452.

Jack, S.L. (2005) 'The role, use and activation of strong and weak network ties: A qualitative analysis', *Journal of Management Studies*, 42(6): 1233–1259. https://onlinelibrary.wiley.com/doi/abs/10.1111/j.1467-6486.2005.00540.x.

Johanson, J. and Vahlne, J.E. (1977) 'The internationalization process of the firm: A model of knowledge development and increasing foreign market commitments', *Journal of International Business Studies*, 8(1): 23–32. https://doi.org/10.1057/palgrave.jibs.8490676

Johanson, J. and Vahlne, J.E. (1990) 'The mechanism of internationalisation', *International Marketing Review*, 7(4): 11–24.

Johanson, J. and Vahlne, J.E. (2009) 'The uppsala internationalization process model revisited: From liability of foreignness to liability of outsidership', *Journal of International Business Studies*, 40(9): 1411–1431.

Johanson, J. and Wiedersheim-Paul, F. (1975) 'The internationalization of the firm: Four Swedish cases', *Journal of Management Studies*, 12(3): 305–323.

Kirzner, I.M. (1979) *Perception, Opportunity, and Profit: Studies in the Theory of Entrepreneurship*. Chicago, IL: University of Chicago Press.

Knight, G. (1999) 'International services marketing: Review of research, 1980–1998', *Journal of Services Marketing*, 13(4/5): 347–360. https://doi.org/10.1108/08876049910282619

Loane, S. and Bell, J. (2006) 'Rapid internationalization among entrepreneurial firms in Australia, Canada, Ireland and New Zealand', *International Marketing Review*, 23(5): 467–485.

Lundberg, H. and Rehnfors, A. (2018) 'Transnational entrepreneurship: Opportunity identification and venture creation', *Journal of International Entrepreneurship*, 16(2): 150–175.

Luostarinen, R. (1994) 'Internationalization of Finnish firms and their response to global challenges'. UNU World Institute for Development Economics Research, Forsa Printing House Ltd. pp. 1–48.

Madsen, T.K. and Servais, P. (1997) 'The internationalization of born globals: An evolutionary process?' *International Business Review*, 6(6): 561–583.

Mesco, M. (2015) 'European malaise hits Italy's food makers, who struggle to export', *The Wall Street Journal*. Available at www.wsj.com/articles/italys-ham-cheese-producers-look-abroad-to-survive-1420234468 (last accessed 27 September 2022).

Mosey, S. and Wright, M. (2007) 'From human capital to social capital: A longitudinal study of technology-based academic entrepreneurs', *Entrepreneurship Theory and Practice*, 31(6): 909–935.

Nahapiet, J. and Ghoshal, S. (1998) 'Social capital, intellectual capital, and the organizational advantage', *Academy of Management Review*, 23(2): 242–266.

O'Farrell, P.N. and Wood, P.A. (1994) 'International market selection by business service firms: Key conceptual and methodological issues', *International Business Review*, 3(3): 243–261.

Oviatt, B.M. and McDougall, P.P. (2005) 'Defining international entrepreneurship and modeling the speed of internationalization', *Entrepreneurship Theory and Practice*, 29(5): 537–553.

Ozgen, E. and Baron, R.A. (2007) 'Social sources of information in opportunity recognition: Effects of mentors, industry networks, and professional forums', *Journal of Business Venturing*, 22(2): 174–192.

Root, H.L. (1994) *The Fountain of Privilege: Political Foundations of Markets in Old Regime France and England*. Berkeley, CA: University of California Press.

Saxenian, A. (1985) 'Silicon Valley and route 128: Regional prototypes or historic exceptions', *Urban Affairs Annual Reviews*, 28(1): 81–105.

Scarborough, N.M. (2014) (Edited) *Essentials of Entrepreneurship and Small Business Management* (7th edn). Harlow: Pearson Education.

Shane, S. (2000) 'Prior knowledge and the discovery of entrepreneurial opportunities', *Organization Science*, 11(4): 448–469.

Solleiro, J.L., Paniagua, J. and Castanon, R. (2006) 'Managing of technology in Mexican firms: The case of Instituto Bioclon', IEEE Conference on Management of Innovation and Technology, 2(1): 1075–1079.

Starr, J. and MacMillan, I.C. (1990) 'Resource cooptation via social contracting: Resource acquisition strategies for new ventures', *Strategic Management Journal*, 11(1): 79–92.

Terjesen, S. and Elam, A. (2009) 'Transnational entrepreneurs venture internationalization strategies: A practice theory approach', *Entrepreneurship Theory and Practice*, 33(5): 1093–1120.

The Year in Trade (2019) *United States International Trade Commission*, https://www.usitc.gov/press_room/news_release/2020/er0831ll1640.htm

Uzzi, B. (1997) 'Social structure and competition in interfirm networks: The paradox of embeddedness', *Administrative Science Quarterly*, 42(1): 35–67.

Zahra, S.A., Korri, J.S. and Yu, J. (2005) 'Cognition and international entrepreneurship: Implications for research on international opportunity recognition and exploitation', *International Business Review*, 14(2): 129–146. https://doi.org/10.1016/j.ibusrev.2004.04.005

6
INTERNATIONALIZATION STRATEGIES OF SMALL FIRMS

CHINESE ENTREPRENEURS: REALIZING CROSS-BORDER DREAMS THROUGH AMAZON

Source: www.needpix.com/photo/907679

China has been exporting goods to the US for decades. Now Chinese entrepreneurs want to sell directly to Americans. American consumers are considered to be prized quarry for Chinese small businesses who perceive Americans as freer-spending than the half a billion online Chinese shoppers. Chinese sellers have flocked to Amazon in a bid to enter into the American market, and directly reach American shoppers. Amazon has sellers from more than 130 countries; however, a significant one-third of Amazon's roughly one million

(Continued)

active sellers are from China. About 250,000 Chinese entrepreneurs joined the site in 2017 alone.

Amazon holds regular conferences in China to promote its platform, and explain the logistics and support services it offers. Additionally, hundreds of training courses have cropped up all over the country to sell Amazon to Chinese entrepreneurs and enable them to realize their cross-border e-commerce dreams. Typically, individual trainers at these institutes are themselves entrepreneurs/small business owners who have prior experience of working with Amazon and international customers. Many of the students at these institutes have small factories producing such products as apparel, LED lamps and outdoor gear for foreign brands. They attend training in order to learn to directly target foreign customers and eliminate the middleman. Trainers help small Chinese sellers to figure out the right keywords and visual marketing techniques for their product listings. Some even recommend inspirational books and listen to podcasts to encourage them.

Despite the support, Chinese entrepreneurs face several hurdles in realizing their cross-border dreams. American shoppers and their favorite e-commerce site are not easy to figure out. Picking the right product is the first challenge. It is not uncommon for sellers to end up with unsold inventories after mis-timing the craze for some products in the American market. Americans are also demanding of product quality. They are not hesitant to complain or post bad reviews to express their dissatisfaction, which Chinese entrepreneurs have to learn to deal with. Learning consumers' shopping habits and culture is especially critical during festive times such as Christmas when the demand for several products is at an all-time high.

Rising production costs in recent years have added to the Chinese entrepreneurs' woes. Also challenging is the influx of several Chinese sellers. Due to competition, profit margins at some small manufacturers have seen a steep drop in recent years. Such intense competition has forced entrepreneurs to diversify their product portfolios and look for alternative products.

Shenzhen-based Agoal, for example, sold about $50,000 worth of products on Amazon in 2017, including a Wi-Fi-equipped smart plug. However, with several hundred Chinese sellers offering products similar to their plug, the firm explored other products, such as measuring tapes or other tools that might appeal to Americans. The firm also considered dog accessories after learning about American consumers' love for animals, and their fetish to dress up their pets.

Source: adapted from Te-Ping (2017)

Learning Outcomes

After studying this chapter, you should be ready to:

- **LO1**: Explain key aspects of small firms' internationalization strategy
- **LO2**: Compare and contrast alternative foreign market entry mode strategies
- **LO3**: Evaluate the role of internal (firm-specific) and external (environmental) factors in international entrepreneurs' choice of foreign market and entry mode strategy

Introduction

Compared to managers of large, established enterprises, entrepreneurs are typically resource-constrained, lacking the knowledge, resources and market power to viably operate overseas. Yet, as mentioned in the last chapter, an increasing number of small firms are pursuing international markets to sell their goods and services.

The implementation of internationalization strategy entails the selection of markets to enter, and entry modes through which to establish in those markets. Traditionally, internationalization among small firms has been synonymous with, and limited to, exporting or selling across national borders typically via domestic or overseas-based intermediaries (Ibeh et al., 2004). However, less than 4% of US small businesses export and, of those that do, 60% sell to only one country (Gerwin, 2014). While an astounding 98% of American exporters are classified as small or medium-sized, these firms' exports represent only about a third of total US exports by value.

Small firms are increasingly using advanced entry modes to penetrate foreign markets. Improvements in production, transportation and communication technologies have led to dramatic improvements in the resources and capabilities accessible to small firms (Bell et al., 2004). Entrepreneurs have become more sophisticated and ambitious in terms of their appreciation of the range of international market entry and development options at their disposal.

The emergence of **micromultinationals (mMNEs)** is testament to this trend. mMNEs are international small and medium enterprises (SMEs) that control and manage value-adding activities in more than one country, using such advanced market servicing modes as international licensing agreements, international franchising, international joint ventures or foreign subsidiaries (Ibeh et al., 2004). What is distinctive about mMNEs is their adoption of export-plus modes for controlling and managing value-adding activities across international markets. Evidence from Scottish small firms shows that size limitations have not prevented them from utilizing more advanced – investment and contractual – modes of servicing foreign markets.

mMNEs are expected to grow in number in the future. They have stronger growth potential relative to exporting firms, and may be vital for the longer term growth and development of national economies (Ibeh et al., 2004). They may also be of greater interest to entrepreneurs with global ambitions due to their stronger growth potential. Policy makers may learn from mMNEs to develop home grown global players, especially in the light of declining foreign direct investment (FDI) inflows.

In this chapter, we explain the core elements of small firms' internationalization strategy, and the factors influencing international entrepreneurs' choice of foreign market and entry mode strategies. First, we describe aspects of foreign market selection and entry mode strategies. Next, we use the framework of the resource-based view (Chapter 5) to evaluate the role of international entrepreneurs' resources, and the external environment that they encounter in home and foreign markets, in their choice of foreign market and entry mode strategies.

Foreign Market Selection

International entrepreneurs' **foreign market selection** has two aspects: the number of markets to enter, and the nature and location of those markets. The number, nature and location of foreign markets for internationalization affect entrepreneurs' ability to coordinate foreign operations (Goerzen and Beamish, 2003). International expansion strategies typically involve either substantial commitment of resources and entry into few markets (concentration) or limited commitment of resources to each market and entry into many markets (dispersion) (Mascarenhas, 1997).

A study of Scottish mMNEs shows that these mMNEs had established offices in at least 40 nations (including the USA, France, the UAE, Germany, Ireland and Hong Kong); manufactured in 27 foreign countries (including the USA, France, Italy, Germany and Holland); formed joint ventures in 33 country markets (including the USA and China); established international licensing agreements in 28 countries; and entered into franchising agreements in at least nine others (including Australia, Holland, Hong Kong, Ireland, Norway, South Africa and Spain) (Ibeh et al., 2004) (Figure 6.1).

Percentage of Overseas Offices

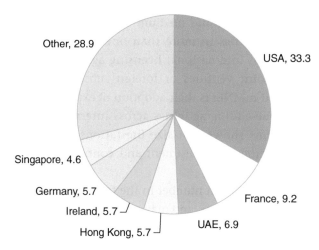

Figure 6.1 Location of overseas offices of Scottish mMNEs

Source: Ibeh et al. (2004)

This finding is particularly interesting in view of the small size of the surveyed mMNEs. It is also revealing that these mMNEs entered the USA, rather than neighboring markets in Europe, as their most common location (Figures 6.2 and 6.3).

Percentage of Foreign Subsidiaries

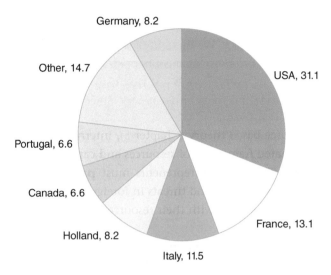

Figure 6.2 Location of foreign subsidiaries of Scottish mMNEs

Source: Ibeh et al. (2004)

Percentage of International Licensing Agreements

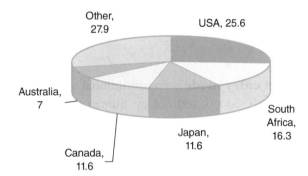

Figure 6.3 Location of international licensing agreements of Scottish mMNEs

Source: Ibeh et al. (2004)

International entrepreneurs' approach to internationalization may be reactive or proactive. Most small firms follow a **reactive** approach to internationalization. They may enter a foreign market because foreign customers initiate the contact. In other cases, they may be pulled into a foreign market due to a new employee.

As Manish Chandra, a Silicon-Valley-based entrepreneur, explained, he did not strategically consider offshoring to another market until the 'iPhone talent' that he found led them to India where their new recruit was based:

It was quite random. We were struggling to find iPhone talent. Somebody told us, this guy is available, we talked to him and he seemed ok. We'd never met him. He was based out of India, my team was skeptical, but I said let's compute the total gamble we are taking. We thought of flying him out. So I said let's take the 10k gamble. What's the worst that can happen? … So we flew him out… Within those four weeks, everyone was just won over. We had an arrangement with him. (Manish Chandra, Founder, Poshmark, Silicon Valley, California)

According to the resource-based theory (Chapter 5), internationalization decisions are taken within a coordinated framework of resources and capabilities, and external environmental conditions. Therefore, entrepreneurs must **proactively** evaluate foreign markets to assess the opportunities and threats in foreign markets, and analyze foreign markets that represent the best fit with their resources, products and services, prior to entering those markets.

A proactive approach to internationalization entails incorporating internationalization into the competitive strategy of a small firm. Adopting a proactive approach makes companies more robust and potentially more successful, with a greater client base and improved scope for growth. Proactive reasons for internationalization include gaining knowledge of other clients and markets, exploiting scale and scope economies, taking advantage of foreign market growth, and moving value-chain activities to more competitive regions.

Foreign Market Entry Mode Strategy

An international market **entry mode** is an institutional arrangement that makes possible the entry of a firm's products, technology, human skills, management and other resources into a foreign country. The easiest way for entrepreneurs to enter foreign markets is by creating a website, followed by exporting. Exporting, contracting (e.g. licensing) and FDI represent the three generic methods of penetrating foreign markets. FDI (e.g. joint ventures, mergers and acquisitions, franchising) entails obtaining a percentage of ownership in the foreign venture related to the amount of investment, nature of industry and rules of host government.

While exporting is the most commonly used entry mode strategy in small firms, there is a rising trend towards small firms' adoption of low-level licensing, strategic alliances and joint ventures, and even franchising. These entry modes are explained below.

Creating a Website

The internet gives even the smallest businesses the ability to sell their goods and services across the world. According to Statista, the worldwide e-commerce share of retail sales has been steadily growing over the years (Clement, 2019). In 2019, e-retail sales accounted for 14.1% of all retail sales worldwide. This figure is expected to reach 22% in 2023.

Creating a **website** is one of the fastest and least expensive modes of rapidly penetrating foreign markets. According to the stages model (Chapter 5), small businesses take incremental steps towards internationalization. They first begin selling locally, and then expand regionally (or nationally) after establishing a reputation. The internet makes that business model obsolete as it provides small firms with a low cost distribution channel that they can use to penetrate foreign markets from the day of inception. Entrepreneurs can extend their reach to anyone, anywhere in the world with a well-designed website. A company's website provides exposure 24 hours a day, seven days a week. The benefit of the internet is that it can be used via a computer, mobile phone, personal digital assistant, games machine, digital TV etc.

Internet users are individuals who have used the internet (from any location) in the last three months. Globally, the number of internet users worldwide increased from only 413 million in 2000 to over 3.4 billion in 2016 (Roser et al., 2020). Approximately more than two thirds of the world population is typically online in developed countries. More and more people are online every year. On any day in the last five years, for example, there were on average 640,000 people online for the first time.

Overall, there are more than 2 billion potential internet customers outside the US. Even for large companies like eBay and Facebook, more than 60% of their total sales are outside of the US. This suggests the potential for entrepreneurial small firms to exploit the power of the internet to tap into an international customer base outside of their home country. When designing their websites, entrepreneurs must 'think local'. They must have a separate domain name for each country. Website design must reflect local culture, customs and language.

Exporting

A large number of small firms are increasingly venturing beyond domestic borders to realize the growth and profit potential of **exporting**. Exporting involves sales and shipping of products manufactured in one country to a customer located in another country. SMEs in the United States are active in international markets via exports. US SMEs with fewer than 20 employees generate 33% of the nation's export sales (Scarborough, 2014).

According to USBA Office of Advocacy (2018), in 2015, 294,834 small businesses in the US comprised 97.6% of exporting firms and generated $1.3 trillion in total exports or 32.9% of the United States' known export value. Canada, the UK, Mexico, China and Japan are the countries that account for the greatest volume of US export businesses (Scarborough, 2014).

According to the US Department of Commerce, the UK is among the top destinations for US SME exports, also serving as a key entry point for US SME exports to the EU (The Year in Trade, 2019). During 2012–16, US SME merchandise exports to the UK grew by an average of 15.9%, compared to a decline of 6.4% for larger firms during the same period.

Exporting can be **indirect** (via trade intermediaries) or **direct** (through agents/ distributors or sales subsidiaries/branches). Indirect exporting involves having a foreign purchaser in a local market or using an export management company. Trade intermediaries are domestic agencies that serve as distributors in foreign countries for domestic companies of all sizes. They include foreign distributors, export management companies (EMCs), as well as resident buying offices that facilitate the purchase of goods in the domestic market on behalf of their foreign governments. Trade intermediaries are becoming increasingly popular among small businesses attempting to branch out into world markets through indirect exports. Small firms can use trade intermediaries to enter foreign markets at relatively low cost. Trade intermediaries also make the transition much faster and easier.

Direct exporting involves the use of foreign distributors or overseas sales offices to sell in foreign markets. A significant number of SMEs in the APEC countries (Canada, Korea, Malaysia, Peru, Philippines, China, Thailand and Japan) participate in **direct exporting** activities (APEC, 2015). However, there are some variations within the region. In 2011, 10.4% of SMEs in Canada were direct exporters of goods and services, accounting for 40% of total exports. In 2013, Korea reported 87,800 SMEs exporting goods and services directly with a value of $95.9 billion. In contrast, only 3.0% of manufacturing SMEs were involved in direct exporting in Japan in 2014.

Licensing

Licensing is the granting of permission by one company to another company to use a specific form of its intellectual property (IP) under clearly defined conditions (Barringer and Ireland, 2015). The company that owns the IP is called the **licensor**, whereas the one that purchases the rights to use it is called the **licensee**. The licensor earns fees in the form of royalty payments in return for permitting the licensee to use their IP. The terms of a license are spelled out through a **licensing agreement**.

Small firms can enter foreign markets by licensing their products or services directly to customers overseas. A study of Scottish mMNEs shows that 21.1% used international licensing to penetrate foreign markets (Ibeh et al., 2004).

Technology licensing is the licensing of proprietary technology that the licensor typically controls through a utility patent. **Merchandise or character licensing** is the licensing of a recognized trademark or brand that the licensor typically controls through a registered trademark or copyright. Entrepreneurial firms like eBay, Starbucks and Yahoo, for example, license their trademarks. In doing so, they earn licensing income as well as promote their products and services to a host of other customers.

Strategic Alliances and Joint Ventures

Formal partnerships take the form of strategic alliances and joint ventures. A **strategic alliance** is a partnership between two or more firms that is developed to achieve a specific goal. A sizeable proportion of Scottish mMNEs employ such contractual modes (Ibeh et al., 2004), with 24.4% of a study sample choosing joint ventures / strategic alliances to enter foreign markets.

Strategic alliances are of two types: technological alliances and marketing alliances. **Technological alliances** feature cooperation in R&D where partners typically produce a product and bring it to market faster and cheaper than either firm could alone. **Marketing alliances** match a company that has a product to sell with a company that has a distribution system in order to increase sales of a product or service.

d.light, a for-profit social enterprise, founded to solve the problem of lack of access to electricity for base-of-the pyramid consumers, entered into a partnership with Total, a French oil and gas company in 2013 (Barringer and Ireland, 2015). d.light sells its solar-powered lamps as part of the company's Access to Energy Program throughout Africa. The partnership and its initiatives throughout the world have enabled d.light to make more than 500,000 solar lanterns per month, up from the initial 20,000 to 30,000 units per month at inception.

A **joint venture** is an entity created when two or more firms pool a portion of their resources to create a jointly owned organization. Unlike strategic alliances that do not involve any exchange of ownership, joint ventures entail the creation of a third, independent entity that is jointly owned by the two partners. Joint ventures can be domestic or foreign.

In a **domestic joint venture**, two or more domestic businesses form a partnership for the purpose of exporting their goods and services. For export ventures, participating companies get anti-trust immunity, allowing them to freely cooperate. The businesses share the responsibility and cost of getting export licenses and permits, and they split the venture's profits. In a **foreign joint venture**, a domestic small business forms an alliance with a company in the target country. The host partner brings to the joint venture valuable knowledge of the local market and its method of operation as well as of the customs and tastes of local customers, making it much easier to conduct business in the foreign country.

Strategic alliances and joint ventures are fraught with some risks. Even though partnerships can be tremendously valuable, setting up and implementing partnership agreements, especially across geographic borders, can be challenging. Selecting the right partner is important to avoiding the risk of opportunistic behavior on the part of the partner and ensuring that their values, goals and standards of conduct are aligned with those of the entrepreneur.

Yet, often the most important ingredient in joint ventures, selecting the right partner is also the most challenging. It can be difficult to identify appropriate partners, structure the terms of the contract and spell out terms and conditions in writing, as well as manage the relationship with a foreign partner. Furthermore, alliances and joint ventures limit the ability to integrate and coordinate activities across national boundaries.

Franchising

Franchising is a form of business organization in which a firm that already has a successful product or service licenses its trademark and method of doing business to other businesses for an initial franchise fee and an ongoing royalty. Popular businesses that have successfully grown using franchising include McDonalds, Kentucky Fried Chicken (KFC), Starbucks and Domino's Pizza.

The **franchisor** is the firm that originates the idea for the business and develops the operational methods. The **franchisee** contributes start-up capital and pays a fee to obtain a franchise from the franchisor. Domino's Pizza, for example, has more than 1100 franchisees worldwide, each franchisee having an average of three stores.

Franchising is of two types. In a **product and trademark franchise**, the franchisor grants the franchisee the right to buy its products and use its trade name (e.g. Toyota Dealerships). In **business format franchises**, the franchisor provides the formula for doing business to the franchisee with training, advertising etc. (e.g. Domino's, Subway).

Unlike licensing, franchising involves sharing knowledge and expertise about the method of doing business with the franchisee. Also, unlike licensing that does not involve any ownership on the part of the licensee, franchising is an equity-based arrangement where the franchisee contributes a small proportion of equity as a condition for obtaining the franchise from the franchisor.

Franchising has become a major export industry for the United States in recent years (Scarborough, 2014). A growing number of franchises have been attracted to international markets to boost sales and profits as domestic markets become increasingly saturated. Domino's Pizza, for example, operates in more than 60 countries and has more than $3 billion in sales worldwide. More than 90% of the company's 9,400 stores outside the US (which exceeds its 5,000 stores in the US) are franchised.

The advantages of a franchise include a proven product or service within an established market, an established trademark or business system, franchisor's training and ongoing support, and technical and managerial expertise. The availability of financing and potential for business growth are other key advantages. At the same time, however, the cost of the franchise, risk of fraud, misunderstandings or lack of franchisor commitment and problems of termination or transfer are among the disadvantages. Poor performance on the part of the franchisees and potential for failure are among the other disadvantages.

Mergers and Acquisitions

Many entrepreneurial ventures enter foreign markets through mergers and acquisitions. A **merger** is the pooling of interests to combine two or more firms into one, whereas an **acquisition** is the outright purchase of one firm by another. In an acquisition, the surviving firm is called the **acquirer**, whereas the firm that is acquired is called the **target**.

Entrepreneurial ventures seek both mergers and acquisitions, but they are more commonly involved with acquisitions than mergers. Often, entrepreneurs use these strategies as they aim to sell to large companies to accelerate their growth. Those funded by investors also sell to create a liquidity event to allow investors to monetize their investment. Among the advantages of acquisitions are reduction of competition, access to proprietary products or services (including an established brand name) and economies of scale.

In some cases, entrepreneurs seek to sell to a large firm due to their inherent dependence on large firms for the execution of their business model. VS Joshi, founder of TrintMe, sought to sell his online dating app to a large social media firm in the same industry after the withdrawal of APIs (Application Programming Interfaces) by Facebook. APIs are a system of tools and resources in an operating ssytem, enabling developers to create software applications. The withdrawal of Facebook's APIs meant that the company's customer base information was no longer available to third parties like Joshi due to privacy issues, which threatened the very basis of TrintMe's existence (Pruthi, 2016). Joshi's location in Silicon Valley, in close geographic proximity to Facebook's headquarters, made it easier for him to approach the company and explore the possibility of acquisition. Facebook was a natural fit because TrintMe's app was built to Facebook's specification and its customer base was already connected to Facebook. Joshi expected that the geographic proximity with Facebook would enable him to more efficiently work with Facebook post acquisition.

Establishing an International Location

Small firms may establish an office or factory to enter foreign markets. Despite their limited size (60.6 mean employees), Scottish mMNEs, for instance, use a variety of advanced, value-creating and control generating market entry modes (Ibeh et al., 2004). Whereas FDI is the most advanced entry mode used by these mMNEs, the establishment of overseas marketing and sales offices is most common (42.6%), followed by setting up foreign subsidiaries (29.9%) and overseas manufacturing (22.5%), respectively (Figure 6.4).

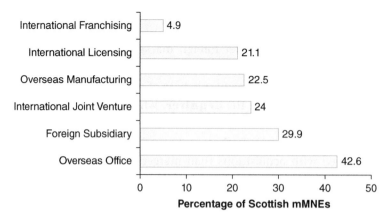

Figure 6.4 Utilization of advanced market servicing modes by Scottish mMNEs

Source: Ibeh et al. (2004)

SMEs in the APEC member countries have also been engaged in foreign direct investment abroad: 0.8% of Canadian SMEs invested abroad in 2015 (APEC, 2015). In the same year, 14,874 Canadian SMEs, equivalent to 3.2% of the total SMEs, outsourced tasks to foreign sub-contractors. Korean SMEs made 4,265 overseas investments and invested in 1,351 new overseas enterprises in 2013. SMEs' total investment abroad was equivalent to $2.4 billion. 13.4% of all SMEs in Japan owned an overseas subsidiary or an affiliated company (investment abroad) at the end of 2011.

Often, entrepreneurs hire local talent to manage an international location. Additionally, they invest in building formal and informal systems to manage their foreign operations. Ravi Kulasekaran, a California-based entrepreneur who established an office in India for his IT venture, Stridus, recruited senior personnel in the US who he formally assigned the responsibility of managing various functional teams in both the US and India. These managers frequently interacted with their India counterparts via phone. They also conducted informal, hands-off conference calls between the US and India every morning.

The local personnel often flew out to India to liaise with their respective teams in the US. Additionally, Ravi devised a web-based collaborative system where people posted pictures and talked about themselves on the company's intranet. He spent about two months in India each year. In the early stages of setting up the India operations, he stayed there until his team understood his thought process and working style, especially in relation to hiring new people and his expectations of the talent pool necessary for the job.

Factors Influencing Choice of Internationalization Strategy

We use the theoretical lens of the resource-based theory to assess the factors influencing small firms' choice of internationalization strategy. Accordingly, we consider the influence of both internal (firm-specific) factors and external (environmental) factors international entrepreneurs need to evaluate in their foreign market and entry mode selection. Whereas internal factors include financial and human resources, external factors refer to the competitive and institutional environments in home or foreign markets.

Financial Resources

Although evidence is mixed, large firms are more likely to internationalize than small firms. Small financial size limits the number of markets served (Calof, 1993). Firms with limited financial resources are ill-equipped to conduct systematic analyses (Papadopoulos and Denis, 1988). Lack of financial resources also constrains small firms' ability to prepare personnel for international operations and provide cross-cultural negotiations training. Larger firms, in contrast, are in a stronger position to contemplate entry into culturally distant markets (Erramilli, 1991).

Often, entrepreneurs enter emerging economies to avail of low product development costs, which makes these locations attractive for business. Pat Krishnan, a Silicon-Valley-based entrepreneur, chose to enter Lithuania as there was a huge cost advantage to building a team there in comparison with hiring a consultant in Silicon Valley:

> The reason is cost advantage. The cost arbitrage. I will have a Lithuania team, again a cost advantage for me. A $15 in Lithuania is huge money, compared to $40 I pay here for the consultant. (Pat Krishnan, Founder, California)

Small firms lacking large resource commitments are more likely to enter into collaborative relationships (Stopford and Wells, 1972). International or foreign licensing, for example, enables small businesses to enter foreign markets quickly, easily, and with virtually no capital investment. Entrepreneurs can collect royalties in return for the sale of their foreign licenses. Although internationalizing SMEs engage in FDI, establishing an office or factory overseas requires substantial investment, which can stretch tight budgets (Erramilli, 1991; Erramilli and Rao, 1993).

Even collaborative entry modes, however, may be difficult to implement without necessary financial resources. Entrepreneurs opting for international licensing, for example, often press for a relatively large initial payment as a way of generating immediate cash to fund operations. Yet, striking a licensing agreement with a large firm can involve tough negotiations.

Human Resources

As discussed in Chapter 5, human resources are tangible resources such as number of employees, and intangible resources such as the owner-founders' tacit knowledge, experience and social networks residing inside the firm. **Firm size** in terms of the number of employees impacts the choice of entry mode strategy. A critical mass of 20 employees is needed to cross the exports threshold (Ibeh, 2012); however, exporting appears not to be correlated with size beyond this point.

Entrepreneurs also exploit their intangible resources in internationalization; alternatively, they seek to fill gaps in the availability of these resources in planning foreign market entry. Entrepreneurs' desire for control and desire to reduce risks are the other aspects of their human resources that influence their choice of internationalization strategy.

Exploitation of Resources

Small knowledge-intensive firms are expected to exhibit higher levels of international activity and enter a larger number of foreign markets than their low-technology counterparts. Yet, evidence about the role of technology intensity in small firm internationalization is mixed. Small firms in traditional sectors can also have a diverse country scope of activities.

Human resource considerations impact entrepreneurs' foreign entry mode choice. International licensing is ideal for entrepreneurial firms whose value lies in their intellectual property. Entrepreneurs may license their patents, trademarks, copyrights, technology, products or processes. Some entrepreneurs earn more money from licensing their know-how from product design, manufacturing or quality control than they do from actually selling their finished goods in a highly competitive foreign market with which they are not familiar. Collaborative entry modes are a particularly feasible method of obtaining incremental income on technology, business systems or other intangible assets by small firms that might otherwise lack the resources to enter foreign markets through more direct methods.

At the same time, entrepreneurs run the risk of losing their proprietary knowledge to their licensees. In contrast, equity-based modes protect the leakage of **knowledge** (Grant, 1996). Entrepreneurial firms are more commonly involved in acquisitions because large firms that acquire them gain by accessing talented employees or new technology to enhance their current offerings.

In some cases, entrepreneurs choose an entry mode strategy to leverage their **prior experience**. Vikas, a Silicon-Valley-based entrepreneur, explained that he did not have any direct investment or physical presence in India, one of the recent foreign markets he had entered. He understood his size constraints as a small firm. He also felt that there were other markets from a business standpoint that he needed to 'hit' before he made any direct investment in India. Even though he well understood India relative to other foreign markets he had thus far entered, he aimed to succeed in India through a channel (resellers) rather than direct investment, given its success as an entry strategy in two other emerging markets, China and Latin America, he had previously penetrated:

> We don't have any direct investment or physical presence in India. The reason
> is we are very small and there are other markets from a business standpoint
> that I need to hit before I invest in India. But there certainly is a presence, it is
> an emerging market like China, Latin America, we have resellers. I try not to

let my emotions play in India, I know India so it's natural for me to penetrate that. We were successful in Latin America through a channel, so my thought process was I should be able to do it in India. (Vikas, Founder, Silicon Valley, California, USA)

Access to Resources

The need to fill resource gaps is a key factor influencing small firms' internationalization strategies. Most small business owners do not have the knowledge, experience or confidence to enter foreign markets all by themselves. Often, entrepreneurs are also unable to undertake all tasks themselves because the majority of tasks needed to build or grow a product or deliver a service are outside their core competencies or areas of expertise.

Furthermore, entrepreneurial firms lack **legitimacy**. They suffer from the liabilities of newness and small size (Venkataraman et al., 1990). This means that they often falter because the people involved cannot adjust fast enough to their new roles and because the firms lack a track record of success.

Often, entrepreneurs consciously select entry modes that allow them **access to strategic resources**. Trade intermediaries can serve as export departments for small businesses lacking foreign market knowledge. Entrepreneurs who are focused on creating novel products but do not have the expertise to build manufacturing capabilities or distribution networks may find it beneficial to use licensing as part of their international growth strategy. Entrepreneurs may also forge partnerships / joint ventures to access vital resources that they rarely themselves possess (Marion et al., 2015). By participating in partnerships, entrepreneurs gain access to resources and benefit from learning from partners. Formerly Ask.Jeeves, Ask.com, for example, has benefitted from access to local markets, knowledge of local customers, media exposure and increased sales through joint venture arrangements.

Despite the benefit of shared control entry modes, in some cases, entrepreneurs need full control modes such as acquisitions or foreign offices of their own to gain access to requisite resources. Entering foreign markets through acquisitions is important to acquiring teams that have the expertise to sell in new markets, as well as seek out new markets to build products at low cost, and hence enable small firms to transform themselves into global ventures in a relatively short period of time.

According to Vas Bhandarkar, a California-based founder, this philosophy was important to growing Global Logic beyond the US and India, the two countries where the company was initially meant to operate. Acquisitions in several other countries including Ukraine, Argentina and Israel helped the top management team to grow the small, 200-person company to a 6,000-person company in a relatively short span of five years.

In other cases, locating in a foreign country may be important to gaining a first-hand understanding of local customers' tastes and preferences. Finding the right team to manage foreign offices is extremely critical to succeeding in foreign markets; however, it can be a challenge for small firms that are usually thinly staffed and cannot afford to send key people abroad, much less employ them in their home market.

Social Networks/ Ethnic Ties

As discussed earlier, social networks play a critical role in internationalization. There is growing evidence that decision makers whose contact networks are internationally spread are more likely to exploit international market opportunities than those lacking such ties (OECD, 2009).

Entrepreneurs' Motivations

Entrepreneurs' **desire for control** can influence their choice of foreign entry mode strategy. The primary disadvantage of using trade intermediaries (vs. direct exporting), for example, is that they require entrepreneurs to surrender control over their foreign sales, which they may be unwilling to accept. Entrepreneurs can avoid these problems by carefully screening intermediaries, maintaining close contact with them, and regularly evaluating their performance.

The potential loss of control over manufacturing and marketing processes is also a possible downside of shared-control entry modes like licensing and partnering. Licensing, for example, runs the risk of creating a competitor if the licensee gains too much knowledge and control. The disadvantages of strategic alliances and joint ventures similarly include loss of proprietary information, management complexities and partial loss of decision autonomy.

In some cases, even full-control modes like acquisitions may require entrepreneurs to compromise control over their product or service offering. This is because potential large firm buyers require possible changes to product/service features that entrepreneurs are often reluctant, or even unable, to make.

Entrepreneurs also seek to minimize their **risk exposure** given their financial and human resource constraints. Thus, they may opt for international licensing, a relatively simple way for even the most inexperienced business owners to extend their reach into global markets with little economic and financial exposure. Licensing spreads the risk and cost of developing new technologies.

In some cases, penetrating foreign markets through acquisitions of former or potential competitors can be a risk-reducing strategy, especially if the acquired company in the foreign market has some connection with the entrepreneur's home country. California-based serial entrepreneur, Raju Reddy, explained the rationale for acquiring a company in China. Raju and his team acquired four companies – two local (in the USA), one in the UK and one in China – prior to being bought by Hitachi.

The first acquisition in Boston was a domestic acquisition that gave them 'a little more of a presence' in the North-Eastern part of their home country, USA, that they did not have. Instead of going and starting on their own in China, Raju and his team subsequently went to China to identify prospective acquisition candidates. He and his CFO considered several companies that they could potentially acquire. Eventually, they settled for a Boston headquartered company, Arai, with operations in China. This was a small company that had been one of their competitors in the US in the early stages. As the company had a physical presence in China, most of their employees were also based in China. Raju felt comfortable with this company as the Arai team in China was already working with a Western management team. He felt their risk was thus reduced. This was their third acquisition and it turned out to be a winning proposition for them.

Competitive Factors

The nature of competition in the foreign market has a direct impact on whether firms choose arms-length contracting or internal organization to undertake business transactions. The greater the volatility of demand in the foreign market, the greater the need for flexibility and the lower the desire to make huge resource commitments (Root, 1994). Firms with many non-dominant competitors in the foreign market are usually favorable to export entry.

Oligopolistic markets with a few dominant competitors or monopolistic markets with a single firm, on the other hand, are more suited to entry through equity investment in production to enable firms to compete against the power of dominant firms. In markets where competition is judged too strong for both export and equity modes, firms turn to licensing or other contractual modes.

Political Factors

Government Support and Intervention

International entrepreneurs are attracted to foreign markets where governments are supportive of foreign investment for generating jobs and boosting the focal industry. As evidence from the APEC region suggests, political risk and corruption, as well as lack of transparency of the rule of law, are the most significant challenges faced by SMEs in external markets (APEC, 2015). Establishing foreign offices can be difficult because of the need to conform with local institutional, legal and regulatory requirements. Setting up an international office can be especially challenging in countries where business infrastructure is inadequate, and securing necessary licenses and permits is often arduous due to the problem of corruption.

Nat Puri, founder of Purico, is a case in point. Purico started as a one-man venture when it was founded. It is now a diversified, paper and plastics multinational enterprise headquartered in Nottingham (UK). Nat closely worked with, and garnered the support of, the local governments in the countries he entered as he grew the business. The Chinese government was one of their major shareholders in China. When Nat first entered China, the condition of the roads around the area where they were setting up their factory was not ideal. The Chinese government rectified the situation, swiftly acting to develop local infrastructure around the factory in a span of just two weeks.

Local mayors of Mexico and Hungary, the other two countries where Purico has a presence, similarly ensured Purico's access to adequate local facilities at the time of setting up and investing in these locations. The Hungarian government 'always checked up' regarding public connections and water supply. In all cases, the local governments in the foreign markets went out of their way to ensure that local operations were properly set up:

> when we wanted to invest in Mexico, in Hungary, in China, the local mayors of the cities, they were enablers… the bureaucrats will go [went] out of their way to make sure that anything that was needed, within the rules of the city, were a) shared and b) helped to achieve. And it was done in a very small time. So our business in Hungary was set up and running in under 16 months. (Nat Puri, Founder, Purico, UK)

Government concessions in the form of income tax exemptions, tariff protections and government-sponsored low-interest loans act as catalysts, creating a decision to look abroad. The compatibility of standards and protection of intellectual property rights are some of the other legal and regulatory factors conducive to the entry of entrepreneurs into foreign markets.

One of the key factors underlying Vijay Parmar's decision to locate his IoT (Internet of Things) start-up, Gainspan, predominantly in Japan, was support from GETRO in the US, further to recommendation from one of his business colleagues. A Japanese government organization under MITI, GETRO has offices in different parts of the world, including the US. The mission of GETRO is to assist entrepreneurs outside of Japan to set up businesses in Japan.

In contrast, legal and regulatory barriers can significantly deter market entry. High compliance costs for the EU's complex rules, for example, are often a prohibitive barrier for small US firms trying to penetrate the EU. Small businesses entering the EU also report serious problems in the EU with trade secrets, patent costs, customs, transparency and industry-specific requirements.

Government regulations also impact the choice between shared and equity-based entry modes. Restrictive foreign investment policies like exchange controls prevent equity entry modes in the manufacturing sector, forcing firms into joint ventures and licensing agreements (Erramilli, 1992). In some cases, shared control arrangements are a government condition for entry into foreign markets. In other cases, foreign governments in host markets place certain limitations on joint ventures, requiring host companies to hold a majority stake in the venture.

Differences in legal and regulatory standards across countries pose a particular challenge to the implementation and subsequent success of direct entry modes such as acquisitions and foreign offices. Raju Reddy, a California-based entrepreneur, explained that their second acquisition in the UK was intended as a 'definite' market entry strategy;

however, this did not work out well due to the difficulty of laying-off people that Raju and his team did not wish to retain post-acquisition. Raju's lack of prior experience of such a situation interfered with his ability to efficiently deal with the challenges faced.

Economic Factors

Level of Economic Development

Emerging economies offer new opportunities to entrepreneurs for selling their products and services. Chris Folayan founded the Mall for Africa in 2012 to enable Africans to purchase items directly from US and UK websites that they were unable to use themselves, using patented technology systems (www.mallforafrica.co.za). Named as the Best Innovation in Fashion Retail in 2017, the company is the first global economy e-commerce infrastructure company of its kind. Recently, the company has launched Mall for the World to globally expand its brand, starting with the Gulf Cooperation Council (GCC) region, comprising Bahrain, Kuwait, Oman, Qatar, Saudi Arabia and UAE.

At the same time, however, the high cost of obtaining information in emerging economies can be a barrier to investment, particularly in less developed countries. The need for special effort to collect information deters choice of such markets. Relatively low labor costs in foreign markets motivate entrepreneurial firms to opt for full-control entry modes in those markets (Dunning, 1993). However, the lack of appropriate market-specific knowledge can exacerbate the risks (Blankenburg and Johanson, 1992).

Socio-Cultural Factors

Cultural differences across countries present opportunities for entrepreneurs. In some cases, entrepreneurs capitalize on cross-country cultural differences to identify business opportunities (Loeb, 2017).

Carl Miller founded the Global Retail Insights Network (GRIN) to help retailers (looking to operate across borders) navigate cross-border cultural challenges. Carl guides companies to test the water – sometimes through social networks, sometimes through internet spots, to understand the local customers and local customs. His experience and contacts are invaluable since he often finds that our tendency to apply our own local idiom is misunderstood and ultimately undermines chances for success. Members of GRIN include eBay, Revolve Clothing and MVMT.

As mentioned earlier, cultural or psychic distance can impact market attractiveness. Differences in work culture across countries, for example, may pose a constraint to the implementation of entrepreneurs' foreign market entry mode strategy in some markets, thus reducing their attractiveness as potential destinations for business.

According to Rajan Raghavan, a US-based serial entrepreneur, although he himself was from India, he found it hard to relate to people and their work style when he first set foot there in the 1990s. People in India were routinely used to being physically present at work and reporting to a line manager higher up in the hierarchy. They were accustomed to strictly following orders from the top. They also expected each and every part of the work to be specified, and did not 'push back' when they were set work assignments. As a consequence, tasks were often not completed within deadlines:

> In hi-tech businesses, you don't ask people what time are you coming, what you produce is more important whether you are physically present or not. In India, I have to tell my boss what time I'm coming, I have to follow certain hierarchical things... Even though I was from India, I found it hard to relate culturally to people in India. For example, I would say let's get this done. People in India would take it as an order... people would expect me to specify every task. (Rajan Raghavan, Serial Entrepreneur, California)

This approach was in stark contrast to that in Silicon Valley. The high-tech sector afforded great flexibility in how work was conducted on a day-to-day basis, and that was especially true of the Valley where the end result was what mattered most. Instead of blindly following orders, employees in the Valley were used to questioning work assignments in order to realistically assess the likelihood of completing them on a timely basis:

> nobody will say 'it cannot be done' or 'this is wrong'. They would just say yes sir. So culturally nobody would push back because people are used to taking orders with the hierarchy in fashion. If the boss told you therefore it has to be done... Initially I did not know that. So when, come 4–5 months I'd asked them how come it's not done. The guy said to us it wasn't possible, how come you didn't tell me, he'd say I don't have the time, but you asked me to do it. This is just an illustration of how things work... Nobody used to think beyond that. (Rajan Raghavan, Serial Entrepreneur, California)

In other cases, entrepreneurs' prior familiarity with a psychically distant country can lower perceived barriers to entry. Vijay Parmar, founder of Gainspan, an IoT venture, had long been going to Japan for business before entering there for Gainspan. He believed Japan was a 'good' place to start up for cultural reasons. Even though it was necessary to find a local partner to build some credibility as a new, foreign entrant, Japanese companies, in his view, were more open than US companies to working with start-ups. They were less demanding than US clients. The Japanese took a long-term view of business relationships and showed extreme loyalty as customers once convinced to sign up:

For start-ups, I find Japan a good place to start. Because if you can convince a Japanese company to be your customer, they'll stick with you for a long time. Interestingly, I find that compared to US, Japanese companies tend to be more open to working with a start-up. The key thing is you must find a local partner, channel partner who can give you some credibility. US companies I know, they would ask me to put my designs in escrow before they would use it. In Japan, they would typically not ask for that. So that's how I started in Japan. (Vijay Parmar, Founder, Gainspan, California)

Locating in a foreign market helps entrepreneurs to deal with local cultural influences on business practices. At the same time, however, cultural attitudes to small firms in some foreign markets and the general aversion to taking up employment at companies without an established brand name can compound the challenges of penetrating those markets. In some countries, there is more prestige attached to working for large, rather than small, firms. In view of such attitudes, the small size of entrepreneurial ventures can present a challenge to recruiting, as well as retaining, employees for entrepreneurs entering those countries.

Vijay Maheshwari, Silicon-Valley-based founder of Verismo Networks, wanted to recruit local people in India to set up his office in the early stages when he first entered there. After a long search, he successfully identified skilled people who were technically well-qualified for the job. However, he discovered that they were reluctant to accept the position. As the venture was in the early stages, there was no formal office and employees were expected to work from home. Unlike large companies like IBM or Infosys, the lack of an established brand name to signal reputation was viewed in an unfavorable light by both potential recruits and their families:

I basically talk to lots of people. Looked at some advertisements... I found two–three good people technically but they were not ready to take the risk of leaving the job and... to work from home. Establish office from scratch. ... people in India are like now you know they have pressure because parents are asking whom they are working with and they say no brand company, then they say you know what is this? If they are working for IBM or Infosys it becomes easier right? So that is the challenge... (Vijay Maheshwari, Founder, Verismo Networks)

In the extreme, Ujjal Kohli, Founder, Rhythm Media, California, was forced to close down his India office two years after first entering there for business. The failure of US management techniques in India due to cultural reasons was one of the key factors for his withdrawal from the country.

RHYTHM MEDIA: CULTURAL CHALLENGES OF OPERATING IN INDIA

Ujjal Kohli, founder, Rhythm Media, California, USA, was forced to close down his India office two years after first entering there for business. He cited the failure of US management techniques in India due to cultural reasons as one of the key factors for his withdrawal from the country:

1. Six months after setting up the office and hiring the first batch of employees, the India manager decided to take the entire group (and their spouses) for an outdoor (white water rafting) event for team building. However, the exercise did not have the desired outcome. In Ujjal's view, such exercises were more of a 'US kind of thing'. It was too early to spend so much money when people had hardly spent time working for the company. He felt local employees exploited the India manager who was perceived as an 'easy take'. An 'ultra-posh' local office equipped with a 2000-dollar remote controlled slide projector and free daily meals for employees led to a snowballing of expenses beyond control.

2. It was common for people to accept the job offer but not show up for work. Typically, people accepted three or four jobs and then finally showed up for the one they ultimately decided to take up. It was important for the local India manager to be savvy enough and know how to 'cut through it'. Ujjal felt that his manager was not equipped to handle that and Ujjal did not have any network in India to navigate these challenges.

3. Small scale was also a big disadvantage in India, especially when it came to hiring young engineers. He felt young talent in India liked to work for big names like Microsoft and Cisco. In a country where arranged marriages are widely prevalent, the reputation of the grooms' employers signaled these individuals' credentials to prospective brides and their families. Thus, people were reluctant to work for small firms no one had heard of and did not have an established brand name. They also demanded salary raises to elevate their standing for matrimonial reasons:

We were actually told that you know I am working for Rhythm, nobody's heard of Rhythm. Who's going to marry me? There were engineers, you know actually this is a true story. You came in and asked for a raise and say 'sir, I have to get a raise sir, because with this salary I am not going to get a wife'. People do that! (Ujjal Kohli, Founder, Rhythm Media, California)

Source: author's own research

Technological Factors

Factors such as the availability of technology infrastructure and technical talent in foreign markets impact entrepreneurs' foreign market strategy.

Availability of Technology Infrastructure

Internet **availability** in foreign markets increases their attractiveness for entrepreneurs, especially if they are willing to use the internet to sell outside their home country. According to Internet World Stats, of a total 4.5 billion internet users estimated in March 2020, only 327 million live in North America; 2.3 billion internet users live in Asia, followed by 727 million in Europe. The top six countries by internet users (and the only countries with over 100 million) in 2016–17 were China (765 million), India (391 million), United States (245 million), Brazil (126 million), Japan (116 million), Russia (109 million). These statistics signal the attractiveness of these markets to US entrepreneurs based on the strength of technology.

The relative lack of technological development of a foreign market can be a constraint to the entry of an entrepreneurial venture in that market due to the lack of availability of complementary products or services. The relative lack of use of smartphones in Vietnam, for example, posed a threat to the growth of the mobile-based GrabTaxi app launched in Vietnam in 2014.

THE CHALLENGE OF TECHNOLOGY FOR GRABTAXI IN VIETNAM

GrabTaxi launched in Ho Chi Minh City, Vietnam, in 2014 after previously launching in Singapore and Thailand. This taxi company is mobile-based and its services are to help people get from place to place by ordering a ride. Vietnam is an attractive market as demand for transportation services is high. GrabTaxi also had first mover advantages as Lyft and Uber had not yet entered the market. GrabTaxi took a financial and operational risk by launching a transportation platform that had not been experimented with before there. However, some critics were apprehensive that GrabTaxi might not grow as fast in Vietnam as people in Vietnam do not use smartphones as much as in other Asian markets.

Source: Do (2014)

Availability of Technical Talent

The **availability of technical talent** in foreign markets to match entrepreneurs' need for specialized technical skills for new product development can drive entry into those markets. The availability of skilled teams in Lithuania and Manila (Philippines), for example, 'provoked' Pat Krishnan, a Silicon-Valley based technology entrepreneur, to think about these geographies for developing his most recent product. He found that teams in these locations were capable of building the technology, and it was more cost effective to work with them as opposed to hiring equivalent talent in the Valley. Pat also planned on building a team in Vietnam for the same reason:

> Lithuania is where we are working with some people. We look at Lithuania because we got a team with whom we are working. They are a very good team actually. For some infrastructure I can use them, and Vietnam would be another area. Philippines – there are some good people out there. With a very low-cost talent – there are some pockets in Manila, which is very good… I outsourced it [product development] to Manila, Philippines, and I have built a relationship with them and found that they are good in the current Helios and Matheson, so one of my development teams is in Manila. So that actually has provoked me to think about those areas. (Pat Krishnan, Technology Entrepreneur, California)

Manish Chandra and Murli Thirumale, both Silicon-Valley-based serial technology entrepreneurs, also reiterated the need to follow skills rather than location per se whilst going abroad. Among the foreign markets Murli entered for his technology venture were Poland, Germany and Canada where he hired independent consultants who had the technical skills to build his products. Often, he searched published research articles to locate the necessary talent in foreign markets. Sometimes, his personal connections also proved to be important:

> We had individual contractors, for example, we had somebody in Poland; we had somebody in Germany… we said 'where is the world's expert in this type of compression?' 'Oh, he happens to be in Poland'. Okay. So we are going to go… It was about finding the right type of people. We just went through research papers and looked at people who had written… research papers on the topic. There were some personal connections too. Our chief scientist… he is based in Florida. And two of the people we ended up hiring were people who were sort of under studies through him… one of them was in Germany. The other guy was in Poland. The third guy was in Toronto. (Murli Thirumale, Founder, Ocarina Networks, California)

Chapter Summary

LO1: International entrepreneurs' **foreign market selection** has two aspects: the number of markets to enter, and the nature and location of those markets. International expansion strategies typically involve either substantial commitment of resources and entry into few markets (concentration) or limited commitment of resources to each market and entry into many markets (dispersion). International entrepreneurs' approach to internationalization may be **reactive** or **proactive**. According to the resource-based theory, entrepreneurs must proactively evaluate foreign markets to assess the opportunities and threats in foreign markets, and analyze foreign markets that represent the best fit with their resources, products and services, prior to entering those markets.

LO2: A **foreign market entry mode** is an institutional arrangement that makes possible the entry of a firm's products, technology, human skills, management and other resources into a foreign country. The easiest way for entrepreneurs to enter foreign markets is by creating a website, followed by exporting. Creating a **website** is the least expensive mode, however entrepreneurs must adapt their website to foreign markets. **Exporting** can be **direct** or **indirect**. However, small firms are no longer restricting their internationalization forays to exporting. Licensing, strategic alliances and joint ventures, franchising, acquisitions and establishing an international location are the other more advanced modes that they use. **Licensing** is the granting of permission by one company to another company to use a specific form of its intellectual property under clearly defined conditions. A **strategic alliance** is a partnership between two or more firms that is developed to achieve a specific goal. **Technological alliances** feature cooperation in R&D where partners typically produce a product and bring it to market faster and cheaper than either firm could alone. **Marketing alliances** match a company that has a product to sell with a company that has a distribution system in order to increase sales of a product or service. A **joint venture** is an entity created when two or more firms pool a portion of their resources to create a jointly owned organization. In a **domestic joint venture**, two or more domestic businesses form a partnership for the purpose of exporting their goods and services. In a **foreign joint venture**, a domestic small business forms an alliance with a company in the target country. **Franchising** is a form of business organization in which a firm that already has a successful product or service licenses its trademark and method of doing business to other businesses for an initial franchise fee and an ongoing royalty. A **merger** is the pooling of interests to combine two or more firms into one, whereas an **acquisition** is the outright purchase of one firm by another. Finally, small firms may establish an **office or factory** to enter foreign markets.

LO3: Both internal factors or **firm-specific resources** including **financial, human (and social capital) resources**, and external factors (foreign **competitive** and **institutional**

(Continued)

environments) influence international entrepreneurs' internationalization strategy. The structure of **competition** in foreign markets affects entrepreneurs' choice of both foreign market and entry mode strategy. Levels of **government support** in foreign markets significantly impact the choice of those markets, as well as the choice between shared and equity-based entry modes in those markets.

Review Questions

1. Compare and contrast any two entry mode strategies that international entrepreneurs can use to penetrate foreign markets. Define each strategy and explain the advantages and disadvantages of each.
2. Explain what you understand by the term 'international franchising'. Explain the advantages and disadvantages of franchising as a way of penetrating foreign markets for international entrepreneurs.
3. What is the importance of acquisitions for small firms? Based on what you have read in this chapter, what factors must entrepreneurs evaluate while selecting an acquisition-based strategy to enter an international market for their venture? Use examples to explain your answer.
4. What is the role of international entrepreneurs' human resources in influencing their choice of internationalization strategy? Give examples to support your answer.
5. Using examples, explain the role of the foreign market political environment in impacting international entrepreneurs' choice of a) foreign market and b) entry mode strategy in that market.
6. How does the level of economic development in a foreign market influence international entrepreneurs' choice of internationalization strategy? Give examples to support your answer.
7. How does the foreign market socio-cultural environment impact the attractiveness of that market for an international entrepreneur? Give examples to support your answer.
8. How does the availability of technological infrastructure in foreign markets impact the attractiveness of those markets for international entrepreneurs? Give examples to illustrate your answer.

Case 6.1

Transputec Limited: The Challenge of India for a British Entrepreneur

Rickie Sehgal: Background and Early Years

As an executive MBA student at Harvard University (US) where he spent six weeks at a time taking classes, Rickie Sehgal juggled work and study with ease. The frequent travel to the US did not bother him, for it was the opportunity to get a 'brain upgrade' and 'have some fun' while growing his UK-based technology business that kept him going.

Born in India, Rickie was one of three children. His father was an Assistant Professor in Biochemistry at the University of London and Chief Chemist at Dr Scholl's in the UK. Before migrating to the UK at the age of 11, Rickie studied in India where he lived with his parents and extended family. He first entered business at the early age of 14 after his father quit paid employment in the UK due to a racist incident at work and set up a small company manufacturing toiletries, shampoos, soaps and astringents in London. Rickie and his brother, Sonny, became 'assistant production engineers' in the venture, doing everything from packing to designing and labeling in their kitchen at home, and driving from shop to shop to sell their products.

Rickie valued the early business experience that gave him the 'confidence to sell' and the 'ability to assess people'. He continued to contribute to the venture as it acquired exclusive customers such as the Dorchester Hotel, eventually becoming one of the first Indian manufacturing companies in the UK at the time. When his father decided to buy a pharmacy after his health took a turn for the worse, Rickie and his wife (a pharmacist, and his fiancée at that time) took it upon themselves to run it.

The Birth and Growth of TL

About the same time, Rickie accepted a job at Chase Manhattan Bank after graduating with a degree in Computer Science & Physics from the University of London. His key responsibility at Chase was to roll out the bank's management reporting software system in Europe. Transputec was born two years later when Rickie and Sonny spun out the business from Chase. Initially running from the back of their pharmacy, the software business soon diversified into hardware and professional services. Transputec Limited (TL) was incorporated when Chase sold off the leasing business in the aftermath of the housing crash four years later.

Rickie and Sonny ventured outside of the UK to conduct business right from the inception. Over time, they acquired several large customers, becoming a 'big player' in the industry. Rickie played an active role in identifying international opportunities. He tracked 'hotspots' on the internet and bid for tenders from organizations such as the United Nations and World Health Organization to execute technology projects in some of the most impoverished places in the world such as Zambia, Ethiopia and North Korea (Pyongyang). He also searched for growth opportunities at international trade exhibitions, and through delegations led by the UK Chambers of Commerce and Department of Trade and Industry. As a member of a political group led by David Cameron, he vigorously campaigned for the internationalization of British businesses.

Rickie was a strong proponent of organic growth through reinvestment of profits, a path he and his brother had chosen for TL over the years. Rickie's aversion to debt finance stemmed from his father's difficult experience with bank borrowing in his manufacturing business. As a small organization, foreign market entry for TL was driven

(Continued)

by considerations of accessing 'the right quality people' and getting 'wide geographic coverage'. Rickie hired local contractors in foreign markets to minimize risk and avoid high fixed costs of setting up an office. He planned to extend the same model to other countries such as Bulgaria and Poland.

Entry into India

Rickie had a strong motivation to drive business into India. He was chairperson of the British Asian Conservative Links, a premier organization with a mission to elect individuals of Asian origin to the House of Commons to promote UK–India business links. Rickie first attempted to do business with India when he liaised with the Indian High Commission to develop an Embassy Consulate Management System, a technology that enabled officials to more efficiently process multiple visa applications. However, he was disillusioned when the deal he had negotiated with the Indian government was terminated after a competitor stole the concept and claimed ownership of the technology. A second attempt to enter the market four years later also failed when the lawyer Rickie had entrusted with a cash deposit to acquire a property lease in Mumbai turned out to be fraudulent.

Rickie's investment in real estate in India ten years later was intended to initiate the process of establishing a back-office for TL. The brothers were attracted to Noida, a township in the suburbs of Delhi. Noida offered good infrastructure and access to skilled labor due to its proximity to several large, high-tech companies and a new private university.

There were also strong emotional reasons underlying the move. Rickie found a partner in his close friend, Harash. As he had lived and worked in the West most of his life, Rickie felt uncomfortable about venturing into India on his own without any local knowledge. He felt it was important to find a partner to deal with the local regulatory environment and adopt local business practices. Born in the UK, Harash had recently relocated to India to set up his own business. Rickie had known Harash and his family since childhood when they were next-door neighbors in India. After drifting apart for many years, they had accidentally re-connected in the UK and decided to collaborate for business. According to Rickie, Harash was the 'real motivation' to enter India. The trust between their respective families provided a strong foundation for the business partnership.

Employing a total of 120 people, the India office of TL was a software development center and service provider for the firm's global client base. Harash provided local infrastructure, and dealt with accounting and tax regulations in India. He also hired staff through local recruitment companies and his own personal social networks. Rickie spoke with Harash every day. He also kept frequent contact with local production and delivery managers. He visited India at least once every year, also directing his top managers in the UK to visit once or twice a year. Local personnel in India were also encouraged to visit the UK office. Inpatriating personnel from India to the UK was deemed important for motivational purposes and for training them in group dynamics.

The Challenge of India

Although successful in the short term, Rickie was much less optimistic about the sustained success of TL's India function. He believed his business relationship with India was under stress because India was out-pricing itself. Growing at 20% per annum, salary expectations in India were unrealistic and unsustainable. He believed an average graduate in India was in a mode of 'decorating' their CVs rather than aiming for a rewarding and stable career at a single organization. The prospects of finding a market for TL in India were also slim. Although India had a large population, and the percentage of internet users was significant, potential customers of TL such as big law firms had their own established IT infrastructure to source similar software at a lower price. In the absence of local connections and lack of critical mass, Rickie feared that TL would be forced to compete with bigger and more established businesses to win customers. Even though the Indian economy was growing in leaps and bounds and small enterprises were struggling to embrace technology, Rickie believed TL's product offering was far ahead of what India was ready for. Rickie felt his product facilitated 'too much transparency', which is also why it was not very welcome in a dual economy like India.

As he contemplated the next steps, he wondered if he should diversify into offering vocational education and training (VET) in India, a cause he was passionate about. He felt he could empower India's youth to shape their future by helping to build their vocational skills. The idea of 'renting out' VET services based on the ETE (Education-to-Education) model appealed most to him as a way to penetrate India in this industry sector. The ETE model allowed large technology firms and educational institutions in the UK to pool, and subsequently access, members' tangible and intangible assets, while retaining profits within the consortium. Rickie aspired for local educational institutions in India to become part of this network. He believed local institutions could benefit from accessing requisite intellectual capital from the UK, even as they locally sourced physical infrastructure and directly engaged with end users. He envisioned a scenario where key training personnel and instructors from India would visit the UK for a period of one or two years to acquire specific training they desired to introduce in India through a cloud application. While in the UK, they would access underlying technological infrastructure including state-of-the-art data centers to enable experimentation and structured learning that was not possible in India.

Rickie was confident about his access to technology to deliver virtual learning environments. In collaboration with Ash Verma, a close friend and former public servant in the UK, Rickie intended to invest in brand recognition to 'bring the commercialists and educationists together' to fulfill this need. As director of the Hertfordshire Regional College Computer Consortium in the UK, he was confident of securing their support for the roll-out. More recently, he had approached the Indian government and representatives of local universities with his proposal.

At the same time, however, Rickie was dissuaded by bureaucracy in India. The Ministry of Labor and Employment's Directorate General of Employment and Training regulated a large part of the VET infrastructure. Rickie felt the favoritism of Indian

(Continued)

politicians towards domestic firms clouded their judgment. The process of negotiating with the Indian government was arduous, with the 'bulk of personnel lower down the spectrum' being unaware of the importance of prudent timekeeping or judicious project management. The reluctance of the Indian government to collaborate with foreign vendors in view of the latter's stringent standards of compliance and transparency was also a reality he was well aware of.

In an environment where both central and state governments in India were unfriendly, the scope for innovation was low and possibility of expropriation of assets was high. Rickie feared 'intellectual shop lifters' were already stealing his ideas, with many new entrants on the scene using brick and mortar modes of service delivery. High administrative costs in an environment tempered by steep inflation and sluggish economic growth translated into extremely high costs of project management and policing for UK-based service providers. Against this backdrop, Rickie wondered if it was worth his time and effort to pursue the Indian market. Should he persist and diversify into VET in order to retain his presence in India? Or should he pull out of India and solely concentrate on growing his technology business in other international markets?

Discussion Questions

1. Why did Rickie want to drive his business, TL, into India? What factors influenced his decision to enter India? Evaluate the role of Rickie's human and social capital, the nature of TL as a product/service and the external environment in India in the internationalization of TL to India.
2. Which entry mode strategy did Rickie use to penetrate India for TL and why? Discuss the internal and external factors that influenced his choice of entry mode strategy in India.
3. What challenges to the growth of TL did Rickie face in India? Evaluate the external, PEST, environment in India to support your answer.
4. Why does Rickie want to offer vocational education training (VET) in India?
5. Should Rickie diversify into VET in order to continue to pursue India, or should he withdraw from India, concentrating on doing business in other markets? Why / why not? What criteria should he consider to justify his choice? Explain.

References

APEC (2015) 'SME internationalization and measurement', *APEC Policy Support Unit – Policy Brief No. 12 March 2015.* 20.500.12592/s80tg2.

Barringer, B.R. and Ireland, D.R. (2015) *Entrepreneurship: Successfully Launching New Ventures.* New York: Pearson.

Bell, J., Crick, D. and Young, S. (2004) 'Small firm internationalization and business strategy: An exploratory study of knowledge-intensive and traditional manufacturing firms in the UK', *International Small Business Journal*, 22(1): 23–56.

Blankenburg, D. and Johanson, J. (1992) 'Managing network connections in international business', *Scandinavian International Business Review*, 1(1): 5–19.

Calof, J.L. (1993) 'The impact of size on internationalization', *Journal of Small Business Management*, 31(4): 60.

Clement, J. (2019) 'E-commerce share of total global retail sales from 2015 to 2023', *Statista*, 30 August. Available at www.statista.com/statistics/534123/e-commerce-share-of-retail-sales-worldwide (last accessed 27 September 2022).

Do, A. (2014) 'GrabTaxi enters Vietnam, intensifying the battle for mobile taxi booking apps', *TechinAsia*, 26 February. Available at www.techinasia.com/grabtaxi-enters-vietnam (last accessed 27 September 2022).

Dunning, J.H. (1993) 'Internationalizing Porter's diamond', *Management International Review*, 33(1): 7–15.

Erramilli, M.K. (1991) 'The experience factor in foreign market entry behavior of service firms', *Journal of International Business Studies*, 22(3): 479–501.

Erramilli, M.K. (1992) 'Influence of some external and internal environmental factors on foreign market entry mode choice in service firms', *Journal of Business Research*, 25(4): 263–276.

Erramilli, M.K. and Rao, C.P. (1993) 'Service firms' international entry-mode choice: A modified transaction-cost analysis approach', *Journal of Marketing*, 57(3): 19–38.

Gerwin, E. (2014) 'Small business exports can drive big growth'. *Small Business Administration (SBA)*. Available at www.sba.gov/page/coronavirus-covid-19-small-business-guidance-loan-resources (last accessed 27 September 2022).

Goerzen, A. and Beamish, P.W. (2003) 'Geographic scope and multinational enterprise performance', *Strategic Management Journal*, 24(13): 1289–1306.

Grant, R.M. (1996) 'Toward a knowledge-based theory of the firm', *Strategic Management Journal*, 17(S2): 109–122.

Ibeh, K. (2012) 'Internationalisation and entrepreneurial business', in S. Carter and D. Jones-Evans (eds), *Enterprise and Small Business: Principles, Practice and Policy* (3rd edn). Harlow: Financial Times Prentice Hall, pp. 430–449.

Ibeh, K., Dimitratos, P. and Johnson, J.E. (2004) 'Micromultinationals: Some preliminary evidence on an emergent "star" of the international entrepreneurship field', *Journal of International Entrepreneurship*, 2(4): 289–303.

Internet World Stats (2020) 'Internet world stats: Usage and population statistics'. Miniwatts Marketing Group. Available at www.internetworldstats.com/stats.htm (last accessed 27 September 2022).

Loeb, W. (2017) 'Going global: Done right, a growth opportunity for all retailers', *Forbes*, 24 July. Available at www.forbes.com/sites/walterloeb/2017/07/24/going-global-done-right-a-growth-opportunity-for-all-retailers/#6df4c1cd42fc (last accessed 27 September 2022).

Marion, T.J., Eddleston, K.A., Friar, J.H. and Deeds, D. (2015) 'The evolution of inter-organizational relationships in emerging ventures: An enthnographic study within the new product development process', *Journal of Business Venturing*, 30(1): 167–184.

Mascarenhas, B. (1997) 'The order and size of entry into international markets', *Journal of Business Venturing*, 12(4): 287–299.

OECD. (2009) 'Top barriers and drivers to SME internationalization'. Report by the OECD Working Party of SMEs and Entrepreneurship. *Paris: OECD*. Available at www.oecd.org/dataoecd/16/26/43357832.pdf (last accessed 27 September 2022).

Papadopoulos, N. and Denis, J.E. (1988) 'Inventory, taxonomy and assessment of methods for international market selection', *International Marketing Review*, 5(1): 38–51, http://dx.doi.org/10.1108/eb008357

Pruthi, S. (2016) 'TrintMe: Perseverance a friend or enemy?' *Journal of Critical Incidents*, 9.

Root, H.L. (1994) *The Fountain of Privilege: Political Foundations of Markets in Old Regime France and England*. Berkeley, CA: University of California Press.

Roser, M., Ritchie, H., Ortiz-Ospina, E. and Hasell, J. (2020) 'Coronavirus disease (COVID-19) – statistics and research'. *Our World in Data*. Available at https://ourworldindata.org/coronavirus (last accessed 27 September 2022).

Scarborough, N.M. (2014) (Edited) *Essentials of Entrepreneurship and Small Business Management* (7th edn). Harlow: Pearson Education.

Stopford, J.M. and Wells Jr., L.T. (1972) *Managing the Multinational Enterprise: Organization of the Firm and Ownership of the Subsidiary*. New York: Basic Books.

The Year in Trade (2019) *United States International Trade Commission*, https://www.usitc.gov/press_room/news_release/2020/er0831ll1640.htm

Te-Ping, C. (2017) 'Chinese entrepreneurs pine for US shoppers on Amazon – merchandise is ready to ship, but sellers first must learn what hooks buyers on website', *The Wall Street Journal*, 17 December. Available at www.wsj.com/articles/will-they-search-for-that-chinese-learn-art-of-hooking-americans-on-amazon-1513539380 (last accessed 27 September 2022).

USBA Office of Advocacy (2018) *Annual Report of the Office of Economic Research, FY 2017*. Available at www.sba.gov/advocacy/2018-small-business-profiles-states-and-territories (last accessed 27 September 2022).

Venkataraman, S., Van de Ven, A.H., Buckeye, J. and Hudson, R. (1990) 'Starting up in a turbulent environment: A process model of failure among firms with high customer dependence', *Journal of Business Venturing*, 5(1): 277–295.

7
MIGRATION AND GLOBAL ENTREPRENEURSHIP

──Learning Outcomes──

After studying this chapter, you should be able to:

- **LO1**: Obtain a critical understanding of the relationship between migration and global entrepreneurship
- **LO2**: Develop a critical appreciation of the underlying trends in migration and global entrepreneurship
- **LO3**: Assess critically the key factors that explain why migration and the movement of people is central to an understanding of the evolution of global entrepreneurship
- **LO4**: Evaluate the different processes that lead to enhanced contributions to global entrepreneurship by migrant communities
- **LO5**: Distinguish between migrants and refugees as distinctive contributors to global entrepreneurship

Introduction

The concern with migration and refugees in recent times has generated the need for the mitigation of negative outcomes of the movement of people. The corollary of this concern is the need to identify support mechanisms for better integration and the significant contribution that migrants do or can make to their new habitats. Since the International Conference on Population and Development in 1994, the issue of international migration and its relation to development has risen steadily on the agenda of the international community (UNPF, 1995). The 2030 Agenda for Sustainable Development (UN, 2016) includes several migration-related targets and calls for regular reviews of the progress toward their achievement using data disaggregated by, inter-alia, migratory status. Two distinctive but related features of the positive aspects of migration include:

1. The transfer of knowledge and skills from countries of origin together with the acquisition of new knowledge and skills in the new country of residence, the amalgamation of which contributes to the labor market specifically and to the economy of the latter more generally
2. The utilization of those skills to mobilize resources and augment personal motivation for setting up new enterprises in the destination country, the experience of which could induce them to set up firms in their countries of origin

This chapter introduces the agenda on migration and its significance for global entrepreneurship. It reinforces the need for understanding and evaluating the role of people and their movement across the world, as a vital component of global entrepreneurship.

The Structure of the Chapter

In this chapter we start by showing how international migration flows have nurtured and enabled entrepreneurship activity. This section analyses the key economic and social trends in international migration that explain the emergence and positive exploitation of entrepreneurial opportunities by migrants. In the second part we describe and analyze the evidence on how migrants have developed entrepreneurial activities both in the countries they chose to migrate to and in their countries of origin. We explain how migrant entrepreneurs face many well-documented barriers of starting up or growing their own ventures, and also the ways in which they have achieved success, part of which is represented by their international and transnational business activity. We move on to Part Three where we discuss some short case studies on global migrant entrepreneurs. Finally, in Part Four we outline some of the challenges faced by different communities of interest – the global migrant entrepreneurs themselves, policy makers and researchers, ending with a summary of prospective policy objectives and suggested ways forward for constructive agendas for the entrepreneurial activities of migrants.

Part One: International Migration Flows and Global Entrepreneurship

The figures for international migration worldwide show rapid and continued growth in recent years, with total numbers reaching 258 million in 2017, up from 220 million in 2010 and 173 million in 2000. Over 60% of all international migrants live in Asia (80 million) or Europe (78 million). North America hosted the third largest number of international migrants (58 million), followed by Africa (25 million), Latin America and the Caribbean (10 million) and Oceania (8 million). Between 2000 and 2015, positive net migration contributed to 42% of the population growth observed in North America and 31% in Oceania. In Europe, instead of growing by 2%, the size of the population would have fallen by 1% in the absence of a net inflow of migrants (UNGA, 2017). Balanced population growth is regarded by most economists as being critical to economic growth. In all OECD countries, migrants are concentrated in certain areas, especially in the poorer neighborhoods and the outskirts of large metropolitan cities. However, not all immigrant groups are concentrated to the same extent, and this is shaped by both geography and historical settlement patterns plus the slow growing awareness of the wide range of technical and entrepreneurial skills that migrants can bring to the host countries.

However, permanent migration flows to OECD countries (the largest group of Western countries but including Japan and South Korea) fell by more than 30% to about 3.7 million in 2020 – the lowest level since 2003. This decline could be as much as 40%, according to the OECD (2021). All categories of permanent migration experienced a drop in 2020, with family migration showing the largest decline. More specifically, even temporary labor migration decreased sharply in 2020. Intra-company transfers of workers fell by 53%. The lowest rate of decline was in the category of seasonal agricultural workers which fell by 9%. Much of the decline in migration can be attributed to the closing of borders in the wake of the COVID-19 pandemic.

Over the two 'COVID years' of 2020 and into 2021, most OECD countries imposed travel restrictions and reduced immigration services, due to the spread of the pandemic. Some temporary measures were implemented to mitigate the pandemic's effects, such as making it possible for migrants affected by the crisis to stay legally past any former deadline, and the use of digital tools for various integration programs, language teaching and outreach services to migrant populations (OECD, 2021).

Different aspects of migration, such as the role of diasporas, have surfaced over time. Entrepreneurial migrants especially are seen as agents of development. Contrary to previously held views about migration contributing to brain drain, research suggests that only some of the poorest countries (Beine et al., 2008; Di Maria and Stryszowski, 2009) suffer from this dilemma. Migration has substantial benefits for highly skilled individuals in terms of gains in income and the acquisition of a higher level of human capital (Gibson and McKenzie, 2012) but also for the host economies (where they have settled) such as the UK, the Netherlands and Germany, which have welcomed their arrival and contributions (OECD, 2011). By way of circular flow, for their countries of origin (Acosta et al., 2007; Adams, 2006; Adams and Page, 2005), the expected development impact of migrant entrepreneurs can be substantial. If we consider just migrant remittances, these are estimated to be around $550 billion annually (more than twice the volume of aid), according to the World Bank (2013). Skills transfers, social remittances (ideas, behaviors, identities) and social capital that flow from receiving to sending country and back (Levitt, 1998; Saxenian, 2002) are enhanced through modern communication methods such as telephone, internet and email, together with return visits by migrants to their origin country. Migrants also contribute to the economy of their host countries through their contributions to the labor market, paying taxes, social contributions and overall economic growth, as shown in Table 7.1 below.

Table 7.1 The benefits of migration for receiving countries

Labor Markets	Public Benefit	Economic Growth
Migrants account for 47% and 70% of the increase in the workforce in the USA and in Europe, respectively.	Migrants receive less in benefits than they contribute in taxes.	Migrants increase the stock of working-age population. The shrinking of the latter in OECD countries is a major economic concern.
Migrants fill important niches in both traditional and fast growing sectors of the economy.	Of all forms of migrants, labor migrants make the most significant positive impact on public resources.	Since migrants arrive with skills they are better able to make a positive impact on the human capital development of the countries that receive them.
Migrants contribute significantly to labor market flexibility, especially in Europe.	Employment is by far the strongest determinant of the fiscal contribution that migrants make to the economy.	Increasingly, and especially in countries such as the USA, UK and Germany, migrants contribute to technology development, innovation and entrepreneurship.
	In 2017, the contribution of immigrants to the financing of pure public goods amounted to $547 billion in the 25 countries included in an OECD report.	

Source: adapted from Westmore (2015)

Given that migration is a worldwide phenomenon, it is not surprising that one aspect of the contribution to the economy manifests itself in entrepreneurial activity both in receiving countries and also globally. The abundant flow of human resources and exchange of ideas or information inherent in the movement of people, globally, has the potential for generating new ideas for creating ventures which could have an intrinsic, international character.

Developed economies such as the USA, the UK and Germany are hosting increasing numbers of successful start-ups and growing firms run by international migrant entrepreneurs. They include sophisticated businesses in high-tech and knowledge-intensive industries started by migrants from a range of regions including Asia, Africa and Latin America. Conversely, migrant entrepreneurs from developed countries are increasingly seeking to exploit opportunities in developing countries. These entrepreneurs typically exploit their connections *in their host and origin countries* to develop stronger businesses that operate in both environments and potentially in third countries as well. These entrepreneurs are engaged in global entrepreneurship which could have important benefits for international business and specifically the successful application of business and technological expertise in both destination and countries of origin.

One interesting statistic that indicates the importance of garnering sufficient confidence among migrants to engage in entrepreneurial activity is their settlement status. In 2019, 2.2 million people became citizens of an OECD country, representing a 12% annual increase from 2018. Although this might decline in countries in the USA because of restrictions in naturalization, the trend is for higher levels of full settlement status as citizens. Europe benefited from the fallout of Brexit in the UK. In 2019, the EU saw the highest number of UK nationals who took up the citizenship of an EU country, a record 15 times the 2015 level before the vote on Brexit. Interestingly, the number of EU citizens who have obtained British nationality has also been on the rise in 2019 like never before (OECD, 2021).

Part Two: Migrant Communities and Entrepreneurial Trajectories

Migrant entrepreneurship is a function of the movement of people across borders. So, the starting point of any consideration of the subject warrants an outline of the key factors in migration that impacts on entrepreneurial outcomes of migrants.

Normative Understanding of Migrant Entrepreneurship

Among the key target groups are migrants and ethnic minority populations. There are large numbers of businesses set up and run by people from migrant and ethnic minority communities in destination countries. In most OECD countries, immigrants set up businesses at the same rate as the native-born population, but in some countries such as Poland and the United Kingdom, they are about 1.5 times as likely as the native-born population to be self-employed (OECD, 2014).

Evidence from research and practice indicates that businesses run by immigrants often operate in highly competitive industries with low barriers to entry and low skill requirements. This includes, for example, restaurants, retail shops and the textile industry. It is, therefore, not surprising to find that these businesses usually have lower survival rates than those operated by native-born entrepreneurs. For example, evidence from France shows that immigrant-operated businesses have survival rates that are 20 percentage points lower than non-immigrant businesses after three years.

In OECD countries, entrepreneurship is slightly higher among immigrants than natives and the total number of persons employed in migrant businesses is substantial, although the survival rate of these businesses is often lower than that of their native counterparts. Migrant entrepreneurship has gone beyond traditional ethnic businesses into a wide range of sectors and innovative areas. Immigrant entrepreneurs often face the same types of barriers as native-born entrepreneurs but are typically held back to a greater extent by these barriers than their local counterparts born and bred in the migrants' host countries.

Both formal and informal institutions can negatively influence business start-up by immigrants because they are typically unfamiliar with the business and regulatory environment. This is especially true when immigrants seek to set up businesses in highly regulated sectors. Access to finance can also be an important barrier to business start-up, particularly for recent immigrants who cannot demonstrate a credit history or have never participated in the formal banking system. As with all entrepreneurs, a lack of entrepreneurship skills can hinder business creation. Particular challenges for ethnic minority and immigrant entrepreneurs are often related to business management skills and ability to speak the language used in the business environment. Migrant entrepreneurs can, therefore, be seen as a group requiring dedicated support to increase the quality of their business start-ups (OECD, 2011).

The Quality, Wealth and Contribution of Migrant Businesses

The quality of businesses started by migrants varies considerably, and some are very successful. There is growing evidence from countries such as the USA and the UK that migrant and/or foreign-born entrepreneurs outnumber their indigenous counterparts in terms of the proportion of people starting up or growing their ventures. A study on migrant business owners published in 2014 by the Centre for Entrepreneurs (CFE), found that no fewer than one in seven British companies turning over at least £1 million a year was founded by someone from overseas. More striking still, these foreign-born entrepreneurs who are contributing so much to the British economy were found to come from a staggering 155 different countries. The top ranking countries that appear to be boosting the entrepreneurial economy include Ireland, India, Germany and the United States. Their sectoral representation is also varied, ranging for example from construction and consumer goods to health care information technology, manufacturing, management consultancy, and media and entertainment (CFE, 2014). The Centre for American Entrepreneurship found that in the USA 43% of companies in the 2017 Fortune 500 were founded or co-founded by an immigrant or the child of an immigrant, and among the top 35, that share is 57%.

The Global Entrepreneurship Monitor (GEM) reports echo the evidence on migrants as vigorous entrepreneurs not least because they show a real interest in taking control of their destiny by launching and growing a new enterprise, both out of necessity and opportunity. It is claimed that first-generation migrants are more active in business start-ups than non-migrants and that start-ups founded by both first- and second-generation migrants are on average more growth-orientated than those of non-migrants across all economic development levels.

The GEM survey by Kelly et al. (2012) indicates that on average 20% of migrant-owned enterprises expected to create ten or more jobs in the next five years, compared to only 14% of non-migrant owned enterprises (Brixy et al., 2013). In the UK, while both white and non-white entrepreneurs increased since 2008 (12.9% were early-stage entrepreneurs in 2017, compared to 8.2% among the UK-born population as a whole (all ethnicities)), for both ethnic minority groups and migrants, the difference from the white and UK-born populations has widened substantially since 2008. The Total Entrepreneurial Activity rate of the white ethnic population in the UK in 2017 was remarkably lower than that of the ethnic non-white population, at 7.9% compared to 14.5%, even if there were no major changes in either group since 2016. As for migrant groups the rate of 12.5% remains well above the rate of 8.2% for UK-born life-long residents (GEM, 2017). In the USA, firms owned and managed by Asians and Latinos generated more than $1.012 trillion in 2015. More than 6.7 million workers earning $212 billion were employed by them, and those businesses which had a majority immigrant ownership employed about one in ten of all workers in private US firms (Kosten, 2018).

This wealth-generating, entrepreneurially enhancing capacity of migrants is a global phenomenon, although most of the data and evidence originates from North America, the United Kingdom, France and Germany.

The successful migrant entrepreneur view tends to be based on three stylized facts or beliefs which hold that:

a. Migrants tend to be more entrepreneurial than natives.
b. Migrant remittances can fund start-ups in the countries of origin.
c. Return migration can bring valuable entrepreneurial skills to developing home countries.

(Naudé et al., 2015; Acosta (2007))

In between the narratives of disadvantage and success lie myriad reasons explaining why and how there might be an entrepreneurial deficit in some quarters or glowing economic success in others. Education, technology adaptation, social capital and extended networks are cited as contributory or constraining factors. One underlying but hitherto under-explored issue that is inherent in the migrant experience is the duality of contextual knowledge, empathy, access to hard and soft resources that stem from what is regarded as their 'dual habitus', an idea drawn from Bourdieu's (1967) work on the interrelationship between social structure and human agency. The 'dual habitus' concept refers to the idea of developing and shaping understandings, attitudes, behavior and learning through the accumulated experience of migrants in two different contexts – their country of origin and their destination country. Together with some of the direct benefits of migration, this transnational knowledge and experience acquired and used in countries of origin and of subsequent settlement have a direct bearing on their ability to exploit simultaneously their connections in host and origin countries in order to grow highly successful international businesses. It is this process that has come to be described as transnational entrepreneurship. For the purpose of this chapter we explore how the very business of migration and people flows is central to global entrepreneurship and how migrants take the unique advantage of using their dual habitus.

Migrants Going Global

When successful migrant business owners in receiving countries start exploring prospects in their countries of origin (COOs) or other overseas markets they have the choice of internationalizing their business through exports or starting different ventures elsewhere. In doing so they engage in the curious task of becoming migrants in their COOs, unless they acquire dual citizenship, or in other nations. The phenomenon of global engagement implies a distinct opportunity structure which enables those migrants who found and maintain businesses to benefit from two or more worlds to break out from stereotypical minority business enclaves, grow their ventures and offer a method for providing competitive advantage (Terjesen and Elam, 2009). Much of the knowledge on this phenomenon is anecdotal or drawn from qualitative research. Commentators identify well-publicized experiences in London, Berlin, Gothenburg, Oslo, Copenhagen, Madrid in Europe, and further afield in Guangdong province and Shanghai in China, and of course Silicon Valley, Boston and the research triangle in North Carolina, offering evidence of extraordinary entrepreneurial endeavors across borders.

What we do know about the global entrepreneurial phenomenon tends also to be drawn from studies on 'high quality' migrant entrepreneurship activities by long-established migrant communities. However, there are also examples of success among new immigrants and among refugees who create enterprises out of 'necessity'. For example, the rise of the Sea Turtles in China (Chinese immigrants in the USA returning to China but also maintaining working links in the USA) and Japanese expatriates in Cambodia.

Table 7.2 summarizes the key features of and the outcomes associated with globally oriented activities of migrant entrepreneurs.

Table 7.2 Key features and outcomes of globally oriented activities of migrant entrepreneurs

Key Features	Outcomes
1. Involves migrant communities.	Could involve immigrants, settled ethnic minorities, refugees.
2. Entrepreneurial activity is distinguished by the formation of at least two ventures in different countries.	The two or more ventures are formed, typically, in the country of residence (COR) or destination, and the country of origin (COO). In some cases it goes beyond the COO to other foreign destinations.
3. Has a distinctive opportunity structure.	Based on the idea of opportunities based on interaction between institutional structure and human agency, in COR and COO.

Key Features	Outcomes
4. Entrepreneurs benefit from both worlds.	The benefits are derived from having knowledge of and experience in both countries, and by being embedded in both environments.
5. Benefits accrue to both global migrant entrepreneurs and the economy.	Benefits in terms of new knowledge, products and services, jobs are obtained in both COR and COO.
6. Migrant entrepreneurs are able to break out from the stereotypical ghetto environment associated with their businesses in COR.	The formation of ventures in more than one country highlights possible strength in business formation and development capacity.

Who are the people who participate in this global entrepreneurship process? Are they the same as immigrant and ethnic minority entrepreneurs? If not what distinguishes them from the latter?

Different Types of Global Migrant Entrepreneurs

Migrant and Ethnic Minority Entrepreneurs

Immigrant entrepreneurship is associated with the members of the first generation of immigrants (foreign-born) who have started their new ventures in the host country. Ethnic minority entrepreneurship encompasses a mix of second, third and further generations of immigrants originating from a given country (including persons already born in the host country), such as those from the broader ethnic minority groups such as Afro-Caribbeans, Asians, Eastern Europeans and Latin Americans. A significant body of research in migrant entrepreneurship has addressed venture creation by ethnic entrepreneurs in their host countries (Basu, 2011; Deakins et al., 2007; Ram and Jones, 2008). Studies have also explored business and technological expertise of returnee entrepreneurs and their role in the development of high-tech industries in emerging economies (Filatotchev et al., 2009; Pruthi, 2014). These immigrant and ethnic minority entrepreneurs are potentially global migrant entrepreneurs but it is not simply their ethnicity or their functioning as immigrants that make them transnational entrepreneurs (TEs).

A comparative analysis carried out by Baycan-Levent and Nijkamp (2007) showed that the overall picture of European migrant entrepreneurship is established by some specific push factors such as high unemployment rates, low participation rates or low status in the labor market, and other factors such as mixed embeddedness (the experience of living and working in the host country together with those of living and working in migrant ethnic niches). There are differences to be found among migrant entrepreneurs in Southern and Northern European countries. While an informal and labor-intensive sector, often associated with an underground economy, and the prevalence of small companies and traditional households, distinguish migrant entrepreneurship in Southern European countries, an overrepresentation of non-Western immigrants among the self-employed, as well as relatively lower income levels of the self-employed among immigrants, relative to both self-employed natives and employed immigrants, are key characteristics of migrant entrepreneurship in Northern European countries. Generalization pertaining to migrant entrepreneurship activity or behavior may be a difficult proposition.

In another study, Levie and Hart (2011) show that people of Black ethnic backgrounds tend to have a higher propensity to either intend or actively be trying to start new businesses, although this inclination does not necessarily correspond to higher levels of actual business ownership.

Global migrant entrepreneurship applies particularly *to* migrant or ethnic entrepreneurs who maintain regular cross-border business activity involving more than one business venture. Their activities can therefore be regarded as an extension or a sub-set of immigrant and ethnic minority entrepreneurship but only where dual country (origin and destination, or more than two countries) economic and social interrelationships are taken into consideration. There is no necessary limitation to the number of countries that they can enter to form new businesses, but the direction of travel generally is from COR to COO and beyond.

There are other migrant entrepreneurs who cross host country borders to commercialize a business idea in their home countries (Drori et al., 2009), representing more traditional international business activities. The differences in the behavior of global migrant entrepreneurs who set up different ventures in more than one country may stem from their unique social networks, market-specific knowledge and experience in both countries (Elo and Volovelsky, 2017; Riddle et al., 2010), or even cultural, linguistic and religious features that represent particular resources and competences for internationalization (e.g. Brinkerhoff, 2016). The global enterprises they form are different from other kinds of international enterprise that are deemed transnational simply because they cross borders, in terms of investments, joint ventures or strategic alliances. Critical is the acquired 'dual habitus' (or 'multiple habitus') context of global entrepreneurship. These entrepreneurs can, therefore, be understood to operate their dual structures between developed economies, between emerging economies, or between developed and emerging economies (Drori et al., 2009; Pruthi et al., 2018).

Migrant entrepreneurs are not passive adherents to institutional constraints; they actively mold them to suit their own unique initiatives. Institutional and other social constraints work in both environments. For example, some of the reasons offered by way of explanation for high rates of failure or low growth ventures started by minorities are, inter-alia, racial discrimination, limited access to information, language difficulties. It is argued that one way of overcoming limitations in the COR is by venture formation in the COO where familiarity with the local language and culture can act as a catalyst for ease of business entry and development. Some research evidence suggests that language and a common culture are often determining factors in the choice of a business in the COO (Sui et al., 2015). This ostensible advantage can be tempered by time away and distance from the COO.

Globally oriented migrant entrepreneurs leverage opportunities arising from their dual fields and networks, optimizing resources where they may be most effective (Drori et al., 2009). Unlike other ethnic minority entrepreneurs established in a COR, they go beyond ethnic enclaves in starting their ventures, using class or national resources to expand business contacts beyond their ethnic group (Gold and Light, 2000). They open up a new frontier to develop insights on the nature of global and local networks that link individual resources at the micro level with institutional structures at the macro level (Chen and Tan, 2009). As employees of multinational corporations (MNCs), diasporas often encourage their employers to investigate the possibility of investing in the diasporan's country of origin (Kotabe and Kothari, 2016; Kothari et al., 2013). This prior experience of entering the home country with a former employer impacts the nature and composition of social capital in venture founding in the home country (Pruthi and Wright, 2017).

Where are the Global Migrant Entrepreneurs?

Globally there are probably a billion entrepreneurs (measured in terms of self-employment) and more than 232 million cross-border migrants (UN, 2013). Unfortunately, no definitive data sets are available for this cohort of entrepreneurs to help us ascertain their strength in numbers.

The significant numbers of cross-border movement of migrants and the resulting growth in population in host countries is a potentially strong indicator of the economic and entrepreneurial dividend that migration yields. For example, the joint London First and PwC report (2015) shows how London's workforce has grown from 4.3 million people in 2005 to just under 5.2 million in 2015. This increase is made up of people from around the UK, the EU and the rest of the world. Of these workers 1.3 million (or 25% of London's total workforce, and up from 1 million in 2005) were born elsewhere in the world in 2015. The analysis indicates that London's 1.8 million migrant workers (including those born in the EU and the rest of the world) generate economic value of £83 billion per year, which represents approximately 22% of the capital's Gross Value Added (GVA). The additional GVA generated by ten jobs from migrant workers will support an additional four jobs in the wider UK economy. Non-EU and Post-2004 Accession country migrants tend to undertake semi-routine and routine work, work in small businesses or are self-employed – often in the construction, tourism or wholesale and retail sectors. Extrapolation in terms of estimates for international entrepreneurial activity is difficult but these people constitute transnational entrepreneurship fodder.

Early research indicates that, depending on particular locations and ethnic groupings, immigrants involved in global entrepreneurship might constitute anywhere between 37.5

to 78.5% of immigrant entrepreneurs (Portes et al., 2002). They tend to have a longer residence experience in host country, better education and have experienced faster occupational advancement. Approximately 10% of the population of developed countries are migrants (Riddle 2008). Some of these migrants can be regarded as being 'transnational' in that they maintain their bond with their country of origin by sending remittances there while developing their careers or businesses in the countries to which they have moved. Remittances make one of the largest contributions to small and low-income developing countries accounting for 30% of its GDP (Mohapatra et al., Ratha and Silwal, 2011).

Zhongguancun is one of the "innovation and entrepreneurial base for overseas talents" conferred by the Central Personnel Work Coordination Group. There are more than 5,000 enterprises with at least 15,000 overseas returnees (Tan, 2006; Zhongguancun Science Park, 2017). Returnees are defined here as scientists and engineers, or students who have trained or studied in OECD countries, and have returned to their native countries to start up a new venture or work for a local company or to start new ventures, while sustaining a venture in the USA (Liu et al., 2010). Similar stories can be found among Indian and Israeli migrants. As Saxenian (1994, 2006) observes, these entrepreneurs tend to move between the USA, China, India and Israel, nurturing businesses in both locations.

An Italian sample of 480 immigrant entrepreneurs found 33% of them (158 entrepreneurs) were transnational entrepreneurs based in Italy. The immigrants declared that their company maintains business ties with their country of origin. Among the 185 respondents for a Canadian study of immigrant businesses, 73 identified themselves as transnational entrepreneurs; the rest were either entrepreneurs whose business was limited to Canada or those who were interested in becoming an entrepreneur in a technology field (Lin and Tao, 2012).

The absence of more systematic data collection undermines the policy capacity to build economic and social advantages from such transnational entrepreneurship.

Since international migration is a global phenomenon we would expect to see global migrant entrepreneurship activity to be occurring around the world. The qualitative evidence available to us suggests that this is indeed the case. The evidence is not restricted to the well-publicized examples of migrant entrepreneurship and their global reach in the USA, UK, France and Germany. There is an increasing awareness of international flows of migrant-led, cross-border new venture creation in and out of Israel, Japan, South Korea, Russia, Cambodia and many other countries.

Part Three: Some Global Case Studies

Let us look at a few cases which normally escape the radar of scholars studying the relation between migration and entrepreneurship.

Case 7.1

Institutions and Capital

In a study of different migrant communities in Israel, Heilbrunn (2019) notes that the idea of the 'Israel Start-Up Nation' is all about global entrepreneurship in practice. Worth noting is the Israeli and Palestinian high-tech communities of entrepreneurs. Entrepreneurs connect between Israel and the countries of origin of legal migrants, adding to the cultural legitimization of 'otherness'. She also found that the differences levels or forms of access to cultural, social, economic and institutional capital acquired in both origin and destination environments, coupled with local institutional arrangements, had a pronounced effect on the entrepreneurs' ability to navigate international environments successfully.

Effective entrepreneurial outcomes across borders were a function of the intersection between the unequal 'capital set' of migrants and the institutional arrangements which were determined by location, legal, political and economic aspects affecting different migrant groups. Relevant locations and actors controlling access are situated mainly within the institutional framework, which shapes not only access but also intentions of migrant entrepreneurs (Heilbrunn, 2019).

Source: adapted from Heilbrunn (2019)

Case 7.2

The Korean Wave

Governments of certain Asian countries have promoted direct and focused initiatives to encourage both diaspora and transnational entrepreneurship activity. The Korean government has a long history of providing public R&D support to many of its high-tech and high-impact sectors. The film industry is one good example. The concept of 'Hallyu' or the Korean wave is based on the rise in popularity of Korean film, television and music, with different governments enabling the entry of the Chaebols to finance growth, or actively supporting the digitization of the industry. (A Chaebol refers to a large industrial South Korean conglomerate owned, run and managed by an individual or family.) A globalized strategic focus to diversify the film and television market into, first, China, was made possible through Korea's Next Entertainment World (NEW) and China's Huace Media Group launching a joint venture – 'Huace & NEW' – to co-produce blockbusters. Apart from the joint production of films this strategy has leveraged the Chinese government's internationalization plans to facilitate cross-border flows of investors, directors and producers, the creation of new firms in the technical service sectors

(Continued)

(including lighting, art, stunts, special effects, and sound mixing), and crucially in the emergence of business-oriented migrant settlement in both countries.

The Korean government's recent drive to wean its economy away from an over-dependence on the Chaebols through its new start-up policy is another illustration of state-sponsored start-up and innovative growth in the country. Emphasis is placed on fintech, the Internet of Things, health care, bioscience, e-commerce and energy. More than 50 co-working spaces, 100 accelerators, incubators and innovation centers have been established with the support of the Ministry of SMEs and Startups and Chaebols such as Samsung and Hyundai. The key elements of such a policy include a sharp focus on technological breakthroughs, international collaboration, Chaebol–government co-operation for funding and campus-based entrepreneurship. The international collaboration element is characterized by the flow of financial capital from Korean migrants, the creation of new start-ups in Korean by the expatriate community in the USA and elsewhere, and facilitation of transnational start-ups, especially of those firms which demonstrate a high-tech capability combined with a social purpose.

This form of state-directed transnationality differs from the organic forms found in North America, Europe and other countries.

Source: adapted from Berg and Hassink (2014)

Case 7.3

Global and Social Consciousness of Nascent Japanese Transnational Entrepreneurs

Traditionally, Japanese companies enjoy a long-term employment system, meaning when university graduates obtain jobs, they are likely to work for the same company until their mandatory retirement. It is Japanese practice that managers within companies decide the professional development of all employees in accordance with corporate strategies. However, these practices have been changing. Increasing numbers of Japanese young people are choosing to navigate their lives using their own initiative, education and experience. As a consequence, many Japanese are choosing to leave Japan and work overseas.

Based on interviews with Japanese self-initiated expatriate entrepreneurs in Cambodia, Indonesia, Myanmar and Vietnam in 2017 and 2018, a recent study (Yokoyama and Birchley, 2018) found that the entrepreneurs set up firms in a variety of fields such as human resources, IT support, publishing, education, tourism and hospitality, amongst others, in the destination countries. The findings suggest that many male Japanese entrepreneurs start their 'expat' businesses in their 30s and women in their late 30s to early 40s, with start-up funds often obtained through savings in Japan. They also have exposure to overseas life and culture during the exploration stage in their career, such as through a study abroad program at university, backpacking, or through foreign friends and colleagues.

In each country, the entrepreneurs are driven by different motivations and experience various barriers to success, supporting the argument about the institutional–capital nexus discussed in the Israeli case above. As an example, in Cambodia, the entrepreneurs appear to be not only entrepreneurial and globally minded but they are also very socially conscious. Cambodia is a small country with a GDP per capita of $1,163 and a population of 15.6 million in 2015. One distinctive case is of a Japanese male who established a university in Cambodia. After discontinuing his PhD program in Japan he started a digital company which competed globally. He eventually sold his company for $240 million and after surveying opportunities throughout South-East Asia he decided to establish a university in Cambodia. He recruited IT teachers from India and language teachers from the Philippines, developing a full board and tuition-free program for Cambodian and Japanese students. He utilized his knowledge, experience and social mindset to make changes in Cambodia. Some of these entrepreneurs are now exploring opportunities to replicate their entrepreneurial drive back in Japan.

The research also found barriers to success in these international contexts. Socio-cultural barriers such as the inability to speak the local language and lack of understanding of religious and cultural norms and expectation could be seen in Indonesia. Additionally, international business people often require in-country partners and nominees in order to set up their businesses which can be prohibitive.

Source: adapted from Yokoyama and Birchley (2018)

Van Gelderen (2007), referring to the entrepreneurial activities of former USSR immigrants in the Netherlands and Israel, found that COO knowledge could help entrepreneurs to recognize unique opportunities. For example, they may start travel agencies providing tour services to people in their COO to visit the COR or take people from the COR to explore the COO. Importing and exporting businesses of hand-made products (e.g. Persian hand-woven carpets) that may be idiosyncratic to the TEs' COO are also another example of opportunities for TEs.

While entrepreneurship is the driving force in all the three cases above, the interest in going international and then using that experience to renew home ties is a constant feature in all the examples. How they accomplish their transnational journeys varies. It is difficult to discern a specific pattern. The different pathways to achieving global entrepreneurial status can be a function of any one or a mix of the following experiences or conditions:

1. The use of the unique human, social and financial capital accumulation experience in the COR to seek new opportunities in countries of origin

2. The search for new horizons back in the COO can be motivated by a sense of nostalgic pull, a fulfillment of social objectives or the opportunity for generating new wealth

3. The pro-internationalization start-up and innovative growth policies of, in particular, certain Asian economic powerhouses such as Korea lubricates the prospect of transnational ventures being created in destination and origin countries

4. In all cases the intersection between institutional structures and human agency in the 'dual habitus' is a key to understanding both the scope of and the variation in global entrepreneurship activity

One set of 'missing entrepreneurs' in the broader migrant category are refugees. They warrant particular attention not simply because of the coverage of their recent plight but also because of the various efforts being made to harness their skills and capabilities for early integration in society. Included in these efforts is a recognition of their trans-national potential.

Refugees and Global Entrepreneurship Prospects

While legal differentiations between migrants (economic) and refugees distinguish the two groups, the latter could be classified as potential migrant entrepreneurs with inter-national experience and capability.

Case 7.4

Refugee Entrepreneurship

European Union refugee statistics for 2021 was 2,858,922.00, a 6.95% increase from 2020. This compares with the statistics for 2020 which showed 2,673,102.00 refugees, a 3.15% increase from 2019. According to Phillippe Legrain, Founder of Open Political Economy Network, 'welcoming refugees is considered to be not only a humanitarian and legal obligation, but as an investment that can yield substantial economic dividends. Welcoming refugees goes beyond humanitarian and legal obligations. It should be seen as an economic investment that can generate substantial benefits to a host country. Many enterprising refugees create new businesses that produce wealth, provide employment for local people, make the economy more dynamic and adaptable by offering new goods and services and adaptable, and help promote inter-national trade and investment.

Refugees differ from migrants, and the difference can have an impact on the ability of the former to act as global entrepreneurs. At the legal level, refugees need work permission in a host country. They have insecure status of residential permission and limited access to home institutions. There are also institutional differences (e.g. unacknowledged documents). From a networking point of view, refugees lack local connections which can only be developed over time. Consequently, they also tend to be disconnected from diaspora networks and ethnic enclaves (Bizri, 2017; Heilbrunn et al., 2019; Wauters and Lambrecht, 2008).

The differences stated above raise two distinctive questions about the global entrepreneurial potential of refugees:

1. What barriers impede refugees from leveraging their entrepreneurial potentials?
2. Can public or private support services for refugees, such as business incubators, support enterprising refugees?

To answer these questions we need to obtain an understanding of the resources that refugees have at their disposal. Harima's 2022 study on refugees in Germany identified these resources, and Table 7.3 drawn from Harima's work provides a framework for identifying the resources at the disposal of refugees. These can be encapsulated in terms of two categories of input variables (the second a summary of the first) which contribute to three key sets of resources – human capital, transnational networks and cultural resources.

Table 7.3 The resources of refugees

First Order Categories: The Resources of Refugees	Second Order (Summary) Categories	Aggregate Themes or Concepts
Work experience at firms in COO	Market and business knowledge	Human capital
Work experience in social projects in COO		
Apprenticeship in COO		
A-Class graduation	Academic capabilities	
Higher education background		
Speak several languages	Linguistic proficiency	
Advanced level of German and English		
Family and friends in COO	Network in COO	Transnational network
Previous colleagues and business partners in COO		
Customers for previous business in COO		
Family and friends in COR	Network in COR	
Civil society in COR		
Business contacts from previous international experience	International networks and contacts	
Investors in other countries		

(Continued)

Table 7.3 (Continued)

First Order Categories: The Resources of Refugees	Second Order (Summary) Categories	Aggregate Themes or Concepts
Ethnic food and culture	Ethnic cultural resources	Cultural resources
Awareness and knowledge of COO social situations		
Intercultural experiences in global context and COR	Intercultural experiences in COR	
Had own companies in COO	Entrepreneurial background	Entrepreneurial resources
Involvement in family business in COO		
Success and failure experiences as entrepreneurs in COO		
Want to realize own dreams	Intention and motivation for enterprise	
Want to solve social problems		
Passion in what he/she is doing		
Identify opportunities in COO and COR		
Self-confidence in own entrepreneurial capabilities	Entrepreneurial traits and characteristics	
Perceiving entrepreneurship in normal career path		
Being a risk taker		
Resilience and optimism		

Source: adapted from Harima (2022)

Against that set of resources there are the critical impediments which can be identified in five different aggregated categories – foreignness, resource scarcity, insufficient skills, emotional disturbance and insufficient external support. Table 7.4 shows how major barriers (identified as 'first order' categories), subsequently summarized as conceptual labels (or 'second order' categories) for those barriers, are developed into the aggregate themes mentioned above.

Table 7.4 Understanding the barriers faced by refugees

First Order Categories Barriers to Enterprise	Second Order (Summary) Categories	Aggregate Themes/Concepts
Bureaucracy	Institutional differences	Foreignness
Legal constraints		
Lack of recognition of COO qualifications		
Tax systems		
Differences in gender roles	Cultural differences	
Different modes and methods of communication in Germany		
Difficulty in understanding German customers		
Work permit issues in Germany	Legal status in COR	
Lack of institutional legitimacy		

First Order Categories Barriers to Enterprise	Second Order (Summary) Categories	Aggregate Themes/Concepts
Use of German technical terms specific to industries	Language difficulties	
Learning German		
Perceived prejudice towards COOs	Prejudice	
Lack of financial capital	Lack of finance capital	Scarce resources
Poor access to financial institutions in both COO and COR		
Absence of financial skills		
Lack of work experience in COR	Lack of business knowledge in COR	
Absence of business and market knowledge in COR		
Premature decision to become entrepreneurs	Entrepreneurial insufficiency	
Lack of entrepreneurial capabilities		
Lack of social capital in COO	Lack of social capital	
Absence of links with diaspora network		
Difficulties in developing business plans	Absence of management skills	Skills insufficiency
Lack of industrial and/or accounting knowledge		
Limited experience of project management		
Lack of IT skills	Lack of IT and social media skills	
Lack of social media skills		
Traumatic experience in COO influencing life in COR	Refugee trauma	Emotional disturbance
Difficulty in adapting to changing circumstances		
Problems in starting a new life from scratch	Settlement difficulties and stress	
Lack of knowledge and access to support services and institutions in COR	Inadequacy of knowledge of support structures	Insufficient external support
Lack of horizontal cooperation between support institutions		
Distrust in COR support institutions		
Insufficient understanding of incubators	Inefficiency in support systems	
Lack of direction and support from incubators		

Source: adapted from Harima (2022)

Framing it along the lines described above allows for a direct comparison of refugees with other migrants. The key distinctive elements are the last four categories mentioned in Table 7.4, with these variables reflecting the fragility of the refugee environment militating against entrepreneurial activity. However, the combination of

(Continued)

human, entrepreneurial, cultural and networking capital provides them with resources that could be tapped into early in their attempts at settlement. It is to this end that the German government has set up specific incubation centers, which alongside business development training, work on the softer aspects of motivation enhancement, and alleviation of anxiety especially to better manage institutional differences. Early recognition and harnessing of their global potential could help to better prospects of both economic integration and economic gain (Harima, 2022).

What is missing is a good stock of relevant data. The absence of more systematic data collection undermines the capacity for studying trends, repeat patterns, generalizations and the development of policy instruments, in order to produce competitive economic and social advantageous policies and strategies.

Why Does Global Migrant Entrepreneurship Merit Attention?

Global migrant entrepreneurship merits attention for a variety of reasons. The migrant entrepreneurs and their actions embrace concepts of ethnicity, race, internationalization and globalization, to name a few, all of which have merited attention in different studies on entrepreneurship and international business. What they bring to bear on business development in general, and international entrepreneurial start-ups and growth in particular, can be regarded as distinctive. We highlight a few overarching issues.

Global Networks of Innovation and New Venture Creation

Research on the subject suggests that migrant entrepreneurship activity is an important source of innovation that contributes to economic development in both host and home countries. Apart from enabling a globalization from below in developed host markets (McEwan et al., 2005), they also make available, locally, a wide range of managerial, technical and international marketing skills through the ventures in different markets (Bresnahan et al., 2001; Parthasarathy and Aoyama, 2006). This results in multiple positive externalities for regions where migrant entrepreneurs operate, and in productive intermediary functions benefiting larger multinational corporations, which make use of their specialism. In a digitized world, there are further advantages to be obtained from this global phenomenon. Vorderwuelbecke (2012) argues that migrant entrepreneurs often maintain strong economic and social ties with their countries of origin by transfer of business and technological know-how, information exchange and remittances.

These global flows of different forms of capital supplement and enhance the capacity for international business, supply chain involvement for SMEs and organizational innovation.

Global Networks of Financial Resources

Direct investment in their home countries is a significant resource. According to Riddle et al. (2010) around 20% of FDI to India between 1991 and 2001 was from its diaspora. Remittance receipt is associated with a reduced likelihood of business operations. It has also been observed that households who already operate a business are more likely to receive remittances from abroad (Amuado-Dorantes and Pozo, 2004). In the case of Mexico, remittances have been found to be a significant source of capital for microenterprises (Lopez-Cordova and Olmedo, 2006). Typically, Mexican households and communities receiving remittances from the United States show that they invest increasingly in business ventures (Woodruff and Zenteno (2007)). SMEs in Mexico gained from being linked financially to migrant networks in the USA.

Fast growing firms established by migrant entrepreneurs are examples of how migrant networks can alleviate financial constraints.

Representation

The exchange and flow of people and capital reflects the established view both in the research literature and in policy circles that migrant communities can help to generate higher volumes of international trade between sending and receiving countries (Vaaler, 2011). It has been pointed out that migrant entrepreneurs may be disproportionately represented, in the United States, amongst high-growth, highly innovative enterprises (OECD, 2011; Saxenian, 2002; Wadhwa et al., 2009), including biotech firms (Stephan and Levin, 2001), high-impact companies (Hart and Acs, 2011) and public venture-backed US companies (Anderson and Platzer, 2006, p. 24). Firms with migrant co-owners and higher levels of migrant workers are more likely to be innovative, and their growth is marked by a decline in the share of new firms started by 'native' entrepreneurs.

Economic and social representation in communities in CORs facilitates economic integration of migrants, legitimacy for economic participation in their COOs, and a growing potential for economic ambassadorial roles for their CORs in the COOs.

New Models of International Firm Creation

We have already established that migrant entrepreneurs have the potential to advance new forms of international business, technology transfer and trade by virtue of their knowledge of and experience in two or more countries. Founded by migrants and continued by their descendants, some family businesses, for example, grow to become leading firms and expand beyond their countries of residence (Discua Cruz et al., 2013). These firms often connect back to their countries of origin from their very outset and involve a collective approach by members of one or several migrant family generations, a process supported by hard to imitate resources nurtured by global family networks from various parts of the world over time (Sirmon and Hitt, 2003). Entrepreneurs that first enter their home country to found a global venture are more likely to found ventures that are 'born global' (McDougall et al., 1994; Oviatt and McDougall, 2005). They offer a fertile opportunity to explore the nature of control and coordination outside the context of MNCs (Dabic et al., 2015; Massingham, 2010). Saxenian and Hsu (2001) suggest that the global linkages of these entrepreneurs may supersede conventional international business relationships, and the MNC may no longer be the preferred organizational vehicle for transferring knowledge or personnel across geographic boundaries. While first-generation migrants may be embedded in their home country based on strong family connections, second-generation migrants are likely to be more integrated with their host country (Bachkaniwala et al., 2001).

New business and social models for entrepreneurship development enhance the capacity for innovation across borders which can facilitate better trade, economic and strategic relationships between countries.

Policy Gains

From a policy perspective, global migrant entrepreneurship can be seen as making direct contributions, inter-alia, to international business creation and growth, international finance and investment, international R&D and innovation, international technology transfer and exchange, international collaboration across regional ecosystems, and international migration. These contributions warrant attention for policy purposes, especially given the rising challenge of migration at political, economic and social levels in OECD countries, alongside the need for embedding inclusive growth agendas nationally and globally.

Table 7.5 lists some of the policy areas where global migrant entrepreneurship can have a potentially positive impact and the potential direction of policy.

Table 7.5 Shaping policy to valorize the impact of global migrant entrepreneurship

Policy Impact Area	Policy Direction
International Business	Ease of trade flows enabled by the global presence of their ventures; cross-border flows of goods and services across multiple countries enabling networked-based policy development
International Finance and Investment	Investment-oriented remittances supplementing and enhancing FDI, and cross-border financial leverage (made easier because of the common pool of global migrant entrepreneurs)
International Entrepreneurship	Higher levels of leveraged international start-ups and early stage growth enabled by new firm formation across borders
International R&D and Innovation	Leveraged R&D activity among and by high-impact global migrant entrepreneurs together with leveraged, cross-border innovation (new products, new services, new processes, hybrid firms), thus supporting collaborative cross-border R&D programs of governments
International Technology Exchange	Promoting and supporting the flow of ideas, technologies and global solutions including complex data analytics
International Ecosystem-Based Regional Collaboration	Enabling regional-level collaboration of ecosystems as between Paris and Dakar, London and Mumbai, California and Herzliya, etc.

Part Four: Challenges and Questions

The different trajectories of global migrant entrepreneurship pose different challenges (Hoskisson et al., 2013; Kiss et al., 2012) for the entrepreneurs, policy makers and researchers.

For Entrepreneurs

Entrepreneurial actions of these entrepreneurs can be constrained by their home country endowments due to variations in home country institutional structures (Yeung, 2009). They also have to cope and adapt to, and form strategies shaped by, institutional constraints, political-economic structures and dominant organizational and cultural practices in both previous and currently adopted countries in which they operate (Portes, 1995; Saxenian, 2005). Rapid fluctuations in the economic and social environments of both COO and CORs makes this management difficult, especially when legislation can change quickly depending on shifts in political power in those countries, geopolitical ramifications and natural disasters. In other words they are susceptible to all the vagaries of international business activity. Familiarity with norms, customs and mores of both economies do not guarantee easier business entry for them and their businesses. The surge in entrepreneurial activity in China and India among returnees has materialized after significant efforts at liberalization of the economies in those countries in the latter part of the 20th and more directly in the 21st century.

For Researchers and Policy Makers

There is a need to understand how varied institutional contexts and differences, rather than merely personal attributes and innovative capacities, shape the way they operate. The literature on different aspects of global migrant entrepreneurs and their ethnic origin in developed markets describes the significance of these communities for the transfer of knowledge back home. However, not all of them form globalized ventures from the position of being based in the country of destination; they can also do so from being based in the home country (Drori et al., 2009).

An understanding of the social and human capital of these entrepreneurs in venture founding opens up the possibility for new insights regarding the behavior and contribution of migrant entrepreneurs (Yang et al., 2012). Yet, little is known about the organization and coordination of their global activities or performance of their ventures (Discua Cruz and Basco, 2018). It may be interesting to understand the way they apportion responsibilities and build social capital in a situation of commitment to two different work units in host, home and other countries (Collings et al., 2009; Harvey et al., 2005).

Little is known about networks and capabilities, locational dynamics, mechanisms and processes that migrant entrepreneurs employ in identifying and exploiting opportunities in multiple institutional contexts (Brinkerhoff, 2016; Tung, 2008). Apart from a few exceptions, international entrepreneurship research on individual founders of international new ventures, or strategies, or the performance of migrant entrepreneurs, is limited generally to studies of the host and home countries (Elo and Freiling, 2015).

Should our understanding of global migrant entrepreneurship be necessarily limited to migrants starting their ventures in CORs, first? There is a wealth of opportunities which have now opened up in countries such as China. In effect, those who avail themselves of these opportunities emerge as global entrepreneurs without the need for migrating physically. Their identity as global entrepreneurs could be regarded as intrinsic to their lives as entrepreneurs, as the words of one of the British entrepreneurs participating at an OECD workshop, who has opened successful firms in China and the USA, indicated: 'I am a British entrepreneur, I work in China every day, I sleep in Cambridge, England every night, What am I?' The possible argument that his actions represent traditional business internationalization may not stand up to scrutiny if and when entrepreneurs like him take advantage of all the digital tools of international venturing that are available today. It may be appropriate to raise such questions if only to enrich the debate about global migrant entrepreneurship and its significance.

Chapter Summary

Global migrant entrepreneurship is an increasingly growing phenomenon among migrant entrepreneurs who have secured an economic foothold in their CORs. In doing so they unleash prospects for policy development and new research which can corroborate or qualify what we know now. What appears to be evident is that migrant entrepreneurship today covers a range of policy issues from migration through to international business and trade and social policy. In circumstances in which the movement of people is a highly contentious arena for policy makers and citizens, there is an urgent need for objective data and information with which to make the case for the productive outcomes of migration and globalization.

The growing phenomenon of global migrant entrepreneurship appears to have escaped the radar of policy makers, technology developers and business strategy analysts. Its multi-faceted prognosis suggests a range of possibilities for new ways of developing and promoting global and entrepreneurial business, the financing of networks of transnational enterprise, and the development of key technologies (using blockchain technology for example) to support the evolving infrastructure for global entrepreneurship.

Of critical importance is the systematic collection of granular data with which to make informed judgments and decisions. The absence of robust data sets makes this a particularly important policy consideration. Action on this front is predicated upon the need for policy makers to understand the value added to the economy and society by the particular actions of the migrant community, and to investigate the implications across each strand of economic and social policy outlined above.

Review Questions

1. Why is the study of migration important for the understanding of global entrepreneurship?
2. How would you define migrant entrepreneurs and what are their unique credentials?
3. What are the different ways in which migrants contribute to the entrepreneurial development of their destination countries?
4. What are the economic, psychological and social barriers that migrants face when they engage in entrepreneurial endeavors?
5. How do refugees make an impact on entrepreneurial activity, globally?

References

Acosta, P. (2007) 'Entrepreneurship, labour market and international remittances: Evidence from El Salvador', in Ç. Özden, M. Schiff (eds.), *International Migration, Economic Development and Policy*. Washington, DC: World Bank and Palgrave Macmillan, pp. 141–159.

Acosta, P., Fajnzylber, P. and Lopez, J.H. (2007) *The Impact of Remittances on Poverty and Human Capital: Evidence from Latin American Household Surveys*, Vol. 4247. Washington, DC: World Bank Publications.

Adams Jr., R.H. (2006) 'Migration, remittances and development: The critical nexus in the Middle East and North Africa', *United Nations Expert Group Meeting on International Migration and Development in the Arab Region*, Beirut, May.

Adams Jr., R.H. and Page, J. (2005) 'Do international migration and remittances reduce poverty in developing countries?' *World Development*, 33(10): 1645–1669.

Amuado-Dorantes, C. and Pozo, S. (2004) 'Workers' remittances and the real exchange rate: A paradox of gifts', *World Development*, 32(8): 1407–1417.

Anderson, S. and Platzer, M. (2006) *American Made*. Washington, DC: National Venture Capital Association.

Bachkaniwala, D., Wright, M. and Ram, M. (2001) 'Succession in South Asian family businesses in the UK', *International Small Business Journal*, 19(4): 15–27.

Basu, A. (2011) 'From "break out" to "breakthrough": Successful market strategies of immigrant entrepreneurs in the UK', *International Journal of Entrepreneurship*, 15: 1.

Baycan-Levent, T. and Nijkamp, P. (2007) 'Ethnic entrepreneurship in European cities: A comparative study of Amsterdam', in Handbook of Research on Ethnic Minority Entrepreneurship: A Co-Evolutionary View on Resource Management, pp. 323–336. Cheltenham: Edward Elgar.

Beine, M., Docquier, F. and Rapoport, H. (2008) 'Brain drain and human capital formation in developing countries: Winners and losers', *The Economic Journal*, 118(528): 631–652.

Berg, S-H. and Hassink, R. (2014) Creative industries from an evolutionary perspective: A critical literature review. *Geography Compass*, 8(9): 653–664.

Berg, S.H. (2018) 'Local buzz, global pipelines and Hallyu: The case of the film and TV industry in South Korea', *Journal of Entrepreneurship and Innovation in Emerging Economies*, 4(1): 33–52.

Bizri, R.M. (2017) 'Refugee-entrepreneurship: A social capital perspective', *Entrepreneurship & Regional Development*, 29(9–10): 847–868.

Bourdieu, P. (1967) 'Systems of education and systems of thought', *International Social Science Journal*, 19(3): 338–358.

Bresnahan, T., Gambardella, A. and Saxenian, A. (2001) '"Old economy" inputs for "new economy" outcomes: Cluster formation in the new Silicon Valleys', *Industrial and Corporate Change*, 10(4): 835–860.

Brinkerhoff, J.M. (2016) 'Assimilation and heritage identity: Lessons from the Coptic diaspora', *Journal of International Migration and Integration*, 17(2): 467–485.

Brixy, U., Sternberg, R. and Vorderwülbecke, A. (2013) *Global Entrepreneurship Monitor 2012: Unternehmensgründungen durch Migranten* (No. 25/2013). Nuremburg: IAB-Kurzbericht.

Chen, W. and Tan, J. (2009) 'Understanding transnational entrepreneurship through a network lens: Theoretical and methodological considerations'. *Entrepreneurship Theory and Practice*, 33(5): 1079–1091.

CFAE (2017) *Entrepreneurship Releases New Study on the Immigrant Founders of Companies in the 2017 Fortune 500*. December 3, 2017. Washington, USA. https://startupsusa.org/press-releases/center-american-entrepreneurship-releases-new-study-immigrant-founders-companies-2017-fortune-500/

CFE (2014) *Migrants behind one in seven UK companies*. https://centreforentrepreneurs.org/releases/migrants-behind-one-in-seven-uk-companies/

CFE. Centre for American Entrepreneurship (2017) *Centre for American Entrepreneurship Releases New Study on the Immigrant Founders of Companies in the 2017 Fortune 500*. December 3, 2017. Washington. Centre for American Entrepreneurship.

Collings, D.G., Scullion, H. and Dowling, P.J. (2009) 'Global staffing: A review and thematic research agenda', *The International Journal of Human Resource Management*, 20(6): 1253–1272.

Dabic, M., González-Loureiro, M. and Harvey, M. (2015) 'Evolving research on expatriates: What is "known" after four decades (1970–2012)', *The International Journal of Human Resource Management*, 26(3): 316–337.

Deakins, D., Ishaq, M., Smallbone, D., Whittam, G. and Wyper, J. (2007) 'Ethnic minority businesses in Scotland and the role of social capital', *International Small Business Journal*, 25(3): 307–326.

Di Maria, C. and Stryszowski, P. (2009) 'Migration, human capital accumulation and economic development', *Journal of Development Economics*, 90(2): 306–313.

Discua Cruz, A. and Basco, R. (2018) 'Family perspective on entrepreneurship', in R.V. Turcan and N.M. Fraser (eds.), *The Palgrave Handbook of Multidisciplinary Perspectives on Entrepreneurship*. Cham: Palgrave Macmillan, pp. 147–175.

Discua Cruz, A., Howorth, C. and Hamilton, E. (2013) 'Intrafamily entrepreneurship: The formation and membership of family entrepreneurial teams', *Entrepreneurship Theory and Practice*, 37(1): 17–46.

Drori, I., Honig, B. and Wright, M. (2009) 'Transnational entrepreneurship: An emergent field of study', *Entrepreneurship Theory and Practice*, 33(5): 1001–1022.

Elo, M. and Freiling, J. (2015) 'Transnational entrepreneurship: An introduction to the volume', *American Journal of Entrepreneurship*, 8(2): 9.

Elo, M. and Volovelsky, E.K. (2017) 'Jewish diaspora entrepreneurs: The impact of religion on opportunity exploration and exploitation', *International Journal of Entrepreneurship and Small Business*, 31(2): 244–269.

Filatotchev, I., Liu, X., Buck, T. and Wright, M. (2009) 'The export orientation and export performance of high-technology SMEs in emerging markets: The effects of knowledge transfer by returnee entrepreneurs', *Journal of International Business Studies*, 40(6): 1005–1021.

Freiling, J., Harima, A. and Heilbrunn, S. (2019) *Refugee Entrepreneurship: A Case-Based Topography*. London: Macmillan.

GEM (2012) *The Global Entrepreneurship Monitor GEM 2011*. Report by Kelley, D.J., S. Singer and M. Herrington., 7: pp. 2–38.

GEM. (2017) *The Global Entrepreneurship Monitor Report*. London: Global Entrepreneurship Research Association, London Business School.

Gibson, J. and McKenzie, D. (2012) 'The economic consequences of "brain drain" of the best and brightest: Microeconomic evidence from five countries. *The Economic Journal*, 122(560): 339–375.

Gold, S.J. and Light, I. (2000) Ethnic economies and social policy. In *Research in Social Movements, Conflicts and Change*. Emerald Group Publishing Limited.

Harima, A. (2022) 'Theorizing disembedding and re-embedding: Resource mobilization in refugee entrepreneurship', *Entrepreneurship & Regional Development*, 34(3–4): 269–293.

Hart, D.M. and Acs, Z.J. (2011) 'High-tech immigrant entrepreneurship in the United States', *Economic Development Quarterly*, 25(2): 116–129.

Harvey, M., Novicevic, M.M. and Garrison, G. (2005) 'Global virtual teams: A human resource capital architecture', *The International Journal of Human Resource Management*, 16(9): 1583–1599.

Heilbrunn, S. (2019) 'Against all odds: Refugees bricoleuring in the void', *International Journal of Entrepreneurial Behavior & Research*, 25(5): 1045–1064.

Hoskisson, R.E., Wright, M., Filatotchev, I. and Peng, M.W. (2013) 'Emerging multinationals from mid-range economies: The influence of institutions and factor markets', *Journal of Management Studies*, 50(7): 1295–1321.

Kelley, D.J., Singer, S. and Herrington, M. (2012) The global entrepreneurship monitor. *2011 Global Report, GEM 2011*, 7, pp. 2–38.

Kiss, A.N., Danis, W.M. and Cavusgil, S.T. (2012) International entrepreneurship research in emerging economies: A critical review and research agenda. *Journal of Business Venturing*, 27(2): 266–290.

Kosten, D. (2018) *Immigrants as Economic Contributors: Immigrant Entrepreneurs.* Available at https://immigrationforum.org/article/immigrants-as-economic-contributors-immigrant-entrepreneurs/ (last accessed 27 September 2022).

Kotabe, M. and Kothari, T. (2016) 'Emerging market multinational companies' evolutionary paths to building a competitive advantage from emerging markets to developed countries', *Journal of World Business*, 51(5): 729–743.

Kothari, T., Kotabe, M. and Murphy, P. (2013) 'Rules of the game for emerging market multinational companies from China and India'. *Journal of International Management*, 19(3): 276–299.

Levie, J. and Hart, M. (2013) 'The contribution of migrants and ethnic minorities to entrepreneurship in the United Kingdom', in M. Minniti (ed.), *The Dynamics of Entrepreneurship*. Oxford: Oxford University Press.

Levitt, P. (1998) 'Social remittances: Migration driven local-level forms of cultural diffusion', *International Migration Review*, 32(4): 926–948.

Lin, X. and Tao, S. (2012) 'Transnational entrepreneurs: Characteristics, drivers, and success factors', *Journal of International Entrepreneurship*, 10(1): 50–69.

Liu, X., Lu, J., Filatotchev, I., Buck, T. and Wright, M. (2010) 'Returnee entrepreneurs, knowledge spillovers and innovation in high-tech firms in emerging economies', *Journal of International Business Studies*, 41(7): 1183–1197.

London First and PwC (2017) *Facing Facts: the impact of migrants on London, its workforce and economy.* London: London First and Price Waterhouse Coopers.

Lopez-Cordova, E. and Olmedo, A. (2006) 'International remittances and development: Existing evidence, policies and recommendations'. Occasional Paper, Inter-American Development Bank.

Macrotrends. (n.d.) *European Union Refugee Statistics 1990–2022.* Available at www.macrotrends.net/countries/EUU/european-union/refugee-statistics (last accessed 20 May 2022).

Massingham, P. (2010) 'Managing knowledge transfer between parent country nationals (Australia) and host country nationals (Asia)', *The International Journal of Human Resource Management*, 21(9): 1414–1435.

McDougall, P.P., Shane, S. and Oviatt, B.M. (1994) 'Explaining the formation of international new ventures: The limits of theories from international business research', *Journal of Business Venturing*, 9(6): 469–487.

McEwan, C., Pollard, J. and Henry, N. (2005) 'The "global" in the city economy: Multicultural economic development in Birmingham'. *International Journal of Urban and Regional Research*, 29(4): 916–933.

Mohapatra, S., Ratha, D. and Silwal, A. (2011) 'Outlook for remittance flows 2012–14: remittance flows to developing countries exceed $350 billion in 2011'. *Migration and Remittances Unit, Development Economics (DEC) and Poverty Reduction and Economic Management (PREM) Network*. Available at https://openknowledge.worldbank.org/bitstream/handle/10986/16182/NonAsciiFileName0.pdf;sequence=1 (last accessed 4 March 2022).

Motohashaia, K. and Yunb, X. (2007) 'China's innovation system reform and growing industry and science linkages', *Research Policy*, 36(8): 1251–1260.

Naudé, W., Siegel, M. and Marchand, K. (2015) *Migration, Entrepreneurship and Development: A Critical Review*. IZA Discussion Papers, No. 9284. Bonn: Institute for the Study of Labor (IZA).

OECD. (2011) *International Migration Outlook 2011*. Paris: OECD.

OECD. (2014) *International Migration Outlook 2014*. OECD Publishing, Paris, https://doi.org/10.1787/migr_outlook-2014-en

OECD. (2021) *International Migration Outlook 2021*. Paris: OECD.

Oviatt, B.M. and McDougall, P.P. (2005) 'Defining international entrepreneurship and modeling the speed of internationalization', *Entrepreneurship Theory and Practice*, 29(5): 537–553.

Parthasarathy, B. and Aoyama, Y. (2006) 'From software services to R&D services: Local entrepreneurship in the software industry in Bangalore, India', *Environment and Planning A*, 38(7): 1269–1285.

Portes, A. (ed.) (1995) *The Economic Sociology of Immigration: Essays on Networks, Ethnicity, and Entrepreneurship*. New York: Russell Sage Foundation.

Portes, A., Haller, W.J. and Guarnizo, L.E. (2002) 'Transnational entrepreneurs: An alternative form of immigrant economic adaptation', *American Sociological Review*, 67(2): 278–298.

Pruthi, S. (2014) 'Social ties and venture creation by returnee entrepreneurs', *International Business Review*, 23(6): 1139–1152.

Pruthi, S. and Wright, M. (2017) 'Social ties, social capital, and recruiting managers in transnational ventures', *Journal of East-West Business*, 23(2): 105–139.

Pruthi, S., Basu, A. and Wright, M. (2018) 'Ethnic ties, motivations, and home country entry strategy of transnational entrepreneurs', *Journal of International Entrepreneurship*, 16(2): 210–243.

Ram, M. and Jones, T. (2008) 'Ethnic-minority businesses in the UK: a review of research and policy developments', *Environment and Planning C: Government and Policy*, 26(2): 352–374.

Riddle, L. (2008) Diasporas: Exploring their development potential. *Journal of Microfinance/ESR Review*, 10(2): 6.

Riddle, L., Hrivnak, G.A. and Nielsen, T.M. (2010) 'Transnational diaspora entrepreneurship in emerging markets: Bridging institutional divides', *Journal of International Management*, 16(4): 398–411.

Saxenian, A. (1994) *Regional networks: Industrial adaptation in Silicon Valley and route 128*. Cambridge, Mass: Harvard University Press.

Saxenian, A. (2002) 'Silicon Valley's new immigrant high-growth entrepreneurs', *Economic Development Quarterly*, 16(1): 20–31.

Saxenian, A. (2005) 'From brain drain to brain circulation: Transnational communities and regional upgrading in India and China', *Studies in Comparative International Development*, 40(2): 35–61.

Saxenian, A. (2006) *International Mobility of Engineers and the Rise of Entrepreneurship in the Periphery* (No. 2006/142). Helsinki: WIDER Research Paper.

Saxenian, A. and Hsu, J.Y. (2001) 'The Silicon Valley–Hsinchu connection: Technical communities and industrial upgrading', *Industrial and Corporate Change*, 10(4): 893–920.

Sirmon, D.G. and Hitt, M.A. (2003) 'Managing resources: Linking unique resources, management, and wealth creation in family firms', *Entrepreneurship Theory and Practice*, 27(4): 339–358.

Stephan, P.E. and Levin, S.G. (2001) 'Exceptional contributions to US science by the foreign-born and foreign-educated', *Population Research and Policy Review*, 20(1): 59–79.

Sui, S., Morgan, H.M. and Baum, M. (2015) 'Internationalization of immigrant-owned SMEs: The role of language', *Journal of World Business*, 50(4): 804–814.

Tan, J. (2006) 'Growth of industry clusters and innovation: Lessons from Beijing Zhongguancun Science Park', *Journal of Business Venturing*, 21(6): 827–850.

Terjesen, S. and Elam, A. (2009) 'Transnational entrepreneurs' venture internationalization strategies: A practice theory approach', *Entrepreneurship Theory and Practice*, 33(5): 1093–1120.

Tung, R.L. (2008) 'The cross-cultural research imperative: The need to balance cross-national and intra-national diversity', *Journal of International Business Studies*, 39(1): 41–46.

UN. (2013) *The Number of International Migrants Worldwide Reaches 232 Million*. New York: Population Facts 2013/12, United Nations Department of Economic and Social Affairs, Population Division.

UN. (2016) Transforming our world: The 2030 agenda for sustainable development.

UNGA. (2017) *United Nations General Assembly 2017: Report of the Special Representative of the Secretary-General on Migration*. Available at www.un.org/en/development/desa/population/migration/events/coordination/15/documents/Report%20of%20SRSG%20on%20Migration%20-%20A.71.728_ADVANCE.pdf (last accessed 4 January 2022).

UNHCR. (2016) *No More Excuses: Provide Education to All Forcibly Displaced People*. UNHCR and Global Monitoring Report. Paris: UNESCO.

UNPF. (1995) International Conference on Population and Development (ICPD), Programme of Action. New York: United Nations Population Fund. (A/CONF171/13/Rev.1). Available at www.unfpa.org/webdav/site/global/shared/documents/publications/2004/icpd_eng.pdf (last accessed 20 March 2022).

Vaaler, P.M. (2011) 'Immigrant remittances and the venture investment environment of developing countries', *Journal of International Business Studies*, 42(9): 1121–1149.

Van Gelderen, M. (2007) 'Country of origin as a source of business opportunities', *International Journal of Entrepreneurship and Small Business*, 4(4): 419–430.

Vorderwuelbecke, A. (2012) *Global Entrepreneurship Monitor - 2012 Global Report, chapter Entrepreneurship and Migration*, pages 42–50. Global Entrepreneurship Consortium.

Wadhwa, V., Saxenian, A., Freeman, R.B. and Gereffi, G. (2009) *America's Loss Is the World's Gain: America's New Immigrant Entrepreneurs, Part 4*. Kansas City, MO: Ewing Marion Kauffman Foundation.

Wauters, B. and Lambrecht, J. (2008) 'Barriers to refugee entrepreneurship in Belgium: Towards an explanatory model', *Journal of Ethnic and Migration Studies*, 34(6): 895–915.

Westmore, B. (2015) 'International migration: The relationship with economic and policy factors in the home and destination country', *OECD Journal: Economic Studies*, 2015(1): 101–122.

Woodruff, C. and Zenteno, R. (2007) 'Migration networks and microenterprises in Mexico', *Journal of Development Economics*, 82(2): 509–528.

World Bank. (2013) *Global Financial Development Report 2014: Financial Inclusion*, Vol. 2. Washington, DC: World Bank Publications.

Yang, X., Ho, E.Y.H. and Chang, A. (2012) 'Integrating the resource-based view and transaction cost economics in immigrant business performance', *Asia Pacific Journal of Management*, 29(3): 753–772.

Yeung, H.W.C. (2009) 'Transnationalizing entrepreneurship: A critical agenda for economic geography', *Progress in Human Geography*, 33(2): 210–235.

Yokoyama, K. and Birchley, S.L. (2018) 'Mindset and social entrepreneurship: Japanese self-initiated expatriate entrepreneurs in Cambodia', *Journal of Entrepreneurship and Innovation in Emerging Economies*, 4(1): 68–88.

Zhongguancun Science Park (2017) *Profile. Nov. 15 2017* https://govt.chinadaily.com.cn/s/201711/15/WS5b77f3be498e855160e89aa1/zhongguancun-science-park.html

8
IMMIGRANT AND ETHNIC ENTREPRENEURS

LEE'S SANDWICHES

Lee's Sandwiches is one of the largest chains of banh mi sandwich shops in the United States and across the globe. The business has more than 60 locations worldwide, with plans of expansion to Taiwan.

Source: www.needpix.com/photo/244857

Chieu Le, the founder of Lee's Sandwiches and the eldest of nine children, was in his second year of law school before the fall of Saigon. In 1975, the Les were forced to flee the country when the Vietcong shut down the Law school, and took over the

(Continued)

family's property and sugar plant business. On a small fishing boat filled with 98 others, the family was among one of the first waves of people to escape Vietnam. Fortunately, their boat avoided disasters like pirate raids and storms that countless others faced.

Chieu Le and his wife arrived safely at a refugee camp in Malaysia where they stayed for 13 months. A month after their first son, Minh, was born, Chieu Le and his wife were on a plane to America. When Le, his parents, four brothers and four sisters finally made it to the US, they settled in San Jose, California. Le began taking night classes to learn English at San Jose High and bought food from a food truck that parked near the school.

Soon, Chieu Le stopped his English classes and began working for the Vietnamese owner of the food truck in order to support his younger brothers and sisters. Within a year, he had saved enough money to buy a truck of his own, and began a family operated food truck business in 1981. He and his brother, Henry Le, the second oldest of the siblings, started Lee Bros. Foodservices after noticing that other immigrant trucks had trouble stocking food and ice. The brothers decided to add an extra letter 'e' behind their name to help others pronounce it. Lee Bros. Foodservices would grow to become the largest industrial catering company in northern California.

In 1983, their parents, Le Van Ba and Nguyen Thi Hanh, asked to sell their traditional Vietnamese banh mi sandwiches on the weekend to students and residents near San Jose State University. The brothers opened their first Lee's Sandwiches location on Santa Clara Street and 6th Street.

Nearly two decades later, the business shifted from being a family business to a growing franchise that expanded out of San Jose. Its second shop opened in Westminster, California, in 2001. Chieu Le's eldest son, Minh, proposed the idea of adding euro-style sandwiches, fresh baked baguettes, desserts, drinks and the famous Vietnamese iced coffee or 'ca phe sua da' to the menu. Thanks to Minh, the family also adopted the principles of American fast-food companies and transformed Lee's into a rapidly growing franchise.

Henry Le is remembered as an entrepreneur who helped grow the family-owned Vietnamese sandwich empire into what it is today. Additionally, the Le family is also known for its philanthropy and charitable activities. Henry Le didn't solely focus on his sandwich shops throughout his life. As a devout Buddhist, he donated to Buddhist temples in the surrounding San Jose area. As an entrepreneur, he also had significant holdings in Biloxi, Mississippi. When Hurricane Katrina hit in 2005, causing damage to his holdings in the region, Henry Le was less concerned about what he had lost and more focused on what he could do to help as many people as possible. He helped fundraise more than $100,000 for the Asian-American community in the Biloxi area in response to the disaster, and provided them with pantry staples such as rice and soy sauce.

He is also remembered as a human rights advocate. That same year, he founded Renew Hope Project, a non-profit organization to assist non-English speaking victims in navigating a system that did not serve them in the Gulf Coast area. He also served as president of the Vietnamese Heritage Society, an organization focused on the preservation and promotion of Vietnamese culture and history, in 2005. Additionally, he co-founded the Vietnamese American National Gala, which is dedicated to promoting the achievements of Vietnamese Americans.

Sources: Constante (2016); Dang (2016)

Learning Outcomes

After studying this chapter, you should be ready to:

- **LO1**: Describe the context and forms of immigrant entrepreneurship
- **LO2**: Explain the distinctive features of ethnic entrepreneurs (EEs) as a class of immigrant entrepreneur
- **LO3**: Explain the paths to immigrant entrepreneurship
- **LO4**: Evaluate alternative theoretical perspectives for the emergence of immigrant enterprise
- **LO5**: Discuss the role of ethnic ties in the founding and growth of EEs' ventures
- **LO6**: Discuss the performance and impact of immigrant entrepreneurship

Introduction

Approximately 3% of the world's population lives in a country different from that of their birth (Kerr et al., 2016). The share of immigrants, as a percentage of population in developed countries, has been rising over the years. According to recent available data, immigrants in the US constitute 15% of the population, up from 12.9% in 2012, and 9.3% in 1996 (Kerr and Kerr, 2016; Simon, 2015; US Census Bureau, 2019).

The general rates of business ownership among the foreign-born are higher than among natives in many developed countries including the US, UK, Canada and Australia (Desiderio and Mestres-Domènech, 2011; Kerr and Kerr, 2016). Immigrants in the US and UK are nearly twice as likely to be entrepreneurs than their native-born counterparts (Hart et al., 2017). In 2013, immigrants in the US created an average of 520 businesses a month per 100,000 people (Simon, 2015). Between 1985 and 2000, migrants in Germany had a higher self-employment rate than non-migrants (Kontos, 2003).

The proportion of self-employed immigrants in economically advanced countries has also witnessed an increase over time (Kerr and Kerr, 2016). Constituting only around

13% of the US population, immigrant entrepreneurs (IEs) launched 28.5% of new businesses in 2014, up from 25.9% a year earlier and just 13.3% in 1996 (Simon, 2015).

There is wide agreement about the positive contribution of IEs to employment and economic growth (Masurel et al., 2002; Wong and Ng, 2002; Zhou, 2004). Immigrant-owned firms in the US generate over $775 billion in revenue, $125 billion in payroll, and $100 billion in income, and employ one out of every ten workers (Wang and Liu, 2015). Between 2000 and 2013, immigrants in 31 of 50 largest metros in the US accounted for all growth in Main Street businesses.

Not all IEs are the same. The population of IEs is heterogeneous. The number of high-skilled immigrant business owners has risen in recent years as more immigrants with advanced degrees have opted to start firms (Simon, 2015). Yet, many self-employed immigrants have a high-school education, or less, and their ventures may be less likely to result in high earnings.

In this chapter, we first present an overview of migration and immigrant communities engaged in entrepreneurship in developed host countries. We then outline the distinctive characteristics of ethnic entrepreneurs (EEs) as a type of IE, and evaluate alternative theoretical explanations for the emergence of immigrant enterprise. This is followed by a discussion of the role of ethnic ties in venture founding by EEs. Finally, we present evidence on the performance and impact of immigrant firms.

Immigrant Entrepreneurs: Context, Types and Paths

Immigrant entrepreneurs are foreign-born owners and operators of business enterprises in their host country or country of residence (Carbonell et al., 2014; Zhou, 2004). They are self-employed individuals hiring family labor as well as those employing outsiders. IEs are majority owner-founders of new ventures.

In the US, immigrants constitute 15% of the general US workforce, but they account for around a quarter of US entrepreneurs and inventors (Figure 8.1) (Kerr and Kerr, 2016). IEs in the US own 22.5% of all businesses; own one of three small, independent businesses.

This immigrant share of entrepreneurship has been increasing dramatically since the mid-1990s, when the immigrant share of founders was closer to 17% (Figure 8.1). This rise in immigrant contributions to entrepreneurship is sharper than the rise in immigrant share of all employees in new firms. In total, 35–40% of new firms have at least one IE connected to the firm's creation.

Immigrant founders launch firms that are smaller than native-founded firms. The average initial employment for firms founded by immigrants exclusively is 4.4 workers, compared to 7.0 workers for firms launched exclusively by natives. When both types of founders are present (i.e. 'mixed founder team'), the average is 16.9 workers.

Immigrant Enterpreneurship Trends in the U.S.

More immigrants are founding businesses and working in new firms.

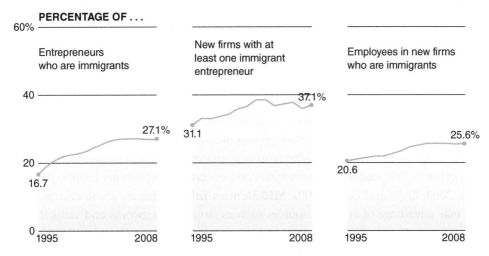

Figure 8.1 Immigrant entrepreneurship trends in the US

Source: Kerr and Kerr (2016)

Research on IEs typically spans immigrants in developed Western **host countries** from developing **home countries**. People from all corners of the world have been heading towards more developed economies to seek better entrepreneurial opportunities since the second half of the 20th century. The US and UK are the most common host countries for IEs, followed by Canada and Europe (in particular, Germany and Netherlands). Immigrant enterprise in the US has been historically prominent for far longer than in Europe (Light, 1984). Australia has a long history of immigrant entrepreneurship with many ethnic groups engaged in the small business sectors of the economy (Zolin and Schlosser, 2013).

The origins of IEs are variable from country to country. Immigrants in North America come from Asia, Africa and the Far and Middle East (Light, 1984; Light et al., 1993). The UK has witnessed immigrant flows from Canada and Europe, South Asia (Basu, 1998), Turkey (Miera, 2008), Korea and Somalia (Kariv et al., 2009; Teixeira et al., 2007).

Asia is the largest source of immigrants to developed countries in the West, with the US, Canada and UK being the three largest receiving countries for Asian migrants in the world, with the most (more than 11 million) immigrants from Asia (Fairlie et al., 2010). Some specific Asian groups, the Chinese and Indians, have large populations in all three countries. Migrants from the Philippines, Vietnam, Korea, Pakistan and Bangladesh are among the other immigrant groups in these countries.

Types of Immigrant Entrepreneurs

The terms 'immigrant entrepreneurs' and 'ethnic entrepreneurs' are often used interchangeably. The term **'ethnic entrepreneurs'** refers to those individuals whose group membership is tied to a common cultural heritage or origin and are known to out-group members as having such traits (Waldinger et al., 1990). EEs are united by a set of sociocultural connections and regular patterns of interaction among people sharing a common national background or migration experience. The enterprises founded by EEs are **ethnic enterprises** or **ethnic businesses**. EEs in Namibia, for example, are Zimbabwean, Zambian, Angolan, European and Nigerian nationals.

The literature on ethnic entrepreneurship analytically distinguishes between two main types of EEs; middleman minorities and enclave entrepreneurs (Bonacich, 1973; Light, 2004; Light and Gold, 2000). **Middleman minorities** are those entrepreneurs who take advantage of ethnic resources such as language, networks and skills to trade between their host and origin societies, while retaining their ethnic identity and non-assimilation stance as an integral part of their business strategy.

Enclave entrepreneurs are spatially clustered within so called **'ethnic enclaves'**, which are bound by a certain location and usually populated by co-ethnics. They focus on exploiting 'ethnic' markets in their host country. 'Ethnic' markets are specific types of opportunities available in the host country, in particular, demand for products and services that are linked to individuals' country or region of origin (Kloosterman, 2010; Waldinger et al., 1990).

Operating within ethnic enclaves, EEs cater to the co-ethnic community's demands that make it more attractive for them to exploit these market opportunities. Their competitive advantage is based on longer opening hours, easily available credit and sale of products in very small quantities (Ram et al., 2012).

EEs are typically found in the retail and service sectors, and rely on the local ethnic community for labor (Bonacich, 1973). Their clustering in ill-rewarded, labor-intensive sectors is a hallmark of ethnic businesses. EEs infuse new life into certain economic sectors; in particular those which require expertise not available in host nations. Common examples from the United States include Korean entrepreneurs for dry cleaners, Vietnamese entrepreneurs for nail care salons, Gujarati Indian entrepreneurs for the motel industry and Punjabi Indian entrepreneurs for convenience stores.

Typically, the term ethnic entrepreneurs is used to include both indigenous minority entrepreneurs belonging to the same ethnic community, and immigrant entrepreneurs. The earliest research on entrepreneurship among certain groups was by sociologists in the 1960s. This research highlighted 'ethnic' characteristics such as race, religion, language, shared history or origin shared by the group members. The terms **'minority entrepreneurs'** or **'ethnic minority entrepreneurs'** in the US and

UK, respectively, refer to entrepreneurs belonging to an ethnic community that shares one or more of these common characteristics.

According to the US Small Business Administration (SBA), 99.9% of small businesses with fewer than 500 employees in the United States are **minority-owned employer businesses** (SBA, 2019). These include businesses owned by Asians, Hispanics, Blacks, Asian-American, African-American, Native Americans, Alaska Natives and Hawaiian and Pacific Islanders.

Minority-owned businesses employed 8.7 million workers at a total annual payroll of $280 billion, amassing $1.3 trillion in total annual receipts in 2016. On average, a minority-owned firm had $1.2 million in annual sales and employed eight workers. Minority-owned businesses in the US are active in a wide range of industries. These include accommodation and food services (2.4 million employees), health care and social assistance (1.4 million employees), and retail trade (863,000 employees). The US states of Hawaii (61%), California (36%), Texas (30%) and New Mexico (27%) have the highest share of minority-owned businesses.

In 2016 there were 555,000 employer businesses with an Asian owner, the highest number of any minority category. The growth pattern of minority-owned businesses in the US suggests that from 2014 to 2016, the overall number of minority-owned employer businesses rose 11%, with Hispanic-owned businesses leading in 13% growth (Figure 8.2).

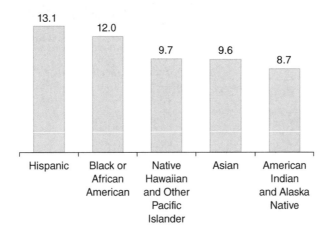

Figure 8.2 Percentage growth in number of employer businesses by owner, 2014–2016
Source: US Census Bureau (2019)

The Latino population in the US has grown at a steady pace and now accounts for 18% of the US population (Figure 8.3). The rate of founding of new Latino firms outpaces Latino population growth.

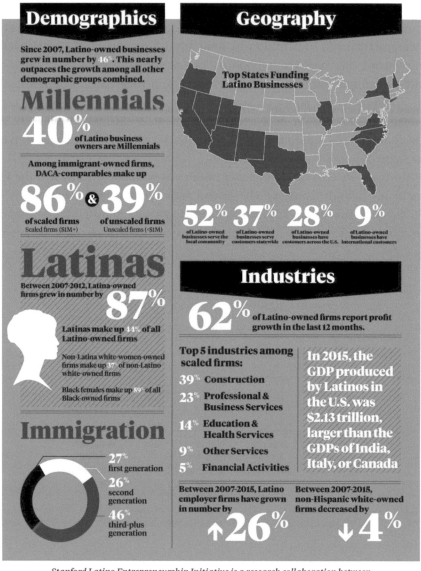

Figure 8.3 Inside the Latino Business Survey

Source: Dolan (2018)

In some variations of the classic EE, EEs may serve the needs of the wider community or even international markets, while relying on the host country's labor for producing their products or services (Basu, 2011). In a further variation, IEs may cater to domestic or international markets, while establishing operations in other countries, including their countries of origin (see the next two chapters for a discussion of transnational and returnee entrepreneurs). In this chapter, we focus on EEs. We adopt a broad definition of EEs to include both classic immigrant entrepreneurs and minority entrepreneurs.

Paths to Immigrant Entrepreneurship

Immigrants take a variety of paths into firm ownership in their host countries (Kerr and Kerr, 2016). Although varied in focus, host country immigration policies are an important factor impacting the inflow of migrants into developed host countries. Since the 1960s, US immigration policy, for instance, has strongly favored family reunification. In Canada, the focus has been on accepting immigrants possessing economic skills required in the country and encouraging immigration of individuals with high education levels. At one time restricted to citizens of the Commonwealth, the UK's immigration policies over the past four decades have shifted toward emphasizing family reunification and employment.

Home country factors also play a role in the likelihood and trajectory of business ownership in the host country. A large portion of refugee/asylum immigrants in the UK is attributed to political events in the former socialist states in Eastern Europe, and wars in the former Yugoslavia and in Turkey. Business ownership can be a self-help strategy for immigrants due to the circumstances surrounding their departure from the home country. Vietnamese refugees who came to California to flee the takeover of South Vietnam by the armed forces of the Communist leader Ho Chi Minh in the 1970s are a case in point. The refugees trained in providing manicure services to overcome their hardship upon deriving inspiration from Tippi Hedren, a famous Hollywood actress, who visited their refugee camp in Hope Village, California, to offer rehabilitation options. Many of the nail technicians in California in the present day are Vietnamese, and they are direct descendants of the 20 women who met with Hedren upon their arrival from Vietnam several decades ago.

Theoretical Explanations for Immigrant Enterprise

Much of the interest in ethnic businesses has tended to focus on the question of why some ethnic groups are more successful than others in starting up in their host country (Waldinger, 1995). Although rates of business ownership among migrant groups vary substantially by country, generally groups with relatively high rates in one country have relatively high rates in the other countries as well, which suggests a marked disparity in the rates of business ownership and self-employment across ethnic groups (Fairlie et al., 2010).

The Latino community in the US has exhibited remarkable growth in terms of new business founding. Latinos found a million net new businesses every five years. Since 2007, Latino-owned businesses in the US have grown by 46% in number. According to a new study from the Stanford Latino Entrepreneurship Initiative, this growth rate outpaces growth in business ownership rate of just about every other ethnic group combined (Orozco et al., 2019). Between 2007 and 2015, Latino employer firms grew in number by 26%, whereas non-Hispanic white-owned firms decreased by 4%.

LATINO BUSINESSES IN THE US

Latinos comprised 17.1% of the US population in 2013, up from 10.6% in 1996. The share of new Latino business owners in immigrant-founded new companies in the US climbed to 22.1% in 2014 from 20.4% in 2013, and just 10% in 1996.

According to data from the Census and the Bureau of Labor Statistics, Mexican self-employment is carrying this growth in Latino business creation. The increase in Latino start-ups likely reflects greater opportunities for Hispanics as entrepreneurs, as well as possible struggles to find salaried employment because of language barriers and other obstacles. In some cases, entrepreneurs may have started up after being laid off in the face of a slow labor market in the US.

Latino entrepreneurs often start 'small mom and pop shops' rather than the fast-growing firms that account for a disproportionate share of US job growth. Latino businesses are also more likely than non-Latino businesses to be family-owned and less likely to secure outside funding. Thus, many Latino entrepreneurs struggle to scale or rapidly expand their businesses.

Latino businesses are smaller than their non-Hispanic counterparts. More than 93% of self-employed Latino immigrants have fewer than ten employees, compared with 88.9% of self-employed non-Hispanic whites. Some even use independent contract workers instead of any full-time staff employees. At the same time, however, approximately 25% of Latino firms get most of their sales from non-Latino customers, a figure that is about the same for young and older firms.

Source: Simon (2015)

In both US and UK, the rate of business ownership among Blacks is relatively lower than those among some other groups. Some ethnic groups like 'business-minded' Koreans in the US, and Asians in the UK, have often been presented as role models for disadvantaged ethnic groups to aspire in their quest for socio-economic advancement.

The immigrant entrepreneurship literature advances various explanations, namely, cultural perspective, reaction model and class resources model for EEs' motivations for business entry in their host country. Although there is no overall consensus, each of these perspectives sheds light on the factors enabling ethnic enterprise.

Cultural Perspective

The **cultural perspective** originates in Bonacich's (1973) concept of middleman minorities. According to this perspective, migrant entrepreneurs regard themselves as sojourners or temporary migrants who remain outsiders in relation to the host society. They reside in self-segregated neighborhoods and rely on their own ethnic community for mutual support and resources. Ethnic and cultural factors such as common race, language and religion, shared history and origin, shared attitudes to education, and values such as hard work and thrift, create a sense of identity, and impact entrepreneurial entry motives within migrant communities.

Immigrant groups like the Jews, Armenians, Chinese and East African Asians, for example, exhibit similarities in entering entrepreneurship and occupying intermediate or middlemen positions in the host country, regardless of where they migrate. A particular 'entrepreneurial spirit' is noted among the South Asians (Dobbin, 1996). Cultural factors also explain the success of some immigrant groups in business as compared to others.

Family is an important cultural influence in EEs' motivation to start up. Family and friends are the most commonly associated type of social network for ethnic enterprises (Ram, 1994). Close family ties are a source of key values such as self-reliance and industriousness. Business family background provides initial advantages in the form of tacit knowledge and exposure to business practices prior to business entry. The commonality of language, culture and adherence to particular authority structures acts as a critical spur to the start and operation of ethnic enterprise.

BEVERLY HILLS MARKET AND DELI:
A FAMILY-OWNED ETHNIC ENTERPRISE

Source: www.needpix.com/photo/519290

(Continued)

Located in the Beverly Hills, California, the Beverly Hills Market and Deli has been the neighborhood's market for more than 30 years. Owned by Shawn Saeedian and his wife, Angela, the store also provides related services including home delivery and special orders for their regular customers, who comprise the large majority of their customers.

Saeedian first arrived in San Francisco as an immigrant from his home country, Iran. He relocated to LA from San Francisco in 1986, drawn by the area's substantial Persian-Jewish population. After first trying to run a large market, the family acquired their current business from a friend's son. Saeedian preferred to run a small business and enjoyed serving local customers in the neighborhood.

When the Saeedians took over the Beverly Hills Market, their main competition was Mrs. Gooch's, a health-food store across the street. They have been the dominant local player in the neighborhood since Whole Foods bought that business. The Saeedians remodeled the store to make it fresher and brighter. They also changed the product mix, with more prepared meals, a deli, good wines and craft beer. Produce accounts for the bulk of the sales, and the Saeedians invest a lot of effort to promote it. They feel they have a competitive advantage due to their relatively lower margins as compared to the big markets.

However, the Saeedians plan to expand their kitchen and deli, partly to satisfy an uptick in catering jobs. They realize that they do just regular sandwiches and they cannot compete with the filet mignon stores. Around 20% of their lunch business comes from other companies seeking an affordable alternative to the city's dining spots.

Moreover, Saeedian takes pride in the fact that his son is a Culinary Institute of America-trained chef, who prepares daily specials to add to their product offering. Three generations of the family have worked at the store over the last 30 years, with 14 of the stores current employees being family members.

Though the Saaedians don't compete with the upscale restaurants nearby, they do sometimes supply them. The local eateries seem to benefit from their long opening hours, staying open until 9 pm in the evenings, which allows them to fill any gaps in their supplies even at the last minute.

Source: Buchanan (2019)

The presence of strong family structures in many ethnic cultures also facilitates access to tangible resources such as cheap capital or labor. Ethnic groups with families in business, therefore, are more likely to choose self-employment and rely on family resources at start-up. In contrast, those that do not have a family tradition of business enter self-employment due to economic motivations, and grow their businesses after gaining a few years of self-employment experience (Basu, 1998).

The relative lack of cultural family resources is considered to be one of the reasons for the 'under-representation' of Blacks in self-employment as compared to the Asians in the UK, for example (Ram et al., 2012). Black families also have a different value base, which does not predispose them to entrepreneurship, unlike their Asian counterparts. Often, they do not have families in business.

The middleman minority model is subject to criticism as it is ahistorical. As starting up is a risky business, sojourners may not necessarily take up self-employment to keep liquid capital. Although important, family is not an unqualified resource for ethnic businesses. Dependence on family restricts access to a wide range of complementary resources otherwise available from non-family sources (Bagwell, 2007).

The role of family in ethnic businesses is often 'double-edged'. This means that while family can make a positive contribution to the business, it can also interfere in the workings of the business (Ram et al., 2012). In his ethnographic study of South Asian employers in the West Midland's clothing sector in the UK, Ram (1994) documents many instances where family members were retained in the business despite a lack of competence. Moreover, the use of informal working relationships and lack of formal contracts act as a smokescreen for unacceptable low pay and long hours, especially for low-skilled workers subject to discrimination in the mainstream labor market.

Middleman minorities may also employ non-co-ethnic labor. Some studies find that ethnic businesses either have no employees, or no family members as employees, and there is no significant difference between ethnic and non-ethnic businesses in their use of family labor (e.g. Zimmer and Aldrich, 1987). Many researchers have not compared their findings to non-ethnic business operations; they have overstated the uniquely 'ethnic' component in resource mobilization.

EEs' ability to tap into family labor in immigrant enterprises is also not critical. This is because all small businesses, not just those managed by family, work long hours. In fact, comparatively high levels of unemployment among the Black community induce self-employment in low-skill, highly competitive and poorly rewarded industrial sectors (Ram et al., 2012). Often, such 'no choice' businesses operate in the informal economy, and, thus, are not accounted for in official statistics, or remain marginal concerns with little prospect of real progress.

Moreover, the role of family varies among immigrant groups that are engaged in self-employment. The interaction between culture and entrepreneurship is stronger for some ethnic groups than others (Light and Gold, 2000). Some ethnic groups like Blacks do not have access to strong family resources because of their pattern of residential settlement (Ram et al., 2012). Unlike Asian communities, Black communities in the UK, for instance, are more dispersed.

More recently, a study of first-generation immigrant entrepreneurs in Norway suggests that their self-employment rates are positively correlated with cultural characteristics like low power distance in the home country, as well as average educational attainment in the home country (Vinogradov and Kolvereid, 2007).

Reaction Model

Although an important influence on the propensity to start up, family cannot be totally separated from the part played by an unfavorable opportunity structure in the wider labor market. According to the reaction model, self-employment is a reaction to **discrimination in the labor market in the host country** (Ram, 1994; Ram et al., 2003). Immigrants often face discrimination in the labor market, and hence potential unemployment in the host country.

Often, contracting job markets in host countries exacerbate this problem. In such circumstances, the decision to establish small businesses is a 'damage limitation' exercise to avoid unemployment. Self-employment offers immigrants the opportunity to rebuild their lives and regain the social status they previously experienced in their home country. By creating their own working environments, they are able to distance themselves from a racist environment.

Thus, the reaction model emphasizes 'push factors' as a motivation for the emergence of ethnic enterprise. This is in contrast with the cultural perspective, according to which ethnic groups are pulled into entrepreneurship by self-selected goals of financial gains and independence.

The reaction model is also subject to criticism. Not all immigrants engage in entrepreneurship due to push factors. It is important to examine the background career histories of individuals on a case-by-case basis to grasp the real dynamics about their motivations to transition from paid to self-employment. Evidence from the UK suggests that Black entrepreneurs have in common with the white owners of small businesses largely positive motivations for entrepreneurship (Ram and Deakins, 1996). Push factors are also less important for some ethnic communities than others due to the presence of pull factors. Indians in the UK, for example, are more highly educated than other Asian communities (Ram et al., 2012). Thus, they are less likely to be pushed into self-employment.

Class Resources

According to the class resources explanation for ethnic enterprise, EEs are more likely to venture into business due to greater access to **opportunities**, and **tangible and intangible resources** to exploit those opportunities, available to them by virtue of their membership in ethnic communities. Many of the values and behaviors that are presented as products of a unique culture related to specific ethnic communities are in fact attributed to a small business class culture (Ram and Jones, 2008).

Light (1984) distinguished between ethnic and class resources to separate purely ethnic from the generic process of resource mobilization. Whereas ethnic resources refer to cultural endowments, **class resources** include entrepreneurs' **financial** and **human capital**. Class resources may refer to personal resources such as education, knowledge, skills and work experience in the home or host countries, fluency in the host country's language, and availability of personal savings at start-up (Min and Bozorgmehr, 2000).

Ethnicity presents unique business opportunities such as demand for ethnic goods and labor-intensive services, or the existence of neglected markets in industries facing unstable market conditions (Waldinger et al., 1990). EEs' knowledge of the needs of their ethnic community provides them with a unique starting niche (Ram, 1994). Moreover, access to tangible and intangible resources including relatively cheap capital and labor derived from ethnic networks, education and their own or their family's business experience enables the exploitation of those opportunities. South Asians in the UK, for example, have a broader socio-economic profile, and therefore greater access to class resources.

Education provides entrepreneurs with a wider range of resources. Educational qualifications provide easy access to informal sources of information. Well-educated migrants (e.g. Asians in the UK) invest their own capital in their businesses at start-up (Fairlie and Woodruff, 2008; Kerr and Kerr, 2016). Prior experience influences the type of businesses EEs choose. In some cases, human capital even substitutes for the lack of social capital (Davidsson and Honig, 2003). Entrepreneurs with demonstrable business and managerial skills have a minimal reliance on social capital in establishing their firms.

The class resources model seems to explain disparities in the rates of business ownership across ethnic groups. Racist consumer behavior and negative stereotyping of Blacks by banks in the UK, for example, has impinged on their capacity to mobilize the necessary financial resources for business (Ram et al., 2012). Comparatively low rates of home ownership among Blacks in the UK also constrain their ability to offer collateral for start-up funding.

According to a recent 500 StartUps poll in the US, out of 250 start-ups and 500 founders, 80 were Asian, 60 were female, 15 were Hispanic and only 9 were Black (see Box below). Early grassroots education, financial support for higher education, engagement in competitions and accelerators can help to pull some of these groups into entrepreneurship. In fact, for non-entrepreneurial families of first- or even second-generation graduates in the US, finding the investments, support and partnerships to engage in entrepreneurship seems to be the biggest challenge, regardless of color or nationality.

EXPLAINING BLACK MILLENNIALS' ENTRY INTO ENTREPRENEURSHIP

Entrepreneurship provides an alternative route to earning a livelihood for those less interested to pursue the traditional job market. For Blacks in the US, however, entrepreneurship does not seem to have the same appeal as for the white population: 60% of all American entrepreneurs are white males. Even in the cohorts of accelerators that help high-potential entrepreneurs to rapidly develop their businesses, Blacks are either in the minority, or sometimes not represented at all. A voluntary poll of participants in

(Continued)

a cohort of 500 Start-Ups, a well-known accelerator program in the US that tracks participant ethnicity and gender, for example, revealed that out of 250 start-ups and 500 founders, 80 were Asian, 60 were female, 15 were Hispanic and only nine were Black.

There are several reasons for this disparity. The majority of the black community takes the government job route instead of starting their own ventures. Few are privileged to attend the country's top universities that foster a culture of entrepreneurship among their students, provide the base knowledge and impart skills to successfully run ventures. Such knowledge and resources can significantly impact individuals' ability to launch their own ventures.

The evidence also shows that having an entrepreneur for a parent increases the probability that a child will become an entrepreneur by 60%. Entrepreneurial parents are better equipped to provide financial, human and social capital resources to support their children's entrepreneurial aspirations. They are a key source of inspiration. Often, they are role models for their offspring. They offer valuable and practical advice, and better understand their children's decision to follow in their footsteps. Perhaps most importantly, they are in a position to introduce their children to the right networks. The presence of few young Black entrepreneurs seems to suggest that even fewer of their parents have taken that route.

At the same time, however, entrepreneurship is a risky option for all, not just for Blacks. Finding the necessary support resources is the biggest challenge for all entrepreneurs, regardless of color or nationality. Non-entrepreneurial families of first- or even second-generation graduates make a big commitment to investing in a college fund. Expensive student loans make it difficult to select the entrepreneurial space over the relatively safer job option. Financial support in higher education, early grassroots education and access to competitions and accelerators can be the way to support potential entrepreneurs from less stable backgrounds who are at a disadvantage.

Ivy League schools in the US, for instance, are switching to free and highly reduced fees for household family incomes below $125,000 in some cases. Reducing personal expenses is key for young entrepreneurs, and institutions that offer these packages directly support the entrepreneurial spirit of their student body.

A focus on networking and outreach in elementary education could train students to seek out the resources they need to implement their ideas early in their lives. Business plan competitions typically offer cash prizes to their participants. More important, they enable participants to connect with judges and industry experts who can provide advice and guidance to stimulate business ideas and build confidence.

Similarly, accelerators not only give young entrepreneurs the financial backing, but also the all-important network they need to branch out, meet investors, and make a real impact in the market and in their communities.

Source: Dennis (2015)

Questions

1. According to the article, why are so many Black millennials missing out on entrepreneurship?
2. What can be done to solve the problem?

Accordingly, policy efforts in the US have been devoted to improving ethnic and minority entrepreneurs' access to tangible and intangible resources. The Small Business Administration (SBA) and Minority Business Roundtable (MBRT) alliance, for example, is intended to strengthen and expand small business development for minority entrepreneurs by providing access to lending and federal contracts.

In 2014, the SBA approved 15,620 minority owned business loans totaling $6.5 billion. In the same year, the number of SBA loans to African Americans grew by roughly 36% from the previous year and 14% for Hispanics and women. Minority-owned businesses continue to account for about 28% of the agency's overall lending and 12.9% of its microloans.

Mixed Embeddedness Perspective

According to the **mixed embeddedness** perspective, the interaction between immigrant entrepreneurs' ethnic resources and the wider **political and social context** in which they are embedded crucially shapes business outcomes (Kloosterman and Rath, 2001, 2003; Kloosterman et al., 1999). Immigrant entrepreneurs' use of ethnic ties depends on the opportunities (or challenges) they face, besides their ethnic group characteristics or historical circumstances (Waldinger et al., 1990).

The utilization of EEs' social networks must, therefore, be set against the broader institutional context in which they operate. EEs enter some sectors and not others due to the fact that government regulation limits the sectors in which many new immigrants may be legally allowed to trade. Social networks often represent a means of negotiating racism rather than a positive strategic choice on the part of small firm owners.

Ethnic ties also lower the transaction costs arising from the difficulties in securing finance or information from formal, mainstream sources like banks. At other times, barriers to obtaining credit may far outweigh the advantages derived from ethnic social capital (Ram and Jones, 2008). Therefore, the external regulatory and institutional environment, including the host country labor market, aids or inhibits immigrant entrepreneurship (Aldrich and Waldinger, 1990; Jones et al., 2014).

The concept of 'mixed' embeddedness implies that immigrant businesses are embedded in multiple spheres, not merely in their ethnic sphere. They are culturally and socially embedded in their ethnic group; in addition, they are embedded in the broader institutional environment in their host economy (Kloosterman and Rath, 2001; Kloosterman, 2010). According to the mixed embeddedness perspective, IEs are embedded in three spheres: microsphere, mesosphere and macrosphere. The **microsphere** refers to the entrepreneurs' ethnic group. It is limited in scope and may constrain immigrant entrepreneurs' growth aspirations, since it can support only a small number of firms in the same industry.

The **mesosphere**, also termed 'opportunity structure', refers to the opportunity structure of immigrants, or competition from other large and small firms, as well as the long-term growth prospects of the market. Opportunities for IEs may be created by established firms leaving a neighborhood or sector because of stiff price competition and unattractive market prospects, or in the case of skilled immigrants, by the broader market allowing them to start innovative businesses.

Finally, **macrosphere** refers to the broader political-legal environment that affects the ability of IEs to operate in the host country. Overall, the mixed embeddedness framework offers a more comprehensive theoretical framework to explain the emergence of immigrant enterprise.

Role of Ethnic Ties in Venture Creation and Growth

EEs actively use their ethnic ties to access start-up finance, personnel, suppliers and markets (Aldrich and Waldinger, 1990; Bagwell, 2007; Waldinger et al., 1990). Ethnic ties substitute for the lack of individual or firm-specific capabilities, and help to deal with fierce competition and limited growth prospects facing ethnic enterprises.

Access to Finance

Some studies find high awareness of formal funding sources in both ethnic and non-ethnic firms (Hussain and Matlay, 2007). Ethnic businesses are not disadvantaged in relation to the volume of start-up finance borrowed from banks and other financial institutions. Moreover, the importance of bank credit, bank finance and venture capital (VC) increases over time.

Other studies find low awareness of formal sources of finance amongst small ethnic businesses (Deakins and Hussain, 1993). Compared to non-ethnic founders, ethnic founders prefer less intrusive and more user-friendly financing options including family and close associates that allow them to remain in control of their businesses. Immigrant founders rely on a single funding source, use bootstrapping as their preferred financing choice, seek funds from small community banks and tend to avoid equity sources of financing as compared to native born entrepreneurs (Moghaddam et al., 2016). Most Latino entrepreneurs in the US, for instance, fund their businesses by tapping friends and family, finding angel investors and venture capital, and using their credit cards (Orozco et al., 2019).

In addition, many Latino business owners feel unqualified to apply for a bank loan at a national bank, and hence some may not be submitting requests for a loan. Limited access to capital hampers the expansion of most Latino-owned businesses in the US. Most Latino-owned businesses remain small, with 98% reporting less than $1 million in annual revenue.

Access to Personnel

EEs use family ties for staffing and gaining access to a cheap pool of labor and trusted information. Typically, ethnic enterprises are partnerships of husbands and wives, fathers and sons or cousins who dominate key positions. Some studies find heavy utilization of family and ethnic ties as a replacement for formal hiring processes in ethnic enterprises (Yang et al., 2011). EEs are more likely to perceive kin as more trustworthy than non-kin, and more frequently assist them than non-kin.

Where families are geographically dispersed, international family links from abroad influence business ideas (Bagwell, 2007). They also positively contribute to start-up operation, and business development and expansion. Vietnamese nail shops in the UK, for instance, sponsor family members from Vietnam to work for them in the UK. Trust between family members is also important for creating effective relationships with suppliers, customers and other businesses.

Access to International Markets

Studies have examined the role of family in the internationalization of immigrant firms (Crick and Chaudhry, 2013; Mustafa and Chen, 2010). Family ties provide both direct and indirect support in the form of access to resources such as finance, office space or even time, both for entry and subsequent development of immigrant businesses in foreign markets. Family members are also more likely to be involved in entry mode and market development decisions. Immigrant founders using family ties to internationalize to their home country are motivated to internationalize early.

Ethnic networks also enable internationalization of EEs' firms to their home country (Chung and Tung, 2013; Filatotchev et al., 2007; Zaheer et al., 2009). Ethnic networks enable EEs to engage in high resource commitments at home at the outset (Saxenian, 2002, 2005). Ethnic ties are particularly useful for conducting business in home countries with volatile political and legal environments where entrepreneurs' social ties can even substitute for the lack of institutionalized law. Ethnic ties have also enabled EEs to import into the host country from their home country. The Zionist ties of British Jews with Israel, for example, have been significant in explaining the flow of Israeli exports into Britain (Ibeh, 2012).

At the same time, however, the use of family ties has some limitations. The lack of diversity of the family network limits access to information and advice, which can inhibit innovation. Fear of displacement of incumbent family members in key managerial positions may prevent professionalization of the business.

For Nat Puri, an immigrant entrepreneur and founder of Purico Limited, a diversified, paper and plastics multinational enterprise headquartered in Nottingham, UK, poor work ethic of his extended family jeopardized his attempts to grow the business in India. Nat first ventured into India in the early 90s to set up a subsidiary after buying another British company. He injected more than £400,000 into the venture; however, his attempts to grow the business were unsuccessful as members of the extended family hired in senior management positions in India did not take their responsibilities seriously. Typically, they were interested in recruiting their own relatives for the company. The culture of favoritism and the tendency to seek favors by recruiting other members of the family resulted in the business serving the family, which was inimical to growth:

> I find they have got their own agenda. The first thing they want is, I've got this nephew, I've got this son, I've got a brother, you know can he have a job? Totally wrong… there are two things that happen in India, if you don't employ relations you're a bad person, if you employ relations it is a disaster… If I was working for somebody in the family, I'll say I haven't got a headache, it doesn't matter, I'm committed I'm going to go. (Nat Puri, Founder, Purico, UK)

Performance and Impact of Immigrant Enterprise
Performance of EEs' Firms

Evidence related to the performance of EEs' firms is mixed. There is no settled view on whether it is advantageous for EEs to work within or without the ethnic economy. Some studies find that IEs' utilization of social networks is a major influence on their performance (Crick and Chaudhry, 2013). Ethnic entrepreneurial firms more involved with their ethnic community have a better rate of return on sales. According to Chaganti et al. (2008), internet firms with ethnic immigrants on their founding team undertake more aggressive growth strategies compared to ventures with non-ethnic, non-immigrants.

Other evidence suggests that ethnic entrepreneurial firms that are less involved with their own ethnic community are larger in terms of number of employees and report slightly better cash flow (Chaganti and Greene, 2002). EEs must tap into customers from outside their ethnic community in order to grow (Ram and Smallbone, 2002). Some researchers conclude that EEs' social capital enables entrepreneurial entry, but human capital facilitates economic success (Valdez, 2008).

Performance also varies among ethnic groups (Masurel et al., 2002). Some ethnic groups have higher rates of business formation than others (Aldrich and Waldinger, 1990). The length of stay in the host country, or EEs' adjustment to the host country labor market, also plays an important role in business performance. More recently, Ndofor and Priem (2011) suggest that the particular alignment of EEs' entrepreneurial (human and social) capital with choice of strategy (ethnic enclave vs. dominant market) shapes the performance of their ventures.

The stage at which immigrants enter the host country also impacts the performance of their firms. Kerr and Kerr (2016) find that immigrants coming to the US as children are more likely to start larger firms than immigrants arriving as adults. Moreover, firms created by immigrants who have grown up in the US are generally associated with better outcomes, in terms of lower closure rates and higher representation among larger firms.

Impact of EEs' Firms

There is general agreement among researchers and policy makers about both positive economic and social impact of immigrant entrepreneurship.

Entrepreneurship in ethnic enclaves creates job opportunities and positive economic returns for EEs who would otherwise be excluded from mainstream labor markets (Kerr and Kerr, 2016; Zhou, 2004; Zhou and Logan, 1989). In doing so, it provides economic resources for EEs' families and children, and empowers group members with economic independence. Both owners and workers in the ethnic economy earn more than if they are unemployed.

Ethnic entrepreneurship also impacts employment outside of the ethnic enclave (Light, 2004; Light et al., 1994). Ethnic enclaves generate spillover effects in terms of new business opportunities for both natives and non-natives (Kerr and Kerr, 2016). Close contact between owners and workers in ethnic enclaves, as well as in spatially dispersed communities, enables potential entrepreneurs to eventually start out on their own.

The economic impact of EEs extends beyond their host country. International EEs have a major share of small businesses in advanced economies. EEs' co-ethnic networks have a positive impact on bilateral trade (Rauch and Trindade, 2002). Co-ethnic networks help to overcome informal barriers to international trade.

Ethnic entrepreneurship contributes to regional and community development. From 2010 to 2013, immigrants accounted for all of the net growth in owners of 'Main Street' businesses such as restaurants, retailers, dry-cleaning services and beauty salons in 31 of the 50 largest US metro areas (Simon, 2015). As they come from different backgrounds, immigrants are able to identify gaps in the market for products or services that benefit their local communities.

Ethnic entrepreneurship also opens up a viable path to social mobility for both individual group members and their group as a whole. Ethnic groups with high rates of self-employment show higher than average rates of educational and inter-generational mobility, and their descendants enjoy individual and family incomes higher than national averages.

Bonds of solidarity and presence of co-ethnic entrepreneurs in small ethnic firms encourage informal business apprenticeships, which have social effects beyond pure economic gain. Ethnic entrepreneurship fosters an entrepreneurial spirit and sets up role models among co-ethnics. It also trains prospective entrepreneurs (Zhou, 2004). Often, immigrant workers are offered training opportunities when they assume supervisory positions at small businesses.

Chapter Summary

LO1: **Immigrant entrepreneurs (IEs)** are foreign-born owners and operators of business enterprises in their host country or country of residence. Research on IEs typically spans immigrants in developed Western **host countries** from developing **home countries**. The US and UK are the most common host countries for IEs; Asia is the largest source of immigrants to developed countries in the West.

LO2: **Ethnic or enclave entrepreneurs (EEs)** are spatially clustered within so called '**ethnic enclaves**', which are bound by a certain location and usually populated by co-ethnics. They focus on exploiting 'ethnic' markets, in particular, demand for products and services in the host country that are linked to their country or region of origin. EEs are typically found in the retail and service sectors, and rely on the local ethnic community for labor. Their competitive advantage is based on longer opening hours, easily available credit and sale of products in very small quantities. Typically, the term **EEs** is used to include both indigenous minority entrepreneurs belonging to the same ethnic community and immigrant entrepreneurs.

LO3: Immigrants take a variety of **paths** into firm ownership in their host countries. Host country immigration policies are an important factor impacting the inflow of migrants into developed host countries. Pre-migration self-employment in home countries increases the probability of self-employment by skilled immigrants in the host country, and boosts their self-employment earnings. In other cases, business ownership can be a self-help strategy for immigrants due to the circumstances surrounding their departure from the home country.

LO4: The immigrant entrepreneurship literature advances various explanations for EEs' motivations for business entry in their host country. According to the **cultural perspective**, migrant entrepreneurs regard themselves as sojourners or temporary migrants who remain outsiders in relation to the host society. The middleman minority model is subject to criticism as it is ahistorical. Also, family is not an unqualified resource for ethnic businesses. According to the **reaction model**, self-employment is a reaction to discrimination in the labor market in the host country. However, not all immigrants engage in entrepreneurship due to push factors. According to the **class resources** explanation for ethnic enterprise, EEs are more likely to venture into business due to greater access to opportunities, and tangible and intangible (**financial and human capital**) resources to exploit those opportunities, available to them by virtue of their membership in ethnic communities. According to the **mixed embeddedness** perspective, immigrant businesses are embedded in multiple spheres besides their ethnic sphere, and the interaction between immigrant entrepreneurs' ethnic resources and the wider **political and social context** in which they are embedded crucially shapes business outcomes. Overall, the mixed embeddedness framework offers a more comprehensive theoretical framework to explain the emergence of immigrant enterprise.

LO5: EEs actively use their **ethnic ties**, including family ties, to access start-up finance, personnel, suppliers and markets. Ethnic ties substitute for the lack of individual or firm-specific capabilities, and help to deal with fierce competition and limited growth prospects facing ethnic enterprises. Family ties also provide both direct and indirect support in the form of access to resources both for entry and subsequent development of immigrant businesses in foreign markets, including EEs' home country. At the same time, the lack of diversity of the family network limits access to information and advice, which can inhibit innovation. In other cases, ethnic businesses might become too large to be managed by family alone, necessitating hiring from outside of the family. Offspring might also not qualify to join the business due to differing interests or expertise lying outside of the family business.

LO6: There is no settled view on whether it is advantageous for EEs to work within or without the ethnic economy. Performance also varies among ethnic groups. The length of stay in the host country, EEs' adjustment to the host country labor market, or even stage of entry into the host country play an important role in business performance. However, there is general agreement among researchers and policy makers about the positive economic and social impact of EEs. EEs provide employment to individuals, improving economic prospects both inside and outside of ethnic enclaves. International EEs also have a major share of small businesses in advanced economies. By virtue of their ability to spot opportunities and create new businesses, EEs also lead to social rejuvenation of local communities, opening up a viable path to social mobility for communities as a whole, beyond pure economic gain.

Review Questions

1. Explain what you understand by the term immigrant entrepreneurs.
2. Explain what you understand by the term ethnic entrepreneurs. What are the distinctive features of EEs as a class of immigrant entrepreneur?
3. According to the chapter, family is one of the hallmarks of ethnic businesses. What are the advantages of the family in ethnic businesses? Are there any disadvantages? Discuss the role of family in the founding and growth of ethnic businesses.
4. According to the reaction model, immigrant enterprise is a response to the disadvantages that immigrants face in the host country labor market. To what extent do you agree/disagree with this statement? Discuss.
5. Explain what you understand by the term 'class resources'. How does the economic opportunity model explain immigrant enterprise? Discuss.
6. Several theoretical models for the emergence of ethnic entrepreneurship are advanced in the chapter. In your view, which of these models best explains ethnic enterprise? Why? Give reasons to support your answer.
7. How do immigrant entrepreneurs contribute to their host country? Explain in relation to a) performance and b) impact of immigrant enterprise.

Sam Sangha: A Story of Success against the Odds

Asiana Foods (AF) is a wholesale and retail food business specializing in oriental foods in the United Kingdom (UK). Founded by Sam Sangha in 2003, the business model is built on importing foodstuffs from China, Vietnam, Taiwan, Korea, Singapore, Hong Kong, Malaysia and the Philippines, and supplying to oriental supermarkets, restaurants and university campus shops in the UK. By 2012, AF owned five retail stores in the cities of Peterborough, Leicester and Nottingham. At the time of writing this case, Asiana had introduced its own brand of oriental food products. Sam had also diversified into real estate, owning Asiana Development, a property development arm for buying and renting commercial property.

Background and Early Years

Sam was born in Surat in Gujarat, India, where his father, originally from Punjab, was briefly stationed as a transport contractor. Sam came to England with his parents, two brothers and a sister in 1966. He was ten years old at the time. It was the year England had won the World Cup in football and India had won the Miss World title. The family's move to England was led by Sam's uncle who first left for England in 1958. As part of the Sikh regiment in the British army in India, Sam's grandfather received an invitation to visit England in 1958, which he passed on to his son.

Sam's uncle arrived in Wolverhampton (also known as the Black Country) in the West Midlands where he took up a job at a foundry. As the birthplace of the industrial revolution, Wolverhampton was home to the steel industry. Sam's uncle intended to stay in England for three or four years and make some money prior to returning to India. In 1962, the British government introduced a voucher scheme to overcome the shortage of migrant labor in the UK. This time, Sam's uncle invited his brother (Sam's father) to England to take advantage of this scheme. Sam's father and several of his uncles followed suit, also taking up employment in the foundries upon their arrival in Wolverhampton.

A Hostile Host Environment

Sam and his family stayed with their uncles when they first arrived in England. In living together, members of the extended family drew comfort from a shared sense of security. There weren't many immigrant families in Wolverhampton at that time. Migrants were mostly first-generation men. Women and children were relatively few. The house Sam's family stayed in was also predominantly men. Eventually, Sam's parents decided to move out.

Sam and his siblings were probably the first Indian children enrolled at the junior school that they attended in Wolverhampton. Although Sam could read and write Punjabi, his native language, English was a challenge. Upon graduating from junior school, Sam was presented with three options regarding the senior school he could attend. He recalled how his father's relative lack of knowledge of the British schooling system as a first-generation immigrant restricted his ability to make an informed decision:

> we were so naïve when we came here, for example, when we came out of our
> junior school, we had a choice of going to say three schools. So we had Park Field,
> Crazely, or Penfields. I didn't know which is a good secondary school or which is
> a bad secondary school. So I asked my father. I said which school do you think I
> should go to? He said, son I don't know. I'm a jack farmer from Punjab, right. I work
> in a factory… go and ask Mr. Sharma who's got a corner shop down the bottom of
> the road. He's an educated man, he will be able to tell you which school to go to.

Even though Sam regretted his choice of senior school, he believed he learned useful skills at his chosen institution, which taught him to withstand challenges later in life:

> it was a rough and tough school. But what it gave us was we were very
> very streetwise. Because it was probably one of the worst schools in
> Wolverhampton but… that school was good for hardship. We learnt a lot…
> it taught us how to look after ourselves… the kids who went to actually that
> school did far better later on in life than the kids who actually went to maybe
> some of the academic schools. Because it gave you different skills in life. We
> were more hands on and we knew how to look after, and the unity was there.

By the time Sam went to secondary school in early 70s, there was more of an influx of migrants as Indians and Afro-Caribbeans came to England to work as laborers. Kids at senior school formed their 'own groups' because they felt comfortable within their own friendships. Sam recalled that he was often beaten up, and forced to beat up others in return in order to defend himself. The work environment in companies and factories was rife with prejudice. Racial abuse was rampant as the indigenous community refused to welcome migrants. The political rhetoric in Wolverhampton was also fraught with hatred for immigrants:

> And in those days in Wolverhampton especially, there was an MP called Enoch
> Powell. He was a conservative MP and there's a speech called the Rivers of
> Blood. He was actually speaking on that and saying get rid of these Indians,
> all of these immigrants. Repatriate these people because we will have rivers of
> blood in this country.

Pre-conceived notions based on race and origin also dictated the career advice Sam received at senior school. The career advisor deemed him fit for a factory job on the basis of his ethnic origin and his father's vocation:

(Continued)

When I went to my careers office I asked 'what do you think I should do'? So you're definitely not going to be a brain surgeon, you're not going to be a doctor. You're definitely not going to be a lawyer as Indian families normally request these. He said what does your dad do? I said work in a factory. I think that's where you're going to go.

At that moment Sam resolved to pursue engineering. He was confident of his capabilities. Even though the West Midlands was a big industrial region, he made a conscious decision to attend college far from home in Dudley after finishing school. His perseverance paid off when he received an offer to do a four-year apprenticeship at British Steel Corporation in Bilston after taking his GCSEs. Sam loved the training but, once again, faced discrimination at the workplace. Indians in England at that time were not seen as engineers. Over 3,000 of more than 5,000 employees at British Steel were from India, but most were laborers, not engineers. Thanks to his training and persistence, Sam survived the harassment and at the end of five years, earned promotion to the role of manager at British Steel:

Lot of problem at work, because the English people wanted you out. They didn't want you as an engineer there. They said listen you are wrong color to do my job. Basically, I think, we knew how to, that's where that school comes in too, we knew how to look after ourselves, we knew how to fight and god knows what but you know what I stuck to it.

Foray into Business

Sam and his wife lived in Wolverhampton where Sam took up a job following the completion of his apprenticeship at British Steel. His father-in-law, a small food business owner in Nottingham, convinced him to move to Nottingham. A bus conductor, when he first came to Glasgow, in 1958, Sam's father-in-law moved to the West Midlands to work in the foundries prior to entering into the oil business with his brother. He moved to Nottingham with his wife and two daughters to set up on his own after separating from his brother.

Sam's father-in-law initiated him into business soon after marriage. Initially, Sam was reluctant to join. He enjoyed engineering, but decided to give business a try upon his father-in-law's insistence. Sam quit his job and moved to Nottingham on a short-term basis. The first attempt was not that successful. He joined his father-in-law and brother-in-law after continued persuasion from his wife's family.

At first, the partners sold Indian and West Indian (Jamaican) foods. Soon, they switched to selling Chinese food to occupy an untapped market niche and satisfy growing demand. A number of Chinese restaurants and takeaways (or 'chopsuey bars' as they were called at that time) were setting up in England in the late 1970s. The partners started to supply these restaurants as they ventured into this market. By the mid-1980s, they began importing Chinese food from Hong Kong and China under their own brand. Soon, they became wholesalers, supplying Chinese food nationally.

By 1990, the business had grown to about £8–10 million in revenue, establishing Sam and his partners as kings of the oriental business:

> We used to sell Indian food and West Indian foods because that was a niche in the market. Mainstream groceries you could go to Tesco's or anywhere but there's a need for Indian food, Chinese food, West Indian food in those days. We had a market stall. From there we found out that the business was growing and we were getting a lot more Chinese customers to us. And we found out there's nobody serving the Chinese market. So rather than do Indian and West Indian foods, West Indian being Jamaican foods, we focused ourselves just doing Chinese food. So now you've got Indians who are coming from India, coming to England and now selling Chinese food.

Although it was growing, the Chinese market in those days was not as big as it is today. The team believed they were too young to retire. They decided to open a cash-n-carry, selling mainstream groceries including Indian, Chinese and West Indian foods. They sold directly to individual customers in exchange for cash. They continued the oriental food distribution business, delivering to supermarkets, restaurants and take-aways. Shop keepers running corner stalls also bought supplies from them.

Even though margins were low, turnover was high, and they grew from £10 million to £40 million, and eventually to over £100 million worth of business. The partners opened some of the largest wholesale food marts in the UK, also building for them-selves a formidable reputation for quality and hygiene. Sam even took up 'category management' for some of the largest UK retailers including Bookers cash-n-carry, advising them on mainstream groceries as well as ethnic foods:

> We had a depot that, I would say was one of the best in UK. People used to say god, these boys knew how to do business. It was so clean, people say we can eat off the floor here. Hygiene levels, we took it to another level. Even the English cash-n-carries looked at us and came and looked and, these people knew how to do business… and eventually we started then supplying, started doing category management for Bookers cash-n-carry. Bookers have 188 depots in UK, they are the biggest cash n carry food. So I would be advising them on Indian foods, Chinese food, West Indian foods, mainstream groceries they understand.

Separation and New Beginnings

By 1998, the business had surpassed all expectations, growing well beyond Sam's father-in-law's vision of two or three small shops. The family was an established market leader and Sam's father-in-law was already in a semi-retired mode. Just then, the fam-ily witnessed a power struggle. Sam's brother-in-law inducted his three sons into the business but objected when Sam desired for his three daughters to join. Sam felt he

(Continued)

was being discriminated against yet again, this time in the form of prejudice against his daughters. He felt it was unfair to discriminate against his children just because they were females. They had a rightful share in the business as he too was a partner in the business just like his brother-in-law. It hurt to accept this kind of treatment at the hands of family after having first experienced it as an immigrant:

> My brother-in-law, basically he brought his son in to the business, I brought my daughter in to the business. It was fine for his son to come in, it wasn't fine for my daughter to come in. Stereotyping Indian girls, going to get married and go away to the boy's house. But hold on, I'm a partner here. So all I'm going to do is bring my daughter here, I'm not going to adopt another son from somewhere else. So we had a family break up. We split up actually in 2003.

Asiana Foods was born in 2003 when Sam exited the partnership to set up a new business with his three daughters. He also trained all three sons-in-law, especially as they came from non-business families. Whereas two of them had grown up in India, one was a Nottingham boy. Sam took great pride in his daughters' contribution to the business. As they had grown up with the family business background, Sam felt that 'they knew the business inside out, back to front. The fact that they were girls made no difference'.

Sam's standing up for his daughters and training them in business was an inspiration to the business community in Nottingham. He set an example by advocating for gender equality and hiring more women at his warehouse. The cause gave a new meaning to his business besides the goal of making money:

> You're probably going to see a lot of girls in the office [laughing]. But er, the three daughters are here and er, I think are here. But I've trained them, they do marketing, selling, they do, they're very confident girls. They are the future here. And they are future of doing other things as well. A lot of other Indian girls are looking at them and thinking, inspirational stuff… you can make a lot of money in this world but there's a different purpose for me in life here now. I'm doing this, it's for a different reason. I'm putting the girls up there now.

Sam was thankful that the mainstream community was recognizing the contribution of businessmen like him, and had set up the British Indian Business Forum (BIBF), an ethnic networking organization for businessmen of Indian origin in the UK.

Looking into the Future…

In the ten years between 2003 and 2013, Asiana Foods grew to £20 million in net worth. Sam took pride in his knowledge of oriental foods despite his Indian heritage. He strongly believed in product innovation as a key strategy for success. Sam was passionate about researching and introducing new products. He was keen on introducing the concept of noodle bars worldwide, which he felt had tremendous potential.

More recently, he had introduced bubble tea into the UK from Taiwan. He had hired a student food scientist at the University of Nottingham to develop the product and refine its nutritional content before rolling it out internationally:

> We teach the Chinese about their foods. We are, even though we are from Punjab Indian, but we know more about the Chinese food than the Chinese do. We teach them about their sources, we do the development and… my daughters are working on a bubble tea concept. Bubble tea comes from Taiwan. It's a bit like a milkshake with tapioca pills at the bottom of it, different flavors, different aromas, different mixtures. But we've got two or three going already. Our idea again is to roll out the bubble tea concept out there. And it's something that we want to look at for India as well.

At the time of writing this case, Sam was working on two beer brands that he was marketing to the US and Australia. One was a pan-Asian beer brewed in Germany and available in Thai, Chinese and Indian restaurants in the UK, and another a Chinese beer that was already selling in the UK, as well as in Scandinavia, Germany, Italy and Greece.

Sam was an asset to the local community. He was appointed a Nottingham ambassador by Nottingham City Council. He was responsible for promoting the city on his extensive travels, attracting inward investment, and hosting senior diplomats on their visit to the city. Recently he represented the city to welcome the armed forces on their return from Afghanistan:

> So that's great if you think back, when you came to England in '66, there's prejudice against you and now you are the city ambassador here. So I'm now coming in and greeting the forces coming back from Afghanistan… if the high commissioner of Indian comes here, or the minister of chief, say Sam can you attend can you meet and greet? And how, and all of a sudden… we're an asset to their country here now. Now they're saying look this guy lives in England, born in India, deals with China, you know.

Another area of interest to Sam was biodegradable compostable packaging, a £250 billion market. He was connecting key participants in London, Italy and Sweden, and bringing them to Nottingham. The city council was ready to provide land to worthy investment opportunities at Sam's behest. He believed there was a real opportunity to create an oriental village in the city given its large Asian student population and relative lack of oriental shopping outlets for food and supplies.

Sam was also keen to forge a business link with India, the country of his origin, but he was wary of making a commitment without a trustworthy partner. He had invested in property in India, adding acreage to the ancestral land left by his grandparents in Punjab. He and his family loved to visit India; however, unlike first-generation migrants,

(Continued)

Sam believed it was unlikely that he or his children would move back to India. Although an important part of his heritage, his loyalty rested with the UK. He was proud to be a British Indian. He felt his roots were 'much deeper' in the UK and he was grateful for the many opportunities that the country had provided to him:

> the ideas of the first-generation Indians, eventually they will move back to India. I don't think that's going to happen because our roots are much much deeper here in this country. Our networks are here, our children, yeah you know we love India we like to go to India for holidays but this is where our roots are. I'm British, I'm very proud to be British Indian… we are Indian also that's our heritage our culture you know. But this country has given us so many opportunities here as well, we should be loyal to this country as well… And, I think, we should be thankful for the opportunities, but the mainstream community here is recognizing us now. We're an asset.

Discussion Questions

1. Trace Sam's early years in the UK. What challenges did he face as an immigrant entrepreneur in the UK? Do you believe Sam's early experiences shaped his success as an immigrant entrepreneur in later years? Why / why not? Discuss.
2. Why did Sam first enter business? Which theoretical model outlined in this chapter best explains Sam's foray into business? Discuss.
3. According to the chapter, the role of family in ethnic businesses is 'double-edged'. To what extent do you agree/disagree with this statement? Discuss the role of Sam's family in the a) founding and b) growth of Asiana Foods.
4. What is Sam's contribution to his host country as an immigrant entrepreneur? Discuss.

Watch the following YouTube video: *080715 Sikh Spectrum: Sam Sangha* (www.youtube. com/watch?v=pXTVZQjFSlc). Who else, besides Sam, is present in the video? What new information other than that described in this case did you learn from this video?

References

Aldrich, H.E. and Waldinger, R. (1990) 'Ethnicity and entrepreneurship', *Annual Review of Sociology*, 16(1): 111–135.

Bagwell, K. (2007) 'The economic analysis of advertising', *Handbook of Industrial Organization*, 3(1): 1701–1844. https://doi.org/10.1016/S1573-448X(06)03028-7

Basu, A. (1998) 'An exploration of entrepreneurial activity among Asian small businesses in Britain', *Small Business Economics*, 10(1): 313–326. https://doi.org/10.1023/A:1007956009913

Basu, A. (2011) 'From "break out" to "breakthrough": Successful market strategies of immigrant entrepreneurs in the UK', *International Journal of Entrepreneurship*, 15(1): 1–23.

Bonacich, E. (1973) 'A theory of middleman minorities', *American Sociological Review*, 38(5): 583–594. www.jstor.org/stable/2094409

Buchanan, L. (2019) 'Even the rich and famous of Beverly Hills need to buy hardware and produce: Here's where they shop', *Inc. Magazine*. Available at www.inc.com/leigh-buchanan/beverly-hills-hollywood-celebrity-favorites-small-business-week-2019.html (last accessed 27 September 2022).

Carbonell, J.R., Hernandez, J.C.P. and Lara García, F.J. (2014) 'Business creation by immigrant entrepreneurs in the Valencian community: The influence of education', *International Entrepreneurship and Management Journal*, 10(2): 409–426.

Chaganti, R. and Greene, P.G. (2002) 'Who are ethnic entrepreneurs? A study of entrepreneursapos; Ethnic involvement and business characteristics', *Journal of Small Business Management*, 40(2): 126–143.

Chaganti, R., Watts, A.D., Chaganti, R. and Zimmerman-Treichel, M. (2008) 'Ethnic-immigrants in founding teams: Effects on prospector strategy and performance in new internet ventures', *Journal of Business Venturing*, 23(1): 113–139.

Chung, H.F. and Tung, R.L. (2013) 'Immigrant social networks and foreign entry: Australia and New Zealand firms in the European Union and Greater China', *International Business Review*, 22(1): 18–31.

Constante, A. (2016) 'Lee's sandwiches co-founder remembered for humility, philanthropy after losing cancer battle', *NBC News*, 13 October. Available at www.nbcnews.com/news/asian-america/lee-s-sandwiches-co-founder-remembered-humility-philanthrophy-after-losing-n665836 (last accessed 27 September 2022).

Crick, D. and Chaudhry, S. (2013) 'An exploratory study of UK based, family-owned, Asian firms' motives for internationalising', *Journal of Small Business and Enterprise Development*, 20(3): 526–547. https://doi.org/10.1108/JSBED-04-2013-0051

Dang, L. (2016) 'Meet the Vietnamese immigrants who created a multi-billion dollar Banh Mi sandwich empire', *Next Shark*, 10 October. Available at https://nextshark.com/lees-sandwiches-founder-vietnamese (last accessed 27 September 2022).

Davidsson, P. and Honig, B. (2003) 'The role of social and human capital among nascent entrepreneurs', *Journal of Business Venturing*, 18(3): 301–331. doi: 10.1016/S0883-9026(02)00097-6

Deakins, D. and Hussain, J. (1993) '*Ethnicity and finance: A case study of the characteristics, requirements and relationships with finance providers of ethnic small businesses in the West Midlands region of the UK*', paper presented at the 23rd European Small Businesses Seminar, Belfast, September, 1993.

Dennis, D. (2015) 'If the new American dream is entrepreneurship, why are so many Black millennials missing out?' *TechCrunch*, 14 September. Available at https://techcrunch.com/2015/09/14/if-the-new-american-dream-is-entrepreneurship-why-are-so-many-black-millennials-missing-out (last accessed 27 September 2022).

Desiderio, V. and Mestres-Domènech, J. (2011) 'Migrant entrepreneurship in OECD countries'. *International Migration Outlook*. Available at www.oecd.org/els/mig/Part%20II_Entrepreneurs_engl.pdf (last accessed 27 September 2022).

Dobbin, C.E. (1996) *Asian Entrepreneurial Minorities: Conjoint Communities in the Making of the World-Economy 1570–1940*. Nordic Institute of Asian Studies (No. 71). London: Psychology Press.

Dolan, K.A. (2018) 'What's fueling Latino entrepreneurship – and what's holding it back: Latinos are starting businesses at a higher rate than other ethnic groups, but scaling remains a challenge', *Stanford Business Entrepreneurship*, 7 February. Available at www.gsb.stanford.edu/insights/whats-fueling-latino-entrepreneurship-whats-holding-it-back (last accessed 27 September 2022).

Fairlie, R.W. and Lofstrom, M. (2014) 'Immigration and entrepreneurship', in B.R. Chiswick and P.W. Miller (eds.), *Handbook of the Economics of International Migration: The Impact*, Vol. 1. Oxford: North-Holland, pp. 877–911.

Fairlie, R.W. and Woodruff, C. (2008) 'Mexican-American Entrepreneurship', *IZA Working Paper* No. 3488. http://dx.doi.org/10.2139/ssrn.1136289

Fairlie, R.W., Zissimopoulos, J. and Krashinsky, H. (2010) 'The international Asian business success story? A comparison of Chinese, Indian and other Asian businesses in the United States, Canada and United Kingdom', in J. Lerner and A. Schoar (eds.), *International Differences in Entrepreneurship*. Cambridge, MA: National Bureau of Economic Research, pp. 179–208.

Filatotchev, I., Strange, R., Piesse, J. and Lien, Y.C. (2007) 'FDI by firms from newly industrialised economies in emerging markets: Corporate governance, entry mode and location', *Journal of International Business Studies*, 38(4): 556–572.

Hart, W., Richardson, K., Tortoriello, G. and Tullett, A. (2017) 'Strategically out of control: A self-presentational conceptualization of narcissism and low self-control', *Personality and Individual Differences*, 114(1): 103–107. https://doi.org/10.1016/j.paid.2017.03.046

Hussain, J. and Matlay, H. (2007) 'Financing preferences of ethnic minority owner/managers in the UK', *Journal of Small Business and Enterprise Development*, 14(3): 487–500.

Ibeh, K. (2012) 'Internationisation and entrepreneurial business', in S. Carter and D. Jones-Evans (eds.), *Enterprise and Small Business: Principles, Practice and Policy* (3rd edn). Harlow: Financial Times Prentice Hall, pp. 430–449.

Jones, K., Sambrook, S.A., Pittaway, L., Henley, A. and Norbury, H. (2014) 'Action learning: How learning transfers from entrepreneurs to small firms', *Action Learning: Research and Practice*, 11(2): 131–166.

Kariv, D., Menzies, T.V., Brenner, G.A. and Filion, L.J. (2009) 'Transnational networking and business performance: Ethnic entrepreneurs in Canada', *Entrepreneurship & Regional Development*, 21(3): 239–264.

Kerr, S.P. and Kerr, W.R. (2016) 'Immigrant entrepreneurship'. *National Bureau of Economic Research*. Available at www.nber.org/papers/w22385 (last accessed 27 September 2022).

Kerr, S.P., Kerr, W., Ozden, C. and Parsons, C. (2016) 'Global talent flows', *The Journal of Economic Perspectives*, 30(4): 83–106.

Kloosterman, R. (2010) 'Matching opportunities with resources: A framework for analysing (migrant) entrepreneurship from a mixed embeddedness perspective', *Entrepreneurship and Regional Development*, 22(1): 25–45.

Kloosterman, R. and Rath, J. (2001) 'Immigrant entrepreneurs in advanced economies: Mixed embeddedness further explored', *Journal of Ethnic and Migration Studies*, 27(2): 189–201.

Kloosterman, R. and Rath, J. (2003) 'Immigrant entrepreneurs: Venturing abroad in the age of globalization', Amsterdam Institute for Social Science Research. Available at https://hdl.handle.net/11245/1.221088 (last accessed 27 September 2022).

Kloosterman, R., Van Der Leun, J. and Rath, J. (1999) 'Mixed embeddedness: (In)formal economic activities and immigrant businesses in the Netherlands', *International Journal of Urban and Regional Research*, 23(2): 252–266.

Kontos, M. (2003) 'Considering the concept of entrepreneurial resources in ethnic business: Motivation as a biographical resource?' *International Review of Sociology/ Revue Internationale de Sociologie*, 13(1): 183–204.

Light, I. (1984) 'Immigrant and ethnic enterprise in North America', *Ethnic and Racial Studies*, 7(2): 195–216.

Light, I. (2004) 'The ethnic economy', in N. Smelser and R. Swedberg (eds.), *Handbook of Economic Sociology* (2nd edn). New York: Russell Sage Foundation, pp. 650–677.

Light, I. and Gold, S.J. (2000) *Ethnic Economies*. San Diego, CA: Academic Press.

Light, I., Bhachu, P. and Karageorgis, S. (1993) 'Migration networks and immigrant entrepreneurship', in *Immigration and Entrepreneurship: Culture, Capital, and Ethnic Networks*, 1st Edition, Routledge, pp. 25–50.

Light, I., Sabagh, G., Bozorgmehr, M. and Der-Martirosian, C. (1994) 'Beyond the ethnic enclave economy', *Social Problems*, 41(1): 65–80.

Masurel, E., Nijkamp, P., Tastan, M. and Vindigni, G. (2002) 'Motivations and performance conditions for ethnic entrepreneurship', *Growth and Change*, 33(2): 238–260.

Miera, F. (2008) 'Transnational strategies of Polish migrant entrepreneurs in trade and small business in Berlin', *Journal of Ethnic and Migration Studies*, 34(5): 753–770.

Min, P.G. and Bozorgmehr, M. (2000) 'Immigrant entrepreneurship and business patterns: A comparison of Koreans and Iranians in Los Angeles', *International Migration Review*, 34(3): 707–738.

Moghaddam, K., Bosse, D.A. and Provance, M. (2016) 'Strategic alliances of entrepreneurial firms: Value enhancing then value destroying', *Strategic Entrepreneurship Journal*, 10(2): 153–168.

Mustafa, M. and Chen, S. (2010) 'The strength of family networks in transnational immigrant entrepreneurship', *Thunderbird International Business Review*, 52(2): 97–106.

Ndofor, H.A. and Priem, R.L. (2011) 'Immigrant entrepreneurs, the ethnic enclave strategy, and venture performance', *Journal of Management*, 37(3): 790–818.

Orozco, M., Tareque, I.S., Oyer, P. and Porras, J.I. (2019) 'State of Latino entrepreneurship report', Stanford Latino Entrepreneurship Initiative. Available at www.gsb.stanford.edu/sites/gsb/files/publication-pdf/report-slei-state-latino-entrepreneurship-2019.pdf (last accessed 27 September 2022).

Ram, M. (1994) 'Managing to survive: Working lives in small firms', Blackwell Business.

Ram, M. and Deakins, D. (1996) 'African-Caribbeans in business'. *Journal of Ethnic and Migration Studies*, 22(1), 67–84.

Ram, M. and Jones, T. (2008) 'Ethnic-minority businesses in the UK: A review of research and policy developments', *Environment and Planning C: Government and Policy*, 26(2): 352–374.

Ram, M. and Smallbone, D. (2002) 'Ethnic minority business policy in the era of the small business service', *Environment and Planning C: Government and Policy*, 20(2): 235–249.

Ram, M., Smallbone, D., Deakins, D. and Jones, T. (2003) 'Banking on "break-out": Finance and development of ethnic minority businesses', *Journal of Ethnic and Migration Studies*, 29(4): 663–681.

Ram, M., Barrett, G. and Jones, T. (2012) 'Ethnicity and entrepreneurship', in S. Carter and D. Jones-Evans (eds), *Enterprise and Small Business: Principles, Practice and Policy* (3rd edn). Harlow: Financial Times Prentice Hall, pp. 199–217.

Rauch, J.E. and Trindade, V. (2002) 'Ethnic Chinese networks in international trade', *Review of Economics and Statistics*, 84(1): 116–130.

Saxenian, A. (2002) 'Silicon Valley's new immigrant high-growth entrepreneurs', *Economic Development Quarterly*, 16(1): 20–31.

Saxenian, A. (2005) 'From brain drain to brain circulation: Transnational communities and regional upgrading in India and China', *Studies in Comparative International Development*, 40(2): 35–61.

Simon, R. (2015) 'Immigrants, Latinos helped drive business creation last year', *Wall Street Journal*, May 27, 8:03 pm ET. https://www.wsj.com/articles/immigrants-latinos-helped-drive-business-creation-last-year-1432771383

Teixeira, C., Lo, L. and Truelove, M. (2007) 'Immigrant entrepreneurship, institutional discrimination, and implications for public policy: A case study in Toronto', *Environment and Planning C: Government and Policy*, 25(2): 176–193.

US Census Bureau. (2019) 'Small business facts: Spotlight on minority-owned employer businesses', US Small Business Administration. Available at https://advocacy.sba.gov/2019/05/23/small-business-facts-spotlight-on-minority-owned-employer-businesses (last accessed 27 September 2022).

Valdez, Z. (2008) 'Beyond ethnic entrepreneurship: An embedded market approach to group affiliation in American enterprise', *Race, Gender & Class*, 15(1): 156–169.

Vinogradov, E. and Kolvereid, L. (2007) 'Cultural background, human capital and self-employment rates among immigrants in Norway', *Entrepreneurship and Regional Development*, 19(4): 359–376.

Waldinger, R. (1995) 'The "other side" of embeddedness: A case-study of the interplay of economy and ethnicity', *Ethnic and Racial Studies*, 18(3): 555–580.

Waldinger, R., Aldrich, H. and Ward, R. (1990) 'Opportunities, group characteristics, and strategies', *Ethnic Entrepreneurs*, 1(1): 13–48.

Wang, Q. and Liu, Y. (2015) 'Transnational activities of immigrant-owned firms and their performances in the USA', *Small Business Journal*, 44(2): 345–359.

Wong, L.L. and Ng, M. (2002) 'The emergence of small transnational enterprise in Vancouver: The case of Chinese entrepreneur immigrants', *International Journal of Urban and Regional Research*, 26(3): 508–530.

Yang, T., Martinez, M.A. and Aldrich, H.E. (2011) 'Entrepreneurship as an evolutionary process: Research progress and challenges', *Entrepreneurship Research Journal*, 1(1). https://doi.org/10.2202/2157-5665.1009

Zaheer, S., Lamin, A. and Subramani, M. (2009) 'Cluster capabilities or ethnic ties? Location choice by foreign and domestic entrants in the services offshoring industry in India', *Journal of International Business Studies*, 40(6): 944–968.

Zhou, M. (2004) 'Revisiting ethnic entrepreneurship: Convergences, controversies, and conceptual advancements', *International Migration Review*, 38(3): 1040–1074.

Zhou, M. and Logan, J.R. (1989) 'Returns on human capital in ethic enclaves: New York City's Chinatown', *American Sociological Review*, 54(5): 809–820. www.jstor.org/stable/2117755

Zimmer, C. and Aldrich, H. (1987) 'Resource mobilization through ethnic networks: Kinship and friendship ties of shopkeepers in England', *Sociological Perspectives*, 30(4): 422–445.

Zolin, R. and Schlosser, F. (2013) 'Characteristics of immigrant entrepreneurs and their involvement in international new ventures', *Thunderbird International Business Review*, 55(3): 271–284.

9
NEW IMMIGRANT ENTREPRENEURS

Growing from just another Silicon Valley start-up into the world's largest media corporation, Google is larger than Disney, General Motors and McDonald's combined. As the world's dominant search engine, used some 300 million times daily, Google hosts an immense amount of data about our collective interests, needs and desires. The $150 billion company achieved these lofty heights by revolutionizing how people surf the internet. Before Sergey Brin and Larry Page, the two co-founders of Google, analyzed the links between web pages to speedily deliver search results based on relevance, looking up information on the Web was not commonplace.

Migration to US and Early Years

Sergey's father, Michael, a mathematics professor at the University of Maryland, and his mother, Eugenia, a research scientist at NASA's Goddard Space Flight Center, migrated to the US from the Soviet Union with Sergey in 1979. Michael was forced to abandon his dream of becoming an astronomer even before he reached college back home in Russia due to the Communist Party that barred Jews from upper professional ranks and denied them entry into universities. He managed to earn a doctorate by studying mathematics on his own, surreptitiously taking evening classes at the Moscow State University and writing research papers. Highly assimilated into Russian culture, the Brins had a circle of university-educated friends.

Sergey was born on August 21, 1973. The family decided to leave the country when he was five years old. The Brins formally applied for an exit visa in Moscow and received papers to leave the USSR in May 1979. Sergey's first memory of the United States when

(Continued)

the family finally landed in America later that year was of sitting in the backseat of the car, observing the giant automobiles on the highway as the family drove to Long Island.

The Brins rented a house in Maryland and enrolled Sergey in Paint Branch Montessori School in Adelphi, Maryland. Sergey spoke with a heavy accent when he started school. Although a shy child, he had the self-confidence to pursue what he had his mind set on and gravitated toward puzzles, maps and math games that taught multiplication. The Montessori environment, which gives students the freedom to choose activities that suit their interests, helped to foster his creativity.

Sergey attended Eleanor Roosevelt High School, a large public school in Greenbelt. He raced through in three years, amassing a year's worth of college credits that later also enabled him to finish college in three years. In the summer of 1990, a few weeks before Sergey's 17th birthday, Sergey accompanied his dad back home to the Soviet Union when his dad led a group of gifted high school math students on a two-week exchange program there. It didn't take long for Sergey, a mature teenager about to enter college, to realize the value of his life in the US and thank his parents for taking him out of Russia.

The Birth of Google

At the University of Maryland, Sergey majored in mathematics and computer science and graduated near the top of his class. When he won a prestigious National Science Foundation scholarship for graduate school, he insisted on Stanford to pursue computer science, specifically data mining, which dealt with extracting meaningful patterns from piles of information. He also took time out to enjoy Stanford social life and a variety of sports including skiing, rollerblading and gymnastics.

Sergey met Larry Page, another computer science student from the University of Michigan, during a prospective student weekend in the spring of 1995. Talking and arguing over the course of two days, they formed an instant intellectual connection. Larry and Sergey soon began working on ways to harness information on the World Wide Web, spending so much time together that they took on a joint identity, 'Larry and Sergey'.

By 1996, Larry had stumbled upon on the idea of using the links between web pages to rank their relative importance. Borrowing the concept of citations in research papers as a measure of topicality and value from academia, he and Brin applied that thinking to the Web: if one page linked to another, it was in effect 'citing' or casting a vote for that page. The more votes a page had, the more valuable it was. A rather obvious concept in retrospect, the principle was groundbreaking at the time. Calling their new invention Google, a misspelling of a very large number in mathematics, Sergey and Larry took leaves of absence from their doctorate program at Stanford to build the company.

Soliciting funds from faculty, family and friends, Sergey and Larry scraped together enough to buy some servers and rent a garage in Menlo Park. Their venture quickly bore fruit when Sun Microsystems cofounder and angel investor Andy Bechtolsheim wrote a $100,000 check to 'Google, Inc.' after viewing a quick demo. Google formally filed paperwork for its initial public offering of stock on April 29, 2004.

Jewish Heritage

Although heavily assimilated in its host country, the company that owes its origins to two Jews maintains a strong home country connection and retains some defining Jewish traditions and characteristics. Among them are the practice of using menorah, rather than a Christmas tree, to decorate the lobby at the start of the winter holiday season and cooking up Jewish delicacies like latkes and matzah ball soup for Hanukkah meals.

Google's first employee and a number of its early hires were Jewish. Google's emphasis on academic achievement, and hiring only the best and the brightest, and employing hundreds of PhDs, is also Jewish. So are its core values as encapsulated in its motto of 'Don't be Evil'. The company's commitment to philanthropy to tackle pressing social and environmental issues such as poverty and renewable energy is reminiscent of the Jewish concept of 'repairing the world'. The founders' tendency to push boundaries without asking permission is perhaps the most extreme of Jewish values at Google. This attitude probably explains why the company is embroiled in lawsuits over many of its new projects such as the display of copyrighted material or aggressive scanning of library books it doesn't own.

Sergey's own Jewish sensibility and sense of being in the minority is grounded in his background and family experience, first as a child of Jewish origin in Russia, and then as a minority Russian immigrant in the US. Being the youngest in his class and significantly ahead in math at school reinforced his feeling of standing apart from the crowd, which is also in some sense a part of the Jewish heritage. Sergey continues to maintain his independence, and being a young billionaire, he's again in a class by himself.

Source: Malseed (2007)

Learning Outcomes

After studying this chapter, you should be ready to:

- **LO1**: Describe the concept and context of the new immigrant entrepreneurs
- **LO2**: Explain the distinctive human and social capital resources of the new immigrant entrepreneurs
- **LO3**: Explain the distinctive characteristics of transnational entrepreneurs (TEs) as a class of immigrant entrepreneur
- **LO4**: Discuss TEs' motivations, and evaluate the role of their human and social capital in the founding of their ventures
- **LO5**: Discuss the performance and impact of the new immigrant entrepreneurs

Introduction

Ethnic entrepreneurship (Chapter 8) refers to small, family-owned businesses founded by immigrant entrepreneurs (IEs) in their host country. However, entrepreneurial activities among immigrants are varied, and IEs are far more heterogeneous in scale and scope (Zhou, 2004).

According to the *Wall Street Journal* (Koh, 2016), about one-fourth of all technology and engineering companies started in the US between 2006 and 2012 had at least one immigrant founder. These companies produced $63 billion in sales and employed 560,000 workers. And 21% of European tech entrepreneurs started their companies outside of their home countries (Michaels and Schechner, 2018).

According to the Center for American Entrepreneurship, the occurrence of first- or second-generation immigrant founders is significantly higher among the largest Fortune 500 companies; 43% of Fortune 500 companies in 2017 were founded or co-founded by an immigrant or the child of an immigrant. Headquartered in 33 of 50 US states, immigrant-founded Fortune 500 firms employed 12.8 million people world-wide, and accounted for $5.3 trillion in global revenue in 2016.

IEs actively look for opportunities and market niches beyond the national boundaries of the host countries. In some cases, they exploit knowledge and networks in both host and home countries for the expansion of investment flows between the two countries. In other cases, they are permanently returning home to found ventures after a period of living or studying abroad (Pruthi, 2014; Wright et al., 2007). The transnational and returnee entrepreneur phenomena are likely to grow at a fast rate as individuals increasingly gain international experience living outside their home countries, pursuing studies or working as managers on overseas projects.

In this chapter, we first review evidence related to the migration of skilled personnel and the emergence of new IEs in developed host countries. We review the distinctive human and social capital resources of the new IEs. Then we introduce the concept of TEs as a class of immigrant entrepreneur (we take up returnee entrepreneurs in the next chapter). We outline the unique features of TEs and review their motivations for the founding of their ventures in the host and home countries. Finally, we discuss the performance and impact of the new immigrant and transnational entrepreneurs.

New IEs: Context and Distinctive Characteristics

New immigrant entrepreneurs are foreign-born founders of high-growth start-ups. Discussions around entrepreneurship in the context of new immigrant entrepreneurs focus on start-ups backed by venture capital (VC) firms and entrepreneurs seeking high-growth opportunities that could result in the next Starbucks, Facebook or Staples.

VC-backed immigrant entrepreneurship is strong in the US, with 31% of VC-backed founders being immigrants, compared to 25% of all entrepreneurs in 2005 (Kerr and Kerr, 2016). According to the National Foundation for American Policy, immigrants have started more than half (50 of 91, or 55%) of America's start-up companies valued at $1 billion or more (Anderson, 2019). Well-known examples include the founders of Uber, WeWork, Houzz, Avant, AppDynamics, Robinhood and Peloton.

One of the founders of Uber, Garrett Camp, is an immigrant from Canada (Neidert, 2018). Camp came up with the idea for Uber after becoming frustrated with taxis while seeing a girlfriend. Adam Neumann, co-founder and CEO of WeWork, came to the United States from Israel as an international student and attended CUNY Bernard M. Baruch College in New York. Houzz was started by a husband and wife team, Adi Tatarko and Alon Cohen, both born in Israel. The idea for Houzz developed out of the couple's frustration with trying to find good information online to renovate their home.

All three founders of Avant arrived in America without wealth or connections when they first entered the country as children. Avant CEO Al Goldstein arrived with his family as an eight-year-old refugee from Uzbekistan; John Sun, the child of an international student, was born in China; and Paul Zhang, born in China, immigrated when his father was sponsored by a family member in the US.

Source: www.needpix.com/photo/1266342

Vlad Tenev, founder of the investor services company Robinhood, is a Bulgarian-born immigrant, and Yony Feng, co-founder of the popular fitness company Peloton, was born in China.

Drastic advancements in communication and transportation technologies have significantly reduced barriers for migrants to not only move from one country to another, but also to connect with people in different locations including their country of origin (Vertovec, 2004). Air transportation and long-distance telephone, fascimile and internet communications, as well as increasingly heterogeneous populations in recent years, have all supported the rise of immigrant transnational activity.

Many skilled immigrants enter the United States for study or paid work and found their company after several years in the country. US immigration law and corporate sponsorship of visas contribute to this career trajectory (Lofstrom, 2002). Pre-migration self-employment in home countries increases the probability of self-employment by skilled immigrants in the United States, and boosts their self-employment earnings (Kerr and Kerr, 2016).

Skilled immigrants in the US have a growing presence in Silicon Valley, California, accounting for one third of Silicon Valley's engineering workforce in most technology firms. In 2013, 56% of STEM workers and 70% of software engineers in Silicon Valley were foreign born.

A large number of foreign-born migrants, including engineers and highly educated professionals, first migrated to the US in the mid-1960s (Saxenian, 2002, 2005). Asian immigration to the US accelerated in the 1990s. Many immigrants started their own companies as they felt that there was a glass ceiling inhibiting their professional advancement despite superior levels of educational attainment compared to their white counterparts. By 1998, close to one quarter of Silicon Valley's firms had Chinese or Indian executives in a Dun & Bradstreet database of technology firms founded since 1980. They have since become increasingly visible as entrepreneurs and investors (Saxenian, 2002).

India and China continue to be the top two sources of skilled migrants in the valley. According to Wadhwa (2012), between 2006 and 2012, entrepreneurs of Indian origin founded one-third (33.2%) of engineering and technology companies started by immigrants in Silicon Valley (Table 9.1). This was followed by founders from China, the UK, Canada, Germany, Israel, Russia, Korea, Australia and the Netherlands.

Table 9.1 Top countries of origin of immigrant founders of billion-dollar companies, and percentage of engineering and technology companies started by immigrants in the US

Country of Origin	Number of Immigrant Founders of Billion Dollar Companies	Engineering and Technology Companies Started by Immigrants, 2006–12 (%)
Australia	2	2.0
Canada	9	4.2
China	6	8.1
Germany	4	3.9
India	8	33.3
Israel	9	3.5
Russia	3	2.4
UK	7	6.3

Sources: Anderson (2019); Wadhwa (2012)

Immigrant founders of recent billion-dollar companies in the US have immigrated from 25 different countries (Anderson, 2019). Table 9.1 summarizes the top countries of origin for these founders.

Human Capital of New IEs

The new IEs are distinctive in terms of their human and social capital resources.

Education

According to Saxenian (2005), new IEs in developed Western countries are highly educated. The education levels of skilled Asian immigrants to the US, Canada and UK are higher than the national average (Fairlie et al., 2010). This is especially true of the US where education levels of Asian immigrants are higher relative to the entire population within the country, and relative to the corresponding population of immigrants in Canada and the UK. Historically, the US alone has hosted close to half of all skilled migrants to OECD countries and one-third of skilled migrants worldwide (Kerr et al.,

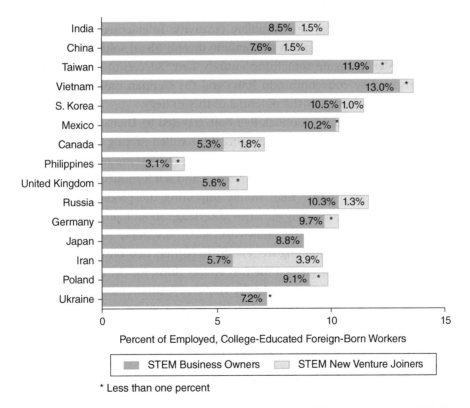

Figure 9.1 Foreign-born workers' rates of participation in STEM entrepreneurship, by country of origin

Source: Blume-Kohout (2016)

2016). The UK is more likely to accept immigrants in the refugee or asylum-seeker category than the US or Canada.

The higher educational credentials of the new IEs are associated with their engagement in STEM entrepreneurship in the host country. Figure 9.1 shows the rates of participation of skilled immigrants by country in STEM entrepreneurship in the US.

The link between higher education and business ownership varies across countries (Fairlie et al., 2010). Higher education is found to be a positive, although not strong, determinant of business ownership in the US and Canada, but not in the UK. Further, the relatively high levels of education among some Asian immigrant groups do not have a large influence on business ownership rates, but have a large effect on business performance at least in the US and Canada, and especially among Indians and Pakistanis.

Immigration / Cross-Cultural Experience

Successful founders of high-growth start-ups in the US share extensive cross-cultural experience (Vandor and Franke, 2016). Cross-cultural experiences increase individuals' capabilities to identify promising business ideas. By living in different cultures, immigrants encounter new products, services, customer preferences and communication strategies, and this exposure allows the transfer of knowledge about customer problems or solutions from one country to another.

Cross-cultural experiences also stimulate creativity. Interacting with two or more cultural contexts helps immigrants to combine diverse ideas, solutions and customer problems in order to create something entirely new. Successful companies such as Starbucks (inspired by coffeehouses in Italy) and the German online retailer Zalando (inspired by Zappos) exemplify the potential of this strategy.

When Dietrich Mateschitz, founder, Red Bull, traveled to Thailand in the 1980s, he observed the popularity of a cheap energizing drink called Krating Daeng among truck drivers and construction workers (Vandor and Franke, 2016). Finding that it helped ease his jet lag, Dietrich decided to license the product and sell it in Austria under the name Red Bull Energy Drink. Rather than simply importing the product, he realized the opportunity to combine the newly obtained knowledge about a product (a drink popular among truck drivers) and the knowledge about his home market (conservative beverages market, growing clubbing scene) into an entirely new business idea. By adapting size, taste and brand, he created the first energy drink for the alternative clubbing scene – something previously unseen in the Thai and Austrian markets.

Social Capital of New IEs

Silicon Valley's new IEs rely on diverse informal social networks to support their entrepreneurial activities (Saxenian, 2002, 2005). In the 1970s and 1980s, these immigrants created social and professional networks among themselves on the basis of shared language, culture and educational and professional experiences. **Ethnic networks** helped to mobilize resources such as capital, skills, information and advice for their technology ventures. They have also contributed to the increased visibility of Chinese and Indian entrepreneurs in the Valley, helped to lower the glass ceiling, as well as attract the attention of venture capital firms for financing IEs' ventures.

Ethnic networks take the form of **professional networking organizations**, and **personal and industry networks**.

Professional Networking Organizations

The professional and technical associations organized by Silicon Valley's Chinese and Indian immigrant engineers during the 1980s and 1990s (Table 9.2) are among the most vibrant and active professional organizations in the region, with membership ranging from several hundred in the newer associations to more than 1,000 in the established ones.

These organizations facilitate professional networking and information exchange within immigrant members for the success of their ventures (Saxenian, 2002, 2005). They support cross-generational mentoring and investment among their members. Older individuals often introduce their younger counterparts to industry experts, offer advice for their ventures and provide informal angel funding for their ventures.

Table 9.2 Professional associations in Silicon Valley

Name	Target Ethnic Group	Year Founded	Mission/ Description	Number of Members
Chinese American Semiconductor Professionals Association (CASPA)	Chinese	1991	Provides networking and business expansion for corporates and individual members; Facilitates collaboration and communication among professionals and companies in the semiconductor industry; Promotes welfare of members by supporting their interests; Exchanges information regarding job opportunities and career development	6,000+
Chinese Institute of Engineers (CIE)	Chinese	1917	Promotes science, engineering, technology and mathematics (STEM) across United States and provide national recognitions to APA professionals	3000+
Chinese Software Professionals Association (CSPA)	Chinese	1988	Promotes leadership, community, and entrepreneurship in technology	6,000+

(Continued)

Table 9.2 (Continued)

Name	Target Ethnic Group	Year Founded	Mission/ Description	Number of Members
German Silicon Valley Innovators	German	2012	Provides German companies tailor-made access to Silicon Valley's startup and innovation ecosystem; Enables German companies to access the local network and experiences and opportunities in Silicon Valley	11–50 employees*
Korean Innovation Center (KIC), Silicon Valley	Korean	2005	Serves as the global frontier for Korean startups and SMEs; Discovers and incubates promising Korean technology startups by providing connections to market enablers, accelerators and training programs	200+
Latino Business Foundation, Silicon Valley	Mexican	2019	Provides empowering resources to existing and future leaders in the business community through long-lasting learning and support; Stirs the entrepreneurial spirit; supports business growth; strengthens local associations and advance leadership	20+
Monte Jade Science and Technology Association (MJSTA)	Chinese	1989	Fosters relationship between technology professionals and corporations on both sides of the Pacific Ocean; Provides an opportunity for professionals to share valuable experiences in business investments, opportunities and management in technology	25+
North American Chinese Semi-conductor Association (NACSA)	Chinese	1996	Strengthens networking among professionals, fosters entrepreneurship among ethnic Chinese, and promotes exchange in the semiconductor and information technology industries	4,000+
North American Taiwanese Engineers Association (NATEA)	Chinese	1991	Promotes science and technology research; provides management and leadership training opportunities for overseas Taiwanese in US and Canada, and their community at large	2,600+
Silicon Valley Indian Professionals Association (SIPA)	Indian	1987	Creates value for its members through programs that foster professional growth and personal enrichment	5,000+

Name	Target Ethnic Group	Year Founded	Mission/ Description	Number of Members
The Indus Entrepreneurs (TiE)	Indian	1992	Fosters entrepreneurship through mentoring, networking, education, funding and incubation; Gives back to the community; Generates and nurtures the next generation of entrepreneurs	15,000
Entrepreneurs' Organization	Philippines	1987	Enables leading entrepreneurs to learn and grow, leading to greater success in business and beyond	13,000+

*membership figures not available

Sources: www.caspa.com/about/introduction; www.cie-usa.org; www.linkedin.com/company/chinese-software-professionals-association/about; https://germaninnovators.com/; www.kicsv.org/home; www.lbfsv.org/ourteam; www.montejade.org; www.nacsa.com/about/background; https://natea.org/about-us; www.sipa.org; https://tie.org/about; www.eonetwork.org/philippines

Founded by Raju Reddy, an immigrant from India in California, and founder of Sierra Atlantic, an IT services company in the US, SIPA (Silicon Valley Indian Professionals Association) is one such example. Raju's main goal in setting up SIPA was to promote business between the US and India in the 1980s when India was not considered a business destination in the US. SIPA was founded to help not just entrepreneurs, but also professionals of Indian origin trying to forge links with their home country:

> I was one of the founders for that. It's a precursor to the TiE organization. TiE started well after SIPA… So the goal was very simple. We just wanted to promote business between India and the US. So it wasn't just focused on entrepreneurship but also professionals of Indian origin who were trying to do that… India was not really considered a business destination here at that time… I'm talking about late 80s. (Raju Reddy, Founder, SIPA)

Personal and Industry Networks

Personal and industry networks are another type of ethnic networks that IEs use in the founding of IEs' ventures. Sarvesh Mahesh, founder of Tavant Technologies, and immigrant founder in the Bay area, explained the importance of **alumni networks** in the founding of his venture. Friendships from school and university were among the strongest in his view. One of his top managers, Rohit, was from the same university as Sarvesh in India. Sarvesh found his co-founder through Rohit as the co-founder was a classmate of Rohit's, also from the same university:

> Rohit is the fellow who I spoke about, he is from Roorkee. Krishnan again, one of our co-founders, he is a class fellow of his… I think, the university is probably the strongest network. The friendships that are made there tend to

be the strongest. Most lasting. But a lot of people, you spend 20 years
with before that, but those five years are when you are very fertile for friends.
Friends made in those five years, tend to last a long time. Even high school,
I was not in a place where I had to move around. I lived in the same place.
Those friends I know them. Some of them came to the same school, so I know
them a lot more. (Sarvesh Mahesh, Founder, Tavant Technologies)

Leveraging personal networks from the home country for venture creation is common
practice for Silicon-Valley-based entrepreneurs. Padman Ramankutty, a serial entrepreneur of Indian origin based in Silicon Valley, California, emphasized the importance of
'small' networks outside of the family. The software developers he found in Dehradun
and Pune, India, for his venture in the US came through referrals from friends.
Locating common connections by asking people about their hometown and place of
origin was an important part of building companies in the Valley:

> Small networks actually work… I found some developers in Dehradun through a
> friend of mine who had these guys do a good job. I found developers in Pune… we
> conscripted them to be an employee and start a company in India in his room in his
> house in Bombay… so these networks are very interesting and in India we always ask
> for that network. Where are you from? What is your thing? … it is not just a family it
> is just about asking that question, Who do you know?, How do you know?, Where
> do you know? and that becomes very much part of the thing that happens in the
> Valley. (Padman Ramankutty, Founder, Bristlecone and Intrigo Systems, California)

Often based on prior work experience, and sometimes originating in the same ethnic community as IEs themselves, **industry networks** also inspire new ventures. Rajan Raghavan,
another IE in Silicon Valley, emphasized their importance. One of Rajan's former colleagues,
Rajveer Singh, introduced him to Thampy who became Rajan's mentor. Thampy invested in
Rajan's second venture. According to Rajan, the 'seed' of other networks that he subsequently
developed came from Rajveer and Thampy, both of whom, like him, were of Indian origin:

> My network evolved from another person, Rajveer Singh. Raj became good
> friends with me because we worked together at Cirrus Logic. He put me in
> touch with Thampy… Raj and Thampy both invested in my second company…
> that's how I started to build my network. They introduced me to people. I also
> started building my network primarily because of selling my ideas. Seed of
> those networks came from Raj and Thampy. (Rajan Raghavan, Serial Immigrant
> Entrepreneur, Silicon Valley, California)

Transnational Entrepreneurs

As discussed in Chapter 6, an increasing number of entrepreneurs are pursuing international markets for selling their goods and services. Many of the new ventures that rapidly traverse geographic borders are started by transnational entrepreneurs.

Drori et al. (2009) define **transnational entrepreneurs** as individuals that migrate from one country to another, concurrently maintaining business-related links with their countries of origin and currently adopted countries. TEs engage in cross-border activities stemming from the very fact that immigration to another country is part of their personal history.

TEs are self-employed immigrants whose business activities require frequent travel abroad and who depend for the success of their businesses on their contacts and associates in another country, primarily their country of origin (Portes et al., 2002). TEs maintain multiple residences in more than one country and leverage social networks in those countries in the founding of their ventures.

Although not all TEs are immigrants, TEs represent a large proportion, often the majority, of self-employed persons in immigrant communities in developed host economies (Portes et al., 2002). As compared to non-immigrant owned firms, immigrant owned firms have significantly higher tendency to be involved in transnational economic activities (Wong and Ng, 2002). As individual IEs, TEs are in a unique position to identify and exploit opportunities that might not otherwise be recognized by entrepreneurs in a single geography.

Instances of transnationalism have been documented among a number of immigrant groups both in the United States and Western Europe (Portes et al., 2002). They are also found among immigrants from Latin America, Asia, the Middle East and Africa.

Tracy Nguyen, founder, Affordable Quality Pharmaceuticals (AQP) in California, US, is one example (see Box below). Tracy founded her venture in the US and Vietnam in 2003 after a visit back to her home country, Vietnam, when she learned about the Vietnamese government incentives for pharmaceutical and biotechnology investments. The company, that makes diagnostic tests for pregnancy and ovulation, is headquartered in the US, with manufacturing sub-contractors located in Vietnam. Tracy, who lives in the US, leveraged her knowledge, education and social networks in the US to start up and partner with the Centre for Disease Control and Prevention, and her knowledge of the local government, as well as language, in Vietnam to find local licensees there.

TRACY NGUYEN
A VIETNAMESE TE IN THE US

Tracy Nguyen came to the US in 1979 as a teenage Vietnam War refugee. She earned a degree in electrical engineering and established a career in the field. Then in 2000, with little working capital, limited English and no pharmacy degree, she started Affordable Quality Pharmaceuticals (AQP) in Garden Grove, California. The 30-employee company, which had revenues of $4 million in 2006, buys large quantities of brand-name and generic prescription drugs and repackages and sells them in smaller packages for retail pharmacies in the US.

On a visit back to Vietnam in 2001, Tracy noticed that the Vietnamese government was opening up and welcoming foreign companies. The government was giving incentives for pharmaceutical and biotechnology investments. Since she knew the language, the 46-year-old entrepreneur wanted to get into the business of pharmaceuticals. It was also her grandfather's dying wish for her before she left for America. In 2003, she decided to set up a biotech company in Vietnam to make diagnostic tests, such as those for pregnancy and ovulation.

Despite pouring nearly $800,000 into the company over two years and getting incentives, including tax breaks and cheap leases, from the government, Tracy decided it was too hard to run the business on her own. The difficulty of finding capable workers and dealing with red tape were among the setbacks. The final straw was an incident in which it took her two months to get a license notarized and approved by different consulates, flying back and forth between Vietnam and the US.

At that point, Tracy changed her business model to a licensing agreement in a cooperative alliance among several Vietnamese pharmaceutical firms. Her company is now widely known by the pharmaceutical industry there, and she maintains close ties with the head of the Ministry of Health.

The lessons learned and connections made from this venture helped her other company, AQP, land a three-year contract in November 2006 with the Centers for Disease Control and Prevention to provide basic medicine-cabinet supplies in Vietnam.

The contract gave AQP the rights to subcontract the manufacturing of generic drugs like aspirin to Vietnamese companies, store them centrally and distribute them to local hospitals. AQP is the only US-based pharmaceutical company licensed in Vietnam to buy and sell drugs there. AQP has been recognized as one of the top 500 woman-owned businesses in the US by DiversityBusiness.com.

From a chain of 18 pharmacies in 4 states, AQP has evolved to become a pharmaceutical wholesaler and is now known as the distributor of AQP prescription drugs throughout the US and Vietnam.

Sources: Raymund (2007); www.aqpharmaceuticals.com

TEs differ from the more traditional ethnic entrepreneurs (EEs) (Chapter 8). The literature identifies distinctive dimensions of TEs, namely: a) frequent travel between host and home countries, b) simultaneous entrepreneurial engagement in at least two countries, c) dual embeddedness in host and home institutional environments, and d) TEs as highly skilled migrants. Additionally, TEs are unique in their motivations and resources as explained below.

Frequent Travel between Host and Home Countries

TEs frequently travel between their host and home countries as they set up their ventures in the two contexts (Vertovec, 2004). European immigrants coming to America at the turn of the 20th century engaged in the same pattern of back-and-forth travel and trans-Atlantic economic ventures linking places of origin and destination.

According to sociologists, TEs are a distinct class of immigrant entrepreneurs who engage in transnational activities on a regular basis and rely on them as their primary means of livelihood (Portes et al., 2002). They travel abroad at least twice a year for business and rely on regular contact with their home country for the success of their firms, however they continue to be based in their host country.

Jega Aravandy, a California-based founder of a technology platform for facilitating air freight service, explained that he took his family to live in his home country, India, for a few months to help to set up the local office and hire people. He returned to California with the family once he had a critical mass of people in India. From that point onwards, he or his colleague frequently traveled to India to manage the India office for short periods of time:

> I went to India for six months to set up the office, hire people… I took my family, my wife and I had one kid at that time. I stayed there for about eight months, hiring people, training them all that… so from six people we got about 50 people in that office and then I came back here, and from then on we had enough people and then we kind of rotated. I would go for some time, my colleague would go for some, but not more than one or two months at a time. And then once you get the initial set going, then it is a little bit more stable over there. (Jega Aravandy, Founder, California)

Even though he frequently traveled back home, Jega continued to live in California on a permanent basis as it was important to be close to clients who were based in the US:

> Yes, I wanted to live in India beyond that eight months, that is what I would have wanted to, but you know we have this thing we call 'opportunity costs', right, the cost of me being there, the cost of me being here. Here is, I can go

to client's place, I can sell more, right. There I really was not selling; I was just setting up the office. Whereas, when you are starting a company, selling is the key, right. You can always figure a way to do it, but selling was important. So it is a tradeoff so I had to come back. (Jega Aravandy, Founder, California)

Although constant travel is a useful part of the definition of TEs, it needs a slight modification due to the changing and advanced nature of technology that makes it possible for TEs to 'virtually' rather than physically travel abroad on a frequent basis in the conduct of their transnational activities.

Simultaneous Entrepreneurial Engagement in at Least Two Countries

TEs build ventures in both their host and home countries at inception (Drori et al., 2009; Yeung, 2009). Their presence in two or more different locations allows them to compare these locations in terms of their suitability for production. This provides them with significant competitive advantages compared to entrepreneurs who are located in only one geographic region.

To that end, TEs organize key activities across those locations early in the founding of their ventures. They may raise capital from their home country, subcontract research and software development in their home country or even sell their products in home country markets. They specialize in dispersing key parts of their value-added activities across their host and home markets such that they can exploit unique skills, resources or other such benefits from their home country.

The nature and form of TE engagement in their host and home countries is varied. Earlier studies point to US-based TEs from Mexico, El Salvador or the Dominican Republic engaging in informal trade in the 1990s. These TEs traveled back and forth to engage in informal activities that bypassed existing laws in both host and home countries, and took advantage of differential demands and prices in both countries (Portes and Guarnizo, 1991). The transnational activities of these migrants seemed to be oriented more toward home countries and tended to be limited to sending remittances back home.

In their study of large Salvadoran and Dominican immigrant populations of Los Angeles, Washington, DC and New York City, Landolt et al. (1999) and Itzigsohn (2000) identified four types of transnational enterprises: **ethnic enterprises**, **circuit firms**, **cultural enterprises** and **return migrant microenterprises**. **Ethnic enterprises** are small retail firms catering to immigrant groups, and depend on a steady supply of imported goods such as foodstuffs and clothing from the home country. **Circuit firms** are involved in the transfer of goods and remittances across countries and range from an array of informal international couriers to large formal firms headquartered in the host country. **Cultural enterprises** rely on daily contacts with the home country and depend on the desire of immigrants to acquire and consume cultural goods from their home country. For example, Salvadoran newspapers are readily available in Los Angeles and Washington as are compact discs and videos with the latest musical hits. Finally, **return migrant microenterprises** are firms established by returnees to the home country that rely on their contacts in the host country. They include restaurants, video stores, auto sales and repairs, laundromats and office supplies.

Miera (2008) discerns four typologies of Polish TEs in Germany based on transnational social networks and embeddedness in host and home environments: TEs using a high degree of personal mobility and differences in purchasing power between Germany and Poland in cross-border trade; TEs recruiting transnational workers; TEs targeting the Polish community as a market; and TEs opening branches in Poland of businesses initiated in Germany.

Vikas, a technology entrepreneur and TE of Indian origin in the US, explained the rationale for locating a sales office, rather than development center, in India for his venture. As a product rather than services firm, they were fast in conducting research and developing new features. A small R&D team located in close proximity to the final market in the US was well-suited to cope with those needs. He would have to build a much bigger R&D team in India in order for it to be as efficient as the team located in the US. It was not worthwhile investing in such a team in India, considering the company's growth potential and the possibility of soon being acquired by another large company. Therefore, it made more sense for them to retain their small development team in the US in order to continue to benefit from high margins from their product-based offering:

> In India we may have an office for sales... I would require a 100 R&D people in India to get the same kind of benefit... We move so fast over here with a very small team that I'm not sure I can do that out of India. Until we grow to that size. More realistically in our life cycle, I think we might get acquired before we get too large... But we are pure product focused and I think that for products nothing like doing it out of here. Our margins are very high our professional services are only 5% of our business and that's the model we want to keep after. (Vikas, Founder, Silicon Valley, California)

TEs need not necessarily have legal entities in both their country of origin and residence (Drori et al., 2009; Portes et al., 2002). Their businesses in both locations may be closely related, but not necessarily formal, in order to offer transnational business value. For example, a TE may hire employees at home through outsourcing to work for a legal entity located predominantly in the host country. They may be socially motivated to hire in their home country in order to uplift the economic status of their home country nationals by offering them employment, without establishing a formal legal entity back home.

Dual Embeddedness in Host and Home Institutional Environments

Embeddedness reflects the degree to which firms are enmeshed in a social network in different situations (Uzzi, 1997). By definition, TEs are simultaneously embedded in at least two institutional environments. This spans their embeddedness in dual legal and regulatory regimes, cultural repertoires, social and professional networks and power relations (Terjesen and Elam, 2009). This dual embeddedness provides valuable, hard to imitate knowledge of, and familiarity with, the two countries, which provides a sustainable competitive advantage in identifying and implementing opportunities.

Legal and regulatory regimes. TEs combine favorable sets of ownership patterns, ease of start-up, established management practices, transparency, intellectual rights protection and resource availability in host and home countries. They may draw on personal resources in countries where formal institutions are relatively less developed, or use resources acquired from other countries through favorable laws or personal networks.

Cultural repertoires describe how individuals operate in differing cultures to access resources and exploit opportunities (Drori et al., 2009). TEs' familiarity with different cultures increases trust and lowers transaction costs associated with doing business across multiple countries. They have an ability to adapt to or adopt existing cultural repertoires and create new ways of doing business.

Social and professional networks provide access to complementary resources such as capital, information and partners in order to enable individuals to establish and run their businesses (Davidsson and Honig, 2003). Social networks enable TEs to develop innovative products and critical resources for direct internationalization and to play an important role as intermediaries for other ventures (Terjesen and Elam, 2009).

Unlike internationalizing firms, TEs' networks span host and home country borders (Drori et al., 2009). TEs differ from EEs in both the nature and scope of their social networks. Unlike EEs, TEs actually avoid close association with their co-ethnics, maintaining that such networks constrain their ability to identify additional resources and otherwise provide novelty, innovation and market excellence. Instead, they expand business contacts beyond their ethnic group (Light and Gold, 2000; Yeung, 2009), which facilitates their 'breaking out' outside of the boundaries of their ethnic environment.

Drori et al. (2009) contend that TE implies three domains for simultaneous network formation – network of origin (ethnic, national), network of destination and network of industry. **Networks of origin** help TEs to select networks of destination, as well as to adapt and acclimatize to the new environment. Immigrants from certain countries and communities favor particular destinations, gradually building on established relationships and the resultant social capital available to them.

Networks of destination provide social capital in the form of affection and trust following immigration. These networks enhance business possibilities and cross-national partnerships. These newly formed networks are also capable of transferring social capital back to their country of origin.

Finally, TEs' professional or **industry networks** span geographic borders (Autio et al., 2004). Often based on prior work experience in the industry, industry networks, particularly in technology, are characterized by a common language (Saxenian, 2002). Within these networks, TEs more quickly raise capital, assemble management teams and develop partnerships across cultural and linguistic boundaries.

Pruthi et al. (2018) show that TEs' use of personal and industry ties in venture founding in host and home countries is contingent on whether TEs have prior experience of entering the home country and implementing the business opportunity underlying the transnational venture (TNV) in the home country, respectively, with a former employer.

Power relations captures the extent to which individuals' specialized human and social capital allows them to formulate sustainable strategies (Terjesen and Elam, 2009). In case of TEs, cultural and institutional artifacts such as awards and keynote presentations in host and home countries confer and reinforce their power and status.

Unlike other types of immigrant entrepreneur, TEs often have access to a greater number of powerful players across multiple institutional environments. They then select individuals and firms to facilitate the trade of their goods. TEs may also be approached by other firms seeking overseas trade, which in turn may enable them to amass greater power.

Even though dual embeddedness is one of the characteristic features of TEs, circular migration is becoming increasingly common. People do not necessarily move from A to B, but from A to B and from B to another country. Immigrants may not necessarily have a relationship with their home country, or the home country may not play a significant role in the business. Thus, immigrants traversing multiple geographic borders may not be embedded in either host or home country, yet business activities may be spread across borders. Overall, transnational entrepreneurial activities need to be considered in a multilateral context, rather than as a bilateral relationship between host and home countries.

TEs as Highly Skilled Migrants

According to Portes et al. (2002), transnational activities are not associated with the recency of arrival or with marginal economic status in the host country. Often, TEs are part of the elite in their respective host communities in terms of education and legal standing, and derive higher-than-average incomes from these activities compared with the wage/salaried majority.

According to research evidence, the higher the educational level, the higher the probability of becoming a TE rather than a local entrepreneur (Portes et al., 2002). Lin and Tao (2012) find that 9.6% TEs in their sample had a PhD as compared to only 4.5% of non-TEs. As compared to 9% in the non-TE group, only 2.7% of TEs had a diploma or a lower educational level.

Countries like the US, Canada and New Zealand give privileged access to skilled migrants who pledge to start new businesses to stimulate economic growth. At the same time, however, TEs are not confined to the high-skilled sectors. They can originate either 'from above' or 'from below' (Drori et al., 2009). Low-skilled migrants from Mexico, El Salvador, Guatemala and the Dominican Republic, for instance, have also shown a tendency toward transnational entrepreneurship (Zhou, 2004).

TE Motivations and Resources

TE motivation and strategy depend on resources available to TEs to navigate host and home country environments (Light and Gold 2000; Portes et al., 2002; Saxenian, 2005). Home country knowledge, prior experience, social and professional networks, as well as the home country's external institutional environment are all influential as explained below.

Knowledge of Home Country

TEs' distinctive knowledge of host and home countries, and prior familiarity with the home country, is a key motivation for establishing operations at home. For Sarvesh Mahesh, a California-based TE and founder of Tavant Technologies, going back home to India was much easier than entering other countries with similar advantages at the time of founding his venture. He considered entering China, but 'couldn't figure out how to make it work'. Vietnam, Brazil, Argentina and the Philippines were other potential candidates, and he was aware of other entrepreneurs who had entered these countries, however he knew very little of them:

> We thought about going to China and went and looked at it but we couldn't figure out how to make it work. One or two experiments we'll do in Vietnam… Vietnam and China from a cost perspective, skill perspective, and number of people who are available perspective are quite big. Another place where people are doing a lot of this is Brazil and Argentina. And Philippines. Philippines not so much for programming but more for call center work… but we know very little of that market and I've heard it's very difficult to set up something in Brazil because they have a very closed system… (Sarvesh Mahesh, Founder, Tavant Technologies)

Prior Experience

Typically, the idea for a TNV originates with migrants' experience in the host country and the investment capital comes from their personal savings (Portes et al., 2002). Often, highly skilled migrants quit well-paying jobs to pursue transnational entrepreneurship. Their goal is to better utilize their skills to reap material gains and maximize their human capital returns (Brzozowski et al., 2014).

Sometimes, TEs have prior experience of entering their home country with a former employer from the host country. MNCs headquartered in the West require their executives to work overseas as a prerequisite for senior leadership positions (Kerr et al., 2015). IBM, General Electric and Siemens, for example, have at least half their workforce employed outside of their headquarter country. Several of these firms also have immigrants as their CEOs. Prominent examples include Google, Microsoft, Clorox, Coca-Cola, Dow Chemical, McDonalds, Pepsi and Pfizer. High-skilled staff and especially senior managers at these corporations are frequently transferred within the firm throughout their careers.

In other cases, many large high-tech companies send recruiting teams to engineering schools in emerging economies (Kerr et al., 2016). Given large absolute numbers of students graduating abroad in countries like China and India (Freeman and Huang, 2015), this traditional flow is quite likely to continue for some time.

This prior work experience inspires TEs to establish a business link with their home country for their own ventures. Vijay Parmar, a US-based TE and founder of Gainspan, wanted to establish a business link with India right at the outset because of his prior experience of entering India as an employee of Arc Media. The experience helped him to understand the significantly lower costs of running operations in India, which is why he decided to set up an India office:

> Right at the outset I wanted to establish something in India. Right. Because I had worked for this company called Arc Media which had the team back in India. So I knew I could do that and I understood that the cost of running operations in India is going to be very lower compared to doing something here. So with that I started off the India office. (Vijay Parmar, Founder, Gainspan, California)

Sarvesh Mahesh said that he 'knew how to make it work' when he decided to set up his venture in India as he had previously entered India as an employee of Tata Consultancy Services (TCS):

> Me, having worked at TCS, I knew how to make it work. If I hadn't worked in TCS, we probably would've waited for longer before we set up our India center. We set up very soon. (Sarvesh Mahesh, Founder, Tavant Technologies, California)

Social and Professional Networks

Cross border networks of TEs in their host and home countries facilitate access to such crucial resources as information, local knowledge, capital, markets and technology in venture creation (Chen and Tan, 2009).

Silicon Valley's new IEs have been instrumental in building links with their home country on the basis of their personal and professional networks (Saxenian, 2002). The region's Chinese and Indian engineers first became key middlemen leveraging their ethnic networks in their home countries to locate R&D and linking their large employers in the US with low-cost expertise back home.

Home country 'ethnic' networks first provided these skilled immigrants an additional advantage over their non-immigrant counterparts in the Valley. Due to their language skills, cultural know-how and contacts, these IEs were able to build business relationships in Asia that transformed into a competitive advantage for their firms.

Sai Gundavelli, founder of Solix Technologies, California, recalled using personal family ties in his home country, India, for first starting up there in the mid-1990s. He invited his father, his brother-in-law, a local government employee and his sister to join him. Sai's father was appointed chairman of this venture. An engineer who did not have many opportunities to grow, his brother-in-law joined as a technical manager, whereas his sister took up an HR-related role. Sai explained that these members of the family became indispensable to setting up and running his local operations, providing the impetus and such vital resources as expertise and infrastructure in the early stages:

> When I first started in 1996, my brother-in-law was working for a government company. So I told him 'Hey, would you like to join me?'… One of them is an engineer… my sister joined more as a HR kind of a function… So they became like my eyes and ears. My father was the chairman. My father-in-law also helped in the initial setting up. He comes from an engineering background. He helped in the infrastructure, the cubicles and the layouts and location and all of that. So my father, father-in-law, brother-in-law, sister, were all kind of a help, initial help to setting up of the system. (Sai Gundavelli, Founder, Solix Technologies, California)

Home Country Institutional Environment

The institutional environment of the home country, including laws and regulations, economic conditions, and specific entrepreneurial culture, is an important determinant of the opportunity structure and form of transnational activity (Brzozowski et al., 2014; Newland and Tanaka, 2010; Riddle and Brinkerhoff, 2011). The stock of human capital in the home country including skilled workers, ease of forming partnerships, knowledge and technology spillovers is likely to support TEs' operations at home, and provides skilled TEs something to return to (Portes and Yiu, 2013).

Vas Bhandarkar, a TE in the San Francisco Bay area, loved working with 'young people'. Additionally, the cost savings from the outsourcing of IT work in India and the ability to leverage time-zone differences between the US and India were the two key reasons for forming a transnational venture in India:

> For me personally, business benefit was secondary. The reason to work with India was I loved working with the young people. I felt like I was making an impact in India. I felt like it was a very decent way to make money. It was like killing two birds with one stone. You are not detrimental to the business yet you are having an impact to the country of your origin. That was the profound reason. Even in SolvVentures, teammates have begun working with India because of the time zone differences. (Vas Bhandarkar, Founder, SolvVentures, California, USA)

Raju Reddy, Founder, Sierra Atlantic, an IT service company in California, USA, was confident about the quality and availability of technical talent in India, which he wished to leverage at the outset in the creation of his own transnational venture in India:

> Partly, the nature of our business was like that because I felt that's where we can differentiate ourselves at Sierra Atlantic....I had that experience with Wipro and Godrej. I mean they were developing those products for Intel and for themselves out of India. So there was never a question in my mind whether India has that talent to develop these kind of products. It's more a matter of leveraging that talent. (Raju Reddy, Founder, Sierra Atlantic, California, USA)

Emotional Reasons

In some cases, TEs maintain links with their home country as a back-up option, an alternative market for their goods or services in case of economic difficulties in the host country (Brzozowski et al., 2014). The home country is perceived as a safe destination in case of a possible return home, as many immigrant entrepreneurs do not intend to permanently remain in the host country (Stark and Bloom, 1985).

In other cases, TEs have strong emotional reasons to forge a business link with their home country at the outset (Riddle et al., 2010; Riddle and Brinkerhoff, 2011). TEs seek emotional satisfaction and recognition from their altruistic activities at home, which is a pressing reason to reconnect with the home country.

Raju Reddy, Founder, Sierra Atlantic, entered India right at inception. He had a strong motivation to become an entrepreneur since migrating from India and working in Silicon Valley. Additionally, he wished to found a business that was connected to India in some way. He emphasized that he probably would not have given up his job at Intel to found a company if it were not for the India component to his venture:

> India was there right from inception, when I started the company. For me there were two things. One, wanting to be an entrepreneur. Again that's sort of the Silicon Valley environment. Clearly that was the big piece of the draw. The second, I definitely wanted to be connected with India in some fashion. Any

business or pursuit. If it didn't have an India component, I would not have left Intel. So connecting with India was very important. (Raju Reddy, Founder, Sierra Atlantic, California, USA)

Role of VC Investors

VC investors also influence TEs' entry into the home country. As Vas Bhandarkar pointed out, top US VC firms, Draper Fisher Juverston and Sequoia Capital, were influential in his career journey, both while working at start-ups and at the time of founding his own ventures. He entered India (his home country) for his ventures as both these VC firms had offices in India:

> This [role of VC investors] is a very important parameter... Draper [VC firm]
> invested in Selectica, and Draper got me on as co-founder of Unimobile. Because
> of Unimobile, I got on the board of Global Logic. Because of the work I did
> at Global Logic, I got to know another investor, Sequoia Capital. Because of
> Sequoia Capital, I founded other ventures. Draper and Sequoia both have offices
> in India. Venture Capital network also plays a big role in our India expansion.
> (Vas Bhandarkar, TE, California)

Overall, TEs' strategies result from the unique intersection and interaction of their habituated mindset, resources and institutional environments that produce a competitive advantage for TEs (Terjesen and Elam, 2009). This model is depicted in Figure 9.2.

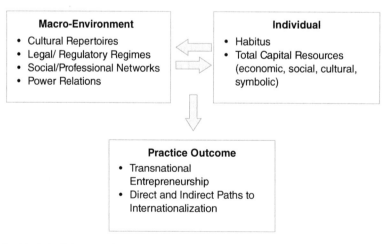

Figure 9.2 Model of theory of practice on firm outcomes

Source: Terjesen and Elam (2009)

Performance and Impact of New Immigrant Entrepreneurs

The new IEs are significant in terms of the performance of their firms, and hence their impact in both host and home countries. TEs make a direct contribution through both job and wealth creation. They also indirectly contribute by facilitating trade flows between their host and home countries, and playing a role in the development of their home countries.

Direct Contribution

Studies have compared the performance of immigrant firms with firms founded by native entrepreneurs in the host country (Kerr and Kerr, 2016). Recent evidence from the US suggests that, on the whole, businesses started by immigrant entrepreneurs perform better than native businesses with respect to employment growth over three- and six-year horizons, especially in high-wage businesses and high-tech sectors.

By contrast, immigrant-founded businesses show no advantages with respect to payroll growth. Immigrant-owned firms with transnational activities also have better performance than non-immigrant firms without transnational activities as measured by employment, total sales and total payrolls (Wong and Ng, 2002).

In her seminal articles, Saxenian (2002, 2005) examines the contribution of skilled immigrants in Silicon Valley. She suggests that these immigrants contribute to the economy both directly and indirectly. As scientists and engineers in the knowledge-based sectors in Silicon Valley, IEs create jobs and wealth, thus making a direct contribution to the California economy. The technology industries in which they are concentrated are California's largest and fastest growing exporters and leading contributors to the state's economic growth.

According to the *Wall Street Journal* (Koh, 2016), more than half of the current crop of US-based start-ups valued at $1 billion or more are founded by immigrants; these 44 companies collectively valued at $168 billion create roughly 760 jobs per company. Immigrants also make up more than 70% of key management or product-development positions at these companies.

With nearly 10,000 US-based employees, Uber, for instance, is valued at $76 billion. The company was listed on the New York Stock Exchange as of May 10, 2019. Founded in 2012, WeWork, which has revolutionized the shared office space concept, is now valued at $47 billion, with more than 6,000 employees. Since its founding in 2016, Houzz has grown from 800 to 1,800 employees and its value has risen to $4 billion. With over 500 employees, Avant has a valuation of $2 billion. In January 2017, AppDynamics was acquired by Cisco for $3.7 billion.

IMMIGRATION AS A SOURCE OF AMERICAN ECONOMIC VITALITY

Intel, Yahoo, Google, eBay and Sun Microsystems are well-known, exceptionally successful high-tech companies. What is less well known is that immigrant entrepreneurs have played a role in founding each one of these, and many other companies.

Over the past 15 years, immigrants in the US have started 25% of US public companies backed by VC firms. These businesses employ some 220,000 people in the US, and have a current market capitalization of more than $500 billion. Nearly half of the founders of the smaller, private venture-backed companies were also immigrants. Almost two-thirds (66 percent) of the immigrant founders of privately held venture-backed companies have started or intend to start more companies in the United States. Rather than stealing jobs from native workers, immigrant entrepreneurs are more likely to expand the job pool.

Yet, skilled migrants to the US face a number of challenges to live and work in the country despite their documented contribution to the US economy. One of the biggest hurdles is that the H1-b visas for skilled workers are currently capped at 65,000 annually. Granted in specialized fields such as computer science and biotechnology, these visas are key to enabling skilled foreign workers to enter and start new, high-growth ventures in the US.

Source: The Wall Street Journal (2006)

While there exist recent studies on the effect of high-skilled immigration on US innovation, a systematic evaluation of how the creation of new firms by immigrant founders contributes to the overall pace and direction of US innovation, and whether these firms produce different types of innovations compared to native-founded firms (e.g. exploration vs. exploitation work), is lacking (Kerr and Kerr, 2016).

Indirect Contribution

New immigrant entrepreneurs also make an indirect contribution, both to their host and home countries. The new IEs facilitate trade and investment links to their countries of origin, even when they choose not to return home on a permanent basis (Saxenian, 2002, 2005). Saxenian (2005) estimates that there is a significant correlation between the presence of first-generation immigrants from a given country and exports from California. For every 1% increase in the number of first-generation immigrants from a given country, exports from California go up nearly 0.5%. This effect is particularly pronounced in the Asia Pacific region where California exports nearly four times more than it exports to comparable countries in other parts of the world.

Spanning national boundaries, TEs' professional and social networks facilitate flows of information and provide contacts, sources of capital and expertise that allow these entrepreneurs to participate in an increasingly global economy. For example, China's entry into the global division of labor was initiated by overseas Chinese entrepreneurs in Taiwan and Hong Kong during the 1980s, before MNCs viewed China as a viable option in the 1990s. Indian employees of large technology firms in the US initiated India's software industry before India turned into a software-exporting powerhouse.

In taking advantage of 'brain circulation' rather than 'brain drain' by traveling across geographic borders (Saxenian, 2005), TEs take advantage of, and benefit from, knowledge that spills over from different environments. Transnational ventures accelerate the long-term integration of TEs with their host country. When TEs orient towards their home countries, they build and strengthen social structures that help enhance their future well-being in the host country (Zhou, 2004).

Further, TEs founding ventures in their home country are better positioned to build partnerships with foreign producers and tap overseas expertise in other markets of the world. TEs' experience of working in a home country context with many institutional voids gives them the confidence to explore markets with similar voids so they are able to capitalize on their knowledge for economic gain (De Silva, 2016). Thus, unlike their non-immigrant counterparts, they have the ability to locate foreign partners quickly, and manage complex relationships across geographic, cultural and linguistic boundaries, thus enabling their small start-ups to be global players from inception.

TEs also contribute to their home countries. Brorzowski et al. (2014) suggest that TEs discover and activate business initiatives that would not otherwise exist. They accelerate capital accumulation, which provides seed capital for business initiatives back in their home countries. Terjesen and Elam (2009) find that TEs act as intermediaries for local firms. Due to their unique position as intermediaries, TEs are able to spearhead innovations and exploit business opportunities.

Thus, TEs' cross-border ties are important for re-directing policy attention towards micro initiatives for promoting the development of entrepreneurship, especially in emerging economies (McEwan et al., 2005; Saxenian, 2005). Lorenzen and Mudambi (2013) argue that decentralized personal ties of individual members of the global diaspora are able to connect entrepreneurial clusters in various parts of the world. Personal relationships facilitate knowledge transfer and spillovers across geographic boundaries, and hence growth and survival of emerging economy clusters. Such cross-border ethnic ties also enable the international growth of new technology ventures inside emerging economy entrepreneurial clusters (Prashantham et al., 2015).

Chapter Summary

LO1: **New immigrant entrepreneurs** (IEs) are foreign-born founders of high-growth start-ups. Immigrants have started more than half of America's start-up companies valued at $1 billion or more. Skilled immigrants in the US have a growing presence in Silicon Valley, California, accounting for one third of the valley's engineering workforce in most technology firms. While India and China remain major sources of immigrant founders of high-growth start-ups in the US, immigrant founders of recent billion-dollar companies have emigrated from 25 different countries.

LO2: The new IEs in developed Western countries are highly **educated**. Higher educational credentials are associated with their engagement in STEM entrepreneurship in the host country. Successful founders of high-growth start-ups in the US also share extensive **cross-cultural experiences** that stimulate creativity and increase individuals' capabilities to identify promising business ideas. Silicon Valley's new IEs rely on a diverse range of informal social and professional networks on the basis of shared language, culture and educational and professional experiences. Taking the form of **professional networking organizations**, and **personal**, **social** or **industry networks**, **ethnic networks** help to mobilize capital, skills, information and advice for technology ventures. **Professional networking organizations** and **personal**, especially **alumni**, **networks** facilitate networking and information exchange within immigrant members. **Industry networks** are often based on IEs' prior work experience and are important for the inspiration to found new ventures.

LO3: **Transnational entrepreneurs (TEs)** are individuals that migrate from one country to another, concurrently maintaining business-related links with their countries of origin and currently adopted countries. The literature identifies four distinctive dimensions of TEs, namely, a) frequent travel between host and home countries, b) simultaneous entrepreneurial engagement in the two countries, c) dual embeddedness in host and home institutional environments, and d) highly skilled migrants.

LO4: There is considerable variability in TE motivations depending on TE resources to navigate host and home country environments, and the institutional environment of the home country. TEs' **knowledge** or prior familiarity with the home country is a key motivation for establishing operations at home. Typically, the idea for a transnational venture originates with migrants' **experience** in the host country and investment capital comes from their personal savings. **Cross-border networks** in host and home countries facilitate access to information, local knowledge, capital, markets and technology in venture creation. The **institutional environment** of the home country is an important determinant of the opportunity structure and form of transnational activity. In some cases, TEs maintain links with their home country as a back-up option, an alternative market for their goods or services in case of economic difficulties in the host country. In other cases, they have strong **emotional reasons** to forge a business link with their home country. **VC investors** also influence TEs' entry into the home country.

LO5: The new IEs have both **direct** and **indirect** impact, and they contribute to both their host and home countries. The new IEs are responsible for building start-ups valued at $1 billion or more. Businesses started by immigrant entrepreneurs in the US perform better than native businesses in high-wage and high-tech sectors. Immigrant-owned firms with transnational activities also perform better than non-immigrant firms without transnational activities. TEs' firms facilitate trade and investment links to TEs' countries of origin.

Review Questions

1. What is the difference between ethnic entrepreneurs (EEs) that you learned about in the last chapter, and the new immigrant entrepreneurs you have read about in this chapter? Explain the distinguishing features of EEs and the new IEs to support your answer.
2. Explain what you understand by the term 'transnational entrepreneurs'. How are TEs different from EEs? Explain.
3. According to Chen and Tan (2009), TE networks are 'glocalized' networks that have both global and local connections. What are the three domains of network formation of TEs, according to the chapter? Explain.
4. What are the motivations of TEs? Why do TEs found ventures spanning their host and home country boundaries?
5. How do TEs use their experience and social networks in the founding of their ventures? Use examples from the chapter to explain your answer.
6. What is the significance of the new immigrant and transnational entrepreneurs? Based on the chapter, discuss the contribution of the new IEs to their a) host country and b) home country.

---Case 9.1---

Abdul-Wahab: Bridging Host and Home Countries to Fill a Gap

Source: www.needpix.com/photo/1614163

Opportunity Recognition

Abdul-Wahab is credited with bringing camel milk to California and the wider US through his Desert Farms company. Abdul-Wahab was raised in Jeddah, Saudi Arabia. An alumnus of the British International School of Jeddah, he continued his education abroad at community college in Santa Monica, California, United States (US). After two years there, Abdul-Wahab transferred to the University of Southern California, where he studied business administration, finance and entrepreneurship, graduating in 2013.

When Abdul-Wahab first arrived in the US in the spring of 2009, he was impressed by how health-conscious the Californian community was. 'Raw and organic' were the be-all and end-all of anything considered healthy and nutritious and a clear indicator of where the market was heading in the US. One summer while Abdul-Wahab was visiting his family in Jeddah, he was approached by a friend with a plastic bag of milk that looked 'really fresh – and tasted so good'. Abdul-Wahab fell in love with the milk and he knew other people would too. He had just discovered camel milk. Proven to be one of the few complete foods available to humans, camel milk contains all of the proteins, carbohydrates, fats and essential vitamins needed to nourish an individual without requiring any additional food or water.

Abdul-Wahab found himself attached to the root cause of improving the health of people around the world. However, despite there being millions of camels in Saudi Arabia, camel milk had not previously been commercialized in the Kingdom. It was mainly seen for medicinal use only, and rarely found in supermarkets. Only the Bedouins sold it. This local community was known for herding camels in Jeddah. For thousands of years, Bedouins and nomads had lived off camel milk for months at a time while trekking through the desert.

Upon his return to the US, Abdul-Wahab realized it was the perfect place to start a camel milk company, and Desert Farms was born. Abdul-Wahab took charge as the company's founder and CEO. As early as 2014, he set up booths at conventions including the Natural Products Expo West at the Anaheim Convention Center in California to enable potential customers to sample his product. After selling camel milk at mosques and ethnic food festivals, Walid's business plan won the Marcia Israel Award from the University of Southern California. He decided to leave his corporate real estate position to begin his camel adventure.

He had discovered a niche in the market for the growing demand for a raw unpasteurized alternative to cow's milk.

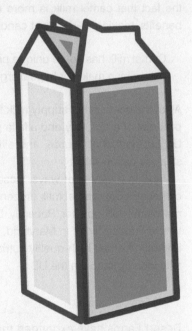

Early demand in the US came from people with gut issues. Others soon began using camel milk to boost their immune system and build good bacteria, which is in fact responsible for 70% of our immune system. Slowly, people who care about healthy foods also became early adopters. Abdul-Wahab believed he introduced a whole new market segment when his company first commercialized camel milk in the West:

> When Desert Farms-commercialized camel milk came to the West, we didn't just bring a new product to consumers, we introduced a whole new market segment.

Returning to California with his newfound love for and knowledge of camel milk, Abdul-Wahab took a tour across the US, from the East Coast to the Midwest, in search of camel farmers who could supply the milk required for his business idea.

Source: www.needpix.com/photo/29664

(Continued)

Building the Business

Abdul-Wahab found his initial business partners within the Amish community of Missouri, US While looking for US camel herders, in the Midwest he came across the Amish community known for being polite and down-to-earth, a group who didn't exist in the Middle East. Watching them work together remained awesome to Walid:

> Networking through social media just isn't the same as teaming up with
> neighbors to build a barn… If you ask an Amish farmer why they're successful,
> don't expect a lot of soul-searching or reflection on what they do right – the
> Amish will likely pin the praise on anyone else but themselves.

Walid felt that the Amish deserved an easier way to bring their products to market. However, as Amish people are reluctant to adopt modern technology, Walid acted as a marketer and distributor for their camel milk, helping to bring its nutritional and medicinal benefits to the wider US.

After extensive market research, Abdul-Wahab attended trade shows where he distributed samples and met potential retailers. A big selling point for Desert Farms was the fact that camel milk is more nutrient-dense than cow's milk and has medicinal benefits, making it an instant candidate as a dairy alternative:

> Camel milk has some unique properties that mimic the health benefits of breast
> milk, which makes it hypoallergenic and unlikely to cause intolerances.

All of the camels that supply milk for Desert Farms are pasture-raised and eat a complex diet of grass, hay and alfalfa pellets. None of the camel milk is imported into the US but bottled at source, and either immediately distributed locally or frozen to be shipped nationwide.

Sold in a variety of ways, Desert Farms offers camel milk in forms including raw camel milk; raw camel milk (frozen); raw camel milk kefir; pasteurized camel milk; and raw camel milk powder. Recently, Desert Farms camel milk has reached the shelves of Whole Foods Market in Maryland, Pennsylvania, DC, Virginia and Ohio. Whole Foods is known for their high-quality nutritious and natural/organic products and environmentally friendly image in the US.

The Path Ahead

Desert Farms have expanded their product line to include camel milk soaps and other camel milk-based beauty products, as well as camel hump fat, which can be used as an alternative to butter and cooking oil. In addition to wanting to share the natural goodness of camel milk, Desert Farms helps to open new markets and build sustainable sources of income for small family farmers. Following its belief in supporting US production, the business helps the best farmers produce the best, and advocates farmer-friendly practices. Among its goals are water and energy efficiency (their Amish farmers are super low energy users), reduced waste production and recycling, all of which translate directly to their reduced carbon footprint. Farmers are also asked to use 'Good Manufacturing Practices' and abide by fair minimum standards to improve their social and environmental performance.

While camel milk continues to increase in popularity in the US, obstacles are ever present. For one, this is an industry where the product animal is far outnumbered: 18,000:1 is the ratio of cows to camels in the US, and the total number of camels in the country is estimated at about 5,000. Additionally, a cow can produce upwards of 40 liters of milk per day, while a camel can produce an average of only 7 liters of milk per day.

Next on the agenda for Desert Farms is venturing into the Saudi market and commercializing the production and distribution of camel milk. Abdul-Wahab also hopes to leverage his home country manufacturing potential to produce for the global market:

> The future will be to set up the world's largest camel dairy in Saudi Arabia and make our region the powerhouse of camel milk production, as well as produce other desert products for the global market.

The business has promising global market potential because of its many health benefits. Nutritionists estimate that anywhere from 65% to 75% of the world population is lactose intolerant, which is why camel milk is proving to be the ideal alternative. As well as containing three times as much vitamin C per serving as cow's milk, camel milk does not contain beta-lactoglobulin, a whey protein found in cow's milk that causes allergic reactions. The amount of lactose in camel milk is so small that a patient suffering from lactose intolerance is able to digest it without discomfort.

Discussion Questions

1. How did Abdul-Wahab identify the opportunity for Desert Farms?
2. How did he build the business model for his venture? What was the role of his background (education/knowledge, experience, social networks) in the a) host country and b) home country in the founding of his venture? Discuss.
3. Visit Desert Farm's website at https://desertfarms.com. Explore their: product range; manufacturing plants/farms in the US; practices; and customer testimonials. Based on the company's website and information presented in the case, do you support Abdul-Wahab's future plans to set up a production facility in Saudi Arabia? Why / why not? Give reasons to justify your answer.
4. Based on this case, what conclusions can you draw about the contribution of the new immigrant entrepreneurs to their a) host country and b) home country?

References

Abdulaziz, A. (2018) 'How a Saudi dairy farmer brought camel milk to the US', *The Arab Times*, 4 June. Available at www.arabnews.com/node/1313456/saudi-arabia (last accessed 27 September 2022).

Anderson, S. (2019) 'Immigrant entrepreneurs prove it doesn't matter where you were born', *Forbes*, 6 May. Available at www.forbes.com/sites/stuartanderson/2019/05/06/immigrant-entrepreneurs-prove-it-doesnt-matter-where-you-were-born/#30fd373a49b7 (last accessed 27 September 2022).

Autio, E., Hameri, A.-P. and Vuola, O. (2004) 'A framework of industrial knowledge spillovers in big-science centers', *Research Policy*, 33(1): 107–126.

Blume-Kohout, M.E. (2016) 'Imported entrepreneurs: Foreign-born scientists and engineers in US STEM fields entrepreneurship'. *US Small Business Administration: Office of Advocacy Report*. Available at https://cdn.advocacy.sba.gov/wp-content/uploads/2019/05/14144122/Imported-Entrepreneurs-Foreign-Born-Scientists-and-Engineers-in-US-STEM-Fields-Entrepreneurship-Report.pdf (last accessed 27 September 2022).

Brzozowski, J., Cucculelli, M. and Surdej, A. (2014) 'Transnational ties and performance of immigrant entrepreneurs: The role of home-country conditions', *Entrepreneurship & Regional Development*, 26(7–8): 546–573.

Chen, W. and Tan, J. (2009) 'Understanding transnational entrepreneurship through a network lens: Theoretical and methodological considerations', *Entrepreneurship Theory and Practice*, 33(5): 1079–1091.

Davidsson, P. and Honig, B. (2003) 'The role of social and human capital among nascent entrepreneurs', *Journal of Business Venturing*, 18(3): 301–331.

De Silva, M. (2016) 'Academic entrepreneurship and traditional academic duties: Synergy or rivalry?' *Studies in Higher Education*, 41(12): 2169–2183.

Drori, I., Honig, B. and Wright, M. (2009) 'Transnational entrepreneurship: An emergent field of study', *Entrepreneurship Theory and Practice*, 33(5): 1001–1022.

Fairlie, R.W., Zissimopoulos, J. and Krashinsky, H. (2010) 'The international Asian business success story? A comparison of Chinese, Indian and other Asian businesses in the United States, Canada and United Kingdom', in J. Lerner and A. Schoar (eds.), *International Differences in Entrepreneurship*. Cambridge, MA: National Bureau of Economic Research, pp. 179–208.

Freeman, R.B. and Huang, W. (2015) 'Collaborating with people like me: Ethnic coauthorship within the United States', *Journal of Labor Economics*, 33(S1): S289–S318.

Itzigsohn, J. (2000) 'Immigration and the boundaries of citizenship: The institutions of immigrants' political transnationalism', *International Migration Review*, 34(4): 1126–1154.

Kerr, S.P. and Kerr, W.R. (2016) 'Immigrant entrepreneurship', *National Bureau of Economic Research*. Available at www.nber.org/papers/w22385 (last accessed 27 September 2022).

Kerr, S.P., Kerr, W. and Nanda, R. (2015) 'House money and entrepreneurship'. Working Paper 15-069. Harvard Business School, Entrepreneurial Management. http://dx.doi.org/10.2139/ssrn.2638045

Kerr, S.P., Kerr, W., Ozden, C. and Parsons, C. (2016) 'Global talent flows'. Working Paper 17-026. Harvard Business School.

Koh, Y. (2016) 'Study: Immigrants founded 51% of US billion-dollar startups', *The Wall Street Journal*, March 17, 9:16 am. https://www.wsj.com/articles/study-immigrants-founded-51-of-u-s-billion-dollar-startups-1458220591

Landolt, P., Antler, L. and Baires, S. (1999) 'From "Hermano Lejano" to "Hermano Mayor": The dialectics of Salvadoran transnationalism', *Ethnic and Racial Studies*, 22(1): 290–315.

Light, I. and Gold, S.J. (2000) *Ethnic Economies*. San Diego, CA: Academic Press.

Lin, X. and Tao, S. (2012) 'Transnational entrepreneurs: Characteristics, drivers, and success factors', *Journal of International Entrepreneurship*, 10(1): 50–69.

Lofstrom, M. (2002) 'Labour market assimilation and the self-employment decision of immigrant entrepreneurs', *Journal of Population Economics*, 15: 83–114.

Lorenzen, M. and Mudambi, R. (2013) 'Clusters, connectivity and catch-up: Bollywood and Bangalore in the global economy', *Journal of Economic Geography*, 13(3): 501–534.

Malseed, M. (2007) 'The story of Sergey Brin', *Moment Magazine*, February–March. Available at https://momentmag.com/the-story-of-sergey-brin (last accessed 27 September 2022).

McEwan, C., Henry, N. and Pollard, J. (2005) 'The "global" in the city economy: Multicultural economic development in Birmingham', *International Journal of Urban and Regional Research*, 29(4): 916–933.

Michaels, D. and Schechner, S. (2018) 'Adyen's IPO success spurs hopes European tech scene has turned a corner', *The* Wall Street Journal, Eastern Edition, September 15, 11:00 am ET. https://www.wsj.com/articles/adyens-ipo-success-spurs-hopes-european-tech-scene-has-turned-a-corner-1537023600

Miera, F. (2008) 'Transnational strategies of Polish migrant entrepreneurs in trade and small business in Berlin', *Journal of Ethnic and Migration Studies*, 34(5): 753–770.

Neidert, M. (2018) 'How 12 immigrant entrepreneurs have made America great'. *Medium.com*, 8 August. Available at https://medium.com/@michael.neidert/how-12-immigrant-entrepreneurs-have-made-america-great-ed178fe9837d (last accessed 27 September 2022).

Newland, K. and Tanaka, H. (2010) 'Mobilizing diaspora entrepreneurship for development', *Diapsoras and Development Policy Project, Migrants, Migration, and Development Program, Migration Policy Institute, USAID (United States Agency for International Development)*, Washington: DC, 1–29.

Portes, A. and Guarnizo, L.E. (1991) 'Tropical capitalists: US-bound immigration and small enterprise development in the Dominican Republic', in S. Diaz-Briquets and S. Weintraub (eds.), *Migration, Remittances, and Small Business Development: Mexico and Caribbean Basin Countries*. Boulder, CO: Westview Press, pp. 101–131.

Portes, A. and Yiu, J. (2013) 'Entrepreneurship, transnationalism, and development', *Migration Studies*, 1(1): 75–95.

Portes, A., Haller, W.J. and Guarnizo, L.E. (2002) 'Transnational entrepreneurs: An alternative form of immigrant economic adaptation', *American Sociological Review*, 67(2): 278–298.

Prashantham, S., Dhanaraj, C. and Kumar, K. (2015) 'Ties that bind: Ethnic ties and new venture internationalization', *Long Range Planning*, 48(5): 317–333.

Pruthi, S. (2014) 'Social ties and venture creation by returnee entrepreneurs', *International Business Review*, 23(6): 1139–1152.

Pruthi, S., Basu, A. and Wright, M. (2018) 'Ethnic ties, motivations, and home country entry strategy of transnational entrepreneurs', *Journal of International Entrepreneurship*, 16(2): 210–243.

Raymund, F. (2007) 'Immigrants gain edge doing business back home; knowledge of culture, personal connections help to open doors', *The Wall Street Journal*, March 20, 12:01 am. https://www.wsj.com/articles/SB117436098462742444

Riddle, L. and Brinkerhoff, J. (2011) 'Diaspora entrepreneurs as institutional change agents: The case of Thamel.com', *International Business Review*, 20(6): 670–680.

Riddle, L., Hrivnak, G.A. and Nielsen, T.M. (2010) 'Transnational diaspora entrepreneurship in emerging markets: Bridging institutional divides', *Journal of International Management*, 16(4): 398–411.

Saxenian, A. (2002) 'Silicon Valley's new immigrant high-growth entrepreneurs', *Economic Development Quarterly*, 16(1): 20–31.

Saxenian, A. (2005) 'From brain drain to brain circulation: Transnational communities and regional upgrading in India and China', *Studies in Comparative International Development*, 40(2): 35–61.

Stark, O. and Bloom, D.E. (1985) 'The new economics of labor migration', *The American Economic Review*, 75(2): 173–178.

Terjesen, S. and Elam, A. (2009) 'Transnational entrepreneurs' venture internationalization strategies: A practice theory approach', *Entrepreneurship Theory and Practice*, 33(5): 1093–1120.

Uzzi, B. (1997) 'Social structure and competition in interfirm networks: The paradox of embeddedness', *Administrative Science Quarterly*, 42(1): 35–67.

Vandor, P. and Franke, N. (2016) 'See Paris and… found a business? The impact of cross-cultural experience on opportunity recognition capabilities', *Journal of Business Venturing*, 31(4): 388–407.

Vertovec, S. (2004) 'Migrant transnationalism and modes of transformation', *International Migration Review*, 38(3): 970–1001.

Wadhwa, V. (2012) *The Immigrant Exodus: Why America Is Losing the Global Race to Capture Entrepreneurial Talent*. Philadelphia, PA: Wharton School Press.

The Wall Street Journal (2006) 'Immigrant entrepreneurs', *The Wall Street Journal*, Institute for International Education, 24 November. Available at www.wsj.com/articles/SB116431825393231459 (last accessed 27 September 2022).

Wong, L.L. and Ng, M. (2002) 'The emergence of small transnational enterprise in Vancouver: The case of Chinese entrepreneur immigrants', *International Journal of Urban and Regional Research*, 26(3): 508–530.

Wright, M., Clarysse, B., Mustar, P. and Lockett, A. (2007) *Academic Entrepreneurship in Europe*. Cheltenham: Edward Elgar Publishing.

Yeung, H.W.C. (2009) 'Regional development and the competitive dynamics of global production networks: An East Asian perspective', *Regional Studies*, 43(3): 325–351.

Zhou, M. (2004) 'Revisiting ethnic entrepreneurship: Convergences, controversies, and conceptual advancements', *International Migration Review*, 38(3): 1040–1074.

10
RETURNEE ENTREPRENEURS

LI GUANJIAO AND ZHOU XIN: RETURNING HOME TO START UP

Source: www.needpix.com/photo/899302

(Continued)

Li Guanjiao, 31 years old, studied for a master's degree in branding at the London College of Communications from 2012 to 2014. Li now owns and runs her own company, BCZW, in Beijing. The company produces decorative Chinese designs that can be screen-printed on a variety of items such as T-shirts, books, clothing and mugs.

Born in Yingkou, a small coastal city in the northeastern province of Liaoning, China, 44-year-old Zhou Xin, the founder of Beijing Define Technology Corp, returned home to start his venture after earning a doctorate in physics from Stanford University, California. Li and Zhou are among the growing number of young returnees in China with experience of studying and working overseas who have returned home to start businesses.

Soon after graduation, Li took up a job in the fashion and design section of a Chinese-language newspaper in London. The role helped her to improve her knowledge and skills in the UK's highly developed fashion, design and printing industry. She had an idea to start her own venture when she returned home. She noticed that countries like the UK and South Korea had iconic painting styles of their own; yet, Chinese cultural images and designs did not seem to match up. Located near the modern Today Art Museum in Beijing, the company has about 20 employees. The location helps Li to promote her products. She also has an online store on Taobao to promote her products.

Zhou took up a job in Los Angeles, California, right after graduation from the doctoral program. His doctoral research examined tunable diode laser absorption spectroscopy technology. Three years later, he had become the company's chief scientist. He liked the job, but not the predictability that came with the ability to envision his career path 20 years down the line. He felt in need of a challenge. He also felt constrained in his ability to express himself freely due to language difficulties.

Zhou had the idea of starting a company in Beijing while he was watching Win in China, a popular TV program about entrepreneurship. His wife, who had an MBA from Stanford, supported the idea, so they relocated to China, bringing their 18-month-old daughter with them. The product they had in mind was an advanced gas-detection instrument for use in coal mines. The device used laser-detection technology, which lowered labor costs and raised the accuracy of detection. Zhou's clients in China are mainly electricity power plants where the device is used to help meet environmental protection standards.

Both entrepreneurs have benefitted from government support in China. Li started her business in an entrepreneurs' incubator established by Renmin University of China in 2015. During her first six months at the incubator, she learned how to approach angel and institutional investors. The incubator also provided training on the basics of entrepreneurship and starting a business. For two and a half years after graduation, she spent every day contacting potential investors, promoting her products and brainstorming design ideas with colleagues. Li received 10,000 yuan ($1,490) from the Beijing government when she started her venture. The seed investment from angels and institutions, as well as subsidy from the government, helped her to jumpstart her business, which was especially important due to the difficulty of producing collateral in order to secure debt capital from banks.

Government policies also helped Zhou as his company was taking shape. He received more than 2 million yuan in subsidies from the central government and the Beijing municipal government. The government of Haidian district also helped by offering him a lower rent for his business premises in Beijing.

Source: Zhang (2017)

Learning Outcomes

After studying this chapter, you should be ready to:

- **LO1**: Describe the concept and context of returnee entrepreneurs (REs)
- **LO2**: Discuss the drivers of returnee entrepreneurship
- **LO3**: Identify the distinctive resources of REs and evaluate the role of those resources in the founding of REs' ventures in their home country
- **LO4**: Discuss the performance and impact of REs

Introduction

As discussed in the last two chapters, the population of immigrant entrepreneurs (IEs) is heterogeneous. As per Drori et al. (2009), ethnic entrepreneurs (EEs), transnational entrepreneurs (TEs) and returnee entrepreneurs (REs) are the three types of immigrant entrepreneur. EEs are the traditional IEs who typically found ventures in their host country (Chapter 8). Others like TEs are the new IEs that establish a connection with their home country in the founding of their ventures (Chapter 9). As a third type of IEs, REs found new ventures upon their return home. Akin to TEs, REs are skilled immigrants returning home to found new ventures; however, unlike TEs who return to their home country on a semi-permanent basis, REs return home on a permanent basis.

Information on return migration is sparse (OECD, 2017). To date, no systematic and representative large-scale data collection has been organized on the subject. Although the rate varies across skilled groups, return migration in recent years has been substantial (Kerr et al., 2016). In China alone, more than 2.65 million students returned home from overseas in 2016 (Zhang, 2017).

A variety of factors including intrinsic motivations, as well as incentives by home country governments, have motivated skilled personnel in developed host countries to return home. Many developing countries are interested in attracting back their compatriots, in particular the highly educated, to benefit from their skills and experience acquired abroad. There is growing evidence that return migrants are more prone to engage in entrepreneurial activities or to be self-employed than non-migrants (De Vreyer et al., 2010; Piracha and Vadean, 2009). By virtue of living and working abroad, REs possess unique skills and experience that they can leverage in the founding of their ventures in the home country (OECD, 2017). Although they face challenges upon their return, REs contribute to innovation, competition and development of communities and entrepreneurial culture in their home country (Avle, 2014; Tynaliev and McLean, 2011).

Research has explored RE motivations and the creation of entrepreneurial ventures by REs. Studies have examined the role of returnees in these ventures, as well as the impact of returnees in their home country. In this chapter, we review these themes. First, we chart broad trends in, and discuss the drivers of, returnee entrepreneurship. Using illustrative examples, we then identify the distinctive human and social capital resources of REs, and evaluate the role of these resources in venture creation by REs. Finally, we discuss the performance and impact of REs.

REs: Trends and Drivers

REs are scientists and engineers, or students who were trained or studied/worked in OECD countries, and returned to their native countries to set up new ventures (Dai and Liu, 2009). According to the OECD (2017), return migrants are individuals who have lived in another country for at least three consecutive months and are now back living in their country of birth. Typically, REs are highly qualified individuals who return home to start up a new venture after several years of business experience and/or experience in another developed country (Drori et al., 2009).

Daniel Shin, American Korean founder of Ticket Monster, a South-Korean-based company, is a case in point. Daniel migrated to Washington, DC with his parents at the age of nine (Chafkin, 2011). He went to a top high school, followed by the University of Pennsylvania's Wharton School, where he studied finance and marketing. Following graduation, he worked in the New Jersey offices of McKinsey & Company, and received a job offer in the New York City office of Apax Partners, a European private equity firm, before returning to South Korea to found his venture.

Kirill Makharinsky and Serge Faguet, co-founders of Ostrovok, a hotel-booking service founded in Moscow, are other examples (Razumovskaya, 2016). The two Russian entrepreneurs returned home to found a venture after studying at Stanford and Oxford universities in the US and UK, respectively. The Russian version of booking.com has raised millions of dollars in venture capital (VC) investment since inception.

Most RE studies are focused on returnees to Asia and, in particular, China, which has facilitated the education of its citizens abroad for many decades (Hao and Welch, 2012;

Huang and Kuah-Pearce, 2014). Reversing decades of exodus, some of China's best and brightest are returning from overseas to take part in the Chinese gold rush. Since 1978, about half of two million students who went abroad returned home, a trend that has rapidly increased in the last few years (Wang et al., 2011). According to China's Ministry of Education, 608,400 students from China left to study abroad while 480,900 returned home in 2017. Nearly 80% of students chose to return to China after graduating overseas in 2017, up from 30% in 2007 and only around 5% in 1987.

According to a report published by the Center for China and Globalization and the Chinese Academy of Social Sciences, enthusiasm for entrepreneurship has soared among returnees in recent years (Zhang, 2017). Returning migrants prefer to enter self-employment in the non-agricultural sectors (Thomas and Inkpen, 2013), and favor capital cities over rural areas for their business activities (McCormick and Wahba, 2003). More than 40% of students who return to China to start businesses opt to work in large cities such as Shanghai and Beijing.

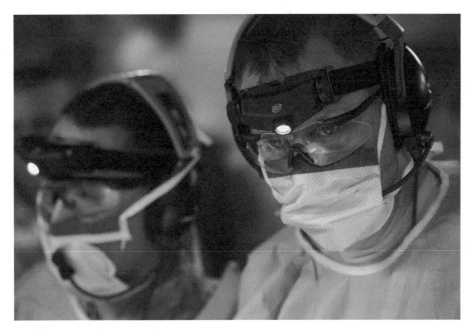

Source: www.needpix.com/photo/394461

Factors Influencing Returnee Entrepreneurship

The motivational process of REs consists of two stages or dimensions which may be separate or intertwined. First, REs are motivated to return to the home country. Second, REs are motivated to start a new venture / engage in entrepreneurial behavior in the home country. These two dimensions may be successive, or they may coincide (Zahra, 2007).

Anu Parthasarathy, a returnee to India from Colorado, USA, first decided to return to India; however, part of the motivation to go back home had to do with starting her own venture, which encouraged her to return right away:

> I think the decision came first to go back to India, but the idea of starting up really motivated us to do it straight away. I mean that was definitely part of the motivation. (Anu Parthasarathy, Founder, RedBug Kreative Kits, India)

Immigrants who decide to return to their home country tend to do so within a reasonably short time period. According to Dumont and Spielvogel (2008), even when a labor market match occurs, 20–50% of skilled immigrants leave their host country within five years of arriving.

The likelihood of return has also been connected to skill level. In some settings, high-skilled immigrants are more likely to return home than low-skilled migrants (Kerr et al., 2016). At the same time, however, whereas high-skilled workers are more likely to return home as a group, those at the very highest skill levels are often less likely to do so. Dumont and Spielvogel (2008) calculate that the United States retains about 65–70% of those who studied for a doctorate at the five-year mark after receipt of degree, higher than university graduates. These migrants with a PhD or high productivity levels are less likely to return migrate than other skilled workers.

In some cases, individuals return home due to intrinsic motivations. In other cases, push and pull factors in REs' host and home countries, respectively, can drive them to go back and found a new venture at home. We examine these factors in turn.

Intrinsic Motivations of REs

Intrinsic reasons for return include personal reasons, or perceptions of attractive market opportunities in the home country. Daniel Shin, founder of Ticket Monster, returned to Korea after living and working in the US due to a strong **personal desire** to start-up on his own (Chafkin, 2011). A graduate from the Wharton School at the University of Pennsylvania, Daniel accepted employment at McKinsey & Company upon graduation. However, he felt restless. He was an entrepreneur at heart, having started two companies while still in college.

While the first, a website for students looking for housing, failed miserably, the second, an internet advertising company which he co-founded with several classmates during his senior year, raised $1 million in venture capital and was bought by Google for $81 million, but only after Daniel had left the company. Even though he was at McKinsey, it did not feel like a career to him as he always wanted to start a business.

Opportunity finally struck when Daniel accepted a job offer in the New York office of Apax Partners, a European private equity firm, on the condition that he could delay his start date until the following year, and that is when he walked out on McKinsey to explore the possibility of starting up on his own in Korea:

> It didn't feel like a career to me. I'd always wanted to start a business… it was my chance to get something off the ground without my parents telling me I couldn't do it… I had about six months. (Daniel Shin, Founder, Ticket Monster)

Personal reasons, such as strong family bonds, also drive the return of skilled personnel who no longer consider the lure of overseas salaries and relative high living standards as enough to make it worth leaving their families.

For Vinita Ananth, who founded Vangal Software and Services upon returning to India from the US, the desire to seek 'change' after spending a considerable number of years living abroad was a key driver underlying her move to India. She did not plan to be an entrepreneur at the time she planned the move back to India. Personal reasons were the predominant influence. Vinita and her husband also wanted their kids to grow up and spend time with their grandparents who lived in India. The fact that markets were opening up in India reinforced these motivations. She and her husband took comfort in the fact that they were US citizens and had the security of going back to live in the US if they wanted:

> When I was moving back I did not plan to be an entrepreneur. We moved for personal reasons, we just said we had been in the US for a good number of years, felt that we wanted a change and heard that the markets had opened up quite nicely in India, that opportunities existed. We also felt that we had the security blanket of always going back to the US if we wanted to because we were US citizens… felt that we wanted our children to grow up in India, and even have some time with grandparents… (Vinita, Founder, Vangal Software and Services)

In other cases, REs return home to start a business due to **perceived opportunities in the home country**. These perceptions stem from their accumulated skills and experiences, and their perceived fit with the opportunities arising from growing market demand at home (Zweig et al., 2006).

Anu explained that she was influenced by green living since childhood. Her experience of living in Colorado, USA, reinforced this culture of eating organic and using eco-friendly toys for her children in a big way. She felt that such a culture was missing in India, especially in relation to children's products, which presented an opportunity upon her return home. Anu's background in the arts reinforced her passion and confidence to start up a venture upon her return:

> Well it's always been a bit of a passion for me, like from the beginning. I think my childhood connecting from the culture quite a bit… the other motivation was living in Colorado… we were influenced regularly by all the type of culture, living green and using eco-friendly toys for my children and eating organic food…, which I think was grossly missing in India, at least when it came to children and children's products… that's something I really miss coming from an arts background… we talked about it a lot when we were there.
> (Anu Parthasarathy, Founder, RedBug Kreative Kits, India)

So did the support of her sister who researched into the market gap in India and validated the gap during her visit to the US:

> And when my sister was here [in the US], she kept saying the kind of access she had to some of the cool stuff here which is not available there [in India]. So I think all that sort of came together. And at the same time thinking of why not do this in India, and then suddenly we located this huge gap… with my sister here [in India] so she would do all the research here as to what's relevant and what's not and then it made sense to come back and do this.
> (Anu Parthasarathy, Founder, RedBug Kreative Kits, India)

Host Country External Environment

The likelihood of return has also been linked to economic conditions, the difficulty of obtaining permanent residency or citizenship in the host country, and the ease of moving across national borders. For some individuals, the choice to return home may be a necessity, rather than an opportunity, due to external push factors in their host country.

For instance, visa regulations, the difficulties of finding employment, or a protective environment for business start-ups in the host country may drive individuals to return home. The slow job market in the US propelled some individuals to return home in the late 1990s / early 2000s. More recently, weakening demand for imported labor in some places like the Middle East is driving the return of Filipinos to their home country (see Box below) (Trefor, 2016).

Home Country External Environment

Job opportunities and institutional reforms in the home country translate into an attractive home country environment for returnees. The availability of job opportunities in the home country attracts individuals, especially those who have lived and worked in developed host countries, back home.

Chinese immigrants to the West who have worked at companies located in the US are in especially high demand in China. Government subsidies in the thriving PC (personal computer) and semiconductor industry in Taiwan in the 1980s created a highly favorable climate to attract and support a large number of its skilled engineers from overseas, especially from the US (Zhou and Hsu, 2010). Small semiconductor companies founded by Taiwanese-Americans moving their bases to Taiwan tapped into the huge reservoir of capital on the island, and attracted skilled Taiwanese graduates in computer and related fields from overseas.

South Korea is another country that is a magnet for returnees of Korean origin (Chafkin, 2011). A country with no mineral resources to speak of, and ranking 117th in the world in terms of arable land per capita, now boasts the world's 12th-largest economy by purchasing power. One of the world's lowest rates of public debt, an unemployment rate of just 3.2% and a per-capita GDP growth of 23,000% over the past half a century, beating that of China, India and every other country in the world, are among the other attractions for returnees.

Often, returnees go back home to take up jobs, only to later quit those jobs to found their own ventures. As the Box below shows, the trend of outward movement of personnel in the Philippines is reversing with talented Filipinos beginning to return home in greater numbers (Trefor, 2016). Averaging 6.2% between 2010 and 2015, economic growth back home (second only to China's among East Asia's major economies) is creating new job opportunities that Filipinos living abroad are returning home to take advantage of. Whereas some are coming back to take senior executive roles at existing companies, others are returning to establish start-ups.

FILIPINOS RETURNING HOME TO TAKE ADVANTAGE OF JOB OPPORTUNITIES

The Philippines has long witnessed significant outflows of its people to foreign lands in search of better opportunities. Since the 1970s, millions of Filipinos in a wide range of professions have left the country due to dismal career prospects at home.

In recent years, this trend is beginning to reverse. After years of exodus, the number of Filipinos living and working abroad has gradually begun to fall. From more than 10.4 million Filipinos living abroad in 2011, the number may be as low as 9.4 million in 2016. Brain drain is slowly giving way to brain gain as skilled Filipinos who once left their country for attractive opportunities abroad are beginning to return home in greater numbers.

There are several reasons for the return journey home. Strong family bonds are a compelling reason for some returnees who are beginning to perceive proximity to their families as more valuable than high salaries and lucrative job offers in the West. In some cases, push factors in the host countries, such as weakening demand for labor in the Middle East, are driving the return home.

In most instances, however, returnees have strong positive motivations based on pull factors in the Philippines. As compared to previous years when corruption was more rampant, recent years have seen more political stability and improved economic

(Continued)

growth in the country. Philippines is second only to China in terms of growth among East Asia's major economies.

Filipinos living abroad are returning home to take advantage of new job opportunities. Many return to take up senior executive roles at existing companies. Others come back to start new ventures. Realizing the renewed dynamism at home, skilled technology workers in the West are not as hesitant to quit successful careers and take the gamble to return to the Philippines and make a difference in their home country. Government efforts to cut the red tape and pump domestic investment into the economy are positive stimuli for these skilled workers.

Valued senior management experience from abroad, followed by relevant work experience upon the return home, also provides a soft landing. Moreover, it contributes to the returnees' ability to eventually quit their jobs and start new ventures. For example, Patrick Cuartero launched Pylon Partners, an umbrella company for a range of business ventures in 2014, three years after resettling in Manila to run Groupon's Philippine operations. Thanks to the rising middle class and demand surges in the bar and restaurant sector in one of his company's areas of interest, he has plans to rapidly expand his workforce to 400 from 100 at inception.

Source: Trefor (2016)

Several emerging economies have undertaken institutional reforms in recent years, which have enhanced the attractiveness of these countries for skilled personnel willing to return home to start up new ventures.

The Chinese government, for example, instituted key policies to attract its skilled migrants back home from overseas (Zweig and Wang, 2013). Coming at the same time as the US economy was stagnating, reforms in China, especially in the early 2000s, convinced some successful Chinese executives to return to hot prospects in their homeland (see Box below). These reforms have included educational initiatives, and provision of funding and incubation space from the government.

THE LURE OF VENTURE CAPITAL FUNDING FOR RETURNING TO CHINA

In 1986, Ying Luo, a top student, left for graduate studies in the US, part of the first large wave of Chinese students to go abroad. Mr. Luo's stipend from the University of Connecticut was $760 a month, more than 200 times his parents' earnings at home, which gave him enough reason to continue to live abroad.

Over the next 15 years Mr. Luo earned a PhD in biomedical science and worked at several California pharmaceutical and biotech companies, including Rigel Inc., in South San Francisco, where he rose to be senior director of Genomics, overseeing 30 people. He became an American citizen and bought a home in Silicon Valley. His salary passed $100,000 a year. His wife, who he met in the US, was a software engineer who had left China in 1991. She was a manager at Cisco Systems Inc., who also earned a six-figure salary, with incentives like stock holdings and options, and planned to retire by the age of 45. The couple had two children who they enrolled in a private school near Stanford University. Mr. Luo's parents moved from China to Berkeley to be near their grandchildren.

Silicon Valley in the 1990s was an entrepreneur-rich environment; however, Mr. Luo was frustrated. He yearned to start his own company, but lacked the necessary contacts. He saw his chances becoming increasingly bleak as the biotech boom turned to bust in the late 1990s. Life in the US was also fairly predictable and monotonous. He felt as if he could predict his career path in technical management for the rest of his life, which did not seem exciting enough to him.

Mr. Luo seized the opportunity to return to China when he was invited to Beijing to give a lecture on genomics with a group of Chinese scientists living in America in 2000. At first Mr. Luo was surprised when soon after the lecture, a Chinese investor proposed to invest $1 million a year in Mr. Luo's potential start-up in China that did not yet exist. The investor was unperturbed as he trusted Mr. Luo and attached tremendous credibility to his being a trained and highly skilled returnee from the US.

Following the encounter, Mr. Luo started realizing that he had knowledge and experience in a sought-after area of expertise that also happened to fall within the Chinese government's investment remit. The Chinese government was targeting biotechnology as an area it wanted to invest in. Mr. Luo was confident about the local 'guanxi' connections that his partner would bring him. He agreed to meet with government officials to further explore the possibilities for setting up shop in China. Mr. Luo's mother also arranged for him to meet with more than 20 government-backed venture capital firms. As soon as he returned to the US, he started writing a business plan. He was so determined that he did not even consult with his family.

Within a few months, Mr. Luo had raised $3.4 million from Chinese government venture capitalists to form Shanghai Genomics. Taking advantage of China's low labor costs, the company did contract genetic research for other companies to find new drugs. Not much later, he returned to rent an apartment in Shanghai; however, his family stayed back in the US as his wife preferred a stable environment for raising their kids.

Whereas in the US, Mr. Luo paid PhD scientists $60,000 a year to do research work, in China he paid Chinese-schooled scientists about $8,000. Despite having grown up in China, being a boss in China and managing people was daunting as his employees expected his involvement to resolve matters even at an operational level. He also missed his family and the calm of the suburbs in the US. Yet, he was not sure about going back to the US, just as a few years ago he did not imagine returning to China.

Source: adapted from Kaufman (2003)

In 2010, China began improving education related to entrepreneurship, and by 2016, the Ministry of Education required all universities to open courses on innovation and entrepreneurship (Zhang, 2017). Many universities, especially those in first-tier cities, also established entrepreneur parks and incubators.

While the dot-com bust in the early 2000s in the US slowed venture-capital funding around the globe, a considerable amount of investment in support schemes and programs attracted prospective entrepreneurs back to China (Dai and Liu, 2009). Until the late 1990s, China didn't have local venture-capital firms. Today it has over 200, most of them backed by government agencies, accounting for about half of all such financing in the country (Yang, 2019).

Offers of free plane tickets, and perks such as free schooling for returnees' children and subsidized office space, have also attracted skilled personnel back to China. Government-funded business incubators for overseas returnees located in high-tech development zones have provided an incentive to individuals of Chinese origin to set up businesses at these locations upon their return.

About a kilometer from the south gate of Beijing Normal University is an entrepreneurs' park the university established for returnees in 2005 (Zhang, 2017). It was one of the earliest facilities designed to help returnees start businesses. At present, about 350 entrepreneur parks around the country house 27,000 companies and 79,000 returnees. The Zhongguancun Science Park is the biggest science park in China and is often seen as a typical example of where REs settle upon their return home (Kerr et al., 2016).

South Korea's embrace of communications technologies and proactive government initiatives has likewise increased the country's appeal as a return destination for its skilled personnel (Chafkin, 2011). In the 1990s, the South Korean government invested heavily in the installation of fiber-optic cables, with the result that by 2000, Koreans were four times as likely as Americans to have high-speed internet access. Koreans still enjoy the fastest internet in the world while paying some of the lowest prices.

In some cases, the home country cultural environment also attracts REs home. Pierre Bi, a 20-something Swiss citizen whose father hails from the Inner Mongolia autonomous region in China, is a case in point. Pierre Bi co-founded Aeris Cleantec, which makes 'next-generation' residential air conditioners in Beijing, upon his return from Europe. According to him, young entrepreneurs were attracted to China because of 'the pace and the people' (Zhang, 2017). Europe was 'too comfortable' in his view. Most people there avoided challenges because they wanted a steady career path. In contrast, people in China were aware of what it meant to work with a start-up:

> Right now, it's summer in Europe, so nothing is really moving. Here, people are aware of what it means to work with a startup, which means long hours and great uncertainty. (Pierre Bi, 2017)

Despite the attractions, the institutional environment for REs in emerging economies leaves much to be desired. Although economies like India and China, for example, have undertaken several reforms in recent years, a restricted environment, power structures, opacity and bureaucracy in these countries have explained the hesitation of skilled persons to return home. Returnees tend to avoid a high degree of regulations and entry barriers (Sheehan and Riosmena, 2013).

In other cases, cultural differences are challenging to navigate. According to the OECD (2017), the length of stay in host countries can play a role in the decision to return and reintegration upon return. Longer stays outside of home countries can make it harder for returnees to reintegrate back into economic, social and political life in their origin countries.

For Ganesh Suryanarayanan, who returned to India from Silicon Valley, California, in the mid-2000s to develop a new technology solution in the energy sector, the relative lack of culture of innovation in India was a challenge. Although rife with several large and small firms, he felt the local ecosystem was deficient in terms of the 'core system for success' – unlike in Silicon Valley – which made it difficult for entrepreneurs to establish credibility for undertaking high-risk ventures:

> in the hi-tech space, doing something on the products side of things is a very risky game. So there's a lot of challenges there to kind of convince people that you're credible and that you can actually do something… the culture for that doesn't exist. For example look at Silicon Valley, right… you have a lot of, you have lot of VCs, and a lot of entrepreneurs… you have good universities, you have the core system for success. Here it's not there… (Ganesh Suryanarayanan, RE in Bangalore, India)

In other cases, REs find it hard to completely disconnect from their host country. Daniel Shin, American Korean founder of Ticket Monster, yearned to do 'one more stint in the States' upon his return to South Korea to found his venture. Even though he successfully sold his company to the social-commerce site LivingSocial for $380 million, he still wanted to go back to the US to find out if he could replicate his success in America's larger, more competitive market. He had learned to speak passable Korean since his return to his home country, yet he never stopped thinking of himself as an American. He anticipated he would likely go 'back and forth' between the two countries.

For some individuals, self-employment at home may be a necessity rather than a promising choice due to a lack of alternatives (Mezger Kveder and Flahaux, 2013). The difficulties of finding employment may contribute to the decision to become self-employed upon the return home. Yet, finding a job at home that is equivalent to returnees' skills is one of the commonly specified challenges for reintegration (OECD, 2017).

Resources of REs

Scholars have explored how REs are different from local entrepreneurs, in particular the link between financial, human and social capital acquired overseas and the probability of self-employment after return.

Financial Capital

Part of the uniqueness of REs stems from their financial capital acquired abroad. Returnees have a high degree of financial capital that is associated with a tendency to create employment due to entrepreneurial activities after return (Lianos and Pseiridis, 2009; Piracha and Vadean, 2009).

Returnees from the developed West have a big competitive advantage as compared to the locals, especially in emerging economies. Savings accumulated abroad can be used as a resource for business establishment at home (OECD, 2017). In fact, return migrants intending to become self-employed or set up businesses on their return are more likely to acquire higher savings abroad; such plans are integral parts of people's migration strategies. They can raise much larger investments from outside of their home country (Chafkin, 2011). The choice of sector by REs is linked to the amount of savings from overseas experiences, among other factors.

At the same time, however, start-up activities may be the last resort, especially for those who were forced to return or whose skills do not match the labor market needs of the country (Mezger Kveder and Flahaux, 2013).

Human Capital

Human capital in the form of education and experiences from abroad is significantly associated with self-employment among returning migrants (Mesnard and Ravallion, 2006). Such capital accumulation from abroad compensates for the loss of social capital in the home country (Martin and Radu, 2012; Wahba and Zenou, 2012). REs cultivate an attitude that is more open to risk-taking as compared to their counterparts in the home country who have not worked or lived abroad. Additionally, they are perceived to be more credible than their local counterparts.

According to Hu Ping at the Shanghai Pudong Service Center for Returned Overseas Students, one of several government agencies that helps returnees cut through bureaucracy in China, China is in need of top-level talent that not only understands China, but also embraces advanced foreign concepts and technologies learned abroad.

Education levels in terms of foreign language proficiency, for example, increase the probability of becoming an entrepreneur with employees rather than being an own-account worker without employees (Piracha and Vadean, 2009). According to Laveesh Bhandari, a returnee from Boston, USA, who founded an economic consulting services venture upon his return to India, the education he acquired abroad exposed him to a range of issues which he had not been exposed to in India. He believed he became better informed, and developed a greater awareness of the happenings in different countries as a consequence of studying and living in the US. This was an important advantage, especially in the days prior to the internet:

the education there did give me an exposure to a range of issues, which I'd not been exposed to here. So that actually helped a lot, it did help me pick up new things… I knew for instance, what's happening in different countries just by reading the newspapers there, as opposed to reading the paper here where you don't know as much. And you know the difference in the coverage right? So that I think was an important difference. Which I think I might be less so now because of the internet. But even then there is a difference, you do get exposed to far more things in the United States and in England, than you would here.
(Laveesh Bhandari, Founder, Indicus Analytics, India)

REs also leverage their **migration, prior work and start-up experiences** in the founding of their ventures at home. According to Vandor and Franke (2016), students who have spent time studying abroad are able to come up with better business ideas due to cross-cultural experience gained abroad. Cross-cultural experience increases the ability to recognize profitable business opportunities.

Vandor and Franke (2016) tested the entrepreneurial capabilities (i.e. ability to identify profitable business opportunities) of 128 students before and after a semester of living and studying abroad by asking them to come up with business ideas in media and food retailing. The researchers did the same for a control group of 115 students who continued their studies at their home university. The business opportunities that all students came up with were rated by four venture capitalists and industry experts blind to the source. The results showed that the group that had gained cross-cultural experience received significantly higher VC and expert ratings on their business ideas after their semester abroad. Experts' ratings of business ideas of students who had studied abroad increased by 17%, whereas those of the control group's business ideas declined by 3% at the end of the semester.

According to Sai Gundavelli, a US-based founder who set up operations in India, returnees are also valued as employees. By virtue of their experience in both host and home countries, they are better able to connect with customers located in the host country, and have understanding of the home country where they are returning to. Sai was thus willing to hire returnees for his own venture:

So I would always look for a person who has returned to India. Because they've already seen the world and they can connect with the US customers really well. Generally people who have worked in the US and go back to India, does increase their value. We are willing to work with them is what I would say.
(Sai Gundavelli, Founder, Solix Technologies, California)

The nature of REs' human capital also influences their location choice in their home country. Evidence from China suggests that REs choose a site that is complementary to their assets (Wright et al., 2008). REs with academic knowledge in the form of patents, for instance, choose to locate on science parks not attached to a university, while those with prior entrepreneurial experience have the tendency to choose university science parks. These location choices are also correlated with the performance of REs' firms.

Although REs' knowledge and experience acquired abroad are invaluable for the founding of their ventures, the lack of local knowledge can pose a constraint. This was true for Zhou Xin, founder of Beijing Define Technology Corp, who returned home to Beijing from San Francisco to start up in 2009 (Zhang, 2017). Zhou's product was an advanced gas-detection instrument for use in coal mines. The device used laser-detection technology, which lowered labor costs and raised the accuracy of detection. Despite those advantages, the device was a failure at first because of Zhou's lack of local market knowledge. He had not researched the Chinese market before launching it. As a result, he did not realize that China's mining industry was accustomed to using old equipment and there was little desire to change. The company also lacked marketing channels. Coal mines were located far from Beijing, so the travel costs to introduce the product were huge.

In addition, the device had to undergo a large number of tests and reviews before it could be used in coal mines, which took far longer than Zhou had expected. Protection of his intellectual property rights in China was another key concern. These factors prompted Zhou to conduct extensive market research upon his return.

Social Capital

Social capital theory is applied to examine the importance and impact of international networks and ties accumulated by REs during their time overseas. Social ties of REs cultivated abroad have implications for venture creation, venture performance and international growth of their ventures (Dai and Liu, 2009; Pruthi, 2014; Qin and Estrin, 2015).

Evidence from developing countries like India shows that a large percentage of REs maintain transnational ties to their host country upon their return, keeping frequent contact with family and friends or former colleagues to exchange information related to customers, technology, job opportunities and business funding (Wadhwa et al., 2011). REs are significantly more likely to rely on social networks built abroad for business leads and financing in venture creation, especially when they are located outside of entrepreneurial clusters in emerging economies (Nanda and Khanna, 2010). These networks help them to circumvent the barriers arising from imperfect domestic institutions in the process of founding their ventures in the home country.

The ties that REs leverage from abroad can be **personal** or **professional**. According to Varun Talwar, a returnee entrepreneur and founder of an early stage venture capital firm in New Delhi, India, his professor's presence on the board of his holding company played a key role in his acceptance into an incubator, which spurred his entrepreneurial journey upon his return to India:

My professor [from the US] is on the board of my holding company, she was the one under whom I learnt, my first business plan there, and she got me in to incubator, that is how my journey began. (Varun Talwar, Co-Founder, Withya Group, India)

Studies also point to the importance of returnees' alumni networks for their likelihood of embracing entrepreneurship. Using a data set of overseas alumni of a top Indian university, Qin and Estrin (2015) find evidence of the strong impact of immediate peer influence on the likelihood of returnee entrepreneurship. Peer ties formed in the early years of university study play a significant role in subsequent career choices and entry into entrepreneurship in the home country.

As the below Box shows, Daniel Shin of Ticket Monster co-founded his venture in South Korea with two of his friends with whom he went to college in the US (Chafkin, 2011). He and his two college buddies came up with the idea after brainstorming in his grandmother's house in Seoul over the course of two months. Daniel also leveraged his college friend's connections in the US to raise capital for his venture. His largest institutional investor was Insight Venture Partners in New York City, where his college roommate worked as an associate.

TICKET MONSTER
A RETURNEE ENTREPRENEUR'S STORY OF STUPENDOUS SUCCESS IN SOUTH KOREA

Born in South Korea, Daniel Shin moved to suburban Washington, DC, with his parents at the age of nine. He went to a prestigious high school, followed by the University of Pennsylvania's Wharton School of Business, where he studied finance and marketing. By 2008, he had secured a high-profile job in the New Jersey offices of McKinsey & Company. Among his perks were all-expenses-paid ski trips. Shin lived in Manhattan where he was comfortable. His parents were proud.

Yet, Shin did not feel entirely content. As someone who had started two companies whilst at college, he yearned to exploit the entrepreneurial streak in him. Whereas the first venture, a website for students looking for housing, had failed miserably, the second, an internet advertising company called Invite Media, which he co-founded with several classmates during his senior year, showed better results. It won a business-plan competition in early 2007 and raised $1 million in venture capital the next year. While Shin left the second venture, his co-founders sold it to Google for $81 million.

(Continued)

Shin desired to start up a venture to complete the unfinished business. However, his parents, who had come to America from Korea to enable their son to attain the heights of success, did not want him to throw the opportunity away for a money-losing start-up no one had ever heard of.

Even though he was restless by late 2009, he did not have the courage to open up to his parents and venture out on his own. When the New York City office of Apax Partners, a European private equity firm, offered him a job, he found a perfect escape route. He negotiated a delayed start to spend the next six months exploring a new business opportunity without telling his parents.

Along with two college buddies, and armed with whiteboards and laptops in his grandmother's house in Seoul, South Korea, where he returned from the US in 2010, Shin brainstormed promising business ideas that would require no start-up capital. Over the course of two months, the team narrowed down their list of 20 initial ideas down to one: a Groupon-style coupon company that would offer deals on restaurants, events and merchandise. Shin liked the business model because it had a built-in financing strategy: cash came in several months before the company would have to pay it out, giving him a supply of free debt. He collected several thousand email addresses, and launched the site in May, naming it Ticket Monster.

Shin raised funding from Insight Venture Partners in New York City, where his college roommate worked as an associate. He felt he had a big competitive advantage in that he could raise much larger investments from outside of Korea as compared to a non-returnee in his shoes. He also benefited from his knowledge of business models in the US, which emerging economies present fertile grounds to successfully replicate. In addition, he felt he had an edge from a cultural perspective as he was more open to risk and less limited to the Korean way of thinking.

Soon, Shin was the CEO of a fast-growing company earning $1 million a month in revenue. By the end of the summer, Ticket Monster had doubled in size, growing to 60 employees. By the end of the year, the company had doubled in size again: 20 months after he quit McKinsey, Shin had 700 employees and roughly $25 million a month in revenue. Soon after, Shin sold his company to the social-commerce site LivingSocial for $380 million. In a radio address to the country, President Lee of South Korea gave Shin's example, urging the youth to follow in his footsteps.

Yet, Shin felt the urge to go back to the US one more time. He was curious to find out if he could replicate his success in America's larger, more competitive market. Even though he learned to speak passable Korean, he never stopped thinking of himself as an American. He envisioned himself traveling back and forth between the two countries even if not going back to the US for good.

Source: Chafkin (2011)

Co-ethnic professional ties developed after migration to the host country also facilitate engagement in returnee entrepreneurship upon the return home. Pierre Bi, co-founder of Aeris Cleantec, which makes 'next-generation' residential air conditioners, relocated to Beijing to found his venture in 2016 (Zhang, 2017). His business partner, Liu Shuo, a 34-year-old Chinese, worked for a Belgian brewing company. The pair met overseas and then decided to move to Beijing because they believed their fledgling company would have a great future in the capital, given China's move away from traditional economic drivers to consumption-led businesses with a strong focus on entertainment and health. In some cases, REs also exploit their professional networks to raise capital from their host country for their ventures founded at home.

The personal and professional networks of REs contribute to their ability to manage across borders (Liu et al., 2010). Due to their 'dual orientation', returnees help to bridge the cultural gap with overseas markets, reducing psychic distance and the likely risks and transaction costs associated with the decision to invest abroad (Rabbiosi and Stucchi, 2012).

Although REs leverage social networks from abroad upon their return home, local networks in the home country are especially crucial for them (Qin and Estrin, 2015). Yet, REs feel 'out of touch' with local networks due to their period of absence from the home country, which is why they predominantly use their networks acquired abroad.

Anu Parthasarathy, a US-returned entrepreneur in India, expressed her frustration due to the lack of local connections in India, and the value of building such connections at home. She remarked that she did not realize the importance of local connections for business until relocating to India. Based on her experience of living in the US, she discovered that in the US it was possible to get things done without necessarily knowing anyone; in contrast, that was difficult to do in India. As it was a lot more cumbersome to start-up in India, she found that it was almost impossible to do anything without knowing anyone:

> the frustration that I couldn't do anything that I could do in the US… but it was so easy there and here we realized it was just a little bit more cumbersome, it is all about contacts. If you don't know anybody in the business world, it's almost impossible to do anything… we didn't know that. I thought you could just walk in to an office and say, there you are, there's my business, can I start, and they say yeah, yeah, come back and then you would never hear from them again. I didn't realize that that's how industry worked here till we actually came back. (Anu Parthasarathy, Founder, RedBug Kreative Kits, India)

At first, Anu's sister helped her to navigate the local environment by locating personnel and space for her venture. Later, Anu moved into a local apartment community, which helped in terms of finding the necessary resources for her venture:

my sister, she lived here five years… so she was able to get in touch with people you know like, like a company secretary, or a CA for the actual physical part of paper work and all that… Contact building work was probably our biggest challenge initially because I came here, I knew very few people in Bangalore… I actually moved in to an apartment community here which was actually a huge deal. That has been my major resource for pretty much all of my contacts we have now… everybody, from writers, to marketing directors, everybody we found right here, within this community. (Anu Parthasarathy, Founder, RedBug Kreative Kits, India)

Legitimacy

REs enjoy a high level of credibility in their home country by virtue of their human and social capital gained abroad, which makes it easier for them to engage in venture creation upon their return home.

Laveesh emphasized the value attached to being a returnee in developing countries like India. Valued more than the training he had acquired abroad, he felt the 'US-returned' brand attached to him upon his return to India provided a great deal of credibility, which opened doors and gave him a higher level of confidence as compared to someone who had not been abroad:

the way things happened in India it was in the masses of people that there are, once you have some sort of a brand as I say with you, then it becomes easier. And the brand was US returned… once people start to give you that little bit of a window, then it becomes easier for you… so the level of confidence that you have is higher than someone who's not actually been abroad… so the most important part was not the training, it was the fact that there is a problem in India, and the US I think it is valued much more than it should be definitely, but that is the way it is. So that was most important. (Laveesh Bhandari, Founder, Indicus Analytics, India)

Sarvesh Mahesh, founder, Tavant Technologies, California, held a different view. According to him, nowadays there was a lot of pride in developing countries, and the novelty of going back as a returnee from the West had waned. It was imperative that REs offered something really unique in terms of skills in order to gain credence over local people and avoid being 'a fish out of water':

So if somebody goes back to India, people expect that they will have a slightly higher position. Now there is a lot of pride in India. Unless you show them something, they are not going to give you any credence because you are back from US. In fact, some of them are fish out of water. They've been for long enough… India, in that case, is a very brutal place… the novelty of going back to India from here is gone. (Sarvesh Mahesh, Founder, Tavant Technologies, California)

Moreover, the difficulties of adapting to the local environment due to cultural challenges after a long period of absence from home could be daunting. According to Sarvesh, people often freeze in time when they first move back from their host country. They are unable to re-connect with the home country upon their return because of being unable to realize that things have moved on during their period of absence:

Some people that have returned from the US are useful for reconciling the cultural differences, some are not… Part of the thing is, they are frozen in the time when they came here [USA]. Then go back there. India has moved on. You are looking for the India that you left and you don't find it. You find that you are sort of not connecting. Some of them have that specially who came for eight nine years who were busy doing their own thing. For eight nine years, you don't really connect that much back. (Sarvesh Mahesh, Founder, Tavant Technologies, California)

Performance and Impact of REs

Studies have investigated returnee firm outcomes, as well as the impact of returnees on industries, economic development, internationalization and knowledge spillovers. Below, we examine both the performance and impact of REs' ventures.

Venture Performance

Returnees are more likely to engage in self-employment than non-migrants (Mezger Kveder and Flahaux, 2013). RE background and characteristics impact the performance of their ventures. Some studies find that in the absence of local ties, returnees have strong incentives to pursue firm efficiency and profitability rather than searching for political connections (Giannetti et al., 2014). Other studies find a positive link between REs' overseas experience and the survival of their ventures (Marchetta, 2012). According to Dai and Liu (2009), due to their technological and commercial knowledge, and international entrepreneurial orientation, especially in high-tech industries, enterprises of REs outperform those owned by local entrepreneurs.

By virtue of their international networks, REs have an international orientation at the outset. Therefore, theoretically, they are well-equipped to follow an early internationalization path for their ventures. As discussed in Chapter 12, international new ventures (INVs) tend to emphasize technologically advanced innovative products and services, and compete in globally integrated industries that are led by internationally experienced entrepreneurs (McDougall et al., 2003; Oviatt and McDougall, 1994), which arguably applies to many returnee-owned firms. As a first step, REs aim to satisfy surging demand in emerging and developing economies where they return to start a new venture.

Different types of learning of REs are positively associated with the performance of their firms (Liu et al., 2015). As compared to non-returnees, REs use novel approaches to operate their ventures due to their exposure to diverse environments and institutional frameworks (Liu and Almor, 2014). At the same time, however, the lack of local network connections can be a constraint. REs may underperform as compared to local firms due to their relative lack of local networks and knowledge. Yet, these disadvantages are less distinct for older ventures, and if REs have state support for their ventures.

Impact of REs

Several studies have shown that REs contribute to the development of local firms, industries and economies (Dai and Liu, 2009; Kenney et al., 2013; Wright et al., 2007; Zhou and Hsu, 2010).

Studies have examined the impact of REs on the high-technology industry in their home country. The findings suggest that REs promote innovation (Liu et al., 2010a; b). REs are instrumental for inspiring new venture creation and advancement of the high-tech industry at home (Chen, 2008). According to Saxenian (2005), REs in China, India and Taiwan have contributed to the initial emergence of the high-technology industry in these countries. REs in these countries have led to the creation of some of the most dynamic private high-tech firms. This is because highly skilled returnees foster two-way flows of capital, skills and information between their host and home countries. They facilitate both direct and indirect knowledge transfer to local firms based on their capabilities, and human and social capital accumulated overseas (Liu et al., 2010a; b).

Others (e.g. Kenney et al., 2013) argue that REs are critical to the continued development, rather than initial emergence, of a high-tech industry in emerging economies. Returning professionals with technological, managerial, marketing or scientific competencies often create new companies, transfer knowledge and increase the human capital stock in their country of origin (OECD, 2017). They can also compensate for the human capital lost through emigration.

FOUNDERS' PERSPECTIVES ON THE VALUE OF RETURNEES AS EMPLOYEES

The best people are I think the ones that are from India, have worked in the US but are still relatively correct in terms of operating in India, have gone back frequently perhaps even worked in India even before they were coming here and working here, they have worked in both places, those are the ideal people to run the India office. (Ujjal Kohli, Founder, Meru Networks, California, USA)

I don't think we have anybody on our team who returned from the US. It's all local talent. I think if we get someone like that, you can relate to them. For us we have the same language with someone here vs. who has spent time in India. Everyone has exposure to US but like deep exposure, I don't think it matters in the end. The level of self-cultural awareness is so high. These kids, they have no barriers in their thought process. They are world class in their thinking. They think they can take on the world. They don't have any inhibitions. They don't think of them as next to anybody. (Manish Chandra, Founder, Poshmark, California, USA)

I am neutral to returnees. I don't have a fear of people who've just worked in India. That kind of a consideration would be important for someone who is not Indian. It would be important for them to partner with someone from India who has moved there from here. (Vas Bhandarkar, Founder, GlobalLogic, California, USA)

Source: authors' own research

REs inspire 'going global' strategy, especially in emerging home economies. They have the potential to impact the globalization of industries and economies (Wang et al., 2011). This is because their international human and social capital, in particular their global networks, are related to internationalization opportunities or, more specifically, to the export orientation of their firms in the home country (Filatotchev et al., 2009; Prashantham and Dhanaraj, 2010).

The social impact of returnees in the home country has also been highlighted. Returnees play a role in shaping the public discourse by transforming the local environment and questioning traditional approaches (OECD, 2017). Return migrants tend to have an influence on electoral behavior, engagement at the local political level as well as on the political engagement of non-migrants. Migration experience influences political attitudes and behavior of return migrants both positively and negatively.

Students studying abroad, for example, form an influential group, transferring demo-cratic values back home on their return from a democratic country (Spilimbergo, 2009). Furthermore, the presence of return migrants tends to increase the electoral participa-tion of non-migrants (Waddell and Fontenla, 2015) as well as to alter electoral behavior within communities (Chauvet and Mercier, 2014). Exposure to different religious, social or political norms abroad can enhance tolerance of diversity in returnees compared to non-migrants (Pérez-Armendáriz and Crow, 2010).

Chapter Summary

LO1: Returnee entrepreneurs (REs) are scientists and engineers or students who were trained or studied/worked in OECD countries, and returned to their native coun-tries to set up new ventures. Typically, they are highly qualified individuals who return to their home countries to start up a new venture after several years of business experi-ence in another developed country. Most studies are focused on returnees to Asia and, in particular, China. Since 1978, about half of two million students who went abroad returned to China, a trend that has rapidly increased in the last few years.

LO2: REs have **intrinsic motivations** to return home. These include personal reasons such as a desire to start up, strong family bonds or perceptions of attractive market opportunities in the home country. REs may also return due to **perceived opportuni-ties in the home country**. These perceptions stem from their accumulated skills and experiences, and their perceived fit with the opportunities arising from growing market demand at home. In other cases, **push** and **pull factors** in both their host and home countries can drive them to go back and found a new venture in their home coun-try. The likelihood of return has been linked to economic conditions, the difficulty of obtaining permanent residency or citizenship in the host country, and the ease of mov-ing across national borders. Job opportunities and institutional reforms in the home country translate into an attractive home country environment for returnees. However, cultural challenges in the home market and the inability of REs to disconnect from the host country might be some hurdles.

LO3: Evidence suggests that returnees are more likely to engage in self-employment than non-migrants due to their distinctive **financial, human and social capital resources**. Return migrants intending to become self-employed or set up businesses on their return are more likely to acquire higher savings abroad. Accumulated **human capital** in the form of education and experiences from abroad is significantly asso-ciated with self-employment among returning migrants. **Education levels** in terms of foreign language proficiency, for example, increase the probability of becoming an entrepreneur with employees rather than being an own-account worker without employees. REs also leverage their **migration, prior work and start-up experiences** in the host country in the founding of their ventures at home. The nature of REs' human capital influences their location choice in their home country. Although REs' knowl-edge and experience acquired abroad are invaluable for the founding of their ventures, the lack of local knowledge can pose a constraint. REs are significantly more likely to rely on **social networks** built abroad for business leads and financing in venture creation, especially when they are located outside of entrepreneurial clusters in emerging economies. REs leverage both personal and professional ties formed abroad in the founding of their ventures. Peer ties formed in the early years of university study play a significant role in subsequent career choices and entry into entrepreneurship in the home country. Although REs leverage social networks from abroad upon their return home, local networks in the home country are especially crucial for them. Yet, REs feel out of touch with local networks due to their period of absence from the home country. Nevertheless, REs enjoy a high level of credibility in their home country by virtue of their human and social capital gained abroad, which makes it easier for them to engage in venture creation upon their return home.

LO4: RE background and characteristics impact the performance of their ventures. Some studies find that in the absence of local ties, returnees have stronger incentives to pursue firm efficiency and profitability rather than searching for political connections. Other studies find a positive link between REs' overseas experience and the survival of their ventures. By virtue of their international networks, REs have an international orientation at the outset. Therefore, they are well-equipped to follow an early internationalization path. REs also contribute to the development of local firms, industries and economies at home. REs inspire 'going global' strategy, especially in emerging home economies. Returnees also have **social impact**. They play a role in shaping the public discourse by transforming the local environment and questioning traditional approaches in their home country.

Review Questions

1. Explain what you understand by the term 'returnee entrepreneurs'. What are the trends in the return of REs to their home country in recent years? Give examples to illustrate your answer.
2. What is the difference between transnational entrepreneurs that you have learned about in the last chapter, and REs that you have read about in this chapter? Explain.
3. Why do individuals return to their home country to found a new venture? Discuss the motivations of REs based on what you have read in the chapter.
4. Using examples from emerging economies (e.g. China, South Korea), discuss the role of the home country institutional environment in returnee entrepreneurship.
5. 'There is something unique about REs that gives them an advantage in venture founding in their home country as compared to local entrepreneurs'. To what extent do you agree/disagree with this statement? Discuss the human and social capital resources of REs to support your answer.
6. What is the significance of REs? Discuss the contribution of REs to the a) economy, b) host country, c) home country.

Case 10.1

Returnee Entrepreneurs in Vietnam: Opportunities and Challenges

Overseas Vietnamese started to return to Vietnam in the early 1990s as Vietnam's Communist Party began to loosen its hold on the economy after the collapse of the Soviet Union. Seattle-raised entrepreneur David Thai moved to Hanoi in the 1990s. He became the first overseas Vietnamese to register a private company and open a chain of coffee shops under the name Highlands Coffee. In the following years, Intel Corp. appointed US national Than Trong Phuc to launch a $2 billion chip factory in Ho Chi Minh City in the early 2000s, while other Vietnamese returned from America, France and elsewhere to set up private businesses.

Source: www.needpix.com/photo/1796320

Henry Nguyen: Background and Early Years

Henry Nguyen is another excellent example. Married to the daughter of Vietnam's prime minister, Henry lives in Ho Chi Minh City with his wife and their twin daughters. A toddler when his family fled Vietnam just before the fall of Saigon 40 years ago, Henry grew up in Virginia's Fairfax County, not far from Washington, DC. His father, a civil engineer, who worked with the old South Vietnamese government, built a new life for his family after leaving Vietnam. Henry describes his upbringing as that of 'a typical suburban kid', playing football and going on dates. At that age, he didn't have much to do with Vietnam at all. The country's language and customs were largely a mystery to him despite his mother's efforts to pass them on to him and his siblings. Despite his family connections, Vietnam was an unknown quantity. His knowledge of the country largely consisted of Hollywood war films. Returning to Vietnam is something he never planned on or anticipated.

Vietnam intervened after a spell at Harvard and postgraduate studies at Northwestern University Medical School and the Kellogg School of Management in Chicago. Henry landed a summer job writing for the student travel guide *Let's Go* and the publisher asked him to go to Hanoi. He set out on the 52-hour journey from Boston via San Francisco, Tokyo, Singapore and Ho Chi Minh City with some trepidation. What he found when he arrived and walked a block or two to Hanoi's Hoan Kiem Lake was a revelation. 'These people spoke the same language my parents spoke at home, they eat the same food. At some level, it was home'.

The Return to Vietnam

Henry returned again to try his hand at business when he was hired by Boston-based International Data Group's (IDG) founder Patrick McGovern, after a chance meeting at a business-community breakfast in Hanoi. Then just 31, Henry was tasked with overseeing the firm's expansion into Vietnam. Subsequently, Henry set up a McDonald's franchise in Vietnam in 2013. The deal was the result of years of lobbying on his part. Henry's association with Vietnam dated back to his teens. In his teens, Henry got a job flipping burgers at a local McDonald's in Virginia, where he fell in love with the brand. He sent a series of reports on Vietnam's progress to McDonald's headquarters in Oak Brook. For a time, Henry was known as 'The Stalker' inside the company's international franchising division.

Vietnam's diaspora have played an important role in expanding the scope and scale of activities in what is expected to be one of the world's next great economic success stories. Viet Kieu, or overseas Vietnamese helped lead the march of foreign investment into the country. Expatriate Vietnamese have invested more than $20 billion in Vietnam, mostly in and around Ho Chi Minh City, the country's economic engine.

Henry was the first franchisee of McDonald's in Vietnam. Since his return in the early 2000s, Henry has become one of the best-known business figures in Vietnam as head of Vietnam operations for fund manager IDG Ventures. From the beginning, he bet heavily on the internet, positioning IDG as a lead investor in Vietnam's emerging start-up scene, funding everything from e-commerce outfits to music-and-entertainment websites. Early successes included funding VNG Corp., a maker of multiplayer video games that morphed into a sprawling internet conglomerate running some of the country's most popular social media sites and messaging platforms. Henry is stepping up IDG's bet on the internet in Vietnam. The firm recently invested in local e-commerce firm Hotdeal. Its chief executive, Nguyen Thanh Van An, said in an interview that his company handles an average of $100,000 worth of transactions a day, with volumes growing at about 15% a month. It already has a team of more than 100 red-and-black-clad drivers zipping through Ho Chi Minh City, delivering orders of women's fashion, children's toys and discount coupons, and plans to diversify into groceries next.

(Continued)

Opportunities in Vietnam

The influx and subsequent success of Vietnamese-born entrepreneurs in Vietnam is attributed to several positive changes in the country since the South capitulated to Communist forces on April 30, 1975. Several individuals are returning to their country of origin to reap the benefits of its economic transition and shift to a more market-oriented economy (Table 10.1). Many economists regard Vietnam as the last Confucian-influenced economy to open up to the rest of the world, following a path already forged by Japan, South Korea, China, Taiwan and Singapore. Foreign direct investment to Vietnam rose nearly fivefold between 2005 and 2013, while inflows to China expanded 1.7 times, according to data from the United Nations Conference on Trade and Development.

Source: www.needpix.com/photo/1796320

Frederic Neumann, co-head of Asian economic research at HSBC, views Vietnam as the best example of a frontier economy benefiting from rising costs in China. Thanks to multibillion-dollar investments from companies such as Samsung Electronics Co. and Intel, exports of smartphones and other electronics now have eclipsed old standbys such as textiles and footwear, leaving the country comfortably higher up the value ladder than cheaper locales such as Cambodia or Bangladesh. One of the three Samsung smartphone plants here is the company's largest anywhere in the world. Already Vietnam exports more goods to the US than Thailand or Indonesia.

Table 10.1　Annual GDP growth in Vietnam, and East Asia and Pacific, 2011–17

	Vietnam (%)	East Asia and Pacific (%)
2011	6	8
2012	5	7.5
2013	5	7
2014	5.5	6.9
2015	5.5	6.5
2016	5.8	6.5
2017	6	6.5

Source: adapted from Hookway (2015)

Table 10.2　Internet penetration rates as a percentage of total population

	US	China	Vietnam	Indonesia	India
2000	40	0	0	0	0
2002	60	5	0	0	0
2004	65	7	10	0	0
2006	68	10	20	5	4
2008	70	25	25	7	6
2010	68	30	30	10	8
2012	65	40	40	17	15

Source: adapted from Hookway (2015)

Vietnam's internet economy is also growing quickly. In a recent report, AT Kearney noted that internet penetration rates in Vietnam are rising faster than anywhere else in the region (Table 10.2). It also has more internet users – more than 40 million – than anywhere else in South-East Asia, including Indonesia, which has a population of more than 250 million.

Demographics are also in favor of Vietnam. A vast majority of the population of Vietnam is young, with a third of the country's 90 million people born in the 1980s or 1990s. Many of them are often seen perched atop motor scooters that weave precariously through the streets of Ho Chi Minh City and Hanoi. The idea of glory being associated with being rich is a Sino-Confucian value.

The Challenges

At the same time, however, the return to Vietnam is fraught with several challenges. Corruption has been rampant in Vietnam in the years following the global financial crisis, which hit the country hard. The country's rapid growth has seen the children and relatives of prominent Politburo members and businessmen quickly rise through

(Continued)

the ranks. The former head of state-owned shipbuilder Vietnam Shipbuilding Industry Group, for instance, appointed his son, brother and brother-in-law to senior positions before the company's debt bubble burst in 2010 and landed him in prison.

Some returning entrepreneurs have found themselves snared in legal disputes, caught out by a legal system ill-equipped to handle civil disputes and where personal contacts sometimes matter more than the rule of law. American citizen Hoan Nguyen spent 14 months, without being charged, in Hanoi's dank B14 prison after a dispute with his Vietnamese business partners in an international school project. He recalled listening to state radio broadcasts booming out in the prison's courtyard each morning exhorting overseas Vietnamese to return to invest in the motherland. He was eventually freed after police concluded he hadn't committed any crime.

For Henry, lack of language skills was a challenge at the beginning. He was 'something of an odd bird to be there in Hanoi', and it was tough to explain to people what he was doing there. His securing a franchise to open the first McDonald's in Vietnam in 2013 was also mired in controversy. He faced allegations of nepotism due to his marriage to the daughter of Vietnam's communist Prime Minister, Nguyen Tan Dung in 2008. Many attacked him on internet sites, accusing him of selling out to Vietnam's communist leaders. 'Henry Nguyen is a communist wearing a Viet Kieu mask', read one anonymous post on a bulletin board catering to the Vietnamese-American community. Despite these challenges, Henry remains optimistic: 'Vietnam hasn't seen a period of peace and stability like this for a couple of centuries. We're still in the very early innings'.

Source: adapted from Hookway (2015)

Discussion Questions

1. What was the process of Henry's return to Vietnam from the US? How did he establish a connection with his home country prior to returning to live there? Explain.
2. What type of venture did Henry establish upon his return to Vietnam? Why?
3. Evaluate the role of the local institutional environment for the return of skilled personnel to Vietnam. What are the opportunities for REs in Vietnam? What are the challenges? What can REs do to navigate these challenges?
4. Do you agree that REs make a contribution to their home country? Outline Henry's contribution to Vietnam to explain your answer.

References

Avle, S. (2014) 'Articulating and enacting development: Skilled returnees in Ghana's ICT industry', *Information Technologies & International Development*, 10(4): 1–13.

Chafkin, M. (2011) 'Born or raised in the US, why are entrepreneurs returning to Korea?' *Inc. Magazine*, 11 December. Available at www.inc.com/magazine/201112/the-returnees.html (last accessed 27 September 2022).

Chauvet, L. and Mercier, M. (2014) 'Do return migrants transfer political norms to their origin country? Evidence from Mali', *Journal of Comparative Economics*, 42(3): 630–651.

Chen, Y.-C. (2008) 'The limits of brain circulation: Chinese returnees and technological development in Beijing', *Pacific Affairs*, 81(1): 195–215.

Dai, O. and Liu, X. (2009) 'Returnee entrepreneurs and firm performance in Chinese high-technology industries', *International Business Review*, 18(4): 373–386.

De Vreyer, P., Gubert, F. and Robilliard, A.S. (2010) 'Are there returns to migration experience? An empirical analysis using data on return migrants and non-migrants in West Africa', *Annals of Economics and Statistics/Annales d'économie et de statistique*, 97(98): 307–328.

Drori, I., Honig, B. and Wright, M. (2009) 'Transnational entrepreneurship: An emergent field of study', *Entrepreneurship Theory and Practice*, 33(5): 1001–1022.

Dumont, J.C. and Spielvogel, G. (2008) 'Return migration: A new perspective', OECD: International Migration Outlook, pp. 161–222. Available at www.oecd-ilibrary.org/social-issues-migration-health/international-migration-outlook-2008/return-migration_migr_outlook-2008-7-en (last accessed 27 September 2022).

Filatotchev, I., Liu, X., Buck, T. and Wright, M. (2009) 'The export orientation and export performance of high-technology SMEs in emerging markets: The effects of knowledge transfer by returnee entrepreneurs', *Journal of International Business Studies*, 40(6): 1005–1021.

Giannetti, M., Liao, G. and Yu, X. (2014) 'The brain gain of corporate boards: Evidence from China', *Journal of Finance*, 70(4): 1629–1682.

Hao, J. and Welch, A. (2012) 'A tale of sea turtles: Job-seeking experiences of hai gui (high-skilled returnees) in China', *Higher Education Policy*, 25(2): 243–260.

Hookway, J. (2015) 'Forty years after fall of Saigon, entrepreneurs return to Vietnam', *The Wall Street Journal*, 30 April. Available at www.wsj.com/articles/forty-years-after-fall-of-saigon-entrepreneurs-return-to-vietnam-1430326981 (last accessed 27 September 2022).

Huang, Y. and Kuah-Pearce, K.E. (2014) '"Talent circulators" in Shanghai: Return migrants and their strategies for success', *Globalisation, Societies and Education*, 13(2): 276–294.

Kaufman, J. (2003) 'Turning back: After years in US, Mr. Luo seeks fortune in China – amid reforms, nation coaxes US schooled executives with perks and funding – leaving his boys behind', *The Wall Street Journal*, 6 March.

Kenney, M., Breznitz, D. and Murphree, M. (2013) 'Coming back home after the sun rises: Returnee entrepreneurs and growth of high-tech industries', *Research Policy*, 42(2): 391–407.

Kerr, S.P., Kerr, W., Ozden, C. and Parsons, C. (2016) 'Global talent flows'. Working Paper 17-026. Harvard Business School, pp. 1–25.

Lianos, T. and Pseiridis, A. (2009) 'On the occupational choices of return migrants', *Entrepreneurship and Regional Development*, 21(2): 155–181.

Liu, X., Lu, J., Filatotchev, I., Buck, T. and Wright, M. (2010a) 'Returnee entrepreneurs, knowledge spillovers and innovation in high-tech firms in emerging economies', *Journal of International Business Studies*, 41(7): 1183–1197.

Liu, X., Wright, M., Filatotchev, I., Dai, O. and Lu, J. (2010b) 'Human mobility and international knowledge spillovers: Evidence from high-tech small and medium enterprises in an emerging market', *Strategic Entrepreneurship Journal*, 4(4): 340–355.

Liu, X., Wright, M. and Filatotchev, I. (2015) 'Learning, firm age and performance: An investigation of returnee entrepreneurs in Chinese high-tech industries', *International Small Business Journal*, 33(5): 467–487.

Liu, Y. and Almor, T. (2014) 'How culture influences the way entrepreneurs deal with uncertainty in inter-organizational relationships: The case of returnee versus local entrepreneurs in China', *International Business Review*, 25(1): 4–14.

Marchetta, F. (2012) 'Return migration and the survival of entrepreneurial activities in Egypt', *World Development*, 40(10): 1999–2013.

Martin, R. and Radu, D. (2012) 'Return migration: The experience of eastern Europe', *International Migration*, 50(1): 109–128.

McCormick, B. and Wahba, J. (2003) 'Return international migration and geographical inequality: The case of Egypt', *Journal of African Economies*, 12(1): 500–532.

McDougall, P.P., Oviatt, B.M. and Shrader, R.C. (2003) 'A comparison of international and domestic new ventures', *Journal of International Entrepreneurship*, 1(1): 59–82.

Mesnard, A. and Ravallion, M. (2006) 'The wealth effect on new business startups in a developing economy', *Economica*, 73(1): 367–392.

Mezger Kveder, C.L. and Flahaux, M.L. (2013) 'Returning to Dakar: A mixed methods analysis of the role of migration experience for occupational status', *World Development*, 45(1): 223–238.

Nanda, R. and Khanna, T. (2010) 'Diasporas and domestic entrepreneurs: Evidence from the Indian software industry', *Journal of Economics & Management Strategy*, 19(4): 991–1012.

OECD. (2017) 'Capitalising on return migration by making it more attractive and sustainable', in *Interrelations between Public Policies, Migration and Development*. Paris: OECD Publishing. http://doi.org/10.1787/9789264265615-12-en

Oviatt, B. and McDougall, P.P. (1994) 'Toward a theory of international new ventures', *Journal of International Business Studies*, 25(1): 45–64.

Pérez-Armendáriz, C. and Crow, D. (2010) 'Do migrants remit democracy? International migration, political beliefs, and behavior in Mexico', *Comparative Political Studies*, 43(1): 119–148.

Piracha, M. and Vadean, F. (2009) 'Return migration and occupational choice'. IZA Discussion Papers, No. 3922. Bonn: Institute for the Study of Labor (IZA). Available at http://nbn-resolving.de/urn:nbn:de:101:1-20090119182 (last accessed 27 September 2022).

Prashantham, S. and Dhanaraj, C. (2010) 'The dynamic influence of social capital on the international growth of new ventures', *Journal of Management Studies*, 47(6): 967–994.

Pruthi, S. (2014) 'Social ties and venture creation by returnee entrepreneurs', *International Business Review*, 23(6): 1139–1152.

Qin, F. and Estrin, S. (2015) 'Does social influence span time and space? Evidence from Indian returnee entrepreneurs', *Strategic Entrepreneurship Journal*, 9(3): 226–242.

Rabbiosi, L. and Stucchi, T. (2012) 'The magic of diasporas: The role of overseas national ownership in outward FDI of emerging market firms', *The Third Copenhagen Conference on Emerging Multinationals: Outward Investment from Emerging Economies*, Copenhagen Business School, Frederiksberg, Denmark, 25 October 2012 to 26 October 2012.

Razumovskaya, O. (2016) 'Russia's venture capital funds look abroad', *The Wall Street Journal*, June 21. https://www.wsj.com/articles/russias-venture-capital-funds-look-abroad-1466529651

Saxenian, A. (2005) 'From brain drain to brain circulation: Transnational communities and regional upgrading in India and China', *Studies in Comparative International Development*, 40(2): 35–61.

Sheehan, C.M. and Riosmena, F. (2013) 'Migration, business formation, and the informal economy in urban Mexico', *Social Science Research*, 42(4): 1092–1108.

Spilimbergo, A. (2009) 'Democracy and foreign education', *American Economic Review*, 99(1): 528–543.

Thomas, K.J. and Inkpen, C. (2013) 'Migration dynamics, entrepreneurship, and African development: Lessons from Malawi', *International Migration Review*, 47(4): 844–873.

Trefor, M. (2016) 'Returning to the Philippines', *The Wall Street Journal*, 3 May. Available at www.wsj.com/articles/for-filipinos-abroad-home-is-calling-1462217402 (last accessed 27 September 2022).

Tynaliev, U.M. and McLean, G.N. (2011) 'Labour migration and national human resource development in the context of post-soviet Kyrgyzstan', *Human Resource Development International*, 14(2): 199–215.

Vandor, P. and Franke, N. (2016) 'Why are immigrants more entrepreneurial?' *Harvard Business Review*. Available at https://hbr.org/2016/10/why-are-immigrants-more-entrepreneurial (last accessed 27 September 2022).

Waddell, B.J. and Fontenla, M. (2015) 'The Mexican dream? The effect of return migrants on hometown development', *The Social Science Journal*, 52(3): 386–395.

Wadhwa, V., Jain, S., Saxenian, A. L., Gereffi, G. and Wang, H. (2011) 'The Grass is Indeed Greener in India and China for Returnee Entrepreneurs. America's New Immigrant Entrepreneurs, Part VI', *Kauffman: The Foundation of Entrepreneurship*, April 2011.

Wahba, J. and Zenou, Y. (2012) 'Out of sight, out of mind: Migration, entrepreneurship and social capital', *Regional Science and Urban Economics*, 42(5): 890–903.

Wang, H., Zweig, D. and Lin, X. (2011) 'Returnee entrepreneurs: Impact on China's globalization process', *Journal of Contemporary China*, 20(7): 413–431.

Wright, M., Clarysse, B., Mustar, P. and Lockett, A. (2007) *Academic Entrepreneurship in Europe*. Cheltenham: Edward Elgar Publishing.

Wright, M., Liu, X., Buck, T. and Filatochev, I. (2008) 'Returnee entrepreneurs, science park location choice and performance: An analysis of high-technology SMEs in China', *Entrepreneurship, Theory and Practice*, 32(1): 131–155.

Yang, J. (2019) 'No more easy profits as China's venture capital boom fizzles', *The Wall Street Journal*, November 14, 5:35 am. https://www.wsj.com/articles/chinas-venture-capital-boom-is-over-leaving-investors-high-and-dry-11573727756

Zahra, S.A. (2007) 'Contextualizing theory building in entrepreneurship research', *Journal of Business Venturing*, 22(3): 443–452.

Zhang, Y. (2017) 'Preferential policies lure returnee entrepreneurs', *China Daily*, 8 August. Available at www.chinadaily.com.cn/china/2017-08/09/content_30383109.htm (last accessed 27 September 2022).

Zhou, Y. and Hsu, J.Y. (2010) 'Divergent engagements: Roles and strategies of Taiwanese and mainland Chinese returnee entrepreneurs in the IT industry', *Global Networks*, 11(3): 398–419.

Zweig, D. and Wang, H. (2013) 'Can China bring back the best? The communist party organizes China's search for talent', *The China Quarterly*, 215(1): 590–615.

Zweig, D., Chung, S.F. and Vanhonacker, W. (2006) 'Rewards of technology: Explaining China's reverse migration', *Journal of International Migration and Integration*, 7(4): 449–471.

11
GLOBALIZATION

Learning Outcomes

After studying this chapter, you should be able to:

- **LO1**: Understand the origins of globalization (did it start everywhere as the term might imply?) and how it has evolved over time
- **LO2**: Obtain a critical understanding of the meaning, scope and significance of the term, 'globalization'
- **LO3**: Evaluate how globalization has opened up opportunities for international entrepreneurship development
- **LO4**: Examine critically the phenomenon of the 'born global firm'
- **LO5**: Work towards developing strategies, policies and actions that could draw on the benefits of globalization while safeguarding against its downsides for entrepreneurship development

Introduction

Let us start with some observations on globalization, as expressed by accomplished thought leaders, academic researchers and other writers.

> The globalization of markets is at hand. With that, the multinational commercial world nears its end, and so does the multinational corporation... The multinational corporation operates in a number of countries, and adjusts its products and processes in each, at high relative cost. The global corporation operates with resolute constancy... it sells the same things in the same way everywhere. (Levitt, 1983)

Levitt's celebration of globalization seems to suggest that it is in the opening up of the markets and the constant supply of homogenous or similar products to the global market-place by multinational corporations that we can find the essence of this phenomenon. In Levitt's globalized world the multinationals conduct one-way traffic of their goods to willing recipients around the world as global corporate lords of the new, connected empire.

This rather narrow perspective typifies arguments about the necessity of exploitation of an extended marketplace, where globalization simply prepares the ground for global corporations. It ignores the emergence of different producers and consumers who are often networked to make and consume goods together. A more nuanced and complex explanation of globalization might, therefore, be helpful.

> At one extreme imagine a world that is a collection of economic islands connected... by highly unreliable and expensive bridges or ferries. At the other extreme, imagine a world as an integrated system where the fortunes of the various peoples inhabiting the planet are highly intertwined. The sneakers that you wear were manufactured in Indonesia... If you agree that over the last 50 years, the world around you has undergone a transformation from something like the first scenario to something like the second one, then we would say that the worldwide economy is indeed undergoing a process of globalisation... globalisation refers to the growing economic interdependence among countries as reflected in increasing cross-border flows of three types of entities: goods and services, capital and know-how. (Gupta et al., 2008)

It is worth considering whether Gupta et al. state anything different from Ted Levitt's assertion about global corporations taking over where the multinationals left.

The reference is to the move from simply buying and selling in foreign markets to integrated and connected operations for firms and even industries. Building and maintaining separate and physically oriented overseas operations is being substituted by alternative cost models based on connections and information and communications technology (ICT) based activities. These connections are characterized by the speed of business transactions covering multiple operations across many countries and varied business units. So, we can assume that bilateral exchange between two or three firms across a limited number of countries has given way to this new form of global connectivity. It is not just goods and services that are being exchanged but the flows of money, know-how and talent too. With Gupta et al. we have moved from global markets to global production processes. So, we could argue that all that we know about business development, from the creating and making of things (and now even services) to their sale of these goods and services, has gone global!

The 'flat earth' belief system appears to have found aficionados from journalists such as Thomas Friedman (2006) in his book *The World is Flat*, to economists like Frances Cairncross (2002 – 'The death of distance'), who have argued for and promoted the universality of technology, organizations, needs and desires of people. Ghemawat (2007) reckons that between 2000 and 2004, more than 5,000 books on globalization regaled policy makers, researchers and ordinary folk dreaming of one world, one love, where they could get together and be alright (with apologies to Bob Marley)!

It is useful to have some deeper understanding of the term globalization than what the definitions above might offer, and raise some questions, such as:

- Is globalization a new phenomenon?
- What is globalization and how is it different from internationalization?
- Is globalization all about large corporations making economic hay whether they are called multinationals or global corporations?
- How has globalization affected entrepreneurship?

These are some of the questions that help us to structure this chapter leading us to answer them carefully and analytically.

Structure of the Chapter

This chapter starts by charting, briefly, the historical trajectory of globalization to better appreciate how this phenomenon may have shaped entrepreneurial activity over time. The second part of the chapter examines its meaning, scope and reach today. In Part Three we examine the born global firm phenomenon, and this is followed in the fourth part by insights into globalization as it affects new forms and modes of venture creation and development. We examine some of the problems that have affected organizations, the entrepreneurship process and the wider economy, globally, in the wake of globalization, and taking a reality check on the scope and impact of globalization. We end the chapter with some concluding observations about the changing shape of globalization today.

Part One: A Historical Snapshot

The narrative of globalization is best told by recounting historical antecedents to the phenomenon today. By going back to history we can make a better economic case for globalization or question its value in both economic and social terms (Darwin, 2007; Hopkins, 2002; Maddison, 2007). Economists typically use the term globalization to refer to international integration in commodity, capital and labor markets (Bordo et al., 2003), and focus on economic growth outside the West, especially in China 'where demand for luxury goods is forecast to quadruple in the next decade, or to considering social change in India, where more people have a mobile phone than a flushing toilet' (Frankopan, 2016, p. xiv). In other words, a significant amount of attention has shifted East and to a scattering of other countries in Asia, Africa and Latin America. This shift marks a form of acceptance of the emergence of a new world order where economic power is moving fast in a direction not monopolized by the so-called 'advanced' nations of the West. At the same time, the emergence of the new world order is often evaluated in terms of how close the East is moving to replicate all the structures, institutions and economic practices of the West, excepting that they may be doing it better now, at least in economic terms. Is this a new phenomenon? We find that interestingly, this shift has historical antecedents which are well worth considering.

What may be particularly useful is to consider what Frankopan (2016) suggests, namely to look at the region between East and West, in countries that have more recently acquired prominence for being politically unstable, making possible threats to global security, running non-democratic governance structures, operating with poor records on human rights, or at best, being peripheral to global interests. Think of countries that have been hitting the headlines recently – Afghanistan, Iraq, Syria and Iran – nations that imperil the West's status quo politically and economically. Consider also, the peripheral states of Kazakhstan, Uzbekistan, Kyrgystan, Turkmenistan and Tajikistan. These countries have been at the center of global affairs since civilization was born. They formed the bridge between East and West where the great ancient cities of Harappa and Mohenjo-daro in the Indus Valley flourished together with the other great centers of Babylon, Nineveh, Uruk and Akkad in Mesopotamia, about 5,000 years ago. Large populations, streets with smart drainage and sewage systems, dazzling architecture, negotiations over trade from far and wide, the emergence of the great religions of Judaism, Hinduism, Buddhism, Christianity and Islam were the notable features of a highly interconnected region with strong global, cultural, economic and political links. The effects of what happened there could be felt in North Africa or Scandinavia, and where the prices of goods were altered as a result of discoveries in America, as networks of merchants, nomads, pilgrims and warriors travelled, exchanging goods, generating prosperity while spreading disease, violence and death. These were the 'Seidenstraβen' or the 'Silk Roads' as named by the German geologist Ferdinand von Richtofen (Frankopan, 2016).

Historians capture the environment of those ancient times as being extraordinarily fertile and rich, ripe enough for a range of entrepreneurial and innovative activities that spread across countries through trade, the exchange of ideas and knowledge sharing. Our purpose here is not to provide a detailed historical narrative but to reflect on events in the past which could help us to obtain proper perspectives of a phenomenon that has had such a huge impact on trade, business, technology and the movement of people across the globe.

The origins of this global phenomenon were in Asia and the region referred to above. Perhaps what was entrepreneurial about that time can be found first in the opening up of both societies and economies that could accommodate changes across the social and economic spectrum of human life. Second, the nature of technological change spawning innovation was generally focused on agriculture and the extractive industries. This enabled a cross-fertilization of ideas, customs and languages as people kept up with the times. Frontier times perhaps, and today the Silk Roads are opening up again with a series of connections as cities, new oil and gas pipelines, technologies and entrepreneurial businesses are proliferating across the spine of Asia, often in countries not aligned to Western forms of political or economic governance (Frankopan, 2016, 2018). This is where we might find the past, present and future of the world.

Dwelling for a little longer to understand Asia's early global dominance both in terms of productivity and competitiveness, we find that a significant amount of specialization and division of labor was responsible for the Indian sub-continent and China being the most advanced economies of Asia and indeed the world. Such specialization resulted from highly developed skills of handicraft workers and various forms of sub-division of the production process, enabled by flexible adaptation to changing demands in the market for types of goods. The industries were on top of the ranking order for both quality and growth of long-staple cotton and in the development of chemical technology together with the industry to dye the cotton. The innovations here were supported by low cost of labor mainly because efficient food production made it possible for food to be supplied cheaply (Gunder Frank, 1998). This combination of technological efficiency and organizational effectiveness engendered spillover effects across industries. Chaudhuri (1990) notes that in addition to the three prominent crafts of Asian countries – textiles, cotton and silk, metal goods including jewelry plus ceramics and glassware – there were a wide range of subsidiary manufacturing capabilities that used early forms of industrial clustering featuring technological prowess and organizational ingenuity based on specialized social and economic functions. Included in that mix were paper, musical instruments, furniture, cosmetics, perfumery, bricks, gunpowder and fireworks. Such excellence in economic and craft-based activities did not simply enrich local societies; they were part of the basket of goods that moved between countries as part of a global operation. Historians such as Chaudhuri (1978), Dasgupta and Pearson (1987), Arasaratnam (1986) and Raychaudhri and Habib (1982), examining world trade flows between 1400 and 1800, confirmed that Asian trade was a flourishing enterprise into which Europeans played only a minor role.

The late 15th and 16th centuries saw the advent of direct maritime contact between Europe and Asia, starting with Vasco de Gama's voyage to India in 1497. The Americas were Europe's bounty land despite significantly higher levels of technological sophistication in the Asian domains of the Ottoman Empire, the Moghul Empire, Saffavid Persia, China and Japan, which of course meant that these blocks were not as vulnerable to conquest as the Aztecs and the Incas were. Asia was also far away from Europe. What made the European venture to Asia possible was, first, considerable developments in European ship design, navigation, naval weaponry. Second, property rights and institutional support from the state facilitated the birth of companies which eventually became behemoths – the East India Company (EIC) and the Dutch Far East Company (VOC) – in the service of the British and Dutch Empires. Third, the lack of interest in European goods in Asia coupled with the latter's imperviousness to succumbing immediately as serfs or underdogs meant that trade in precious metals obtained from the Americas was vital for entry to the Asian continent. Underpinning these three key factors was the significant rivalry of European countries for the spoils of other nations. With armed ships and sophisticated weaponry pitched against groups of people with virtually no opposing force, the practice of free trade and most-favored nation treatment spearheaded by the EIC and VOC was turned into an imperialist project of territorial hegemony by 1820.

Fast forwarding the historical narrative, Baldwin and Martin (1999) trace at least two episodes of globalization since the mid-19th century. The first episode began around the mid-19th century and ended with the commencement of World War I. The second episode which began in the aftermath of World War II continues today, although we see variations on the theme (see Chapter 13). What happened in both episodes was a rapid growth in trade and economic output coupled with changes in the size of the economies which became involved in globalization. It is not as if there was a smooth transition from one episode to another. There were patterns of ebb and flow, with periods of accelerated integration (in the 19th century and in the second half of the 20th century) followed by periods of dramatic reversals (as in the inter-war period or during the financial crisis of 2008, and as we are witnessing now because of COVID-19), sometimes with highly expensive consequences.

What does this very brief and cursory tale of history tell us about globalization and entrepreneurship?

First and foremost, there is the confirmation of the historical trajectory of globalization. Recognizing this trajectory should help us to understand that most phenomena have antecedents, and that it is through the ebb and flow of technological development, organizational capabilities and spillover effects that we can find how opportunities are identified and realized in different parts of the globe at alternate times. Globalization is often discussed as a very specific 20th century phenomenon offering opportunities for an advanced West to grab from the rising East. The West's subsequent dominance of the economic order was built on trade and knowledge exchange with the East, not forgetting of course the egregious nature of war, colonization and empire that accompanied the West's ascendancy.

Second, we find that globalization is unequal in that there is this element of localized or regional concentration of production, crafts, technology and organization together with the availability of natural resources (sometimes) which provides for a competitive advantage in both enterprise creation and development and trade flows.

Third, obtaining a historical context allows us to examine the changes that are occurring now, with on the one hand the resurgence of the East, and on the other the ubiquitous power of technology in enterprise creation and connectivity between firms and nations.

Fourth, we can interpret globalization as a phenomenon affecting all countries and firms, albeit in different ways. History gives us a perspective of globalization which is the essence of the phenomenon, namely that it is not firm-specific. Unlike internationalization it is not a process with which a firm engages in order to buy or sell goods and services outside its own country.

We turn now to look at globalization as it plays out today.

Part Two: Scope and Meaning of Globalization in Recent Times

Analyses of the various effects of globalization on the prospects of people to search for opportunities have been mixed, leading to different interpretations of its value to both firms and the economies of different countries. We provide short sketches summarizing the general features of the 'globalized world' as understood in its current stage of development. Table 11.1 provides this summary.

Table 11.1 Features of a globalized world

1.   A Single Global Market

The emergence of a common or single global market for goods widely used as intermediaries for manufacturing or as end products for individual or corporate use, together with the supply of capital, credit and financial services chasing the most productive markets around the world.

2.   Intense Cross-Border Interactions

Dense and intense interaction between both neighboring and geographically distant countries whose interests have become global, and not simply regional.

3.   Culture, Media and Brands

The global organization of media and its use of cultural props and commercial brands to penetrate disparate or common cultures by globally organized media and claim the ubiquity and inseparability of the products and their message.

4.   Migration

Large flows of migration including so-called economic migrants and refugees (the highly contentious distinction notwithstanding), the emergence of diasporas, leading to the creation of networks and connections that rival the impact of the great European out-migration of the 19th century, or obversely the appropriation through the Atlantic slave trade.

5.   New World Order

The demise of the Cold War and its 'bi-polar age' (1945–1989) and the rise of a single 'hyperpower', the United States of America (though many question its fading economic hegemony in the 21st century), whose economic and military strength far exceeds that of any other in modern world history.

6.   China and Emerging Economies

The rise and rise of a resurgent China, technologically, militarily and in terms of manufacturing and trade, followed distantly by India and the other emergent nations such as Brazil and South Africa, resulting in dramatically increasing world output and tilting the balance of the world economy. Many have compared the economic mobilization of their vast populations to the opening up of vast new lands of the 19th century.

Source: adapted from Darwin (2008)

A simplistic reading of the features mentioned above might suggest that the resulting economic interdependence makes for a flat world of business commerce, R&D and talent sharing. Some observations tend to reinforce this view implying that firms, industries, regions and countries are becoming fully integrated.

Friedman (2005) for instance notes that this flattening process has not only happened quickly because of digitization, but that it has influenced the roles and relationships between firms, countries and governments. The corollaries of digitization are virtulalization and automation which have generated gains in productivity with the adoption of digital technology tools. Crucially, Friedman believes that more and more people around the world will have access to these tools and be able to be part of a globally linked community of innovators, collaborators, and even as terrorists!

Friedman's richly anecdotal panegyric to flat world globalization refers to a form of integration of markets and countries which is not necessarily borne out in reality. Historical, cultural, political, social and technological factors are diverse across different countries, regions and firms. Moreover, it is this very diversity which informs the purpose of doing business, sharing know-how and resources across borders. Additionally, different countries have adopted varied speeds to integrate globally.

We will discuss the features of globalization further in the paragraphs that follow.

Adopting Globalization

Gupta et al. (2008) offer an interesting explanation of what it means to globalize across different units of analysis – the country and the industry.

The Country Unit

For a country the extent of interlinkages of the economy of a particular country with the rest of the world is what describes globalization. While countries such as Cuba remain isolated and others such as Iran are threatened with sanctions, a cabal of emerging economies such as the BRICS countries have made rapid strides in globalization as measured by the share of their GDP of exports and imports, inward and outward flows of foreign direct investment and portfolio investment and inward and outward flows of royalty payments associated with technology transfer.

Let us look at some random data on exports and imports of goods and services in 2021. Exports represent the value of all of these goods and a range of market services provided by individual countries to the rest of the world. The World Bank data shown in Table 11.2 includes the value of merchandise, freight, insurance, transport, travel, royalties, license fees and other services, such as communication, construction, financial, information, business, personal and government services. They exclude some other financially oriented services which used to be called factor services.

Table 11.2   Exports and imports of goods and services (% of GDP), 2021

Countries	Exports	Imports
Brazil	20.1	19.1
United States	10.9	14.6
Russian Federation	30.9	21.3

Countries	Exports	Imports
United Kingdom	27.9	28.7
China	20.0	17.4
India	21.4	23.9
France	29.4	31.4
Germany	47.0	41.7
Belgium	86.9	85.8
Korea Rep.	42.0	38.5
Bhutan	31.8	52.7
Dibjouti (2020)	115.8	107.3
Hong Kong SAR, China	203.5	198.7
San Marino (2020)	164.5	140.4

Source: adapted from World Bank national accounts data, and OECD National Accounts. All figures are for 2021 except as indicated

The figures reflect the varying level of dependence that different countries have on their exports. Smaller countries might be more dependent on exports (subject to goods and services being saleable in the global market) but they might equally be banking on imports partly due to limited capacities for local production of specific goods. Large countries with substantial internal markets tend to be less reliant on exports. But here too the level of sophistication of that internal market can make a difference as it does in the USA. This macro-level picture is important because it does not necessarily reflect the arguments put forward at the micro level about the propensity of firms to export being a measure of their innovative capacity and growth. Therefore, the impact individual firms have on the economy might be limited to the large global or medium-sized firms as opposed to their smaller counterparts. Critically, obtaining an understanding of the macro picture of globalization also offers insights into business strategy making, especially when it comes to identifying appropriate environments for the flow of goods and services. On the surface, trade may not appear to have any direct impact on the establishment of a new cross-border business, but such a view belies the importance of the relative ease of movement of goods and services for entrepreneurs and their aspirations for the growth of their ventures in different markets.

The Industry Unit

At the industry level globalization refers to the degree to which a firm within that industry relies on its competitive position being interdependent with the competitive position of another country. This global interdependence allows it to leverage technology, manufacturing, prowess, brand names and capital across borders. This degree of interdependence tends to favor larger firms such as Motorola, Samsung, Sony, Coca Cola, Pepsi, Cadbury and Schweppes (Gupta et al., 2008). However, not to be outdone, small innovative firm may also distinguish themselves with their international presence. This is evinced in:

1. The sub-contracting role many small firms play which involves them in work with larger firms.

2. The reversal of the sub-contracting role when small firms adopt a leadership position by granting licenses to larger firms to manufacture products based on their intellectual property associated with design work. Before its global presence transformed the firm's capacity, size and attractiveness as an ideal firm to acquire, Arm Ltd. was a small smartphone, Internet of Things and network equipment chip design firm in the UK, licensing its technology to large chip manufacturers such as Hewlett Packard, Apple, Samsung, Qualcomm, CISCO and others. A small royalty for each device was its income source. Arm Ltd. was purchased by the Japanese telecoms group Softbank (SBG) for £24.3 billion in 2016.

3. The opportunities for fairly small players to enter the global market independently through the internet and through portals and platforms such as EBay or Amazon, and increasingly through apps using web-based technologies and cloud computing. Theoretically, this new phenomenon enables technologically savvy individuals to enter global markets armed with their laptops and their ingenuity.

4. The idea or the phenomenon of 'born global firms', which suggests that firms start their business in the global market with global customers on day one of their business. We will return to 'born global' firms later in the chapter.

5. Small firms' owner-managers engaging in internationalization by using their private knowledge about entering global markets, and accessing and mobilizing cross-border knowledge networks, often using their international or transnational social capital. (Acedo and Jones, 2007; Aspelund et al., 2007; Cavusgil and Knight, 2009; Rialp et al., 2005)

The last two points deserve special attention because they have become part of the established phenomena of globalization. Let us start with born global firms.

Part Three: Born Global Firms

Can firms have a global birthplace? Asking this question reflects a concern with its conceptual significance. Traditionally new firms start local. They tend to draw their resources (people, money, technologies) locally. They know their local customers and they are more likely to depend on local suppliers, distributors and networks. A so-called 'born global' enterprise starts and grows its business activities in at least two different countries from its inception (or very close to its start). In other words the start-up process is globalized. Where then can we make a start with what research and scholarship have to say about the born global firm?

Rennie (1993) states that firms which begin operating globally within their first six years can be regarded as born global firms. Rennie is arguing on the basis that the average gestation period of these mainly high-tech-driven firms is around six years. For these firms, many of their products and services tend to be the same across different geographical market spaces, although contextualized in terms of either manufacturing or marketing to suit local conditions and customs. Central to the adoption of a global presence at inception is the utilization of the global information technology infrastructure. While internationalization is a process adopted by firms to enter different markets, globalization enables firms to gain competitive advantage in many countries at the same time. Oviatt and McDougall (1994) sum it up neatly: a born global firm is 'a business organization that, from inception, seeks to derive significant competitive advantage from the use of resources and the sale of outputs in multiple countries' (p. 124).

Developing this line of argument further, Knight and Cavusgil, explain a born global firm as follows:

> The distinguishing feature of these firms is that their origins are international, as demonstrated by management's global focus and the commitment of specific resources to international activities… these early adopters of internationalization begin with a global view of their markets, and develop the capabilities needed to achieve their international goals at or near the firm's founding. (Knight and Cavusgil, 2004, pp. 124–125)

In other words a born global firm does not only seek competitive advantage; it has a global view and it sets international goals at or close enough to the start of operations.

Yet another definition by Servantie (2007) corroborates what we know already:

> Companies of which we can observe, earlier than usual, a capacity to develop and coordinate regular links with the international.

This unique group of firms derives competitive advantage via access to and use of global resources; they tend to generate rapid turnover across the globe early on in their lives, which marks them out as being very different to an average firm internationalizing its business after they have established themselves in their home countries (Mitra, 2020).

In common with most new phenomena, new labels extend the scope of conversation and research. In addition to born globals we have 'global startups' (Oviatt et al., 1995), 'instant internationals' (Fillis, 2001) and 'international new ventures' (Oviatt and McDougall, 1994). We see the emergence of a typology of born globals.

A Typology of Born Globals

Developing a typology suggests that that born global firms do not have a common set of universal characteristics. They might be referred to as born global, but they are spread across a spectrum of different types of start-up operations, often in a combination of exporting and foreign direct investment activities.

The four categories of born globals considered by Oviatt and McDougall (1994) are:

- 'Import-export start-up' – internationalized trading activity.
- 'Multinational trader' – a large corporate trading firm operating across several countries.
- 'Geographically focused start-ups' – start-ups that concentrate their activities in specific countries, by choice.
- 'Global start-ups'.

These distinctions might blur our understanding of the specific type of born global firms we are attempting to understand. The important point, however, is to note that they offer us a chance to distinguish between process and phenomena. The first three types are process-oriented firms, interested in buying and selling their goods in different international markets. Only the last type might be regarded as the genuine article.

In a nuanced, empirical article on several hundred firms, Knight and Cavusgil (2005) identified four broad clusters of born global firms. A first group of firms has a strong entrepreneurial and strategic focus differentiating their products, services and operations, by design, from others (Porter, 1980). A second group is distinguished by their technological leadership coupled with being product differentiators. A third, more functional group, relies on cost leadership but, as Knight and Cavusgil (2005) claim, firms in this group are not always as profitable as the others. The peculiarity of being global requires perhaps a greater emphasis on innovation in terms of the use of strategies, technology, design and business models (Mitra, 2020).

Born Global Capabilities

Does attention to the capabilities of born globals help us to obtain more clarity about these firms and what they represent? Weerawardena et al.'s (2007) account of the critical capabilities of born global players is based on the theory of capabilities propounded by Nelson and Winter (1982) and Teece et al. (1997) among others. These capabilities comprise market-focused learning and firm-focused learning alongside networking capabilities. The capability for such learning and networking is a function of the entrepreneurs' qualifications and competencies and prior international experience. These capabilities are absorbed by the firm helping it to develop high-value-added products that facilitate early internationalization (De Clercq et al., 2012; Knight, 2015).

Most born-global firms are, by definition, new small businesses. Their presence in international markets early in their gestation challenges the orthodoxy of some scholars and opinion-formers that only established home-based firms of a certain age and a certain size, with adequate resources and years of experience, can have purchase in international markets. The tendency, however, is for many of them to be high-tech-based firms. A good list of such firms include Logitech, Skype, Mojang AB, Spotify and HTC – all good examples of firms which targeted international markets from the very beginning with their high-tech prowess, and strategic and learning capabilities. The high-tech dividend is also what makes born globals more profitable than their domestic high-tech counterparts (Tanev, 2012).

Accident, Choice, Conditions

We have by now some idea of the historical trajectory of globalization. But that knowledge does not explain whether being born global is an accidental offshoot of that phenomenon, or a specific entrepreneurial choice, based on the identification of new opportunities arising in a technologically transformed economic environment. The fact that firms grow and operate in international markets dispenses in various ways with the idea of an accident. Analyzing the emergence of born globals from a choice perspective is reflective of what we find in the entrepreneurial literature (Moen et al., 2008). Adopting a choice perspective could lead us to explore the conditions in which these firms start and grow successfully.

Taking the comments about typologies and capabilities discussed above, we find that our born global firms tend to rely on certain conditions for their successful operations, and have certain features. Table 11.3 highlights these.

Table 11.3 Conditions for and features of born global firms

Descriptors	Conditions For and Features
Sector	Born global firms tend to operate in a knowledge-intensive or high-technology sector.
Size	Limitations of size and depth of the home market makes it difficult for some firms with global-standard technologies, products and services to rely on the local market for their emergence or survival.
Market	The customer potential can be found mainly overseas and generally among other foreign, multinational firms. This seems obvious especially if the domestic market is limited. Multinationals operating in other markets are typically the best early buyers of technologies or intermediary products made by born globals.
Customer Profiles	Customer profiles in terms of needs and tastes are fairly standard across the firm's potential country-markets. This is partly because of the ubiquity of many electronic products and internet-based business activities. In certain situations there is a high-cost issue associated with personal products catering to a high-end market, as in health care or beauty products affordable by particular income groups.
Technology	The more technology advanced and differentiated the offering, the greater the likelihood of born globals securing competitive advantage, as the apps world illustrates.
Products and Services	The products or services on offer have high value relative to the costs of transportation and logistics.
Barriers to Trade	Trade barriers to the products or services made or offered by these firms tend to be few and far between unless there are political sensitivities in question within certain sectors as in telecommunications or utilities.

(Continued)

Table 11.3 (Continued)

Descriptors	Conditions For and Features
Strategy	There are significant first mover advantages and also gains from networking externalities. This is especially true of internet-based products or services.
Internationalization	They are dependent on their major competitors being internationalized already or are in the process of early internationalization. The internet is not limited to specific countries although large-scale penetration in terms of usage by the wider population affects poorer or remote nations and regions.
Ownership and Management	The owners and managers of these firms are experienced in the art of international business, especially in the high-tech sector. This point could be regarded as contentious because many of the born global players are rookie entrepreneurs engaged in commercial activity for the first time.

Sources: adapted from Rialp et al. (2005); Tanev (2012); Mitra (2020)

We could argue that the above list of features suggests a rather deterministic appraisal of born global firms. That could be in the nature of post hoc analysis when we start attributing aspects of a phenomenon after its occurrence or emergence. How all these features cohere is often because of a set of circumstances or a personal motivation for being part of a solution to a problem. Such circumstantial and personal aspects need to be factored into any analysis for us to obtain a more robust picture of these types of ventures. We will look at a short case study of a Korean start-up to try to capture the different dimensions of creating and growing a born global firm.

SOCIALLY DRIVEN, HIGH TECH, BORN GLOBAL

Mandro is a Korean high-tech venture which makes and distributes 3D printed, light-weight, low-cost, myoelectric prosthetic hands for Syrian refugees. Led by a young computer science doctorate, Lee Hang-So, the new venture was created in 2014, growing eventually to a firm of ten people and with sales of slightly over $100,000 in 2018, operating in Korea, the Middle East and various parts of Africa.

The realization of markets outside Lee's home country was driven less by market conditions in other economies and more by a humanitarian concern for injured Syrian refugees fleeing the brutalities of war in their homeland and caught in the cross-fire of different political ideologies. In fact, there was no market to consider in Syria. The refugees were seeking shelter and hope, carrying severe injuries and with little or no money in different countries (notably in Jordan). These realities underline Lee Hang-So's vision that no one should suffer because of lack of money and, given the excessive cost of prosthetic limbs, that no one should miss out on using functional prosthetic hands because of money.

A linear model of personal development would show that nothing would have pre-pared him for the development of his product for refugees from a war-torn country.

Working at the Samsung Electronics Software Center and having completed a stint as a visiting researcher at Stanford University in the USA, Lee Hang-So was interested in developing his personal hobby of 3D printing by setting up his new venture, a classic example of an enthusiast turned entrepreneur. Being a one-man band did not deter him from applying for and obtaining 40 million won (approximately $32,000) from the Korean Entrepreneurship Development Agency to grow his new 3D printing business. His objective was to network with as wide a group of people as possible in order to obtain legitimacy for his venture and announce his plans for augmenting the benefits of 3D printing. Participating in exhibitions in the field of 3D printing and creating his own unique 3D events, he gradually started making a name for himself in the Korean technology space. There were no refugees in Korea and the country had no program to accommodate refugees there.

It was in January 2015 that he came across a severely disabled person who had lost both hands due to an accident. The experience prompted him to think outside of the 3D-printing box about the possibility of making 'prosthetic hands' which could help people like the person he met. Saddened by the circumstances of a man of a similar age, Lee Hang-So started working on the first version of the goal of donating a prototype of the 'prosthetic hand in the form of talent donations. He received initial funding from the Korean government to help leverage additional resources.

There were three factors that Lee had to consider. First, talent donations were an interesting idea, but they were not popular events in Korea. Second, existing prosthetic hand products cost tens of thousands of dollars. Both the form of raising awareness of the need for prosthetic hands and the prospect of developing such a product using available technology made the possibility of developing new but similar products a difficult proposition. Relying on benchmarking incumbents would not have allowed for much by way of innovation, especially when manufacturing costs were so high. Third, the economics of prosthetic hands at that time meant that users did not have enough sway in the market because their purchasing power was insufficient. The need in society might have been high, but the market had other ideas. If Lee was to equate social need with market supply, then he had to innovate and seek alternative solutions. By this time Lee had switched his objectives from simply advancing a technology to developing it for a very specific and social cause for which there was a genuine need. In the meantime, the horrors of Syria and both the flight and plight of refugees were televised or broadcast through social media regularly.

The news and pictures of the daily horrors in Syria and the dystopian lives of the refugees sparked an interest in him to use his knowledge, experience and personal interest to develop a product that would be effective, efficient and user friendly, both in terms of usage and cost. If that idea could be channeled through a new venture, then that could change the lives of many. Lee's goal was to make a prosthetic hand at the price of a smartphone. To this end he worked on eight different incremental models, following 850 trials in partnership with Swiss Limbs – a specialist company in Switzerland. In July 2016, he produced the world's first 'myoelectric' hand, weighing only 0.8 kg and with a grasp force of 3 kg, at a price of only $1,000 (excluding the cost of any sockets).

(Continued)

> To ensure that the products were available to refugees where it mattered most, he set up an office in Jordan, the country which saw the largest influx of refugees from Syria. This socially driven, technology-based born global venture attracted attention from a wide group of international stakeholders, including funding of 1.8 million from the Korean government and the Bill and Melinda Gates Foundation. Such a venture could not have had a more successful start to fulfill its social and economic goals.
>
> *Source:* adapted from Berg and Mitra (2021)

The Mandro case study offers an interesting mix of a strong socially driven personal motivation for change and technical and academic expertise, which are deployed in alleviating disability in an external social environment with global market prospects for scaling up and development. While no single case study allows for a reasonable form of generalization, we can identify features that are both peculiar to the Mandro case study and potentially common to all successful born globals. Table 11.4 outlines these features in terms of their uniqueness and by way of their common, born global elements.

Table 11.4 Mandro's born global features

Features	Uniqueness to Mandro	Common to Born Globals
Personal motivation	Strong social motivation	High technology for the global market
Opportunity formation	Serendipitous and unexpected circumstances	Ability to identify prospects for utilization of opportunity
Ecosystem encouraging innovation and venturing	Korean government funding for unique, high technology products – government strategy	Attractiveness to global market and support of wider ecosystem stakeholders
Approach	Collaborative – local and international and socially driven business venture	Collaborative
Resourcing	Competitions, national government and international funding	Competitions, international funding

Individual globally minded entrepreneurs have numerous opportunities to discover, form, assess and exploit different scenarios of entrepreneurship spread across different parts of the globe. These opportunities lend themselves to achieving both economic outcomes and urgent solutions to pressing social challenges (Alvarez and Barney, 2007; Elkington and Hartigan, 2008; Perrini, 2006). If some entrepreneurs are driven by the need to find necessary solutions to serious social challenges, then their socially driven ventures are likely to internationalize when they possess the capabilities to serve a universal social need. As Zahra et al. (2008, p. 125) comment: 'Internationalization facilitates the efficient and timely transfer of these capabilities, thereby meeting the needs of affected individuals and groups in other countries'.

Prahalad and Krishnan (2008) had argued some years ago that the modern, internationally focused business is less concerned with owning all the assets necessary for business growth, and more with strategically accessing resources from a wider pool of independent assets, adding value to their own international endeavors by entering into strategic alliances (Mitra, 2020) and relying on technological capabilities (Mitra, 2019) that can increase the pace of internationalization. Socially driven ventures operating at an international level find that they have to create innovative structures and employ cooperative strategies in order to connect with different resources around the world (Zahra et al., 2008). Learning with strategic international partners to accumulate knowledge in the form of networking is one of the primary strategies to grow, adapt and evolve.

Organizations Evolving

Born globals that succeed in remaining global have pioneered a movement that impugns traditional mores of international business practice and standards. The phenomenon has influenced the structure and organization of existing large firms, which have dismantled large, centralized structures by setting up locally centered organizations in different countries focusing on niche activities reflecting the availability of local assets and expertise, such as R&D, the use of just-in-time modes of local production, local warehousing and mass customization techniques. Good examples are the usual large firm suspects of Amazon, Apple, Google and Microsoft. Many other large manufacturing firms such as Nestlé and Proctor and Gamble have also restructured their organizations. This is not the standard form of internationalization following a linear process of gradual change but rather a needs-oriented, strategic disruption of the organization, often leading to the emergence of spherical sub-sets rather than hierarchical structures. These sub-sets are spread out across different geographies with sufficient levels of autonomy to make critical decisions about business design, attracting customers and signing deals locally.

Networking is fundamental to the emergence of new firm structures and operations. The smaller new firms interact with medium and larger firms for the creation of new products, new ventures and sometimes new forms of organization. Technological change, and in particular digitization today, drives globalization, as firms and governments have sought to restructure competitiveness for their businesses and the economy of their countries. It is to these new landscapes and the process of digitization that we turn our attention in the next part.

Part Four: Emergent Landscapes of Globalization

The rapidly changing landscape of business over the past two decades for high-technology and innovative firms is characterized by the novel methods used to pursue entrepreneurial activities, especially in the way that they source, produce and develop ideas, skills, technologies, intermediary products and services as part of a collaborative ecosystem, often made up of networked centers of excellence, where access to resources requires a high level of computational and organizational skills (as in supply/demand chain management and IT-enabled logistics). Where does all this complex form of development lead to? Some authors argue that the confluence of connectivity and digitization, together with the convergence of different technology sectors such as IT and electronics, bio-technology, bio-informatics, medical technologies and communications, are engendering new dynamics between consumers and businesses (Mitra, 2020; Nambisan and Sawhney, 2008; Prahalad and Krishnan, 2008), and between producers and end-users (Von Hippel, 2005). The added layer of complexity is offered by the development of global, network-centric, open innovation environments and ecosystems consisting of large and small firms, and a host of other organizations participating in 'free' (not necessarily pecuniary or transactional but shared forms) modes to enhance services, the development of new products and crucially business models for a wide variety of 'verticals' or industry sectors.

These developments alter our understanding of entrepreneurship in that they identify new opportunities in previously unknown and highly uncertain environments. That entails the generation of economic value that is not necessarily associated with growth, for example in terms of market share, but in terms of better value propositions for users of such products and services (Mitra, 2009, 2020). A significant part of these entrepreneurial activities take place across borders, between firms that are networked with each other.

Take the example of the production of Apple's iPods, iPhones and iPads. The entire process of design, production and use of these devices are based on a form of diversity that depends on inputs of knowledge and skills at various stages of production from multiple sources. The product is personalized to meet the individual customer's preferences and usage patterns, with a high specification product characterized by co-creation with customers, suppliers and distributors. In Prahalad and Krishnan's (2008) conceptualization, $N = 1$ where the sale of every iPod is a unique proposition based on the individual customer, and where $R = G$ in the sense that all resources are more or less sourced globally (Prahalad and Krishnan, 2008; Mitra, 2013).

Network-Centric Models

Nambisan and Sawhney (2008) argue that with the advent of the internet have come various phenomena such as the 'Open Source software movement, electronic R&D marketplaces, online communities and a whole new set of possibilities to reach out and connect with innovative ideas and talent beyond the boundaries of the corporation' (p. 11). Innovation itself is increasingly being described in different ways, as 'open', 'democratic', 'distributed' and 'community-led'. There is a shift in the language, the processes and in the construct of innovation. It tends to exist almost 'outside' the organization, a far cry from the methods used in the past to engineer growth, either through vertical growth models or through mergers and acquisitions (M&As). The legendary failure of M&As (Nambisan and Sawhney, 2008, refer to between 70% and 80% of M&A initiatives ending in failure) does, thankfully, have an alternative in the new quest for growth based on new forms of innovation and connectivity.

The term 'network-centric' applies to a wide range of subjects, from computing through to warfare, operations, enterprise and advocacy of social movements. In applying the term to innovation, Nambisan and Sawhney (2008) define network-centric innovation as being externally focused on innovation, relying on drawing on the resources and capabilities of external networks and communities to enhance reach, speed and quality of production of innovative products, services and organizations.

Readers may be suspicious of an entirely organic process of progression in innovation from traditional models of innovation to network-centric models of recent times. That suspicion would be unfounded because there are certain principles that apply to such network-centric approaches and formats. For any network to succeed there is an acceptance (not often made explicit) of shared goals and objectives by members of communities of practice or the adoption of specific architectures of participation among more disparate groups of dispersed players due to geography, or even indirect interests. Consider the possibility of an auto components firm in Coimbatore, India working with a jewelry firm in Birmingham, specializing in costume jewelry, to make car dashboards out of titanium.

The adoption and effective use of principles requires innovators and businesses to adopt different models and operational infrastructures to have control over issues such as intellectual property and talent sourcing (see Mitra, 2020 for an overview of the tools of open and collective forms of innovation in entrepreneurial organizations).

Global Networks and the Geography of Distributed Innovation Processes

It might be evident from the discussion above that network-centric activity among firms in global communities of practice is potentially synonymous with a distributed innovation process. In other words, innovation is enabled by a distributed network of firms. This is not simply about tracking the value chain in a traditional, linear process of innovation where the downstream firms take the kudos for innovating. Rather, firms networking across borders, especially as part of a cluster of differentiated firms and supporting institutions, innovate at different points in the value chain, connect with other value chains and engage in collective forms of learning to enable firms to manage external relationships, albeit at various levels for different types of firms. In this scenario the locus of control for innovation and internationalization has shifted in part from the independent firm to outside the boundaries of the firm. This has the potential for the emergence of alternative forms of management, based on new innovative business models enabling firms to avail of the benefits of creativity, diversity and compatibility of partners, (Sawhney and Prandelli, 2003). However, the learning process inherent in this change can become complicated. Intended or unintended learning and productivity gains can follow from what is in effect a global pipeline of knowledge, creativity, production processes, products and services.

Global Pipelines

Berg (2015, 2018) suggests that the global pipeline and the 'local buzz' (the generation of information gained from intended and unintended learning processes just by 'being there') have helped to establish a useful platform for knowledge creation and diffusion in specific industries. Bathelt (2005) has argued that these pipelines are a function of knowledge transferred from external linkages between firms, often across borders. The pipelines are designed and maintained by firms and supporting institutions all as part of decentralized structures to maximize the effectiveness of the transfers across varied spatial scenarios generally by means of strategic coalitions. Trust, investment in human capital and high-end communication links coupled with both hard and soft infrastructure provision are used to overcome the inherent uncertainty in interactions between the agents and the agents and principals.

Building on various economic geography studies, (Lorenzen and Mudambi's (2013)) work on the decentralized network structure of the Bollywood film cluster, Vang and Chamnidae's (2007) examination of local–global linkages for the development of indigenous production in cultural clusters in Toronto, Canada. Berg reflects critically on the Korean film and TV industry and its ability to target the wider Asian market, export Korean talent overseas, expand co-production and joint ventures, explore new markets and gain international recognition.

Changing Geographies of Innovation

Readers will be sufficiently astute to glean from the points made above that any talk about global networks embraces the idea of connected spaces or geographies of innovation. Historically, we have been able to identify innovation hotspots, the hegemony of corporate behemoths in the innovation process, located largely in developed nations in the West, and the uses of contributing ideas, human capital, natural resources and technologies to the powerhouses of innovation (see below in the section 'A Reckoning' how theoretical notions of development reinforced the idea of a linear model of development spearheaded by the West). Linkages between different countries were characterized by trade and strategic alliances to promote each other's goods or work together on specific production plans. The bastions of innovation continued to retain their positions of power and control over the innovation and its diffusion. In terms of high-tech development, for example, the Silicon Valley's position as the fountain head of such technology, enables it to attract and host the mega stars of high-growth and high-value technology.

From 1939 to 2009 we witnessed the emergence and ramping up of firms such as:

- Hewlett Packard at Paolo Alto (founded in 1939)
- Intel at Mountain View (1968)
- Apple at Los Altos (1976)
- Google at Menlo Park (1998)
- Facebook – moving from Cambridge, Massachusetts to Silicon Valley (2004)

Money sniffing around high-growth, high-risk, high-yield, high-tech firms led to a third of venture capital (VC) investment in Silicon Valley. The clustering of these firms meant that by 2011, when there were only 27 unicorns in the world, 20 of them were in the USA, and that subsequently, Silicon Valley boasts 136 unicorns (The Economist, 2022), with other estimates suggesting a higher figure of 174 (Who are the The Unicorns of Silicon Valley?

Things have not remained the same; the geography of innovation has changed and is changing continually. Researchers had relied on the traditional factors of economies of scale and scope, transportation costs and the level of savings, to elucidate the distribution of economic activity across space. They emphasized the role of cities as being the places most conducive to the generation of ideas, talent, clustering of flourishing, innovative firms in close proximity and the related economic and social benefits of metropolitan life. But as we have noted earlier new technologies supporting knowledge flows have created new global networks accompanied by dispersed urban agglomerations across the world carrying the same or similar features of innovative clustering.

An ambitious study by the World Intellectual Property Organization (WIPO, 2019) used patent data from 1970 to 2017 across 168 patent offices and 9 million 'patent families' (or groups of patents associated with a specific underlying invention) listing 22 million inventors. Geo-coding the addresses of all the inventors and 24 million authors of scientific papers (from 1998–2017), they developed an algorithm to identify two types of networks – innovation hotspots and specialized innovation clusters. Innovation hotspots are areas with the highest density of inventors and authors, while specialized or niche innovation clusters are also places with a high density of innovation but lower than the hotspots, according to WIPO.

WIPO identified 174 hotspots. Not surprisingly, Silicon Valley is seen as one of the most advanced and acclaimed global innovation hotspots, while the area of Neuchâtel, Biel, Bern and Fribourg in Switzerland is an example of a specialized cluster, one among 313 other such niche environments. Taken together, these hotspots and clusters are overwhelmingly concentrated in North America, Western Europe and East Asia. As of 2018, China had announced 100 clusters (BSA, 2018) with 19 city super-clusters built by 2020 (China Briefing, 2018). Apart from China, and to a lesser extent, Brazil and India, there are far fewer hotspots in middle-income economies. While there are no innovation hotspots in Africa, there are a number of specialized niche clusters.

All the hotspots and most niche clusters are located typically in highly populated, urban, often coastal areas in the USA and in China. Clusters are by definition network-centric super organizations including firms and institutions. There is, therefore, a built-in expectation of cooperation and collaboration among the cluster members. However, the interesting story is about the nature of international collaboration for innovation. Comparing two different periods of 1999–2002 and 2011–2015, WIPO (2019) found that both co-inventing and scientific collaboration across borders were on the increase, especially among global innovation hotspots: 22% of the global co-inventions are accounted for by the innovation hotspots of Silicon Valley, New York, Frankfurt, Tokyo, Boston, Shanghai, London, Beijing, Bengaluru and Paris. What accounts for this development? Gone are the days of solo inventors or single scientific authors as the essential arbiters of scientific knowledge development and innovation. Different types of teams which tend to grow in size are becoming visibly significant in pushing scientific research forward, with more than one-fifth of scientific publications having six or more authors especially in the 'pure' science areas. The levels of technological complexity contributing to the development of products and services, the dispersion of varied talent across countries possessing the appropriate set of knowledge and skills to both augment their individual skills sets and combine with those of others, are probably the key factors explaining international collaboration for technology development and innovation.

The entrepreneurial agents for international collaboration for innovation are the multinational corporations (MNCs) of different countries. Judging by an analysis of patent documents (WIPO, 2019), MNCs have spread their global R&D activities across their global value chains through, for example, activities such as international patent sourcing, which involves a patent applicant in one jurisdiction listing inventors from other countries. This was a common practice among companies and inventors in high-income economies in the 1970s and 1980s, but more recently the sharing has shifted to encompass counterparts from middle-income countries, with China and India being the most prominent among them. Companies such as Didi from China, Infosys from India and Embraer in Brazil work closely with inventors from the United States and Western Europe. This form of dominance by MNCs of the collaborative global innovation arena reflects prescient observations made by Schumpeter (1943) about the stronger, resource-secure large firms making innovation breakthroughs at the expense of smaller firms.

Patents and scientific writing do not necessarily translate easily for the actual development of products and services in different industries. However, there are significant examples of direct links between science, technology and industry together with collaboration across hotspots and clusters, for example in the car industry (autonomous vehicles) and in agriculture (agricultural biotechnology or ag-biotech). Developments in this industry are engendering new players in particular industries. Information technology (IT) companies are challenging established car manufacturers and their suppliers (consider Google's driverless cars) in the same way that Apple threatened the music industry with iTunes.

Scientific breakthroughs have always influenced applied innovation. CRISPR (clustered regularly interspaced short palindromic repeats), which is a family of DNA sequences found in the genomes of prokaryotic organisms such as bacteria and archaea, has been used to cut the cost of gene editing and promises to unleash new genetic improvements in crops and livestock. Universities and public research organizations, particularly in developing economies, are often the main sources of innovation in the ag-biotech industry but collaboration is also important for the sector's growth where large amounts of private investment for commercialization is required or where there is a need for an early roll out of technological support to farmers (WIPO, 2019).

Mushrooming Global Start-Ups

As we noted earlier, unicorns are no longer confined to the USA. They can be found in 45 countries with over 1,000 of them around the globe. For instance, the rapid growth of unicorns in Bengaluru (previously and popularly known as Bangalore) in 17th Cross Road, part of the city's HSR Layout,[1] has earned it the moniker of 'Unicorn Street', or 'Unicorn neighborhood' suggesting the creation of a technology hub. It is the regions of countries, and more specifically, their cities which curate the start-up scene. They include the mature hubs of London, Tel Aviv and Beijing which have always had a global outlook, and the early-stage counterparts of Bengaluru in India, Singapore, Sao Paolo in Brazil (The Economist, 2022), and the more recent or nascent places such as Lagos in Nigeria, Nairobi in Kenya and Medellin in Colombia. These places have all the common features of clusters, namely a pool of talent, good research institutions or other support services, a technical talent pool, access to local and international venture capital, and significant connectivity. Just as the WIPO (2019) report identified differences between various types of clusters and hotspots, we can find distinctive characteristics. The mature hubs including London and Cambridge in the UK and Tel Aviv in Israel are at the vanguard of advanced technologies such as artificial intelligence, machine learning and other software, with corporations across the world as their customers. The Beijing cluster is, however, almost focused fully on the domestic market, while the hubs in Sao Paolo, Bengaluru and Singapore tend to have a distinctive regional focus, adapting business models elsewhere to local conditions rather than engaging in breakthrough technology developments. The latter are also more consumer oriented. They represent what Anand Daniel of Accel, a VC from Silicon Valley, refers to as the 'X' of 'Y' playbook, so Flipkart (e-commerce) is the Amazon of India, Ola and

---

[1]The Hosur-Sarjapur Road (HSR) Layout is a well-known residential locality in Bengaluru developed by the Bangalore Development Authority in 1985 in the southeastern part of the city. The HSR Layout has seen a phenomenal growth in residential housing because of its proximity to the commercial areas of the city (Magic Breaks), near where high-tech start-ups, microbreweries and traffic congestion and pollution are part of the norm of local development.

Grab (ride-hailing) are the Uber of India and South-East Asia, and Nubank (fintech) is the Revolut of Brazil. Fintech and consumer internet services account for around 70% of South-East Asian and 80% of Latin American unicorns (The Economist, 2022).

We are all knowledgeable about the availability of tools such as cloud computing, driving the accelerated global adoption of the internet and smartphones, and the growth of start-ups. However, it is the COVID-19 pandemic which has prompted a 'pandemic' in internet usage, the growth of direct consumer interest in technology-based services (such as home delivery of groceries) and an increase in earnings of several orders of magnitude for the provider firms. Could this rise, and further rise of creation, access to and use of technology, suggest a democratization of technology such that netizens and high-tech and high-growth firms are emerging uniformly in countries? Unfortunately, inequalities abound in the high-tech space. The Economist (2022) finds that in ten countries with the highest number of billion-dollar start-ups, 40% of them are concentrated in the top start-up urban agglomeration (city). The fuel of VC funding, so essential to high-growth firms, grew from below 50% to approximately 70% in London, from 24% to 60% in Berlin, and 15% to 34% in Bengaluru.

Policy Matters

Beyond the fundamental ingredients of successful start-up hubs (talent, VC, research institutions and successful entrepreneurs turned business angels and VCs), effective policy making matters. A city such as Tokyo with its giant technology firms such as Sony and Rakuten, together with the overpowering presence of the Keiretsu conglomerates (Mitsubishi, Toyota and others), does not have any clear policy framework for start-ups. South Korea and its capital Seoul also have the Chaebol conglomerates of Samsung, LG and Hyundai, hindering start-up formation and development until recently, when a series of corporate scandals and a more pronounced effort by the government started providing fertile ground for the rookie innovative technology-based firms. A policy open to migrants in countries has also been a factor in the shaping of high-tech spaces of economic growth and cultural emancipation. The USA and the UK have always struggled with the 'bogeyman' of immigration but have failed to deny the fact that foreign-born entrepreneurs are key players in stimulating local economies. Approximately 60% of the most successful technology firms in the USA were started by immigrants or their children. Refer also to the groundbreaking story about there being at least one immigrant key founder in 25.3% of all engineering and technology companies created between 1995 and 2005 in the USA (Wadhwa et al., 2008). The estimate that followed indicated that the club of immigrant-founded companies generated more than $52 billion in turnover and just under 450,000 jobs as of 2005 (Wadhwa et al., 2007).

There is both a technology and a cultural buzz in cities such as London, Berlin and Paris, each with more than ten unicorns (The Economist, 2022). China substitutes foreign founders with 'sea turtles' or returning Chinese students or technology workers to provide for a technology sizzle in cities such Shanghai, Shenzhen, Chengdu and Beijing.

Mazzucato (2013) explained the significant role that governments can play in fostering the entrepreneurial drive that makes it possible to develop some of the most important technologies, well beyond its classic role of attending to market or system failures, a favorite reasoning of neo-classical economists. The Apple iPhone in the USA and the funding for the global renewable energy sector (particularly in China) are good examples of the private sector intervening only after the initial high-risk investments. Schemes attracting investors and founders are common to many countries as part of their inward investment strategies, but Israel and Singapore stand out as exemplar nations. The latter's entrepot status, the creation of a very direct pro-business environment and continuing political stability are also given as reasons for their success but they are all part of the public infrastructure of support for enterprise in general. Climate can play a part too. California is generally sunny, and the move to the Bahamas by FTX, a cryptocurrency exchange, might suggest the value of sitting back and letting the sun, sea and sand do all the talking and provide the inducements.

Often evidence points to the failures of governments in imposing start-up developments. Germany's Bavarian cluster initiative made a mess of $1.6 billion and so did the Malaysian government's BioValley complex at a cost of $150 million (The Economist, 2022). Josh Lerner (2009) argues that for each government intervention, there might be dozens or even hundreds of failures, thus questioning the poor value for money of public sector venturing or risk taking. But arguments that cast doubt on governmental start-up initiatives ignore the failures of private sector risk capital investment; 75% of start-ups fail in the USA, in that they do not return investors' capital (Ghosh, 2012), based on a survey of over 2000 start-ups receiving more than $1 million dollars each, between the years of 2004 and 2010. In the UK, VC funds aim for no more than one in ten investments to exit profitably (success measured in terms of payback to investors or an initial public offering. The successful exit of one out ten firms is profitable enough to cancel out the losses made on the other nine.

How governments can or should determine policy is not an easy consideration. Governments have to weigh up the public mood, consider drastic changes in policies when uncertain conditions prevail as during the financial crash of 2008 or the more recent COVID-19 pandemic, and as we write, the devastating war in Ukraine. Political ideologies also shape the direction of government policy and start-ups can fall out of favor, especially when government are seeking easy electoral gains from low hanging fruit in terms of large numbers of people being employed by larger firms, or succumbing to populist measures like reducing migration. However, none of this chaos necessarily precludes the creation of a strategy for both start-ups with a technology focus and innovative ways of fostering collaborative innovation across the regions of the world.

At the heart of the developments discussed above is digitization and its global manifestation. We focus on digitization and globalization exclusively in Chapter 13, but first let us take a reality check on some of the claims that industry, researchers and policy makers make about globalization.

A Reckoning or a Reality Check

Even technology luddites do not deny the forces of globalization. They campaign against the ostensible benefits of globalization pointing to its discontents and negative externalities. The purveyors of globalization call for deregulated and integrated markets even after the financial crash of 2008 and the economic fallout across the world of the COVID-19 pandemic, not forgetting other market, systemic and institutional failures. Much of the motivation for banking on globalization stems from the legacy of the 'Washington Consensus', a set of ten economic policy prescriptions regarded as the 'standard' reform package promoted for developing countries by Washington, DC based institutions such as the International Monetary Fund, World Bank and the United States Department of the Treasury. First used in 1989 by the English economist John Williamson, the idea was to determine global development in the image of the US and other Western economies, pursuing an aggressive form of free market economics, including liberalizing the economy by opening up the market, wider macroeconomic stabilization and the general uplift of market forces in the economy.

The Washington Consensus found life with the rise of the internet and mobile telephony, with believers in a 'flat world' (Friedman, 2006) or 'the death of distance' (Cairncross, 2002) arguing that ubiquitous technological developments spearheaded in the West would sweep the world. The rest of the world are, therefore, expected to be ready followers as users, and in some cases, linked producers. Internationalization in a flat, globalized world became code for an easier form of value appropriation than what was possible in earlier historical periods. This line of argument would suggest that emerging nations in the South were seen as providers of cheaper mass production of goods made by unskilled labor.

A nuanced view is explained by Audretsch et al. (2021), who develop a three-stage product life cycle model characterized by new, mature and off-shored production. The model helps to assess the impact of a shock in the supply of unskilled labor in the South (mainly in the form of job losses in the North), a fall in the level of political risk associated with outward foreign direct investment (manifest in off-shoring) and the diffusion of a general purpose technology, developed in the West, such as ICT, across the globe (Mitra, 2020).

The changes assumed in the model lead to an endogenous allocation of entrepreneurial activity, where the outcome generates a shift in the comparative advantage of developed countries towards new varieties corresponding to activities in the early stages of the product life cycle. Since the agency function between life cycle stages is attributable to the entrepreneur, his or her value-added increases due to globalization and technical change. The basic factors of production employed in the mass-production-based, mature stage of the life cycle – namely, low-skilled labor in developed economies – become less valuable there. The model predicts the emergence of a new knowledge-driven entrepreneurial economy in advanced nations while the less developed emerging economies of the South open up to trade and manufacturing, as the late-20th-century 'Made in China' and the more recent 'Made in India' models and public marketing slogans would confirm (Mitra, 2020).

There is a very specific problem with the adaptation of the model. It assumes a linear trajectory of growth based on the Rostow, Easterly and Porter models of development of countries which clearly delineate the lowest form of economic growth in agrarian economies (mostly in Africa and Asia), the mass manufacturing economies of middle-income countries (such as China) and the knowledge-based economies of the advanced nations of the West. But as we have noted before, whether in history or in our digital era, whole nations do not grow uniformly. There are considerable intra-country inequalities. In the fastest growing country over the last two decades, China, regions take their turn as people in Shanghai and Tianjin may testify. Moreover, there is the question of resource availability, allocation and distribution. Assumptions behind the notion that advanced nations are resource rich and, therefore, better able to appropriate such resources to make their countries great again, lies at the heart of a retreat from globalization as exemplified in the Trump era in the USA or the Brexit decision to decouple the UK from the European Union.

The realities of the 21st century point to an increased dependence on globalization which disrupts the notion of linear flows of development and of the firms creating wealth through global products and services. Take BMW's manufacturing of the Mini car – a German car manufactured in Britain. Nearly 60% of its components are made by a mix of small, medium and large firms around Europe and the globe, and its sales are of course dependent on global markets. Consider a small component manufacturer of 'air spindles' which drills holes in printed circuit boards (PCBs) for all our high-tech gadgets: 80% of the market is in the hands of two small companies in Poole in the UK, which are dependent on drilling machines made in Germany and Japan, which in turn are reliant on Taiwan and China for the PCBs and the gadgets. Add to that the continuing flow of talent from highly skilled engineers and analysts from emerging countries to solicitous advanced countries, often in direct contrast to the populist measures of immigration control (Mitra, 2020).

The dependence of the knowledge economy on resources scattered across the globe makes the argument of leading and deficient economies a rather shallow one. The statistics will surely allow for rankings based on growth in domestic productivity, increased and advanced stocks of technology or cutting edge talent, and new high-tech firm crea-tion rates. These statistics will always favor the ranking of advanced nations. But that does not help to obtain a more nuanced and critical understanding of the dynamics of globalization and the heterogeneity characterizing the nature of knowledge production and enterprise creation today.

Noting the flows of both cross-border and local activities and computing the interna-tional component of the aggregate value of activities show some interesting results. Making use of data such as the cross-border component of mail and phone calls to pro-vide evidence of communication that underpins international activities, Ghemawat (2007) estimates that only 1% of letters actually mailed in the world cross borders! The percentage of telephone calling minutes involving international calls is less than 2%. Approximately 17 to 18% of all internet traffic, between 2006 and 2008, was indeed being routed across a national border. An international magazine such as *Time* has a readership of only about 20% outside the USA, and international news coverage was only 21% for the US and 38% in Europe. Of the total number of patents filed in the advanced OECD countries, only 15% of the patents are foreign-owned and the number involving international co-operation research is half of that. However, as we have noted above, international collaboration is on the increase, although the mix of countries actu-ally involved in collaboration is skewed in favor of the few technologically developed countries. Despite all the political hue and cry over immigration, first-generation immi-grants account for only 3% of the world's population, while university students studying overseas are around 2% of all university students. Against that their contribution to the economies of their destination countries remains considerable (see Chapter 7).

Following Ghemawat we find that the four key components of cross-border activity – information, trade, funds and people flows – do not have as wide a spatial reach as advocates of globalization might enthuse about. Ghemawat (2007) also refers to issues of cultural, administrative, geographic and economic sensitivities, which are all 'distance' issues related to Krugman's conclusion about the need for an integrative perspective on borders and dis-tance. Both matter (Mitra, 2020). Flows tend to decline with distance and they are also 'subject to discontinuous drop-offs at borders of various sorts' (Ghemawat, 2007).

What contributes to this geographic distance are the lack of or entrenchment of land borders, time zone differences, extent to which countries are landlocked, climatic varia-tions and physical size, as well as cultural distance sensitivities, such as different languages, work styles and systems, alternate values, administrative distance issues such as varied institutions, institutional, economic distance, such as purchasing power, differ-ent consumer income profiles, and availability of resources, and of course geographic distance. In terms of entrepreneurship, geographic, administrative, cultural and economic barriers impact on firms being born global, new firms and innovation across borders.

There has been considerable further disruption to cross-border flows as a conse-quence of the COVID-19 pandemic. According to the DHL study on global connectedness (DHL, 2020), the world's level of global connectedness declined in 2020 after holding steady in 2019 because of the COVID-19 pandemic. But the effect is unlikely to be so bad as to fall below the 2008–09 levels noted during the global financial crisis. Migration or the flows of people crossing borders declined dramatically as countries closed borders to stop or mitigate the spread of the virus. Consequently, international travel might have to fall back to its 1990 level. However, international trade rebounded with vigor after a sharp drop at the beginning of the pandemic, even though the proportion of global output crossing national borders fell a little in 2020. Capital flows were hit harder than trade, although these flows have begun to recover since strong recovery plans by governments and central banks have attempted to stabilize the markets globally. The up and down story of cross-border flows finds its apotheosis in the data on information flows. In contrast to early signs of a possible slowdown before the pandemic, the globalization of information flows and telephone calls bounced back not least because banned in-person interactions made people become eager enthusiasts for all things digital. Contrary perhaps to expectations, Europe boasts its position as the world's most globalized region, leading on trade and people flows. Eight of the ten most globally connected countries are located in Europe. North America is the top-ranking region for information and capital flows, suggesting a 'tangible and intangible' continental divide. Disaggregated information indicates that The Netherlands is currently the world's most globally connected, but the second ranked nation is Singapore in Asia where the size of its international flows is disproportionately high considering the level of its domestic activity. Other smaller South-East countries such as Cambodia, Singapore, Vietnam and Malaysia also show heft in the performance of their regional supply chains.

The rather topsy-turvy picture of globalization captured by the DHL data is to some extent a function of global geopolitical tensions and a resetting (or fracturing) of the world economy along regional lines, and the continuing dependence of global entrepreneurial collaborations to mitigate the seriously negative effects of climate change, global pandemics, poverty and other major disconnects posing an existential threat to all humanity.

Chapter Summary

LO1 and **LO2**. This chapter provides the reader with theories and empirical information with which to understand critically the nature and shape of globalization from its origins to the present. A historical appreciation of the globalization phenomenon offers insights into its evolutionary nature with continuous changes in both the interactions between countries and organisations, the dominance of different countries in certain countries at different times, and how these historical antecedents allow us to obtain specific perspectives (historical, regional, technological) about them and obtain a critical overview of the meaning, scope and significance of the term, 'globalisation'.

(Continued)

LO3: The different sections of the chapter have been written to help evaluate how globalization has opened up opportunities for international entrepreneurship development at the level of the individual, the firm, the region and of nations. These levels point to the complexity of the global phenomenon, not least because each of these levels have a bearing on each other. If an individual in the UK connects with a counterpart in Vietnam and exchanges goods, services or information with each other for the purpose of a commercial transaction, both individuals are probably using platform technologies designed by a leading technology firm such as Amazon sourcing those goods, services or information from different regions and countries.

LO4: More specifically the chapter examines critically the phenomenon of the 'born global firm' as an outcome of the phenomenon where both the individual and the firm could be considered to be 'globalised'. The global knowledge and connections of the individuals starting new ventures are assumed to be central to the development of these firms.

LO5: Finally in this chapter, the reader has the opportunity to consider strategies, policies and actions that could draw down on the benefits of globalization while safeguarding against its downsides for entrepreneurship development. Equally, the depth and breadth of globalization is examined in terms of the variations that occur between countries and their contributions to the global pool of knowledge, resources and people, noting that we also need to be realistic about the reach of globalization in that it might be more about countries in regions being more closely associated with each other rather than a free flow of opportunities across the globe.

Review Questions

1. What do we mean by 'globalization' and how does it differ from the term 'internationalization?
2. What does the history of globalization have to tell us about the driving forces of global entrepreneurial activity?
3. Explain the born global phenomenon?
4. In what way has globalization changed in the world today?
5. How does globalization today impact on entrepreneurship and what are its limitations?

References

Acedo, F. and Jones, M. (2007) 'Speed of internationalization and entrepreneurial cognition: Insights and a comparison between international new ventures, exporters and domestic companies', *Journal of World Business*, 42(3): 236–252.

Alvarez, S.A. and Barney, J.B. (2007) 'Discovery and creation: Alternative theories of entrepreneurial action', *Strategic Entrepreneurship Journal*, 1(1–2): 11–26.

Arasaratnam, S. (1986) *Merchants, Companies and the Commerce of the Coromandel Coast 1650–1740*. Delhi: Oxford University Press.

Aspelund, A., Madsen, T. and Moen, O. (2007) 'A review of the foundation, international marketing strategies, and performance of international new ventures', *European Journal of Marketing*, 41(11–12): 1423–1448.

Audretsch, D., Sanders, M. and Zhang, L. (2021) 'International product life cycles, trade and development stages', *The Journal of Technology Transfer*, 46(5): 1630–1673.

Baldwin, R.E. and Martin, P. (1999) 'Two Waves of Globalisation: Superficial Similarities, Fundamental Differences', *NBER Working Paper 6904*. Cambridge. Massachusetts: National Bureau of Economic Research.

Bathelt, H. (2005) 'Cluster relations in the media industry: Exploring the "distanced neighbor" paradox in Leipzig', *Regional Studies*, 39(1): 105–127.

Berg, S.-H. (2015) 'Creative cluster evolution: The case of the film and TV industries in Seoul, South Korea', *European Planning Studies*, 23(10): 1993–2008.

Berg, S.-H. (2018) 'Local buzz, global pipelines and Hallyu: The case of the film and TV industry in South Korea', *Journal of Entrepreneurship and Innovation in Emerging Economies*, 4(1): 33–52.

Berg, S.H. and Mitra, J. (2022) 'Good Tech and Social Good: Value Creation by Korean Social and High-Tech Oriented Start-Ups', *Journal of Entrepreneurship and Innovation in Emerging Economies*, 8(1): 29–45.

Bordo, M.D. and Flandreau, M. (2003) 'Core, periphery, exchange rate regimes, and globalization.' In *Globalization in Historical Perspective* (pp. 417–472). University of Chicago Press.

BSA. (2018) *Best 100 Chinese Industrial Clusters + Complete Guide + Tips*. Best Sourcing Agency (BSA). Available at www.bsasourcing.com/best-100-china-industrial-clusters-map-complete-guide-tips (last accessed 10 March 2022).

Cairncross, F. (2002) 'The death of distance', *RSA Journal*, 149(5502): 40–42.

Cavusgil, S.T. and Knight, G. (2009) *Born Global Firms: A New International Enterprise*. New York: Business Expert Press.

Chaudhuri, K.-N. (1978) *The Trading World of Asia and the East India Company 1660–1760*. Cambridge: Cambridge University Press.

Chaudhuri, K.-N. (1990) *Asia before Europe: Economy and Civilisation of the Indian Ocean from the Rise of Islam to 1750*. Cambridge: Cambridge University Press.

China Briefing. (2018) *China's City Clusters: The Plan to Develop 19 Super-Regions*. China Briefing. Available at www.china-briefing.com/news/chinas-city-clusters-plan-to-transform-into-19-super-regions (last accessed 10 March 2022).

Darwin, J. (2008) *After Tamerlane: the rise and fall of Global Empires, 1400–2000*. Penguin UK.

Darwin, J. (2020) *Unlocking the World: Post Cities and Globalization in the Age of Steam, 1830–1930*. London: Allen Lane.

Dasgupta, A. and Pearson, M.N. (eds.) (1987) *India and the Indian Ocean 1500–1800.* Calcutta: Oxford University Press.

De Clercq, D., Sapienza, H.J., Yavuz, R.I. and Zhou, L. (2012) 'Learning and knowledge in early internationalization research: Past accomplishments and future directions', *Journal of Business Venturing*, 27(1): 143–165.

DHL. (2020) *DHL Global Connectedness Index, 2020.* By S.A. Altman and P. Bastion. Deutsche Post DHL Group in partnership with NYU Stern. Available at www.dhl.com/gci (last accessed 1 February 2022).

The Economist. (2022) 'The geography of innovation: A new atlas'. *The Economist*, April 16. pp. 59–61.

Elkington, J. and Hartigan, P. (2008) *The Power of Unreasonable People: How Social Entrepreneurs Create Markets that Change the World.* Boston, MA: Harvard Business Press.

Entrepreneur Handbook. (2012) 'Venture capital firms in the UK & London'. James Pursey. November 29. Available at https://entrepreneurhandbook.co.uk/venture-capitalists (last accessed 10 January 2021).

Fillis, I. (2001) 'Small firm internationalisation: an investigative survey and future research directions', *Management Decision*, 39(9): 767–783.

Frank, A.G. (1998) *ReOrient: Global economy in the Asian age.* California: University of California Press.

Frankopan, P. (2016) *The Silk Roads: A New History of the World.* London: Bloomsbury.

Frankopan, P. (2018) *The New Silk Roads: The Present and Future of the World.* London: Bloomsbury.

Friedman, T.L. (2006) *The World Is Flat: A Brief History of the Twenty-First Century.* London: Macmillan.

Ghemawat, P. (2007) *Redefining Global Strategy: Crossing Borders in a World Where Differences Matter.* Boston, MA: Harvard Business School Press.

Ghemawat, P. (2007) 'Managing differences: The central challenge of global strategy', *Harvard Business Review*, 85(3): 58–68.

Ghosh, S. (2012) 'Why most venture-backed companies fail'. *The Wall Street Journal*, 10 December. Available at www.hbs.edu/news/Pages/item.aspx?num=214 (last accessed 10 January 2021).

Gupta, A.K., Govindarajan, V. and Wang, H. (2008) *The Quest for Global Dominance: Transforming Global Presence into Global Competitive Advantage* (2nd edn). New Delhi: Wiley.

Harvey, M., Novicevic, M.M. and Garrison, G. (2005) 'Global virtual teams: A human resource capital architecture', *The International Journal of Human Resource Management*, 16(9): 1583–1599.

Hopkins, A.G. (2002) 'The history of globalisation – and the globalisation of history?' in A.G. Hopkins (ed.), *Globalisation in World History.* London: Pimlico, pp. 11–46.

Hoskisson, R., Wright, M., Filatotchev, I. and Peng, M. (2013) 'Emerging multinationals from mid-range economies: The influence of institutions and factor markets', *Journal of Management Studies*, 50(7): 1295–1321.

Investopedia. (2021) *Companies Owned by Facebook (Meta)*. www.investopedia.com/articles/personal-finance/051815/top-11-companies-owned-facebook.asp (last accessed 10 January 2021).

Knight, G.A. and Cavusgil, S.T. (2004) 'Innovation, organizational capabilities, and the born-global firm', *Journal of International Business Studies*, 35(2): 124–141.

Knight, G.A. and Cavusgil, S.T. (2005) 'A taxonomy of born-global firms', *MIR: Management International Review*, 45: 15–35.

Knight, G. (2015) 'Born global firms: Evolution of a contemporary phenomenon', in S. Zou, H. Xu, L. Hui Shi (eds.), *Entrepreneurship in International Marketing* (Advances in International Marketing, Vol. 25). Bingley: Emerald Group Publishing, pp. 3–19.

Kudina, A., Yip, G.S. and Barkema, H.G. (2008) 'Born global'. *Business Strategy Review*, 19(4): 38–44.

Lerner, J. (2009) *Boulevard of Broken Dreams: Why Public Efforts to Boost Entrepreneurship and Venture Capital Have Failed – and What to Do about It*. Princeton, NJ: Princeton University Press.

Levitt, T. (1983) 'The globalization of markets', *Harvard Business Review*, (61): 92–102.

Lorenzen, M. and Mudambi, R. (2013) 'Clusters, connectivity and catch-up: Bollywood and Bangalore in the global economy', *Journal of Economic Geography*, 13(3): 501–534.

Lund, S., Manyika, J. and Bughin, J. (2016) 'Globalization is becoming more about data and less about stuff', *Harvard Business Review*, 14 March. Available at https://hbr.org/2016/03/globalization-is-becoming-more-about-data-and-less-about-stuff (last accessed 12 April 2022).

Maddison, A. (2007) *Contours of the World Economy, 1–2030 AD: Essays in Macro-Economic History*. Oxford: Oxford University Press.

Mazzucato, M. (2013) 'Financing innovation: creative destruction vs. destructive creation', *Industrial and Corporate Change*, 22(4): 851–867.

Mitra, J. (2009) 'Learning to grow: how new, small, high technology firms acquire cognitive and socio-political legitimacy in their regions', *International Journal of Technology Management*, 46(3): p. 344.

Mitra, J. (2013) *Entrepreneurship, Innovation and Regional Development: An introduction*. Abingdon: Routledge.

Mitra, J. (2020) *Entrepreneurship, Innovation and Regional Development*. Abingdon: Routledge.

Moen, Ø., Sørheim, R. and Erikson, T. (2008) 'Born global firms and informal investors: Examining investor characteristics', *Journal of Small Business Management*, 46(4): 536–549.

Nambisan, S. and Sawhney, M. (2008) *The Global Brain: Your Roadmap for Innovating Faster and Smarter in a Networked World*. Hoboken, NJ: Pearson and Wharton School Publishing.

Oviatt, B.M. and McDougall, P.P. (1994) 'Toward a theory of international new ventures', *Journal of International Business Studies*, 25(1): 45–64.

Oviatt, B.M. and McDougall, P.P. (1995) 'Global start-ups: Entrepreneurs on a worldwide stage', *Academy of Management Perspectives*, 9(2): 30–43.

Perrini, F. (ed.) (2006) *The New Social Entrepreneurship: What Awaits Social Entrepreneurial Ventures?* Cheltenham: Edward Elgar Publishing.

Porter, M.E. (1980) 'Industry structure and competitive strategy: Keys to profitability', *Financial Analysts Journal*, 36(4): 30–41.

Prahalad, C.K. and Krishnan, M.S. (2008) *The New Age of Innovation*. New York: McGraw-Hill Professional Publishing.

Raychaudhri, T. and Habib, I. (eds.) (1982) *The Cambridge Economic History of India*, Vol. 1: c. 1220 – c. 1750. Cambridge: Cambridge University Press.

Rennie, M.W. (1993) 'Born global', *The McKinsey Quarterly*, 4: 45.

Rialp, A., Rialp, J. and Knight, G. (2005) 'The phenomenon of early internationalizing companies: What do we know after a decade (1993–2003) of scientific inquiry?' *International Business Review*, 14(2): 147–166.

Sawhney, M., Prandelli, E. and Verona, G. (2003) 'The power of innomediation', *MIT Sloan Management Review*, 44(2): p. 77.

Schumpeter, J.A. (1943) *Capitalism, Socialism and Democracy*. London: Allen and Unwin.

Silicon Valley Centre. Infographic February 18 2020) (https://siliconvalley.center/blog/infographic-unicorns-of-silicon-valley

Statista. (2022) 'Facebook: Number of monthly active users worldwide 2008–2021'. Statista Research Department, February 14. Available at www.statista.com/statistics/264810/number-of-monthly-active-facebook-users-worldwide/ (last accessed 18 February 2022).

Tanev, S. (2012) 'Global from the start: The characteristics of born-global firms in the technology sector', *Technology Innovation Management Review*, 2(3).

Teece, D.J., Pisano, G. and Shuen, A. (1997) 'Dynamic capabilities and strategic management', *Strategic Management Journal*, 18(7): 509–533.

Vang, J. and C. Chaminade (2007) 'Cultural clusters, global-local linkages and spillovers: Theoretical and empirical insights from an exploratory study of Toronto's film cluster, *Industry and Innovation*, 14/4: 401–420.

Von Hippel, E. (2005) 'Democratizing innovation: The evolving phenomenon of user innovation', *Journal für Betriebswirtschaft*, 55(1): 63–78.

Wadhwa, V., Saxenian, A., Rissing, B.A. and Gereffi, G. (2007) *America's New Immigrant Entrepreneurs: Part I*. Duke Science, Technology & Innovation Paper No. 23. Available at http://dx.doi.org/10.2139/ssrn.990152 (last accessed 20 November 2021).

Wadhwa, V., Saxenian, A., Rissing, B.A. and Gereffi, G. (2008) 'Skilled immigration and economic growth', *Applied Research in Economic Development*, 5(1): 6–14.

Weerawardena, J., Sullivan Mort, G., Liesch, P.W. and Knight, G.A. (2007) 'Conceptualizing accelerated internationalization in the born global firm: a dynamic capabilities perspective', *Journal of World Business*, 42(3): 294–306.

Weerawardena, J., Mort, G.S., Salunke, S., Knight, G. and Liesch, P.W. (2015) 'The role of the market sub-system and the socio-technical sub-system in innovation and firm performance: A dynamic capabilities approach', *Journal of the Academy of Marketing Science*, 43(2): 221–239.

Winter, S.G. and Nelson, R.R. (1982) 'An evolutionary theory of economic change', *University of Illinois at Urbana-Champaign's Academy for Entrepreneurial Leadership Historical Research Reference in Entrepreneurship*.

WIPO. (2019) *The Geography of Innovation Local Hotspots, Global Innovation*. The World Intellectual Property Organisation (WIPO) Report, 2019. Geneva: WIPO.

World Bank (2021) *Exports of Goods and Services (% of GDP)*. Available at Exports: https://data.worldbank.org/indicator/NE.EXP.GNFS.ZS Imports: https://data.worldbank.org/indicator/NE.IMP.GNFS.ZS?view=map (last accessed 1 February 2023).

Zahra, S.A., Rawhouser, H.N., Bhawe, N., Neubaum, D.O. and Hayton, J.C. (2008) 'Globalization of social entrepreneurship opportunities', *Strategic Entrepreneurship Journal*, 2(2): 117–131.

12

INTERNATIONAL NEW VENTURES AND GLOBAL START-UPS

UBER TECHNOLOGIES INC.
A CAB-HAILING REVOLUTION AT INCEPTION

Uber is an on-demand ride-hailing smartphone app. The Uber mobile phone app lets users request a ride and a driver-contractor is routed to pick them up, with Uber getting a cut of the fare. Its unique service provides reliable drivers to pick up riders and transport them to their destinations. Uber does not own any of the cars that transport its customers. Using proprietary software, Uber's app links clients with the nearest available drivers, with Uber taking a 25% share of the total fare. Uber gives riders the opportunity to view the estimated cost of their ride prior to travel. To avoid the hassle of cash changing hands, customers are charged through their credit card. Each driver is rated on a 1–5-star scale with comments available for viewing. The opportunity to provide feedback gives an incentive to the drivers to maintain cleanliness and provide a professional experience to their riders.

Geographic Spread and Scope

Headquartered in San Francisco, Uber has entered over 65 countries and more than 450 cities worldwide since inception. The service is available in North America, parts of Central and South America, parts of Europe, the Middle East, Africa, East Asia, South Asia and Australia and New Zealand. Many people use Uber because of the convenience that it offers. Uber provides riders with a fast and safe mode of transportation

(Continued)

that is more convenient than public transportation, especially in high population density cities where public transportation often means cramming into trains. Uber's service is also attractive to people whose lifestyle includes a very active nightlife. For example, in cities like Seoul and Tokyo, it is very common for office workers to spend the evenings drinking together. In such situations, it is not always easy or safe to find a taxi.

The Founding Team

Now popularly known as Uber, UberCab was founded by Travis Kalanick and Garret Camp in 2009. A resident of San Francisco, Kalanick is often described by investors as passionate, quirky and ruthless. Kalanick studied computer engineering at the University of California, Los Angeles (UCLA) before dropping out in 1998 to create Scour. Scour was a multimedia peer-to-peer search and file exchange service. Scour was very controversial as it enabled users to share copyrighted material between themselves. Eventually, the company was sued by both the Motion Pictures Association and the recording industry, leading Kalanick to file for bankruptcy to avoid the suit. Kalanick then started another file sharing company called Red Swoosh. Red Swoosh was almost exactly like his former venture, and its launch caused a lot of backlash from critics about copyright infringement. Red Swoosh was later sold to Akamai Technologies.

Born in 1978, Garrett Camp is a Canadian national who is famous for his ground-breaking technology ventures. He is ranked no. 422 on Forbes magazine's list of global billionaires for 2018, and at no. 8 in Canada. Camp completed his Bachelor of Science in Electrical Engineering from the University of Calgary between 1996 and 2001, followed by Master of Science in Software Engineering from the same institution between 2001 and 2005. While at university, Camp launched StumbleUpon in November 2001. StumbleUpon is an online content discovery portal that works like a web search engine, but it is personalized to match the interests of the user by using recommendations from connected peers and social networks. StumbleUpon moved to the San Francisco area in 2006, after successfully securing funding from investors. eBay acquired StumbleUpon in 2007 for $75 million, and the company again became independent after a successful spin-off in 2009. As CEO of the company, Garrett led StumbleUpon to a five-fold increase in its user base that crossed 25 million users by 2012.

Other lesser-known initiatives of Camp include Expa and Mix. Founded in May 2013, Expa serves as a global network of entrepreneurs who help peer-supported creation of businesses and companies. Since inception, Expa has successfully launched more than a dozen ventures and raised funding worth $150 million. In October 2015, Camp made a fresh attempt at content discovery, launching Mix.com, a portal 'to discover the most compelling content' on the web for users. Clubbing the user's preferences along with the recommendations from friends and subject matter experts, the online content is served to the user's mobile or computer. Mix was launched under the Expa initiative and continues to work in parallel to StumbleUpon.

More recently, Camp launched a new initiative, Eco, in the cryptocurrency space. Eco attempts to address the pain points of the existing virtual currency systems like bitcoin and Ethereum. It is designed to fix such problems as regulatory concerns due to the anonymous nature of cryptocurrency participants, issues of high-power consumption linked to mining activities and concerns around (un)fair sharing of block reward for miners.

Kalanick and Camp met at the LeWeb Tech conference. Camp realized the potential of sharing economies and wanted to reduce the cost of direct transportation to the average consumer. Kalanick and Camp invested $200,000 as seed money when they founded Uber. This was followed by $1.25 million in angel capital by First Round Capital. After building a reputation and bringing another series of inventors into the company, Uber was ready to roll over the hump and finally be a big-time company. Uber was first launched in San Francisco in 2011. Paris was the first city outside of the US where Uber's service began to operate, in December the same year, prior to the international LeWeb Tech conference. The company expanded to Canada in March 2012. In July 2012, the company launched its app in London, and in November it was introduced in Australia following a six-week test period. Sydney was Uber's first launch in the Asia Pacific region and the band Art vs. Science participated in an early promotion.

Continuous Growth

The soft launch of Uber in Singapore began in January 2013 after Kalanick expressed an intention to expand into Asia in early 2012. Uber's service was launched in the South Korean capital city of Seoul in August 2013. In accordance with standard practice, Uber Seoul started as a test phase. Uber's launch in Bangalore on August 29, 2014, was the company's first day of operation in India. Indian musicians Raghu Dixit and Vasundhara Das participated in the promotion for the launch of the UberX service. On September 4, 2013, Uber announced its first sports deal. The company held a promotion with the NFL Players Association to promote safe rides for NFL players. By March 2015, Uber's service was available in 55 countries and more than 200 cities around the world.

Uber listed its shares on the New York Stock Exchange on May 10, 2019. The company's service offering since the early days has been expanded to include different variants, namely UberX, Uber SUV, and UberTAXI. Focused on reducing the cost of cab rides, Camp also launched a ride-sharing option in early 2013. Camp continues to serve as the chairman of Uber, which is known for being among the leaders that revolutionized the cab-hailing service across the globe.

Sources: Henshall (2017); Hoffman (2016); Manangi (2017); Pullen (2014); Seth (2019)

After studying this chapter, you should be ready to:

- **LO1**: Explain the concept and distinguishing features of international new ventures (INVs)
- **LO2**: Describe key elements of the theory of INVs
- **LO3**: Compare and contrast different types of INVs
- **LO4**: Explain the distinguishing features of a global start-up
- **LO5**: Explain the factors underlying the emergence of INVs and global start-ups
- **LO6**: Discuss the role of immigrant entrepreneurs in the founding of INVs and global start-ups

Introduction

As discussed in Chapter 5, small firms are no longer confined to the domestic market; they are significant players in the international landscape. However, the population of small firms is heterogeneous. Whereas some small firms struggle to enter foreign markets due to their financial and human resource constraints, others rapidly internationalize to dominate the world economy within a few years of their founding.

As profiled in the opening case, Uber is one such example. Founded in 2009, the firm crossed 50 million users by 2012, selling its stock on the public market in 2019, within ten years of its founding. Airbnb, Facebook, Amazon and the like display similar trajectories. Each of these entrepreneurial small firms internationalized early in its life, and attained significant scale and scope in a relatively short span of time.

The study of cross-border entrepreneurial behavior focuses on how actors discover, enact, evaluate and exploit opportunities to create future goods and services. Clearly, some entrepreneurial behavior crosses national borders with greater speed than others. As we know from Chapter 9, many of these rapidly growing firms are founded or co-founded by highly skilled immigrant entrepreneurs who have a link with another country outside of their country of origin.

The phenomenon of rapid internationalization is important to explain as it has performance advantages. That is, the earlier in its history that a firm internationalizes, the faster it seems to grow. Several models inform our understanding of how the process works. The stages model of internationalization and the common emphasis on organizational scale as an important competitive advantage in the international arena (Chapter 5) is one possible explanation. However, the stages model is inappropriate to explain multinational business activity for new ventures that are instantly international.

In this chapter, we draw on Oviatt and McDougall's (1994) seminal work to explain the phenomenon of rapid internationalization of new and small firms. First, we outline the distinguishing feature of international new ventures (INVs). Then we explain key elements of the theory of INVs. Using examples, we then compare and contrast different types of INVs. Finally, we explain the distinguishing features of global start-ups as a special type of INV.

International New Ventures: Concept and Distinguishing Features

Oviatt and McDougall (1994) define an **international new venture** as a business organization that, from inception, seeks to derive significant competitive advantages from the use of resources and sale of outputs in multiple countries. The key distinguishing features of INVs pertain to their age at internationalization, speed of internationalization, proactive internationalization strategy, innovative product or service and minimal ownership of assets, as described below.

Age at Internationalization

The distinguishing feature of INVs is that their origins are international, as demonstrated by the significant commitments of resources (e.g. material, people, financing, time) in more than one country, early in their life. In contrast to large multinational firms that typically first enter foreign markets years after their founding, INVs are international at inception.

Consumer health care company Johnson & Johnson (J&J), consumer electronics giant Sony, and clothing retailer the GAP are examples of late internationalizers (Isenberg, 2008). J&J set up its first foreign subsidiary in Montreal in 1919 – 33 years after its founding in 1886. Established in 1946, Sony took 11 years to export its first product to the United States, the TR-63 transistor radio. Founded in 1969, the GAP opened its first overseas store in London in 1987.

In contrast, the focus in the case of INVs is on the **age** of firms when they become international, not on their size. The entry timing of INVs into foreign markets is relative to the age of the venture itself, not the order of entry of other firms into particular foreign markets, or a comparison between first mover and follower advantages. Thus, INVs are **early internationalizers**, even if they are the last entrant into a particular foreign market, as long as they entered the market at a young age (Autio et al., 2000). They would be late internationalizers only if they were old.

Speed of Internationalization

A characteristic feature of INVs is the speed with which they internationalize or enter foreign markets. Oviatt and McDougall (2005) identify three vital aspects of **internationalization speed**: First, the **time** between the discovery or enactment of an opportunity and its first foreign market entry. Typically, rapidly growing high-tech ventures are less than six years old, have fewer than ten employees and have entered their first market within three years of inception (Coviello, 2006). Second, the speed with which **country scope** is increased, that is, how rapidly entries into foreign markets are achieved and how rapidly are countries entered that are physically distant from the entrepreneur's home country. Third, the **speed of international commitment**, that is, the rate of increase of the percentage of foreign revenue increases due to international activities.

Proactive International Strategy

In contrast with organizations that gradually evolve from domestic firms to multinational enterprises (MNEs), INVs begin with a proactive international strategy. According to Autio et al. (2000), INVs have '**learning advantages of newness**'. Early venturing across borders establishes a self-reinforcing pattern that implants into the firm a proactive culture, enhancing the ability to see and realize foreign opportunities, and the willingness to do so. As firms get older, they develop learning impediments that hamper their ability to successfully grow in new environments. The relative flexibility of newer firms allows them to rapidly learn the competencies necessary to pursue continued growth in foreign markets.

Innovative Product or Service

INVs typically offer an innovative product or service marketed through a strong network, and a tightly managed organization focused on international sales growth. The product-service innovation provides a unique source of competitive advantage for rapid growth in global markets. Although high-tech ventures are the most commonly researched small and new type of small firms, INVs are not limited to technology. They appear in a wide range of industries including services.

   As Vijay Maheshwari, a technology entrepreneur, and founder of Verismo Networks, California, explained, it takes a lot of research for a new and small entrepreneur to identify a market gap and offer a radically innovative product different from other product offerings on the market:

You have to do lot of homework to figure out if you are taking a particular field right? Really research what is there, what each companies' plus minus are, and what you bring to the table and you have to assume that the other companies will eventually catch up on some of this stuff. So, you have to really look at something. (Vijay Maheshwari, Founder, Verizmo Networks, California)

When Vijay first started his video company, he capitalized on the dramatically rising speed of the internet, an emerging phenomenon at that time, to offer a novel product that brought internet directly to the television. He was able to penetrate a large number of foreign markets at inception based on the strength of his product:

So when we started this video company. There was no product at that time which could bring internet directly to the TV… they were getting it on the PC, but not on the TV. So that is the differentiation we had… we capitalized on that… Usually most of the things happen because there is a technology breakthrough… and you see how you can apply that to your things. So what we realized was that the speed of the internet was increasing dramatically. Previously people were just able to send email dial modems and… speeds didn't increase. So we said, how do I use this speed, excess speed for doing something. (Vijay Maheshwari, Founder, Verizmo Networks, California)

Minimal Ownership of Assets

INVs do not necessarily own foreign assets. In other words, **foreign direct investment** is not a requirement for entry into foreign markets. Often, these ventures enter into **strategic alliances** in order to use foreign resources such as manufacturing capacity or marketing. Thus, the definition of INVs is concerned with value added, not assets owned.

To this end, INVs share common characteristics with **mMNEs** or **micromultinationals** (Chapter 8). However, unlike mMNEs, INVs are defined by their speed or pace of internationalization, not just their tendency to enter a diverse set of foreign markets or adopt advanced market entry modes to penetrate those markets. INVs are also different from mMNEs in their sector focus. Whereas a vast majority of mMNEs operate in traditional or low-tech sectors, INVs prevail mainly in high-tech or knowledge-intensive sectors.

Theory of INVs

In their seminal paper, Oviatt and McDougall (1994) argue that stages theory, used to explain the internationalization of firms, is not applicable to the case of INVs. According to the **stages theory of internationalization** (Chapter 5), firms proceed in small, incremental steps to cope with risk and uncertainty inherent in the internationalization process (Johanson and Vahlne, 1977). Small steps make sense because they allow firms to learn from, rather than to be destroyed by, their mistakes.

However, the stages model of internationalization and the common emphasis on organizational scale as an important competitive advantage in the international arena are inappropriate explanations of multinational business activity for new ventures that are instantly international.

The stages theory best applies to the early stages of internationalization with three exceptions (Oviatt and McDougall, 1994). First, firms with large resources are expected to take large steps toward internationalization. Second, when foreign market conditions are stable and homogeneous, learning about them is easier. Third, when firms have considerable experience with markets that are similar to a newly targeted foreign market, previous experience may be generalizable to the new arena.

Yet, none of these exceptions seems to apply to INVs. First, INVs are constrained by their young age and usually by their small size. INVs are almost always small organizations. Although an important source of advantage for some MNEs, large size is only one among many ways to compete internationally. In order to understand the rationale for the existence of INVs, it is important to appreciate that large MNE size may be a concomitant, not a cause, of other more elemental sources of competitive advantage.

Second, INVs operate in markets that are among the most volatile. Typically, INVs compete in the knowledge-based industries where competition is stiff and the pressure to rapidly commercialize the product/service innovation is extremely intense. Finally, by definition, INVs have little or no experience in any market. They either skip stages of international development, or may not internationalize in stages at all. In their study of rapidly internationalizing high-tech start-ups, Autio et al. (2000) find that the number of years of foreign operating experience is not correlated with foreign growth of new and small ventures.

Therefore, stage theory is not applicable to INVs as it stands. The age at first foreign entry may affect a new and small business's internationalization mode. It may also impact its pace of resource commitment to foreign markets. Likewise, individual founders may play a key role in creating and sustaining entrepreneurial activity in a firm in the early stages.

Oviatt and McDougall (1994) propose a new framework to explain the existence of INVs. Their framework has four key elements – internalization of some transactions, alternative governance structures, foreign location advantage and unique resources. We explain each in turn.

Internalization of Some Transactions

The first element of INV theory is **internalization of transactions**. Internalization in MNE theory is often used to explain foreign direct investment; that is, ownership of assets located in foreign countries. According to **transaction cost economics**, organizations form when economic transactions are inefficiently governed by market prices; in other words, where market imperfections exist (Williamson, 1991). The transaction costs of contracting in an open market, or monitoring the conduct of independent transactions between different parties, are high due to the presence of **asset specificity**, and hence the risk of **opportunism**. The internalization of transactions reduces these costs.

Organizations come into existence when the internalization of transactions reduces the costs of constructing and executing contracts, and monitoring the performance of the contracting parties. Transactions are said to have been internalized within an organization and its hierarchical authority is chosen as the governance mechanism when the costs of executing and monitoring contracts are at their lowest, and these costs outweigh the transaction costs on an open market. Internalization is the defining element of all organizations, whether new or established, domestic or multinational.

Organizations must own assets in order to minimize the transaction costs of using those assets when they are located outside of the organization. Thus, according to the first element of INV theory, INVs are organizations that must own some assets, else they will have nothing of value to exchange in economic transactions. However, unlike MNEs or large organizations, ownership of foreign assets is not a defining characteristic of INVs. New ventures commonly lack sufficient resources to control many assets through ownership. The result is that new ventures tend to internalize, or own, a smaller percentage of resources essential to their survival than do mature organizations.

Alternative Governance Structures

Even though INVs must own some assets, they are different from established organizations in the minimal use of internalization and greater use of **alternative governance structures**. In the absence of ownership of many vital assets, INV founders rely on alternative modes of controlling those assets, which distinguishes them from other organizations. Under conditions of moderate asset specificity, hybrid structures such as licensing and franchising offer useful alternatives to both internal control and market control over the exchange of resources (Williamson, 1991). So does the use of contractual foreign market entry modes like strategic alliances. In some cases, founders also enter into acquisitions to acquire critical resources. Overall, INVs are strategic in relying on a combination of foreign entry modes.

Started by David Kranzler, Hands-On Mobile, a Silicon-Valley-based developer of the mobile versions of Guitar Hero III, Iron Man and other games, provides an interesting illustration of the use of alternative governance structures by new and small internationalizing ventures (Isenberg, 2008). When the company started in 2001, the markets for mobile multimedia content were developing faster in Asia and Europe than in the United States, and gamers were creating attractive products in China, South Korea and

Japan. Kranzler realized that his company had to acquire intellectual property and design capacity overseas in order to offer customers a comprehensive catalog of games and the latest delivery technologies. Therefore, Hands-On Mobile picked up MobileGame Korea, as well as two Chinese content development companies, which helped it become a market leader.

A powerful alternative to internalization for new ventures is the **network structure**, or use of contractual arrangements with other parties, without directly owning them. For example, contracting the purchase of raw materials from suppliers outside of an organization without building those parts in-house. As entrepreneurs are resource constrained, they use network structures even when the risk of asset expropriation by partners is high. Networks depend on the social (i.e. informal) control of behavior through trust and moral obligation, rather than formal contracts. As business and personal reputations are at stake, cooperation in network structures dominates opportunistic behavior. A network structure also provides greater flexibility and keeps costs low.

Sai Gundavelli, Founder, Solix Technologies, California, explained the rationale for entering into **partnerships** with large companies for rapidly penetrating a large number of foreign markets early in the life of his venture. According to Sai, as a small venture, there was no way he could outperform his large industry competitors like IBM. Neither did he have financial resources nor the capacity to hire as many people as them. Unlike his established competitors, he was also limited in his ability to build a large number of relationships. Therefore, partnering with the 'competitors of his competitors' was the only way to compete with some of the biggest names in the industry:

> IBM is a multi-billion dollar company. I can never ever become IBM. Neither I have the financial resources nor the clout to be like that. So we said the only way to compete with an IBM like organization is have IBM's competition work with us… I will never be able to hire 100,000 sales persons by myself. I never had all the relationships that IBM already had. So, it gave us no choice other than to partner with their competition like CAC who resell our product. They've done business with us, WIPRO does business with us. So we said, 'Hey CAC, can you work with us? WIPRO you are competing with IBM Global Services, can you partner with us?' So we targeted the competition of our competition to see if they could partner with us. We had a very clear focus to hire them as partners, tell them, educate them why they needed to be our partners and that worked. (Sai Gundavelli, Founder, Solix Technologies, California)

Foreign Location Advantage

The third key element of the theory of INVs postulates that **private knowledge** creates differentiation or cost advantages for INVs. Private knowledge simultaneously overcomes the advantages of indigenous firms in many countries (Oviatt and McDougall, 1994).

According to MNE theory, firms are international because they find advantage in transferring some moveable resources (e.g. raw materials, knowledge, etc.) across national borders to be combined with immobile, or less mobile, resources or opportunities (e.g. raw material, a market etc.) in the foreign markets that they enter. MNEs rely on advantages of large size to overcome such obstacles as barriers to trade and incomplete understanding of local institutional contexts in foreign countries, vis-à-vis indigenous firms. In contrast, small and new ventures derive foreign location advantages from the novelty, complexity and sophistication of their knowledge resources, which explains the speed of their internationalization.

Bell et al. (2003) classify firms into three types depending on their reliance on knowledge and subsequent speed of internationalization: traditional firms, knowledge-intensive firms and knowledge-based firms. **Traditional firms** adapt well-understood technologies to new foreign markets and usually internationalize incrementally. **Knowledge-intensive firms** use complex knowledge to design a new product, an improved production method or more efficient service delivery. These firms are less constrained by distance or national boundaries. They serve a broader scope of international markets and have a more rapid pace of internationalization. They internationalize faster because they usually hold a competitive advantage that can be exploited in multiple countries. These firms seek to exploit narrow windows of opportunity and gain first mover advantages (McNaughton, 2001, 2003). Finally, **knowledge-based firms** are dependent on some novel complex knowledge for their existence. This type of firm is likely to have the most accelerated internationalization because it has a unique sustainable advantage that may be in demand in a number of countries.

Autio et al. (2000) detail two reasons for the 'amplifying' effects of knowledge on internationalization: first, the mobility of knowledge provides a location advantage for INVs in foreign markets. As knowledge, explicit knowledge in particular, is a **mobile resource**, it provides a flexible platform for international expansion. Knowledge is inherently mobile as it can be combined with fixed assets, such as distribution channels or manufacturing resources, in foreign markets at relatively low costs. Knowledge-intensive firms exploit international growth opportunities more flexibly through such combinations than firms that are dependent on fixed assets alone.

Second, firms focusing on knowledge creation and exploitation as the source of advantage are more likely to develop **learning skills** useful for adaptation and successful growth in new environments than are firms more dependent on tangible resources. These firms' ability to learn about a new host country moderates the speed of internationalization to exploit an entrepreneurial opportunity.

For entrepreneurial firms competing in international markets, the learning process is critical in helping them to overcome their **liabilities of foreignness** (Zaheer, 1995). Using panel data from the Finnish electronics industry, Autio et al. (2000) conclude that as firms get older, they develop learning impediments that hamper their ability to successfully grow in new environments. The relative flexibility of newer firms allows them to rapidly learn the competencies necessary to pursue continued growth in foreign markets.

The **learning advantages of newness** thus represent a counterpoint to the widely accepted concept of '**liability of newness**' for young organizations. Although it can apply to all entrepreneurial firms, the concept of the learning advantages of newness is particularly valuable for entrepreneurial firms that are seeking accelerated internationalization.

Knowledge and learning are also important determinants of INV growth. Together with age at entry, knowledge about international markets and operations, as well as the efficiency with which such knowledge is learned, is an important determinant of international sales growth, especially for high-technology start-ups (Autio et al., 2000). The earlier in their development these firms venture into international competition, the more rapidly they grow internationally.

Altogether, unique foreign location advantages explain why new ventures with valuable knowledge are propelled to instant internationalization. When firms introduce valuable innovative goods or services, they signal the existence of their special knowledge to competitors. Competitors then try to uncover the secret of this knowledge. New ventures confronted with such circumstances must be international from inception or be at a disadvantage to other organizations that are already international.

Unique Resources

The fourth element of the theory of INVs is that INVs possess **unique resources** that are the basis of their sustained competitive advantage in foreign markets (Barney, 1991). Additionally, it is important for them to limit the use of these resources by competitors in many countries in order for the resources to have commercial value. Oviatt and McDougall (1994) propose four conditions that limit the use of proprietary knowledge of INVs: intellectual property (IP) protection, imperfect imitability, licensing and use of alternative governance structures.

IP protection through the use of patents, copyrights or trade secrets helps to keep knowledge proprietary, prevents imitation and slows the development of substitutes. **Imperfect imitability** refers to a unique organizational history, socially complex knowledge and ambiguous causal relationships between knowledge and the competitive advantage it provides such that unique resources are difficult for competitors to copy or imitate. The unique management style and organizational culture of new venture founders also offers advantages. INVs form because internationally experienced and alert entrepreneurs have a unique vision from inception. Entrepreneurial knowledge and vision are the keys to aggressive international opportunity seeking. Additionally, entrepreneurs are able to link resources from multiple countries to meet the demand of markets that are inherently international.

In contrast with multinational firms, knowledge in entrepreneurial firms tends to be more individualized to the founder or entrepreneurial team. Firms in which the founder or entrepreneurial team has lived abroad or has prior work experience in international markets exhibit speedier entry and/or commitment to internationalization. Thus, entre-preneurial firms led by founders or management teams who have a greater wealth of personal international knowledge are more likely to exploit entrepreneurial opportuni-ties earlier. Their greater **absorptive capacity** makes these firms able to readily accumulate additional foreign knowledge, which reduces the uncertainty of operating abroad and increases their likelihood of entering additional countries and increasing their commitment to internationalization (Autio et al., 2000).

Licensing helps to limit the use of a venture's knowledge outside of the INV. When demand is strong for expropriable knowledge, but its valuable life is believed to be short (e.g. some personal computing innovations), high fees may be used to extract maxi-mum rents over a short period. Finally, as discussed above, INVs frequently used **network governance structures**, which limit the expropriation of venture knowl-edge. Although strategic alliances with complementary organizations risk expropriation, the network structure tends to control the risk due to the high personal and economic value inherent in network relationships among internationally experienced team mem-bers, which inhibits them from usurping the venture's knowledge.

Types of INVs and Global Start-Ups

According to Oviatt and McDougall (1994), INVs are heterogeneous based on a) number of value-chain activities that are coordinated and b) number of countries entered. They identify new international market makers, geographically focused start-ups and global start-ups as the three main types of INVs (Figure 12.1).

Figure 12.1 Types of international new ventures

Source: Oviatt and McDougall (1994)

New international market makers specialize in creating new markets by discov-ering imbalances of resources between countries (Figure 12.1, Quadrants I and II). Their competitive advantage depends on their unusual abilities to identify new business opportunities and expert knowledge of markets and suppliers. They also have the ability to attract and maintain a loyal network of business associates. New international market makers typically internalize the value-chain activities related to systems and knowledge of inbound and outbound logistics. Direct investment in any country is typically kept at a minimum.

New international market makers may be either **export/import start-ups** or **multinational traders**. Importers and exporters profit by moving goods from nations where they are to nations where they are demanded, typically serving a few nations with which the entrepreneur is familiar. In contrast, multinational traders serve a large number of countries, constantly scanning for trading opportunities where their networks are established, or where they can quickly be set up.

Geographically focused start-ups derive advantages by serving the specialized needs of a particular region of the world through the use of foreign resources (Figure 12.1, Quadrant III). Like export/import start-ups, their geographic scope is limited to the location of the specialized need; however, unlike both export/import start-ups and multinational traders, they coordinate more than just the activities of inbound and outbound logistics. Their competitive advantage is found in the coordination of multiple value-chain activities, such as technological development, human resources and production. Successful coordination may be inimitable because it is socially complex or involves tacit knowledge. That advantage may be further protected by a close and exclusive network of alliances in the geographical area served.

As the most advanced form of INVs (Figure 12.1, Quadrant IV), **global start-ups** derive significant competitive advantages from the dispersal of multiple value-chain activities across the globe, *and* extensive coordination of those activities in multiple countries. Knight and Cavusgil (2004) define born globals as business organizations that, from or near their founding, seek superior international business performance from the application of knowledge-based resources to the sale of outputs in multiple countries. Born global firms are often described as highly innovative, with global technology competence.

Global start-ups respond to globalizing markets. Many ventures must globalize some aspects of their business – manufacturing, service delivery, capital sourcing or talent acquisition – the moment they start up in order to be competitive (Isenberg, 2008). Additionally, they are founded by entrepreneurs who proactively act on opportunities to acquire resources and sell outputs wherever in the world they have the greatest value. Instead of buying raw materials from nearby suppliers or setting up factories close to their headquarters, global entrepreneurs search for the best available manufacturing locations across the world.

In the words of Vas Bhandarkar, co-founder of Global Logic, Silicon Valley, California, it is important to acquire teams that have expertise in selling into new markets, and also in markets where one's products can be built, in order to build a truly global business. As a company that was initially founded in the US and India, Global Logic acquired offices in Ukraine, Argentina and Israel, growing from $7 million to $250 million in revenue, and from a 200-person company to a 6000-person company, in just five years:

> If you want to build a truly global business, you want to acquire teams that have expertise in selling into new markets but also where your products can be built… So that was the philosophy behind Global Logic… I joined the company when it had $7 million revenue. Today it has $250 million revenue. When we started the company, it was called Indus Logic, CEO changed the name to Global Logic because we wanted to be beyond just the US and India. Then we acquired a company that had offices in Ukraine. Then we acquired a company that had offices in Argentina. Then we acquired a company that had offices in Israel. So before you know it, a small company, a 200 person company, is now in five years, it has become 6000 person company. (Vas Bhandarkar, Co-Founder, Global Logic, California)

Global start-ups also scout for talent across the globe, tap investors wherever they may be located and learn to manage operations from a distance – the moment they go into business. As they disperse their activities in multiple geographic locations, global start-ups face the challenge of coordinating those activities.

When the husband-and-wife team of Andrew Prihodko, a Ukrainian studying at MIT, and Sharon Peyer, a Swiss-American citizen studying at Harvard, set up an online photo management company, Pixamo, they struggled to decide where to domicile the company (Isenberg, 2008). Ukraine, which had a simple and low tax structure, was one option, but it had a problematic legal history. Although taxes were higher in Switzerland, the legal system was well established. Delaware was attractive because most US start-ups were domiciled there, even though taxes were higher. Prihodko and Peyer eventually chose to base the company in the relatively tax-friendly Swiss canton of Zug, a decision that helped shareholders when they sold Pixamo to NameMedia in 2007. We discuss more on the challenges of managing global start-ups in the next chapter.

Factors Influencing the Emergence of INVs

According to Oviatt and McDougall (2005), the internationalization process begins with a potential entrepreneurial opportunity. Internationalization speed is then collectively determined by four forces, namely, entrepreneur knowledge and networks, competition, and technology (Figure 12.2). We classify these influences into internal and external factors that influence the speed of internationalization of new and small firms. Whereas internal factors refer to the role of the entrepreneur, and their human and social capital resources such as knowledge, experience and networks, external factors include the influence of competition and technology.

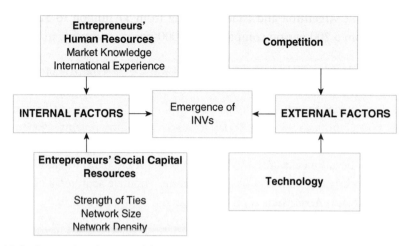

Figure 12.2 Internal and external factors influencing the emergence of INVs

Entrepreneur's Human Resources

Founders play a particularly important role in global start-ups. Entrepreneurs must be able to identify opportunities, gather resources and strike deals (Isenberg, 2009). They all must possess soft skills like vision, leadership, and drive and passion to succeed, as well as positive psychological traits such as risk-taking propensity in order to compete in global markets.

Knowledge of entrepreneurs includes both market knowledge, and knowledge intensity of the product or service (as explained earlier in this chapter). As INVs tend to emphasize technologically advanced innovative products and services, and compete in globally integrated industries, they are led by internationally experienced entrepreneurs (McDougall et al., 2003). Additionally, global entrepreneurs are able to coordinate value-chain activities in different parts of the world.

As Raju Reddy, a serial entrepreneur in Silicon Valley, and founder of Sierra Atlantic, which was acquired by Hitachi Consulting, explained, he was used to running all employee meetings from different world locations. These meetings were especially important for announcing new acquisitions to their 2400 odd employees, 1800 of which were located in India and 250 or so were in China:

> When we were 2400 employees, 1800 or so were in India, China was about 250 something. The rest was in US, UK and other countries. I used to run especially with acquisitions, whenever we acquired a company, always used to run an all employee meeting from their location. So I ran it from Boston, from China, wherever. So that way the 2400 people in my company know that the new company we've acquired is very important. Because I'm physically present there. (Raju Reddy, Founder, Sierra Atlantic, California)

Entrepreneurs' Social Capital Resources

Additionally, entrepreneurs use established social network connections that cross national borders to explore where and how quickly the opportunity can be exploited in foreign locations. Involvement in networks to facilitate rapid internationalization is a key distinguishing feature of INVs (Coviello and Munro, 1995, 1997).

Network resources are essential to INVs' pre-internationalization, pre-growth and even pre-commercialization, that is, from the time of conceiving the new business idea (Coviello, 2014). Networks have both a positive and negative impact on the pace and patterns of market selection and entry mode strategy for INVs.

McDougall et al. (1994) explain that networks help founders of INVs to identify international opportunities, establish credibility and often lead to strategic alliances and other cooperative strategies. Network relationships generate social capital for INVs – a resource that enables entrepreneurial firm mobilization. Increased social capital for INVs includes better access to resources and international opportunities. It also provides a means by which to overcome the liabilities of newness and foreignness. External social capital, in the form of management contacts, customers and suppliers, positively impacts upon foreign market knowledge and, in turn, the international growth of new ventures (Yli-Renko et al., 2002). INVs also collaborate to access resources and enhance their reputation.

According to Oviatt and McDougall (2005), all three key aspects of networks – strength of network ties, network size and density – influence the speed of internationalization of INVs. The existence of cross-border weak ties positively and significantly moderates the speed of venture internationalization. If an entrepreneur already has weak ties when he or she discovers or enacts an opportunity, the initial foreign entry may occur with unusual speed. As explained in Chapter 5, the more direct or indirect cross-border weak ties that an entrepreneur has established, the greater the potential country scope of internationalization and the greater possible speed for increasing that scope.

Larger entrepreneurial networks are associated with faster venture internationalization and more rapid increases in country scope. Furthermore, with a large network in place, a relatively large portion of venture revenue comes rapidly from foreign sources, and the venture, therefore, has more rapid commitment to internationalization. Finally, as trust in dense networks is established by their monitoring potential of actors linked by weak ties, dense cross-border networks provide relatively efficient support for internationalization. Entrepreneurs who have already established such networks can internationalize rapidly.

Personal and industry ties also influence the rapid internationalization of high-tech start-up ventures (Sharma and Blomstermo, 2003). No one pattern explains the nature of ties in INV networks. Although network ties are consistently found to facilitate INV internationalization, they are not able to be easily categorized. The literature provides diverse arguments regarding the patterns of network structure and interaction as they pertain to INVs. Some studies suggest that whereas personal ties, for example, are influential in the early phases of growth, they become less important over time (Chetty and Wilson, 2003). Once the INV start-up process is complete, organizational needs become more complex and necessitate non-social relationships.

Other studies find that initial ties might be economic (industry/business) rather than social (personal) ties if the INV's emphasis is on managing for growth from the outset (Coviello, 2014). Yet other evidence suggests that economic ties dominate INV networks regardless of stage. This is particularly true of high-tech start-ups that are not family businesses but are conceived by founders based on their business knowledge and experience, especially as it relates to their knowledge at start-up.

The INV literature also offers mixed evidence in respect of proactive and reactive growth stance. The literature generally takes the position that INVs are proactive and strategically aggressive. However, some studies suggest that they may be reactive, reliant on previously established ties for growth (Sharma and Blomstermo, 2003). They found that the history of network ties shapes the INV's future. Unplanned and serendipitous ties can be influential (Crick and Spence, 2005). Yet others suggest that INVs' approach to building networks is a mix of both unintended occurrences and proactive design.

Recent studies find that INVs' network and resultant growth patterns are characterized by change with time. In particular, the range of INVs' networks increase, while the density of these networks decreases, over time (Coviello, 2014). Technology-based INVs, in particular, are niche marketers that seek to rapidly internationalize, and either act or respond rapidly when building contacts beyond their initial network, which tends to increase network size and decrease the density of ties. Overall, a small dense network is perhaps beneficial at the conception stage to generate initial resources from trusted sources; the overall changes in network structure lead to an increase in social capital for the INV.

Finally, evidence suggests that the network relationships that INVs develop are somewhat volatile. They enter relationships as and when the need arises, which indicates that some relationships are more opportunistic, while others are deterministic.

Immigrant Entrepreneurs' Human and Social Capital Resources

Immigrant entrepreneurs (IEs) are an important force behind global start-ups. Evernote, Google, WhatsApp, SlideShare, NYX Cosmetics, eBay, Instagram and Udemy are all examples of global start-ups that are founded by immigrant entrepreneurs (see Box below).

IMMIGRANT FOUNDERS OF GLOBAL START-UPS

Phil Libin – Evernote

With 200 million users, Evernote, one of the companies that Phil Libin founded, is valued at $1 billion. It is one of the technology entrepreneur's two ventures that he sold for $26 million and $24 million before the 1990s were over. Phil Libin emigrated to the United States from the Soviet Union. His family settled in a rough Bronx neighborhood when they first arrived from St. Petersburg. Libin took up several well-paid programming jobs due to his knack for computers, before earning a spot at Boston University.

Sergey Brin – Google/Alphabet

With a net worth of $56.3 billion, Sergey Brin is the President of Alphabet and one of the two well-known founders of Google. He is also an angel investor, with Tesla Motors and Mosa Meat, a lab-grown meat start-up, being among his portfolio companies. Born in the former Soviet Union, Sergey first arrived in the US as a child with his parents to escape Jewish persecution at the hands of the Communist Party. Far ahead in his class as a math student at school, Sergey attended Stanford University in California where he met the co-founder of his future venture, Google.

Jan Koum – WhatsApp

Founded in 2009, WhatsApp was acquired by Facebook for $19 billion. A philanthropist at heart, WhatsApp's founder and Facebook board member, Jan Koum, donated $555 million in Facebook shares to the Silicon Valley Community Foundation shortly after selling WhatsApp. A San Jose State University dropout, Jan Koum failed to be hired at Facebook in his early days despite his enthusiasm for computers. Few know that Jan Koum arrived in the US with his family to flee persecution in Ukraine where he first started his life.

Rashmi Sinha – SlideShare

Founded in 2006, SlideShare, a unique technology-based product that combines the power of social media and information sharing to facilitate slide sharing on the internet, was acquired by LinkedIn for just over $118 million in 2012. SlideShare's female founder, Rashmi Sinha, has impressive credentials as the creator of several successful technology businesses in the Bay Area prior to SlideShare. She also holds a PhD in Cognitive Neuropsychology from Brown University that she joined after first earning an undergraduate degree in her native India.

(Continued)

Toni Ko – NYX Cosmetics

L'Oreal purchased NYX Cosmetics, a cosmetics company that takes on luxury brands at affordable prices, for $500 million in 2014. The purchase followed a smashing sales record in the aftermath of the 2008 financial crisis when shoppers searched the shelves of major retailers for more affordable products. Working in her family's cosmetics business since the age of 13, Toni Ko founded NYX in a rented 600 square foot storefront. After selling NYX Cosmetics, she launched her next business, PERVERSE, a sunglasses brand in 2016. Of South Korean descent, Toni Ko immigrated to Southern California with her family of entrepreneurs.

Pierre Omidyar – eBay

Worth around $11 billion, Pierre Omidyar is the founder of eBay, one of the most visited sites on the internet that changed how people buy and sell. Pierre Omidyar built the platform to help his future wife buy collectible Pez dispensers online, and the rest is history. Born in Paris to Iranian immigrant parents, Pierre Omidyar first arrived in Baltimore because of his father's medical residency at Johns Hopkins University. His early entrepreneurial attempts did not yield much success, while his interest in computers grew. He now continues to inspire and support other entrepreneurs through his venture capital firm, Omidyar Technology Ventures.

Mike Krieger – Instagram

Instagram, a photo and location-sharing app that was first called Burbn, was purchased by Facebook for $1 billion. The immensely popular app caused Facebook's servers to crash upon launch due to excessive downloads. Technology entrepreneur Mike Krieger, who immigrated to the US from Brazil to study at Stanford University, partnered with Kevin Systrom to found this gem of a venture. At one point, immigration hurdles and H1-B visa complications almost forced him to abandon his entrepreneurial aspirations in the US.

Eren Bali – Udemy

Udemy educates 24 million students around the globe through its 35,000 instructors. An online course and learning platform, Udemy found success after more than 50 rejections by venture capital investors. Founded and developed in Turkey for more than six years before moving to Silicon Valley, Udemy is the brainchild of Eren Bali, a child who was curious about math and science while growing up in a small Turkish village. Bali felt that internet learning platforms helped him to overcome his frustrations in a crowded one-room schoolhouse, leading him to later take second place in the International Math Olympiads.

Source: Neidert (2018)

On average, compared to native entrepreneurs, IEs are more likely to have the human resources needed to start INVs (Zolin and Schlosser, 2013). They are also more likely to develop international connections. IE-founded firms are more likely to report that they have a strategic relationship with a foreign firm. These social networks, including their ties in their home countries, provide social capital that helps founding teams of INVs to overcome initial resource constraints.

Moreover, as part of INV founding teams, IEs positively influence new ventures' internationalization efforts by fostering international attention of the firm in the market (Drechsler et al., 2019). Founders from foreign nationalities play a key role in the international attention efforts of newly founded US firms by aligning available resources with the international operations of new ventures. Thus, immigrants can be seen as a special kind of entrepreneur, a kind that not only dares to start a new company in his or her home country, but in a foreign country as well.

We discussed transnational entrepreneurs (TEs) in Chapter 9. As IEs who cross host and home country borders in venture founding, TEs are more likely to establish ventures that are born global. Although initially focused on business exchange between their host and home countries, they soon include additional country markets after inception (Lundberg and Rehnfors, 2018).

Many TEs take advantage of ethnic networks to formulate and execute a global strategy. The culture, values and social norms members hold in common forge understanding and trust, making it easier to establish and enforce contracts. Through home country networks, TEs can quickly gain access to information, funding, talent, technology – and, of course, contacts.

Chinese TEs, for example, are able to build supply chain networks through their cross-border ethnic networks (Alvarez et al., 2018). These supply chain networks horizontally integrate production and distribution between manufacturers and traders, and help the TEs to expand their market and international operations. These TEs enter the global market, including their host country.

Vikas, an immigrant founder of Indian origin in California, explained that he entered China, Korea, Singapore and Latin America only after he got success in his home country, India:

> India we entered two and a half years ago. I would go back and I would try and meet people and pitch to them. After I got success there, after three months, we ventured into China, Singapore. Interestingly we skipped Europe. I don't know why but it just seems the emerging market in Korea, China, Singapore at least seemed more reasonable and attractive to go into. Same for Latin America, which is why we skipped Europe. (Vikas, Entrepreneur, Sunnyvale, California)

According to Isenberg (2008), entrepreneurs who most successfully exploit their home country immigrant networks to found global ventures are able to map their networks and identify organizations that can help. The members of a diaspora often cluster in residential areas, public organizations or industries. Americans in Tokyo, for example, tend to work for professional service firms such as Morgan Stanley and McKinsey, live in Azabu, shop in Omotesandō and hang out at the American Club. They also reach out to overseas offices that facilitate trade and investment, and they open their doors to people visiting from home. These organizations can provide names of influential individuals, companies and informal organizations, clubs or groups. Informal organizations of ethnic entrepreneurs and executives are usually located in communities where immigrant professionals are concentrated. In the United States, for instance, they thrive in high-tech industry neighborhoods such as Silicon Valley or universities like MIT.

Finally, IEs identify mentors to guide them in their entrepreneurial journey. It can be difficult to identify people who have standing with local businesses and also within the diaspora network. A board member or coach that both show respect is an invaluable resource for a global entrepreneur.

Theoretically, returnee entrepreneurs (REs) (Chapter 10), just like TEs (Chapter 10), are well equipped to follow an early internationalization path by virtue of their international experience and networks cultivated abroad. However, REs may aim to satisfy surging demand in emerging and developing economies where they return to start-up as a first step. Their internationalization process may be more gradual in accordance with stage theories. Moreover, inward internationalization based on engagement with foreign suppliers or through international R&D by REs upon their return to the home country may precede subsequent outward internationalization based on a staged, step-wise process.

Competition

Entrepreneurs can be encouraged, or even forced, to enter foreign markets due to competition. Many entrepreneurs are motivated to take pre-emptive advantage of technological opportunities in foreign countries because they fear competitors will quickly respond to a new product introduction and prevent them from eventually going international if they initially competed only in their home country. As in Vijay's case, selling only in the domestic, home market also restricts the growth potential of technology-based global start-ups.

Technology

Technology is a key factor enabling rapid internationalization among new and small firms. Technology drives the emergence of INVs in more than one way. First, technology has made possible rapid movements of people and goods over long distances. It has also lowered the costs of these movements, which has revolutionized the way in which entrepreneurs can reach foreign markets. Faster and more efficient air and container freight transportation are cases in point. Dramatic improvements and cost reductions in digital technology have also made high-quality and rapid communication feasible, which is important for entrepreneurs to control and coordinate their operations across borders.

Chapter Summary

LO1: An **international new venture (INV)** is a business organization that, from inception, seeks to derive significant competitive advantages from the use of resources and sale of outputs in multiple countries. The key distinguishing features of INVs pertain to their age at internationalization, speed of internationalization, proactive internationalization strategy, innovative product or service and minimal ownership of assets. The origins of INVs are international, as demonstrated by the significant commitments of resources in more than one country, early in their life. In contrast with large multinational firms that typically first enter foreign markets years after their founding, INVs are international at inception. A characteristic feature of INVs is the speed with which they internationalize or enter foreign markets. Three aspects of **internationalization speed** are characteristic of INVs: first, the **time** between the discovery or enactment of an opportunity and its first foreign market entry; second, the speed with which **country scope** is increased; and third, the **speed of international commitment**, that is, the rate of increase of the percentage of foreign revenue increase due to international activities. In contrast with organizations that gradually evolve from domestic firms to multinational enterprises (MNEs), INVs begin with a proactive international strategy. INVs typically offer an innovative product or service marketed through a strong network, and a tightly managed organization focused on international sales growth. INVs do not necessarily own foreign assets; in other words, **foreign direct investment** is not a requirement for entry into foreign markets. Often, these ventures enter into **strategic alliances** in order to use foreign resources such as manufacturing capacity or marketing.

LO2: Oviatt and McDougall (1994)'s theory of INVs has four key elements – **internalization of some transactions**, **alternative governance structures**, **foreign location advantage**, and **unique resources**. INVs are organizations that must own some assets, else they will have nothing of value to exchange in economic transactions. However, unlike MNEs or large organizations, ownership of foreign assets is not a defining characteristic of INVs. In the absence of ownership of many vital assets, INV founders rely on alternative (e.g. contractual) modes of controlling those assets, which distinguishes them from other organizations. INVs derive foreign location advantages from the novelty, complexity and sophistication of their knowledge resources. The mobility of knowledge provides a location advantage in foreign markets. Knowledge-intensive / knowledge-based firms also develop learning skills useful for adaptation

(Continued)

and successful growth in new environments than are firms more dependent on tangible resources. INVs possess unique resources that are the basis of their sustained competitive advantage in foreign markets. It is important for them to limit the use of these resources by competitors through intellectual property (IP) protection, imperfect imitability, and licensing and use of alternative governance structures.

LO3: INVs are heterogeneous based on a) the number of value-chain activities that are coordinated and b) the number of countries entered. New international market makers, geographically focused start-ups, and global start-ups are the three main types of INVs. **New international market makers** specialize in creating new markets by discovering imbalances of resources between countries. Their competitive advantage depends on their unusual abilities to identify new business opportunities, and expert knowledge of markets and suppliers. They typically internalize the value-chain activities related to systems and knowledge of inbound and outbound logistics. Direct investment in any country is typically kept at a minimum. New international market makers may be either **export/import start-ups** or **multinational traders**. **Geographically focused start-ups** derive advantages by serving the specialized needs of a particular region of the world through the use of foreign resources. Like export/ import start-ups, their geographic scope is limited to the location of the specialized need; however, unlike both export-import start-ups and multinational traders, they coordinate more than just the activities of inbound and outbound logistics. As the most advanced form of INVs, **global start-ups** derive significant competitive advantages from the dispersal of multiple value-chain activities across the globe, and the extensive coordination of those activities in multiple countries.

LO4: **Global start-ups** are the most advanced form of INVs. They are founded by entrepreneurs who proactively act on opportunities to acquire resources and sell outputs wherever in the world they have the greatest value. Global entrepreneurs search for the best available manufacturing locations across the world. They also scout for talent across the globe, tap investors wherever they may be located and learn to manage operations from a distance – the moment they go into business. As they disperse their activities across multiple geographic locations, global start ups face the challenge of coordinating those activities.

LO5: Both internal and external factors influence the speed of internationalization of new and small firms. Whereas internal factors refer to the role of the entrepreneur, and their **human resources** and **social capital resources** such as knowledge, experience and social networks, external factors include the influence of competition and technology. Entrepreneurs must be able to identify opportunities, gather resources and strike deals. They all must also possess soft skills like vision, leadership, and drive and passion to succeed, as well as positive psychological traits such as risk-taking propensity, in order to compete in global markets. Knowledge of entrepreneurs includes both market knowledge and knowledge intensity of their product or service. INVs tend to be led by internationally experienced entrepreneurs. Additionally, entrepreneurs use established social network connections that cross national borders to explore where and how quickly the opportunity can be exploited in foreign locations. Networks have both a positive and negative impact on the pace and patterns of market selection and entry mode strategy for INVs. Entrepreneurs can be encouraged, or even forced, to enter foreign markets due to competition. Technology drives the emergence of INVs by enabling rapid movements of people and goods over long distances, lowering transportation costs, and allowing entrepreneurs to control and coordinate their operations across borders.

LO6: Immigrant entrepreneurs who cross host and home country borders in venture founding are more likely to establish ventures that are born global. Immigrant entrepreneurs can take advantage of ethnic networks to formulate and execute a global strategy. Entrepreneurs who most successfully exploit their home country immigrant networks to found global ventures are able to map their networks and identify organizations that can help. Finally, immigrant entrepreneurs identify mentors to guide them in their entrepreneurial journey. Theoretically, both REs (Chapter 10) and TEs (Chapter 10) are well equipped to follow an early internationalization path.

Review Questions

1. Explain what you understand by the term international new ventures. What are the distinguishing features of INVs as described in this chapter?
2. What are the key elements of the theory of INVs? Briefly explain each of the four elements to support your answer.
3. What are the different forms of INVs identified in this chapter?
4. Explain what you understand by each of the following terms. Give one example of each to illustrate your answer.

    i.   International new market makers
    ii. Geographically-focused start-ups
    iii. Global start-ups

5. How are global start-ups different from other types of INV? Explain the distinguishing features of a global start-up. Give examples to illustrate your answer.
6. Is Uber Technologies Inc., the firm profiled in the opening case, a global start-up? Why / why not? Give reasons to explain your answer.
7. What is the role of founders in the rapid growth and expansion of global start-ups? Based on the opening case of Uber Technologies Inc., explain the contribution of the two co-founders to the rapid growth and success of the company.
8. What is the role of immigrants in the founding of global start-ups? Give examples to support your answer.

Case 12.1

Inverness Medical Innovations: Born Global

Born in Israel, Ron Zwanziger spent his childhood and youth in Cyprus after his family relocated there. He began boarding school in the UK at age 16 and subsequently attended Imperial College of Science and Technology in London. Upon graduating, Zwanziger teamed up with a UK entrepreneur who had designed a new wind turbine. Deciding that an MBA degree would help him bring the technology to market, he chose Harvard Business School (HBS) over MIT and started class. During his first few months at Harvard, instead of reading cases, he spent his time flying around the country trying to get funding for the wind-turbine venture, but failed. He learned that the large fuel companies were investing in alternative energy just as a politically correct cover; they were not really committed to energy.

The Founding of Genetics International (mid-1980s)

At the beginning of his second year at HBS, Zwanziger invited three of his classmates to start a venture in genetic engineering. He did not have a clue as to what genetic engineering was, however, he intended to revolutionize health care by taking major health diagnostic and monitoring functions out of the doctors' offices and clinical labs, and putting them into the hands of patients. He knew diseases existed everywhere and were not related just to the size of the economy.

After one of his friends opted out of the venture, the remaining three identified 13 problems that might conceivably be solved by genetic engineering. Their plan was to persuade scientists around the world to work on these problems, and grant Genetics International commercialization rights and share in the future profits of the solutions. They flew around the US and the UK and found scientists who, in exchange for options, would give them the rights to future developments in these areas. In the meantime, they used the names of the 13 labs to raise $120,000 in seed funding from a dozen section-mates at HBS, in exchange for approximately 10% of Genetics International.

In order to have some working capital, Zwanziger and team approached large pharmaceutical and medical device companies and sold contract research. They obtained three $600,000 contracts and paid each of the labs working on the project $150,000. Professor John Higgins led one of their contracted labs at the Cranfield Institute of Technology north of London. Higgins's lab had developed a unique electrochemical process that the team believed could be used to develop a revolutionary new blood-glucose monitor. The monitor would give diabetes patients, who put drops of blood on a proprietary, disposable strip, immediate indications of their blood-glucose levels. Genetics International would make and sell both the monitors and disposable strips. Zwanziger and his team dropped the other 12 projects to focus on this electrochemical testing project.

Zwanziger convinced Dave Scott, a bright scientist at Higgin's lab, to join his team. He hired another recruit, Jerry McAleer, from the outside. An HBS classmate, James

McCann, who was on the founding team since early on, moved back to the UK to manage the operation, which eventually included setting up a research facility.

MediSense: A New Name for Genetics International

In the early years, Zwanziger and his team had bruising battles with suppliers. They had many setbacks, but they learned a lot and aged in experience by 30 years. Genetics International set up a hardware design center in Boston to develop the electronic glucose monitor that would analyze the strips being designed in the UK, and Genetics International changed its name to MediSense.

MediSense was funded by commercial contracts and a large research grant from the British government. Zwanziger also succeeded in raising 'first serious capital' by selling, for $5 million, 20% of the company to the medical devices giant Baxter, which later also loaned MediSense $13 million. As part of the financing, MediSense granted Baxter worldwide distribution rights to its glucose-monitoring products. Subsequently, Zwanziger raised $20 million from European and American funds.

When MediSense launched its first product, its major competitor, Miles Laboratories, dropped the prices of its monitors by $100; MediSense could not match Miles's prices. Fortunately, it had been selling in Japan. The monitor price in Japan was $300, and the product was 'massively profitable'. A similar situation prevailed in Germany at the time. Profits from these two countries kept MediSense liquid.

Zwanziger lost McCann, the last remaining HBS section-mate, when he promoted Scott from a relatively low position in the R&D organization to manage the entire UK research operation. By then, MediSense's revenues had reached $30 million, and the company was rapidly gaining market share. As sales increased, Zwanziger received a proposal from Novo Nordisk to acquire them for $350 million. However, the board turned down the acquisition offer, and he was forced to quit.

The Founding of Selfcare Inc. (early 1990s)

Zwanziger founded his second venture, Selfcare Inc., after leaving MediSense. He immediately built a board of trusted directors. Selfcare's initial strategy was to exploit Zwanziger's extensive acquaintance with the international supply and distribution channels to generate cash quickly by buying, repackaging and selling home-care self-diagnostic tests made and developed by third parties. In parallel, Zwanziger searched for intellectual property, products and companies related to home health care and self-diagnostics that could be bought cheaply. Among his acquisitions was a company that was developing a blood-glucose monitor.

Zwanziger reunited with his old friends, Dave Scott and James McAleer, at Selfcare after Scott was fired from MediSense and McAleer left MediSense. The three partners, together with Higgins, set about developing a new blood-glucose monitor that could compete with MediSense's. Soon, they developed a prototype that consisted of a

(Continued)

glucose meter and disposable strips and began soliciting government agencies to fund a manufacturing plant. Ground was broken for Selfcare's plant in Inverness, Scotland, after the Scottish government proposed the best deal.

Zwanziger, meanwhile, concluded that Johnson & Johnson's (J&J's) Lifescan division would be the most relevant marketing partner for Selfcare's new product. He teamed up with six scientists and nine production people to design and develop a new glucose system and manufacturing process, including clinical trials for US FDA approval, in a short span of 120 days. It was a very ambitious goal, but one they succeeded in achieving as planned.

As always, Zwanziger showed tremendous audacity in partnering with J&J. Before Selfcare appeared on the scene, J&J Lifescan was the market leader in the US with its own blood-glucose system, but was coming under increasing pressure from new technologies. Zwanziger told them that they were losing market share and ran the risk of losing the entire market. He persuaded the CEO and other officers to come to the UK to see their prototype. The tone of Ron's pitch was interesting: he indicated that Selfcare was developing a new glucose system on its own, and they would allow J&J to purchase an option to distribute the product. He was selling an opportunity to J&J, not asking for J&J's financial and marketing support.

That audacity led to a deal with J&J even before they had a product. The J&J deal consisted of $21 million in financing, to be paid upon the company's reaching designated milestones. In return, J&J received worldwide marketing rights for Selfcare's proprietary monitor and strips. The signing of the agreement triggered the first $7 million payment from J&J.

Subsequently, Zwanziger and team filed for FDA approval, triggering the second milestone payment of $6.7 million. They soon went public on AMEX on the strength of their trading revenues and, in particular, their relationship with J&J, raising $10.4 million. The FDA cleared the monitor and strips for sale, triggering the third and final milestone payment of $7 million and, along with J&J, the company announced its worldwide distribution agreement, causing conversion of J&J's first two milestone payments (originally structured as loans) into equity and giving J&J approximately 10% ownership of Inverness Medical Technologies (IMT) (the new name for Selfcare).

From Inverness Medical Technologies to Inverness Medical Innovations (2001)

Zwanziger and Scott met with J&J's Lifescan division to discuss the possibility of a merger. Eight intense weeks of meetings and negotiations followed, culminating in the signing of a definitive split-off and merger agreement. Following the deal, IMT shareholders received approximately two-thirds of a share of J&J stock, and one-fifth of a share of Inverness stock, for each share of IMT stock they held prior to the split-off and merger.

As per the agreement, Inverness Medical Innovations was organized as a wholly owned new company that owned all of IMT's non-diabetes-related activities, assets and subsidiaries in the US, UK, Ireland, Israel, Belgium and other countries. These included Inverness Medical Canada Inc., a sales and distribution network for Inverness's women's health products; Inverness Medical Benelux BVBA, a similar organization in Europe; and Cambridge Diagnostics Ltd. in Ireland and Orgenics Ltd. in Israel, both of which had been acquired by IMT (for less than $20 million in the aggregate) for their strong diagnostic technologies in infectious diseases. The company offered a product line that included pregnancy self-testing, nutritional supplements and doctors' diagnostic kits for chlamydia.

On the day of its creation, Inverness Medical Innovations was already listed on the American Stock Exchange. It had first-half 2001 revenues of $24 million; net income of $1.5 million; and earnings before interest, taxes, depreciation and amortization of $4.5 million. The company had $40 million in cash and approximately 300 employees, with a market capitalization of $137 million.

Approximately 80% of its employees and management team, including Scott and McAleer, were situated outside of the US. Zwanziger knew selling consumer products and global manufacturing was critical to operate, and sourcing from the location with the lowest cost was imperative for setting up a successful business. He also knew that it was not important where people were located geographically – they could function perfectly well in a globally dispersed fashion.

To attract and retain the best people, they set up and built technology centers where the people were, where their homes and families were, and built the business around them. That way, people could keep their homes, keep their children in the same schools, let their spouses keep their jobs. They also avoided the expense of relocation. Thus, they located their meter design group in California, where the head of design was located. He happened to be Chinese and also helped them think about how to exploit low-cost manufacturing in China. Jerry and Zwanziger were in the UK, where their families and roots were.

As a company, Inverness Medical Innovations did not have a formal communication infrastructure determined by reports and protocols. They believed a core of a few dozen people could do anything as long as there was vision, understanding, commitment and trust. It did not matter where they were. Communication among team members was frequent, mostly one-to-one, and usually via telephone and email. Videoconferencing and teleconferencing were less commonly employed.

To be really successful, a company must be international in concept. Technology developments must be global, otherwise getting the best is not possible. Marketing, of course, has to be global. Only two weeks old, Inverness was 'born global', its executive team split between the UK and the US, and its people and operations spread throughout the world.

Source: Isenberg (2009)

Discussion Questions

1. What is unique about the product/service offering of Inverness Medical Innovations? To what extent is this unique offering responsible for the rapid growth of the venture?
2. What role did Ron Zwanziger play in the founding and growth of his ventures? Discuss the role of Zwanziger's human and social capital resources to explain your answer.
3. Among other factors, a global start-up is characterized by extensive coordination of value-added activities in different parts of the world. To what extent does Inverness Medical Innovations satisfy this criterion? Discuss.
4. Based on what you have learned in this chapter, is Inverness Medical Innovations a global start-up? Why / why not? Give reasons to justify your answer.

References

Alvarez, S., Carayannis, E.G., Dagnino, G.B. and Faraci, R. (2018) 'Introduction: Entrepreneurial ecosystems and the diffusion of startups', in *Entrepreneurial Ecosystems and the Diffusion of Startups*. Cheltenham: Edward Elgar Publishing. 1–10.

Autio, E., Sapienza, H.J. and Almeida, J.G. (2000) 'Effects of age at entry, knowledge intensity, and imitability on international growth', *Academy of Management Journal*, 43(5): 909–924. https://doi.org/10.5465/1556419

Barney, J.B. (1991) 'Firm resources and sustained competitive advantage', *Journal of Management*, 17(1): 99–120. https://doi.org/10.1177/014920639101700108

Bell, J., McNaughton, R., Young, S. and Crick, D. (2003) 'Towards an integrative model of small firm internationalisation', *Journal of International Entrepreneurship*, 1(4): 339–362. https://doi.org/10.1023/A:1025629424041

Chetty, S.K. and Wilson, H.I. (2003) 'Collaborating with competitors to acquire resources', *International Business Review*, 12(1): 61–81. https://doi.org/10.1016/S0969-5931(02)00088-4

Coviello, N.E. (2006) 'The network dynamics of international new ventures', *Journal of International Business Studies*, 37(5): 713–731. https://doi.org/10.1057/palgrave.jibs.8400219

Coviello, N.E. (2014) 'How to publish qualitative entrepreneurship research in top journals', in A. Fayolle and M. Wright (eds.), *How to Get Published in the Best Entrepreneurship Journals*. Cheltenham: Edward Elgar Publishing. https://doi.org/10.4337/9781782540625.00016

Coviello, N.E. and Munro, H.J. (1995) 'Growing the entrepreneurial firm', *European Journal of Marketing*, 29(7): 49–61. https://doi.org/10.1108/03090569510095008

Coviello, N.E. and Munro, H.J. (1997) 'Network relationships and the internationalisation process of small software firms', *International Business Review*, 6(4): 361–386. https://doi.org/10.1016/S0969-5931(97)00010-3

Crick, D. and Spence, M. (2005) 'The internationalisation of "high performing" UK high-tech SMEs: A study of planned and unplanned strategies', *International Business Review*, 14(2): 167–185. https://doi.org/10.1016/j.ibusrev.2004.04.007

Drechsler, I., Savov, A. and Schnabl, P. (2019) 'How monetary policy shaped the housing boom. No. w25649. National Bureau of Economic Research. Available at https://rodneywhitecenter.wharton.upenn.edu/wp-content/uploads/2019/12/18-19.Drechsler.pdf (last accessed 27 September 2022).

Henshall, A. (2017) 'The aggressive processes uber uses for global expansion'. *Process.st*, 21 April. Available at www.process.st/global-expansion (last accessed 27 September 2022).

Hoffman, A. (2016) 'Uber and the sharing economy: Global market expansion and reception'. *Havard Business Review*, 19 February. Available at https://hbr.org/product/uber-and-the-sharing-economy-global-market-expansion-and-reception/W04C79-PDF-ENG (last accessed 27 September 2022).

Isenberg, D. (2007) 'Government in search of cover: Private military companies in Iraq', in Chesterman, S. and Lehnardt, C. (ed.), *From Mercenaries to Market: The Rise and Regulation of Private Military Companies*, New York: Oxford University Press.

Isenberg, D. (2008) 'The global entrepreneur'. *Harvard Business Review*. Available at https://hbr.org/2008/12/the-global-entrepreneur (last accessed 27 September 2022).

Isenberg, D. (2009) 'Inverness medical innovations – born global (A)'. Case No. *9-806-177*. Boston, MA: Harvard Business Publishing.

Johanson, J. and Vahlne, J.-E. (1977) 'The internationalization process of the firm – a model of knowledge development and increasing foreign market commitments', *Journal of International Business Studies*, 8(1): 23–32. https://doi.org/10.1057/palgrave.jibs.8490676

Knight, G.A. and Cavusgil, S.T. (2004) 'Innovation, organizational capabilities, and the born global firm', *Journal of International Business Studies*, 35(2): 124–141. https://doi.org/10.1057/palgrave.jibs.8400071

Lundberg, H. and Rehnfors, A. (2018) 'Transnational entrepreneurship: Opportunity identification and venture creation', *Journal of International Entrepreneurship*, 16(2): 150–175. https://doi.org/10.1007/s10843-018-0228-5

Manangi, S. (2017) 'Uber's global expansion strategy – "think local to expand global" – will it work for startups?' 31 July. Available at www.linkedin.com/pulse/ubers-global-expansion-strategy-think-local-expand-work-manangi (last accessed 27 September 2022).

McDougall, P.P., Shane, S. and Oviatt, B.M. (1994) 'Explaining the formation of international new ventures: The limits of theories from international business research', *Journal of Business Venturing*, 9(6): 469–487. https://doi.org/10.1016/0883-9026(94)90017-5

McDougall, P.P., Oviatt, B.M. and Shrader, R.C. (2003) 'A comparison of international and domestic new ventures', *Journal of International Entrepreneurship*, 1(1): 59–82. https://doi.org/10.1023/A:1023246622972

McNaughton, R.B. (2001) 'Determinants of time-span to foreign market entry', *Journal of Euromarketing*, 9(2): 99–112. https://doi.org/10.1300/J037v09n02_06

McNaughton, R.B. (2003) 'The number of export markets that a firm serves: Process models versus the born-global phenomenon', *Journal of International Entrepreneurship*, 1(3): 297–311. https://doi.org/10.1023/A:1024114907150

Neidert, M. (2018) 'How 12 immigrant entrepreneurs have made America great'. *Medium*, 8 August. Available at https://medium.com/@michael.neidert/how-12-immigrant-entrepreneurs-have-made-america-great-ed178fe9837d (last accessed 27 September 2022).

Oviatt, B.M. and McDougall, P.P. (1994) 'Toward a theory of international new ventures', *Journal of International Business Studies*, 25(1): 45–64.

Oviatt, B.M. and McDougall, P.P. (2005) 'Defining international entrepreneurship and modeling the speed of internationalization', *Entrepreneurship Theory & Practice*, 29(5): 537–553.

Pullen, J.P. (2014) 'Everything you need to know about uber'. *Time*, 4 November. Available at http://time.com/3556741/uber (last accessed 27 September 2022).

Seth, S. (2019) 'Meet Garrett camp, uber founder and crypto inventor', *Investopedia*, 25 June. Available at www.investopedia.com/tech/garrett-camp-uber-founder-crypto-inventor (last accessed 27 September 2022).

Sharma, D.D. and Blomstermo, A. (2003) 'The internationalization process of born globals: A network view', *International Business Review*, 12(6): 739–753. https://doi.org/10.1016/j.ibusrev.2003.05.002

Williamson, O.E. (1991) 'Comparative economic organization: The analysis of discrete structural alternatives', *Administrative Science Quarterly*, 36(2): 269–296.

Yli-Renko, H., Autio, E. and Tontti, V. (2002) 'Social capital, knowledge, and the international growth of technology-based new firms', *International Business Review*, 11(3): 279 304. https://doi.org/10.1016/S0969-5931(01)00061-0

Zaheer, S. (1995) 'Overcoming the liability of foreignness', *Academy of Management Journal*, 38(2): 341–363. https://doi.org/10.5465/256683

Zolin, R. and Schlosser, F. (2013) 'Characteristics of immigrant entrepreneurs and their involvement in international new ventures', *Thunderbird International Business Review*, 55(3): 271–284. https://doi.org/10.1002/tie.21543

13
DIGITIZATION, GLOBALIZATION, TRADE AND ENTREPRENEURSHIP: THE CURRENCY OF THE 21ST CENTURY

Learning Outcomes

After studying this chapter, you should be able to:

- **LO1**: Appreciate critically the trajectory of digitization in global trade and entrepreneurship and the connection between the two
- **LO2**: Identify the key technologies that are driving digitization and their importance for global entrepreneurship
- **LO3**: Understand critically the new combinations occurring among small and larger firms as a consequence of digitization and their potential impact on business model innovations
- **LO4**: Distinguish critically the scope of digital entrepreneurship and its implications for different units of analysis
- **LO5**: Understand critically how entrepreneurial firms could reset their strategies and functions to operate innovatively in emerging ecosystems

Introduction

This chapter is based in the 'here and now'. Consequently, not everything that is discussed here has evolved to offer a concrete base for post-hoc assessment and evaluation. Digitization and all its contents are in the process of engendering prospects for different applications of goods, services, processes, and alternative forms of interactions between individuals, firms, institutions and governments. Much of what is being made crosses borders effortlessly. Much of what crosses borders in a digital world is intangible. Much of what crosses borders in a digital world is insubstantial, namely intangible data. In doing so the digital goods and services throw up opportunities for new ways of opportunity recognition closely linked to trade. Successful innovation and entrepreneurship in any country has generally been associated with the ability to export and function effectively in the competitive global trading system. That has followed a linear route from growth at home to subsequent internationalization. Competition still prevails but digitization creates non-linear patterns of cooperative interaction for production and trade among multiple user groups and individuals that were never contemplated before with other technologies.

In the previous century cross-border trade in goods and services was led mainly by multinationals. They created large supply and value chains which connected different regions across the world. That large firm hegemony over international trade has 'flattened' out in the new millennium (Freidman, 2000, 2006) with the emergence of new technologies outside any single geographical domain, nimble born globals and small and medium-sized enterprises (SMEs) with high impact, as we touched on in Chapter 11 on Globalization. To recap, globalization has moved on from the increasing integration of input, factor and final product markets mainly at the behest of multinational enterprises and cross-national value-chain networks to a digital frontier where digital technology is integrated into all facets of production, sales, marketing and increasingly new forms of data-driven business creation, together with socialization and personal entertainment.

Much of the early period of modern globalization, the 30 years overlapping the end of the 20th and the first two decades of the 21st century, saw changes in the global economic order accompanied or enabled by key political landmarks such as the fall of the Berlin Wall, suggesting a marked decline of Communism, and the shift of power from the last remnants of colonial fiefdom to Chinese control in Hong Kong. These and many other dramatic political movements from uprisings to wars, often aided and abetted by digital technologies, have created a hiatus in the global political and economic landscapes. That hiatus is characterized by a considerable amount of uncertainty and noise, leading almost simultaneously to a retrenchment in global economic activity on the one hand and decentralization of some of the structures of such activities, as we can find in the world of finance, with the advent of 'fintech' and blockchain technologies.

More recently, and especially with the COVID-19 pandemic and the rise of populist politics across countries around the world, there have been calls for either a cancellation or a reversal of globalization, as countries have sought to focus on its discontents by restructuring trading relationships accompanied by ideas of 'bringing back' production facilities from offshore locations. The USA led the charge during the Trump era with a particular focus on withdrawals from China. While the UK Brexit vote has echoes of withdrawal from key networks such as the European Union, which are instrumental in negotiating the best collective deals in the global marketplace, Brexit proponents have argued that it has released the country from EU trading and business constraints to pursue more innovative trade deals globally. The rallying cry of 'Take Back Control' among Brexit supporters has an anomalous relationship with the realities of doing business in the world.

The question is whether globalization has really reversed. According to Lund et al. (2016), globalization has not really reversed but has gone digital. When we look at cross-border data flows, which only registered in terms of global trade accountability at the beginning of the 21st century, we find that it has grown by a factor of 45 since 2005. Projections suggest that the cross-border bandwidth is likely to increase over time as flows of information, searches, communication, video, transactions and intracompany traffic continue to surge. We note two complementary dimensions of the digital globalization process:

1. First, we have the phenomenon of transmission of valuable streams of data and information and ideas.
2. Second, these data flows are facilitating the movement of goods, services, finance and people in a more enhanced way than before.

Almost every type of cross-border transaction now has a digital component. The world is perhaps more connected than ever, with a significant digital twist to the nature and scope of the connections that firms, regions and countries make (MGI, 2016), with intangibles such as data and information taking center stage alongside tangible goods and services. In its wake, entrepreneurial opportunities for business, in terms of both the processing of goods and services for global consumption, and the creation of new digital products and services, have unleashed a scramble for innovative outcomes in different economies around the world.

But then the Ukraine crisis happened and suddenly the imposition of sanctions on Russia and the reaction by the latter to freeze shipments of grain has turned everything that we know about global trade and entrepreneurial outcomes on its head. Whether or not this major setback has upturned all developments flowing from digitization, however, is a different question. But first, we need to obtain a clear appreciation and a critique of the digitization process enabling global entrepreneurship today.

Structure of the Chapter

In this chapter we examine the way in which digital and related technologies are transforming the global dimensions of business engagement today, with trade as a background to the development of international entrepreneurship and innovation. In the first part we describe the digital landscape for global business and trade activity. This is followed in Part Two with an overview of some of the important digital technologies and how they are driving changes in enterprise creation, innovation and global trade. In Part Three we stop briefly to consider the implications for digitization and entrepreneurship in services. We move to Part Four where we explore how digitization is energizing existing and promoting new stakeholders of enterprise creation, globally. In Part Five we focus attention on how entrepreneurial firms can develop new strategies and models for operating in a global and digitized world. Finally, in Part Six we speculate (with the help of empirics) on the future of the digitized global economy and the prospects for entrepreneurship and innovation, before concluding the chapter.

Part One: The Digital Landscape for Global Trade and Enterprise

In the second decade of the 21st century the quantum of global flows of goods, services, money, people and data is said to have contributed approximately 10% of world GDP. A whacking $7.8 trillion was added in 2014 alone. Around 36% (or $2.8 trillion) of this value is attributable to data flows (UNCTAD, 2022). This distinctive element of global business activity is in itself a marker for new entrepreneurial activity across borders based simply on data creation, retrieval, interpretation, visualization and storage services with a plethora of technologies from cloud to artificial intelligence (AI) and augmented and virtual reality supporting the data infrastructure. The impact of data on global trade rather than physical goods, is, therefore of considerable importance to various stakeholders involved in global trade (Lund et al., 2016).

Digital Trade

By digital trade we refer to digitally enabled transactions of trade in goods and services that can be delivered either digitally or physically (OECD, n.d.). These transactions have been made possible because of the involvement of firms, governments and users or consumers. This involvement takes different forms from that in traditional trade. Governments are responsible for ensuring an effective digital infrastructure working closely with larger telecommunications and digital technology firms, but firms and users often swap roles as is the case in the platform technology ecosystem which we shall discuss later. But note that because goods and services can be delivered digitally or physically, not all digital trade is digitally delivered even though all types of digital trade are made possible by digital technologies. Online purchase of consumer items such as clothes or books or the booking of hotel accommodation is a good example of an exchange of goods and services which is *digitally enabled but delivered physically.*

Central to an understanding of digital trade is the importance of data and its movement in trade flows. For some time now data has become integral to the production process, and with new developments in machine learning and cyber-physical forms of production where machines work as co-producers with humans, data inputs have become critical to the production process and its outcomes. But data is not only a means of production. Data is also an asset. It can be traded and used as a means through which global value chains are organized and services are delivered. Physical trade is also facilitated by data exchange. With the advent of critical new technologies such as cloud computing, the Internet of Things (IoT) and additive manufacturing, data is very much at the heart of new and fast-growing service supply models. We could argue that with so much change occurring in how we trade today, it is effectively leading to a new form of mobilization of resources (mainly data but not exclusively so), and the creation of new channels of production, storage, distribution and sales of goods and services. We could argue, further, by stating that the trade ecosystem, and not just individual firms, is demonstrating a high level of entrepreneurial capability.

Changes and Innovations in Trade Due to Digitization

Digitization is a relatively easy concept to understand. It is the process of converting information into a digital format, or what we refer to as bits and bytes. When we refer to a 'digital version' of goods and services we are explaining how an object, image, sound, document or signal (usually an analog signal) is generated through a series of ones and zeroes and can be exchanged automatically machine-to-machine without manual intervention. Digitization aims to create the favorable conditions for 'digital transformation', a catch-all term for describing the implementation of new technologies and processes to improve business operations through the arrangements of bits and bytes.

Digitization has made possible several changes to how we do trade in the world today, and as a consequence created several prospects for new enterprise creation:

1. First, digitization increases the volume (scale), reach (scope) and timing (speed) of trade.
2. Second, it allows firms to bring new products and services to a larger number of digitally connected customers across the globe.
3. Third, it allows firms, especially entrepreneurial small ones, to use new and innovative digital tools to overcome barriers to growth, by facilitating payments,

making collaboration possible, helping to avoid investment in fixed assets through the use of cloud-based services, and even using new and alternative funding mechanisms such as crowdfunding to raise necessary and sometimes smaller amounts of investment as appropriate.

Not all digital

Overall, UNCTAD (2022) global trade grew to $28.5 trillion in 2021, an increase of 25% on 2020 and 13% higher than 2019 (UNCTAD, 2022). But not all of this growth was digital! UNCTAD's Global Trade Report (2022) shows that in the fourth quarter 2021, the volume and value of imports and exports for all major trading economies increased significantly, demonstrating a major turnaround from the pre-pandemic levels in 2019. Interestingly, it was the developing economies which were the key players in this resurgence in the trade of goods. This development is not new. South–South trade (broadly, trade between developing and emerging countries) outperformed both world trade and South–North trade, with trade in goods amounting to about $5 trillion in 2013, or approximately a quarter of world goods trade. If we take the financial crisis of 2008 and the COVID-19 pandemic surfacing 12 years later, we find that it is essentially South–South trade which has helped to revive the global economy after both crises. While exports of the developing economies grew by 30%, those of the richer nations was half of that at 15% over the same period in 2020. Two features of such growth stand out: first, commodity-exporting enjoyed the highest rates of growth because of a surge in commodity prices following the gradual slowing down of the COVID-19 pandemic, and second, the growth in trade between developing countries or South–South trade registered a 32% year-on-year increase which was well above the global average (UNCTAD, 2022). We are witnessing a geo-spatial ordering of trade which reflects in part the new landscapes of innovation and entrepreneurship discussed in Chapter 11.

We do not know whether the increase in the share of overall global trade among countries of the South can be directly related to the growth in capacity and capabilities for innovation and entrepreneurship. But we can see a marked difference in the way trade is done between countries and where opportunities for underpinning entrepreneurial activity lie.

But let us return to things digital and explore the underpinning technologies and emerging structures of digitization that allow global trade activity to be underscored by digitization.

Part Two: Digital Technologies and Structures

In 1976, the eminent Harvard sociologist Daniel Bell predicted the impending arrival of the Information Age, well before the advent of the PC or the internet. This age was referred to as the fourth industrial revolution (or Industry 4.0) leading to major structural changes in organizations and in the wider economy in which they operate. Four decades after Bell's forecast, and with the continued doubling of transistors of Moore's law, the new age ushered in the creation of a $2 trillion information technology industry (and growing) based on the technological advances of minicomputers, relational databases and the Web. Now the internet, the smartphone, the cloud and additive manufacturing, among others, follow three industrial revolution curves that have yielded an extraordinary mass of technologies, and with that the possibility of disruptive and significant changes to our lives.

There are about ten technological components of the new technology infrastructure of digitization; namely, autonomous robots, simulation, system integration, the IoT, cybersecurity, cloud computing, additive manufacturing, virtual reality, augmented reality and big data. These components power the new digital infrastructure with their variegated impact on different industries and on global entrepreneurial activity. Much of the focus of attention of different governments is on this ICT-oriented economic strategy and on actively competing or cooperating with their counterparts in other countries.

Let us look at just a few of the more well-known, overarching technologies such as AI and technology structures such as online platforms that are permeating almost all forms of business creation, growth and trade within and across borders.

Artificial Intelligence

AI drives many of the technological components, which together with machine learning, involves computers crunching large quantities of data to find patterns and make predictions without being explicitly programmed to do so. AI enables the preparation of large amounts of data, thousands of layers deep with billions of parameters, intensive monitoring of sophisticated algorithms, lots of customization, and massive computing power. You can imagine extremely large groups of statisticians with unlimited time and resources, delivering data-based solutions more cheaply and efficiently. The likelihood of the use of AI in this way, leading to a dramatic drop in the cost of making predictions, concentrates the minds of both the researcher and the innovator. In some respects, AI could be compared to electricity in a previous technology era which made lighting more affordable.

At what is referred to as the 'edge' computing level, AI provides for the direct ability to process information by smartphones, wearable devices and cars instead of communicating with a central cloud or server. Large firms such as Qualcomm, Apple and NVIDIA are working with start-ups to build chips for 'edge' services. Apple released the A11 Chip for iPhones, which is capable of machine learning tasks at up to 600 billion operations per second. Similar developments include Qualcomm's $100m AI fund for on device AI; Intel's Myriad X and NCS2 (Neural Compute Stick); and NVIDIA's Jetson AGX Xavier.

The global AI market size was valued at $93.5 billion in 2021. Thanks to continuous research by both corporates and governments, the trend is towards a growing adoption of AI technologies across industries as diverse as automotive, health care, retail, finance and manufacturing. The projected rate of expansion is at a compound annual growth rate (CAGR) of 38.1% from 2022 to 2030 (Grand View Research, 2021). The largest proportion of revenues comes from AI for the enterprise applications market. AI's radical push helps to leverage significant investment in R&D, with the big names such as Amazon, Google, Apple, Facebook, IBM and Microsoft aiming to make AI more accessible for enterprise use-cases. For many companies, especially those that are service focused, AI technology offers the opportunity to provide a more nuanced and better customer experience. These investments often take the form of swift acquisitions of smaller firms that could be located at places different from that of the purchaser. In March 2020, the global US food brand McDonald's, for example, made a novel and its most largest investment of $300 million to acquire the AI start-up Tel Aviv to provide a personalized customer experience using AI. These investments cut across sectoral interests, while the key AI technology players can be found in a variety of different countries. Grand View Research's firm coverage included a mix of known and unknown names such as: Advanced Micro Devices; AiCure; Arm Limited; Atomwise, Inc.; Ayasdi AI LLC; Baidu, Inc.; Clarifai, Inc; Cyrcadia Health; Enlitic, Inc.; Google LLC; H2O.ai.; HyperVerge, Inc.; International Business Machines Corporation; IBM Watson Health; Intel Corporation; Iris.ai AS.; Lifegraph; Microsoft; NVIDIA Corporation; Sensely, Inc.; and Zebra Medical Vision, Inc.

If the global market for AI is on a roll, and if we have a combination of small, large and cross-sectoral firms, all involved in its entrepreneurial evolution, then it might be interesting to see whether there is a global geographical presence of AI.

Private consulting and market research organizations suggest that only six nations are leading the charge on AI. The Asia Pacific region is expected to be the fastest growing region in AI over the next decade. The People's Republic of China has been at the forefront of AI with high ambitions for technology leadership. It is already regarded as a world leader in AI Research with its scholars publishing more research papers on deep learning than any other country in the past few years. State Council has identified its goal to become a $150 billion AI global leader by the year 2030, using the phenomenal supply of data generated by its internet-using population of around 750 million people. The United States could be regarded as having an equally favorable climate for AI. Driving the race here is the long established venture capital oriented tech culture in various parts of the country. Approximately $10 billion in venture capital has been directed towards AI in recent times, but this largesse has to be contrasted with funding reductions for AI, increased education costs and restrictive immigration policies for international R&D professionals. Unlike China, the US is dependent on both immigrant researchers and entrepreneurs for its technology-driven growth (see Chapter 7). Overall, however, North America was the largest region in the AI market in 2019 (Lynch, 2019; Pandya, 2019).

In Europe the UK is the clear leader in AI with 121 AI firms. Recent estimates point to the UK's GDP growing 10% higher as a result of AI by 2030, which translates as a monetary increase equivalent to approximately $266 billion. Given the downward pressures on the UK economy caused by other factors such as Brexit it is not surprising to see the UK government taking an active interest in promoting AI. Back in November 2017, it announced the budgeting of $78 million to fund research into robotics projects and AI. At another level, Norway, a minnow in the European scene, is moving away from its oil-drilling and fishing image of the past by creating in 2017 an $11 million fund and accelerator program for the development of a technological hub. The industrial powerhouse of Europe, Germany now looks at Industry 4.0 and AI to establish a fresh cyber-physical identity merging its tradition of technical efficiency with technical innovations. The 'Cyber Valley' near Tübingen and Stuttgart was created in 2016 as a collaboration among universities, major private firms and a leading research organization. Berlin has become Europe's leading hub for AI talent, and the country is well-set to become a leader in robotics, autonomous vehicles and quantum computing. The Swedes appear to be accommodating AI and robots into their economic and social lives with both corporations and trade unions viewing AI positively as a game changer for developing new skills (Lynch, 2019).

This is important for four critical reasons:

1. The extent to which AI builds on what we know about new technology and innovation spurring on different economic territories to claim advances in the wider ecosystem with significant ramifications across cyberspace, geospace and/or space (CGS).
2. The emergence of artificial intelligence (AI) as a significant technology disrupter undermining governance, management and growth models of enterprises and countries, and the way in which AI is breaking concepts and policy boundaries defined by human decision makers.
3. How AI is blurring the dividing lines between human intelligence and machine intelligence, and between what is real and fake in terms of outputs and outcomes.
4. The shift in the power dynamics from a select few nations of the 'North' and away from humans to, entirely in some cases, algorithms. This shift calls into question the criteria upon which geopolitics, trade, innovative solutions to global issues and entrepreneurial activities are framed (Pandya, 2019).

Pandya argues that traditionally, a country's technological trajectory (and, therefore, its capacity for innovation and entrepreneurship) has been determined by a Ricardian notion of geography and existing infrastructure. The rapid growth of digital infrastructure, digital data and the rapidly evolving artificial intelligence infrastructure is, however, forcing us to re-evaluate that spatial or geographical advantage in determining a nation's trajectory of innovative and entrepreneurial growth. Only a few countries – Australia, Canada, China, Denmark, Finland, France, Germany, India, Italy, Japan, Kenya, Malaysia, Mexico, New Zealand; and countries in the Nordic-Baltic Region such as Estonia, Latvia and Lithuania, Poland, Russia, Singapore, South Korea, Sweden, Taiwan, Tunisia, the UAE, UK and US have begun to develop policies for AI development. It is possible that lack of financial and human capital, coupled with inadequate infrastructure, education systems and leadership, are thwarting other nations.

Online Platforms

As stated earlier, digitization is having a direct impact on how goods are traded. Presently, only a tiny fraction of companies participate in trade with foreign countries. In 2014, the total value of US exports was $1,620.5 billion. Of that total, about 90% or $1,447.3 billion of those exports were managed by a group of firms referred to as 'identified exporters', firms to which the Census Bureau was able to match specific export transactions. There were 305,213 identified exporters in 2014 out of the roughly 7 million firms in the USA. That number went down to 179,000 in 2017 and 178,000 in 2018. Statistics for other countries are similar. The reason why only a tiny percentage of firms engage in international trade is that it requires a considerable effort to deal with authorities in the export market, conform to regulations, build a retail network, etc.

Online retail platforms such as Amazon or Alibaba have an important effect on trade. Their emergence alleviates some of these thresholds to trade, since the need to build up their own retail network abroad, hire staff etc. no longer exists – it is sufficient to create an account and trade through the platform. This implies that trade through these platforms – and therefore trade flows in general – are likely to increase, as is the number of firms engaging in international trade and the number of productions available to consumers. Increased competition and transparency is also going to result in lower prices which will benefit the consumers. The precondition for successful participation in online retail platforms is – again – a suitable physical and digital infrastructure. Typically, online platforms make it possible to sell smaller packages across international borders more frequently. This is a good example of how digitization technology induces innovation and, in its wake, upends the way trade is done, bringing in different players in the trading game, necessitating, as appropriate, policy changes by governments. For example, the physical management of parcel trade now demands separate arrangements for handling smaller parcels. At the same time, there are implications for risk management when we take into consideration possible counterfeit goods or the maintenance of biosecurity standards. Governments have to deal with the headache of revenue collection from taxes and tariffs which may need distinctive arrangements for different forms of packaging, weightage and content. Readers will not be surprised to know how issues such as these are plaguing the smooth implementation of the UK government's Brexit strategy, the problems relating to which are compounded by governance issues and political and ideological differences between the EU and the UK governments. With the emergence of the new frontier of digitization, old trade issues may have new consequences – such as the impact of cumbersome border procedures on parcel trade, or restrictions on newly tradable services. New considerations for trade policy are also being taken on board by government agencies such as variegated regulations among nations in relation to data flows. Further understanding of the nature and extent of these changes is needed to help policy makers create an environment that nurtures innovation and promotes digital trade in goods and services.

We might consider the wealth of possibilities being created by platform firms and their technologies to be central to a kind of disruptive change in the global entrepreneurship development process. The disruptive change affects firms and their networks, the direction of ownership of these firms and the constant resetting of boundaries and thresholds of international activity. The mini case study that follows throws some sharper light on this process of disruptive change

THE PLATFORM COMMUNITY METAMORPHOSIS

Introduction: The Facebook Model

The community of Meta (Facebook) users is larger than the population of China. Back in 2016, the McKinsey Global Institute (MGI, 2016) estimated that 914 million people had at least one international connection on social media. Over 360 million take part in cross-border e-commerce activities which includes eBay and numerous other platforms, both global and local. This represents 12% of the global trade in goods.

Consider a more up-to-date statistic. By the fourth quarter of 2021 Facebook had approximately 2.91 billion monthly active users, making Facebook the highest ranked online social network worldwide. The 2 billion mark was exceeded by the second quarter of 2017, taking just over 13 years to reach this milestone. Compare that with Instagram's timeline for the same target and we are looking at 11.2 years, while Google's YouTube took a shade over 14 years to achieve this landmark. These figures represent Facebook's global reach with their leading audience base in India, with almost 350 million users, as of October 2021. Its country of origin, the USA, has a little over half the number with approximately 193 million users, while nation states with significant numbers of users flying the Facebook flag include Indonesia and Brazil, with well over 100 million users in both countries.

Facebook has now metamorphosed, and its recently renamed parent company is appropriately called Meta. Meta had a grand total of 3.59 billion core product users by the final quarter of 2021. Meta is a genuine digital platform conglomerate, an aggregation of the most popular and technologically advanced social media platforms. Table 13.1 below shows the Facebook's trajectory of aggregation and method.

(Continued)

Table 13.1 Social media aggregation – the way Facebook grew

Social Media Firm	Type of Digital Service	Cost of Acquisition	Date of Acquisition
Beluga	Messaging	Undisclosed	March 2011
Instagram	Photo and video sharing app	$1.0 billion	April 2012
Onavo	Mobile web analytics	$100–200 million (estimated)	October 2013
WhatsApp	Mobile messenger	$19.0 billion	February 2014
Occulus	Virtual reality technology	$2.0 billion	March 2014

Source: adapted from Investopaedia (2021) cited in Mitra (2022)

This aggregation is no mean achievement for five Harvard students, Mark Zuckerberg, Eduardo Saverin, Andrew McCollum, Dustin Moskovitz and Chris Hughes, who created Facebook in 2004, taking the name from the face book directories that are generally handed out to students of US universities. The speed of acquisition is one thing. The range of technologies amassed by one player is staggering, not just because of the spread but the capacity enhancement for Facebook to traverse commerce, entertainment, web and related technology spaces, all at the same time, a procedural prelude to the creation of the 'Metaverse'. Add to that the earlier observation of Facebook's global reach.

The Large and Small Firm Mix in an Open, Digital Environment

These platforms are open, creating an efficient and a large-scale base of customers. With half the world's traded services having gone digital, the players in this new landscape are a mix of large firm players actively competing and cooperating with nimble start-ups and small and medium-sized enterprises around the world (Lund et al., 2016). This apparent easy flow of interactions is possible because digital technologies enable both types of firms to globalize in a leaner and less capital-intensive way. Entering and operating in global markets take the form of virtual teams of agile, small and larger firms collaborating remotely and expanding into new markets. Flexibility allows for the easier hiring of specialized talent following demand trends wherever they can be found. Different services by different sized firms complement each other. For example, in the case of people management issues, self-service digital platforms and intranets provide consistency on overarching issues; local regional managers control decisions such as hiring. Global hubs can be formed for typical 'backbone' operations together with smaller sales and marketing teams around the world.

Source: adapted from Mitra (2022)

The Role of 3D Printing

One of the most disruptive effects on international trade could be attributed to the growing use of 3D printing. 3D printing, first developed in the 1980s, is a process in which material is layered up in an automated process until a 3D structure emerges. These printers are now capable of working with a range of materials from plastic, to concrete and even metal. We could imagine a world of both producers and consumers working with multiple materials to download printing plans and print their products on their own printers at either the office/factory or at home. With the growing interest in decentralized patterns of work and the home as the work-base, we could foresee the emergence of different scenarios for innovation and entrepreneurial outcomes.

3D printing could play a significant role for goods produced in batch numbers of small amounts and for goods which require a high level of customization. While it may not be able to compete in terms of costs with the economies of scale generated by standardized production, they might prove to be more efficient than other means of production. Consider the prospect of 3D printing playing a key role in the production of spare parts or in remote places where delivery could take too long. Leaving aside raw materials and some goods which may not be printable, trade might be dealt a heavy blow. There would hardly be the need for any trade. However, it is perhaps too early to evaluate (even ex-ante) any negative effect on the volume of trade flows.

It is outside the scope of this chapter to delve deep into the world of 3D printing or indeed other related digital technologies such as Artificial Intelligence or Augmented Reality. Our purpose is to identify some of the key technologies that are upending industries and generating new types of firms. Of equal importance is the way these technologies are creating new canvasses for entrepreneurial activity. In line with most new digital technologies these canvasses are global. They are composed of significantly large amounts of data, the effective use of which is dependent on sophisticated levels of ICT-related technical expertise. Since the value of their use cuts across sectoral lines, the need for cooperative engagement of analogue-era businesses (from manufacturing to services) with high-end technology firms is critical to the application of the technologies, the development of new products and services, and the creation of networked-based firms as opposed to traditional hierarchies. Given the newness of these technologies and their uses, there is an increasing need to consider whether traditional protocols and standards associated with goods, services and technologies can inform government policy making. For example, while the Chinese government exercises strict controls of ethical and social uses of social media and other digital technologies, the US has a more open approach to their uses with potentially fragile outcomes for different user groups.

These monumental changes in trading activity and global production processes, often buffeted by political winds of unrest, might suggest a change in the process and institutional structures of entrepreneurship and innovation. Could it be that we have entered an interregnum which could lead to a paradigm shift in what we know about global entrepreneurship and, crucially, how it is done?

Part Three: What about Services?

It has been argued in conventional terms that most services are globalization-proof. Since services typically require geographic proximity, it is difficult to take advantage of cheaper factor prices elsewhere. While going to the barbers in Mexico City is certainly cheaper than in London, it is unlikely that anyone would fly to Mexico just to find a Mexican barber or have the barber visit the person in London. This may be true for haircuts, but digitization enables other types of services to be performed or delivered at locations large geographic distances from where they are commissioned. Several decades ago, financial firms in the USA and in Europe began to outsource their accounting activities to Indian subcontractors.

New technologies and alternative business models are impacting on how services are produced and supplied, impugning the traditional distinctions between the different modes of delivery of goods and services. ICT-enabled services now provide the critical network infrastructure underpinning the digitization of other types of services. New technologies have also facilitated the rise of digitally enabled services that are supported by a range of new services building on data-driven innovative solutions such as cloud computing. In some situations, we see the emergence of new combinations of goods and services. Take the example of a smart fridge with a sensor built into it to provide continual data relating to the goods inside the fridge, and the maintenance of the fridge. Two markets are in operation at the same time, one for the good, for example the fridge and the food products used in the fridge, and the other for the embedded data service. Food is ordered digitally but delivered or collected physically. But a sensor in the refrigerator can collect information on the goods and the level of stock being held by the consumer to help alert the supermarket to obtain early information on projected supplies. Or note how 3D printing enables a small firm to provide a cross-border design service by sending a copy of a design of a piece of equipment which is then turned into a good once the equipment is manufactured. In the past the design service would be integrated with the production and be valued as part of the same item.

We should distinguish between digitally tradable services – which includes most business services – and services that are not digitally tradable. Not much is going to change in the service provision of haircuts, unless you imagine automation creating a new army of robo-barbers. However, some digitally tradable services – accounting, R&D, health services – have already come under stronger competition from different regions with a good technological capability, because it is technically possible to outsource them to low-cost countries. This has begun to provide for an important source of economic growth for developing and emerging economies, provided they have strong digital infrastructure and human capital. But strong legal protections of some services, as well as other barriers to services trade, can be found in the provision of legal services which remain protected by enshrined requirements – both against outsourcing and automation – in many countries. There could be special entry requirements for the legal profession and personal liability that may be unlikely to be conferred to machines. While many legal services could in fact be automated or outsourced, restrictions could take the form of these services being performed by a human being in a given country to protect legal professionals there.

Implications for Global Trade

Interconnectedness, the speed of transactions, the equation of goods and services, the growing volume of trade, the reach of goods and services and just-in-time delivery methods in a digitized global world call for a reorientation of trade. This is not simply a matter of anticipated or incremental change. Reliability, security and confronting a new reality in trade needs innovative approaches to how trade is managed and governed, and how entrepreneurial both firms and governments need to be to implement a transformative agenda. Discussions and actions for the need to clarify, update or reformulate existing trade rules and commitments have been part of policy agendas for most governments. As we noted before, traditional trade rules and conventions have relied on identifying products as either goods or services, and which borders they cross. But, in the digital era, these distinctions may not always be clear cut. Since it is now possible for firms to apply flexible operation methods from different and distanced locations to bundle goods with services, in response to 24/7 demand cycles, there are inevitable questions about the application of specific rules to particular transactions (OECD, n.d.).

The pattern of global trade depends on the availability and price of production factors. Since automation and digitization are already changing the prices of the production factors involved, it is only natural that we see a change in global production patterns. While automation is capital-intensive, it reduces the impact of labor costs on the location of production. Digitization lowers information and communication costs and makes both the capital and the labor parts of production more efficient.

How are firms, especially the smaller or medium-sized entrepreneurial ones, responding to the challenge of AI and the related gamut of digital technologies?

Part Four: Digital Stakeholding – Entrepreneurial Firms and Individuals

The McKinsey Global Institute (MGI) (2016) offers a scenario in which SMEs worldwide are making use of what they describe as the 'plug-and-play' infrastructure of internet platforms to position themselves right in the front of the global customer base. Around two million third-party SMEs are hosted by Amazon alone, and eBay-based exporting by SMEs is higher than exporting done offline, not to mention PayPal's intermediary role for SMEs in facilitating cross-border transactions and payments! Small micro firms increasingly rely on crowd platforms such as Kickstarter, Indiego, Seeders and others to raise capital. Approximately 3.3 million people from all over the world made pledges in 2014 on these platforms.

When it comes to trade, we find that the ascendancy of the SMEs in the global marketplace is accompanied by a gradual drop in the share of exports by the larger multinational corporations (MNCs). For example, in the United States, the MNC share of exports dropped from 84% in 1977 to 50% in 2013. However, the SME picture is a mixed one. According to the OECD (n.d.), the growth of the share of exports by the smallest group of firms (that is less than 50 employees) is prevalent in only 10 out of the 16 countries that were studied. This is not necessarily a size-related issue because MGI's own survey of very early-stage high-tech start-ups across 19 countries (and firms) shows that even the smallest and youngest enterprises can have at least one cross-border activity (86%), have users or customers in other countries (two-thirds) or recruit skilled personnel from other countries.

The digital landscape is both highly competitive and unpredictable. Yet another innovative variation to the theme is the accelerator-type initiatives of firms such as Amazon, Alibaba and eBay which are directly supporting and empowering firms of any size across the globe to make, market and sell products in completely new markets. The unpredictability and high levels of competitiveness are also reflected in the way pricing pressures are mounting, product cycles are being shortened and global labor markets are being created. The collaborative process ensures that it is not so much the acquisition of physical assets but rather the access to them via a rich digital asset base that makes firms competitive. Digital technology offers both economies of scale and scope in international markets (Lund et al., 2016).

Outside governments, regions and firms, the digital landscape has empowered another community quite dramatically to play an active part in shaping the discourse and practice of digitization. This is the community of individuals worldwide.

Individuals

Social media and the internet have ushered in a new class of 'globalist', namely the individual who exchanges data across borders. MGI (2016) estimates that 914 million people around the world have at least one international connection on social media, and 361 million participate in cross-border e-commerce. The numbers suggest exponential growth in individual-level internationalization when we look at Facebook and other social platform users, especially in emerging economies.

There is a two-pronged outcome resulting from the facilitation of individual participation in international, entrepreneurial activity. First, there is the provision of a digital platform of users and producers exchanging roles as appropriate to both buy and sell goods in an expanding market, and second there is the possibility of a structural shift in the methods and modes of international entrepreneurship. On the one hand we have products, both old and new, going viral on an enormous scale, especially as the new digital customer and provider come together on these platforms. Adele's song 'Hello' picked up 50 million views on YouTube in its first 48 hours, and her album *25* achieved a record sale of 3.38 million copies in the United States in the very first week of its release, more than any other album in history (MGI, 2016). On the other hand, we have individuals finding new ways to share information, learn, collaborate with other individuals, businesses and social groups, acquiring new skills on the way and promoting themselves.

The incidence of the individual freelancer on the global stage is also part of the rise of the so-called 'sharing economy', in which digital platforms such as Facebook, LinkedIn and Upwork provide the basis of sharing information, goods, services and personal data.

To summarize, this new era of digitization is marked by a sharp rise in the flows of data from different corners of the world, which calls into question the hegemony of both large multinational companies and their homes in developed economies. While large multinational incumbent firms have the resources to continue to dominate this new landscape, the new era ushers in the presence of formidable players among niche SMEs, start-ups and individual consumers, user-producers and citizens. Out of all technology based start-ups, 80% are supposed to be 'born globals' with foreign customers, access to financing and suppliers drawn from the global marketplace from day one or very early in their life cycle. This quantum of global flows could lead to a tenfold increase in GDP (MGI, 2016). We might be witnessing here a new world order of how business and trade is done with firms, individuals, institutions and governments directly involved in both interactive innovation and in the determination of new agendas for production, individual choices regarding work and play and public governance systems.

Some Implications of the New World Order

It is possible to note a differentiated form of linkage between larger firms and smaller medium-sized counterparts. This is not simply a sub-contracting issue as would be the case in previous eras of mass manufacturing and globalization agendas marked by flows of goods and services only. The sources of data flowing globally are numerous and various and so are their uses. The technologies in use to generate the data – communication, automation and virtual fabrication, including machine learning and artificial intelligence – are also capable of development and use in varied production units, large, medium and small. Crucially, it also involves individuals and citizens who can be part of the community of makers globally (Mitra, 2017).

Arthur (2009) and McAfee and Brynjolfsson (2017) suggest that radical technological advances do not stem from linear improvements within a single subject or a specific domain of expertise, but generally from the combination or recombination of seemingly disparate inventions and disciplines. As Arthur (2009) has noted, the overall mix of technologies bootstraps itself, growing from the few to the many and from those that are simple to others that are complex.

These issues raise questions about the structure of firms. If individuals can make significant products, from clothes to food to furniture and music and films, thanks to 3D printing and various forms of digital fabrication, and also share the data emanating from these products and their use with fellow citizens, then that has potential ramifications for the structure of organized business entities, and how those entities work with each other and with individual, freelancing genius.

Part Five: Digital Era Globalization and Strategies for the Entrepreneurial Firm

Technological and structural shifts demand a different, entrepreneurial approach to management of tasks and the firm. This might entail either a reordering of the objectives set within the last decade or two or an imaginary leap into uncharted territory to find and combine a new set of intellectual, experiential, creative and integrative challenges, often involving a consideration of practices and norms across the globe. Managing this reset requires an entrepreneurial management mindset to develop new strategies with a defined, new, global purpose (Mitra, 2020).

The entrepreneurial manager has to contend then with a very different approach to running the internationally driven entrepreneurial firm. Table 13.2 shows the strategic shift in an approach to globalization in the digital era, explained in terms of 'flows', which probably explains the pattern of exchange, of goods, services, data, information, knowledge and people. This pattern of flows engenders a different calibration and understanding of how goods and services are developed in the 21st century than the older, binary language of the 20th century of exchange of imports and exports or goods and services.

Table 13.2 Managing global flows: Directions for the entrepreneurial manager

Global Flows	20th Century	21st Century
Goods and Data Flows	Tangible (of physical goods)	Intangible (a mix of physical goods but also, critically, data and information)
Space and the Geography of Flows	Between advanced economies in the main	Growing participation by emerging economies
Capital Flows (Economic and Social)	Capital and labor intensive	Knowledge intensive

Global Flows	20th Century	21st Century
Organizational Flows	Driven by multinationals	More pronounced but selective involvement of SMEs and individuals
Infrastructure for Flows	Transportation dependent	Greater importance of digital infrastructure alongside physical infrastructure
Content of Flows	Monetized transactions	Increases in exchange of free content and services
Ideas and Knowledge Flows	Slow diffusion across borders	Immediacy of global access to data and information
Innovation Flows	Transfer from advanced to emerging economies	Innovation in both/multiple directions
People Flows	Highly regulated and needs oriented	Paradox of managing high regulation vs. talent attraction and recruitment for creativity and technical capability

Source: adapted from MGI (2016)

The entrepreneurial manager's approach to digitization is not predicated on considering either the strategic issues discussed above or in looking at different opportunities for new products and services which are driven by data. A major new management and innovation frontier is that of business models innovation. As firms start working with other businesses (B2B), consumers and users (B2C) and facilitating interaction between consumers (C2C), they are obliged to explore different business models, often running with more than one business model at the same time for different stakeholder interests. Among some of the emergent business models are those based on:

1. The firm as a 'service'
2. The firm as a 'marketplace'
3. The firm as a 'platform'

Table 13.3 below explains the models and the benefit that can be derived from each of them.

Table 13.3 Emergent business models

Emergent Business Models	Model Explanation	Benefits
Firm as a Service	Rent; Subscribe; Gift Offer products or services on demand or as a subscription service model	Develop a long-term customer relationship and help deliver products in the hands of new customers (examples include: Coursera in education, ZipCar for car rentals)

(Continued)

Table 13.3   (Continued)

Emergent Business Models	Model Explanation	Benefits
Firm as a Marketplace	Resell; Co-Own; Exchange; Gift Creating a community around the firm enabling customers and other partners to resell or co-purchase products, exchange goods related to the brand, or even facilitate lending or gifting for no monetary exchange	Adding value to customer relationships (examples include: Airbnb and Etsy)
Firm as a Platform	Co-Ideate; Co-Build; Co-Fund; Co-Distribute; Co-Market; Co-Sell; Co-Revenue Share Enable customers to generate ideas, build products and new services as partners	Build connection with customers, stabilize that relationship by connecting customers with each other, improve the products and reduce costs (examples include Kickstarter; Yerdle; Flipkart)

Source: adapted from Market Revolution (2019)

All three models are sharply focused on the customer and in developing relationships that go well beyond customer relationship management (CRM), although the idea of a firm as a service is close to what we know about CRM. In recognizing the firm as a market we introduce notions of exchange and gifts beyond monetary considerations that generally fall outside the ambit of commercial firms. One of the reasons for this shift in the way one does business is because of the participatory involvement of the end-user/ customer who is no longer a passive recipient of goods (however vocal he/she might have been in articulating complaints or demanding better service delivery). We see a step change with the 'firm as a marketplace' model with customer involvement at a different level, which is augmented by a considerable degree by the 'firm as platform' model. In the latter model, customers and sellers are not limited to a binary exchange of goods and services. The platform can be used in multi-directional ways with customers connecting to other customers and exchanging information or gifts, and in some circumstances changing roles. If a company uses open-source methods to co-design a car under a commons license, then the vendor can enable the users to share the design with other vendors or customers for similar or different applications. At the heart of all this is data and its flows. What we note in the business model is also the need to undergo innovative change to make the best use of new, digitally-enabled and data-driven goods and services.

Should we dare to speculate on the future of new goods, services, firms, business models and economies? How else could we be entrepreneurial?

Part Six: The Prospective Patterns of Future Trade, Place and Global Entrepreneurial Activity

As we stated earlier there appears to be a shift in the process of industrialization from widespread production networks – or offshoring – to onshoring, suggesting a return of industrial production to the developed world. If technology can help with the automated production of goods then there is less of a need for using low labor costs as a justification for offshoring production. Part of this thinking is based on the notion that if most of the consumption of goods takes place in the developed world then factors such as the time to market and delivery to the customer become more important than labor costs in our automated world. What customers want is mass specialization, in the form of customized goods and services. So, all our Nike and Adidas trainers need to be customized for individual use, and if they cannot cater to that in enough numbers then Balance, Puma and new players in the trainers space could absorb the demand. Produced locally, firms can save both time and shipping costs. Note, however, bringing production back home entails the organization of both technology, especially digital technology supporting the automation process, and the more analogue development of physical space, in other words both the digital and the physical infrastructure. The developed world, especially in large countries such as the USA, has a distinct advantage in offering both solutions.

What happens to that larger physical mass, called the developing or emerging world? It is possible that emerging nations could gear production towards their domestic markets and cease to be the production centers of the world in the way China has been for over three decades. This shift is evident already in large and fairly well-established domestic markets such as China, while a country such as India which is trying to position itself as a global production center might find it too late to establish its economic credentials in the same way. It is possible, therefore, that if modern, specialized production moves back to the developed world, the developing nations will continue to offer large volumes of unspecialized goods from commodities to clothing.

Herein lies the economic and entrepreneurial rub. Do emerging nations have to be part of the international economic order simply as second tier economies serving the interests of developed nations and their consumers? Does the nature and scope of their transformation of their capacities through the proliferation of digital technologies need to be aligned to the demands of the developed world? The larger emerging countries such as China, India, South Africa, Nigeria and Brazil, for example, could focus attention on their increasingly sophisticated citizenry and large internal markets to produce goods and services for domestic consumption. Equally, there is no reason to believe that with advances in digitization capabilities in those countries, key modern industries that have high global purchase might not be more competitive in terms of production of both the underpinning technologies and the products or services. China is by far the exemplar country with their significant lead in key technology areas from lithium batteries to solar and wind energy, electric vehicles and social media. Korea's softer technology power through K-Pop, for example, sits alongside its substantial electronics industry production. As things stand today, Asia is on course to become the world's hub of innovation (production) and consumption (markets).

ASIA AS THE GLOBAL HUB OF PRODUCTION AND CONSUMPTION

Asia is by far the most populated continent in the world. This fact alone makes the region a natural hub of consumption, access to talent and extensive labor markets, and the combination of these two factors with technology makes it potentially a major player in the innovation space. When we look at population figures in depth, we find more data that supports such an argument. According to Worldometers (2022), the population of Asia, based on the latest estimates of the United Nations, is 4,720,237,664 as of July 3, 2022, or 59.76% of the total world population. The median age is 32 years.

The World Economic Forum (2019) estimates that by 2030, the region is expected to contribute roughly 60% of global growth. Asia Pacific will also be responsible for the overwhelming majority (90%) of the 2.4 billion new members of the middle class entering the global economy.

The bulk of that growth will come from the developing markets of China, India and throughout South-East Asia and it will give rise to a host of new decisions for businesses, governments and NGOs. The pressure will be on them to guide Asia's development in a way that is equitable and designed to solve a host of social and economic problems.

Size, demographics, age and space, all regarded as significant contributors to innovation and entrepreneurship, offer Asia a distinctive innovation-driven competitive advantage. Add to that the changing face of technology in Asia.

Technology Leadership

A 2019 roundtable discussion of the *Business Times of Singapore* – moderated by Genevieve Cua, its wealth editor, and involving leading stakeholders: Yash Patodia, partner and portfolio manager, Wellington Management; Fan Cheuk Wan, chief investment officer, Asia Private Banking and Wealth Management, HSBC; Julie Koo, managing director head of Citi Investment Management Sales, APAC Citi Private Bank – throws up some interesting data:

1. Asia has the highest number of small and medium-sized technology companies. These are not the behemoths of the US and Europe, but the nimbler, entrepreneurial firms, over 1,400 companies in Asia Pacific that are

below $5 billion in size. It is likely that these are not founded in the volatile but fertile ground of globally diversified technology funds.

2. As a global hub of technological innovation, the leaders – namely, China, Japan, Korea, Taiwan and Singapore – are accepted as world leaders in the development of artificial intelligence, big data, semiconductors, fintech, automation, health sciences and 5G technology.

3. The powerful and pivotal technology supply chain of Asia is supported by over 80% of global installed semiconductor manufacturing capacity. Fabless semiconductor companies of the US are almost exclusively reliant on Asian producers for the most advanced 7-nm-and-below chip production. Note that Asia's hegemonic position in the global technology supply chain is due in part to the size of its domestic market.

4. On the revenue side, around 60% of global semiconductor sales is accounted for in Asia, with China alone capturing over 30% of global semiconductor revenues. Since 2016, China has become the world's biggest buyer of semiconductors. The extent of dependency on Asia, and in particular China, is evinced in the fact that most of the 15 largest global semiconductor companies generate more sales from China than the US. The big firms of the West cannot ignore the large markets in China and Asia. It does not require much imagination to understand that Asia does, therefore, has a distinctive scale advantage for attracting technology investment and innovation.

5. The gradual expansion of data generation enabled by digital technologies is expected to provide the building blocks for faster networks, more data centers and new neural networks, replacing older central processing units. Unlike Europe and the US, the absence of too many legacy systems in Asia opens up possibilities for countries to jump the curve to emerge as leaders of innovation. In other words the combination of technology and the availability of technology ecosystems unburdened by historic constraints creates a climate conducive to the emergence of robust digitally driven industries.

6. The consumer market allows for the absorption of digital technologies with the acceleration in the use of smartphones. For many consumers in Asia this is the first time they have access to a computing device in their hands and pockets, with a greater dependence on online services bundling the usage of data and services for both work and pleasure. The consequence is the rapid emergence and scaling up of many new internet companies.

Other Soft, Secular Factors

As we have noted earlier, critical secular factors support technological innovation and entrepreneurship in Asia, from the decisive government policy support for enhancing digital transformation through to the continuing and sustained re-investment of corporate

(Continued)

cashflows into capital expenditure and R&D spending. These favorable framework conditions are buttressed by high-quality human capital. Fresh graduates in China in 2020 amounted to a record high of around eight million students, a number nearly double that of the total number of degrees earned at all levels of higher education in the United States (Statista, 2021). This growth in higher education is expected to break all records with over 9 million in 2021. Approximately 40% of these high achievers are science and engineering graduates. With many of them studying and researching in the US and in Europe, they form a solid global community of highly skilled and specialized labor forces fostering a strong competitive edge for Asia but equally a major contributor to the rest of the world. There is a circularity in this 'graduates phenomenon' in that Asian graduates are forming a major pool of talent sought after across the world, a completely new development in the world of global technological advantage. Understanding this transformation in the global innovation landscape helps researchers and policy makers to consider how best to devise work and policies that are not hamstrung by simplistic notions of specialization and competitive advantage. At another level, it also allows us to figure out how transnational entrepreneurs in the high-tech industries create new possibilities for entrepreneurial activity.

Political Tensions

We have alluded before to political interventions which could scramble and upset the trajectory of technological advancement and innovation. Nowhere is this more prominent than in the recent tensions between the USA and China. This may lead to first China looking for alternative sources of technology rather than relying on the US, and second to the setting up of two technology standards, something which has been reflected upon in the use of the dollar as the principal currency for trade. China will find alternative sources. The US is by far the leader in semiconductor chip design and fabrication equipment, a significant advantage in the emergent 5G world. This could hamper China's competitively advantageous push in areas such as high-end smartphones and its space exploration program. The ostensible rift may be impugned as we see other advances in modern computing. Indeed China and the US have already started to make progress in quantum computing technology.

Chapter Summary

LO1 to **LO3**. What we are witnessing is a change in the process and the geography of technology development and innovation. The past may have been characterized by the spillover of technical knowhow from the relocation of production of high-tech goods from the advanced economies to the developing world, as part of a catch-up proposition in economic growth theory and policy. The past saw a dominance of Western countries in the innovative start-up market. It is unlikely that underpinning growth and firm creation theories and the policies that were based on these myopic ideas will be available for use. The opposing forces of fragmentation in the production of technologies and the ubiquity of both production and development might mean a resetting of our ideas for a multipolar world of global entrepreneurship and innovation.

One positive outcome from the COVID-19 pandemic was the boost in the digitization of interactions and operations in many sectors of society and across different units of economic activity – the individual, the firm and the public sphere.

Challenges remain especially in terms of adoption of digital technologies, which in turn constrain the opportunities for entrepreneurial endeavor. The lack of coordination of digitization efforts especially among the big-ticket players has resulted in multiple 'digital islands', each with its own set of standards and rules regarding how to digitize the data and exchange it. Think about operating systems or mobile data exchange. While it is possible to connect one-to-one, it may be too expensive and complex to connect one-to-many.

This chapter could be considered to have a more futuristic approach than many of the others in this book. That is in part due to the uncertainty over the technologies which are in their infancy or are continually subject to changes. While we can observe the emergence of opportunities for new venture creation globally, we also witness the gradual hoovering up of firms with digital and economic heft, the larger firms appearing to have either an addiction for the acquisition of nimble, agile start-ups and early-stage firms or a smart approach to facilitate their growth through the creation of accelerators. We will need more time to learn.

Review Questions

1. How is globalization being transformed today by digitization?
2. What are the different forms of entrepreneurial endeavor that we can find as a result of digitization, globally?
3. Why is digitization affecting global trade and how does that lead to different types of entrepreneurial outcomes?
4. Why is digitization disrupting what we know of entrepreneurship and innovation across the world?
5. Who are the different stakeholders in the digital environment across the globe?
6. What are some of the key digital technologies affecting new venture creation, growth and global trade?

References

Arthur, W.B. (2009) 'The Nature of Technology: What It Is and How It Evolves.' New York: Simon and Schuster.

Business Times. (2022) 'Asia's big digital transformation'. 19 May. Available at www.businesstimes.com.sg/focus/asia-tech-insights/asias-big-digital-transformation (last accessed 1 July 2022).

Friedman, T.L. (2000) 'The Lexus and the olive tree: Understanding globalization'. NewYork: Anchor Books.

Friedman, T.L. (2006) 'The World Is Flat: A Brief History of the Twenty-First Century'. London: Macmillan.

Grand View Research. (2021) 'Artificial Intelligence Market Size, Share & Trends Analysis Report by Solution, by Technology (Deep Learning, Machine Learning, Natural Language Processing, Machine Vision), by End Use, by Region, and Segment Forecasts, 2022–2030'. Available at www.grandviewresearch.com/industry-analysis/artificial-intelligence-ai-market (last accessed 27 September 2022).

Lund, S., Manyika, J. and Bughin, J. (2016) 'Globalization is becoming more about data and less about stuff'. *Harvard Business Review*, 14 March. Available at https://hbr.org/2016/03/globalization-is-becoming-more-about-data-and-less-about-stuff (last accessed 12 April 2022).

Lynch, M. (2019) 'Six countries leading the AI race'. *The Techedvocate*, February 25. Available at www.thetechedvocate.org/six-countries-leading-the-ai-race/ (last accessed 15 March 2022).

Market Revolution. (2019) 'NEWS Un sabbatico per Market Revolution'. 24 May. Available at https://www.facebook.com/marketrevolution.it/ (last accessed 20 April 2020).

McAfee, A. and Brynjolfsson, E. (2017) 'Machine, Platform, Crowd: Harnessing our Digital Future'. New York: W.W. Norton & Company.

MGI. (2016) 'Digital globalization: The new era of global flows'. *Report by the McKinsey Global Institute*. February 24. Available at https://www.mckinsey.com/capabilities/mckinsey-digital/our-insights/digital-globalization-the-new-era-of-global-flows (last accessed 25 April 2020).

Mitra, J. (2018) 'Sharing, Giving and Taking: Enabling Citizen Entrepreneurship. In Exploring the Culture of Open Innovation' (pp. 69–106). Emerald Publishing Limited.

Mitra, J. (2022) 'SMEs, climate change and digitisation'. Briefing Paper for the 21st International Network for SMEs (INSME) Annual Summit. Sofia, Bulgaria, 8–9 July.

OECD. (n.d.) Digital Trade. *Paris: Organisation for Economic Cooperation and Development*. Available at www.oecd.org/trade/topics/digital-trade/ (last accessed 14 April 2022).

Pandya, J. (2019) 'The geopolitics of artificial intelligence'. *Forbes*, 28 January. Available at www.forbes.com/sites/cognitiveworld/2019/01/28/the-geopolitics-of-artificial-intelligence/?sh=71509d8d79e1 (last accessed 21 February 2022).

Statista. (2021) 'Number of college and university graduates in China 2010–2020'. 24 November. Available at www.statista.com/statistics/227272/number-of-university-graduates-in-china/ (last accessed 24 March 2021).

The World Economic Forum. (2019) 'In 2020 Asia will have the world's largest GDP: Here's what that means'. *World Economic Forum*, 20 December. Available at www.weforum.org/agenda/2019/12/asia-economic-growth/ (last accessed 20 March 2022).

UNCTAD (2022). TRADE AND DEVELOPMENT REPORT 2022 Development prospects in a fractured world: Global disorder and regional responses. United Nations Conference on Trade and Development. Geneva. Available at https://unctad.org/system/files/official-document/tdr2022_en.pdf (last accessed 20 April 2022).

Worldometers. (2022) 'Asia's population (live)'. Available at www.worldometers.info/world-population/asia-population/ (last accessed 3 July 2022).Concluding Summary

14
VENTURE CAPITAL

ANGEL INVESTMENT VIA THE INTERNET

Entrepreneurs nowadays are reaching out to investors via a range of online funding platforms and websites. One such online platform that connects founders with business angels (BAs) via the internet is AngelList. The tool is free for both investors and entrepreneurs to use.

AngelList invites select start-ups to list on its website. Entrepreneurs are required to create a profile to inform investors about their product/service and expected funding needs. They are also encouraged to describe their background and track record using portfolio websites, social-media profiles, news coverage or product reviews of their companies. Ninety-five accredited individual investors are allowed to commit as little as $1,000 each. Each investor has a net worth of more than $1 million, or annual income exceeding $200,000 for more than two consecutive years. In the past, AngelList offered founders the opportunity to only create a profile and share information. More recently, it has become possible for interested investors to invest in start-ups that pique their interest.

Although terms vary per company and per deal, unlike rewards-based crowdfunding platforms like Kickstarter, people who invest through AngelList get a stake in the start-up. AngelList is an equity-based funding site. Also unlike other platforms, AngelList investors must commit a minimum amount of $1,000. AngelList works with New York-based SecondMarket, a licensed broker-dealer approved by the Financial Industry Regulatory Authority and Securities and Exchange Commission, to form a single security fund for each deal such that start-ups do not need to follow up with each individual investor to collect the money.

Double Robotics (DR), a young Silicon Valley start-up, is an example of a start-up that has raised equity investment in this manner. DR, that developed a roving teleconferencing robot in 2013, turned to AngelList to seek $300,000 of equity funding for starting to ship its new device. David Cann, the 31-year-old co-founder of DR, created a profile on the platform. He mentioned the nearly $2 million of pre-orders and that he and his co-founder had received. He also explained the engineering background of the two co-founders, and the elite program for entrepreneurs that they had participated in. David attracted the attention of about 50 BAs who poured money into his venture.

(Continued)

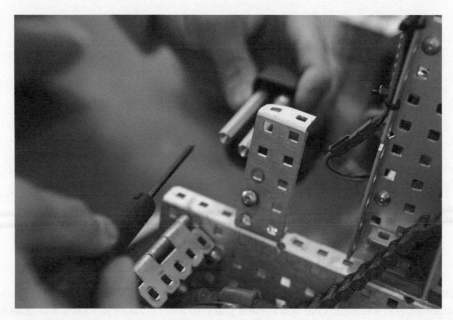

Source: www.needpix.com/photo/1834023

New angel investing services such as AngelList have made it possible for BAs to invest in start-ups situated far away, opening up many exciting possibilities for both investors and entrepreneurs. In the past, the reach of BAs was limited to investment opportunities within their personal network or geographic area. They found it impossible to identify and invest in high-growth prospects located far away from them. Online funding platforms have mitigated these challenges, allowing the relatively smaller BAs to co-invest alongside larger investors in deals that they believe are investment worthy. Founders also benefit, for they are spared the trouble of meeting with their investors in person.

At the same time, however, the arrangement is not without shortcomings. Some critics argue that websites like AngelList add a whole new layer of risk to an already very risky investment class. They believe it is not wise to make investment decisions based on online research and tools, without meeting or talking to the entrepreneurs involved in person. According to experienced investors, it is important to spend at least 20 hours of face time with the founders and team prior to committing money in order to assess managerial capabilities and group dynamics. AngelList warns investors that it does not verify the information posted by start-ups on its platform. Thus, it might even be necessary to conduct additional due diligence on the founders outside of the information provided on the platform. Some investors even look up the other investors who have already committed to a start-up in order to check their domain expertise and validate the quality of the start-up in question.

Source: Needleman and Kolondny (2013)

—Learning Outcomes—

After studying this chapter, you should be ready to:

- **LO1**: Explain the meaning of venture capital (VC) as a form of equity finance for rapidly growing start-ups
- **LO2**: Explain the distinctive resources of VC firms
- **LO3**: Explain VC firms' investment strategy
- **LO4**: Explain the stages of the VC investment process
- **LO5**: Explain the meaning of business angels (BAs) as a form of equity finance
- **LO6**: Compare and contrast VCs and BAs as forms of equity finance for entrepreneurial firms
- **LO7**: Discuss the significance of VC for the development of entrepreneurship

Introduction

High-growth entrepreneurial start-ups demand large infusions of capital to develop their competitive advantage and rapidly attain scale. They also need ongoing investor involvement to tide over situations of high uncertainty. Raising funding is thus one of the critical roles of founders of potentially global start-ups.

Traditional sources of finance like loans are unsuitable for high-growth prospects. Venture capital (VC) firms are specialized investors that meet the complex funding needs of global start-ups. Google, the gold standard for search on the internet, is a case in point in this kind of funding. Founded by Larry Page and Sergey Brin in 1998, Google went public in 2004, within six years of its founding. The start-up that revolutionized search engine technology completed a $25 million round of equity funding led by Sequoia Capital and Kleiner Perkins Caufield & Byers in 1999.

VC firms are not the only providers of equity investment. Individual equity investors or business angels (BAs) step in even earlier than VCs. Prior to receiving funding from equity investors, Google received $100,000 from Andy Bechtolsheim, co-founder of Sun Microsystems, and Ram Shriram, Vice President of Business Development at Amazon. com. More recently, as the opening profile suggests, angel investors are also willing to invest over the internet.

In this chapter, we explain VCs and BAs as forms of equity finance for rapidly growing entrepreneurial start-ups. First, we explain VC firms' distinctive resources and investment strategy, and key stages of the VC investment process. In the second part of the chapter, we outline the distinguishing features of BAs, and compare and contrast BAs with VCs. Finally, we evaluate the significance of VC for the development of entrepreneurship.

Venture Capital: Concept and Definition

Venture capital refers to investment by professional investors of long-term, unquoted, risk equity finance in new firms where the primary reward is an eventual capital gain, supplemented by dividend yield (Wright and Robbie, 1998). VCs share the returns from the investment in the form of a capital gain at the end of the life of the investment.

Formed in 1972, Sequoia Capital, for example, is the original founding investor in companies including Cisco Systems, Apple Computer, and Yahoo! It provided the original start-up financing for companies that now control more than $1.4 trillion of combined stock market value.

Another of Silicon Valley's most famous VC firms, Kleiner Perkins Caufield and Buyers, has backed entrepreneurs in over 900 ventures since inception. Formed in 1972, the firm has served as a lead investor in five of the top ten new internet companies, including Amazon.com and America Online.

VCs risk losing their investment if the business fails, which is why they restrict their investments to businesses with the potential to achieve rapid growth and significant size. As financial intermediaries, VC firms attract investments from financial institutions (banks, pension funds, insurance companies), large companies, wealthy families and endowments into fixed-life investment vehicles ('funds') with a specific investment focus in terms of location, technology and stage of development. The money is then invested in young, growing businesses that offer the prospects of high reward.

The investors in VC funds are limited partners; VC fund managers (or investment executives) are general partners. The function of general partners is to identify promising investment opportunities, support them through the provision of advice, information and networking, prior to ultimately exiting the investment. The proceeds from the liquidity event are returned to the limited partners.

Resources of VC Firms

Financial Resources

One of VC firms' most important resources is money raised and managed. **Fund size** refers to the total amount of **funds raised/managed** by VC firms. **Funds invested** is the total amount of funds invested in portfolio companies. Closing on $8 billion, Sequoia Capital's Global Growth Fund earned the title of largest venture fund on record in 2018.

The United States is the largest VC industry in the world, with $70 billion deployed in more than 8,000 start-ups each year between 2014 and 2018 (NVCA, 2019).

An additional third indicator of industry size is the total number of VC firms. At the end of 2018, 1,047 venture firms were in existence in the US, managing 1,884 venture funds, and translating to approximately $403 billion in assets under management.

VC firms that are small in terms of fund size often co-invest with large firms (Wright and Robbie, 1998). This phenomenon is called VC **syndication**. Syndication reduces risk and information uncertainties while enabling larger VC firms to fill gaps in smaller firms' investments. Syndication also allows for pooling of information with other investors in order to establish a fair price for the next round.

Additionally, syndication is useful for providing complementary expertise and social networks to VC firms in subsequent funding rounds. Finally, a syndication strategy reduces the burden of playing a hands-on role for the partners by giving them the choice of active involvement only when they are the lead investor in an investment.

In some cases, entrepreneurs prefer to obtain funding from a VC syndicate to reduce their dependence on a single investor. Murli Thirumale, a serial, California-based entrepreneur who founded and exited two ventures, Net6 and Ocarina, post-2000, raised money from three different VCs in the founding of one of his ventures:

> This venture was VC funded even though it was a tough time to raise money from VCs post 2000 but we raised about 17 million from three different VCs over just two rounds. At one point the two of them were in the syndicate. The first round Series A were two persons and I added a third. I believe in syndicates as you don't want to be in the grip of just one VC. I think it is not a prudent thing to do. (Murli Thirumale, Founder, Net6, California)

Human Resources

Human resources include both the **quantity** (number) and **quality** (expertise) of people (Bygrave, 1987). VC firms typically have a flat organization structure with a small number of investment executives.

With about 40 investment executives in the UK, Barclays Private Equity (BPE), a strategic business unit within Barclays Bank, UK, is an example. Although there is a distinction between investment executives and support staff, it is a flat structure overall. By virtue of their small size, VC firms like BPE are regarded as a 'permanent partner' by the portfolio companies:

> People at 3i tend to get promoted and move on. So they may be in one office for 2–3 years and in another later, at a higher level. Often, they have 2–3 different investment executives over a period of five years, while BPE has the same. The advantage of being small is that portfolio companies regard BPE as more of a permanent partner than the others. (Tom Lamb, Barclays Private Equity, UK)

Of particular relevance to VC firms is the quality of their investment executives, which typically refers to their **international or industry experience**. Specialized knowledge of innovations is also crucial for identifying the highest potential reward deals (Wright and Robbie, 1998).

Michael Moritz and John Doerr, general partners of Sequoia Capital and Kleiner Perkins Caufield & Buyers, respectively, who joined the board of Google at the time of its first VC funding in 1999, had a track record of funding and advising several high-growth technology ventures. Whereas Michael Moritz had prior experience as director of Yahoo, John Doerr had served as a director of several high-growth internet companies, including Amazon.com and Sun Microsystems.

VC Investment Strategy

VC firms are heterogeneous in terms of the size of their investment deals and investment stage preferences (Table 14.1). They also vary by ownership type and industry sector of activity.

Deal Size

VC firms differ in their investment range, both at the time of initial investment, as well as over the life of the investment. Benchmark Capital, for example, typically invests $3 million to $5 million per company in the initial round, and $5 million to $15 million over the life of the investment (Bose, 2008). As the following quote illustrates, VC firms' competitive advantage can be a function of their deal size:

> Competitive advantage in the UK is a function of our deal size. We do a lot of deals that are £10–25–30 million level now. (Michael Needley, Sovereign Capital, UK)

Investment Stage Preferences

Entrepreneurial ventures typically evolve through multiple stages of development (Jarvis and Schizas, 2012). Each stage has its own capital requirements. VC assumes importance once the business model, product and management capabilities have been proven, market acceptance has been demonstrated and uncertainties about market size and profitability have been reduced.

The earliest stage which signals the emergence of new ventures is the **seed stage**. Ventures at this stage are in the process of undertaking R&D and solving key product development issues. Ventures at the **start-up** stage demonstrate commercial viability and secure initial sales for the product/service. The **initial growth** stage is

Table 14.1 Investment strategy of VC firms

VC/ PE Firm	Website	Investment Range (US $) Min–Max	Investment Stage	Ownership Type	Industry Sector	Exits
Altria	www.altria.com/pages/default.aspx	2m–12.8b	Early & Late	Corporate	Tobacco	Juul; Cronos Group; Omada
Andreessen Horowitz	https://a16z.com/	4m–2b	Seed to Late	Private	Technology (consumer, enterprise, bio/fintech)	AnyRoad; Hipcamp; Omada Health
Bleu Capital	www.bleucap.com/	2.8–22.5m	Seed	Limited Partnership	Retail	For Days; Cargo; Oliver
Canvas Ventures	www.canvas.vc/	100k–20m	Early	Private	Fintech, marketplaces, digital health, new enterprise	Flowspace; Luminar; Kidbox
Chevron Technology Venture	www.chevron.com/technology/technology-ventures	10–68m	Early & Late	Corporate	Technology (auto industry)	Carbon Engineering; ChargePoint; Mission Secure
Fidelity Investments Inc.	www.fidelity.com/	13–600m	Late	Private	Finance, e-Commerce	Lyft; Reddit; CollegeVine
Sequoia Capital	www.sequoiacap.com/	1.5–621m	Early & Late	Limited Partnership	Technology	Bird; Google; RobinHood; Against Gravity
SoftBank Group Corp.	www.softbank.jp/en/corp/	4m–9b	Late	Corporate	Telecom services	Uber; Clip; Kabbage
Shareworks	www.shareworks.com/	1.5–756m	Early & Late	Corporate	Information technology services	Dropbox; Capshare
York Capital Management	https://services.intralinks.com/branding/707992947/?clientID=707992947	2.7m–1.8b	Late	Limited Partnership	Hedge funds	Snapchat; InSightec; Blue Sphere
OPIC (Overseas Private Investment Corporation)	www.opic.gov/	500k–350m	Debt	Government Office	Clean tech, finance, government, security, venture capital	Proximity Finance; ReNew Power; Orb Energy; Yes Bank

Source: NVCA (2019)

characterized by a product or service that is in demand, with much of owner-manager founders' efforts devoted to improving product quality, lowering unit costs and developing new products. Although businesses at this stage may be reaching profitability, it is insufficient to fund additional working capital, space and staff to meet the demands of growth.

Whereas VCs are receptive to funding ventures at the growth stage, they usually step in after initial, smaller resource needs have already been met (NVCA, 2019). Most growth equity investments are characterized by a proven business model and positive cash flow, profits or approaching profitability.

In some cases, sudden growth spurts due to unanticipated external environmental factors can stimulate investor interest and justify further cash infusions. The new coronavirus in early 2020, for example, saw increased investor interest in health care, and in particular in smoking cessation start-ups, in the US (Haverstock, 2020). The crisis served as a wake-up call to more than 1 billion smokers worldwide at higher risk of contracting a serious case of COVID-19, causing pneumonia or other potentially deadly complications.

As a result, VC-funded smoking cessation start-ups such as Pivot, Quit Genius and Lucy witnessed surging demand. As founders unveiled free versions of their mobile apps, they strongly signaled their growth prospects and, in turn, saw increased investor interest from their private investors including Octopus Ventures, Vice Ventures and RRE Ventures.

Source: www.needpix.com/photo/1133006

Ventures that continue to grow enter the **sustained growth** stage (Jarvis and Schizas, 2012). These ventures can expect to grow beyond $10–20 million in sales and 100 employees. Although profits and cash flow are sufficient to meet the majority of their capital requirements, additional finance may be required to explore new growth possibilities. VCs funding such ventures are specialists in development capital and provide investment with a view to ultimately listing these ventures on the stock market.

A commonly used distinction for VC investment stage preferences is between early- and late-stage investors. **Early-stage investors** typically specialize in investing in technology-oriented, young and rapidly growing entrepreneurial companies in the seed/ start-up and expansion/development (or early growth) stages. **Late-stage investors** fund companies across the whole spectrum of development stages right from inception through to established companies demanding restructuring types of investments.

In contrast with the US where the origins of VC have been synonymous with early- stage investment, in Europe, the term **private equity** (PE) refers to equity investment by long-term investors in already established companies. **Management buy-outs (MBOs)** and **management buy-ins (MBIs)** are the two most common forms of PE investment referring to funding of incumbent or incoming management teams, respec- tively, to buy companies from their owners to run as independent businesses.

Historically, venture capital and MBO/MBI investments have been regarded as entirely different industries in the US, with the term 'venture capital' reserved for investments in new or recently started companies. More recently, VC and PE have often been used interchangeably.

Ownership Type

Ownership type refers to the way VC firms are organized and their sources of finance. VC firms raise finance from a variety of sources such as pension funds, insurance com- panies, banks, wealthy individuals, corporations, overseas investors, government agencies, endowment funds and foundations, and public share issues (Dixon, 1991; Robinson, 1987). Accordingly, VC firms are captives, independents (or private / limited partnerships), corporates and even public-sector.

Captive and Independent VCs

VC firms may be **captive** or **private (independent)**. **Captives** are subsidiaries of financial institutions (e.g. banks). Captives draw on resources of larger financial institu- tions of which they are a part. They are open-ended funds that do not have a limit on the amount of capital available for investment (Dixon, 1991; McNally, 1994). In con- trast, **private** VCs raise finance from a number of financial institutions. They are different from both captives and affiliates in that they are closed-ended, with the amount available for investment being fixed by the parent.

Most VC firms are **independent organizations or limited partnerships**. Typically, VC firms create a limited partnership (LP) with their investors as limited partners and the firm itself as the general partner (NVCA, 2019). Examples of LPs include public pension funds, corporate pension funds, insurance companies, family offices, endowments and foundations. Each 'fund', or portfolio, is a separate partnership.

Corporate Venture Capital

A few large non-financial companies, particularly technology companies, have their own VC subsidiaries that invest to complement their own internal R&D activities for strategic reasons. This is called **corporate venture capital (CVC)**.

For example, Airbus Group SE, Europe's largest aerospace company, established a $150 million early-stage venture capital arm in Silicon Valley in 2015 to independently fund and support start-ups impacting the aerospace industry (Wall, 2015). The arm was set up to maintain a technology edge and ward off competition from traditional competitors like Boeing Corp., as well as newcomers like SpaceX that have already made inroads into the aerospace industry.

Orange Digital Ventures, a €150 million early-stage opportunity launched by the French Telecommunications Company, Orange, targets entrepreneurs from across the globe developing businesses related to services and technologies that are in line with Orange's fields of expertise.

The role of CVC has become increasingly evident in the past decade (IFC, 2018). The proportion of CVC activity as a percentage of overall VC activity grew from 16 to 20% from 2013 to 2017. Three of the ten largest venture investments in 2018 were corporate deals (NVCA, 2019). Corporations were involved in more than a third of deals in Asia in 2017 (Lucas, 2018).

Large corporations use their experience and in-house expertise to work with early-stage companies to stay competitive and abreast of fast-moving, disruptive developments (IFC, 2018). Unlike standard VC funds, CVC groups are not bound by closed-end, roughly ten-year fund lives. CVC thus brings patient capital to allow breakthrough companies to develop at their own pace rather than racing through to an exit.

Public Sector Venture Capital

Public sector venture capital refers to the provision of equity capital by the government to fill perceived gaps in the supply of venture capital (Carter and Jones-Evans, 2012). In some countries, governments use their own money to provide investment funds as a strategic policy initiative. Labor-sponsored VC funds in Canada and Venture Capital Trusts (VCTs) in the UK are examples of government VC funds.

In other cases, governments use the tax system or other financial incentives to alter the risk-reward ratio for private investors. Small Business Investment Companies (SBICs) in the US and Regional Venture Capital Schemes in England are investment funds created as a result of government co-investment alongside private money but on less favorable terms.

In some cases, government funds are structured as limited partnerships, co-investing alongside the private sector. Created to support innovation in SMEs dedicated to green and sustainable techologies in France, The Ecotechnologies Fund, for example, is a public VC/PE fund structured as a limited partnership. Focused on early and growth stage investments in SMEs of less than 250 employees, the fund has two limited partners, ADEME and the French public banking institution, BPI France, that collectively provide policy actions and state aid to help develop the portfolio innovations. Private sector investments alongside the fund's minority stakes are expected.

Industry Sector of Investment

VC firms choose to specialize in technology, or invest across a broad spectrum of industry sectors. Whereas the former are **specialists**, the latter are called **generalists**.

Michael Needley at Sovereign Capital, UK, specified the non-technology investment focus of his VC firm. Sovereign Capital is a generalist VC firm; they do not invest in technology as they do not understand technology; it lies outside of their area of expertise. Nevertheless, their non-technology sector focus, according to Michael, had paid them well in the long run:

> We don't invest in tech-related sectors, we have experience and expertise in
> the four sectors that I mentioned, and if we decided to go into other sectors, it
> would be a serious disadvantage to us... when technology was very popular two
> or three years ago... our investors then may have asked us, why don't you invest
> in technology... because we don't understand it and it's not our expertise...
> (Michael Needley, Sovereign Capital, UK)

In the US, VC firms are known for their historical focus on technology-based investments. The software sector continues to attract the lion's share of VC activity in the US, comprising 36% of capital invested and 42% of deal count in 2018 (NVCA, 2019). Exploding in popularity during the 2010s, the fintech industry continues to birth unicorns at a rapid rate (Pitchbook, 2020).

VC Investment Process

VC firms render their services in a multi-stage, sequential investment process. This is because they need to mitigate concerns of adverse selection and moral hazard. Agency theory provides a framework to understand the risk and uncertainty in the VC investment process.

An agency relationship exists when one individual (principal) engages another individual (the agent) to perform a service on their behalf (Jensen and Meckling, 1976). The separation of ownership and control creates the risk that the agent will make decisions that are not in the best interests of the principal.

This possibility of opportunistic behavior on the part of the agent creates two types of risk for the principal – **adverse selection** and **moral hazard**. **Adverse selection** arises out of information asymmetries: the agent is better informed about their true level of ability than the principal. **Moral hazard** means that in situations where it is not possible for the principal to observe the behavior of the agent, the agent may shirk, engage in opportunistic behavior that is not in the interests of the principal or pursue divergent interests rather than those of the principal.

As principals, VCs are vulnerable to the risks of adverse selection and moral hazard from their investees (agents). Additionally, every investment decision involves market risk, the risk that the business will perform less well than anticipated on account of competitive conditions.

VCs perceive information asymmetries as less costly compared to other investors. They achieve expertise and economies of scale in locating and financing potentially successful ventures on the basis of their multi-stage, sequential investment process comprising deal generation, screening and evaluation, investment appraisal, deal structuring, post-investment monitoring and service provision, and finally investment realization, exit and re-contracting (Hall and Hofer, 1993; Tyebjee and Bruno, 1984; Wright and Robbie, 1998). Each of these stages is explained below.

Deal Generation

Deal generation is concerned with access to viable projects that generate target rates of return (Wright and Robbie, 1998). Deal generation is linked with VCs' preferences with respect to investment stages and deal size. VC firms follow two approaches to access investment opportunities. The first is **unsolicited deal flow**, and the second is **active deal seeking**.

As they are listed on various directories and websites, VC firms are very visible. VCs' trusted networks of intermediaries are also a key and highly regarded source of deal flow. Entrepreneurs' own professional contacts are considered a valuable means of obtaining referrals to VCs, especially because of the importance of industry-specific experience as a criterion for VC funding.

According to Vijay Maheshwari, co-founder of Verismo Networks, California, cold calling VCs by individual entrepreneurs is extremely unlikely to work. As VCs believe in investing in entrepreneurs they know or are able to trust, it is best for entrepreneurs to leverage their professional networks to approach VCs:

VCs definitely need somebody they know or can trust. So it's difficult cold calling VCs. It's almost impossible. It has to be through people you have worked with, who can vouch for you. Only then can you get inside and go for it. (Vijay Maheshwari, Co-Founder, Verismo Networks, California)

VCs also engage in **proactive deal seeking** to identify exceptional innovators (Bygrave and Timmons, 1986, 1992). They typically recruit investment executives with specific skills and network connections to seek out transactions. The investment executives then work with investees to turn ideas into investable business propositions.

Investment Screening and Evaluation

VC firms typically conduct a two-stage evaluation process comprising an **initial screening**, followed by a **detailed evaluation** of deals that pass the initial test (Jarvis and Schizas, 2012). Recent studies find that for every company in which a VC firm eventually invests, the firm considers roughly 100 potential opportunities (NVCA, 2019). The median VC firm closes about four deals per year.

VC firms **initially screen** a large number of deals with a view to weeding out prospects that do not meet their investment criteria (Muzyka et al., 1996). The amount of equity held by the entrepreneurial team and the personal wealth committed to the business are some signals that potentially influence VCs' early decision making (Busenitz et al., 2005). Missing information in the business plan can also be grounds for rejection at the initial screening stage.

The deals that pass the initial stage are then subject to more **detailed scrunity**. VC firms consult with both inside and outside sources to gather in-depth information about the credentials of the management teams and prospects of the investment (Dixon, 1991; Hall and Hofer, 1993). **Due diligence** is the detailed investigation of the merits of an investment proposal based on gathering extensive information from a variety of sources. VCs meet with the management team, review financial statements, interview suppliers, customers, bankers, other investors and industry experts.

VCs use a number of criteria to evaluate investment proposals. These include size of the opportunity, length of the exit horizon, and expected rate of return (NVCA, 2019). The most important factor in VC investment screening is nature of the management team. Research shows that quality of the entrepreneur ultimately determines the investment decision. VCs prefer to invest in individuals who have personal integrity and exhibit strong leadership skills. Also of importance is the nature of entrepreneurs' prior, in particular industry, experience.

According to Vijay Maheshwari, co-founder of Verismo Networks, California, VCs are unlikely to fund entrepreneurs starting up in an industry that is new to them in terms of their area of expertise. Vijay was able to succeed in finding an equity investor due to his years of prior work experience in the field where he eventually ended up starting-up:

So, I was in the video field in the DVD player but was still in the video field. When I came here, I knew a bunch of people who belonged to the video industry, who were good at video but didn't know much of the internet. So I could relate to them and continue forward. It has to be a continuum. You have to be in a particular industry for many years to really understand it and make a difference there. You cannot, 'I am going to make the next Facebook' before even having an idea about social networking. If I try to do so, no VC is going to fund me. (Vijay Maheshwari, Co-Founder, Verismo Networks, California)

Additionally, it is important for entrepreneurs to emphasize their contribution as a team in order to establish credibility with VC investors on an individual basis:

If you go and look at the research of VCs and figure out why they are funded, it has to be that they directly know that person or through some other person… If you do not put so much emphasis as a team they would not fund you… once you get success with one company then it's easier to tell them that I have got success and can establish some credibility and then it's easier to get funded… (Vijay Maheshwari, Co-Founder, Verismo Networks, California)

Most businesses do not meet VC investment criteria. Either they do not have proprietary products, or are not the first or second entrant into the market. Often, it is challenging for VCs to identify competent management teams to build and manage a growing company due to which VC rejection rates are very high.

Deal Structuring, Investment Valuation and Assessment

The initial screening and subsequent selection of proposals for investment is followed by negotiation of the terms and conditions of the investment (Jarvis and Schizas, 2012). **Deal structuring** entails drawing an investment agreement to specify the terms and conditions of the investment. The overall objective of the investment agreement is to minimize risk.

VC investment agreements typically include such key elements as investor control over key decisions, a seat on the board of directors, a compensation scheme to align investor interests with those of the management team, and investment instruments for downside risk protection. VCs seek the power to replace management or approve investee expenditures by assuming a seat on the board of directors. They also incentivize the management team using a combination of financial instruments such as salaries and stock options.

Finally, VCs stage their investments. They provide funds in stages, subject to the completion of specific milestones, rather than all at once. Staging investments helps VCs to avoid losses in funding their investments. VCs can increase their capital commitments if the management team shows evidence of meeting key milestones; and they can withdraw in the event key milestones are not met or new information about the prospects of the business is not favorable.

Post-Investment Activities

VCs perform two key roles in their investee companies post-investment – **post-investment monitoring** and provision of **value-added services**. VCs spend around half their time monitoring and supporting the companies in their portfolio (Gorman and Sahlman, 1989). A typical VC investment executive is responsible for nine portfolio companies and sits on the boards of five of those companies.

Post-Investment Monitoring

VCs use a variety of **formal** and **informal mechanisms** to monitor the progress of their investee companies. They request frequent, **formal** accounting statements from their portfolio companies.

According to Tony May at Charterhouse Development Capital (CDC), UK, each of their portfolio companies produces monthly accounting statements. It was important to request these statements in order to avoid last-minute surprises:

> Each month, each of our companies produces monthly management figures, the profit-loss account, the balance sheet, the cash flow, broken down by divisions, broken down by countries, putting some commentary on how they are doing everywhere… and each month, our co-investors would be sent this information… In Charterhouse, we don't give any surprises, we don't suddenly say, God, we haven't heard from this investment for six months, how are they performing, we are in contact with these companies on a regular basis. (Tony May, CDC, UK)

VCs use a combination of **informal** monitoring methods including personal visits and face-to-face meetings, telephone calls, video-conferences and emails to engage with their investee companies (Gorman and Sahlman, 1989). A typical VC visits each company 19 times per annum and spends 100 hours in direct contact with them.

According to Michael Needley, Sovereign Capital, UK, they encourage their investees to make phone calls to contact them. That was the easiest way to track investee companies' progress, both, initially, as well as in follow-up funding rounds. Theirs being a small and non-hierarchical firm made it easier for founders to approach them:

> where we make investments initially, or for follow-on investments, it's very easy for any of our investee companies to just get on the phone and call us. We'd rather take a phone call and get a heads-up for what's going on than

hear nothing at all. And that's generally quite easy to do because being a small company, we've got rid of lots of hierarchy and if you need to talk to some person making a decision you can get hold of that person directly. Call the directors themselves (four), and as the director of the company, they are in a position to recommend. (Michael Needley, Sovereign Capital, UK)

Value-Added Service Provision

By definition, VCs are active investors. They play an active, hands-on role in the companies in which they invest. VC firms' small size in terms of investment executives enables them to make quick decisions and intervene on a timely basis. Evidence suggests that VC-backed boards are generally more active than those of non-VC backed firms (Fried et al., 1998).

VCs provide a variety of value-added contributions to their investee companies. They help to recruit and compensate key individuals, work with suppliers and customers, establish strategic goals, raise capital and structure transactions (e.g. mergers and acquisitions) that the company might make. They may also introduce entrepreneurs to other key members of their co-founding and top management teams.

Manish Chandra, a California-based entrepreneur and founder of Poshmark, an online platform for second-hand fashion, met one of his co-founders through his VC investor. His VC investors at Mayfield first introduced him to Tracy, a fashion expert, in the early stages of founding his venture when he was searching for industry expertise on his co-founding team. Manish struck a chord with Tracy and invited her to join at the incubation stage:

> Tracy, I ended up meeting her through my VC firm, Mayfield... I knew I was going to do something fashion and I wanted someone who truly understood fashion, not the Silicon Valley fashion converts. So I ended up meeting a lot of people. Tracy and I just clicked and she became a part of my incubation and brainstorming process... she was one of the first people I brought in and she loved it. So she decided to join the venture. (Manish Chandra, Founder, Poshmark, California)

For Vas Bhandarkar, a Silicon-Valley-based serial entrepreneur, VCs were a very important source of funding for all his ventures. VC investors provided valuable introductions to the co-founding teams of his start-ups:

> Investors have always played a very important role in financing me. Because VCs like Draper invested in Selectica, I got the job at Unimobile. Draper invested in Selectica, and Draper got me on as co-founder of Unimobile. Because of Unimobile, I got on the board of Global Logic. Because of the work I did at Global Logic, I got to know another investor, Sequoia Capital. Because of

Sequoia Capital, I founded other ventures. (Vas Bhandarkar, Founder, Global Logic, California)

VCs add most value by acting as a sounding board for their investees and serving as consultants for their investee companies (MacMillan et al., 1989; Rosenstein et al., 1993). However, VCs are heterogeneous in their nature and level of involvement (MacMillan et al., 1989). VC Partners at Sovereign Capital, UK, for example, are 'quite involved' with their investee companies. They sit on the boards of their investee companies, attend all meetings and actively engage in each financing round.

In other cases, the degree of involvement is contingent on the level of VCs' expertise and experience, stage of investment, as well as performance of the business (Bruton et al., 1997). Some VC firms are more involved at a **strategic** level, whereas others are more active on an **operational** basis.

Apax Partners, UK, for example, refrain from operational involvement in their investee companies. As Toby Wyles, former partner at Apax Partners explained, they did not manage their portfolio companies on a day-to-day basis; their intervention mainly took the form of providing money and devising exit strategies for their ventures:

> If I make an investment in a company, if I lead an investment in a company, I would go on the board, so APAX generally takes a board seat, and it's generally pretty involved in making strategic decisions with management about the company. We don't manage the company, that's not our strategy, but we do help manage the strategy, and we are hands-on. The APAX director has a lot of discretion in setting our strategy, in driving the business, etc. (Toby Wyles, Managing Partner, Virtuvian Partners, and Former Partner, Apax Partners, UK)

Investment Realization and Exit

VC firms hold their investments for a finite time period (typically seven to ten years). This time period is called the **investment horizon** of the VC firm in question. The exit allows VC firms to realize returns and distribute the proceeds to investors, raise a new fund for future investment, and invest in the next generation of companies. Typically, VCs seek to take their investees public through an **initial public offering (IPO)**. Alternatively, they may **sell** to larger entities (NVCA, 2019).

IPOs

Gaining a listing on a public stock market through an **IPO** is one of the main forms of exit for VC firms. In 2010, Tesla rang in the decade with the first IPO for an American automaker in more than 50 years. The success of the company sparked a decade in which autonomous driving and electric transportation became the hottest technologies in venture capital. Tesla's stock was up more than 100% in the first 50 days of 2020.

Cloud-based file storage provider Dropbox (the largest IPO of 2018), drug discovery company Moderna Therapeutics (the largest biotechnology IPO on record) and e-signature provider DocuSign are among other top VC-backed companies achieving recent IPOs. Venture-backed companies accounted for 40% of all IPOs in the US in 2018, a 15-year high (NVCA, 2019).

An IPO is an important way through which founders and other shareholders of the company, notably equity investors, realize returns in the form of capital gains. In some cases, VCs sell shares in the portfolio companies to institutional and private investors to raise additional finance following a stock market listing. A public listing also enables entrepreneurial firms to raise debt finance or make acquisitions (Jarvis and Schizas, 2012).

At the same time, however, an IPO is expensive to achieve and maintain. In some cases, the private-to-public transition may not be smooth. VC-funded entrepreneurial firms find it difficult to leave the VC cocoon and deal with a much large investor base that is less familiar with their operations.

After going public in March 2017 with an initial valuation of over $19 billion, Snap's stock, for example, sunk dangerously low in the first two years after its IPO before recovering in 2019 (Pitchbook, 2020). As a VC-backed camera and social media company founded in California, Snap was dealing with a much larger investor base after the IPO that was much less familiar with how the company operated.

Not all VC-funded start-ups are necessarily 'the next big thing'. For example, Blue Apron, the meal-kit start-up, raised more than $190 million in VC before its IPO in 2017 that resulted in a valuation of about $1.9 billion (Pitchbook, 2020). However, problems with supply chains, customer retention and profitability quickly mounted, resulting in a loss of more than 97% of the company's value in less than three years.

More recently, high-growth prospects have been resisting an IPO due to a surge in late-stage investments to fund high-growth start-ups from private rather than public sources. LPs have been flooding the VC market with cash drawn by incredible returns that the biggest start-up winners can generate, which is allowing start-ups to stay private for longer.

At the time of its offering in May 2012, Facebook had already been valued above $1 billion for nearly five years and had raised multiple nine-figure rounds (Pitchbook, 2020). Founded in 2010, Uber has also capitalized from this trend. Uber's round of funding in December 2014 pushed its valuation to the highest for any company backed by venture capitalists. The company finally went public in May 2019 after years of mega-rounds, scandals and breakneck growth, raising $8.1 billion and resulting in an initial market cap of some $70 billion.

Trade Sales / Acquisitions

VCs may sell their portfolio companies to large investors at the end of their investment horizon. In 2018, trade sales were the most prominent exit route in the UK, followed by sale to another private equity firm, and public offering, respectively (www.bvca.co.uk).

In the US, VC firms backing financial tech start-ups such as Galileo Financial Technologies, Plaid and CreditKarma have recently achieved exits by selling these companies to large financial firms such as SoFi, Visa and Intuit (Pitchbook, 2020). The Galileo acquisition marks a significant exit for VC firms Accel and Mercato Partners as lead investors in the firm, with Accel expected to earn a more than fourfold return on its investment at the time of the sale.

Business Angels

Business angels are high net-worth individuals who directly invest their own personal capital in unquoted companies in which they have no family connection (Jarvis and Schizas, 2012). Unlike VC firms, BAs are individual investors. They are typically 45–65 years old, which reflects the length of time required to build significant personal net worth and greater discretionary wealth of this age group.

It is impossible to be precise about the number of BAs or their investment. Available estimates suggest that there are approximately 300,000 to 350,000 BAs in the US. Annual angel investment activity in the US is about $24 billion each year, contributing to the growth and success of more than 64,000 start-ups. The equivalent estimate for the UK is 20,000 to 40,000 business angels investing 0.5 million to 1 billion pounds in 3000 to 6000 companies. Approximately 5–10% of BA investments are economically profitable and achieve positive exits.

Angel groups invest in a variety of industries, with roughly two-thirds of deals in information technology and health care (Timmins et al., 2019) (Table 14.2).

Around 78% of BAs are males, most commonly with prior experience in technology (Huang et al., 2017). However, the number of women entering the angel investment market appears to be growing, with 30% of angels who started investing within the last two years being women.

Resources

BAs have unique motivations, skills, experiences and networks that differentiate them from formal VC firms.

Motivations

Unlike VCs, BAs have strong personal motivations to engage in equity investment. Becoming investors after their own entrepreneurial journey helps BAs to remain occupied and economically active after a career spanning several decades. More crucially, BAs derive considerable satisfaction from mentoring entrepreneurs. They feel rejuvenated by working with new, young talent, and providing guidance and advice based on their own experience of founding and growing ventures.

Table 14.2 Angel investment by industry, seed round, investment stage and co-investment type in the US

Industry	No. of Deals (%)	Amount Invested (%)	Investment Range	Average Amount Invested (%)	Investment Stage	No. of Deals (%)	Amount Invested (%)	Co-Investment Type	Deals by Co-Investment Type (%)
IT	38	35	<99K	28	Pre-Seed	3	2	Not syndicated at all	32.3
Healthcare	25	30	$100K to $249K	41	Seed	60	55	Syndicated with only other angel groups	31.3
Consumer Discretionary	13	10	$250K to $499K	24	Series A	25	21	Syndicated with angel groups and VCs	29.3
Industrials	8	8							
Consumer Staples	6	3	>500K	7	Series B	4	4	Syndicated with VCs only	7.1
Energy	3	4							
Financials	3	2							
Manufacturing	1	1			Series C and Later	9	8		
Materials	2	2							
Real Estate	1	4							

Source: adapted from Timmins et al. (2019)

Skills and Experience

BAs have specialist professional or industry experience, often stemming from prior senior management roles at large organizations. Unlike VCs, however, the majority of BAs have a prior track record of successfully founding and exiting entrepreneurial ventures. Evidence suggests that 55% of angel investors were previously a founder or CEO of their own start-up (Huang et al., 2017).

Networks

BAs have diversified networks for deal flow (Huang et al., 2017). The Angel Capital Association (ACA) is the leading US professional and trade association connecting angels interested in high-growth, early-stage ventures with entrepreneurs. With a membership of over 14,000 angels and 275 angel groups, accredited platforms and family offices, the association offers valuable networking, information and support resources to enable BAs to make better investments and generate results. The top ten angel groups in the US with the highest dollars invested are shown below (Table 14.3).

Table 14.3 Top angel groups in the US (by deals)

Angel Group	Year Founded	Members	Mission
Central Texas Angel Network	2006	100+	Provides quality early-stage investment opportunities for accredited angel investors; Assists entrepreneurs and early-stage growth companies by providing funding, mentorship, strategic advice and educational resources
Charlottesville Angel Network	2015	70+	Fosters a business environment where entrepreneurs grow, thrive and enrich the community; Strives to educate investors and entrepreneurs, and cultivate and attract new business ideas
Golden Seeds	2004	285+	Achieves lasting impact by propelling women entrepreneurs
Houston Angel Network	2001	100+	Develops the innovation ecosystem in Houston, Texas by supporting founders and start-ups with financial resources and mentorship
Keiretsu Forum	2000	2500+	Creates interlocking relationships (of both individuals and small companies) with partners to produce the highest quality deal-flow and investment opportunities
Launchpad Venture Group	2000	150	Provides human and financial capital to help entrepreneurs build successful companies
Northern Ontario Angels (NOA)	2005	10	Facilitates essential business connections between Northern Ontario's entrepreneurs and accredited angel investors; Stimulates increased investment capital into Northern Ontario companies to help them succeed

(Continued)

Table 14.3 (Continued)

Angel Group	Year Founded	Members	Mission
Pasadena Angels	2000	100+	Creates a unique investment community of successful business and professional leaders to identify promising start-up ventures and provide capital and counsel necessary for success
Portland Seed Fund	2011	5	Provides opportunities for entrepreneurs to connect with local investors and service providers, as well as with a family of early-stage company CEOs who can provide guidance and support
Tech Coast Angels	1997	400+	Builds Southern California's economy into a thriving center of technology and entrepreneurship

Sources: https://ctan.com; https://cvilleangelnetwork.net; https://goldenseeds.com; www.houstonangelnetwork.org; www.keiretsuforum.com; www.launchpadventuregroup.com; www.newyorkangels.com; www.northernnontarioangels.ca/en; www.pasadenaangels.com/about; http://portlandseedfund.com/whypsf; www.techcoastangels.com/tag/tech-coast-angels

Friends and associates are the next significant sources of deals, followed by direct contact with entrepreneurs, and online and crowdfunding platforms. There is also an increasing trend toward angels investing alongside other funding vehicles, especially crowdfunding platforms, with 16% of angels reporting the use of a digital platform for at least one investment.

Investment Strategy

Like VCs, BAs are heterogeneous in the number and size of their investments, level of involvement with investee companies, and return targets and equity stakes.

Number, Size and Stage of Investments

As individual investors, BAs have a much smaller investment range than VCs, typically between $10,000 and $500,000, and a much smaller number (typically between two and five) of portfolio companies (Timmins et al., 2019). Table 14.2 shows the average amount invested by angel groups in seed rounds. According to the ACA, nearly 70% of angel investments in the seed round are less than $250,000.

Unlike VCs, BAs are willing to invest in seed and start-up stages even before ventures have attained proof of concept. The funds they provide are beyond what entrepreneurs can raise from their own sources, and below the minimum threshold of VC funds. California-based Band of Angels (www.bandangels.com), for example, provides the first 'organized' money into start-up companies, either a series Seed or Series A. Investments are in the range of $300,000 to $750,000.

A study by ACA suggests that angel groups also invest in follow-on rounds just over half the time (Timmins et al., 2019) (Table 14.2).

BAs are often constrained in the total amount available for investment, and end up collaborating with other angels, angel groups or VCs to co-invest in a single investment. Co-investing allows BAs to diversify their portfolios. At times, however, it makes it challenging for entrepreneurs to manage the syndicate as a group.

Manish Chandra, founder of Poshmark, felt fortunate to have really powerful angels. However, it took a 'lot of energy' to manage them as they built a 'confederation' to pool their financial resources for the purpose of the investment:

> Whenever I needed the money, it was always available. But it came from eight ten people as opposed to one person, which takes a lot of energy. It was all angels. We had Guy Kawasaki, Ron Conway, Jeff Clavier and Kanwal [Rekhi]. Mayfield took the lead, but we took angel from my previous angel. Angels are really a confederation. You have to manage a group. With VCs you have one or two powerful people which is almost like having a boss, someone you can count on. You have one powerful voice so you can make decisions very rapidly…
> (Manish Chandra, Founder, Poshmark, California)

Level of Involvement

Just like VCs, BAs play an active, hands-on role in the businesses in which they invest. The goal of the Band of Angels, for example, is to provide as much value as possible to all companies that pitch to them. Owing to the networks of more than 165 of their expert investor members, entrepreneurs are able to garner important business development opportunities, referrals for excellent employees, and valuable advisors or board members, even if they do not eventually succeed in raising money from the Band.

Unlike VCs, BAs adopt a more personalized approach to investment. Companies that get to the Deal Dinner presentation at the Band of Angels, for example, have been put through a diligence and review process that includes several hours of speech and presentation coaching and feedback from experienced venture investors. Unlike VCs, BAs typically do not have standard contractual agreements in place due to the high costs involved.

At the same time, however, BAs are heterogeneous in the level of their involvement (Huang et al., 2017): 60% of BAs with an entrepreneurial background, for instance, take an advisory role and 52% take a board seat in their investee companies.

Rate of Return Targets

Just like VC firms, BAs invest for a capital gain and financial return on their investments. However, BAs are not as aggressive as VCs in their rate of return targets. Vijay Maheshwari, co-founder of Verismo Networks, California, emphasized that he had to develop a product prototype in order to obtain funding from VCs. He also had to convince investors of his prior successful track record as VCs are reluctant to invest in entrepreneurs who are starting from scratch:

VCs don't normally fund you just like that. You have to go and develop a product. It may not be like a final product, but at least developed to a point where they can feel and they can see. In this case, we developed some product and being able to show some sort of a demo and customer interest and so that's how we got funding… (Vijay Maheshwari, Co-Founder, Verismo Networks)

Equity Stakes

BAs are much less demanding of equity stakes from their investees as compared to VCs. They also place less emphasis on control and reporting requirements than VCs.

Ravi Kulasekaran, a California-based serial entrepreneur, was already doing five million dollars in business for his first venture, Simplify, an ERP (Enterprise Resource Planning) solution, when one of his customers encouraged him to raise money from external sources. The VC money that Ravi subsequently raised gave them a launch pad and visibility in the market; however, it came at the expense of compromising a majority equity stake in the venture.

By the time Ravi founded his fourth venture, Colabus, an internet-based enterprise collaboration tool to create and share a document repository and contact information for employees, he wanted to be sure to run the venture on his own, without any VC support. He preferred to use internal finance to scale his venture as he did not want to submit to VCs' demands for a large equity stake even if that meant slower growth:

I wanted a company where I enjoy the freedom of creating various stuff, not necessarily worry about taking it IPO. So even if I built this company at a steady pace and if I do something good, then I can still exit selling the whole company to somebody else, rather than try to run at an insane, breakneck speed and walk away with peanuts. So that is not the goal! It was a conscious choice that I made. I was able to afford it. I can play my own VC. (Ravi Kulasekaran, Founder, Colabus)

Significance of Venture Capital

VCs provide equity finance designed for use in risky settings. VC/PE firms fund innovative solutions and disruptive business models (IFC, 2018). They support early stage companies that cannot access debt financing and are too small for securities markets.

Finance from family and friends is typically inadequate for high-growth prospects. Debt finance is usually inappropriate from a cash management perspective. Banks are traditionally risk-averse. They are not experts at assessing or dealing with information asymmetries inherent in start-up investments. The difficulty of obtaining reasonable collaterals on loans to start-ups that have few tangible assets severely restricts banks' willingness to bear the additional risks.

Unlike banks and other lenders, VCs achieve economies of scale in locating and financing potentially successful ventures (Amit et al., 1998). Compared to consultants who provide strategic advice only, VCs provide both money and guidance (Barry, 1994). The injection of VC money into the likes of Facebook, Amazon, Google and Uber very early in their lives has enabled these companies to grow much faster than proceeds from sales revenue alone. At the end of 2018, venture-backed companies in the US accounted for five of the six largest publicly traded companies by market capitalization: Microsoft ($780 billion), Apple ($746 billion), Amazon ($737 billion), Alphabet ($727 billion) and Facebook ($374 billion).

VC is rare among asset classes in that success is truly shared among several different stakeholders including entrepreneurs, employees, VC investors and institutional investors (NVCA, 2019). Entrepreneurs benefit when their companies achieve successful exits. Both founders and employees benefit from appreciated stock price and options. Investors in VC funds split capital gains with VCs.

VC/PE firms are an engine of jobs and innovation. Venture-backed companies in the US have generated high-skilled jobs and trillions of dollars of benefit for the US economy (NVCA, 2019). High-growth, VC-backed start-ups account for as many as 50% of gross jobs created, and 2.9 million average net jobs created annually between 1980 and 2010.

Gornall and Strebulaev (2015) found that of 1,339 US companies that went public between 1974 and 2015, 556 (or 42%) were venture-backed. These 556 companies represented 63% of the market capitalization and 85% of the total R&D of those 1,339 companies.

Chapter Summary

LO1: Venture capital refers to investment by professional investors of long-term, unquoted, risk equity finance in new firms. VC firms attract investments from financial institutions. The money is then invested in young, growing businesses that offer the prospects of high reward at a liquidity event.

LO2: Fund size refers to the total amount of **funds raised/managed**. **Funds invested** is the total amount of funds invested by VC firms in their portfolio companies. VC firms that are small in terms of fund size often co-invest with other large firms, especially at the second and subsequent funding rounds. This phenomenon is called VC **syndication**. The human resources of VC firms include the **quantity** (number) as well as **quality** (expertise) of their people. VC firms are relatively small in terms of the number of investment executives that they employ. The **international or industry experience** of VC investment executives is instrumental for the conduct of the VC investment process. Another key aspect of VC firms' human resources is their **incentive structure**.

(Continued)

VC firms maintain alignment of interests by tying the compensation of VC/PE fund managers to the success of their portfolio companies.

LO3: VC firms are heterogeneous in **size** of investment deals, **investment stage** preferences, **ownership type** and **industry sector preferences**. Whereas **early-stage investors** specialize in investing in technology-based companies in early growth stages, **late-stage investors** fund companies across the spectrum of development stages right from inception through to established companies. The term **private equity (PE)** refers to equity investment by long-term investors in already established companies. **Management buy-outs (MBOs)** and **management buy-ins (MBIs)** are the two most common forms of PE investment. Whereas **captives** are subsidiaries of financial institutions (e.g. banks) that do not have a limit on the amount of capital available for investment, **independent** or **private** VCs are closed-ended funds that raise finance as **limited partnerships**. Large non-financial, particularly technology, companies have their own VC subsidiaries. This is called **corporate venture capital**. **Public sector** VC refers to the provision of equity capital by the government to fill perceived gaps in the supply of venture capital. VC firms choose to specialize in technology, or invest across a broad spectrum of industry sectors. Whereas the former are **specialists**, the latter are called **generalists**.

LO4: VC firms render their services in a multi-stage, sequential **investment process** to mitigate concerns of **adverse selection** and **moral hazard**. VC firms may receive unsolicited deal flow or proactively seek deals. VC firms typically conduct a two-stage evaluation process comprising an **initial screening** and **detailed evaluation** of deals. **Due diligence** is the detailed investigation of the merits of an investment proposal based on gathering extensive information from a variety of sources. **Deal structuring** entails drawing up an investment agreement to specify the terms and conditions of the investment. VCs perform two key roles – **post-investment monitoring** and provision of **value-added services** post-investment, and use formal and informal mechanisms to monitor their investments. Whereas some VC firms are more involved at a **strategic** level, others engage on an **operational** basis. VC firms hold their investments for a finite time period called the **investment horizon**, and take their investees public through an **initial public offering** or **sell** to larger entities.

LO5: **Business angels (BAs)** are high net-worth individuals who directly invest their own personal capital in unquoted companies in which they have no family connection. BAs are individual investors. They are typically 45–65 years old.

LO6: BAs have unique motivations, skills, experiences and networks that differentiate them from formal VC firms. Unlike VCs, BAs have strong personal motivations to engage in equity investment, and a prior track record of successfully founding and exiting entrepreneurial ventures. BAs have a much smaller investment range and much smaller number of companies (typically between two and five) in their portfolio than VC firms. They have a much lower minimum investment threshold, and are willing to invest in seed and start-up stages even before ventures have attained proof of concept. Just like VCs, however, BAs play an active, hands-on role in supporting the businesses in which they invest. BAs also invest for a capital gain and financial return on their investments; however, they are not as aggressive as VCs in their rate of return targets or required equity stakes.

LO7: VC is high-risk capital that is credited with filling the equity gap for small and innovative firms. VC firms yield high returns to other stakeholders and investors and contribute to economic growth through job creation.

Review Questions

1. Explain what you understand by the term venture capital. What is the difference between venture capital and private equity? Define each term and give examples to illustrate your answer.
2. What are the distinctive resources of VC firms? Explain VC firms' a) financial resources and b) human resources.
3. Some VC firms are specialists, whereas others are generalists. Explain what you understand by each of the two terms. Give examples to illustrate your answer.
4. What are the reasons for the sequential nature of the VC investment process? Use the concept of agency theory to explain your answer.
5. How do VC firms add value to their investees a) pre-investment and b) post-investment? Explain your answer.
6. Explain what you understand by the term business angels.
7. How are BAs different from VC firms? Compare and contrast BAs and VCs in terms of their resources and investment strategy.
8. What is the significance of venture capital finance? Explain the economic impact of venture capital finance.

Case 14.1

Sovereign Capital Partners: A Mid-Market PE Firm in the UK

Sovereign Capital Partners (SCP) is a PE firm headquartered in London, UK. Founded in 2001 by entrepreneur Michael Needley and managing partner Andrew Hayden, SCP started as a small independent firm in the UK, committing funds available for investment from their limited partners.

SCP has partnered with over 50 businesses since inception to deliver more than 300 follow-on transactions. The firm has an impressive track record of success.

(Continued)

Several of their portfolio companies that they have successfully exited have won top performance awards in the UK. These include Contractor UK (Reader Awards for Best Contractor – Accountant Large – 2018), Asset Control (Data Management Awards 2018 for Best Sell-Side Enterprise Data Management Platform), NursePlus (The Health Investor Awards – Recruitment Services – Winner) and Optionis (The Sunday Times Grant Thornton Top Track 250 Award, 2019).

More recently, their largest ever and most successful exit of the Linnaeus Group to Mars Petcare's Veterinary Health Group fetched them the 'UK Mid-Cap Exit of the Year' award at the British Private Equity Awards in 2019. This was their second award for the exit of Linnaeus, which won 'UK Mid-Cap Deal of the Year' at the Private Equity Awards earlier the same year.

DataManagement
Awards 2018

 Asset Control
Best Sell-Side Enterprise Data Management Platform

Investment Strategy

As a PE firm, SCP does not invest in the seed/start-up stages. The firm invests in the late-stages, namely, development capital, and MBOs and MBIs, for companies that were acquired but were trying to expand. SCP is considered as a 'Buy and Build specialist', helping their portfolio companies to achieve transformational growth. The firm specializes in providing strategic investment to enable their investees to find innovative ways to create value, organically, through acquisitions, or via a combination of both strategies.

Buy and Build Strategy

Buy: Strategic acquisition rapidly accelerates a company's growth. By adding new geographies, clients and expanding the service offering, businesses can rapidly scale and consolidate market share.

Build: SCP supports intensive organic growth. This enables businesses to rapidly roll-out new sites; invest in systems, technology and infrastructure; optimize their sales & marketing; recruit key talent and a whole lot more. They back businesses where we believe our expertise, network and active partnership can significantly enhance their opportunities.

SCP's largest exit, Linnaeus, is an example of the success of their Buy and Build strategy. Linnaeus saw 21 acquisitions completed, significant organic growth via roll-out funding and an increase in earnings before interest, taxes, depreciation and amortization of more than 700%. The company came to be recognized as one of the UK's leading veterinary services providers.

Linnaeus Group: A Successful Exit

Goal: To build a market leading high-quality veterinary group through organic growth and strategic acquisition.

Strategy: SCP's origination and investment team worked with management to identify and acquire 21 veterinary businesses, expanding Linnaeus' service offering and geographic reach. At the end of Sovereign's investment in June 2018, the Group had five referral hospitals, over 82 first-opinion practices, and more than 1,400 staff.

Result: Linnaeus was recognized as one of the largest and most highly regarded small animal specialist veterinary operators in the UK.

> Our expansion has been pacey but exciting. It's not just that Sovereign supported our M&A activity, their commitment to investing in the best, and focusing on what really matters, was fantastic. (Lynne Hill, CEO, Linnaeus Group)

SCP's competitive advantage in the UK is a function of their deal size. In order to differentiate themselves from competition, the firm concentrates on the lower-end of the midmarket, doing deals in the £20–30 million range. According to Michael Needley, founding partner of SCP, market saturation at the upper end made it difficult to compete with the big players. Investing in the lower-end of the mid-market, so that they did not have to do £50 or £100 million deals and compete with the likes of 3i (one of the biggest PE firms in the UK), gave them a competitive advantage in the UK, at least in the near term.

At the time of inception, the sector specialism of SCP was limited to health care, waste and environmental, and education and sports services. Unlike some of their competitors that invested in technology, SCP called themselves 'mainstay VC investors' in the early years. Michael Needley reiterated that they did not have the expertise or experience in technology, which is why they did not invest in technology then, and it worked well for them at the time:

> We don't invest in tech-related sectors, we have experience and expertise in the four sectors that I mentioned, and if we decided to go into other sectors, it would be a serious disadvantage to us. But the whole premise

(Continued)

of our competitive advantage is that we don't. And we had on lever to
technology people when technology was very popular two or three years
ago and our investors then may have asked us, why don't you invest in
technology... because we don't understand it and it's not our expertise.
And I think in the long term that proved well for us. (Michael Needley,
Founding Partner, SCP)

Also in the early years, SCP's investment strategy was UK-based as the firm's expertise
was primarily in the UK. Hence, their competitors, including their largest competitor
Gresham and other venture capital firms, were all UK-based. They believed they had
good opportunities in the UK to invest locally. There were no decisions on internationalization in the early years, although they expected for that to change in the next five
years when they possibly raised more money from their investors:

There's no strategy that's spelt out. You always have ideas in your head
but there's nothing... we're a small company, and we have always done
the same thing, and our investors like to give us money to keep on doing
it. In five years when we raise our next fund, things may change. We've just
finished raising a fund, that's our largest fund yet, a £120 million, which is
quite a lot of money and we are in the process of investing that right now.
We are hands full for the next couple of years. (Michael Needley, Founding
Partner, SCP)

Over the years, SCP has expanded their industry sector and geographic scope preferences. SCP's preferred industry sectors in 2020 include education and training,
business services, lifestyle, leisure travel, technology and information services, financial services and insurance, and the health care and pharma services sector.

SCP has also evolved in its geographic scope. They add value by partnering with
talented management teams and high-quality businesses to deliver accelerated growth
in specific service-based sectors, both in the UK and internationally.

Resources

SCP needs to have both financial and human capital resources to implement their
investment strategy, whether it is doubling their fund management side, or investing in
(or expanding outside of) their current sectors. In 2020, SCP managed close to £1 billion
of funds. The firm attracted £120 million in capital for its maiden fund in 2001. Two
subsequent funds, launched in 2005 and 2010, raised £275 million and £290 million,
respectively. SCP launched its latest fund, a £395 million buyout vehicle, in 2014. At the
time of writing this case, SCP were raising their fifth fund.

SCP does not often syndicate. As a firm, they do not have strategic alliances with
other VC firms from a co-investment perspective. Occasionally, one or two institutional investors in their fund, if they liked a particular deal or expressed an interest in a particular sector, directly invested in those deals as co-investors along with

SCP partners. Thus, 'piggy-backing' as they call it, happens in some circumstances depending on the sector, the individual limited partner and their preferences and the size of the potential investment. SCP's motivation to co-invest in those cases is due to the interest of their limited partners who wish to have an opportunity to invest alongside the general partners, rather than due to financial constraints per se:

> We don't select our co-investors, our co-investors come to us through the limited partnership agreement so they ask for it, but in a sense you could say we do select them because if we want to take their money or more, we have to allow for them to come with us… So it would be a company that we would want to have along, to have a relationship with. Relationships… yes, I mean if they give us £15–20 million, they become quite important to us. (Michael Needley, Founding Partner, SCP)

Underlying SCP's Buy and Build strategy is one of the largest investment and specialist research teams in their market. According to Michael Needley, SCP was at an 'optimal level' of resourcing and staffing in the early years. They were at a 'very good size' in the amount of funds deployed; however, they would have to bring in the expertise if they sought to diversify in the future. As per the vision of their founding partner, SCP had grown from just seven investment executives at inception to a team of 37 over the years.

Senior partners at the firm currently include Andrew Hayden, Dominic Dalli, Alex Hay, David Myers, Jeremy Morgan, Matthew Owen, Andrew Pars and Kevin Whittle. Of a large senior partner team of eight, five have worked together for 14 years or more. This means they have the expertise and deep sector knowledge to help deliver the growth strategy that was right for their portfolio companies. They have always invested in some of the strategies in similar sectors, so certainly their experience was long and it supported them throughout the process. It is also something that they market quite heavily.

Recently, however, the firm lost several executives to competition as it prepared to raise its fifth buyout fund. Over the past 18 months, eight people in the SCP investment team have left the firm following the retirement of founding partner Michael Needley in 2017. The most recent departure was that of partner Neil Cox, who had worked at SCP for more than a decade and became a partner in 2015 at the time of his promotion. Cox led SCP's largest ever exit in 2019. He worked on the acquisition and sale of veterinary company Linnaeus Group, increasing its earnings before interest, taxes, depreciation and appreciation by 700% in four years and completing 21 bolt-on acquisitions.

Other senior executives who left SCP included director Sunil Jain in February 2019, after seven years within the firm. He joined London-based private equity firm Synova Capital. Investment director Simon Jobson left in 2018 and joined Duke Street, according

(Continued)

to Duke's website. Jobson worked at Sovereign for less than two years. Jobson and another director, Dyson Bogg, left for personal reasons. Bogg left to join Kerogen Capital in January 2019. Director Jose Cesenas left in May 2019, according to Companies House. He worked at Sovereign for 15 years, according to his LinkedIn profile. Earlier in 2020, investment executive Oliver Hedley-Whyte left to join Australian buyout firm Odyssey Private Equity as an investment manager.

Another investment executive, Alexander Postlethwaite, left in March 2019. He joined former investment manager, Ravi Aujla, who left after three years at SCP, at rival private equity firm TPA Capital, according to TPA's website. The firm was formerly known as Capitis Consulting but lately rebranded, according to Private Equity News.

Staff turnover is not rare when private equity firms are planning to or are raising new funds. This is because buyout funds typically last for at least a decade requiring long-term commitments from management. As per SCP's spokesperson, these moves were part of the 'natural evolution' of the firm. 'It's natural that as the firm evolves and matures that there is change'. By mid-2020, SCP is expected to announce two new appointments to the investment team, who will join the four already hired since May 2018.

SCP also took pride in its rich and diverse network of contacts. Their contacts included industry experts in their portfolio companies, some notable examples being Lynne Hill, the highly experienced industry CEO and veterinary surgeon, and Paul Coxon, who SCP had previously backed for their highly successful investment in CVS, UK. They also had a pool of advisors such as Lincoln International, Pinsent Masons, Alvarez & Marsal, Spectrum CF, Mansfield Advisors and Grant Thornton, with whom they consulted in the process of investing their financial capital in portfolio companies. Additionally, SCP had strong ties with their financial institutions that they also got loan funding from as part of the package that they invested.

Investment Process

The investment directors at VC/PE firms are the executives who sit on the investment committee and make investment decisions. Being a small firm, there were fewer layers of bureaucracy at SCP, which was a key competitive advantage. The directors made a collective decision, such that there was only one overall layer of approval for each investment.

However, prospective investees are required to make several presentations while seeking investment funds and the investment committee went through several stages in the process of reviewing those presentations. At first, the investment committee goes through an 'approval stage'. This is followed by a 'preliminary paper', and then a 'due-diligence paper'. These different papers are required to be completed before the investment executives commit to making an investment and deciding whether or not to devote resources to a particular investment.

At the screening stage, SCP sought from their investees a differentiated market positioning, potential for expansion in the UK or internationally, and operations in the service-based sectors. SCP structured deals that suited the interests and ambitions of their portfolio companies. They did not just put the money in; they also support their investees post-investment. A lot of SCP's successes in the past had come from the fact that they were highly involved with the investee companies. Investment executives worked with their investees throughout the investment period to realize their business's potential. They also ensured any follow-on acquisitions that their investee companies made were seamlessly integrated with the core functions at those companies.

The level of control that SCP exerts within the investee firms, post-investment, has both formal and informal components. It was important to put in place formal controls in the early stages post-investment to ensure that all of SCP's criteria were satisfied. Thus, SCP made it mandatory for their investees to adhere to certain policies and procedures from the protocol point of view. They had to make sure that all appropriate reviews and due diligence had been duly done, which could be quite formal at that stage.

At more advanced stages, SCP's level of involvement was a function of their deal size. They were hands-on in terms of their investment style, which meant that they not only sat on all the board meetings, but also attended meetings related to all the financing rounds they were involved in. Quite quickly, they understood if there were any development concerns or obstacles to recovering their portfolio companies.

At an informal level, it was quite easy for their investee companies to get hold of them when needed. In the early years, as SCP, like their investees, were locally based in the UK, they did not have people in different countries needing to fly over in order to support them. The same went for their decision making. As there were only four people on the investment committee, investment decisions on follow-on investments or support companies were typically made quite quickly:

> A lot of our successes in the past have come from the fact that we can be quite involved with the investee company… we just don't put the money in… we're so hands-on and our investment style, we not only sit on all the board meetings, but also on all the financing rounds we're involved in. Quite quickly, we understand if there are any development concerns, or obstacles to recover the company; it's quite easy for investee companies to get hold of us when they need us… Because there's only four people on the investment committee, we can make investment decisions on follow-on investments, or supporting a company typically quite quickly. (Michael Needley, Sovereign Capital, UK)

This informal approach has continued to be a hallmark of SCP's post-investment strategy to the present day. It is very easy for any of SCP's investee companies to just get

(Continued)

on the phone and call them, whether at an early stage or during follow-on investments. The partners believe that it is important for them as a firm to hear from their investee companies rather than not hear at all, which is why phone calls are deemed important. It is also generally easy for SCP partners to do this being a small, non-hierarchical firm. Investees can call the directors themselves who are in a position to make recommendations for every investment:

> We'd rather take a phone call and get a heads-up for what's going on than hear nothing at all. And that's generally quite easy to do because being a small company, we've got rid of lots of hierarchy and if you need to talk to some person making a decision you can get hold of that person directly. Call the directors themselves, and as the director of the company, they are in a position to recommend. Every investment that we make, a director is responsible for that. (Michael Needley, Founding Partner, SCP)

Sources: author's personal interview with Michael Needley; Alves (2019); www.sovereigncapital.co.uk

---

Discussion Questions

1. What type of firm is Sovereign Capital Partners (SCP)? How does SCP differentiate itself from the competition? Explain each of the following aspects of SCP's investment strategy:
   i. Ownership type
   ii. Stage preferences
   iii. Industry sector preferences
   iv. Geographic preferences
2. What are the distinctive resources of SCP? How do these resources contribute to SCP's competitive advantage? Explain.
3. How do the partners at SCP add value to its investees post-investment? What mechanisms do they use to add value and why? Explain the nature of their a) monitoring and b) involvement with their investee firms, post-investment.
4. Go to the NVCA website (www.nvca.org) and find at least one direct competitor of SCP. Study their investment strategy. Would you recommend changing any aspect of SCP's investment strategy based on this information? Why / why not? Give reasons to justify your answer.

References

Alves, J. (2019) 'Sovereign capital loses investment executives as it preps new fund', *The Wall Street Journal*, 23 June. Available at www.penews.com/articles/sovereign-capital-loses-investment-executives-as-it-preps-new-fundraising-20190723 (last accessed 27 September 2022).

Amit, R., Brander, J. and Zott, C. (1998) 'Why do venture capital firms exist? Theory and Canadian evidence', *Journal of Business Venturing*, 13(6): 441–466.

Barry, C.B. (1994) 'New directions in research on venture capital finance', *Financial Management*, 23(3): 3–15.

Bose, K.R. (2008) 'Benchmark capital: The international expansion of a Silicon Valley venture capital firm'. Case E-218. Stanford Graduate School of Business, 9 November. Available at www.gsb.stanford.edu/faculty-research/case-studies/benchmark-capital-international-expansion-silicon-valley-venture (last accessed 27 September 2022).

Bruton, G., Fried, V. and Hisrich, R. (1997) 'Venture Capitalist and CEO Dismissal', *Entrepreneurship Theory and Practice*, 21(3): 41–54.

Busenitz, L.W., Fiet, J.O. and Moesel, D.D. (2005) 'Signaling in venture capitalist – New venture team funding decisions: Does it indicate long–term venture outcomes?' *Entrepreneurship Theory and Practice*, 29(1): 1–12. https://doi.org/10.1111/j.1540-6520.2005.00066.x

Bygrave, W.D. (1987) 'Syndicated investments by venture capital firms: A networking perspective', *Journal of Business Venturing*, 2(2): 139–154. https://doi.org/10.1016/0883-9026(87)90004-8

Bygrave, W.D. and Timmons, J.A. (1986a) 'Networking among venture capital firms', *Frontiers of Entrepreneurship Research*, 437–456.

Bygrave, W.D. and Timmons, J.A. (1992) *Venture Capital at the Crossroads*. Boston, MA: Harvard Business School Press.

Carter, S. and Jones-Evans, D. (2012) *Enterprise and Small Business: Principles, Practice and Policy* (3rd edn)., Harlow: Financial Times Prentice Hall.

Dixon, R. (1991) 'Venture capitalists and the appraisal of investments', *Omega*, 19(5): 333–344.

Fried, V.H., Bruton, G.D. and Hisrich, R.D. (1998) 'Strategy and the board of directors in venture capital-backed firms', *Journal of Business Venturing*, 13(6): 493–503. https://doi.org/10.1016/S0883-9026(97)00062-1

Gorman, M. and Sahlman, W.A. (1989) 'What do venture capitalists do?' *Journal of Business Venturing*, 4(4): 231–248. https://doi.org/10.1016/0883-9026(89)90014-1

Gornall, W. and Strebulaev, I.A. (2015) 'The Economic Impact of Venture Capital: Evidence from Public Companies', *Stanford Graduate School of Business*, Working Paper No. 3362, 1–22.

Hall, J. and Hofer, C.W. (1993) 'Venture capitalists' decision criteria in new venture evaluation', *Journal of Business Venturing*, 8(1): 25–42. https://doi.org/10.1016/0883-9026(93)90009-T

Haverstock, E. (2020) 'As pandemic provides a wake-up call, smokers turn to startups to quit', Pitchbook, 31 March. Available at https://pitchbook.com/news/articles/as-pandemic-provides-a-wake-up-call-smokers-turn-to-startups-to-quit (last accessed 27 September 2022).

Huang, L., Wu, A., Ju Lee, M., Bao, J., Hudson, M. and Bolle, E. (2017) 'The American angel: The first in-depth report on the demographics and investing activity of individual American angel investors'. Harvard Business School Report, November. Available at https://www.hbs.edu/faculty/Pages/item.aspx?num=57843 (last accessed 27 September 2022).

International Finance Corporation (IFC) (2018) 'Sustainability report redefining development finance'. Available at www.ifc.org/wps/wcm/connect/3aa05003-d634-40f9-8af4-35b8c8a87248/IFC-AR18-Full-Report.pdf?MOD=AJPERES&CVID=moNw5we (last accessed 27 September 2022).

Jarvis, R. and Schizas, E. (2012) 'Finance and the small business', in S. Carter and D. Jones-Evans (eds), *Enterprise and Small Business: Principles, Practice and Policy* (3rd edn). Harlow: Financial Times Prentice Hall, pp. 362–385.

Jensen, M.C. and Meckling, W.H. (1976) 'Theory of the firm: Managerial behaviour, agency costs and ownership structure', *Journal of Financial Economics*, 3(4): 305–360.

Lucas, L. (2018) 'Asia close to eclipsing US as world's biggest VC market', *Financial Times*, 10 January. Available at www.ft.com/content/ccd356f6-f67d-11e7-88f7-5465a6ce1a00 (last accessed 27 September 2022).

MacMillan, I.C., Kulow, D.M. and Khoylian, R. (1989) 'Venture capitalists' involvement in their investments: Extent and performance', *Journal of Business Venturing*, 4(1): 27–47.

McNally, K.N. (1994) 'Sources of finance for UK venture capital funds: The role of corporate investors', *Entrepreneurship & Regional Development*, 6(3): 275–297. https://doi.org/10.1080/08985629400000016

Muzyka, D., Birley, S. and Leleux, B. (1996) 'Trade-offs in the investment decisons of European venture capitalists', *Journal of Business Venturing*, 11(4): 273–287. https://doi.org/10.1016/0883-9026(95)00126-3

National Venture Capital Association (NVCA) (2019) *Yearbook*. Data provided by Pitchbook. Available at https://nvca.org/wp-content/uploads/2019/08/NVCA-2019-Yearbook.pdf (last accessed 27 September 2022).

Needleman, S.E. and Kolondny, L. (2013) 'Risks abound, but investors search for promising startups'. *The Wall Street Journal*, 23 January. Available at www.wsj.com/articles/SB10001424127887323301104578258651038480358 (last accessed 27 September 2022).

Pitchbook. (2020) *Pitchbook Data*. Available at https://pitchbook.com/blog#all (last accessed 27 September 2022).

Robinson, P.B. (1987) 'Prediction of entrepreneurship based on attitude consistency model', Unpublished doctoral dissertation, Brigham Young University. *Dissertation Abstracts International*, 48: 2807B.

Rosenstein, J., Bruno, A.V., Bygrave, W.D. and Taylor, N.T. (1993) 'The CEO, venture capitalists, and the board', *Journal of Business Venturing*, 8(2): 99–113. https://doi.org/10.1016/0883-9026(93)90014-V

Timmins, R., Flaim, S., Shipley, T., Bolle, E., Angold, E. and Hudson, M. (2019) 'Angel funders report: The ACA report on angel group investment and the startups they support'. Angel Capital Association. Available at www.angelcapitalassociation.org/angel-funders-report (last accessed 27 September 2022).

Tyebjee, T. and Bruno, A. (1984) 'A model of venture capital investment activity', *Management Science*, 30(9): 1051–1066. https://doi.org/10.1287/mnsc.30.9.1051

Wall, R. (2015) 'Airbus to create venture capital arm, innovation center in Silicon Valley', *The Wall Street Journal*, May 29, 1:11 pm. https://www.wsj.com/articles/airbus-to-create-venture-capital-arm-innovation-center-in-silicon-valley-1432919479

Wright, M. and Robbie, K. (1998) 'Venture capital and private equity: A review and synthesis', *Journal of Business Finance & Accounting*, 25(5–6): 521–570. https://doi.org/10.1111/1468-5957.00201

15
INTERNATIONAL VENTURE CAPITAL

CHINESE VENTURE CAPITAL INVESTMENT IN ISRAEL

Source: www.needpix.com/photo/737090/

(Continued)

Chinese investors have recently joined their American, European and Russian counter-parts to target high-tech prospects in Israel, a country also known as the exit nation due to the strength of its high-tech workforce and R&D talent. In fact, China is expected to surpass the US as Israel's biggest collaborator in the number of joint government-backed development projects. In 2014, deals between Chinese and Israeli firms were $300 million, up from $250 million in 2013.

Chinese companies like Ping An Insurance (Group) Co., Baidu, and Alibaba Group Holding Ltd. are making investment inroads in Israel. Ping An Ventures had made eight investments in Israeli start-ups by 2014. Baidu, a leading Chinese online search and e-commerce company, invested an undisclosed sum in Israel-based venture fund Car-mel Ventures. In May 2014, it announced its first investment in an Israeli start-up: a $3 million investment in Pixellot Ltd., which develops remotely controlled video cameras to provide footage of sports and music events. The company recruited two Israeli technology scouts to search for possible tech investment and acquisition opportunities in Israel.

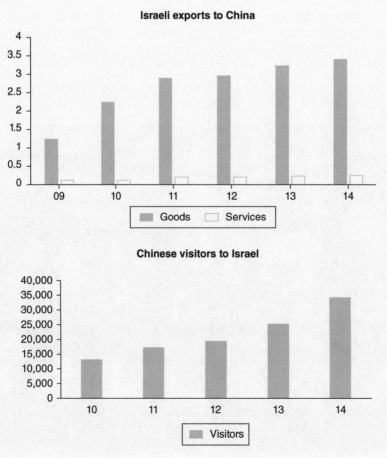

Figure 15.1   Israeli exports to China and Chinese visitors to Israel

Source: adapted from Hirschauge (2014)

Alibaba Group Holding Ltd. invested in, and acquired, Visualead, a 15-person start-up that specializes in QR code generation, in 2015. More recently (March 2019), the company acquired another Israeli start-up, Infinity Augmented Reality, after investing in it in 2016. InfinityAR will join Alibaba's Israel Machine Vision Laboratory.

Chinese investors are seeking new technologies in alternative energy, agriculture and water management that they can usefully apply at home with a view to addressing some of the issues caused by China's rapid urbanization. The deal-making extends to Israel's biotech sector. As Israeli technology companies are still much smaller than their counterparts in Silicon Valley, Chinese VC investors have kept their investment to a few million dollars per deal, sometimes alongside non-Chinese venture-fund partners.

Chinese investment in Israel is good for Israeli start-ups that need Chinese investors and partners. Israel entrepreneurs have begun to view China as a viable option for both growth and exit strategies (Figure 15.1). Investors perceive Israeli entrepreneurs as easier to work with in some cases. Unlike their Silicon Valley counterparts that are keen on disruptive technology, Israeli entrepreneurs take a more practical approach to building their companies.

Sources: Hirschauge (2014); Levingston (2019)

Learning Outcomes

After studying this chapter, you should be ready to:

- **LO1**: Analyze patterns and trends in the international development of venture capital
- **LO2**: Evaluate the role of the external (political, economic, socio-cultural and technological) environment in the international development of venture capital
- **LO3**: Identify trends in cross-border flows of venture capital and discuss reasons for the internationalization of VC firms
- **LO4**: Discuss the challenges to the conduct of Western VC firms' investment operations in emerging markets

Introduction

In Chapter 14, we explained the distinguishing features of venture capital (VC) firms and their role in the funding of rapidly growing new ventures that have the potential to cross geographic boundaries early in their lives. The last two decades have seen the rise of VC Associations in several parts of Asia and the developing world, outside of developed Western markets (IFC, 2018).

There has also been a commensurate rise in cross-border VC investment flows. These flows are no longer limited to outward investments from developed to developing markets. As the opening case shows, even developing countries like China are emerging as active players in their capacity as investors in innovative, high-technology ventures outside their borders.

The development of a VC industry is contingent on the broader institutional environment (Jeng and Wells, 2000; McDougall and Oviatt, 2000). The balance of political, economic, socio-cultural and technological factors in foreign markets also impacts the attractiveness of those markets as potential investment destinations for VC investment, as well as their conduct of operations in those markets. Western VC firms entering developing markets, for example, may be forced to adapt their investment operations in those markets.

In this chapter, we compare and contrast the international environment for the development of venture capital. Using illustrative examples, we evaluate the role of the external environment in the emergence of VC. For high-growth entrepreneurs seeking equity finance, an assessment of external conditions for equity finance can help them to select an optimal location for founding their ventures. For policy makers, a comparative assessment of the external environment can help to identify gaps in the underlying conditions for the development of VC and take steps to address those gaps.

The structure of this chapter is as follows. We first chart broad trends in the international development of VC, and evaluate the role of the external environment in the development of VC. Next, we identify trends in cross-border VC investment flows. We then discuss reasons for the internationalization of VC firms. Finally, we review challenges to the conduct of VC firms' operations in foreign markets.

International Development of VC: Patterns and Trends

The United States is the birthplace of the VC/PE industry. According to the National Venture Capital Association (NVCA), 257 US VC funds closed on $54 billion in capital commitments in 2018 (NVCA, 2019). The US share of global fundraising remained strong, accounting for two-thirds of total funds raised and 51% of global VC investment in 2018.

At the same time, however, the US share of global capital invested and exited has dropped precipitously over the past 15 years. In 2018, the US share of global VC investment was well below its 84% global share in 2004, and almost 90% share in the 1990s. At 40%, US share of total capital exited also dipped below 50% for the first time in 2018.

Over the years, VC has become a conduit for the flow of capital and ideas on a global basis (Patricof, 1989). According to PricewaterhouseCoopers, global VC funding increased nearly 50% year on year to more than $164 billion invested across 11,042 deals in 2017 (Lucas, 2018). Globally, $254 billion was invested across nearly 15,300 deals in 2018 (NVCA, 2019).

Table 15.1 VC associations

Country	VC Association/ Website	Year Founded	Members (VC Firms)	Mission Statement
USA	National Venture Capital Association (NVCA) www.nvca.org	1973	780+	Venture capital has enabled the United States to support its entrepreneurial talent by turning ideas and basic research into products and services that have transformed the world.
UK	British Venture Capital and Private Equity Association (BVCA) www.bvca.co.uk	1983	500+	The BVCA exists to connect all of the internal components of the private equity and venture capital industry – investors, fund managers, entrepreneurs and companies, advisers and service providers – to each other, and to represent their interests to government, parliamentarians, officials and regulators, the media, other sections of the business community and society at large.
India	Indian Venture Capital Association (IVCA) www.ivca.in	1993	15+	IVCA as an industry representative body aims to develop and promote India's private equity sector and actively demonstrate its impact to the government, media and the public at large, establish high standards of ethics, business conduct and professional competence and serve as a platform for investment funds to interact with each other and develop the ecosystem of India's PE/VC industry.
China	Chinese Venture Capital and Private Equity Association (CVCA) www.cvca.org.cn	2002	50+	Supports the sustainable development of venture capital and private equity industry in the Greater China region; fosters the understanding of the importance of venture capital and private equity to the vitality of the Greater China economy and global economies; promotes government policies conducive to the development of venture capital and private equity; promotes and maintains high ethical and professional standards; facilitates networking and knowledge sharing opportunities among members; provides research data, publications and professional development programs for members; provides quality informational/networking services between members and entrepreneurs.
Singapore	Singapore Venture Capital and Private Equity Association (SVCA) www.svca.org.sg	1992	40+	To foster greater understanding of the importance of venture capital and private equity to the economy in support of entrepreneurship, innovation and growth, and to represent the interests of members in the broader VC and PE community.
South Korea	Korean Venture Capital Association (KVCA) www.kvca.or.kr	1970	160+	To promote a more favorable system and vibrant investment environment for the development of the venture capital industry, but also to enhance awareness and understanding of the importance of venture capital to the Korean economy. Furthermore, it facilitates interaction among its members as well as communication between the members and key industry participants including institutional investors, entrepreneurs, policy makers and so on.
Malaysia	Malaysian Venture Capital and Private Equity Association (MVCA) www.mvca.org.my	1995	100+	To promote and develop the venture capital and private equity industry in Malaysia, and advocate policies that enhance the environment for venture capital and private equity activities.

Sources: https://nvca.org; www.bvca.co.uk/about-us; www.eesc.europa.eu/en/about; https://ivca.in; http://cvca.org.cn; www.svca.org.sg/history; www.kvca.or.kr; https://mvca.org.my

Originating in the US, there are VC Associations throughout the UK, Western Europe, France and Japan (Table 15.1). While Australia created the atmosphere for the growth of VC through the deregulation of its financial markets, state-dominated economies like Sweden have also witnessed the emergence of this form of finance. Asian countries like China and India have started to think of ways risk capital can help to solve their development problems. Following a drastic drop in public equity values in the aftermath of the stock market crash of the early 2000s, institutional investors have turned to international VC to diversify their portfolios.

VC/PE in UK

VC/PE began to develop in Western Europe in the early 1980s, first in the UK, and then on the Continent. Toby Wyles, Managing Partner, Virtuvian Partners, and former partner, Apax Partners, UK, recalled the role of Alan Patricof, one of the American founding partners of Apax Partners, to bring VC (and private equity), and even limited partnership structure, to Europe:

> when we started, it was so long ago, it was in the 1980s, the only place in the world where venture capital existed was America. So Alan Patricof, one of our partners who had created the firm was American, and he had managed some private equity money. So when he teamed up with the other partners (in the UK and France), he was really bringing venture capital to Europe. At that point, in Europe, the only venture capital firm was 3i. (Toby Wyles, Managing Partner, Virtuvian Partners and Former Partner, Apax Partners, UK)

Until the 1990s, the VC industry in Europe was small and inactive. As in the US, PE in Europe was concentrated in geographic pockets, the three most active countries in terms of fundraising being the UK, France and Germany. Driven by financial success and improvements in public stock markets, prospects improved in the 2000s (Bose, 2008). Accounting for approximately 75% of the European VC pool, the UK VC/PE industry is one of the largest in Europe and second in importance globally to the US (Tyebjee and Vickery, 1988).

Total fundraising in the UK reached £34.12 billion, with 94 funds raising new capital in 2018 (BVCA, 2018). Over the years, the UK industry has gravitated towards VC fundraising and investment. VC investment in 2018 increased by 21%, more than doubling since 2015. There was a corresponding 8% fall in later stage investments.

VC in Emerging Markets

VC in emerging markets such as Central and Eastern Europe and Asia began to appear only in the 1990s. Emerging markets have exhibited strong growth in recent years (Hammer, 2018).

As Figure 15.2 shows, VC has emerged in Latin America, the Middle East and North Africa (MENA) region, sub-Saharan Africa, as well as South Asia, outside of the developed West. As of May 2018, emerging market-based VC fund managers located in these economies closed nearly 600 VC funds and secured an aggregate $47 billion in the past decade (Hammer, 2018).

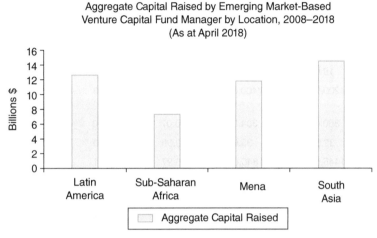

Figure 15.2 Aggregate capital raised by emerging market-based venture capital fund manager by location, 2008–18

Source: Hammer (2018)

Asia

Asia is closing in on the US as the biggest home for venture capital (Table 15.2) (Lucas, 2018). In the ten years from 2010–2020, Asia-focused funds have grown 30% a year, on average, compared to 9% annual growth for their North America-centered counterparts (Loh, 2019). Whereas funding in the US rose 17% year on year, it more than doubled in Asia.

Table 15.2   Annual global VC financing trend: Asia

Year	Deals (#)	Investment ($b)
2012	765	5.66
2013	1040	7.87
2014	1500	22.36
2015	2020	42.20
2016	2020	32.75
2017	2938	70.86

Source: adapted from Lucas (2018)

Australia, Hong Kong / China, Singapore, Taiwan, Thailand and Vietnam saw a rise in both capital under management and new funds raised in 2018 over the corresponding levels in 2017 (Table 15.3). The percentage increase in capital under management is especially stark in Hong Kong / China, Singapore and Taiwan.

Table 15.3   Capital under management and new funds raised in Asia (2017–18)

Country	Capital Under Management (2017) (USD $b)	Capital Under Management (2018) (USD $b)	Percentage Change (%)	New Funds Raised (2017) (USD $b)	New Funds Raised (2018) (USD $b)	Percentage Change (%)
Australia	18.05	21.06	0.17	0.21	0.91	3.33
Hong Kong / China	4200.00	7400.00	0.76	13.63	35.00	1.57
India	360.00	334.82	−0.07	0.90	2.30	1.56
Indonesia	32.61	35.61	0.09	3.00	2.12	−0.29
Japan	1445.57	1840.00	0.27	2.51	1.21	−0.52
Malaysia	188.62	180.69	−0.04	1.70	1.48	−0.13
Singapore	2409.64	3200.00	0.33	1.20	7.50	5.25
South Korea	899.51	883.00	−0.02	0.60	6.81	10.43
Taiwan	202.00	246.46	0.22	4.65	17.00	2.66
Thailand	162.79	164.06	0.01	0.11	0.13	0.18
Vietnam	1.55	1.44	−0.07	0.29	0.89	2.05
Total	9920.33	14307.15	0.44	28.79	58.34	1.03

Sources: http://tvca.or.th/resources; www.sitca.org.tw/ENG/SitcaData/SD1003.aspx?PGMID=SD0103; Asia Asset (2019); Australian Investment Council (2019); Beyond Ventures (n.d.); Bhattacharya (2018); Cheok (2018); EMPEA (2019); FINSMES (2018); IBEF (n.d.); IBEF (2018); Lee (2018); PricewaterhouseCoopers (2018); Securities Commission Malaysia (n.d. a, b); Straits Times (2019); Vietnam Briefing (2019); VinaCapital (2017); Yi (2018); Young-sil (2019a, b)

VC funds that have successfully raised capital in emerging markets have been over-whelmingly early-stage focused (Hammer, 2018). In 2017–18, the MENA region took the lead in terms of the proportion of funds raised for early-stage investment, followed by South Asia and Latin America. However, pre-IPO bridge funding and funding that is necessary for achieving scale has been lacking. Such a gap has hindered the potential for growth in these markets, posing a significant developmental obstacle for entrepreneurial ventures operating there.

Factors Influencing the International Development of Venture Capital

Each country has its own institutions and policies that shape its VC industry (Mason and Harrison, 1999; Ooghe et al., 1991; Wright and Robbie, 1998). The level of political and economic stability, development of the stock market, culture of entrepreneurship and attitudes to risk, and size of the technology sector are all crucial. Much of VC's success in the US, for example, comes from policies that encourage new company formation, the protection of intellectual property, and financial recognition of success and talent (NVCA, 2019).

An understanding of the external environment for VC is important for VC firms seeking new investment opportunities in foreign markets, as well as for their selection and implementation of foreign market entry strategies in those markets. Varied fiscal and economic environments in developing countries, for example, have implications for VC firms' strategies as they embark upon internationalization, especially from developed into developing markets. For entrepreneurs, an appreciation of differences in the international development of VC can help them to compare and contrast the attractiveness of different countries for founding and growing new ventures.

In this section, we use the PEST (political, economic, socio-cultural, technological) framework to review the external environment for the international development of VC.

Political and Regulatory Environment (P)

Government policy measures can enhance the supply of venture capital. In contrast, legal and regulatory barriers such as the lack of relevant legislation, discretionary nature of existing rules, and over regulation can impede the development of a VC market (IFC, 2018). A lengthy and complex competition approval process, for example, can prove to be both expensive and time consuming for small VC/PE funds, especially if countries are under a regional market and multiple regulatory bodies are responsible for competition policy.

A host of legislative changes and conscious government initiatives like the Business Start-Up Scheme in 1981, and the Unlisted Securities Market in London in 1980, fostered the rapid growth of VC/PE in the UK (Wright et al., 1992). They also led to the emergence of specialized late-stage investments in the form of management buy-outs.

Historically, complex fiscal and regulatory contexts of many European states have been responsible for stifled demand for, and supply of, VC (Martin and Sunley, 2018). Double taxation of dividends and greater tax deductions for interest expenses than dividends paid in Italy and France, for example, has been detrimental to the growth of VC. High capital gains and equity taxes, as well as complex company laws in several other states, have been obstacles to equity trading and buy-out activity. Fragmented patent laws, bankruptcy laws and demanding company registration procedures have all limited the demand for VC.

In recent years, there has been some progress in improving the institutional infrastructure and presence of intermediaries in the European states (Martin and Sunley, 2018). In addition, specific policy measures in some member states have been targeted at increasing the supply of VC. The Dutch industry, for instance, was significantly boosted by the provision of a public guarantee of 50% of VC investments. A similar measure was also introduced in Denmark.

Likewise, public subsidies to VC in Germany have acted as a magnet for private funding. On the demand side, initiatives such as changes to capital gains rules for start-up founders and visas for foreign entrepreneurs in France, some launched almost a decade ago and given new energy by President Emmanuel Macron, have cut red tape and boosted enthusiasm around entrepreneurship (Michaels and Schechner, 2018).

ROLE OF GOVERNMENT IN THE DEVELOPMENT OF VENTURE CAPITAL IN ISRAEL

The Israeli government took several initiatives to provide equity finance as well as create a market for domestic VC/PE funds in Israel in the 1990s (IFC, 2018). In 1991, the government created a technological incubator program that provided selected entrepreneurs with tools, professional guidance and seed capital. In return, the government incubator could take up to 20% of the start-up and receive royalties of 3% of the company's eventual sales.

In 1993, the incubator created the Yozma Group with $100 million of capital by the Israeli government to anchor up to 40% (or $8 million) of qualifying VC funds' total commitments alongside additional private capital of $12 million. Co-invested with ten funds from outside of Israel, and modeled as limited partnerships, as in the US, the group originated from an Israeli government program aimed at promoting VC investments in high-growth companies in strategic sectors, namely communications, information technologies, and life sciences where the country had demonstrated world leadership. Within five years of the initial launch of the Yozma Group, 60 VC funds were active in Israel, managing over $10 billion.

By 1998, Israel had attracted over $3 billion in VC investment – a 30-fold increase in less than three years – and had over 3,000 start-up companies, or one for every 2,000 inhabitants. The group is considered as one of the key factors underlying the country's entrepreneurial success. Other investors in this fund were required to pay the government only nominal interest on its money, but had the option to buy out the government's original investment after a few years. This feature was very attractive to investors since it left them the majority of the economic benefits after the government had borne the phase of greater risk. The requirement to include foreign capital in the qualifying funds resulted in the participation of significant pools of overseas capital (mostly from the US, Japan and Germany). The investment expertise of these funds contributed to capacity building in the Israeli market.

Source: IFC (2018)

Governments in several emerging economies have also taken proactive action and introduced positive reforms for developing VC. Recognizing the economic benefits from entrepreneurial start-ups, the government in Argentina, for example, passed Argentina's Entrepreneurship and Venture Capital Law (IFC, 2018). The law created the Fiduciary Fund for the Development of Venture Capital (FONDCE), which allocates public finance to qualifying investments via loans, direct equity investments, and investments in funds, among other instruments. This law set up the Simplified Stock Companies, a business organization type that offers greater flexibility, and makes it simpler and quicker to register a company. Three state-sponsored funds have been established to participate in different parts of Argentina's capital markets that need to be developed or scaled.

Economic Environment (E)

The state of the economy, availability of stock markets and commercial banks are all influential for the development of VC. The problems of severe recession, coupled with the subsequent need for conglomerates to reverse earlier diversification policies in the early 1980s in the UK, for example, were, in large part, responsible for the growth of VC/PE in the country (Wright et al., 1992). The wave of restructuring accompanying the process of transformation to a market economy in the 1990s offered fresh avenues for the development of VC in the Central and Eastern Europe region.

Key to building any VC/PE ecosystem is providing the possibility of exits through liquid stock markets (IFC, 2018). Financial markets that offer diverse capital sources the ability to participate in exit opportunities allow VC/PE managers to commit capital, and create value alongside a deepening pool of skilled labor.

Historically, cumbersome regulatory structures and the lack of exit routes and stock options have militated against a sufficient supply of risk capital in Europe (Martin and Sunley, 2002). European stock markets have been too small and fragmented to provide the necessary liquidity. Between 1992 and 1997, for example, there were 1,200 venture-backed IPOs in the US, compared to 244 in the UK and only 156 in the rest of Europe.

Before the 1980s, SMEs had difficulty obtaining equity finance because there were few second-tier equity markets, and the first-tier markets had over-demanding listing requirements. The creation of the UK's AIM, France's Nouveau Marche, Frankfurt's Neuer Markt and Milan's Nuovo Mercato in the mid-1990s improved the situation. The creation of EASDAQ in Europe was meant to remedy the lack of a pan-European market for raising liquidity for small, high-technology companies; however, it remained too small to attract large numbers of European entrepreneurs.

Few markets in developing countries have the scale and sophistication to support native VC/PE markets that offer the depth and deal selectivity necessary for a VC/PE ecosystem to evolve (Lucas, 2018). In China, one-time start-ups such as handset maker

Xiaomi have recently been eyeing the public markets, where liquidity is abundant. On the one hand, China's tech titans, Tencent and Alibaba, are seeing their prices propelled higher. On the other hand, a number of recent stumbles deflating the value of high-profile start-ups, including WeWork, and disappointing IPOs for companies such as Uber and Lyft, are expected to reduce valuations (Loh, 2019). Economic challenges and relatively shallow capital markets in countries like Argentina have similarly curtailed the natural growth of the country's entrepreneurial activity (IFC, 2018).

Socio-Cultural Environment (S)

Socio-cultural factors such as attitudes to risk and social networks play a role in the development of a VC market.

Attitudes to Risk

Traditional attitudes to firm ownership have been one of the major factors explaining the immaturity of many European VC markets (Martin and Sunley, 2002). Historically, many firms in Europe have been family owned and most have preferred bank loans to equity finance. Entrepreneurs' desire for control and reluctance to part with equity have impacted the development of risk capital.

Although Berlin is unusual by German standards in tolerating business failure (Michaels and Schechner, 2018), firms in Germany have been overwhelmingly reliant on banks (Martin and Sunley, 2002). Compared to 50% in the US and UK, the ratio of equity to total assets in Germany has typically been less than 20%. Entrepreneurs in Italy have been very reluctant to take equity partners because of the fear of undesired external influence and the possible loss of control.

Searching for equity capital has also been potentially damaging to reputation in Europe and Latin America. European entrepreneurs have found themselves to suffer from a relatively low social status. Although this image is now changing, unlike in the US, bankruptcy in many European states remains tainted with stigma and failure. Translated as 'risk capital' in Spanish, VC generates negative connotations for both entrepreneurs and prospective investors in Argentina (IFC, 2018). Local policy makers in Argentina have started to refer to VC as 'entrepreneurship capital' to overcome this perception issue, and generate broader appeal and acceptance for VC for all kinds of entrepreneurs.

Social Networks

Social networks and enterprise demographics influence receptivity to VC. Small firms in India, for example, make as much or more use of equity finance than large firms primarily through informal networks of family, friends and business contacts. Because their ownership is not dispersed, the mass of small and medium-sized firms benefit from lower information asymmetries and lower agency costs.

Representing up to 70% of the private economy, family businesses in the MENA region, similarly, are known for raising equity funding within tightly knit family circles (Mahroum, 2016) (see Box below). At the same time, however, the conventional wisdom of drawing on friends and family fosters a risk-averse business culture. Keeping businesses in the family also reduces their disruptive potential, even when they do manage to innovate.

ENTERPRISE DEMOGRAPHICS AND THE CHALLENGE OF RISK CAPITAL IN THE MIDDLE EAST AND NORTH AFRICA REGION

The MENA region's start-up scene is coming of age. The successes of the region's start-ups should not be underestimated. According to Wamda, a regional accelerator platform, more than a dozen start-ups – including Bayt, Careem, MarkaVIP, Namshi, News Group, Propertyfinder and Wadi.com – now have estimated valuations above $100 million. With a valuation above $1 billion, Souq.com, a 3,000-employee company founded in 2005, is poised to be the region's first 'unicorn'.

Yet, MENA entrepreneurs face serious structural impediments to progress. The regional environment remains far from conducive to entrepreneurship. One of the key problems relates to enterprise demographics. According to some estimates, family businesses represent up to 70% of the MENA private-sector economy – a higher share than in any other region. This means that a large segment of the business community raises funds, shares equity and manages operations within small, tight-knit social circles.

The conventional wisdom of drawing on friends, family and fools for new business endeavors seems to translate in the MENA region as, 'If you are not a friend or family, you must be a fool'. While this might help to contain risk, it also fosters a risk-averse business culture. And yet, a willingness to take risks is pivotal to innovation and entrepreneurship. Moreover, keeping businesses in the family reduces their disruptive potential, even when they do manage to innovate.

This family-oriented, or 'tribal', business culture is the result of a long history of inefficient commercial judicial systems, arbitrary nationalization programs, and a lack of effective corporate governance. While most countries have made improvements on these fronts, the tribal business tradition remains entrenched, and will take time to dislodge.

Source: Mahroum (2016)

Technological Environment (T)

Innovative technology companies are magnets for VC finance. In the US, for example, artificial intelligence attracted increasing financing, up to $5 billion in 2017, while $2.5 billion went into genomics in the same year (Lucas, 2018). Coupled with fiscal incentives like loss guarantee programs of the government, the large size of the technology sector has also been instrumental for the development of the VC industry in the UK (Jarvis and Schizas, 2012).

Historically, the difference in the size of the technology sector in the UK relative to the US has shaped the evolution of VC/PEs in these markets. As discussed in Chapter 14, VC in Europe is different from its namesake in the US. Compared to the US, VC in Europe is less technology oriented and more focused on mature and later-stage deals rather than young, rapidly growing entrepreneurial companies (Jarvis and Schizas, 2012).

However, as the Box below shows, the recent public listing of some successful technology start-ups like the Dutch payments company Adyen NV, that handles payment processing for the likes of Facebook Inc., and Uber Technologies Inc., has sparked excitement in Europe's tech start-up scene (Michaels and Schechner, 2018). The rousing listing of the company is offering investors hope that Europe's tech scene is finally fertile enough to generate a stream of successful start-ups.

HIGH-TECHNOLOGY ENTREPRENEURSHIP AND THE DEVELOPMENT OF VENTURE CAPITAL IN EUROPE

The number and variety of technology start-ups in Europe has ballooned in recent years. As compared to the last two decades when the European tech scene had some false starts, recent high-growth prospects have attracted a growing amount of venture capital money. At $8.7 billion, equity funding in VC-backed start-ups went up 13% in Europe in the first half of 2018 over the same period a year earlier, and up 44% from five years ago.

Cities such as London, Paris and Berlin already have developed tech ecosystems, with growing numbers of local VC firms and incubators. London has many fintech firms like Revolut Ltd. and Funding Circle Holdings Ltd. Established firms in Paris include carpooling service BlaBlaCar, as well as a sprawling new start-up campus called Station F. The start-up factory Rocket Internet SE has spawned several successful ventures.

Other European cities are aiming to replicate that formula. The success of the music-streaming service Spotify Technologies SA in Sweden has inspired others like payments firm iZettle, which was bought earlier this year by PayPal Inc. just before it was going to go public. The Estonian creators of Skype have helped promote Tallinn as a tech hub with successes like fintech start-up TransferWise Ltd.

Several tech ventures have also gone public in Europe in recent years. These include Zalando SE, Delivery Hero AG and HelloFresh SE in Berlin. Founded in 2006, Adyen, a platform that handles payment processing for companies including Netflix Inc., Facebook Inc. and Uber Technologies Inc., is a star example. The venture achieved its initial public offering (IPO) in 2018. The IPO was one of Europe's largest that year. The company's shares were up 156% since the IPO, valuing the company at more than $25 billion.

Launched by two entrepreneurs with a track record of successfully exiting two fintech start-ups, the Adyen IPO serves as a role model to other entrepreneurs at high-growth tech companies in many ways. The two co-founders are among a growing European wave of serial tech founders who are tapping experience, connections and capital from earlier ventures to establish and finance new ventures. The success of the start-up signals the greater willingness of technology investors to invest in a more mature and dynamic European ecosystem as a whole.

Source: Michaels and Schechner (2018)

Technological capabilities are also a factor for the emergence of the newer VC markets such as India and China that have now built a track record of successful technology-driven exits. Many innovative companies that have driven China to the forefront of sustainable industries, including electric vehicles, shared asset business models and information marketplaces have been backed by domestic VC/PE funds (IFC, 2018). These companies have efficiently used resources, reversed the country's crippling levels of pollution and meaningfully reduced carbon emissions.

According to Jixun Foo, managing partner at GGV Capital, which has offices in Beijing and Shanghai, rising disposable incomes and mobile phone penetration in the country offer compelling business opportunities for a new wave of tech start-ups (Loh, 2019). Additionally, there is no shortage of entrepreneurs targeting basic infrastructure-building, payments, lending and logistics – a breeding ground for new business model innovation in China.

Internationalization of Venture Capital Firms

The globalization of venture capital has seen increasing cross-border activity both from and into developed Western markets. In 2018, UK PE firms invested £7.44 billion into UK portfolio companies and £6.05 billion into overseas portfolio companies (BVCA, 2018). Portfolio companies in the UK also received equity investment from overseas amounting to £2.34 billion.

Cross-border investment activity has been characterized by investment flows both within developed markets, and into less developed markets elsewhere. US investors, for instance, are showing an increasing interest in European companies. US-based investors are the largest source of capital for VC/PE funds globally (IFC, 2018).

Particularly significant in recent years is the growth of international VC investments into emerging markets such as China and India. Top-tier innovation hubs such as Beijing and Shanghai dominate the surge in Asia-focused investment, with the ten largest Asia-based VC funds headquartered in China (Loh, 2019).

New opportunities are also beginning to appear in other more fringe, regional markets, such as Latin America, South-East Asia, and, to a lesser degree, Africa and the Middle East (Hammer, 2018). Major US VC firms are setting up posts in places such as Singapore and Mexico City so they can be closer to the markets that interest them (NVCA, 2019).

In 2019, the global investment team of the Silicon Valley Bank spent time in Mexico, Brazil and Australia, among other places, to link investors with opportunities in those countries. US VCs such as Andreessen Horowitz, Accel and Foundation Capital are collaborating with local VC firms to finance Mexico-based technology.

Reasons for VC Firm Internationalization

The reasons for the internationalization of VC firms include the historical origins of VC/PE firms, and investors' preferences. The rise in cross-border VC investment flows is also attributed to both 'push' and 'pull' factors in home and foreign markets, respectively.

Historical Origins

In some cases, internationalization is embedded in VC firms' historical origins. According to Toby Wyles, former partner at Apax Partners in London, UK, their firm had been international since inception because of its origins in the US, UK and France. The partners at Apax had plans to expand beyond those geographies very early in their life as they believed that the VC industry would evolve to become a global industry.

Likewise, HSBC (Hong Kong Shanghai Banking Corporation) Private Equity, UK, opened offices in New York, Buenos Aires and the Middle East, all outside of London, by virtue of the fact that their parent company, HSBC, had international operations as part of its history:

> We've had international offices for a long long time, say 30 years. So, that's more a result of our parent company internationalizing. So we internationalized because we're part of an international operation with international history. And one asks oneself historically, if we hadn't belonged to HSBC, would we have offices in Hong

Kong, Middle East, New York? The answer is probably not. We set ourselves up from the start as an independent organization in Europe. We probably still would operate within Europe. (Brian Denman, HSBC Private Equity, UK)

Investors' Preferences

VC firm internationalization can also be client-driven, where 'client' refers to investors in VC funds. As Julian Knott at Electra Partners Europe explained, being a captive organization that was wholly controlled by their parent, the Electra Investment Trust, who was also their principal investor, they had to reflect the wishes of their parent. They sought to internationalize their business as their parent desired exposure outside of the UK to Europe, the USA and the Far East:

> Our internationalization was client-driven [investor-driven]… we used to manage money really principally for one client – Electra Investment Trust (EIT). EIT did not just want to be exposed just to the UK PE market. It wanted an exposure first in mainland Europe, and the USA, and then it wanted to begin to put a toe in the water in the Far East. And that's principally why we internationalized our business. At that time, we were very much a captive organization, commercially or totally controlled by our investor and, therefore, we effectively were just reflecting the wishes of our parent, which had to be our principal client. (Julian Knott, Electra Partners Europe)

Push Factors in Domestic Markets

Domestic market saturation in traditional VC markets has led VC firms abroad. Following domestic economic turmoil and intense competition in Silicon Valley in the late 2000s, both US and international VC investors began to look for new markets abroad (Hammer, 2018). Valuations in high-growth potential start-ups in developed markets have become increasingly stretched, making it more difficult to generate returns.

As Michael Needley, Sovereign Capital, UK, noted, the availability of attractive opportunities in the home market can be a deterrent to internationalization. The partners at Sovereign Capital chose to focus on the domestic market in order to capitalize on the abundance of investment opportunities in the UK in the early 1990s. Their investors were also convinced of their domestic UK market expertise and focus, and hence their intention to stay local.

In other cases like Russia, domestic VC funds are shifting their gaze to outside the country due to exacerbated political and economic risks in the country. The loss of value of the ruble against the dollar since Russia's annexation of Crimea, and, more recently, invasion of Ukraine in 2022 and the imposition of Western sanctions have made the local investing climate less attractive to investors.

THE FLIGHT OF RUSSIAN VENTURE FUNDS OVERSEAS

A robust start-up scene emerged in Russia after the collapse of the Soviet Union, and venture capital funds followed closely behind. However, Russian VC funds are now shifting their gaze to outside of Russia, contributing to an exodus of capital from the country. Many funds are opening offices abroad or focusing on foreign companies. Moscow-based venture capital fund, Maxfield Capital, for instance, opened offices in Tel Aviv, London and New York earlier this year.

Russia's central bank projected the country would suffer relatively low capital flight of $30 billion to $40 billion in 2016; however, the figures did not reflect the full picture. According to the Bank of Russia, $56.9 billion in capital left the country in 2015, including some from funds that invest in new technology companies. For Emery Capital, for example, Russia-based investments 'historically' accounted for about 30% of its portfolio. Now that share is nearly zero. The fund focuses on Israel.

Political and economic risks are contributing to the exodus of venture capital from Russia. The atmosphere in Russia is considered to be 'depressing', and the state is perceived as rather aggressive, pushing society to reject anybody who thinks differently. This thinking was becoming increasingly difficult for VC investors to accept.

Russia's annexation of Crimea in 2014 and the imposition of Western sanctions led to a loss in the value of the ruble against the dollar by almost 50%. While the currency has somewhat recovered, it remains vulnerable to swings in oil prices. The drop in capital investment in the country mainly reflects Russia's inability to borrow on global capital markets due to sanctions. But money continues to flow abroad, despite the government's attempts to attract investment.

Some VC firms are choosing to leave Russia altogether, saying the country does not allow entrepreneurship to thrive. Some investors believe that Russian founders often see their start-ups as a part-time activity, not feeling responsible for investors' money. The quality of ideas is also not the best, especially compared to Israel and Northern Europe. The search for growth, liquidity, bigger rounds and exits and more dynamic ecosystems has propelled them to leave.

Source: Razumovskaya (2016)

Pull Factors in Foreign Markets

The **availability of attractive investment opportunities** in foreign markets pulls VC investors abroad. For example, the attraction of France and Germany as the two most active PE markets outside of the UK in Europe, led Electra Partners UK to these markets:

the reason why we went into France and Germany was because they are the two most active private equity markets besides UK in Europe. (Julian Knott, Electra Partners UK)

Investment executives at Apax Partners, UK, likewise, chose to enter Germany in the 1990s to take advantage of Germany's attraction as a PE market driven by the size of the economy, the presence of technology companies, and large, family-owned companies that they could re-structure:

> We chose Germany as we felt that if this is prospering in time in the UK
> and France, then it should prosper in time in Germany. It took a long time
> to get going, but the German market took off towards the end of the 1990s.
> The decision to go into Germany was driven by the size of the economy, by
> the fact that Germany had technology companies, and a lot of large, family
> owned companies, which have succession issues, and they had some very large
> corporates we had to restructure. (Toby Wyles, Managing Partner, Virtuvian
> Partners, and Former Partner, Apax Partners, UK)

The presence of attractive investment opportunities and radical reforms in many developing nations has made them conducive VC/PE investment destinations in recent years. In a process known loosely as 'geo-arbitrage' or 'tropicalization', VC funds began to back start-ups that take an established business model and adapt it to an emerging market (Hammer, 2018). This phenomenon has been especially evident in China and India in recent years. Flipkart (an Indian e-commerce site similar to Amazon), Baidu (a Chinese internet company similar to Google) and Alibaba (a Chinese online auction site comparable to eBay) are some examples of this trend.

Emerging economies allow VC firms from developed markets more room to operate simply due to the presence of a smaller number of players (Hammer, 2018). Fast-growing start-ups like ride-hailing services Grab and Go-Jek, both of which enjoy valuations in excess of $10 billion, have raised the profile of South-East Asia among VCs (Loh, 2019).

Vijay Maheshwari, a US-based entrepreneur and founder of Verismo Networks, California, recalled that VCs were not very supportive of having a team in India when he first entered there to set up an office in the early 2000s. Therefore, he made no mention of his India team when he approached VCs for fundraising. However, the situation has recently been reversed, with VCs increasingly wanting Silicon Valley entrepreneurs to have teams outside of the country:

> It is funny that in the early 2000s VCs were not very supportive of having team
> back in India. We had engineering team here, we had engineering team in India
> but when we talk to VCs we never mention about the team back then... but
> now it's the reverse... VCs want you to have a team outside of Silicon Valley.

> And that change I think was the dot.com. Things went down in 2003. Things started to change... (Vijay Maheswari, Founder, Verismo Networks, California)

At the same time, however, VC/PE investments in developing countries, especially for offshore funds, can be made more complicated and time consuming (IFC, 2018). The regulatory framework and investment guidelines for domestic pension funds or insurance companies in some developing countries are biased towards investments in the country, and specifically in government securities or listed markets, making it difficult for mostly offshore VC/PE funds to attract domestic capital. These regulations also restrict the ability of long-term domestic investors, such as pension funds, to invest in VC/PE funds.

VC Investment Behavior in Foreign Markets

There exist wide variations in the nature of VC firms' operations between developed and emerging markets. Internationalizing VC firms entering foreign markets need to adapt their investment behavior in those markets. For entrepreneurs seeking VC investment in foreign markets, a comparison of foreign and domestic VC firms' investment operations can help them to decide whether to approach a foreign or domestic VC firm for funding their ventures.

As the history of VC in emerging economies is relatively shorter than in developed economies, and cross-border investment flows have originally characterized outflows from developed to emerging markets, we examine the investment behavior of VC firms originating in developed markets. In this section, we examine US firms' investment behavior predominantly in China.

In the early stages of development of the VC/PE industry in China, US dollar denominated funds with capital from international investors played a significant role in China (IFC, 2018). Managed by foreign expatriates, these funds were mainstream in the 1990s and early 2000s, and helped create/spin-off a new generation of Chinese VC/PE managers.

Although Renminbi (RMB)-denominated VC/PE funds now dominate the investment landscape in China, US dollar denominated VC/PE funds are expected to continue to pioneer investments in certain sectors and play an important educational role in China, especially concerning best practices in governance, corporate social responsibility and sustainable investing. Below, we examine US VC firms' investment behavior in China at key stages of the VC investment process.

Deal Generation

As discussed in the last chapter, the identification of exceptional innovators with relevant expertise in developed markets entails active deal seeking through the use of executive search agencies, or attendance at conventions, trade fairs and conferences

(Bygrave and Timmons, 1986a, b; Tyebjee and Bruno, 1984). Inter-firm competition for initial buy-out transactions, especially in the UK and Continental Europe, induces investors to be more proactive in creating and identifying new types of deals (Wright and Robbie, 1998). In contrast, high associated costs and a dearth of appropriate technical and financial skills of VC executives in emerging markets deter such an approach.

Investment Screening and Evaluation

VCs in the West rely on financial and accounting information contained in the business plan to initially evaluate proposals and assess the risk of proposed ventures (Wright et al., 1992).

An unsteady regulatory environment and weak corporate governance in emerging markets, in contrast, raises the issue about which firms to fund. VCs investing in emerging markets need to understand the local setting while screening investments. Therefore, they focus on a limited region of the country in initial screening of proposals. They are less likely to use industry sector as a screen than in the West (Fried and Hisrich, 1994). VCs also seek entrepreneurs who have established some track record and have at least a couple of years of financials.

VC firms in China, for instance, try to fund firms in close geographic proximity (Bruton and Ahlstrom, 2003). They must also build relationships with local authorities in order to get things done. Chinese entrepreneurs are less likely to engage in opportunistic behavior when their ventures are located in close proximity to their friends and family.

One of the top criteria for investment evaluation in the West is the quality of the management team (Tyebjee and Bruno, 1984). Assessing the people leading the investment is difficult in emerging economies. It is challenging to obtain all necessary information about top management due to the nature of the legal and cultural environment. Entrepreneurs in China, for example, are extremely private (Bruton and Ahlstrom, 2003). They find it awkward to share information with people they do not know or have relationships with.

The evaluation of investment proposals in the West is based on information presented in the business plan (Wright and Robbie, 1996). In emerging markets, in contrast, timely, useful and accurate information about investee companies' performance is hard to obtain. Therefore, VCs need to exercise extra caution in using and interpreting financial statements and related information presented to investors.

In China, for instance, accounting rules significantly deviate from international accounting standards (Bruton and Ahlstrom, 2003). This is because local accounting rules are aimed at managing production rather than asset valuation. Regulations are often not clearly defined and are not widely enforced. As a result, items such as assets and accounts receivables can often be of questionable nature. Additionally, the definition of terms differs across different industries and regions. Therefore, it is critical for VCs to ensure that investees are aware of international accounting standards. It may also be prudent for VCs to request financial information in a form that can be interpreted.

VCs in the West typically use consulting firms to conduct an in-depth investigation of the merits of the investee company. In emerging countries, the support activities on which VCs typically rely to conduct due diligence in the West are not present.

Regulations in China, for example, do not require the same level of disclosure of public information to the government or other regulatory bodies as in the West (Bruton and Ahlstrom, 2003). A centrally planned political regime means that crucial information about the market and local regulatory environment is in control of select bureaucrats and government officers who carefully dispense it to obtain favors.

Therefore, VCs evaluating potential investments in China need to obtain knowledge of the entrepreneurs' connections with the government and other organizations. They must invest greater time and effort to help locate and aggregate a greater range of information, which can substantially prolong the due diligence process as compared to the West.

Post-Investment Monitoring

Level of Monitoring

VCs in the West actively monitor their investments (MacMillan et al., 1987; 88). VCs in emerging markets must maintain greater vigilance in monitoring funded firms to meet performance expectations and take swift action in the event the investment agreement is violated.

VCs in the US commonly assume that they share the goals of growth and profit maximization with the funded firms' management (Bruton and Ahlstrom, 2003). In emerging markets, the goals of VCs may be significantly different from those of their investees. Government agencies in these countries wield considerable influence over the conduct of investee firms.

Chinese firms, for instance, are often encouraged by the state to maximize employment and production (Bruton and Ahlstrom, 2003). VC-funded private ventures in China thus often end up with extra workers on their payrolls that are surreptitiously moved to these firms. The resultant overproduction of goods and unsalable inventory can lead to severe losses for VCs.

Monitoring investees in emerging markets, moreover, needs more personalized attention than in the West. This is because the uncertain nature of the local institutional environment in emerging economies increases the likelihood of opportunistic behavior on the part of the entrepreneurs.

In China, for example, setting up competing businesses to the funded venture to sell the same product lines at a lower price in order to beat the competition is not uncommon (Bruton and Ahlstrom, 2003). Therefore, VCs need to be extremely careful in drafting term sheets and legal agreements to clearly list the roles and requirements of all parties. It is not uncommon for VCs to make frequent, often unannounced, visits to their funded firms to see how things are going, and to speak with employees and customers. Selecting investments in close proximity helps to keep a direct oversight of their investee firms and mitigate some of these risks.

Financial Reporting

VCs in the West use a range of mechanisms including periodic financial reporting and a seat on the board of directors to monitor their investees (Gorman and Sahlman, 1989; Sapienza and Gupta, 1994). They also place contractual restrictions on managerial actions. In emerging markets, investees may be more likely to misreport sales or understate inventories, necessitating active VC intervention to validate financial reports.

Board Membership

In the West, VCs typically take a seat on the board of directors of the funded firms in order to monitor them (Fried and Hisrich, 1992; Sapienza, 1992). VCs in emerging markets increasingly require a seat on the boards of their investee companies. However, the power and information provided to board members is less than in US firms. Investee companies are more likely to withhold information from the board. The influence of outside directors is also weaker than in the West.

In countries like China board members are typically not nominated by commercially oriented owners or their representatives, but by government bodies (Bruton and Ahlstrom, 2003). These groups end up safeguarding the state's interests rather than those of shareholders. Investees are also more likely to share information with insiders who have more credibility with them rather than outsiders. Thus, VCs need to remain close to their invested firms to obtain the desired information and ensure its accuracy, rather than depending on a board seat for it. They must also make a conscious effort to get to know their investee companies and get involved with them.

Post-Investment Involvement

VCs in the West frequently interact with their investees during the monitoring process (Bygrave, 1987). They add value by providing strategic and operational advice, connecting the firm with buyers and suppliers (Fried and Hisrich, 1995; Macmillan et al., 1988). VC firms in the US are very involved in serving as a sounding board to the entrepreneurial team, and in financially oriented activities.

Providing advice is also increasingly the case with venture capital in emerging markets (Bruton and Ahlstrom, 2003). Involvement in strategic and operational areas like soliciting customers and distributors, formulating marketing plans or negotiating remuneration issues are also typical of emerging markets. However, the level of involvement and the nature of advice provided to investee firms in emerging markets is different from than in the West. This is because the level of managerial sophistication in funded ventures in these markets is often low.

Managers contemplating the sale of their company, for example, may solely value the firm based on the firms' physical assets (Bruton and Ahlstrom, 2003). They may ignore intangibles like brand name, distribution channels or customer contacts. They may be unacquainted with accounting packages and perpetually struggle to establish cash flow. In such situations, VCs may be forced to get involved at a very basic level, and educate senior managers on how to value their firm or more effectively manage day-to-day operations.

Additionally, VCs in emerging markets must make introductions to potential customers and suppliers, and assist with marketing plans. This is because relative to developed markets, marketing problems, coupled with the inability of investors to compete effectively, are rated very highly in emerging markets (Gorman and Sahlman, 1989; Wright et al., 1999).

In the US, advice provided to CEOs of funded firms is often very direct, and may occur in regular interactions (Fried and Hisrich, 1995). However, in some emerging markets, especially Asia, VCs must also deal with cultural issues such as 'saving face'. In China, for example, VCs must put forth their ideas as suggestions or even questions, and do so in private in order for the managers to feel in charge and take credit for the changes if successful (Bruton and Ahlstrom, 2003).

Additionally, VCs in emerging markets must invest time and effort in building connections with key individuals both inside and outside of the firm in order to provide value to their funded firm (Bruton and Ahlstrom, 2003). Such informal relationships are especially important in countries like China where 'guanxi', or the unwritten social rules about norms of conduct, is more pervasive than economic or legal controls or institutions. VCs need to build relationships with relatives and educators, for instance, who are considered more significant than government officials in their ability to influence others, and can thus enable VCs to exert control over their funded firms.

Investment Realization and Exit

The highest return exits in developed VC markets are realized through **IPOs** (Black and Gilson, 1998). As most VC firms in the West are organized as limited partnerships, their goal is to ultimately to exit their investments through IPO before the partnership is terminated (Sahlman, 1990).

Exiting through IPOs can be problematic in emerging markets. Owing to very few public companies, VC firms in emerging markets have very little experience with taking firms public (Ray, 1991). A host of laws on securities markets, disclosure and accounting standards may also not be in place.

Several exit mechanisms exist in China; however, options are more constrained and fraught with greater complexity than in the West. Numerous rules exist about working with offshore partners, and transferring capital overseas. Moreover, the selection of which firms may list on the stock market is a state decision in China (Bruton and Ahlstrom, 2003). The government has a position that VC-funded firms possess the relevant resources, and hence should not need more capital through a stock market listing; stock market listing should instead be directed toward state enterprises that are in desperate need of funds. Therefore, many VC-funded firms are forced to seek listings on foreign exchanges such as the NASDAQ, or look for other exit options like finding strategic buyers.

Strategic buyers may be the most likely exit option in such situations. However, even finding suitable strategic partners may be problematic. Strategic partners often demand majority stakes in the venture, which may be difficult for entrepreneurs in some countries, especially in Asia, to accept. As a result of these difficulties, the returns for many VC firms exiting their investments in emerging markets have not been very high (Bruton and Ahlstrom, 2003). Private equity firms in China, for example, typically target a 20–30% return, but the actual returns for many funds have been much lower.

Chapter summary

LO1: The United States is the birthplace of the VC/PE industry. The US is home to Silicon Valley, the world's oldest, most successful and largest entrepreneurial ecosystem. At the same time, the dominance of the US in global venture investment has been falling. VC has become a conduit for the flow of capital and ideas on a global basis. Originating in the US, there are **VC Associations** throughout the UK, Western Europe and Japan. The UK PE industry is one of the largest in Europe and second in importance globally to the US. While Australia has created an atmosphere for the growth of VC through the deregulation of its financial markets, state-dominated economies like Sweden also witnessed the emergence of this form of finance. Countries like China and India also started to think of ways risk capital could help to solve their development problems. Following a drastic drop in public equity values in the aftermath of the stock market crash of the early 2000s, institutional investors also turned to international venture capital to diversify their portfolios.

LO2: The development of the VC industry hinges on a number of features of the external environment. Each country has its own institutions and policies that shape its VC industry. Legal and regulatory barriers to the development of VC can take various

(Continued)

forms, including the lack of relevant legislation, discretionary nature of existing rules, and over-regulation. The level of economic stability and development of the stock market, the culture of entrepreneurship and attitudes to risk, and size of the technology sector are also crucial.

LO3: The **globalization** of venture capital has seen increasing cross-border activity both into and within **developed markets** and into less developed markets elsewhere. Following domestic economic turmoil and intense competition in Silicon Valley in the late 2000s, both US and international VC investors began to look for new, attractive opportunities in markets abroad. There is increasing interest among US investors in European companies. Particularly significant in recent years is the growth of international VC investments into **emerging markets** such as China and India. New opportunities are also beginning to appear in other more fringe, regional markets, such as Latin America, South-East Asia, and, to a lesser degree, Africa and the Middle East. There are multiple reasons for the internationalization of VC firms and cross-border investment flows, especially from developed to developing markets. These include the historical origins of VC/PE firms, and investors' preferences. The rise in cross-border VC investment flows is also attributed to both 'push' and 'pull' factors like domestic market saturation and availability of attractive investment opportunities in home and foreign markets, respectively.

LO4: Internationalizing VC firms entering foreign markets adapt their investment behavior in those markets. There exist wide variations in the nature of VC firms' operations between developed and emerging markets. Unlike in developed markets, high associated costs and a dearth of appropriate technical and financial skills of VC executives in emerging markets deter active **deal seeking**. VCs in the West rely on financial and accounting information contained in the business plan to initially **evaluate** proposals and assess the risk of proposed ventures. An unsteady regulatory environment and weak corporate governance in emerging markets, in contrast, raises the issue about which firms to fund. VCs in the West actively **monitor** their investments. Active oversight is also needed for both government and private enterprises that are funded in emerging markets. However, VCs in emerging markets must maintain greater vigilance than in the West in monitoring funded firms to ensure that their performance is in line with expectations. They also need to take swift action in the event the investment agreement is violated. The highest return **exits** in developed VC markets are realized through **IPOs**. Most VC firms in the West are also organized as limited partnerships with a limited life. Therefore, their goal is to ultimately exit their investments through IPO before the partnership is terminated. Owing to very few public companies, VC firms in emerging markets have very little experience with the process of taking firms public. A host of laws on securities markets, disclosure and accounting standards may also not be in place.

1. According to the chapter, there has been a fall in the dominance of the US in global venture capital investment. To what extent do you agree/disagree with this statement? Provide evidence to support your answer.

2. What are the external (environmental) factors that impact the international development of venture capital? Based on what you have read in this chapter, explain the role of any two external environmental factors in explaining the development of venture capital in any country of your choice. Give examples to support your answer.

3. Explain the trends in the cross-border flows of venture capital as outlined in this chapter.

4. What are the reasons for the internationalization of VC firms? Explain.

5. What challenges do international VC firms face in investing in foreign markets? Based on the material covered in this chapter, how do VC firms respond to those challenges? Explain at least two ways in which VC firms from developed markets adapt their investment operations in emerging foreign markets.

Case 15.1

i2 India: Internationalization Challenges of a British Venture Capital Fund

Chris Mathias: Beginnings

Chris Mathias came to the UK to attend boarding school at the age of 16. It was the same school where his older brother had completed his A levels and his younger brother was soon to attend. Chris's mother was spending a year building a family house in India before joining her husband in Saudi Arabia where he had recently moved.

After completing his accountancy training at Arthur Anderson, Chris went on to earn an MBA from INSEAD, France. He then took up a job as a consultant at Bain & Company, but soon realized that he 'did not like working for someone else'. At the same time, a turnaround on a fuel card company that he did for a group of venture capitalists turned out to be 'ridiculously profitable'. It was probably 'the investment of the year' back then. When another turnaround on a group of marketing services businesses called Marketing Choice was also 'very successful' the following year, Chris decided to 'go off' and do it on his own. He was confident of his capabilities given his recent track record and the availability of a large number of troubled businesses at the time:

(Continued)

So the phone rang all the time. Chris we've got this, Chris we've got that, come and do this turnaround, come and do that turnaround and er, so yeah. I believed the, my own hype and whatever anyone else told me that I was great at doing turnarounds so obviously I went and did turnarounds.

In June of the same year, Chris bought Tanners, a bankrupt envelope manufacturing business in the UK that he turned around and profitably sold at the end of 14 months. He owned 51% of another loss-making marketing services company just prior to his departure from Bain. Chris grew the business into an internet consulting firm, and one of the three biggest in Europe at the time of its sale. By then, he had started two other companies, also profitably selling them, and taking the total number of ventures owned since his first turnaround to 40.

The Idea of i2 India

Chris travelled to India on a regular basis to visit with family and 'a huge network' of friends. i2 India was conceived at a drinks reception for diplomats in Delhi to which he was invited during one such visit. The then Minister of Science & Technology referred to Indians as the 'cyber coolies' of the world, a word that struck a chord with Chris. He realized the shortcomings of the local innovation ecosystem in India and took it upon himself to change it:

> I went home and I was like… we're not going to be the cyber coolies of this world we're going to do more than that… and then I started figuring out to do more than that we really have to change some fundamental things in India… or Indians' ability to dream up new ideas and make them into a reality… and rather than sit around and moan, I'm going to do it.

Chris knew that it was rare for academics to commercialize the innovations they had developed themselves. As a big believer in the profit motive, he set out to create 'real incentives' for Indian scientists to generate valuable intellectual property (IP). He visited Silicon Valley, California, and met with experts at top US universities such as Stanford, MIT and Harvard to understand their role in innovation. His alumni network from a top business school, and reputed accounting and consulting firms, also came in handy. A good friend made introductions at Stanford, while Harvard Business School was one of Chris's biggest clients in Boston during his consulting days:

> talking to people in Silicon Valley, the stuff that's easy. You know, pick up the phone and they'll all talk to you. Yeah, I mean you just need to know somebody. Or if you've been to Insead and Andersons and Bane just look through the book and there's always somebody who's working there, there's some connections, it's not hard it's really not hard, and so no I never really considered it to be a challenge, and it wasn't.

After extensive research, Chris ended up choosing the 'Imperial College model'. He felt the ecosystems in the US were way too advanced to replicate in India. The Imperial College model was more likely to work given his focus on commercializing IP generated in universities. As the charter founder of the Indian Institute of Technology (IIT), India's top engineering institute, Imperial College London had a good brand image in India. Imperial also had a good relationship with the Indian Institute of Science, another of India's top research institutes in Bangalore.

Chris phoned Tidu Maini, Pro Rector, Public & Corporate Affairs, at Imperial regarding his proposal. An old acquaintance, Tidu quickly agreed to partner with Chris, and Imperial Innovations India (or i2 India) was formed as a joint venture with Imperial College London. The mission of i2 India was to enter into Memoranda of Understanding (MOUs) with Indian universities over a 12–15-year period with a view to commercializing their ideas. The company was a 'co-promoter', expecting to have an equity relationship with the businesses that it helped to commercialize.

Raising Investment

Chris leveraged his personal connections in India to raise investment for his venture. Friends or former colleagues who he had not previously worked with in this capacity came on board to fund i2 India. As investors of repute, they all believed in the cause of innovation in India and trusted Chris's ability to deliver a return on their investment without compromising his high ethical standards:

> The investors are people who are organizations with really good names, deep pockets and some connection with me. All of them have invested on the basis of trust because it was a complete, this has never been done before in India. You know I can't promise you any other than I'll try. And I can promise you two things, one is I'll try, and two is whatever happens I guarantee I will spend your money… they were people who believed in a) what I was doing was important for India, b) that I would do it with honesty and c) that there was an outside possibility that they would make money out of it.

Chris also approached the Tata group for investment, one of the biggest and oldest business conglomerates in India, whose ethical standards he held in high regard. Following a referral from one of his former colleagues in the UK, he spoke with Cyrus Mistry, a top executive at Tata. More than the money, he valued the credibility that they lent to his venture, especially in the early stages:

> They're an investor, they're great actually, they're a good investor… and they're very helpful. And I ask them to, can you do this and they always say yes, and they do it. That's a very useful Indian group and provides really good air cover if I need it. I didn't want the money I wanted the brand… it does make life so

(Continued)

much easier you know. We're okay now, now we can get to speak to anyone we want to and it's fine. But early on it just helps a lot if you can say oh Cyrus, can you drop this guy an email please, and the door opens straight away.

Building the Team

Chris established a physical location in Bangalore in September 2009. He hired Egon Zehnder, one of the world's top three executive recruitment companies, to search for a CEO for the India office. Deepak Mishra, a scientist of Indian origin in the US, who desired to return to India, was deemed perfect for the job:

It was great, I love him to bits he's fabulous, he's a proper scientist and he had kind of been involved in a couple of commercial start-ups there. Where really he was a researcher. And he really wanted to come back to India and do the same thing. And Egon Zehnder found him and Deepak and I got on great.

Vincent, a former employee at CDC Ventures, a British PE firm, headed by one of Chris's close friends, Donald Peck, in India, was the second hire at the local office. Vincent was responsible for looking into operational issues such as those related to infrastructure, including water, electricity etc. Altogether, there were eight people on the top management team in India, and 7–25 people in the office on any given day depending on the number of start-up teams using the office space at a premium location in Bangalore.

The Challenge of Culture in India

Cultural attitudes influenced both deal generation as well as the management of operations in India. At the outset, Chris relied on the Imperial brand to bridge the local network gap as he was not plugged into academic connections in India:

I don't think anyone that I know, has tremendous academic connections, which is what I needed in the first instance. I didn't need commercial connections, I needed academic connections. And I didn't, I wasn't very well plugged in to that so, that Imperial really had to fill that one for me.

He also hired a local firm called Sun Shadow to do the initial IP research and locate sources of patent filings. The firm's connections with local scientists and innovators were extremely helpful in the beginning. Additionally, Chris directly reached out to local scientists and innovators at India's top research institutions. However, his efforts met with resistance. Cultural attitudes to risk and innovation in India interfered with his ability to generate local deal flow. It was not easy to convince academic founders and innovators to commercialize their ideas, as knowledge was considered sacrosanct in India and the idea of attaching a monetary value to learning was deemed to be in conflict with this core value:

So getting around IIT Delhi, IIT Mumbai, CSIR, ISSC, IT Chennai, oh god IIM Ahmedabad whatever you know. You could pick about eight institutions… that cover 75% of India's patent findings… getting around them… that was not easy… that was the hardest getting into, those guys are difficult… one of the Deans said to me, Chris, Lakshmi [goddess of wealth] and Saraswati [goddess of learning and wisdom] should not meet. And I'm sitting across the table and that was just so deep in him. He didn't even want to talk to me… and this is the problem. It's kind of right through the fabric of academia in India.

In Chris's view, there was a relative lack of 'high-quality people' staying in India to conduct research with the potential to make a 'significant difference in the world'. While he had ended up keeping the process 'ticking over', the unfortunate reality was that i2 India was increasingly bringing in IP from abroad and commercializing that 'as specific to large Indian needs' in India.

The responsibility for the India operations of i2 India was entirely delegated to Deepak.

Deepak is the CEO, he does everything, his key responsibility is to do everything and to make it work. I'm the chairman he's the CEO, his job is to make it work, not mine. Because my job was to dream up the idea which I did. Get it off the ground which I did. Find him which I did. Raise the money which I did. And help him when he needs it which I do.

Chris often visited the India office for a week, typically arriving on a Monday morning, and spending all week with Deepak and his various teams. In most cases, he carved out an agenda, calling Deepak ahead of time to discuss key issues of strategic importance he needed to resolve during his visit. Once on the ground, Chris stepped in as necessary, hiring a new recruit or talking to potential customers. At other times, he mentored the founding partners he was working with to resolve their strategic problems and guide them in their growth path:

I spend all week with him, with the various teams… sometimes, I'm hiring helping them recruit someone. Sometimes I'm talking to a potential customer who's worried about them because they are a start-up, and I'm saying don't worry it's going to be fine. A lot of time I am working with them on whatever their issues are, they're facing right then in their growth. If it's marketing or technology or strategically what should we do here or there? How do we price this?

Yet, Chris was forced to intervene at an operational level, often on an ongoing basis. He had a strong stand in matters of business ethics, for example, and felt inclined to communicate his aversion to bribery with his India staff. Culturally ingrained attitudes

(Continued)

to hierarchy and deference for authority based on caste or age were other issues he felt strongly about. A lot of his time was thus spent reinforcing the importance of ethical conduct and building a flat organization to facilitate rational decision making devoid of any pre-conceived cultural biases:

> Some of it is cultural like banging home a couple of really core messages… for example, the understanding that it takes two to corrupt, one to pay one to receive and that the payer is just as corrupt as the recipient. And that is behavior in which we will not participate at all. People in India don't see it that way. So you've got to keep reinforcing that and banging it out, and that's one example. I mean there are others: Indians are incredibly hierarchical, incredibly deferential to people they consider either from a social point of view, caste point of view, age or hierarchy, if in any of those categories you're considered above someone then they're considered incredibly deferential to you. This is not a helpful attitude in a) their deferential upwards and b) the boss tends to be quite autocratic downwards. And these are not attitudes that I find helpful. And so a lot of what I need to do is cultural as I say.

According to Chris, i2 India covered between 75 and 80% of India's innovations, of which three had been commercialized since its inception in 2005. Yet, eight years since founding, the venture had yet to make any money.

Source: authors' own research

Discussion Questions

1. How did Chris Mathias generate the idea for i2 India? How did he validate his idea?
2. What was Chris's vision for i2 India? To what extent do you believe Chris's personal background and human and social capital resources influenced his decision to set up an India-focused fund / enter India as an investor? Discuss.
3. How did Chris set up i2 India? What financial and human capital resources did he need? How did he acquire these resources?
4. Evaluate the success of i2 India in India. What challenges does Chris face in the process of a) generating deals and b) adding value to his investments in India? What steps must Chris take to overcome these challenges? Outline your recommendations.

References

Asia Asset. (2019) 'Thailand mutual fund industry assets up marginally in 2018'. Available at www.asiaasset.com/post/14096-decaimc-gte-0107 (last accessed 27 September 2022).

Australian Investment Council. (2019) *Australian Private Equity & Venture Capital Activity Report.* Available at https://docs.preqin.com/reports/AIC-Preqin-2019-Yearbook-Australian-Private-Equity-and-Venture-Capital-Activity-Report.pdf (last accessed 27 September 2022).

Beyond Ventures. (n.d.) 'Financial insight: Venture capital'. Available at www.beyondventures.hk/Uploads/pdf/2019-03-11/5c85bc5441c39.pdf (last accessed 27 September 2022).

Bhattacharya, A. (2018) 'Investors are chasing fewer but more valuable startup deals in India'. Available at https://qz.com/india/1490981/vcs-are-investing-more-money-in-fewer-indian-startups (last accessed 27 September 2022).

Bose, K.R. (2008) 'Benchmark capital: The international expansion of a Silicon Valley venture capital firm'. Case E-218, Stanford Graduate School of Business, 9 November. Available at www.gsb.stanford.edu/faculty-research/case-studies/benchmark-capital-international-expansion-silicon-valley-venture (last accessed 27 September 2022).

British Private Equity and Venture Capital Association (BVCA) (2018) *BVCA Report on Investment Activity 2018.* Available at www.bvca.co.uk/Portals/0/Documents/Research/Industry%20Activity/BVCA-RIA-2018.pdf (last accessed 27 September 2022).

Bruton, G.D. and Ahlstrom, D. (2003) 'An institutional view of China's venture capital industry: Explaining the differences between China and the West', *Journal of Business Venturing*, 18(2): 233–259. Available at https://doi.org/10.1016/S0883-9026(02)00079-4 (last accessed 27 September 2022).

Bygrave, W.D. (1987) 'Syndicated investments by venture capital firms: A networking perspective', *Journal of Business Venturing*, 2(2): 139–154. https://doi.org/10.1016/0883-9026(87)90004-8

Bygrave, W.D. and Timmons, J.A. (1986a) 'Networking among venture capital firms', *Frontiers of Entrepreneurship Research*, 437–456.

Bygrave, W.D. and Timmons, J.A. (1986b) 'Venture capital's role in financing innovation for economic growth', *Journal of Business Venturing*, 1(1): 161–176.

Cheok, J. (2018) 'Singapore startups to step up 2018 fund-raising for global expansion: KPMG'. *Business Times*, 4 June. Available at www.businesstimes.com.sg/technology/singapore-startups-to-step-up-2018-fund-raising-for-global-expansion-kpmg (last accessed 27 September 2022).

EMPEA. (2019) *Emerging Markets Private Capital Fundraising and Investment.* Available at www.empea.org/app/uploads/2019/02/EMPEA-Industry-Statistics-YE-2018-Official-Public.pdf (last accessed 27 September 2022).

FINSMES. (2018) 'Venture investment spending in Japan reaches new heights'. Available at www.finsmes.com/2018/03/venture-investment-spending-in-japan-reaches-new-heights.html (last accessed 27 September 2022).

Fried, V.H. and Hisrich, R.D. (1992) 'The role of the venture capitalist in the management of entrepreneurial enterprises', *Journal of International Business and Entrepreneurship*, 1(1): 75–96.

Fried, V.H. and Hisrich, R.D. (1994) 'Toward a model of venture capital investment decision making', *Financial Management*, 3(3): 28–37. www.jstor.org/stable/3665619

Fried, V.H. and Hisrich, R.D. (1995) 'The venture capitalist: A relationship investor', *California Management Review*, 37(2): 101–113. https://doi.org/10.2307/41165791

Gorman, M. and Sahlman, W.A. (1989) 'What do venture capitalists do?' *Journal of Business Venturing*, 4(4): 231–248. https://doi.org/10.1016/0883-9026(89)90014-1

Hammer, M. (2018) 'An introduction to venture capital in emerging markets'. Wharton University of Pennsylvania, Public Policy Initiative (PPI), 2 December. https://publicpolicy.wharton.upenn.edu/live/news/2745-an-introduction-to-venture-capital-in-emerging (last accessed 27 September 2022).

Hirschauge, O. (2014) 'Israeli tech start-ups attract Chinese investors', *The Wall Street Journal*, 16 December.

IBEF. (n.d.) *Domestic Investment in India*. Available at www.ibef.org/economy/domestic-investments (last accessed 27 September 2022).

IBEF. (2018) *Financial Services*. Available at www.ibef.org/download/Financial_Services-August-2018.pdf (last accessed 27 September 2022).

International Finance Corporation (IFC) (2018) 'Sustainability report redefining development finance'. Available at www.ifc.org/wps/wcm/connect/3aa05003-d634-40f9-8af4-35b8c8a87248/IFC-AR18-Full-Report.pdf?MOD=AJPERES&CVID=moNw5we (last accessed 27 September 2022).

Jarvis, R. and Schizas, E. (2012) 'Finance and the small business', in S. Carter and D. Jones-Evans (eds.), *Enterprise and Small Business: Principles, Practice and Policy* (3rd edn). Harlow: Financial Times Prentice Hall, pp. 362–385.

Jeng, L.A. and Wells, P.C. (2000) 'The determinants of venture capital funding: Evidence across countries', *Journal of Corporate Finance*, 6(3): 241–289. https://doi.org/10.1016/S0929-1199(00)00003-1

Lee, E. (2018) 'Venturing beyond to South Korea', *Medium*, 30 August. Available at https://medium.com/venture-beyond/venturing-beyond-to-south-korea-b4996f7061a4 (last accessed 27 September 2022).

Levingston, I. (2019) 'Alibaba buys Israeli AR start-up amid China investment scrutiny', *Bloomberg*, 24 March. Available at www.bloomberg.com/news/articles/2019-03-24/alibaba-buys-israeli-ar-startup-amid-china-investment-scrutiny (last accessed 27 September 2022).

Loh, D. (2019) 'Asia set to eclipse US as world's venture capital powerhouse', *Nikkei Asian Review*, 21 October. Available at https://asia.nikkei.com/Business/Business-trends/Asia-set-to-eclipse-US-as-world-s-venture-capital-powerhouse (last accessed 27 September 2022).

Lucas, L. (2018) 'Asia close to eclipsing US as world's biggest VC market', *Financial Times*, 10 January. Available at www.ft.com/content/ccd356f6-f67d-11e7-88f7-5465a6ce1a00 (last accessed 27 September 2022).

Macmillan, I.C., Zemann, L. and Subbanarasimha, P.N. (1987) 'Criteria distinguishing successful from unsuccessful ventures in the venture screening process', *Journal of Business Venturing*, 2(2): 123–137. https://doi.org/10.1016/0883-9026(87)90003-6

Macmillan, I.C., Kulow, D.M. and Khoylian, R. (1988) 'Venture capitalists' involvement in their investments: Extent and performance', *Journal of Business Venturing*, 4(1): 27–47. https://doi.org/10.1016/0883-9026(89)90032-3

Mahroum, S. (2016) 'The triumphs and struggles of Arab start-ups', *Project Syndicate*, 4 May. Available at www.project-syndicate.org/commentary/startups-entrepreneurship-middle-east-by-sami-mahroum-2016-05?barrier=accesspaylog (last accessed 27 September 2022).

Martin, R. and Sunley, P. (2018) 'Towards a developmental turn in evolutionary economic geography?' *Regional Studies*, 49(5): 1–21. doi: 10.1080/00343404.2014.899431

Martin, R. and Sunley, P. (2002) 'Taking risks in regions: the geographical anatomy of Europe's emerging venture capital market', *Journal of Economic Geography*, 2(2): 121–150.

Mason, C. and Harrison, R. (1999) 'Editorial: Venture capital: Rationale, aims and scope', *Venture Capital: An International Journal of Entrepreneurial Finance*, 1(1): 1–46. https://doi.org/10.1080/136910699295974

McDougall, P.P. and Oviatt, B.M. (2000) 'International entrepreneurship: The intersection of two research paths', *Academy of Management Journal*, 43(5): 902–906. https://doi.org/10.5465/1556418

Michaels, D. and Schechner, S. (2018) 'Adyen's IPO success spurs hopes European tech scene has turned a corner', *The Wall Street Journal, Eastern Edition*, September 15, 11:00 am ET. https://www.wsj.com/articles/adyens-ipo-success-spurs-hopes-european-tech-scene-has-turned-a-corner-1537023600

National Venture Capital Association (NVCA) (2019) *Yearbook*. Data provided by Pitchbook. Available at https://nvca.org/wp-content/uploads/2019/08/NVCA-2019-Yearbook.pdf (last accessed 27 September 2022).

Ooghe, H., Manigart, S. and Fassin, Y. (1991) 'Growth patterns of the European venture capital industry', *Journal of Business Venturing*, 6(6): 381–404. https://doi.org/10.1016/0883-9026(91)90027-B

Patricof, A. (1989) 'The internationalisation of venture capital', *Journal of Business Venturing*, 4(4): 227–230. https://doi.org/10.1016/0883-9026(89)90013-X

Pitchbook. (2020) *Pitchbook Data*. Available at https://pitchbook.com/blog#all (last accessed 27 September 2022).

PricewaterhouseCoopers. (2018) 'US PwC'. *Asset & Wealth Management Market Intelligence Digest Taiwan*. Available at www.pwc.com/sg/en/asset-management/assets/market-research-centre/sample-reports/sample-report-tw.pdf (last accessed 27 September 2022).

Ray, D.M. (1991) 'Venture capital and entrepreneurial development in Singapore', *International Small Business Journal*, 10(1): 11–26. https://doi.org/10.1177/026624269101000101

Razumovskaya, O. (2016) 'Russia's venture capital funds look abroad', *The Wall Street Journal*, June 21. https://www.wsj.com/articles/russias-venture-capital-funds-look-abroad-1466529651

Sahlman, W.A. (1990) 'The structure and governance of venture-capital organizations', *Journal of Financial Economics*, 27(2): 473–521. https://doi.org/10.1016/0304-405X(90)90065-8

Sapienza, H.J. (1992) 'When do venture capitalists add value?' *Journal of Business Venturing*, 7(1): 9–27. https://doi.org/10.1016/0883-9026(92)90032-M

Sapienza, H.J. and Gupta, A.K. (1994) 'Impact of agency risks and task uncertainty on venture capitalist–CEO interaction', *Academy of Management Journal*, 37(6): 1618–1632. https://doi.org/10.5465/256802

Securities Commission Malaysia. (n.d. a) *Annual Report 2017*. Available at www.sc.com.my/api/documentms/download.ashx?id=097e62ec-8464-46a2-a3e0-9cb4ee164ca7 (last accessed 27 September 2022).

Securities Commission Malaysia. (n.d. b) *Annual Report 2018*. Available at www.sc.com.my/api/documentms/download.ashx?id=69b9ad2a-13c7-40bf-b0d3-341951a62278 (last accessed 27 September 2022).

Straits Times (2019) 'CapitaLand tops for Asia-Pacific real estate assets under management with US$55.9b'. *Straits Times*, 22 May. Available at www.straitstimes.com/business/property/capitaland-tops-asia-pacific-with-us559b-of-real-esate-assets-under-management-as (last accessed 27 September 2022).

Tyebjee, T. and Bruno, A. (1984) 'A model of venture capital investment activity', *Management Science*, 30(9): 1051–1066. https://doi.org/10.1287/mnsc.30.9.1051

Tyebjee, T. and Vickery, L. (1988) 'Venture capital in western Europe', *Journal of Business Venturing*, 3(2): 123–136. https://doi.org/10.1016/0883-9026(88)90022-5

Vietnam Briefing. (2019) 'Investments in Vietnamese startups tripled in 2018'. Available at www.vietnam-briefing.com/news/investments-vietnamese-startups-tripled-2018.html (last accessed 27 September 2022).

VinaCapital. (2017) 'Vietnam Wealth Management Forum'. VinaCapital. Available at http://pdf.hubbis.com/pdf/eventAgenda/vietnam-wealth-management-forum-2017-2017-9-7-Driving+diversity+via+mutual+funds.pdf (last accessed 27 September 2022).

Wright, M. and Robbie, K. (1996) 'Venture capitalists, unquoted equity investment appraisal and the role of accounting information', *Accounting and Business Research*, 26(2): 153–168. https://doi.org/10.1080/00014788.1996.9729506

Wright, M. and Robbie, K. (1998) 'Venture capital and private equity: A review and synthesis', *Journal of Business Finance and Accounting*, 25(5/6): 521–570. https://doi.org/10.1111/1468-5957.00201

Wright, M., Thompson, S. and Robbie, K. (1992) 'Venture capital and management-led leveraged buy-outs: A European perspective', *Journal of Business Venturing*, 7(1): 47–71. https://doi.org/10.1016/0883-9026(92)90034-O

Wright, M., Karsai, J., Dudzinski, Z. and Morovic, J. (1999) 'Transition and active investors: Venture capital in Hungary, Poland and Slovakia', *Post-Communist Economies*, 11(1): 27–46. https://doi.org/10.1080/14631379996039

Yi, W.K. (2018) 'Singapore's asset management industry clocks strong growth; AUM up 19% to $3.3 trillion in 2017'. *The Business Times*, 25 October. Available at www.businesstimes.com.sg/government-economy/singapores-asset-management-industry-clocks-strong-growth-aum-up-19-to-s33 (last accessed 27 September 2022).

Young-sil, Y. (2019a) 'S. Korean asset management firms struggle with deficit in 2018'. *Business Korea*, 14 March. Available at www.businesskorea.co.kr/news/articleView.html?idxno=29964 (last accessed 27 September 2022).

Young-sil, Y. (2019b) 'New venture investment in South Korea tops 6.4 Tril. won in 2018', *Business Korea*, 5 June. Available at www.businesskorea.co.kr/news/articleView.html?idxno=32590 (last accessed 27 September 2022).

INDEX